Marketing Strategy and Management

FOURTH EDITION

Michael J. Baker

palgrave
macmillan

First edition 1985
Reprinted three times
Second edition 1992
Reprinted three times
Third edition 2000
Reprinted seven times
Fourth edition 2007
Published by
PALGRAVE MACMILLAN
Houndmills, Basingstoke, Hampshire RG21 6XS and
175 Fifth Avenue, New York, N.Y. 10010
Companies and representatives throughout the world

PALGRAVE MACMILLAN is the global academic imprint of the Palgrave Macmillan division of St. Martin's Press, LLC and of Palgrave Macmillan Ltd. Macmillan® is a registered trademark in the United States, United Kingdom and other countries. Palgrave is a registered trademark in the European Union and other countries.

ISBN-13: 978–1–4039–8627–6
ISBN-10: 1–4039–8627–4

This book is printed on paper suitable for recycling and made from fully managed and sustained forest sources.

A catalogue record for this book is available from the British Library.

A catalog record for this book is available from the Library of Congress.

10 9 8 7 6 5 4 3 2 1
16 15 14 13 12 11 10 09 08 07

Printed in China

MARKETING STRATEGY AND MANAGEMENT

Books are to

Also by Michael J. Baker:

Marketing New Industrial Products (1975)*
Market Development: A Comprehensive Survey (1983), Harmondsworth: Penguin Books
Marketing: An Introductory Text (4th edn) (1985)*
Marketing: An Introductory Text (6th edn) (1996), English Language Book Society
The Strategic Marketing Plan Audit (1998) Cambridge: Cambridge Strategy Publications
The Marketing Manual (1998), Oxford: Butterworth Heinemann
Business and Management Research (2003), Helensburgh: Westburn Publishers
Marketing: An Introductory Text (7th edn) (2006), Helensburgh: Westburn Publishers
Marketing Strategy and Management (4th edn) (2007)*

Edited by Michael J. Baker:

Marketing in Adversity (1976)*
Industrial Innovation: Technology, Policy, Diffusion (1979)*
Perspectives on Marketing Management, Vol. 1, 1991; Vol. 2 1992; Vol. 3 1993; Vol. 4 1994, Chichester: John Wiley and Sons
Marketing: Theory and Practice (3rd edn) (1995)*
The Companion Encyclopedia of Marketing & Advertising (1995), London: Routledge
Dictionary of Marketing and Advertising (3rd edn) (1998)*
Encyclopedia of Marketing (1999), London: International Thomson Business Press
Marketing Theory (2000), London: International Thomson Business Press
Marketing: Critical Perspectives on Business and Management, 5 Volumes (2001), London: Routledge
The Marketing Book (5th edn) (2003), Oxford: Butterworth Heinemann

Co-authored by Michael J. Baker:

Baker, M. J. and McTavish, R. (1975) *Product Policy and Management**
Parkinson, S. T. and Baker, M. J. (1986) *Organizational Buying Behaviour**
Baker, M. J. and Hart, S. (1989) *Marketing and Competitive Success*. Oxford: Philip Allan
Ughanwa, D. O. and Baker, M. J. (1989) *The Role of Design in International Competitiveness*. London: Routledge
Baker, M. J. and Hart, S. J. (1998) *Product Strategy and Management*. Hemel Hempstead: Prentice-Hall, (2nd edn) (in press) 2007
Baker, M. J., Graham, P. and Harker, D. and M. (1998) *Marketing: Managerial Foundations*. Sydney: Macmillan

* Published by Palgrave Macmillan

To my family

Brief contents

Full contents

List of figures

List of tables

Preface to the fourth edition

The first edition of *Marketing Strategy and Management* was largely written while I was the Crowther Foundation Distinguished Visiting Scholar at the Chinese University of Hong Kong in 1983. This break from the routine administrative duties of my appointment at Strathclyde University enabled me to commit to paper the essentials of a course which I have taught for many years as the capstone to an honours degree in marketing. The book thus assumes that the reader has already pursued one or more introductory courses in marketing, such as the Chartered Institute of Marketing's Certificate/Diploma courses or an undergraduate programme in business studies, and so is familiar with the descriptive aspects of the subject, as well as possessing a reasonable overview of it as a whole. It is quite likely, therefore, that the intended reader of this book will have already read one or more of the many comprehensive textbooks which are now available. Indeed, in the case of the honours year students at Strathclyde they will probably have read several of them, as well as having studied many sub-areas of marketing, such as advertising, organisational buying behaviour, market research, product development etc. in some depth.

While positioned originally as an advanced text for undergraduates, adoptions and use of the text indicate that it is widely used on Master's programmes – both in marketing and more broadly based MBA courses. Given the emphasis on professional practice in these programmes, and the CIMs Postgraduate Diploma, the content and approach have been found to work well with more experienced students seeking an authoritative overview of the subject. Accordingly, the purpose of this book is to build upon this knowledge by opening in Part 1 with an analysis of the nature of marketing strategy and strategic marketing planning (SMP).

The scope of Part 1 remains very similar to that in earlier editions and opens with a Prologue which is intended to provide an overview of the book as a whole, of the perspective adopted by the author and the manner in which this is to be developed. Chapter 2 takes a wide-ranging look at the nature of competition and the role which marketing has to play in contributing to organisational success. Much new material has been incorporated into this chapter to reflect the many changes which occurred in the 1990s. Among these were the emphasis on skills and competences and the notion of the learning organisation together with a revival of interest in the resource-based theory of the firm. Chapter 3 explores the relationship between corporate strategy and marketing strategy and comes to the conclusion that in all but the largest multidivisional organisations they amount to the same thing. This theme is expanded in Chapter 4 with a consideration of what is involved in formulating an effective strategy through the process of strategic marketing planning.

Chapter 5 explores a number of key concepts which experience has shown are of fundamental importance in defining the strategic alternatives available to the firm. Several of the techniques involve the use of matrix analysis whereby the decision-maker seeks to reduce complex issues to simple ones. Although this approach has been widely criticised as 'oversimplified' by many academics there can be little doubt that these techniques are widely used by practitioners.

The final chapter in Part 1, Research for marketing, appeared much later in earlier editions. However, on the basis that Part 2 is concerned with the analysis of information it seemed more logical to explore the methods and techniques at the manager's disposal for collecting data before describing the kind of data required.

Part 2 of the book comprises seven chapters which I have called The Marketing Appreciation. Essentially this section explores all the areas which the marketing decision-maker needs to consider in choosing a marketing strategy. The section opens with a discussion of the macro-environment which determines the courses of action available to all competitors in the marketplace. This is followed by a series of micro-environmental analyses of industries and competitors, customers and the firm itself. Taken together these analyses provide the raw materials for identifying those market opportunities which offer the greatest potential to the organisation in terms of its aspirations and goals and paying due regard to the assets, skills and resources it has available to it. This process is termed 'matching' as the objective is to match the firm's strengths with opportunities while seeking to avoid potential threats and remedy any perceived weaknesses (the SWOT analysis).

The final two chapters in Part 2 explore three processes central to the development of an effective marketing strategy – segmentation, positioning and branding. Obviously, if customers are to develop preferences for and loyalty towards an organisation and its products/services they must be able to distinguish and differentiate its output from all those other competitors offering near or perfect substitutes for that output. It is here that the ability to define precisely the existence of subgroups or 'segments' within a market in terms of the specific wants of these segments will enable the seller to create offerings with a sustainable competitive advantage.

Part 3 is concerned with the management of the marketing mix. While it is fashionable in some quarters to question the validity of the mix concept, and especially the notion of the four Ps (product, price, place and promotion) which underpin it, I believe that it offers a robust and useful technique or approach for reducing the complexity of operational marketing to manageable proportions. By the same token, while I have taken the opportunity in preparing this fourth edition to extensively revise and update the content, I have not felt it necessary to discard some of the older material which has withstood the test of time. Many of the key concepts and ideas about marketing were first articulated in the 1950s and 60s by pioneers like Alderson, Ansoff, Drucker, Howard, Kotler, Levitt, McCarthy etc. With the rapid growth of the discipline much of this pioneering work became buried and lost to view – a tendency which has provoked frequent calls to get ' back to the basics'. In the process much orig-

inal material is being rediscovered but, in my opinion, this hardly seems a sufficient reason to discard the original sources in favour of the new disciples. Hopefully, the reader will find an appropriate mix of both the old and new.

In dealing with the marketing mix, and following the traditional 4Ps framework, I have concentrated on the policy issues as these define the alternative courses of action from which the decision-maker must choose in seeking to develop a unique mix of their own. Those requiring more detailed and descriptive material will need to consult the specialised literature which deals with topics such as product development, personal selling, advertising etc. as subjects in their own right. (Recommendations for further reading are given at the end of every chapter.)

Part 4 – Implementing Marketing – explores a number of issues involved in converting objectives and ideas into effective action. In recent years a great deal of research has been undertaken into the nature and sources of competitive success.

While numerous prescriptions have been proposed it has become clear that there is no single, simple solution. Perhaps we should not be surprised at this given that competition is a dynamic activity in which rivals seek to gain an advantage over one another. What has become clear is that there are numerous conditions which are necessary for success but they are rarely if ever sufficient to guarantee it. The necessary conditions are described in some detail in this book and many like it. If you ignore the available advice there is a very high likelihood of failure. But, if you follow it it will only put you on a level playing field with everyone else who is familiar with the same advice. What differentiates degrees of success and failure appears to depend upon the quality of implementation. Some aspects of implementation, such as the preparation of a marketing plan and the measurement of performance against objectives, may be defined and quantified. But others, and probably the more important aspects, are more difficult to capture and define. They tend to be more subjective and qualitative in nature and embrace issues such as organisational culture and customer care and service. Both these topics are discussed in some detail.

Finally, I have included a chapter called Current issues and future trends and conclude with a summary chapter which highlights some of the key issues which have emerged in the book as a whole.

As with the earlier editions, the opportunity has been taken to include a significant amount of new material. This process was assisted by the comments of three anonymous reviewers and many of their suggestions have been incorporated. Both structure and content have also benefited from using the text on a number of Executive Development and MBA programmes and the feedback received from these. In addition, editing two major textbooks – The *IEBM Encyclopedia of Marketing* (International Thomson Business Press)

and *The Marketing Book* (5th edn) (Butterworth Heinemann) – has provided me with an unparalleled opportunity to benefit from the latest thinking of some of the most distinguished marketing writers in the world. As you will see from the recommendations for further reading, these are seminal sources for any serious student of marketing.

While the compilation of the book has benefited greatly from the inputs of others, in the final analysis the responsibility for its merits and failings rests with the author.

MICHAEL J. BAKER
January 2007

Acknowledgements

The author and publishers wish to thank the following for the use of their material within the text:

A.D. Little Inc., for Figures 4.6 and 4.7.

Administrative Science Quarterly, for Figure 21.3, from P. R. Lawrence and J. W. Lorsch, Differentiation and integration in complex organizations (1967).

Allyn & Bacon, for Figure 3.1, from R. A. Kerin and R. A. Peterson (eds) *Perspectives on Strategic Marketing Management* (1983); Table 9.2, from P. J. Robinson, C. W. Faris and Y. Wind, *Industrial Buying and Creative Marketing* (1967); Table 14.1, from R. A. Kerin, *Perspectives on Strategic Marketing Management* (1980).

AMACOM, for Figure 17.4, from A. Oxenfeldt, *Pricing Strategies* (1975).

American Management Association, for Table 4.4, from E. S. McKay, *Marketing Mystique* (1972); Figures 20.3 and 20.4, from T. A. Gannon (ed.) *Product Service Management* (1972).

Appleton-Century-Crofts, for Table 12.4, from C. R. Wasson et al., *Competition and Human Behaviour* (1968).

Booz, Allen & Hamilton Inc., for Figures 15.5 and 15.6.

Butterworth Heinemann, for Figures 6.1, 14.4 and Table 17.2, from M. J. Baker (ed.) *The Marketing Book* (4th edn) (1999).

CACI, for extract and Figure 12.3, from the *ACORN User Guide* (www.caci.co.uk).

California Management Review, for Figure 11.1, from R. M. Grant The resource-based theory of competitive advantage: implications for strategy formulation (1991).

Chicago Tribune, for Table 12.2.

Collier Macmillan, for Figures 13.5 and 13.7, from R. D. Buzzell and B. T. Gale, *The PIMS Principles: Linking Strategy to Performance* (1987); Figure 13.6, from T. Levitt, *The Marketing Imagination* (1983).

Cranfield School of Management, for Tables 19.1 and 19.4, from D. Corkindale and S. Kennedy, *The Evaluation of Advertising Objectives* (1974).

Design Council, for Table 15.1 and Figure 15.1, from R. Rothwell, P. Gardiner and K. Schott, *Design and the Economy* (1983).

DTI, for Table 8.8, from *Closing the Gap* (1998).

European Journal of Innovation Management, for Table 8.1, from Hart et al., The effectiveness of marketing information in enhancing new product success rates (1999).

European Journal of Marketing, for Figure 15.2, from L. G. Shostack, How to design a service (1982)

George Allen & Unwin, for Figure 7.3, from J. J. van Duijn, *The Long Wave in Economic Life* (1983); Table 19.2 from J. O'Shaughnessy, *Competitive Marketing: A Strategic Approach* (1984).

Goodyear, for Figure 12.1, from B. M. Enis, *Marketing Principles* (1977).

Government Actuary's Department and the Office of National Statistics, for Figure 7.1.

Gower, for Table 10.2, from J. Stapleton, *How to Prepare a Marketing Plan* (1989); Figure 8.1, from J. Saunders, *The Marketing Handbook* (1989).

Harvard Business Review, for Table 5.3, from N. Dhalla and S. Yuspeh, Forget the product life cycle concept! (1976); Table 19.3, from S. R. Fajen, More for your money from the media (1978); Figure 2.2, from M. E. Porter, How competitive forces shape strategy (1979); Figure 2.3, from M. E. Porter, The competitive advantage of nations (1990); Figures 3.2 and 15.3, from I. Ansoff, Strategies for diversification (1957); Figure 6.5, from J. F. Magee, Decision trees for decision making (1964); Figure 15.4, from S. C. Johnson and C. Jones, How to organize for new products (1957).

Harvard Business School, for Table 4.2, from M. Salter, *Course notes*, MBA Program (1968).

Harvard Business School Press, for Table 2.2, from G. Hamel and C. K. Prahalad, *Competing for the Future* (1994).

Heinemann, for Figure 4.4, from M. H. B. McDonald, *Marketing Plans* (1984).

Houghton-Mifflin, for Figure 2.1, from F. M. Scherer and D. Ross, *Industrial Market Structure and Economic Performance* (1990).

Hutchinson Business Books, for Figure 14.3, from P. Guptara, *The Basic Arts of Marketing* (1990); Figure 4.2, from A. Campbell, M. Devine and D. Young, *A Sense of Mission* (1990).

Intercollegiate Case Clearing House, for Table 4.1, from C. W. Hofer, *Conceptual Constructs for Formulating Corporate and Business Strategies* (1977).

International Thomson Business Press, for Tables 1.1 and 4.5, from M. J. Baker (ed.) *Encyclopedia of Marketing* (1999).

Intertext, for Figure 6.4, from B. M. Enis and C. L. Broome, *Marketing Decisions: A Bayesian Approach* (1973).

Irish Marketing Review, for Figure 20.2, from D. Carson and A. Gilmore, Customer care: the neglected domain (1989).

Irwin, for Table 23.1, from J. A. Howard, *Marketing Management* (1963); Figure 23.7, from E. A. Helfert, *Techniques of Financial Analysis* (1982).

J. Walter Thompson Co., for Figure 19.2, from T. Joyce, *What Do We Know about How Advertising Works?* (1967).

John Martin Publishing, for Figure 14.2, from J. Martin, The best practice of business, *Marketing Planning* (1978).

John Wiley, for Figure 14.1, from H. A. Lipson and J. R. Darling, *Introduction to Marketing: An Administrative Approach* (1971).

Journal of Business and International Marketing, for Figure 17.5, from B. J. Coe, Strategy in retreat: pricing drops out (1990).

Journal of Business Strategy, for Figure 5.16, from G. Day, Gaining insights through strategy analysis (1983).

Journal of Marketing Management, for Figure 21.1, from P. Doyle, What are the excellent companies? (1992); Figure 22.1, from J. W. Leppard and M. H. B. McDonald, Marketing planning and corporate culture (1991); Table 13.4, from L. de Chernatony and F. Dall'Olmo Riley (1998).

Journal of Marketing, for Table 12.3, from R. I. Haley, Benefit segmentation (1968); Figure 12.4, from

D. W. Twedt, How important to marketing strategy is the 'heavy user'? (1964).

KPMG, for Figure 24.1, from *Electronic Commerce* (1999).

Long Range Planning, for Figure 4.8 and Table 4.6, from T. G. Marx, Removing the obstacles to effective strategic planning (1991).

Macmillan, for Tables 15.1 and 18.1, from J. R. Evans and B. Berman, *Marketing* (1982).

McGraw-Hill, for Figure 5.15, from *Business Week* (28 April 1975); Figures 13.9 and 13.10, from *Business Week* (August 2005); Figures 5.21 and 15.3, from I. Ansoff, *Corporate Strategy* (1965).

McKinsey Quarterly, for Table 15.3, from R. C. Bennett and R. G. Cooper, The misuse of marketing: an American tragedy (1982); and Figures 20.5, 20.6, and 20.7.

Modern Textiles Magazine, for Figure 5.6, from J. P. Yale, Innovation of new products postpones the time of total maturity – nylon industry (1964).

Palgrave Macmillan, for Figure 3.7, from M. E. Porter, *The Competitive Advantage of Nations* (1990); Figures 5.7 and 5.8, from M. J. Baker, *Marketing New Industrial Products* (1975); Figure 6.2, from M. J. Baker, *Research for Marketing* (1991); Table 17.3, from M. J. Baker (ed.) *Marketing: Theory and Practice* (1996).

Paul Chapman Publishing, for Figures 13.1, 13.2 and 13.3, from G. Davies and J. Brooks, *Positioning Strategy in Retailing* (1989).

Penguin, for Table 23.4 and Figures 23.5 and 23.6, from J. Sizer, *An Insight into Management Accounting* (1979).

Philip Allan, for Tables 13.1, 13.2 and Figure 2.4, from M. J. Baker and S. Hart, *Marketing and Competitive Success* (1989).

Prentice Hall, for Table 5.5, from D. F. Abell and J. S. Hammond, *Strategic Market Planning* (1979); Figure 5.4, from P. Kotler, *Marketing Management* (1980); Figure 7.2, from K. Albrecht, *Stress and the Manager* (1979); Figures 13.4, 15.5 and 15.7 and Tables 15.4, 15.5 and 15.6, from M. J. Baker and S. Hart, *Product Strategy and Management* (1998).

Prism, for Figure 20.8, from T. J. Erickson, Beyond the quality revolution: linking quality to corporate strategy (1991).

Quarterly Review of Marketing, for Table 12.1, from M. Thomas, Market segmentation (1980).

Routledge, for Tables 7.2 and 7.3, from M. J. Baker (ed.) *Companion Encyclopedia of Marketing* (1995).

Shell International Chemical Co., for Figure 5.12, from *The Directional Policy Matrix: A New Aid to Corporate Planning* (1975).

Sidgwick & Jackson, for Figure 13.8, from D. K. Clifford and R. E. Cavanagh, *The Winning Performance: How America's High-growth Midsize Companies Succeed* (1985).

Sloan Management Review, for Table 10.1, from P. Kotler, W. Gregor and W. Rogers, The M.A. comes of age (1977).

Society of Management Accountants and National Society of Accountants, for Figure 18.1, from D. M. Lambert, *The Distribution Channels Decision* (1978).

Sociological Review, for Table 6.1, from P. Halfpenny, The analysis of qualitative data (1979).

The Marketing Review, for Table 12.5, from S. Dibb, Market segmentation implementation barriers and how to overcome them (January 2005).

University of Alabama, for Table 18.2, from D. L. Brady, *An Analysis of Factors Affecting the Methods of Exporting Used by Small Manufacturing Firms* (1978).

University of Bradford, for Table 5.1, from C. Firth, *New Approaches to Strategic Marketing Planning* (1980).

University of Bradford Management Centre, for Table 5.4, from G. J. Hooley, *MBA Core Course Lecture Notes 1979/80;* Tables 25.1 and 25.2, from J. Lynch, G. Hooley and J. Shepherd, *Effectiveness of British Marketing* (1988).

University of Illinois Press, for Figure 19.1, from W. Schramm, *The Process and Effects of Mass Communication* (1955).

University of Strathclyde, for Table 17.4, from H. Said, The relevance of price theory to pricing practice: an investigation of pricing policies and practices in UK industry (1981); Table 4.3 and Figure 4.1, from L. Gunn, *Teaching Notes* (1991).

West Publishing, for Figure 4.3, from C. W. Hofer and D. E. Schendel, *Strategy Formulation: Analytical Concepts* (1978).

Every effort has been made to trace all the copyright holders but, if any have been inadvertently overlooked, the publishers will be pleased to make the necessary arrangements at the first opportunity.

Acronyms

ADL	Arthur D. Little	IP	internet protocol
AID	automatic interaction detector	IPR	intellectual property rights
AIDA	awareness, interest, desire and action	ISP	internet service provider
AIO	attitudes, interests and opinions	IT	information technology
ASP	application service provider	JND	just noticeable difference
B2B	business-to-business	JV	joint venture
B2C	business-to-consumer	KAM	key account management
BCG	Boston Consulting Group	MDA	multiple discriminant analysis
BSC	balanced scorecard	MDS	multidimensional scaling
C2B	consumer-to-business	MEU	maximise [the] expected utility
C2C	consumer-to-consumer	MIS	management information system
CAC	cognitive, affective and conative	MkIS	marketing information system
CAD	computer-aided design	MSI	Marketing Science Institute
CAM	computer-aided manufacturing	NIC	newly industrialising country
CLV	customer lifetime value	NPD	new product development
CPI	customer perception index	OE	operational effectiveness
CRC	child-resistant container	OEM	original equipment manufacturer
CRM	customer relationship management/ customer relationship marketing	P2P	peer-to-peer
		PIMS	profit implications of market strategy
CS	customer service	PLC	product life-cycle
CSF	critical success factor	R&D	research and development
CSM	customer satisfaction management	R-A theory	resource-advantage theory
CSR	corporate social responsibility	RB	resource-based
CUGs	currently useful generalisations	RFID	radio frequency identification
DPM	directional policy matrix (Shell)	ROA	return on assets
DPS	Direct Payment Solutions	ROI	return on investment
DSL	digital subscriber lines	SBU	strategic business unit
DTI	Department for Trade and Industry (UK)	SCA	sustainable competitive advantage
EDI	electronic data interchange	SDA	sustainable differential advantage
EMV	expected monetary value	SIC/NTIC	standard industrial classification
FMCGs	fast moving consumer goods	SME	small- to medium-sized enterprise
GE	General Electric	SMP	strategic marketing planning
GM	genetically modified	SSoD	single sets of data
HOBO	human behaviour in organisations	SWOT	strengths, weaknesses, opportunities, threats
HRM	human resource management		
IBP	integrated brand promotion	TC	transaction cost
ICT	information and communication technology	USP	unique selling proposition
		VMS	vertical marketing system
IFC	institutions for collaboration	WOM	word of mouth
IMC	integrated marketing communication	WOMM	word of mouth marketing
IMP	Industrial Marketing and Purchasing Group		

MARKETING STRATEGY

CHAPTER 1 | Prologue

INTRODUCTION

Prologues, like overtures, are intended to achieve at least three objectives:

1. To establish the point of departure
2. To indicate the direction in which one is to proceed
3. To introduce some of the themes which will be encountered as the plot unfolds.

These, then, are the basic goals of this chapter in which we shall seek to define the general scope of the book, the audience for which it is intended, the information and learning objectives to be pursued, and the structure to be followed in attempting to meet these objectives.

THE POINT OF DEPARTURE

Writing in the spring 1983 issue of the *Journal of Marketing*, two well-known American professors of marketing, Yoram Wind and Thomas S. Robertson, offered the opinion that marketing had reached a point of discontinuity in its development as a discipline from an emphasis upon marketing management to a broadened perspective concerned with marketing strategy.

The early emphasis upon marketing management and the marketing functions – particularly advertising and selling, distribution, market research and product development – is not surprising. The manipulation of these elements of the marketing 'mix' allows tactical responses to the prevailing conditions in the markets in which one is competing. However, tactical manoeuvres tend to be sufficient to cope only with short-term and localised conditions and circumstances. They are only effective in the long term and on a large scale if they are coordinated and integrated within a more broadly based strategic framework. As the markets of the advanced industrialised economies of the Western world gradually moved from an endemic condition of undersupplied markets to one of potential oversupply, it was clear that marketing practices had to change. Tactical management was not able to cope with the intense competition of the new market conditions; something more was required. It was this recognition that led to what I have chosen to characterise as the 'rediscovery' of the marketing concept.

While most authors and commentators date the statement of the marketing concept to the 1950s and identify its articulation with the General Electric Company, it is obvious that such identification is purely a matter of convenience. Marketing did not just happen in the 1950s – its functions had been in daily use in some shape or form from the beginnings of trade and commerce way back in antiquity. What happened was that the changing balance resulted in the conclusion that supply is the servant of demand. Of course this has always been true, but under conditions of general scarcity demand tends to be basic and obvious. One does not require a sophisticated intelligence and planning system to identify attractive market opportunities. Rather one requires the most cost-effective production and distribution system. This encourages the production and sale of standardised products, which can minimise cost thus satisfying more customers. But the combined effects of technological innovation, increased competition, both national and international, and a slowing of growth in population (to mention but a few long-term trends) have resulted in a much more complex and competitive marketplace. In this environment survival, let alone success, calls for a new philosophy of business in which the process of manufacture or supply creation should be seen to start with a clear statement of customer needs – the marketing concept.

THE STRATEGIC PERSPECTIVE IN MARKETING

The adoption of the marketing concept and a marketing orientation (discussed in detail in Chapter 21) does not create or bring into existence new business functions but it does call for a change in both focus and emphasis, and it is this change of focus and emphasis that has led to the need for marketing-oriented strategy. In Wind and Robertson's view it was this strategic emphasis or perspective that was missing from the development of both marketing thought and practice. Specifically, they identified seven key limitations within the marketing field that are a direct consequence of the emphasis on management as opposed to strategy, namely:

1. A fixation with the brand as the unit of analysis
2. The interdisciplinary isolation of marketing
3. The failure to examine synergy in the design of the marketing programme
4. Marketing's short-run orientation
5. The lack of rigorous competitive analysis
6. The lack of an international orientation
7. The lack of an integrated strategic framework.

At the time, many thought that Wind and Robertson's criticisms were exaggerated but, 10 years later, many other commentators were questioning both the role and function of marketing in the organisation. Taken together, these criticisms were characterised by McKinsey & Co. (1993) as 'Marketing's mid-life crisis'. We shall return to these issues in Chapter 2 when addressing the question 'What is marketing?' but, for now, it should be stated that when the first edition of this book appeared in 1985 it was very much concerned with developing a strategic perspective of marketing. At the same time, it was also felt that to explore the nature of marketing strategy on its own without examining its relationship to marketing management would perpetuate the deficiency of a partial treatment which Wind and Robertson had criticised in the first place. Accordingly, in this book we seek to show how a strategic approach to marketing can be implemented through management of the marketing function.

At the outset, however, it will be useful to help distinguish between *strategic* and *tactical* (or managerial) decisions. Steiner and Miner (1977) suggest that this may be done along eight dimensions, namely:

1. *Importance:* Strategic decisions are significantly more important than tactical ones.
2. *Level at which conducted:* Strategic decisions are usually made by top management.
3. *Time horizon:* Strategies are long term, tactics short term.
4. *Regularity:* The formulation of strategy is continuous and irregular, tactics periodic and fixed time, e.g. annual budget/plan.
5. *Nature of problem:* Strategic problems are usually unstructured and unique and so involve considerable risk and uncertainty. Tactical problems are more structured and repetitive and the risks easier to assess.
6. *Information needed:* Strategies require large amounts of external information much of which relates to the future and is subjective. Tactical decisions depend more on internally generated accounting or market research information.
7. *Detail:* Strategy broad, tactics narrow and specific.
8. *Ease of evaluation:* Strategic decisions are more difficult to make.

Similarly, Weitz and Wensley (1984) distinguish between levels of strategic decision-making: 'Strategic decisions at the corporate level are concerned with acquisition, investments, and diversification', i.e. the management of a portfolio of businesses or strategic business units (SBUs).

> At the business or SBU level, strategic decisions focus on how to compete in an industry – or product – market. Business level strategy deals with achieving and maintaining a competitive advantage. Strategic decisions at the business level are concerned with selecting target market segments and determining the range of products to offer.

It is with these issues that *Marketing Strategy and Management* is mainly concerned.

MARKETING ORGANISATION AND MANAGEMENT

Much of the discussion about marketing's 'mid-life crisis' prompted by a McKinsey article in 1993 and Webster's (1992) 'The changing role of marketing in the corporation' came about as a result of changes in the role of marketing within the organisation. Conventionally, discussions of organisation for marketing focused upon the existence of a marketing department responsible for management of the various mix functions. However, as a result of increasing competition through the 1970s and 80s the emphasis changed from the manipulation of the mix functions to a view which saw marketing's role as one involving the entire organisation. Thus, Piercy and Cravens (1999) observed: 'Marketing organisation has become a fundamental strategic issue concerned with intra-organisational relationships and inter-organisational alliances, and the management of critical boundary spanning environmental interfaces.' In Webster's (1997) view this represents the fourth stage in the evolution of marketing organisation. To begin with, marketing was equated with sales and demand generation activities. In the second phase, bureaucratic and hierarchical organisational forms are developed to plan and control the performance of specialists. In turn, this leads into a third phase where marketing becomes identified as a function in its own right responsible for the development of integrated marketing strategies. Nowadays, however, in response to competitive pressures, marketing competence has become integrated with other business functions in team centred organisational processes focused on the customer.

Much of the debate on organisational structure is reflected in the distinction between 'marketing orientation' and 'market orientation'. Superficially, this may appear a semantic quibble but the distinction is much more than this. In essence, a marketing orientation assumes the dominance of the marketing function in managing the organisation's interfaces with its markets, whereas a market orientation mirrors Drucker's (1954) original conceptualisation of the role of marketing as the need to focus all the organisation's efforts on the needs of customers and markets.

Piercy and Cravens (1999) distinguish four different levels of organisational strategy and suggest that each of these calls for a different kind of analysis, as reflected in Table 1.1. They cite a number of examples to underline the speed of change in the organisation of marketing. Thus, 'in 1997, IBM announced its global initiative customer relationship management in which most marketing activities are embedded. The goal is to coordinate customer relationships by focusing management on core business processes instead of traditional functions.' Similarly, Procter & Gamble adopted a 'customer business development structure' while the Unilever-owned Elida Faberge 'abandoned its conventional brand management and marketing management roles by creating customer development and brand development as centres of expertise, with category management

TABLE 1.1 Levels and focus of organisational analysis in marketing

Strategic level	Unit of analysis	Examples of major issues	Examples of new organisational forms
FUNCTIONAL	Marketing subsystems	Organising and coordinating sub-functions of marketing such as advertising, marketing research, sales operations	Channel management. Logistics/services specialists. Information/technology specialists
BUSINESS	Marketing department	The departmentation of marketing and internal structure of the marketing department. The integration of marketing sub-functions Relationships with other functions	Sector/segment management. Trade marketing. Investment specialists. Venture/new product departments
CORPORATE	Divisional marketing responsibilities and group-wide marketing issues	Centralisation/decentralisation of marketing decision-making and relationships between central and peripheral marketing units	Marketing exchange and coalition companies. Network organisations
ENTERPRISE	Strategic alliances and networks	External relationships and boundary-spanning with strategic marketing partners. Marketing 'make-or-buy' choices	Partnerships Alliances

SOURCE: Piercy, N. and Cravens, D. W. (1999) Marketing organization and management, in M. J. Baker (ed.) *Encyclopedia of Marketing*. London: International Thomson Business Press, p. 191

working with retailer customers as part of the sales organisation'.

Piercy and Cravens also cite extensively from a Marketing Science Institute (MSI)-sponsored publication *Reflections on the Futures of Marketing* (Lehmann and Jocz, 1997) to which George Day and Frederick Webster made important contributions on marketing organisation.

While there was an element of overstatement in Wind and Robertson's claims they had a point and this book represents an attempt to meet the criticisms they voice by providing both a description and analysis of the nature of marketing strategy. But to write a book on marketing strategy without examining its relationship to marketing management would seem to perpetuate the deficiency of a partial treatment which Wind and Robertson criticised in the first place. Accordingly, this book seeks to show how a strategic approach to marketing can be implemented through management of the marketing function.

However, before describing how this is to be attempted in any detail, it will be helpful if we anticipate our own advice and spell out:

1. What is the need to be satisfied?
2. What is the objective to be achieved?
3. What assumptions underlie the approach and method selected?

NEEDS

From the preceding section it should be clear that the basic need to be satisfied is a formal description and analysis of both the strategic and managerial aspects of marketing. However the vital question is, how has this need been identified?; for there can be little doubt that few if any practitioners responsible for marketing strategy and management have expressed a demand for a book on the subject. Indeed many practitioners would readily tell you that marketing is an art or craft which you practise and that it is practice or experience, not theorising or book-learning, which makes you proficient.

I reject this lack of overt demand on at least three counts. First, as will become clear in Chapter 4 when discussing the environment, there has been a radical change in recent years to the extent that the prevailing and likely future conditions differ radically from those of the 1970s and 80s when most senior managers were acquiring their experience. While some have been able to adjust to the changed conditions the overall sluggishness of the economy and the number of business failures suggest that the majority have not.

Second, the adoption of a marketing orientation is well advanced and no longer confined to the fast-moving consumer goods (FMCG) companies where it originated. All kinds of manufacturing companies now subscribe to the marketing approach as do service organisations in both the public and private sector whether for profit or not-for-profit. This widespread acceptance has resulted in a massive increase in demand for people to fill marketing appointments and it would seem sensible to try and prepare and train young persons to fill such posts rather than pursue a policy of trial and error learning through experience. Third, the body of knowledge based upon experience has now become so extensive that it makes sense to try and distil and codify it so that it can be communicated formally through books and other media. If experience, synthetic or real, is the key to the identification and solution of problems, who needs a book on the subject? Clearly this is an overstatement, for if everyone subscribed to this view there would be no book, nor a reader for these words. As in most things, the truth probably lies between the two extremes – managerial decision-making cannot be learned from books alone, but it is equally unlikely that it can be learned without them other than possibly by a gifted few with an intuitive flair for it.

A balance of formal learning and practice in application is required. Skills such as driving a car certainly fall into this category – flying aeroplanes even more so, for they involve three dimensions as opposed to two. In fact, flying aeroplanes provides a good analogy with managing an organisation – much of the activity is routine and can be handled satisfactorily in an almost reflex manner, thus leaving the practitioner free to concentrate upon two factors critical to continued success in executing the skill – anticipation and planning – while still maintaining the integrity of the system through a feedback and control system.

Like flying, management has become much more complex in this century. Speed is an obvious example and requires very sophisticated systems to maintain the integrity and safety of the machine. Everything must be done to much finer tolerances and the pilot must depend upon aids to his skill which were unknown and unnecessary in the early days of flying. The substitution of radar for visual observation is but one example of a situation where science and technology are required to give sufficient advance warning of hazards to permit evasive action to be taken. Of course, as many near misses bear witness, in the final analysis it is the pilot's observation and skill which are critical. In the management context, speed is the speed of change and demands elaborate forecasting systems to predict the future conditions likely to be met by the organisation. Similarly, size and complexity have increased markedly and require more extensive and more intricate systems to maintain control.

Without wishing to labour the analogy, the point being made is simply that managerial decision-making is a blend of routine and predictable events with occasional but potentially very hazardous interruptions. Therefore, it makes good sense to define and describe the routine occurrences and to develop standard operating procedures to deal with them. By doing so, it will be possible to delegate responsibility for routine to a lower level of management (or to a mechanical or electronic control system) and leave time free for the anticipating and planning functions. It also makes good sense to accept that if standard operating procedures evolve then they should be formalised and codified into a 'rule book' to which reference can be made as appropriate.

OBJECTIVES

And so to the justification for this book. In the author's opinion managerial decision-making itself is amenable to description, definition and codification. Hence, standard procedures for identifying and solving problems may be created. However, it cannot be overemphasised that providing a framework for managerial decision-making cannot automatically guarantee correct or 'good' decisions. The selection of data to be used and their interpretation is still in the hands of the decision-maker.

The real point is that everyone is fallible. For

those who are skilled decision-makers this book will provide an aide-memoire – a cockpit checklist. While everyone likes to think that the pilot can get his jumbo jet off the ground without such assistance (and, even more important, back down again), it is comforting to know that use of a checklist prevents him omitting a vital step in the procedure.

For those less gifted or less experienced, the purpose of the book is the same – to provide a structured approach to managerial problem-solving – but its contribution is likely to be greater. Indeed I would claim that, as many management problems are of a recurrent type and require the exercise of only a minimal amount of judgement, then following the procedures and methods prescribed in this book will lead to a successful outcome in 95% of the problems one is likely to meet. This is not to decry judgement – far from it – merely to put it into perspective.

In light of the above arguments the objective to be achieved may be stated as:

- To provide a comprehensive and integrated framework for the direction and management of the marketing function.

It must be stressed that it is the framework that is claimed to be comprehensive and integrated. While it is hoped that the overall treatment is integrated also, it manifestly cannot be comprehensive. However, references to more specialised sources will enable the reader to follow up on topics on which they require more detail.

ASSUMPTIONS

Assumption 1 is that readers have read a basic textbook on the subject and/or have some business experience. As the author of a basic textbook I have tried to make this work complementary and avoid duplication as far as possible. Of course there are situations where repetition is essential for clarification and desirable for reinforcement, but, in general, *Marketing* (Baker, 2006) is primarily descriptive while this book is analytic and normative.

Assumption 2 is that there is a 'wheel' of management which revolves through a sequence of conceptualisation, planning, implementation, evaluation and feedback. Assumption 3 is that diagnosis must precede prognosis and Assumption 4 is that while firms may be at any stage of the management wheel it will simplify the analysis if a clean sheet start-up is assumed and so start with conceptualisation and diagnosis before proceeding to planning, prognosis, etc., in an ordered sequence (the organising principle for the book as a whole). Assumptions 5 to 8 are:

5. That the majority of cases are in existing organisations/institutions and that action plans must be based on realistic proposals for the transition from the present to the desired future state.
6. That the broad means of achieving one's objective is a strategic decision and that awareness of broad strategic alternatives must precede the formulation of action plans.
7. That the translation of plans into action is a managerial responsibility and that marketing has a primary role to play.
8. That planning and management are iterative and interactive so that measurement of performance, feedback, control and adjustment are essential elements of the managerial task.

While the above assumptions are the ones on which this book has been developed, it is important to recognise an important qualification – in order to be comprehensive many of the practices and procedures described may be neither relevant nor appropriate for the small to medium-sized enterprise (SME). As presented in standard textbooks, the normative theory of marketing almost invariably adopts a 'big business' perspective. Given that more than 90% of people work for organisations with less than 200 employees (SMEs), one should not automatically assume that they are either relevant or applicable in such firms. This issue was examined in some detail by Lancaster and Waddelow (1998) in an article in which they explored specifically the role of strategic marketing planning in SMEs.

A review of existing literature indicates that both the concept and implementation of marketing planning appear to be at variance with the philosophy and practice of small firms. In order to test this perception delegates at a management seminar were interviewed to see whether or not their companies had a formal strategic marketing plan. Of the 20 respondents only three (15%) had such a plan but they regarded it as a chore rather than an ongoing process. The remaining 85% did not have a marketing plan and explained this away with a variety of 'reasons', which may be summarised as:

■ Lack of focus (market orientation, direction, consensus)
■ Lack of capability (knowledge, skills, resources)
■ Lack of will (desire, faith, commitment, motivation).

Clearly, what is called for is adaptation of the normative theory as applicable to the large organisation in order to meet the needs of SMEs.

The importance of doing this was underlined in as report entitled 'Marketing success in fast growth SMEs' published as a result of work by the Marketing Council and Warwick Business School's SME Centre (1997). Based upon a series of case studies, the report identifies nine fundamental lessons about how marketing can work for growing SMEs. These lessons were identified as:

■ *Professional advice:* outside professionals can act as a catalyst, to focus the business on the importance of marketing.
■ *Basic techniques:* simple techniques are required, e.g. segmenting the market, or using existing information.
■ *Customer focus:* this will improve business performance because you will be better able to give customers what they really want.
■ *The need to plan:* the discipline of putting the customer first brings with it a range of benefits, e.g. systematic planning, prioritising and measuring effectiveness, all of which aid performance.
■ *New focus changes other factors:* focusing on customer needs changes the whole outlook of the business as it reviews all its functions in a new light.
■ *New rules create new markets:* legislation and regulations have created new opportunities for those actively seeking them. This is a real growth area.
■ *Competitive advantage:* by focusing on customer needs and marketing issues, SMEs can establish a competitive advantage, as they target their operations on what is really required of them by the customer.

- *Changed outlook:* marketing can become the central business function, which increases the firm's competitiveness.
- *Staffing changes:* staff need to change to adopt the new philosophy.

As will become clear in later chapters, this advice might just as well have been offered to senior managers in large companies. In other words, the principles are the same but their implementation will be a matter of scale and degree appropriate to the complexity of the organisation and the issues it is addressing.

ANALOGY AND METAPHOR

Everett Rogers (2003) argues that the speed with which people will be willing to modify their current behaviour and adapt to change is the function of five factors or characteristics which he identified as:

- Relative advantage
- Complexity
- Compatibility
- Communicability
- Trialability.

Of these five factors the first four are perceptual and depend on the knowledge, attitudes and experience of the decision-maker. They will also be influenced by the specific context and situation in which a decision is to be made.

In simple terms *relative advantage* reflects the scale and nature of the additional benefits that will arise from the changed behaviour. *Complexity* represents the degree of difficulty perceived in adoption and is closely linked to *compatibility* – how similar or different the new thing is to the established way of doing things – and *communicability* – the degree of ease or difficulty experienced in explaining the innovation to others. The final characteristic of *trialability* measures the ability of the potential user to experience the innovation without final commitment to it. It is essentially objective but may also be perceived subjectively.

In the case of physical objects, evaluation of an innovation is facilitated by the existence of phys-

ical evidence and the ability to demonstrate performance. For intangible objects such as services and ideas, this is more problematic and innovators frequently have to resort to analogy and metaphor in order to communicate the nature of and potential benefits associated with their innovation. The case of strategic marketing planning is a case in point and provides a good example of the barriers to the adoption of a new (and recommended) managerial practice. It also helps explain why textbooks such as this are written the way they are and why readers must interpret them in the context of the situation in which they find themselves. We will address the latter point first.

The purpose of a textbook is to summarise the current and accepted body of knowledge for the subject with which it is concerned – in the present case marketing strategy and management. Depending upon the scope (length) of the textbook, it may be more or less comprehensive than others but, in terms of the core ideas and principles with which it is concerned, it should not differ to any significant degree from any other textbook on the same subject. Further, the structure and development of the subject matter is likely to follow a similar pattern. This is so because the authors of textbooks are concerned with the normative theory that represents current perceptions and beliefs about the subject, and the best way of applying it in practice.

However, this creates a dilemma when one considers the context in which the normative theory is to be applied and requires the author to make certain assumptions. If one believes one is dealing with an unsophisticated audience and/or one which wants an unequivocal treatment of the subject, then the treatment is likely to be prescriptive. Conversely, if the audience is more sophisticated and has more knowledge and/or experience of the subject, then the author may acknowledge the need to question or qualify certain generalisations or prescriptions contained in the current theory. I have assumed this book is addressed to the latter audience!

One further issue needs to be resolved. While it is true that over 90% of all people work for SMEs with less than 200 employees, there is little evidence of strategic marketing planning within these companies as was highlighted in the

Lancaster and Waddelow (1998) paper referred to earlier. Whether this accounts for the higher failure rate of SMEs is an issue on which the reader will have to form their own opinion having considered the evidence in this book.

THE PRACTICE OF MARKETING

Yoram (Jerry) Wind (1997), of the Wharton School, identified a number of key issues concerning the practice of marketing in the twenty-first century.

As has been noted elsewhere, with the growing recognition of marketing as the key business philosophy, it has become necessary to reappraise the role of the marketing function. Wind suggests that,

> In considering these required changes and their implications, management may want to consider 12 interrelated questions:
> 1. Is marketing and its focus on meeting and anticipating customer needs widely accepted as a key business philosophy?
> 2. Are your business and corporate strategies focused on creating value to all your stakeholders?
> 3. Do your objectives include customer satisfaction and the creation of value?
> 4. Is the marketing function integrated with the other functions of the company as part of the key value creating processes?
> 5. Are the key marketing positions market segment (or key accounts) managers?
> 6. Are products viewed as part of an integrated product and service offering that delivers the desired benefit positioning for the target segment?
> 7. Is your marketing strategy global in its scope?
> 8. Are you utilising market research and modelling for generating and evaluating your marketing and marketing driven business strategies?
> 9. Are you relying on information technology as an integral part of your marketing strategies?
> 10. Does a significant part of your marketing efforts constitute innovative practices not previously used by you and your competitors?
> 11. Are you forming strategic alliances for co-marketing activities and are you building your market-

> ing strategies on the development of long-term relationships with your clients?
> 12. Are you focusing your attention and resources on message effectiveness (instead of media power) and value-based pricing (instead of discounting)?

Wind concludes that in order to succeed in the twenty-first century, it is not sufficient to answer 'Yes' to these 12 questions. To be successful it is necessary to involve the whole organisation in the integration of these activities into a focused and market-oriented strategy. These are themes we address throughout the book. But, if marketing is everybody's interest do we still need a dedicated marketing function?

WHY MARKETING STILL MATTERS

The above heading was the title of an article by Kamran Kashani (1997), which was itself a summary of a longer report that had appeared in *Long Range Planning*. In summary, the report led to the conclusion that:

> The marketing function in companies may appear to be under threat from 'own label' products, re-engineering, and advances in information technology. But it is alive and well and has undergone important shifts in recent years so as to provide a better service for top management. It has frequently become more of a line than a staff responsibility, it has developed a strategic bias, and it has become diffused throughout the organisation.
>
> Increasing price competition, more (general) competition and the growing role of customer service are among the most important changes facing marketers generally ... Four key management tasks stand out: Improving product quality, developing new products, keeping up with customers and improving customer service. The three most relevant competencies for marketers are: Strategic thinking, communication capability and sensitivity to customers. Specialist marketing skills appear to be among the least important.

We believe these conclusions still apply and endorse them.

SCOPE OF THE BOOK

To provide a perspective of the book as a whole, Chapter 2 addresses the subject of 'Marketing and competition'. Beginning with a definition of 'competition' and the role it performs in ensuring that scarce resources are used to maximise satisfaction, we then examine the role which marketing plays in this process. The concept of 'market structure' is then introduced both as a consequence of and an influence upon the conduct and performance of firms in competition with one another. The concept of international competition is then introduced and supported by an extended review of Michael Porter's discussion of *The Competitive Advantage of Nations* (1990). Next, we offer a broadly based assessment of the contribution of marketing to competitive success and conclude with an assessment of what will be necessary to compete successfully in the future – essentially a knowledge-based, learning organisation.

Chapter 3, 'Marketing and corporate strategy', seeks to establish the point of departure by defining the development of the marketing orientation and the nature of marketing strategy, and comparing the latter with the broader concept of corporate strategy. The conclusion is that the two are very similar, although marketing strategy may be seen as a subset of corporate strategy responsible mainly for anticipating and planning. The larger concept embraces issues of organisation design and control which go beyond marketing per se. Then, it is proposed that there is only a small set of strategic options open to the decision-maker and these are defined as a backcloth for an examination of basic marketing strategies. The chapter concludes with a statement of the functions of marketing management – analysis, planning, implementation and control – which serves as an introduction to the extended treatment of the topics in the remainder of the book.

Chapter 4, 'Principles of strategic marketing planning' (SMP), looks first at the evolution of management systems and the role of mission, vision and strategic intent before moving to the heart of the issue by proposing definitions, a framework for SMP and some basic principles to be observed in developing and implementing a strategic marketing plan. It is then argued that the need for SMP is continuous, in the sense that every

innovation contains within itself the seeds of its own destruction, and will increase the user's awareness and expectations which will prepare the way for new and improved substitutes. Thus marketers need to formulate strategy in terms of the underlying needs and satisfactions of customers rather than the specific products or services which serve as the means of delivery of these satisfactions. Equally they must be sensitive to the inevitability of change summarised in the concept of the product life-cycle (PLC), an analysis of which leads to a proposal to use it as a key element in the process of SMP.

Chapter 5, 'Analytical frameworks for strategic marketing planning', builds upon the foundations introduced in Chapter 4 and suggests techniques and procedures for implementing SMP. To begin with we look at demand curves and the product life-cycle (PLC) concept. We propose that the latter provides a highly useful framework for organising our thinking about the evolution of products, firms and industries, and the appropriate strategies and tactics associated with the phases of birth, growth, maturity and decline. The inevitability of this progression prompts the view that an organisation should seek to develop a portfolio of products which are at different stages of the cycle and so ensure the firm's long-term survival. The ideas of the product portfolio and portfolio analysis are extended to examine analytical approaches developed by successful companies such as Shell and GEC, and the techniques of gap, scenario and SWOT analysis, all of which help the decision-maker structure and implement strategic marketing plans. We also take the opportunity to introduce Baker's Box as an introduction to the ideas of segmentation, targeting and positioning which are the subject of extended treatment later in the book.

Chapter 6, 'Research for marketing', was placed much later in earlier editions as an element of the marketing mix, and a specialised aspect of the management of the marketing function. Experience with using the text suggests that it would be more appropriate to discuss research methods used in marketing before exploring the kinds of data the manager requires in developing a focused marketing strategy and plan. The chapter opens with a discussion of the factors that create particular difficulties in seeking to apply formal analytical procedures to marketing decisions, namely:

- Many marketing problems are more or less unique
- Buyers can think for themselves
- Most marketing problems are very complex.

To help overcome these difficulties, it is argued that the first step must be to establish just what information is available or may be acquired, to assess its worth, and then combine it with one's own experience and judgement to reach a decision. A review of sources of secondary and primary data leads naturally into a discussion of data reduction and analysis as a means of imposing structure and meaning on what otherwise might constitute an 'information overload'.

The chapter concludes with a review of decision-making under uncertainty and the ways in which decision-makers may combine objective 'facts' with their own subjective judgement to reach a decision using a Bayesian approach.

Part 2, 'The Marketing Appreciation', contains seven chapters. Chapter 7, 'Macro-environmental analysis', is based on the proposition that the external environment constitutes the ultimate constraint upon the firm and dictates the boundary conditions within which it must operate. Following a review of the major forces that influence and shape the environment – demographic, social, cultural, political, economic and technological factors – attention is focused on the argument that there are discernible cyclical and secular trends in the overall pattern of business activity. An analysis of four basic kinds of economic cycle and broad theories of economic growth lends support for the existence of an underlying process or life-cycle and reinforces the use of the PLC as a basic organising principle. The need to take account of the nature of competition in the marketplace, discussed in Chapter 2, is reviewed, with particular emphasis on the importance of non-price competition and the implications this has for marketing strategy. Finally the chapter provides some guidelines for the commissioning and execution of an environmental audit as an essential prerequisite to the formulation of a marketing strategy.

Chapter 8, 'Industry and competitor analysis', builds upon the macro-discussion of competition in Chapter 2 by exploring in more detail, and from a micro-perspective, competition between the individual players in the industry. The chapter opens with a review of the nature and importance of competitor analysis before introducing the notion of the value chain as a model that helps to highlight the interdependencies between producers, their suppliers and their customers – a perspective which helps explain the growing interest in networks and relationships in recent years. This leads naturally into a review of critical success factors, and the skills and competencies that firms need to succeed against the competition. Three further topics included in Chapter 8 are benchmarking, the identification of 'best practices' and the growing importance of strategic alliances, all of which have assumed growing importance in recent years.

Chapter 9, 'Customer analysis', addresses the nature of 'buyer behaviour' and poses the fundamental question 'How do buyers choose?' Following a limited and eclectic review of four different disciplinary explanations of choice behaviour, six concepts are examined because of the light they throw on the basic issue of how individuals and organisations choose between alternatives, namely:

- Selective perception
- The hierarchy of needs
- The hierarchy of effects
- Dissonance
- 'Buy tasks' and 'Buy phases'
- The characteristics of goods.

In and of themselves, none of the basic models, or the key concepts, appears sufficient to reflect the complexity of real-world purchase decisions. So a composite model of buyer behaviour is proposed that seeks to incorporate and synthesise both objective and subjective considerations.

The need for a composite model of buyer behaviour rests essentially on the fact that the total demand for a product is the aggregate of the demand of all the individuals who have a need for it backed up by purchasing power. In that each of these individuals will bring to the purchase decision their own values and perceptions, we have to allow for these when presenting the 'facts' about our product to them. However, with limited exceptions, very few suppliers can afford to tailor their output to the precise needs of the individual customer (even services have to be standardised to some degree), and it follows that to compete successfully one must steer a careful course between complete homogeneity and total heterogeneity. To achieve this compromise marketers have developed an extensive range of techniques for aggregating individual demands or, conversely, disaggregating total demand, into worthwhile groupings or segments. To do so calls for a 'customer audit' and 'market segmentation' that is the subject of Chapter 12.

In Chapter 10 the analysis is directed inwards to identify and quantify insofar as possible the firm's assets, resources, skills and competencies through the execution of a marketing audit. In Chapter 11 the outputs of the marketing appreciation are pulled together in what we call the 'matching' process. Matching represents a more balanced view of strategy formulation and execution than that implied by the structure, conduct performance approach popularised by Michael Porter that tends to emphasise external factors as those determining the firm's strategy. While we have acknowledged that the environment, competition and customers all proscribe the firm's freedom of action, they don't control it. If they did there would be no need for managers as the course of action available would be predetermined. Because it is not, management can exercise control, and this it what it seeks to optimise by matching its strengths with opportunities, avoiding threats and correcting potential or actual weaknesses. The view that organisations have a degree of control over their destiny is implicit in the resource-based view of the firm and we look at this as background to the conduct of a SWOT analysis.

In Chapter 12 we pick up the idea of market segmentation and a wide range of different approaches is considered in some detail – demographic, locational, psychographic and behaviouristic – as a basis for suggesting how and when segmentation should be used as an appropriate strategic approach.

Chapter 13, 'Positioning and branding', recognises the fact that a sustainable competitive advantage depends increasingly upon the seller's ability to develop a distinctive personality and reputation in the perception of prospective buyers. Key concepts such as positioning, branding, perceptual mapping, niche marketing and the augmented

product are defined and described and the chapter concludes with a discussion of the view that increasingly companies will come to be seen as brands. This chapter also completes Part 2 and prepares the way for Part 3 'Managing the Marketing Mix'.

In Chapter 14, 'The marketing mix', we recognise that marketing planners have a number of key factors or variables which they can manipulate in seeking to devise a distinctive and differentiated marketing plan. Several approaches to classifying the mix elements from the basic 4 Ps of product, price, promotion and place to Borden's extended listing of 12 elements are considered. The chapter concludes with an examination of the management of the marketing mix and acts as an introduction to Part 3 in which we explore each of the major mix elements in some detail.

Chapter 15, 'Product policy and management', begins with a reminder that most business is transacted by existing organisations with commitments to both products and customers. It follows that a preoccupation with one's product is not a negation of the marketing concept, but an essential precondition of survival. Similarly, it is argued that the emphasis upon user needs and product benefits has distracted attention from the product's physical characteristics, and it is contended that a more even balance needs to be struck between the two. The interaction between product and market is implicit in the four core strategies considered earlier – market penetration, market development, product development and diversification – each of which is reviewed in terms of the most appropriate product policy, and in the idea of the product portfolio. To a lesser or greater degree all require development of the product, which leads naturally to a discussion of the role and nature of the new product development process and alternative forms for achieving this. Depending upon its stage in the life-cycle, the product will require differing degrees of emphasis upon the other elements, and these are summarised in terms of the four major stages – introduction, growth, maturity and decline. The chapter concludes with a discussion of ways and means of monitoring the product's performance.

'Packaging' (the subject of Chapter 16) does not always receive separate treatment in marketing texts, despite the fact that it may provide 'the just discernible difference' on which so many choice decisions hinge. In part this may be because packaging is considered an intrinsic element of the product and treated as such, in part because it is seen as a promotional tool and the subject of passing reference alongside the detailed discussion of advertising. The chapter opens with some definitions of packaging that underline the different roles it plays in protecting and selling goods, and is followed by an extended discussion of the five criteria to be considered in developing a package – appearance, protection, function, cost and disposability. To round off the chapter the issues and steps involved in developing a pack are reviewed.

Chapter 17, 'Pricing policy and management', acknowledges that, while firms prefer to compete on dimensions other than price, nonetheless price is of critical importance in the buying decision and calls for a high level of attention. Accordingly, while marketers might deprecate the economists' overwhelming emphasis upon price as the mechanism for adjusting supply and demand in the marketplace they can learn many useful lessons from price theory. A number of key concepts such as elasticity, fixed, variable, marginal and opportunity costs are considered, as are some of the major limitations of price theory as an explanation of the real world, e.g. its assumption of profit maximisation, lack of dynamism, neglect of subjective factors, etc. Pricing objectives are examined, together with the three broad approaches to price determination – cost plus, flexible mark-up and marginal cost. Finally, the role of pricing in the marketing mix is explored as are the three basic strategies – skimming, penetration and value based.

The comparative neglect of 'Distribution and sales policy' provides the introduction to Chapter 18. Given the functions performed by channels of distribution and the important role these play in the creation of time, place and possession utilities, such neglect is seen as surprising. The composition and structure of alternative channels, and the factors that influence them, are described, as are the considerations that condition channel selection decisions. In the latter context much will depend upon whether the producer wishes to pursue an undifferentiated, differentiated or concentrated marketing strategy and intends to push or pull the product through the distribution channel. All these alternatives receive attention. The chapter

concludes with a brief summary of the personal selling function.

Chapter 19 deals with the final element of the marketing mix – 'Promotion policy and management'. Like distribution, promotion and particularly mass-media advertising is often regarded as a cost-creating function which adds little or nothing to the value of a product – a viewpoint which finds little or no support in the evidence presented here. Starting with the argument that awareness is a necessary prerequisite to purchase, Schramm's model of the communication process is reviewed to clarify the essential point that all information has to be transmitted by a sender to a receiver. While personal communication may be the most direct method, it is by no means always the most efficient or cost-effective, and it is here that the impersonal and indirect methods classified collectively as 'promotion' have an important role to play. Ever since Lord Leverhulme offered the opinion that half his advertising expenditure was wasted, marketers have been increasingly concerned with the problem of determining which half. To solve this conundrum one must first have some working hypothesis as to how advertising works and the two major schools of thought – that attitudes cause behaviour and vice versa – are analysed to throw light on the problem. Once one has formed an opinion as to how advertising works it becomes possible to formulate objectives and state policies for their achievement. In turn this leads to a discussion as to how one should set an advertising appropriation and measure the effectiveness of the expenditures incurred.

The chapter concludes with a look at the problems involved in choosing between the various promotional alternatives in order to develop an optimum promotional mix. This chapter concludes Part 3 and introduces Part 4 'Implementing Marketing'.

Since the publication of the first edition in 1985 the importance of service has become much more widely recognised, to the point that specialised textbooks are now available concerned solely with this aspect of the marketing mix. Within a general text it is not possible to give the topic extended coverage but Chapter 20 explores some of the key issues of customer care and their contributions to competitive marketing strategy. The chapter concludes with a discussion of how one should offer and price customer services.

Chapter 21, 'Developing a marketing culture', opens with a discussion of the relationship between organisational structure and strategy formulation. As recognised elsewhere in the book, most strategies are developed by organisations which already exist. Only rarely does management have the opportunity of the clean sheet start-up situation so easily assumed in the textbooks. Accordingly, strategy formulation must take place within the constraints of existing structures, and the existing values and attitudes associated with them. While marketers naturally emphasise the importance of a marketing orientation, it is quite clear that other functional aspects of business may colour an organisation's overall orientation – R&D, production, sales and finance. The nature of these orientations is examined together with the underlying concepts of organisational climate, corporate personality and culture as the basis for determining what is required to develop a marketing-oriented organisation. The chapter concludes with a review of the issues involved in implementing marketing.

Chapter 22 takes a brief look at the nature of the short-term marketing plan. The need for formal plans is justified and a normative framework proposed. The conditions necessary for producing market plans are spelt out, as are the key elements in the marketing plan itself.

Within the constraints imposed by the environment, the firm will seek to control its own actions in order to achieve its corporate objectives in the most effective and efficient way, and control is the theme of Chapter 23. The primary concern of marketers must be to optimise the marketing mix and to do so they must attempt to quantify and measure the contribution of its different parts. To this end cost–volume–profit relationships are examined, as are the concepts of cash flow and present value. Finally, in order to assess both one's own and one's competitors' performance, a brief look is taken at the interpretation of corporate accounts through the use of management ratios.

Chapter 24, 'Current issues and future trends', is an overview of some of the 'hot topics' in marketing at the time of writing and includes coverage of information technology and marketing, electronic commerce, ethics in marketing, green marketing, corporate social responsibility, globalisation and marketing strategy, and guerilla tactics in marketing.

Chapter 25, 'Recapitulation', is just that. Unlike this introduction, which is designed to give a broad overview of the scope and coverage of the book as a whole, the final chapter is more eclectic, in that it seeks to tease out what I regard as the key lessons to be learnt from a reasonably extensive and rigorous review of the field as a whole.

REFERENCES

Baker, M. J. (2006) *Marketing* (7th edn). Helensburgh: Westburn.

Drucker, P. (1954) *The Practice of Management*. New York: Harper & Row.

Kashani, K. (1997) Why marketing still matters, in *Mastering Management*. London: Financial Times Management, pp. 165–70.

Lancaster, G. and Waddelow, I. (1998) An empirical investigation into the process of strategic marketing planning in SMEs: its attendant problems, and proposals towards a new practical paradigm, *Journal of Marketing Management*, **14**(8): 853–78.

Lehmann, D. R. and Jocz, K. E. (eds) (1997) *Reflections on the Futures of Marketing*. Cambridge, MA: Marketing Science Institute.

McKinsey & Co. (1993) Marketing's mid-life crisis, *The McKinsey Quarterly*, **2**: 17–28.

Piercy, N. and Cravens, D. W. (1999) Marketing organization and management, in M. J. Baker (ed.) *Encyclopedia of Marketing*. London: International Thomson Business Press, pp. 186–207.

Porter, M. E. (1990) *The Competitive Advantage of Nations*. Basingstoke: Macmillan – now Palgrave Macmillan.

Rogers, E. (2003) *Diffusion of Innovations* (5th edn). New York: Free Press.

Steiner, G. and Miner, J. (1977) *Management Policy and Strategy; Text, Readings and Cases*. New York: Macmillan.

The Marketing Council/Warwick Business School SME Centre (1997) Marketing success in fast growth SMEs, *Marketing Business* (October).

Webster, F. (1992) The changing role of marketing in the corporation, *Journal of Marketing* (October).

Webster, F. (1997) The future role of marketing in the organization, in R. D. Lehmann and K. E. Jocz (eds) *Reflections on the Futures of Marketing*. Cambridge, MA: Marketing Science Institute, pp. 39–66.

Weitz, B. A. and Wensley, R. (1984) *Strategic Marketing*. Boston, MA: New-Publishing.

Wind, Y. and Robertson, T. S. (1983) Marketing strategy: new directions for theory and research, *Journal of Marketing*, **47**(spring): 12–21.

Wind, Y. (Jerry) (1997) Big questions for the 21st century, in *Mastering Management*. London: Financial Times Management, pp. 209–11.

| # Marketing and competition

There are only two functions of a business – innovation and marketing.

PETER DRUCKER

After reading Chapter 2 you will be able to:

✔ Define competition and the role it performs in ensuring that scarce resources are used to maximise satisfaction.

✔ Appreciate that good theory usually reflects best practice and why learning through knowledge acquisition is more cost-effective than learning by experience.

✔ Understand the nature and scope of marketing.

✔ Know why marketing is a discipline that *synthesises* knowledge derived from empirical generalisations.

✔ Answer the question 'What is strategy?'

✔ Appreciate the ways in which market structure and performance influences and is influenced by the conduct of suppliers and their interaction with users.

✔ Perceive how these interactions help determine marketing strategy.

✔ Recognise and be able to describe the impact of international trade on competition.

✔ Understand and be able to describe Porter's concept of the 'Diamond of National Advantage'.

✔ Identify the influence of government policy on competitive activity.

✔ Define the nature of competitive advantage and how this leads to the creation of 'clusters' of successful firms and industries.

✔ Appreciate the contribution that marketing makes to the achievement of competitive success.

✔ Recognise the key issues facing firms in the future.

✔ Understand why *knowledge* is likely to be the key to success in the future.

INTRODUCTION

In Chapter 1 we drew attention to Wind and Robertson's (1983) criticisms of the absence of a strategic emphasis in marketing. Central to these criticisms were the interdisciplinary isolation of marketing, the lack of rigorous competitive analysis and the lack of an international orientation. In this chapter, we seek to address all three of these perceived deficiencies.

To begin with we acknowledge the fact that modern explanations of competitive behaviour in the marketplace draw on over 200 years' rigorous and detailed analysis by economists. While the extent of this dependency has only recently become recognised generally through the writings of people like Michael Porter (1980), it is clear that marketing is indeed a synthetic discipline in the sense that, like medicine and engineering, it depends fundamentally upon other disciplines. Where the new discipline of marketing adds value is in its willingness to cross the (artificial) boundaries which are necessary to define the single discipline and link ideas and concepts from a number of disciplines in order to provide a more comprehensive explanation of the complexity of the real world. First, however, it is important to understand precisely what insights the single discipline can offer, so we open the chapter with arguments in favour of getting back to the basics before attempting a more sophisticated and more complex analysis.

Next we attempt a short answer to the question 'What is marketing?' to provide both content and perspective for the book as a whole. Essentially, we argue that the success of an economy in using and allocating resources may be judged in terms of the satisfaction given by their consumption. It follows that it is the consumers' perception of value which is fundamental to the whole concept of economic and business success.

A further section 'Market structure, conduct and performance' offers a conceptual framework from the field of industrial economics which helps explain how performance in the marketplace is the consequence of the interaction between the basic forces of demand and supply as mediated by the structure and operation of the market.

The following section 'International competition' recognises that technological change and a revolut-

ion in communication has transformed the preoccupation with the operation of national economies to a consideration of their global interdependence.

Finally, we address the issue of central concern to readers of a book of this kind – the contribution of marketing to competitive success. It was Kenneth Boulding who coined the memorable doggerel about 'innovation' 'for which we could easily substitute "marketing"':

> We all know innovation
> Benefits both world and nation.
> The question we must answer later,
> Is, 'will it help the innovator?'

In 'Marketing and competitive success', we report the findings of a major survey into this question. The answer, and justification for the book, is that marketing is a necessary, albeit not a sufficient, condition for competitive success.

COMPETITION

In their seminal text *Industrial Market Structure and Economic Performance*, Scherer and Ross (1990) open their analysis with the observation that:

> Any economy, whatever its cultural and political traditions may be, must decide what products to supply and how much of each to produce, how scarce resources will be apportioned in producing each, and how the end products will be divided up or distributed among the various members of society. There are three alternative methods to solve this bundle of problems. First, decisions can be made to conform with tradition. The economic organisation of manors in Europe during feudal times and the caste system of occupational selection in India are prominent examples. Second, the problem can be solved through central planning. Illustrations include output and input planning for most industries in the Soviet Union and the elaborate controls the US Department of Defense imposes over its contractors.
>
> Finally, there is the market system approach, under which consumers and producers act in response to price signals generated by the interplay of supply and demand in more or less freely operating markets.

With the growth of democracy throughout the world, the collapse of the Soviet economy in the early 1990s and the abandonment of communism, it is clear that the market system approach offers the best solution to the central economic problem of maximising satisfaction through the consumption of scarce resources. The process by which this is achieved is *marketing*.

Clearly, the process and function of marketing has existed since the time when man first discovered that by exchanging surpluses with others he could improve his overall satisfaction – an insight which was to lead to acceptance of task specialisation and exchange as the foundation for increased productivity and higher standards of living. From 1776, and the publication of Adam Smith's *Wealth of Nations* (1970[1776]), to 1960, and Ted Levitt's 'Marketing myopia' (1960), the formal study of the nature of competition remained the province of the professional economist. As a consequence, and in common with many other professions, much of the substance of the body of knowledge which distinguished the field of study was poorly communicated to others who might have benefited considerably from the insights it was able to offer to the solution of real-world problems. Indeed, few managers appreciate that the essence of Michael Porter's (1980, 1985, 1990a) influential writings on competition and competitive advantage are derived directly from the subfield of economics known as 'industrial organisation' or 'industrial economics'.

The point that we are seeking to make is that there is a tradition of more than 200 years' concentrated analysis on the subject of competition. As such, it would be negligent to ignore the contribution such analysis might make to solving contemporary problems as experienced by the managers of individual and independent firms competing one with another.

In this spirit we shall revisit some of the key ideas developed by industrial economists as a basis for determining how they can help us better understand the nature of competition and its implications for the formulation of strategy at the level of the individual firm. A word of caution is appropriate here. Over 40 years' experience as a teacher confirms that the biggest danger faced by decision-makers is a tendency to dismiss facts or evidence on the grounds that 'I know all that'

and/or 'That's all very well in theory but in practice ...'. The point about 'theory' is that it is usually distilled wisdom based upon observation and documentation of real-world experience, i.e. it is what works in practice. So, before you dismiss the explanations of social scientists as 'academic', bear in mind that these capture the essence of what seems to work or not work in the field of business management. These are the basic relationships that offer structure and understanding for the solution of particular problems and, therefore, of much greater value than the passing popularity of most of the current management bestsellers.

Before reviewing the nature of competition, it will be useful first to address the question 'what is marketing?' A little earlier we claimed that marketing is the process through which economies address the central problem of allocating resources in a manner that will maximise the satisfaction of the members of that economy. However, 'marketing' has many other connotations – most often those associated with selling and advertising – so some justification of this claim seems called for.

WHAT IS MARKETING?

Marketing is an enigma. At the same time it is both simple and complex, straightforward and intricate, a philosophy or state of mind and dynamic business function; it is new and it is as old as time itself. Cynically, we might observe that marketing is therefore precisely what you want it to be, and thereby everything or nothing. In attempting to resolve this paradox, the views expressed must be those of the author, although they clearly owe much to the influence and thinking of others. Similarly, the reader will have to draw his or her own conclusions concerning the boundaries and parameters of marketing. Fundamentally, however, it is felt to be of little consequence whether the reader thinks or agrees that the concept and processes discussed in this book are the province of marketing or of some other discipline or orientation. What is important is the credibility and conviction that can be attached to them.

While the science of economics is founded essentially upon analysis of the interaction of supply and demand, and the causes and consequences of this interaction – one might say the issues of what will be produced and how – so the art of politics is concerned mainly with who will receive what share of the resultant output. From the viewpoint of marketers, it could be restated somewhat as follows:

> The economic problem is to maximise the satisfaction arising from the consumption of scarce resources. Accordingly, we are concerned with consumer satisfaction, and the best judge of such satisfaction is the individual consumer. This must be so, for satisfaction is a subjective concept that varies between individuals and even within individuals over time. We are concerned, therefore, with consumer sovereignty[1] founded upon the basic proposition that supply must be a function of demand.

In essence, therefore, the marketing concept is concerned with exchange relationships in which the parties to the exchange are seeking to maximise their personal satisfaction. This proposal is fundamental to the discipline of economics, but goes beyond it in its emphasis upon the subjective rather than the so-called rational or objective measurement of satisfaction. The importance of this distinction is made clear by Lawrence Abbott in his book *Quality and Competition* (1955), in which he asserts that 'what people really desire are not products but satisfying experiences'. He then goes on to say:

> what is considered satisfying is a matter for individual decision: it varies according to one's tastes, standards, beliefs and objectives – and these vary greatly depending on individual personality and cultural environment. Here is a foundation for a theory of choice broad enough to embrace Asiatic as well as Eastern cultures, non-conformists as well as slaves to convention, Epicureans, Stoics, Cynics, roisterers, religious fanatics, dullards and intellectual giants alike.

Basically, the marketing concept is very simple. It is built upon the basic principle of economic organisation which is 'to maximise satisfaction through the utilisation of scarce resources'. While technological innovation has had a major impact upon both the availability and productivity of scarce resources, on a global scale millions of people still eke out an existence below the poverty level. Clearly, there is a long way to go before

poorer people in developing economies can enjoy the abundance available within the advanced economies. But, irrespective of which kind of economy one lives in, the challenge remains the same – maximising satisfaction. To do this it is essential that we define precisely what we mean by 'satisfaction'. To do so, it is important to recognise that fundamentally satisfaction is a highly personalised construct which is particular to the individual. It is derived from their culture, values, attitudes and experience and is relative to the current standard of living which they enjoy. If, therefore, we wish to increase satisfaction it would seem obvious that we need to ask customers to define this in their own terms. To do this producers/sellers need to make a genuine effort to establish a dialogue with prospective customers and seek to develop an ongoing relationship with them.

Understanding of this 'marketing concept' was implicit in some of the earlier definitions of it which emerged in the 1950s and early 1960s. For example, Peter Drucker in his seminal *Practice of Management* (1954) observed that:

> Marketing is not only much broader than selling, it is not a specialised activity at all. It encompasses the entire business. It is the whole business seen from the point of view of its final result, that is, from the customer's point of view. Concern and responsibility for marketing must therefore permeate all areas of the enterprise.

And later, 'Marketing is the distinguishing, unique function of the business.' These themes were developed at considerable length in Theodore Levitt's 'Marketing myopia' (1960) in which he attributed the failure of firms and industries to their emphasis upon the products which they made rather than the needs which they served.

Despite this clear and widely shared understanding of the philosophy behind marketing its implementation through the marketing function diverged widely from it. This was particularly the case in the paradigm of marketing which dominated education and much academic research for almost 30 years (1960–90). This paradigm was enshrined in what is now known as the 'marketing management model' with Philip Kotler's *Market-*

ing Management: Analysis, Planning, and Control (1967) as its bible.

While the American Marketing Management School represented the received doctrine, heretics in Europe and particularly Scandinavia were developing a dogma of their own based around concepts of interaction, networks and relationships. The essential difference between these two creeds is that the marketing management model seeks to understand consumer needs better so that it can manipulate the elements of the marketing mix more effectively and so bend demand to the available supply. It tends to emphasise the transaction and sees exchange largely as a zero sum game in which there are inevitably winners and losers. Needless to say, it is the seller who intends to win. In other words, it is concerned with what marketing can do *to* buyers. By contrast, relationship marketing reflects the marketing concept much better. Relationship marketing is built upon the creation and maintenance of mutually satisfying exchange relationships. It enjoys a win–win perspective and sees the role of a producer as doing things *for* customers.

As a result of accelerating technological change and global competition during the 1980s, the failings of the marketing management model began to become apparent even in its heartland, the US. The extent and nature of this changed perspective was encapsulated in an authoritative review of the marketing management school in Frederick E. Webster Jnr's 1992 article 'The changing role of marketing in the corporation'. In his own words:

> The purpose of this article is to outline both the intellectual and the pragmatic routes of changes that are occurring in marketing, especially marketing management, as a body of knowledge, theory and practice and to suggest the need for a new paradigm of the marketing function within the firm.

In the turbulent and recessionary environment which characterised the early 1990s Webster's call for a new approach to the practice of marketing was widely echoed, particularly in practitioner publications. Among the more influential of these was McKinsey's (1993) observation that marketing was experiencing a 'mid-life crisis'. In simplified terms the argument ran that if exchange was concerned with relationships between individuals

and organisations then marketing must be everybody's business and not the preserve of a privileged few to be found within a formal marketing department. This perception was probably magnified by the fact that several important developments in managerial thinking, such as benchmarking, total quality management, strategic alliances, globalisation and strategic thinking, might properly be considered the primary concern of marketers. These fields had been preempted by others.

In the 2000s, marketers appear to have recovered some of their confidence and are able to take a more balanced view of their discipline. It is now generally accepted that the relationship marketing approach has effectively extended the marketing concept into areas such as services and business-to-business marketing, which were poorly served by the marketing management model, based as it was upon concepts of mass production, mass distribution and mass marketing essentially of packaged consumer goods. At the same time, it has also been appreciated that many marketing exchanges are based upon low involvement and transactions, and that the two distinct approaches can coexist together. Simultaneously, a clearer distinction is being drawn between the philosophy of marketing, which is encapsulated in a marketing orientation that can be held by everybody, both internal and external to an organisation, and the market-oriented organisation that is customer-oriented and market-driven. The marketing-oriented organisation is committed to the philosophy of mutually satisfying exchange relationships, while the market-oriented company is focused on how to achieve this through the professional practice and management of the marketing function.

MARKETING AS A SYNTHETIC DISCIPLINE

A little earlier we suggested that the discipline of marketing is directly concerned with solving issues of supply and demand which lie firmly within the domain of economics. Indeed, the history of marketing is inextricably linked with the history of economic development. In the beginning there was *barter*. People discovered that they could increase their consumption opportunities by exchanging surpluses of goods they did not require for other people's surpluses for which they had a need. To facilitate exchange a designated place was agreed upon where all those with goods to exchange could meet with one another. This place was the *market* from which it follows that the practice of marketing antedates recorded history.

Given the opportunity to exchange surpluses it made sense for the individual to *specialise* in producing those goods or services where they enjoyed some natural aptitude or advantage because, by doing so, they maximised their productivity. Thus, *task specialisation* borne out of marketing was the first step in economic development. It was conceived from a concept of mutual advantage and freedom of choice, in other words 'mutually satisfying exchange relationships'.

Recorded history traces the stages of economic development with marketing as the peaceful solution to satisfying human needs, and warfare and conquests as its antithesis. With the Enlightenment of the eighteenth century, and the Industrial Revolution that accompanied it, mass production led to mass distribution and mass markets. In turn, the quest for scarce resources led to colonisation and the opening up of new international markets culminating in the 20th century with what we now call globalisation.

While industrialisation and internationalisation have undoubtedly given rise to enormous economic growth and greatly enhanced standards of living, it has not been without a cost. Mass production and mass distribution resulted in a *physical* and *psychological separation* between producer and consumer to the point that under the marketing management model of exchange producers became preoccupied as to how they could shape consumer demand through the manipulation of the marketing mix rather than letting this demand shape their production decisions. The dialogue and interaction that is inseparable from the barter exchange, and was still largely present in the craft industry that preceded the Industrial Revolution, had largely disappeared in what has come to be identified as the *Anglo-Saxon* version of capitalism on which the marketing management model is based. In his *Wealth of Nations*, Adam Smith (1970[1776]) observed: 'Consumption is the sole end and purpose of production.' Having stated this self-evident truth, he felt no need to revert to it elsewhere in his

work, concentrating instead on the obvious problem of increasing output to meet unsatisfied demand. In this process the precise needs of the consumer began to be taken for granted with producers assuming they knew best what their customers really wanted. The fallacy of this assumption becomes apparent when conditions of oversupply begin to develop and competition between suppliers intensifies as they try to persuade consumers to prefer their output to that of their rivals. Out of this ever-intensifying, now global, competition has come the realisation of the need to return to first principles. To listen to the voice of the market and shape production to the needs of consumers.

This recognition of the need to pay attention to consumers – their needs, wants and behaviour – led to an inevitable broadening of the scope of the marketing discipline. To better understand buyer behaviour, widespread borrowing from other social sciences took place. The origin of this borrowing is frequently attributed to the migration of many European social scientists to the US during the 1930s to escape Hitler and his fascist policies. On arrival in the US, however, many established social scientists from fields such as psychology and sociology found only limited opportunities for academic employment. By contrast, the growing field of business studies offered opportunities and led to the integration of many behavioural concepts into the field of study previously dominated by economic concepts.

It is for this reason that we regard marketing as a synthetic discipline which, in turn, is strongly related to a professional practice. In using the word 'synthetic' we do so in the original sense of something which integrates and pulls together related ideas into a more powerful and holistic explanation of a phenomenon. This integrative function is a defining characteristic of professional practices such as architecture, engineering and medicine. Like marketing, all of these synthetic disciplines are dynamic and subject to continuous change. One consequence of this is that they are not easily amenable to the kind of definitive statement and explanation characteristic of the physical sciences. By contrast, managerial disciplines depend much more upon empirical generalisation or what, at my time at the Harvard Business School, we called CUGs – *currently useful generalisations*. Much of the content of this book consists of CUGs for which the appropriate test would seem to be 'does this seem to work?' If so, then one has a currently useful generalisation which can be depended upon until it is shown not to work. If and when this occurs it is far easier to jettison a CUG than to worry how one is to rewrite the textbook.

Of course, many of the CUGs which will be deployed throughout the book are regarded as accepted theoretical explanations by social scientists and others from whom they have been borrowed. But, rather than enquire into the reasons why they have achieved this standing, our focus will be on how the insights and conceptual frameworks offered can help improve managerial analysis and decision-making. In other words, how can we use this knowledge to do our job better?

Recent years have seen growing interest in empirical generalisation which Bass (1995) has defined as 'patterns or regularities that recur over different circumstances, and which therefore are amenable to mathematical, graphical or symbolic representation'. An alternative definition offered by Uncles et al. (1995) is that empirical generalisations are concerned with 'the establishment of law-like relationships'. In other words, the existence of 'association' which may or may not be causally related. In light of these definitions, Mark Uncles (1997) makes the point that empirical generalisations are not anecdotes (what Lillien and Pras (1994) have called 'factoids'), they are not one-off cases nor are they isolated empirical or experimental studies. Indeed, empirical generalisations would probably come somewhere around the middle of a hierarchy of generalisations, which might be as follows:

- Myths
- Rules of thumb
- Analogy/metaphor
- CUGs
- Empirical generalisations
- Normative theory
- Axioms, laws and universal truths.

Because of its dynamic nature and because human beings – the subject of our enquiry – tend to change their behaviour as a result of being 'experimented' upon, it seems unlikely that marketing is ever going to achieve the status of axioms, laws

and universal truths. Nonetheless, the formulation of generalisations is fundamental to the generation of knowledge that may be systematically established as applying over a range of conditions. Much knowledge provides a basis for the generation of further knowledge, and also acts as a guard against unsubstantiated claims to knowledge – or what Ehrenberg (1994) has termed 'sonking', which he defines as the 'scientific presentation of non-knowledge', a status common to many fashionable managerial panaceas!

In answering the question 'Do empirical generalisations exist in marketing/management?' Uncles observes that they must in that the answer 'No' is itself an empirical generalisation! On the other hand, it is also clear that there are not many effective generalisations in marketing as insufficient effort has been given to identifying them. Such effort as has been made is largely concerned with reviews of the existing literature and content or meta analysis. These approaches are often flawed from a scientific point of view because the studies included in such reviews were not intended to be compared or related to one another in the first place. In the experimental sciences the acid test for a theory is the ability to replicate it exactly. Because of its dynamic nature this is extremely difficult to achieve in marketing, added to which there is little incentive or encouragement given to scholars to undertake replication studies. Instead, the research methodology used in marketing is predominantly concerned with single sets of data (SSoD) where significance is looked for within a unique data set using inferential statistics.

Despite these difficulties many of the explanations and analytical frameworks offered in this text are considered by the author to be useful generalisations. As such, they have been seen to be useful in the past and are expected to continue to be so in the future. However, if they don't seem to work for you, remember that you can always discard them and look for a better generalisation yourself.

WHAT IS STRATEGY?

The above question was used as the title of an article by Michael Porter (1996). In Porter's opinion, events of the previous two decades have led managers to adopt a remarkable number of management tools and techniques in their quest for productivity, quality and speed. Amongst these may be numbered total quality management, benchmarking, time-based competition, outsourcing, partnering, re-engineering and change management. But, according to Porter, while all of these may have helped improve operational effectiveness, they have distracted management from the importance of strategic thinking and so have not improved their competitive position. In reality, what is needed is a combination of both.

In Porter's words:

> Operational effectiveness (OE) means performing similar activities *better* than rivals perform them. Operational effectiveness includes but is not limited to efficiency. It refers to any number of practices that allow a company to better utilise its inputs by, for example, reducing defects in products or developing better products faster. In contrast, strategic positioning means performing *different* activities from rivals or performing similar activities in *different ways*.

However, improvements in operational effectiveness arising from the new tools and techniques are easily available to anyone who cares to adopt them. While failure to do so will result in declining competitiveness and their take-up will enhance efficiency and productivity, this will merely represent a new base line for competition at a higher level. In other words, the espousal of new managerial tools and techniques is a necessary but not sufficient condition for competitive success. In Porter's view the latter depends upon strategic positioning. 'Competitive strategy is about being different. It means deliberately choosing a different set of activities to deliver the unique mix of values.' However, Porter distinguishes strategic positioning in terms of the customers served, which is the conventional view of positioning first developed by Ries and Trout (1982) (see Chapter 13) in favour of a definition of strategy based on activities:

> But the essence of strategy is in the activities – choosing to perform activities differently or to perform different activities than rivals. Otherwise, a strategy is nothing more than a marketing slogan that will not withstand competition.

In making this assertion, Porter appears to over-look the direct link between the selection of activities and the satisfaction of specific customer needs. This, despite the fact that when he comes to discuss strategic positions, he perceives these as being based on customers' needs, customers' accessibility or the variety of a company's products or services. In our view, it is because of the existence or potential to develop different customer responses that sellers have the opportunity to differentiate themselves from competitors through their activities.

Once the strategic position has been identified then trade-offs are invariably required to sustain that position. 'Trade-offs occur when activities are incompatible. Simply put, a trade-off means that more of one thing necessitates less of another.' Put differently, the choice of one course of action will necessarily exclude or modify other courses of action. This view leaves Porter to conclude that

> strategy is making trade-offs in competing. The essence of strategy is choosing what *not* to do. Without trade-offs, there would be no need for choice and thus no need for strategy. Any good idea could and would be quickly imitated. Again, performance would once again depend wholly on operational effectiveness.

In addition to recognising the importance of trade-offs, Porter also re-emphasises the importance of *fit*. In the pursuit of concepts such as core competencies, critical resources and key success factors, many managers appear to have lost sight of the fact that it is the combination of all its activities into a coherent whole that yields synergy and, potentially, sustainable competitive advantage. According to Porter there are three types of fit although they are not mutually exclusive. These are identified as *consistency*, *reinforcement* and *optimisation* of the chosen activities. Given the difficulty of matching identically any given activity, it follows that the greater the number of activities combined into a system, the less likely it becomes that a competitor will be able to replicate that strategy.

According to Porter: 'The pursuit of operational effectiveness is seductive because it is concrete and actionable.' By contrast, much strategising may appear abstract and inactionable and so is ignored by managers who mistake action for results. While Porter does not say so explicitly, his analysis is a rejection of the idea of 'emergent strategy' popularised by Mintzberg and Waters (1985). Practitioners of emergent strategy are easily diverted from their chosen course of action by events as they unfold. By responding to these events a series of incremental changes can result in the loss of the distinctive factors which were the original source of competitive advantage. In other words, managers fail to recognise the trade-offs associated with frequent change and the loss of a long-term strategic objective.

To sum up, Porter offers two alternative views of strategy. The first, an implicit strategy model of the 1990s, comprises five attributes:

1. One ideal competitive position in the industry
2. Benchmarking of all activities in achieving best practice
3. Aggressive outsourcing and partnering to gain efficiencies
4. Advantages rest on a few key success factors, critical resources, core competencies
5. Flexibility and rapid responses to all competitive and market changes.

By contrast, his own view is that sustainable competitive advantage will only accrue when a company identifies a unique competitive position for itself that tailors its activities to its strategy and makes clear trade-offs and choices vis-à-vis its competitors. In turn, competitive advantage is derived from the fit between the activities, while sustainability comes from the activity system as a whole rather than the individual parts. Finally, to maintain a sustainable competitive advantage, operational effectiveness is taken as given.

'What is strategy?' is included in Michael Porter's book *Competition* (1998), a collection of his most important articles published over the previous 20 years. The review of this book and an interview with Porter appeared in *Fortune*, which is seen by the author James Surowiecki (1999) as 'counter intuitive':

> At a time when strategic thinking is as fragmented as it's ever been and when pronouncements of permanent revolution are in the air, Porter's faith in enduring strategy truths runs strikingly against the grain.

The report continues:

For Porter, much of what has passed for management thinking in the past decade may have been important, but it wasn't strategy – and it isn't nearly as crucial as good strategy. 'Strategy is not accidental. It is a purposeful process', he says. 'Luck is alive and well. Intuition is alive and well. But human beings have some control over their own destiny. And you can improve your odds of making better judgements ... operational effectiveness means you are running the same race faster', Porter says. But strategy is choosing to run a different race because it's the one you've set yourself up to win.

We return to these issues in Chapter 3.

SOURCES OF COMPETITIVE ADVANTAGE

Marketing literature (Turnbull et al., 1997; Hakansson et al., 2004; Narayandas and Rangan, 2004) in the past two decades has increasingly reflected the need for building bonds with suppliers, consumers and other related constituents. Webster (1992) urges marketers to broaden the *agenda* of the marketing field, and suggests that:

> Theory development must be accompanied by aggressive programs of empirical research ... survey research should be guided by strong theoretical frameworks from allied social science disciplines. Top priority should be given to analysis of the forces and factors that cause firms to move along the continuum from transactions to long-term relationships to strategic alliances and, perhaps, back again.

Based on a review of past research, eight themes were identified (Oburai and Baker, 2005) that seek to explain the nature and sources of competitive advantage.

It is argued that traditional notions of competitive advantage need to be supplemented with views from relational and resource-based theories. Sources of competitive advantage may well lie outside firms' boundaries. The fields of strategy, organisational theory and marketing have several distinct and interrelated explanations that are examined below for their central orientations, assumptions and implications. The eight themes to be discussed are distinctive in some senses and overlapping in others. What may be needed is an integration of the different ideas to form a coherent and complete model that is workable.

TRANSACTION COST ANALYSIS AND EXPLANATIONS

Transaction cost (TC) economics and analysis are concerned with economic organisation. Williamson's (1975) work is 'principally concerned with the institutions of governance'. Williamson sketches his core arguments: 'Intuition tells us that simple governance structures should mediate simple transactions and complex governance structures should be reserved for complex transactions' (1996, p. 3). A deeper exploration of the foundations reveals that TC relies on selection arguments at the level of transactions or tasks. TC arguments regularly omit the perspective of competence or capabilities. This seriously *limits the applicability* to a few contexts. Value generated from relation-specific interaction is ignored due to the static nature of the formulation.

GAME THEORY

Game theoretic approaches are stylised versions of interactions between and among parties, and depict interdependencies. They serve to highlight the *relatedness of goals*, *expectations*, *choices and outcomes*. Excellent summaries of the concepts involved in understanding game theory are stated in Kay (1993). Three main games are described, each of which corresponds to the most important objectives of commercial relationships, which are:

- *Cooperation:* joint activity towards a shared goal
- *Coordination:* the need for mutually consistent responses
- *Differentiation:* the avoidance of mutually incompatible activities.

Game theoretic approaches ignore many contextual details and hence the outcomes depicted in these games represent extremes. Even in the context of the games' rules, it may be generally noted that the main issue appears to be that of *information asymmetry*, which is a result of lack of communication but is amenable to remedies.

MARKET POWER AND INDUSTRY STRUCTURE EXPLANATIONS

Porter is the most popular and leading advocate of this strand. Although his later works also draw on resource-based explanations (Porter, 1985), in his *Competitive Strategy* Porter (1980) draws heavily on industrial organisation theory (Oburai and Baker, 1999a), and on the Bain-Mason paradigm and oligopoly theory. Industry characteristics and a firm's bargaining power determine a firm's performance:

> The goal is to find mechanisms to offset or surmount these sources of suppliers' power ... purchases of an item can be spread among alternate suppliers in such a way as to improve the firm's bargaining power. (Porter, 1980 p. 123)

Competition is the main anchor for Porter. The product–market focus and agenda about building strong market positions that characterised the early writings in the field of strategy have changed, with attention being paid to sources of competitive advantage external to firms as well. This has led to the development of evolutionary and resource-based explanations.

EVOLUTIONARY THEORIES

Biological reasoning permeates a variety of management and social science disciplines. Darwinian evolution depends on random mutation and hard selection. Since mutation is inherently involuntary and hence uncontrollable, the reasoning depends much on the effect of the external environment. Nelson and Winter's (1982) evolutionary theory focuses on routines or sequences of activities or patterned responses that firms generate, modify, acquire, imitate and use. These routines of organisations are analogous to the skills of individuals and form the organisational memory and reservoirs of knowledge and experience. Firms inherit routines and, in an attempt to adjust to the environment, when needed adapt them through research. Routines are the equivalent of genes. Evolutionary and resource-based explanations have much in common and a synthesis has been proposed in some quarters.

RESOURCE-BASED EXPLANATIONS

Strategy literature is now replete with resource-based (RB) views (Penrose, 1959; Wernerfelt, 1984). RB theories attempt to explain inter-firm differences in performances and attribute them to the possession of unique and lasting resources. Competitive advantage is the result of internal firm organisation and hence managerial discretion is an important aspect considered. The endogenous orientation is necessary to explain *firm-level differences* unlike the market power and evolutionary theories. Hunt (1997) puts forward a resource-based theory with an explicit marketing perspective. In a sense, the resource explanations are still all about competition where the firm's boundary ends and are seen to be relevant to the study of large and diversified firms, whereas evolutionary arguments may be more suited to the study of small and growth firms.

INTERACTION AND NETWORK THEORIES

Interaction and network views are mainly the contribution of the Industrial Marketing and Purchasing Group (IMP) team. This is a vast and growing collection (Turnbull et al., 1997). The IMP group interaction model (Hakansson, 1982) recognises that interaction may lead to the institution of relationships. However, this dyadic focus is now giving way to network views of the firm and its context. This highlights a perspective that is not provided by other theories. An actors–activities–resources framework is used to depict firms. Network theories recognise the importance of the environment and hence take a more realistic perspective of firms (Axelsson and Easton, 1992). Networks bind as well as blind; they enable and constrain. While network centrality is seen as an important attribute, the ability to influence other firms in a network may not be a straightforward possibility. Interlinkages among multiple actors and memberships in different networks are some issues (Mattsson, 1997). The redundancy of common linkages (Granovetter, 1973) and associated transaction costs are issues that may need to be resolved. This perspective also draws on earlier and ongoing developments in sociology and related fields. Studying networks is argued to be problematic (Easton, 1995). Multiple members and links are difficult to explore and hence methodological issues are the main hurdles that may need to be overcome.

COMPLEXITY THEORIES

Organisations are not machines, but complex, overlapping sets of dynamic, non-linear systems. The behaviour of complex adaptive systems is unpredictable and the precision of linear relations between cause and effect cannot be obtained in these systems (Waldrop, 1992). Complexity theories recognise and advance the view that the nature of evolution is essentially unpredictable and explicitly make allowances for massive, sudden transitions, and the emergence of internal order. This makes complexity views compatible with the evolutionary and resource theories, but also provides room for radical and sudden transformations. A main contribution of complexity theories is the concept of attractors that captures the idea that evolution is varied but limited in its patterns.

RELATIONAL VIEWS

Relational views are perhaps among the most influential ones in currency across business disciplines, and the marketing discipline, with its fundamental notions concerning the *primacy of exchange relationships* and *external orientation*, is the leading contributor in this group of theories. Overlapping themes are to be found in both the industrial and services marketing concepts and in the field of relationship marketing. The interaction and network perspectives do capture several of these important notions. This paradigm evolution is a journey towards embracing the reality of connectivity of firms.

Clearly, it is not possible to deal with all these theoretical explanations in detail. Accordingly, in the following pages, we concentrate on a discussion of the models that enjoy the widest currency in the marketing literature.

MARKET STRUCTURE, CONDUCT AND PERFORMANCE

The field of economics concerned with market structure, conduct and performance is generally designated as 'industrial organisation' and, in the opinion of Scherer and Ross (1990), who are leading authorities on the subject, is concerned with the 'market systems' approach to solving economic problems. According to Scherer and Ross, the market system operates through producer and consumer responding to the price signals, which result from the interplay of supply and demand in more or less freely operating markets, in an attempt to 'make the best of the market conditions he or she faces'. As a result of this interaction between supply and demand, a chain of events is created in which these forces result in the evolution of a particular

market structure, the nature of which has significant effects upon the conduct of suppliers and their consequent performance. The causal relationship between the factors is shown in Figure 2.1. As Scherer and Ross (1990) acknowledge, 'The broad descriptive model of these relationships was conceived by Edward S. Mason of Harvard during the 1930s and elaborated by numerous scholars'. They explain the key elements of the model as follows (pp. 4–5):

> Performance in particular industries or markets is said to depend upon the conduct of sellers and

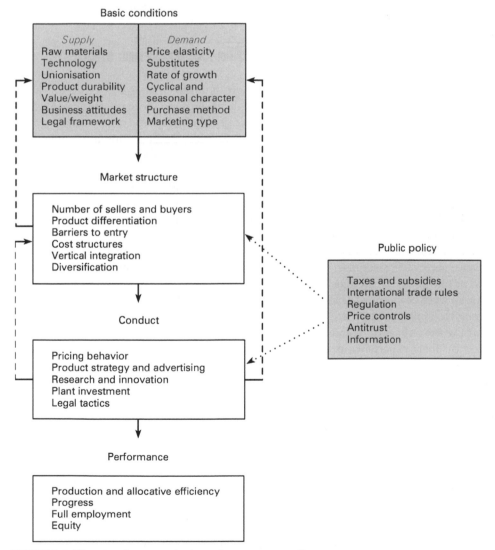

FIGURE 2.1 The structure–conduct–performance paradigm

SOURCE: Scherer, F. M. and Ross, D. (1990) *Industrial Market Structure and Economic Performance* (3rd edn). Boston, MA: Houghton Mifflin

buyers in such matters as pricing policies and practices, overt and tacit interfirm cooperation, product
line and advertising strategies, research and development commitments, investment in production facilities, legal tactics (for example, in enforcing patent
rights), and so on. Conduct in turn depends upon the
structure of the relevant market, characterised by the
number, size and distribution of sellers and buyers,
the degree of physical or subjective differentiation
distinguishing competing sellers' products, the presence or absence of barriers to the entry of new firms,
the shapes of cost curves, the degree to which firms
are vertically integrated from raw material production to retail distribution, and the extent of the firms'
product line diversification (conglomerateness).

Market structure is in turn affected by a variety
of basic conditions. These basic conditions are
summarised as falling into two categories – supply
and demand – and a number of aspects of each is
contained in Figure 2.1.

The study of industrial organisation and the
thrust of Scherer and Ross's book is concerned
with the causal flows represented by the solid
black arrows with the objective of seeking to
predict ultimate market performance from the
observation of structure, basic conditions, and
conduct. However, Figure 2.1 differs in two important respects from that which appeared in the first
edition (Figure 4.3). First, it contains feedback
loops (the dotted lines) and, second, it recognises
the role and influence of public policy in mediat-
ing the 'free operation' of market economies. The
feedback loops thus acknowledge that markets are
dynamic systems and that the forces of supply and
demand will be modified by their experience or
performance in the marketplace with satisfactory
outcomes leading to reinforcement and repetition,
and unsatisfactory outcomes to the selection of
alternative courses of action. Similarly, the inclusion of public policy issues recognises that, while in
theory 'good economic performance should flow
automatically from proper market structure and
the conduct to which it gives rise' (Scherer and
Ross, 1990), in practice it does not, and government agencies may feel it necessary to intervene to
improve performance in accordance with public
opinion as to what is the acceptable face of capitalism. This is clearly apparent in the UK in the
creation of regulatory agencies like OFTEL, which

are charged with monitoring competitive performance in ologopolistic industries dominated by a
few players.

Ultimately it is true that all firms are in competition with one another. But, for practical purposes,
most analyses are concerned only with firms which
are competing directly with one another in the
context of other suppliers producing similar end-
use goods or services (an industry) for sale to
consumers with closely related needs (the market).
It follows that in proceeding from the general to the
particular the strategist must move from general
considerations of competition and market structure
to the specific conditions that characterise the
industry or market in which their firm is to operate.

COMPETITION AND MARKETING STRATEGY

While there is an extensive economic literature
that deals with industrial organisation, comparatively little of this has received any consideration
from businessmen. Perhaps this is because businessmen have an intrinsic distrust of economics
(often with good cause) but, more likely, it is
because they have failed to perceive the potential
contribution of academic theory to their practical
problems. The publication of Michael Porter's
book *Competitive Strategy* (1980) did much to
redress this deficiency. In this section we will draw
heavily upon Porter's exposition (which is
strongly recommended as a source book) as it
represents a comprehensive review of the applied
economist's view of competition. In doing so,
however, we would not wish to overlook the existence of a very well-developed and extensive literature dealing with competition that is to be found
classified in a library under 'Economics' rather
than under 'Business' or 'Management'. Equally,
one needs to take account of other analysts whose
contributions will be located under the latter headings and reference will be made to these following
the discussion of Porter's views.

One of the crucial decisions which faces the
industry analyst is precisely where to draw the
boundaries that define an 'industry'. As we shall
see, similar difficulties exist in terms of defining a
'market', and the parameters which one uses will
have a major bearing upon the applicability of
most, if not all, of the tools and techniques that

have been developed to aid management. In particular, therefore, the firm's definition of its industry and its market will be critical to the formulation of its own competitive strategy and the success or otherwise of that strategy. In general, however, and as a prerequisite to such specific definition, it is useful to assume that the industry has been defined so that attention can be concentrated upon the determinants of competition.

Porter uses the economists' concept of substitutability when he offers a working definition of an industry as 'the group of firms producing products that are close substitutes for each other'. In order to define the interaction or state of competition between these firms, economists have developed definitions of a continuum of competitive states ranging from zero (monopoly) to absolute ('perfect'). While the theoretical implications of these states are conceptually important (see Baker, 2006, Chapter 4 and the preceding discussion) it will suffice here if we appreciate that the nature of competition is to ensure that the marginal rate of return on capital

will be the same everywhere. Thus the forces of competition work to ensure that capital will flow from less efficient firms in an industry to more efficient firms and from less efficient industries to more efficient industries. The ultimate aim of every strategist should therefore be to have the most efficient firm in the most efficient industry. However, this rarely if ever is done, as is clear from John Kay's (1993) analysis.

In 'How competitive forces shape strategy' (1979), Michael Porter distinguishes five basic forces that govern competition in an industry – the threat of new entrants, the threat of substitution, the bargaining power of suppliers, the bargaining power of customers and rivalry between current competitors – and depicts their interaction as in Figure 2.2. It will be noted that these are very similar to the factors in the Market structure box in Figure 2.1, which is hardly surprising as Porter studied Industrial Economics at Harvard College before moving to the Business School. Porter describes the key features of these five forces along the following lines.

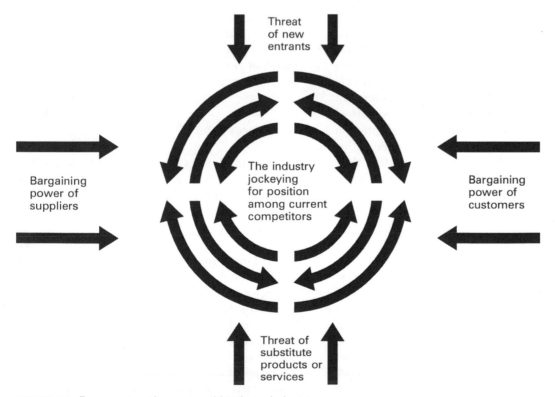

FIGURE 2.2 Forces governing competition in an industry

SOURCE: Porter, M. E. (1979) How competitive forces shape strategy, *Harvard Business Review* (March–April): 141

THE THREAT OF NEW ENTRANTS

Freedom of entry to an industry is widely regarded as a key indicator of an industry's competitiveness, such that in the case of a monopoly by definition no other firm can enter, while in the case of 'perfect competition' there are no barriers to entry. From the firm's viewpoint the greater the barriers to entry the less the threat from new competitors and the more secure its own position.

Seven major barriers to entry are proposed by Porter:

1. Economies of scale (concentration)
2. Product differentiation
3. Capital requirements
4. Switching costs
5. Access to distribution channels
6. Cost disadvantages independent of scale
7. Government policy.

A full discussion of these factors is to be found in Porter, and at this juncture we wish only to underline a point to which we will return many times: namely, that product differentiation has become the key competitive factor. Simplistically, the reason why this should be so is that if one owns a product which is perceived as differentiated by users then one has a monopoly and so is not exposed to competition for as long as one can maintain this position of the perceived difference. As we shall see in Chapter 8, perception is a subjective state and one which can be influenced significantly by marketing activities, thus explaining the current importance attached to the subject.

THE THREAT OF SUBSTITUTION

As Porter notes: 'Identifying substitute products is a matter of searching for other products that can perform the same function as the product of the industry', a point which underlines our assertion that if your product is sufficiently differentiated to be perceived as unique by a sufficient number of users to comprise an economically viable market, the threat of competition is latent rather than active. Given such a position, the danger lies in complacency, for change is inevitable, if only

because the act of consumption will change the consumers and so make them susceptible to improved products.

THE BARGAINING POWER OF SUPPLIERS

According to Porter, a supplier group is powerful if the following apply:

- It is dominated by a few companies and is more concentrated than the industry it sells to
- It is not obliged to contend with other substitute products for sale to the industry
- The industry is not an important customer of the supplier group
- The supplier's product is an important input to the buyer's business
- The supplier group's products are differentiated or it has built up switching costs
- The supplier group poses a credible threat of forward integration

Porter also makes the important point that 'labour must be recognised as a supplier as well, and one that exerts great power in many industries' – a point even more true of the UK economy than that of the USA, albeit of diminishing importance in recent years.

THE BARGAINING POWER OF CUSTOMERS

Many of the factors that apply here are corollaries of those cited as applying to the power of suppliers. Eight specific conditions are proposed by Porter where a buying group will exercise power:

1. The buyer group is concentrated or purchases large volumes relative to seller sales, e.g. Marks & Spencer vis-à-vis its suppliers, or the multiple grocery chains like Tesco or Sainsburys.
2. The products it purchases from the industry represent a significant fraction of the buyer's costs or purchases.
3. The products it purchases from the industry are standard or undifferentiated, e.g. basic chemicals, steel, aluminium, etc.
4. It faces few switching costs.

5. It earns low profits, i.e. it will be active in seeking cost reductions in bought-in supplies.
6. Buyers pose a credible threat of backward integration.
7. The industry's product is unimportant to the quality of the buyers' products or services, e.g. most packaging materials.
8. The buyer has full information.

RIVALRY BETWEEN CURRENT COMPETITORS

'Jockeying for position' is the phrase that Porter uses to describe the tactical moves employed by firms to seek an advantage over their competitors. Clearly, the greater the degree of skirmishing between the rivals the more active and volatile is the competitive state. The intensity of this rivalry is a function of numerous factors, of which Porter distinguishes eight:

1. Numerous or equally balanced competitors (a basic condition for a state of 'perfect' competition).
2. Slow industry growth, e.g. retail food sales.
3. High fixed or storage costs. On this point Porter makes the important observation that 'The significant characteristic of costs is fixed costs *relative to value added* (emphasis added), and not fixed costs as a proportion of total costs.'
4. Lack of differentiation or switching costs.
5. Capacity augmented in large increments, e.g. steel, shipbuilding.
6. Diverse competitors, particularly international rivals.
7. High strategic stakes.
8. High exit barriers, e.g. specialised assets with low liquidation values, redundancy costs, social implications, etc.

Porter comments:

> When exit barriers are high, excess capacity does not leave the industry, and companies that lose the competitive battle do not give up. Rather, they grimly hang on and, because of their weakness, have to resort to extreme tactics. The profitability of the entire industry can be persistently low as a result, cf. the world automobile and steel industries.

INTERNATIONAL COMPETITION

Until recently most analyses of competition have focused upon competition within a single national economy. Of course the importance of international trade is recognised and prompted Ricardo to articulate his theory of comparative advantage as long ago as 1817. More recently, however, there has developed a recognition that we are now concerned with a global economy and global competition. Developing the ideas introduced in *Competitive Strategy* (1980) and *Competitive Advantage* (1985), Porter extended the scope of his analysis from companies and industries to countries with the publication of his book *The Competitive Advantage of Nations* (1990a). Contrary to the views of classical economists, who attribute national prosperity to a country's natural endowment of land, labour and capital, Porter asserts that prosperity is created, not inherited, and depends on its industry's capacity to innovate and upgrade:

> A nation's endowment of factors clearly plays a role in the competitive advantage of a nation's firms, as the rapid growth of manufacturing in low-wage countries such as Hong Kong, Taiwan, and more recently, Thailand attests. But the role of factors is far more complex than is often understood. The factors most important to competitive advantage in most industries, especially the growth in advanced economies, are not inherited but are created within a nation, through processes that differ widely across nations and among industries. Thus, the stock of factors at any particular time is less important than the rate at which they are created, upgraded, and made more specialised to particular industries. (p. 74)

Firms create competitive advantage by perceiving or discovering new and better ways to compete in an industry and bringing them to market, which is ultimately an active innovation. Innovation is here defined broadly, to include both improvements in technology and better methods or ways of doing things. It can be manifested in product changes, process changes, new approaches to marketing, new forms of distribution, and new conceptions of scope. Innovators not only respond to possibilities for change, but force it to proceed faster. Much innovation, in practice, is rather mundane and incremental rather than radical. It depends more on accumulation of small insights and advances than on major techno-logical breakthroughs. It often involves ideas that are not 'new' but have never been vigorously diffused. It results from organisational learning as much as from formal R&D. It always involves investment in devel-oping skills and knowledge and usually in physical assets and marketing effort (p. 45).

Frequently, innovation occurs when firms iden-tify a new market opportunity or a segment of a market which has been neglected by those serving the market as they understand it. Thus the Japanese success in world auto markets (both cars and motorcycles) was based upon the production of small, high-quality, high-performance machines when the prevailing fashion was for large, compar-atively low-performance machines. By definition, innovation consists of doing something new and so must overcome the inertia of the old, established and hitherto successful way of doing things. It is for this reason that radical innovation is often precipit-ated by an 'outsider' or a 'newcomer' who is unaware of the thousand and one reasons why the existing way of doing things cannot be changed.

Basically, however, humans possess only a limited range of needs (q.v. Maslow's, 1943 needs hierarchy) so that innovation represents an improved way of serving an existing and known need. It was for this reason that Ted Levitt (1960) exhorted suppliers to define markets in terms of the need served such as transportation, entertain-ment, 'fast food', convenience, etc. rather than in terms of the current products through which these needs were served. Thus the vast majority of innovations are substitute products which offer a more satisfying way of meeting a consumer need. Given that consumers are motivated more by self-interest than by supplier loyalty, it is unsurprising that innovations will displace existing products or ideas if they offer enhanced satisfaction.

It follows that a necessary condition for compet-itive success is that one's own product is at least equivalent to that of one's competitors. Thus the ultimate goal of competition is usually seen as having a 'better' product than one's competitors. Indeed, it is a truism that no company can survive unless a sufficient number of customers hold that view so as to ensure that it can achieve a profitable sales volume. Overall 'better' reflects a combin-ation of both objective and subjective factors as

implied by Rogers' (2003) definition of 'relative advantage'. In most cases the objective characteris-tics of a product are a sine qua non of the intend-ing consumers' willingness even to consider it – if you want to buy a washing machine you don't look in a car showroom! However, the value attached to particular objective features of a prod-uct will vary significantly according to the intend-ing users' attitudes, knowledge, discretionary purchasing power etc. In other words, they are *situation-specific*. They also change over time.

The paradox for both users and suppliers is, therefore, that while they resist change they can improve their (competitive) position only by accepting it. The problem is more acute for supp-liers than it is for users and, the more successful a supplier is, the more acute the dilemma – if for no other reason than that they appear to have least to gain and most to lose from changing the status quo. As Porter (1990) observes:

> Successful companies tend to develop a bias for predictability and stability; they work on defending what they have. Change is tempered by the fear that there is much to lose. The organisation at all levels filters out information that would suggest new approaches, modifications, or departures from the norm. The internal environment operates like an immune system to isolate or expel 'hostile' individ-uals who challenge current directions or established thinking.

THE 'DIAMOND OF NATIONAL ADVANTAGE'

Porter's thesis is that in order to explain how firms may overcome this inertia or complacency one must examine what he terms the 'diamond of national advantage'. As illustrated in Figure 2.3, the 'diamond' is defined by four sets of attributes, which Porter describes as follows:

1. *Factor conditions:* The nation's position in factors of production, such as skilled labour or infra-structure, necessary to compete in a given industry.
2. *Demand conditions:* The nature of home-market demand for the industry's product or service.
3. *Related and supporting industries:* The presence or absence in the nation of supplier industries and

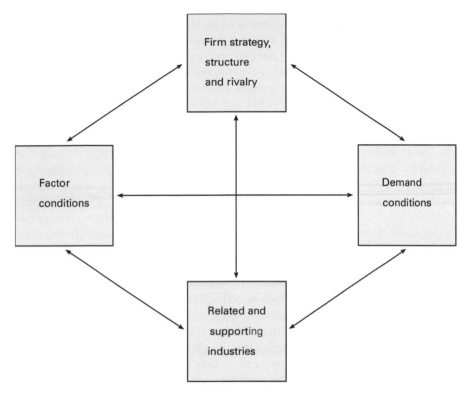

FIGURE 2.3 Determinants of national competitive advantage

SOURCE: Porter, M. E. (1990b) The Competitive Advantage of Nations, *Harvard Business Review*, (March–April): 72

other related industries that are internationally competitive.

4. *Firm strategy, structure and rivalry:* The conditions in the nation governing how companies are created, organised, and managed, as well as the nature of domestic rivalry.

According to Porter, the classical theory of comparative advantage based upon the concept of factor endowment 'is at best incomplete and at worst incorrect' as an explanation of the competitive advantage of nations. As noted earlier, this is not to say that the factor conditions are unimportant but to emphasise that their contribution depends more upon their utilisation than their mere existence. Indeed, there is much evidence in international competition in the second half of the last century to suggest that factor deficiencies act as a spur to innovation rather than a deterrent, e.g. Japan's development of just-in-time techniques to economise on expensive space, and the development of steel mini-mills in northern Italy. Porter

also emphasises that the most important factors are those that involve sustained and heavy investment and are specialised, e.g. advanced education and R&D.

The second factor which has a major bearing upon a nation's competitiveness is the home-market demand, and *Best of Business* summarises its influence as follows:

The nature of domestic demand shapes the way companies interpret and respond to customer needs. Nations gain advantage in industry or industry segments where home demand gives local companies a clearer or quicker picture of buyers' needs than foreign rivals can have. Countries also gain advantage when customers push local companies to innovate faster.

Such highly sophisticated and demanding buyers provide a window into the most advanced and stringent customer needs. For example, hot and humid summers make air conditioning highly desirable in Japan. But Japanese homes are small and tightly packed, and a bulky, noisy air conditioner is unacceptable. This, along with the high energy costs, pushed Japanese companies to pioneer energy-saving rotary compressors. A consequence is that Japanese companies have penetrated international markets with their compact, quiet units. Domestic market conditions in Japan have led to an intense effort to innovate by creating products that are *kei-haku-tan-shou*, or 'light, thin, short, small'. The result is a constant stream of compact, portable, multifunctional products that are accepted internationally.

The third point of Porter's diamond is related and supporting industries. Few, if any, industries are completely vertically integrated and the strength of any firm in the value chain, which stretches from the extraction of raw materials through to after-sales service, depends significantly on the quality of the firms with which it interacts, particularly on the supply side. Supplier companies which are at the forefront of their own industries act as a catalyst for the transfer of new technology and methods to their customers and, in doing so, enhance and extend both their own and their customers' competitive edge. Examples include the Swiss pharmaceutical industry that grew out of its success in the manufacture of dyestuffs, the Japanese facsimile industry based upon its success with copiers, and Swedish strengths in fabricated steel products like ball bearings and fasteners derived from superior performance in the manufacture of specialty steels.

Finally, firm strategy, structure and rivalry complete the model. Much of the work into international competitiveness in the 1980s came to the conclusion implicit in Porter's model – namely, there is no single source of success. Rather, success depends upon a combination of factors which are appropriate to the needs and context which exist at a point in time: as Shakespeare observed 'There is a tide in the affairs of men, which taken at the flood leads on to fortune' (*Julius Caesar*, 4, 3). So it is with business. We can define and describe the circumstances that are auspicious but the key issue is whether anyone will recognise and be able to take advantage of an opportunity when it arises. It is for this reason that so much attention has come to be focused on the concepts of organisational climate and culture and the managerial systems

and practices through which values and attitudes are translated into competitive behaviour. Given his background as an economist, Porter tends to write of management systems rather than cultural differences between nations, although these are reflected in his descriptions of the Italians' penchant for strategies that stress focus, customised products, niche marketing, rapid change and breathtaking flexibility, while the German system 'works well in technical or engineering-oriented industries – optics, chemicals, complicated machinery – where complex products demand precision manufacturing, a careful development process, after-sales service, and thus a highly disciplined management structure'.

National 'character' also influences attitudes to risk and capital formation, and one of the most trenchant criticisms of UK and US competitive performance over recent decades has been the tendency to go for short-term, more certain and immediate payoffs rather than adopt a long-term view and 'nurse' emerging technologies and industries through their often difficult formative years. Thus companies and industries that focus on a particular business – 'stick to the knitting' in Peters and Waterman's (1982) terms – and confine any diversification to closely related activities are seen as succeeding more than those which pursue unrelated diversification strategies.

Another factor strongly associated with international competitive advantage is the presence of strong domestic competition. In the absence of domestic rivalry and with protected markets, the evidence suggests that firms and industries become complacent and flaccid and unable to withstand the rigours of competition from either within or outside their own home market. Given strong competition, firms are forced to innovate and look to the market as the basis for distinguishing specific segments that they can seek to dominate through differentiated products and marketing mixes. Further, the pace of innovation quickens as firms imitate each other's developments and seek to buy in expertise through their hiring policies that enhance labour mobility and the transfer of know-how.

In addition to the four basic determinants of competitive advantage, Porter acknowledges the existence of two additional variables which may have an important influence – government and chance.

THE ROLE OF GOVERNMENT AND CHANCE

As with so many theories developed in the social sciences the academics' attempt to define the boundaries of their subject often leads to greater attention being given to the extreme conditions in their 'purest' form and so being diverted from the intermediate states which are typical of the great majority of cases. Certainly this is so with the concepts of perfect competition and monopoly which rarely, if ever, exist. In the case of government's role in economic affairs and the stimulation of competitiveness (efficiency) the same tendency is apparent in the dichotomy between centrally planned and free market economies. Porter observes:

> Both views are incorrect. Either, followed to its logical conclusion, would lead to the permanent erosion of a country's competitive capabilities. On one hand, advocates of government help for industry frequently propose policies that would actually hurt companies in the long run and only create the demand for more helping. On the other hand, advocates of a diminished government presence ignore the legitimate role that government plays in shaping the context and institutional structure surrounding companies and in creating an environment that stimulates companies to gain competitive advantage.

Porter (and many others) believe that Japan's government has grasped the role governments should play better than any other country. While this is not to say Japan has not made any mistakes it has stimulated the pursuit of both quality and advanced technology which are seen as critical to the forces of the 'diamond'. Thus, while Japanese politicians have not been averse to attempting to manage industry structure, to protect domestic markets and to condone inefficiency to secure political support, they have tempered these typical political responses with a longer view than most other countries. In doing so, they have favoured the policies that Porter argues are vital to nations seeking to gain competitive advantage:

- A focus on specialised factor creation
- Non-intervention in factor and currency markets

- The enforcement of strict product, safety and environmental standards
- The restriction of direct cooperation among industry rivals
- The promotion of goals that lead to sustained investment
- The deregulation of competition and the enforcement of strong domestic antitrust policies
- The rejection of managed trade, i.e. attempts to negotiate levels of trade between markets.

As for 'chance', its effect is important because it creates discontinuities. Discontinuities disrupt the established pattern of doing things and create opportunities for innovation – from both established players and newcomers alike.

THE DEVELOPMENT OF 'CLUSTERS'

If, then, one regards the 'diamond' as a system, on which chance and government influence impinge, it would appear that competitive industries within a country occur as 'clusters'. Clusters occur as a consequence of both vertical relationships with suppliers and customers and also as a result of horizontal relationships based upon shared technologies and common customers. Numerous examples demonstrate that clustering is a pervasive phenomenon:

- In Denmark, the agricultural dairy-food cluster
- In the USA, leadership in consumer goods contributed to pre-eminence in advertising
- Japanese strength in consumer electronics skewed strength in semi-conductors towards memory chips and integrated circuits
- German chemical companies promoted the growth of the pump industry.

Best of Business summarises the impact of clustering as follows:

> Once a cluster has formed, the whole group of industries becomes mutually supporting. Benefits flow forward and backward. Aggressive rivalry in one industry tends to spread to others in the cluster, through the exercise of bargaining power, spin-offs and related diversification by the established companies. Information flows freely, and innovations

diffuse through the conduits of suppliers and customers that have contact with multiple competitors.

The presence of a cluster magnifies and accelerates the process of factor creation. Companies from an entire group of interconnected industries all invest in specialised but related technologies, information, infrastructure and human resources, and numerous spillovers occur. The scale of the cluster encourages greater investment and specialisation. Government and university attention is heightened, and the pull of size and prestige in attracting talent to the cluster becomes more insistent. The nation's international reputation in the field grows. The cluster of competitive industries thus becomes more than the sum of its parts.

Once again Japan provides a compelling example of the impact of the emergence of clusters on a country's competitive advantage. In Japan keiretsu have developed around the major banks and comprise loose groupings of companies with shareholding connections as a result of which cooperation and interaction are encouraged. However, while such collaboration ensures that members of the cluster exchange information and ideas about market needs they are not allowed to dull rivalry or prevent members looking outside the group for more attractive sources of supply or custom. Several other examples of national clusters are given by Porter and it is interesting to note that the 'mechanisms which facilitate interchange within clusters are generally strongest in Japan, Sweden and Italy and weakest in the UK and the US' (*Best of Business*).

THE CREATION OF COMPETITIVE ADVANTAGE

Porter's analysis of the factors that give rise to competitive advantage is reflected throughout history in the rise and fall of nation states. Companies and economies appear to grow and prosper by confronting adversity and overcome it through innovation and application. By the same token, they decline and decay as a consequence of self-satisfaction and complacency, which dull sensitivities and the ability to recognise that change is inevitable as those with a lesser level of advantage seek to improve upon the status quo. The phenomenon is reflected in

the North Country saying 'Clogs to clogs in four generations'. The origin of the saying dates from the time of the Industrial Revolution when the lowest paid mill workers wore clogs that, thereby, represented the working class. Members of this class with ambition would seek to improve their lot by sacrificing current consumption to invest in the education of their children who then became white-collar workers in the lower paid administrative and professional jobs. In turn they invested in the education of their children who secured top jobs. However, the fourth generation would be brought up in an insulated environment in which everything was provided for them and with no particular pressure to improve themselves. Accordingly, they would squander their inherited wealth leaving their offspring to fend for themselves and initiate another cycle.

Levitt's 'Marketing myopia' (1960) and the rediscovery of marketing emphasise the dangers of complacency, the inevitability of change and the fact that continued success and prosperity depend upon continuous monitoring of one's environment both to anticipate and respond to change. Thus firms and nations lose competitive advantage due to the absence of the reasons which encourage and enhance it. The absence of demanding customers, a deterioration in factor inputs or changes in their relative importance due to technological change, the development of short-termism and a preoccupation with present pleasures to the neglect of long-term investment all initiate the downward spiral from success to failure. Unfortunately, the systemic nature of the 'diamond', which means that improvements in one area can initiate and amplify improvements in the others, works in reverse, too. It is also apparent that homeostasis or equilibrium is very difficult, if not impossible, to achieve.

What is one to do? There is a large measure of truth in the view that people get the politicians and government they deserve – in other words that democratic governments reflect the views and aspirations of the majority. While oppositions may propose and even stimulate change, the gradual convergence of policies in most Western democracies suggests that there is more to be gained by swimming with the tide of popular opinion rather than against it. If this is so then change must be initiated by individuals and groups of like minded individuals who organise around them. In terms of economic growth and competitive performance, companies represent the key unit for change. As Porter observes: 'Ultimately, only companies themselves can achieve and sustain competitive advantage'. In order to do, so there appear to be five basic lessons to be learnt.

THE FUNDAMENTAL SOURCE OF COMPETITIVE ADVANTAGE IS INNOVATION

Innovation can take many forms from the first radical or 'discontinuous' innovation such as Sony's use of the transistor to build a smaller and lower cost radio. (The transistor was invented at the Bell Laboratories in the USA in 1947. Akio Morita, the president of a small Japanese company, paid $25,000 for a licence to produce it and two years later introduced the first portable transistor radio which weighed one-fifth of radios then on the market and cost one-third the price. Morita was the innovator and within three years dominated the American market and within five years the world market.) Perhaps more important is the capacity for continuous or incremental innovation which can be seen in Sony's strategy of portable entertainment systems.

COMPETITIVE ADVANTAGE INVOLVES THE ENTIRE VALUE SYSTEM

Stoddard Carpets Limited maintained both volume and profitability in 1989/90 when the UK market crashed as a result of high interest rates. It did so because it combined skills in wool buying with strengths in spinning (which has a major impact upon both design and construction) and weaving, together with excellence in design and marketing, both recognised by national awards. Weakness in any one of these elements would have dulled its competitive edge not only in the carpet market but in all the other consumer durable markets with which it competed for the consumers' discretionary purchasing power. Subsequently, a change of top management, and a failure to understand the nature of the company's competitive advantage, led to the failure of the firm.

COMPETITIVE ADVANTAGE IS SUSTAINED ONLY THROUGH RELENTLESS IMPROVEMENT

It has been estimated that any innovation is fully diffused and understood within 18 months of its first introduction. Similarly, it is claimed that 10 years after graduation 80% of the knowledge used by a scientist or engineer will have been discovered since they graduated. The message is clear – you cannot afford to stand still but must strive continuously to improve upon the currently successful solution to the markets' needs.

TO SUSTAIN AN ADVANTAGE REQUIRES CONTINUED INVESTMENT OVER TIME

Because objective factors which give rise to competitive advantage can be replicated, imitated or acquired, long-run advantage tends to reside in less tangible subjective factors which together constitute what might be termed 'reputation' and occasionally are reported in a firm's balance sheet as 'goodwill'. It is these assets which comprise skills and competencies. In the same context competitive advantage is more often to be found in marketing, distribution and service than in R&D and manufacturing. This is not to say that the latter are less important. On the contrary, investment in them is a necessary condition for success. It is just that, for the reasons given above, they are not sufficient to guarantee long-run success.

A GLOBAL APPROACH TO STRATEGY IS REQUIRED

While it is true that successful firms must dominate their domestic market, it is also true that it is the challenge of international competition which maintains the competitive edge. Only by continuously testing one's abilities with the most difficult suppliers and demanding customers in the most competitive markets can the firm be sure that it is avoiding complacency and pursuing excellence. In welcoming international competition, however, it is vital to remember that the core strength comes from the domestic market and development of the 'diamond' here must not be neglected.

Finally, however, Porter comes to much the same conclusion as many other analysts of competition in recent decades. As Baker and Hart (1989) put it (in the words of the song), 'it ain't what you do it's the way that you do it'. In other words, there is no royal road to success – one can identify a multiplicity of factors positively associated with success. But while in many instances one can point to the fact that the absence of particular 'critical success factors' (CSFs) will almost certainly lead to failures, one cannot guarantee success even if all the CSFs are present. The reason, quite simply, is that competition is a dynamic state in which two or more adversaries vie for the patronage of customers. Obviously one will seek to develop objective and measurable advantages over one's rivals but, for the reasons touched on earlier, these tend to be short lived unless continuously improved upon. Thus, from the customer's point of view choice exists when there are two or more equally acceptable alternatives – if there is only one solution then the 'choice' is 'take it or leave it'. The customer's problem is to distinguish between closely similar alternatives and to do so they will draw on previous experience, attitudes (a predisposition to behaviour) and the recommendations of others. It follows that the successful firm or nation is the one that can achieve pre-eminence on performance grounds through innovation and then sustain it.

To sustain competitive advantage demands vision and leadership: vision to be able to perceive the need for continual improvement and change, and leadership to inspire and motivate others to respond to the challenge. 'Leaders believe in change. They possess an insight into how to alter competition, and do not accept constraints in carrying it out. Leaders energise their organisations to meet competitive challenges, to serve demanding needs and, above all, to keep progressing. They find ways to overcome the filters that limit information and prevent innovation' (*Best of Business*).

MARKETING AND COMPETITIVE SUCCESS

In the preceding section reference was made to a study by Baker and Hart published in 1989 as *Marketing and Competitive Success*. Given that this book is concerned primarily with marketing strategy, it will be useful here to summarise some of the key findings of this broadly based empirical study

into the contribution of marketing to overall competitive success.

In the post-war period there was a significant acceleration in the scope and intensity of international competition. During the late 1940s and the 1950s much economic effort was devoted to making good the losses occasioned by the war so that the emphasis was upon the restoration of national domestic economies. In parallel with the post-war reconstruction taking place in Europe and Japan, a number of developing countries sought to improve their economic performance through industrialisation leading to the establishment of a new group of NICs (newly industrialising countries).

Initially much of the increased output of countries like West Germany, Japan, Hong Kong, Singapore, Taiwan, etc. was consumed domestically. But, as growth slowed, these countries began to look to international markets in order to sustain economic growth. Thus, the 1960s and early 1970s witnessed the steady growth of international trade and a marked change in the standing of traditional trading countries such as the USA and the UK. From the mid-1970s onwards the 'threat' of this increasing competition resulted in more and more attention being given to the sources of competitive advantage and the nature of competitive success.

The nature of the threat and the appropriate response are to be found documented in two seminal publications. The first, 'Managing our way to economic decline' by Bob Hayes and Bill Abernathy, appeared in the July/August 1980 issue of the *Harvard Business Review*. In drawing attention to the USA's decline in competitiveness in international markets and the import penetration of domestic markets, such as automobiles and electronics, which it had 'invented', Hayes and Abernathy pointed out that even the UK had outperformed the USA in terms of economic growth over the past two decades. The diagnosis? – an overemphasis on a financial/sales orientation, the key features of which may be summarised as:

- The emphasis tends to be upon short-range profit at the expense of growth and longer range profit. Budgeting and forecasting frequently pre-empt business planning.
- Efficiency may outrank effectiveness as a management criterion.
- Pricing, cost, credit, service and other policies

may be based on false economy influences and lack of marketplace realism.

■ The business focus is not on the customer and market but on internal considerations and numbers.

The other seminal publication which could be seen as a response to Hayes and Abernathy's concern was the bestselling *In Search of Excellence* by Thomas Peters and Robert Waterman (1982). The subtitle of the book – *Lessons from America's Best Run Companies* – helps to explain how this book captured the imagination of American managers. This was the real thing, an insight into how eminently successful and widely admired corporations managed their affairs. As Baker and Hart (1989) note, the success of *In Search of Excellence* and other such bestsellers is that they themselves conform to a formula for success, namely:

■ They assert the superiority of American management and systems.

■ They stress entrepreneurial values and the money-making ethic which had been so strongly challenged by the consumerist movement in the 1960s and 70s.

■ They are based upon the analysis of the practice and procedure of firms or people who are leaders in their field and manifestly successful.

■ They reduce the ingredients of success to simple catechisms or formulae.

■ They emphasise that the essential catalyst and hero of the piece is the manager himself.

But the managerial bestsellers were not without their critics. Based upon an extensive review of the literature, Baker and Hart (1989) (Chapter 4) came to a number of conclusions concerning a real understanding of the possible relationship between marketing and competitive performance:

1. While a number of suggestions have been made regarding the practical nature of a 'marketing orientation', the majority of writers have been content with a broad and general statement that a marketing orientation enhances success.

2. There is a tendency for many authors to focus solely on the organisational dimensions of marketing: the trappings rather than the substance.

3. Empirical work has often been concerned with only one or two factors and their effect on corporate success. This means that having carried out a literature review, a broad view is gained of how important the variable under consideration is to the success of the company, but no indication is obtained of the relative importance of each variable in the total number of factors. A more comparative investigation of the variables would greatly improve knowledge in the area.

4. Empirical studies, where they have been undertaken, have often been confined to one industry, which limits the findings to the industry under investigation.

5. A large number of authors write normatively, and this widens the gulf between theory and practice. That theorists and practitioners do not see some managerial issues in the same way is an indication of the work that needs to be done by researchers.

6. The various articles dealing with this subject have been written in different countries at different times and pertain to the economic and social environments which existed at the time the study was executed. Such environments, in many cases, are no longer applicable to marketing today.

7. A number of key empirical studies have identified the characteristics of successful design companies, successful exporting companies, all-round successful companies, etc. without attempting to verify if such characteristics are also present in less successful companies. Some progress towards defining what is exclusive to successful firms would consolidate findings that would otherwise remain uncontested and unvalidated.

It was against this background that Baker and Hart undertook a survey with a rigorous design to try and remedy the weaknesses noted in earlier work. Readers requiring the full details of this study must refer to Baker and Hart's (1989) original book. However, it will be helpful here to present the multifactor model that guided both a consideration of other work and the survey of actual practice. In Figure 2.4 it can be seen that five sets of factors – environmental, strategic, marketing, organisational and managerial – are generally invoked in seeking to explain business performance. All but managerial factors are the subject of more extended discussion in this book. Based upon extensive qualitative research involving in-depth interviews with industry leaders, government officials, management writers and other academics, a formal questionnaire was developed for administration to a representative sample of companies with the overall objective of measuring the contribution of marketing factors to competitive success.

In order to avoid the criticisms levelled against earlier studies, it was decided to sample both growth and mature or declining industries (sunrise and sunset). Within these industries respondents were selected who were successful or less successful within the industry by comparison with three performance indicators – sales growth, average profit margin and average return on capital employed. The details of the final sample composition and the findings of the survey are contained in Baker and Hart's (1989) Chapter 6. Based on our analysis, the overriding conclusion was that, contrary to the impression gained from many earlier commentators, 'unsuccessful' companies

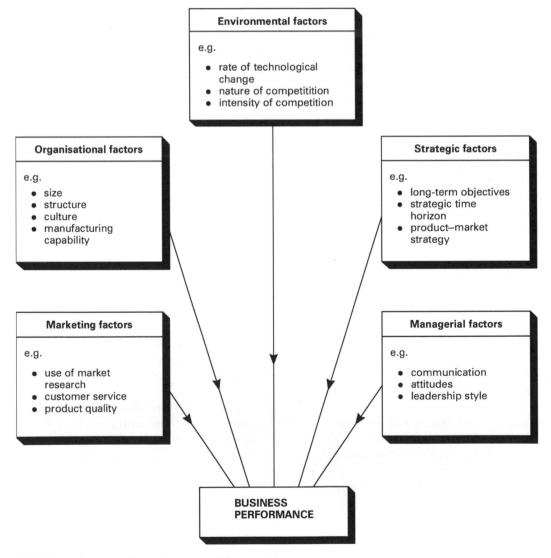

FIGURE 2.4 Factors influencing competitive success

SOURCE: Baker, M. J. and Hart, S. J. (1989) *Marketing and Competitive Success*. London: Philip Allan

deserve more credit than they are usually given. Given that the data were collected following a major recession in the late 1970s and early 1980s, all the respondents satisfied the minimum criterion of success, which was that they had survived. Further, our analysis confirmed that knowledge and use of modern management ideas and techniques were widely diffused and accepted in the 'less successful' companies. Specifically, we found that:

> At the structural level, however, the existence of a particular department's or board titles is as much related to size as to any other factors. In other words, it is fruitless to look at obvious indicators of commitment to marketing. It is therefore necessary to look at more subtle factors, like the extent to which marketing personnel communicate with top level decision-makers, or the extent to which there is a clear and defined responsibility for marketing.

At the strategic level, the studies identified a few factors that seem to distinguish between above- and below-average companies: a long-term approach, specific strategic objectives, linking strategic plans closely with changes in markets, and a continuous commitment to new product development are all activities apparent in more successful companies rather than less successful ones.

At the tactical level, market research, market segmentation, and certain promotional techniques are more common in successful companies.

Overall, it is possible to say that relatively few of the factors studied actually accounted for differences in performance. However, the fact that these tightly controlled studies failed to find more factors which distinguish the successful from the less successful is, in itself, very important. Both studies covered a wide range of issues, from the McKinsey 'Southern' Framework in Pascale and Athos (1981) and the simultaneous loose–tight structures of Peters and Waterman (1982) to the managerial style reported as being important by Wong et al. (1992).

Clearly, in order to sustain and improve their competitive edge, managers seek information and advice on best practice and seek to incorporate it in their planning and execution. Ultimately, it is clear that it is the quality of implementation that differentiates most between more and less successful competitors. But it is important to emphasise

that the quality of implementation will become determinant only provided that the initial analysis and planning is of equivalent quality. It is only when one has taken full advantage of the analytical procedures and techniques described in the managerial literature that the quality of implementation will become important. Otherwise, an excellent plan executed by average management will always outperform a below-average or non-existent plan executed by above-average managers. Without this belief there would be little if any justification for a book of this kind, the great majority of which is concerned with describing and explaining methods and techniques that are known to improve performance.

COMPETING FOR THE FUTURE

Two of the most influential writers on strategic issues during the 1990s were Gary Hamel and C. K. Prahalad. Much of their thinking was incorporated in their book *Competing for the Future* (1994) and is summarised briefly here. Hamel and Prahalad start from the proposition that:

> Substantial challenges face any organisation intent on getting to the future first. The first challenge, how to navigate from here to there, arises as both public and private institutions struggle to plot a course through an increasingly *inconstant environment*, where experience is rapidly devalued and familiar landmarks no longer serve as guideposts. (p. ix)

The authors' basic premise is that whereas economy, efficiency and effectiveness are important in protecting today's businesses, it is imagining and creating the future that is important for tomorrow. In today's competitive environment they perceive that most performance indicators such as ROI consist of two components: a numerator of net income and a denominator consisting of investment, net assets or capital employed. Faced with such a ratio the quickest way to increase or improve performance is to cut the denominator rather than grow the numerator. In their words 'Denominator management is an accountant's shortcut to asset productivity' (p. 9). This was the case in the early Thatcher years of the 1980s when Britain's manufacturing output only increased by 10% in real

TABLE 2.1 The new strategy paradigm

Not only	But also
The competitive challenge	
Re-engineering processes	Regenerating strategies
Organisational transformation	Industry transformation
Competing for market share	Competing for opportunity share
Finding the future	
Strategy as learning	Strategy as forgetting
Strategy as positioning	Strategy as foresight
Strategic plans	Strategic architecture
Mobilising for the future	
Strategy as fit	Strategy as stretch
Strategy as resource allocation	Strategy as resource accumulation and leverage
Getting to the future first	
Competing within an existing industry structure	Competing to shape future industry structure
Competing for product leadership	Competing for core competence leadership
Competing as a single entity	Competing as a coalition
Maximising the ratio of new product 'hits'	Maximising the rate of new market learning
Minimising time-to-market	Minimising time to global pre-emption

terms but employment was slashed by 37%. It appeared that manufacturing productivity was increasing faster than in any other major industrialised country except Japan when, in reality, the UK was simply selling market share profitably.

In common with many other observers Hamel and Prahalad see that in the future quality alone will no longer be enough. It will be merely the price of market entry. Under these conditions it is innovation that will create the competitive edge. In their view, top management's primary task is reinventing industries and regenerating strategy. Creating the future involves one or more of three things:

1. Changing the basis of competition
2. Redrawing the boundaries between industries
3. Creating entirely new industries.

In Hamel and Prahalad's opinion getting to the future first calls for a new view of strategy.

Pathbreaking is a lot more rewarding than benchmarking. One doesn't get to the future first by letting someone else blaze the trail. At a broad level it requires four things: (1) an understanding of how competition for the future is different; (2) a process for finding and gaining insight into tomorrow's opportunities; (3) an ability to energise the company top to bottom for maybe a long and arduous journey toward the future; and (4) the capacity to outrun competitors and get to the future first, without taking undue risks. ... what is needed is a *strategic architecture* that provides a blueprint for building the competencies needed to dominate future markets. (p. 25)

These features are incorporated in Table 2.1, The new strategy paradigm.

In order to get to the future first, Hamel and Prahalad identify three distinct but overlapping stages. The first they see as being involved in establishing intellectual leadership and foresight into industry trends and developments. Second, there is a need to speed up the process of getting to the newly desired position before the competition – what they call the management of migration paths. And, third, there is active competition to secure their market position and increase market share. These three phases are summarised in Table 2.2.

Hamel and Prahalad express a preference for the concept of *foresight* rather than vision, which is a term widely used in the management literature. In doing so they anticipated the UK government's Foresight project. The distinction between the two concepts is important. The word 'vision' has overtones of dreams or apparitions, whereas 'foresight' implies more than a single flash of

TABLE 2.2 Three phases of competition for the future

Intellectual leadership

Gaining industry foresight by probing deeply into industry drivers

Developing a creative point of view about the potential evolution of:

- Functionality
- Core competencies
- Customer interface

Summarising this point of view in a 'strategic architecture'

Management of migration paths

Pre-emptively building core competencies, exploring alternative product concepts and reconfiguring the customer interface

Assembling and managing the necessary coalition of industry participants

Forcing competitors on to longer and more expensive migration paths

Competition for market share

Building a worldwide supplier network

Crafting an appropriate market positioning strategy

Pre-empting competitors in critical markets

Maximising efficiency and productivity

Managing competitive interaction

SOURCE: Hamel, G. and Prahalad, C. K. (1994) *Competing for the Future.* Boston, MA: Harvard Business School Press

---

insight. In a conference held in 1995 to assess the progress of the Foresight initiative, Anderson and Fears (1994) suggested the following definition:

> Foresight is often defined by what it is not. It is not 'picking winners'; it is not forecasting; it is not predicting the future. Foresight is a more active process, in which possible futures are envisaged and attempts are made to steer reality towards one or more of these imaginary worlds: shaping the future. In contrast to forecasting, foresight does not assume there is one set future; rather there are many possible futures, depending on the actions taken today.

Unlike forecasting and scenario-building, which tend to extrapolate forward from the present, the exercise of foresight involves the identification of desired futures and then works back to the present to establish what needs to be done to secure that desired future. Such a perspective

assumes that management can exercise a degree of control over the future and so be proactive rather than simply reactive. This theme will occur in several places and marks the distinction between *deliberate* and *emergent strategy* (see Chapter 3) and is central to the *resource-based view* of the firm (Chapter 11).

Another important distinction made by Hamel and Prahalad that has attracted considerable support is to define organisations in terms of their 'core competencies' which reflect the benefits they offer customers e.g. 'user friendliness' at Apple, 'pocketability' at Sony and 'untethered communications' at Motorola. This approach is, of course, congruent with the marketing concept and quite different from the product–market focus that is more typical of a production/marketing management orientation.

At the same time, while Hamel and Prahalad acknowledge the importance of a customer orientation, they believe that tomorrow's companies must go beyond being customer-led. In their view, customers are notoriously lacking in foresight and they cite Akio Morita of Sony in endorsing his view that, as the public does not know what is possible whereas the company does, it is the company's responsibility to define this carefully, create a product, and then educate customers by communicating its benefits for them. They also take the view that if one is consistently customer-led, then inevitably one is doomed to be a perpetual follower. It also begs the question of who customers are, and emphasises that tomorrow's customers may be quite different from today's. With a simple 2 × 2 matrix of needs and customer types, they highlight that unexploited opportunities exist in going beyond the articulated needs of served customers. (This matrix page bears a striking similarity to Ansoff's growth vector matrix – see Chapter 3.)

A recurrent theme in Hamel and Prahalad's writing, which is also reflected in the writings of John Kay (1993), is that of strategic architecture. In their words:

> Strategic architecture is basically a high level blueprint for the deployment of new functionalities, the acquisition of new competencies or the migration of existing competencies, and the reconfiguring of the interface with the *customers*. (p. 118)

Hamel and Prahalad (1994, p. 121) go on to say:

> A strategic architecture identifies 'what we must be doing right now' to intercept the future. A strategic architecture is the essential link between today and tomorrow, between short term and long term. It shows the organization what competencies it must begin building *right now*, what new customer groups it must begin to understand *right now*, what new channels it should be exploring *right now*, what new development priorities it should be pursuing *right now* to intercept the future. Strategic architecture is a broad *opportunity approach* plan. The question addressed by a strategic architecture is not what we must do to maximize our revenues or share in an existing product market, but what must we do today, in terms of competence acquisition, to prepare ourselves to capture a significant share of the future revenues in an emerging opportunity arena.

Of the Fortune 500 companies in 1970, less than 40% existed in the same form in 1991. In Hamel and Prahalad's view great companies fail due to their inability to escape the past and an inability to invent the future. (Another example of 'Clogs to clogs in four generations' discussed earlier, but on a much larger scale!)

To succeed in the future an organisation must have strategic intent:

> Whereas the traditional view of strategy focuses on the 'fit' between existing resources and emerging opportunities, strategic intent creates, by design, a substantial 'misfit' between resources and aspirations (p. 142).

Thus, strategic intent may be thought of as the distilled essence of a firm's strategic architecture which conveys both a sense of direction and a sense of discovery. Further, it conveys a sense of destiny so that direction, discovery and destiny are seen as the attributes of strategic intent. This view is intrinsic to the resource-based view of the firm that we discuss in some detail in Chapter 11.

In discussing strategy as leverage, Hamel and Prahalad (1994, Chapter 7) paint a familiar picture of two firms competing in the same industry. Alpha is the industry leader and has a wealth of resources of every kind. It has no particular aspiration other than to maintain its status quo. By contrast, Beta is much smaller and more ambitious. While it is resource-poor, it is aspiration-rich. 'The gap between Alpha's resources and aspirations can be described as "slack"; the gap between Beta's resources and aspirations is what we have termed "stretch"' (p. 165). Given the disparity between their existing positions and resources, Alpha's inclination is to overwhelm opposition by sheer weight of numbers whereas Beta appreciates that to succeed it must adopt the tactics of guerrilla warfare. Central to such tactics might be:

> A view of competition as encirclement rather than confrontation, a propensity to accelerate the product development cycle, tightly knit cross-functional teams, a focus on core competencies, close links with suppliers, programmes of employee involvement (p. 169).

All these, of course, are central to the strategy pursued by the Japanese in the post-war era. Collectively, they amount to what Hamel and Prahalad term 'resource leverage'. Adopting a resource-based view of the firm as a portfolio of resources as well as a portfolio of products or market focused business units, Hamel and Prahalad argue that future success will ultimately be determined by the success an organisation has in leveraging its resources. These themes are discussed further when considering the idea of a value chain (Chapter 8).

The development of a sustainable competitive advantage depends upon one or more of the three things identified earlier:

1. Changing the basis of competition
2. Redrawing the boundaries between industries
3. Creating entirely new industries.

Innovation in technology, processes and organisational stuctures is necessary to achieve this. But, as we shall see, many innovations can be benchmarked and copied by competitors and so do not confer any lasting or sustainable advantage. Lasting advantages reside in what Hamel and Prahalad call 'core competencies'. This idea is at the heart of current thinking about competitive strategy and calls for explicit definition:

A core competence is a bundle of skills and technologies that enables a company to provide a particular benefit to customers. At Sony that benefit is 'pocketability', and the core competence is miniaturization. At Federal Express the benefit is on-time delivery, and the core competence, at a very high level, is logistics management. Logistics are also central to Wal-Mart's ability to provide customers with the benefits of choice, availability, and value. At EDS the customer benefit is seamless information flows, and one of the contributing core competencies is systems integration. Motorola provides customers with the benefits of 'untethered' communications, which are based on Motorola's mastery of competencies in wireless communication. (p. 219)

They continue:

A competence is a bundle of skills and technologies rather than a single discrete skill or technology ... A core competence represents the sum of learning across individual skills sets and individual organizational units. Thus, a core competence is very unlikely to reside in its entirety in a single individual or small team. (p. 223)

In order to be considered as a core competence, a skill has to meet three tests. First, it must make a disproportionate contribution to value as perceived by customers. Second, it must give competitor differentiation and be competitively unique. And, third, it must be extensible in the sense that it may be applied in new areas. In identifying core competencies, it must be recognised that they are not assets in the accounting sense of the word. Further, whereas all core competencies are sources of competitive advantage, not all competitive advantages are core competencies. Likewise, every core competence is likely to be a critical success factor, but not every critical success factor will be a core competence. (p. 229)

It is also important to recognise that the nature of core competencies changes over time: 'Quality, rapid time to market, and quick-response customer service – once genuine differentiators – are becoming routine advantages in many industries' (p. 233). In essence then, core competencies represent the difference between an organisation's asset value and its market value. This difference, which traditionally was identified as 'goodwill' is, in fact, the organisation's core competence embodied in the skills of its people and the franchise it enjoys in the marketplace.

What elsewhere we have termed 'trial and error marketing', Hamel and Prahalad identify as 'expeditionary marketing'. 'What counts most in expeditionary marketing is not hitting a bull's eye the first time, but how quickly one can improve one's aim and get another arrow on the way to the target. Little is learned in the laboratory or product development committee meetings.' This idea is endorsed by management guru Tom Peters when he exhorts management 'Ready, Fire, Aim'. We return to this need to engage in trial and error when discussing emergent strategy in the next chapter.

KNOWLEDGE AND THE LEARNING ORGANISATION

Hamel and Prahalad's analysis echoes ideas and a school of thought crystallised in Peter Senge's book *The Fifth Discipline* (1990). In this Senge argues that in the future it is knowledge that will determine competitive performance and the organisation with the greatest capacity to learn will dominate its chosen sphere of activity. The importance of knowledge and knowledge management was the subject of an issue of *Prism*, Arthur D. Little's (ADL) in-house magazine in 1998.

Traditionally, business schools have stressed the management of labour and capital with less emphasis on 'land' as the third resource element to which value was added through the deployment of the first two. More recently, attention has been focused on ways and means of improving the efficiency and effectiveness of the value adding process such as business process re-engineering, organisational design and value chain optimisation. Less attention has been given to ideas, skills, competencies and knowledge until recently when these 'soft' assets have resulted in far higher valuations for companies that possess them by comparison with firms based on 'hard' assets (multiples of 20, 30 or 40 compared with 5–10). Human capital in the shape of competencies, ideas, brands, relationships and networks, strategic alliances and the like are based on knowledge and it is recognition of this which has given rise to the current interest in knowledge management. 'Knowledge, after all, is the only resource that increases through use.' (ADL, 1998, p. 6)

A learning organisation is one skilled in acquiring, creating, transferring, and retaining knowledge – as well as transforming that knowledge into improved performance or innovative products and services. (p. 6)

Knowledge may be either explicit or tacit. Explicit knowledge is the kind which may be communicated formally through traditional educational processes. Tacit knowledge is more difficult to capture and resides in the skills and practices of individuals or groups who are demonstrably superior in the performance of given tasks. An essential element of knowledge management is the conversion of tacit knowledge into explicit knowledge that can be learnt (and applied) without the direct involvement usually called for in experiential learning.

ADL find it useful to think about knowledge management in terms of four integrated dimensions: content, culture, process and infrastructure (p. 8).

With regard to *content*, it is important to be selective and identify those aspects of knowledge which are strategically relevant and avoid information overload by collecting everything which might possibly be relevant. A knowledge audit is a useful means of mapping an organisation's knowledge base and determining what it knows and, more importantly, what it needs to know.

Culture has been shown by research to be the principal determinant of success in knowledge management but it is also the most neglected aspect (p. 10). Two aphorisms – 'Knowledge is power' and 'Ignorance is bliss' sum up the fundamental reasons why people hoard knowledge and refuse to share it or resist its acquisition for fear it will require them to change, making earlier knowledge and skills redundant and obsolete. It follows that knowledge transfer and management is inextricably tied in with change management.

ADL propose a five-step knowledge management *process*:

1. Define knowledge objectives and organisational core knowledge and describe future knowledge needs
2. Identify available knowledge
3. Save knowledge
4. Disseminate knowledge

5. Use knowledge.

The golden rule concerning the *infrastructure* to support knowledge management is that it must be adapted to the company's needs and not vice versa. It needs to be accessible, flexible and up to date and contain the strategically relevant information identified through the knowledge audit.

Ultimately, the objective of knowledge management is to encourage and enhance innovation. Research by ADL indicates that 'at least half the competencies that will determine their firms' competitive position will come from outside the company' (p. 32). It follows that one needs to define precisely what knowledge and skills the firm has, what it needs, and how to fill the 'gap' from external sources. According to ADL's 1997 *Global Innovation Survey*, getting such information is the biggest obstacle to effective innovation:

> Any competence that will be relevant to your business in the next five years already exists. If you don't have it now, you can't 'invent' it in time. You have to find it wherever it currently resides, acquire it, and integrate it into your business. (p. 34)

Auditing and benchmarking are key.

A good starting checklist in knowledge management includes these eight practices:

- Map knowledge management directly to the business strategy and support it clearly with the technology strategy.
- Develop processes for continuously linking major decisions with the knowledge management system.
- As with any other major initiative, get senior management's commitment (including that of the CEO).
- Build an intelligence system by first focusing on a few intelligence topics and achieving short-term successes. This allows processes to be refined, generates momentum, and provides lessons for subsequent efforts.
- Establish legal and ethical guidelines for your intelligence activity early. The bounds of behaviour must be understood by everyone.
- Remember the 'soft skills' that enable innovation – the ability to negotiate a win–win deal

with an outside firm to obtain a piece of intellectual capital is just as important as the skills to develop a technology internally.

- Get human resources involved early, often, and actively in understanding the knowledge needs of the organization and striving, through training and recruiting, to maintain and enhance them.

- Develop and use performance metrics to evaluate both the results (examples: incremental earnings from new or first-to-market products introduced over the previous five years that stemmed from new technology knowledge, or number of plants that adopt a new technology and the time it takes them to implement it in production) and the process itself (example: number of queries to database and percentage that can be associated with technical and/or commercial successes).

Chapter summary

The main purpose of this chapter has been to provide a context in which to consider the detailed issues that comprise the substance of the book. As the title indicates, the primary concern has been to describe the nature of competition and the role which marketing has to play in determining the outcome of competition between firms, industries and national economies.

The chapter opened with recognition of the fact that the subject of competition has been central to the formal study of economies for over 200 years. We also observed that, as we move into a millennium, the market economy has emerged as the principal and preferred mechanism for solving the basic economic problem of maximising satisfaction from the consumption of scarce resources. In parallel with our summary of the key factors which industrial economists have identified as having a major influence on the nature and outcome of competition between firms we warned of the dangers of the implied distinction between theory and practice.

Frequently, theory and practice are presented as if they were polar opposites with little or no relationship to one another. In reality theory (or at least 'normative' theory) should reflect our understanding of real world relationships and so enable us to predict how events will turn out in the future, given particular and clearly defined sets of circumstances. Knowledge, from which theory is derived, represents distilled experience. While knowledge can never be a complete substitute for experience, its sheer volume predicates that no individual could ever hope to acquire directly the kind of understanding and insight which can be achieved through education as opposed to experiential learning. But, rather than digress into a polemic on the importance of theory per se, we recommend the pragmatic test adopted by the Harvard Business School in its use of 'currently useful generalisations' (CUGs), namely: 'Does this seem to work?' If it does, then the practitioner would be best advised to use the 'theory', 'concept', 'paradigm' or whatever to its best advantage, and leave it to the academics to argue over the niceties of the distinctions between the meaning of these terms.

On the assumption that readers of textbooks are inclined to accept this advice, the remainder of the chapter has reviewed and described some of the more important ideas necessary to an understanding of the nature of competition. First, we explored the view that the interaction between supply and demand (sellers and buyers) resulted in the development of specific markets. The structure of these markets will both influence and be influenced by the actions of suppliers as they compete for patronage of customers. Their success in this competitive activity will be reflected in their performance, and the performance of the industry vis-à-vis other industries that are seeking to attract consumers' disposable income.

Within an industry, competition is governed by five main forces – the threat of substitutes for the industry's output, the bargaining power of customers and suppliers, the threat of new entrants and the 'jockeying' for position between current competitors. Each of these factors was examined with a view to establishing how they contributed to the creation of competitive advantage. In turn we explored how competitive advantage could be seen to influence and shape marketing strategy.

The analysis of competition was then broadened from the single economy to the case of international trade and exchange. Considerable attention was given to Michael Porter's work, *The Competitive Advantage of Nations*, in which he develops a modern explanation of the theory of comparative advantage as first proposed by Ricardo (1817) in the early nineteenth century. This analysis led to an extended statement of the sources of competitive advantage.

Next, the chapter reviewed the question of the role played by marketing in achieving competitive success. From this review it was apparent that while marketing alone is not a sufficient guarantee of success it is certainly an important and, therefore, necessary factor contributing to it.

To conclude the chapter we looked at the work of Hamel and Prahalad who promote a resource-based view of competition which stresses the importance of skills and competencies and, particularly, the role of knowledge as the ultimate source of a sustainable competitive advantage. In turn, this led to a brief consideration of the nature of the knowledge-based organisation and the learning company.

Having established the context within which marketing occurs, we proceed in Chapter 3 to define more precisely what marketing is, and its relationship to corporate strategy.

Recommended reading

Baker, M. J. and Hart, S. J. (1989) *Marketing and Competitive Success*. London: Philip Allan.

Porter, M. E. (1980) *Competitive Strategy: Techniques for Analyzing Industries and Competitors*. New York: Free Press.

Prahalad, C. K. and Ramaswamy, V. (2004) *The Future of Competition: Co-creating Unique Value with Customers*. Boston: Harvard Business School Press.

Saunders, J. (ed.) (1994) *The Marketing Initiative*. Hemel Hempstead: Prentice Hall International (UK) Limited.

Scherer F. M. and Ross, D. (1990) *Industrial Market Structure and Economic Performance* (3rd edn). Boston: Houghton Mifflin.

REFERENCES

Abbott, L. (1955) *Quality and Competition*. New York: Columbia University Press.

Anderson, J. and Fears, R. (eds) *Shaping Things to Come*. Report on a meeting 'Planning National Research Priorities: Foresight and the Science Base in Wealth and Health Creation', organised by SmithKline Pharmaceuticals, 31 May–2 June, 1994.

Arthur D. Little (1997) *Global Innovation Survey*.

Arthur D. Little (1998) Knowledge management: reaping the benefits, *Prism*, (2).

Axelsson, B. and Easton, G. (1992) *Industrial Networks: A New View of Reality*. London: Routledge .

Baker, M. J. (2006) *Marketing* (7th edn). Helensburgh: Westburn.

Baker, M. J. and Hart, S. J. (1989) *Marketing and Competitive Success*. London: Philip Allan.

Bass, S. (1995) Empirical generalisations and marketing science: A personal view, *Marketing Science*, **14**(3), Part 2, G6–G19.

Brady, J. and Davis, I. (1993) Marketing's mid-life crisis. *McKinsey Quarterly*, (2): 17.

Drucker, P. (1954) *The Practice of Management*. New York: Harper & Row.

Easton, G. (1995) Methodology and Industrial Networks, in K. Moller and D. T. Wilson (eds) *Business Marketing: An Interaction and Network Perspective*. London: Kluwer Academic Publishers, pp. 411–92.

Granovetter, M. S. (1973) The strength of weak ties, *American Journal of Sociology*, **78**(6): 1360–80.

Hakansson, H. (1982) *International Marketing and Purchasing of Industrial Goods: An Interaction Approach*. New York: John Wiley & Sons.

Hakansson, H., Harrison, D. and Waluszewski, A. (2004) *Rethinking Marketing: Developing a New Understanding of Markets*. Chichester: John Wiley & Sons.

Hamel, G. and Prahalad, C. K. (1994) *Competing for the Future*. Boston, MA: Harvard Business School Press.

Hayes, R. and Abernathy, W. (1980) Managing our way to economic decline, *Harvard Business Review* (July/August).

Hunt, S. D. (1997) Competing through relationships: grounding relationship marketing in resource-advantage theory, *Journal of Marketing Management*, **13**(5) (special issue): 431–46.

Kay, J. (1993) *Foundations of Corporate Success*. Oxford: Oxford University Press.

Kotler, P. (1967) *Marketing Management: Analysis, Planning and Control*. Englewood Cliffs, NJ: Prentice Hall.

Levitt, T. (1960) Marketing myopia, *Harvard Business Review* (July–August): 45.

Lilien, G. L. and Pras, B. (1994) Research Traditions in Marketing. Boston, MA: Kluwer.

McKinsey and Co., *The Winning Performance of the Midsized Growth Companies*, American Business Conference (May). London: McKinsey and Co.

Maslow, A. (1943) A theory of human motivation, *Psychological Review*, **50**.

Mattsson, L.-G. (1997) 'Relationship Marketing' and the 'Markets-as-Networks Approach' – A comparative analysis of two evolving streams of research, *Journal of Marketing Management*, **13**(5) (special issue): 447–62.

Minzberg, H. and Waters, J. A. (1985) Of strategies deliberate and emergent, *Strategic Management Journal*, **6**: 257–72.

Narayandas, D. and Rangan, V. R. (2004) Building and sustaining buyer–seller relationships in mature industrial markets, *Journal of Marketing*, **68**(July): 63–77.

Nelson, R. R. and Winter, S. G. (1982) *An Evolutionary Theory of Economic Change*. Cambridge, VA: Harvard University Press.

Oburai, P. and Baker, M. J. (1999) Strategic alliances and supplier partnersips, in M. J. Baker (ed.) *Encyclopedia of Marketing*. London: International Thomson Business Press, pp. 238–50.

Pascale, R. and Athos, A. (1981) *The Art of Japanese Management*. New York: Warner Books.

Penrose, E. (1959) *The Theory of the Growth of the Firm*. Oxford: Oxford University Press.

Peters, T. and Waterman, R. (1982) *In Search of Excellence: Lessons from America's Best Run Companies*. New York: Harper & Row.

Porter, M. E. (1979) How competitive forces shape strategy, *Harvard Business Review* (March–April).

Porter, M. E. (1980) *Competitive Strategy: Techniques for Analyzing*

Industries and Competitors. New York: Free Press.

Porter, M. E. (1985) *Competitive Advantage: Creating and Sustaining Superior Performance*. New York: Free Press.

Porter, M. E. (1990a) *The Competitive Advantage of Nations*. London: Macmillan – now Palgrave Macmillan.

Porter, M. E. (1990b) The Competitive Advantage of Nations, *Harvard Business Review* (March–April).

Porter, M. E. (1996) What is strategy? *Harvard Business Review*.

Porter, M. E. (1998) *Competition*. Boston, MA: Harvard Business School Press.

Ries, A. and Trout, J. (1982) *Positioning The Battle for Your Mind*. New York: McGraw-Hill.

Rogers, E. M. (2003) *Diffusion of Innovations* (5th edn). New York: Free Press.

Scherer, F. M. and Ross, D. (1990) *Industrial Market Structure and Economic Performance* (3rd edn). Boston, MA: Houghton Mifflin.

Senge, P. M. (1990) *The Fifth Discipline: The Art and Practice of the Learning Organisation*. New York: Doubleday/Currency.

Smith, A. (1970[1776]) *An Enquiry into the Nature and Causes of the Wealth of Nations*. Skinner, A. (ed.) Harmondsworth: Pelican.

Surowiecki, J. (1999) The return of Michael Porter. *Fortune*, 1 February.

Turnbull, P., Ford, D. and Cunningham, M. (1997) Interactions, relationships and networks in business markets: an evolving perspective, *Journal of Business & Industrial Marketing*, **11**(3/4): 44–62.

Uncles, M. (1997) Seminar, Monash University.

Uncles, M. D., Ehrenberg, A. S. C. and Hammond, K. (1995) Patterns of buyer behaviour: regularities, models and extensions, *Marketing Science*, **14**(3), Part 2, G6–G19.

Waldrop, M. M. (1992) *Complexity: Life at the Edge of Chaos*. New York: Simon & Schuster.

Webster, F. E. (1992) The changing role of marketing in the corporation, *Journal of Marketing*, **56**: 1–17.

Williamson, O. E. (1975) *Markets and Hierarchies: Analysis and Antitrust Implications*. New York: Free Press.

Williamson, O. E. (1996) *The Mechanisms of Governance*. New York; The Free Press.

Wong, V., Saunders, J. and Doyle, P. (1992) The effectiveness of marketing implementation: functional managers' views of practices in their firm, in Baker, M. J., *Perspectives on Marketing Management*, vol. II. Chichester: John Wiley.

NOTE

1 We cannot claim consumer democracy unless it is possible with disproportionate representation, for different consumers have widely different claims or titles to economic wealth. But sovereignty does exist, albeit in the negative sense that consumers within controlled supply economies choose not to consume, rather than accept someone else's interpretation of what constitutes a satisfying product.

CHAPTER 3 | # Marketing and corporate strategy

No wind blows in favour of the ship with no port of destination.

MONTAIGNE

After reading Chapter 3 you will be able to:

✔ Describe the function of marketing.

✔ Recognise the concept of need satisfaction in the development of a marketing orientation.

✔ Understand the role of corporate strategy and be able to describe its constituent elements.

✔ Define a business in terms of the need served.

✔ Distinguish the four factors which create the cycle of business-growth and decay.

✔ Identify four alternative strategies of the growth vector components and understand the concept of limited strategic alternatives.

✔ Appreciate the PLC as a planning tool and be able to use the concept.

✔ Describe three basic marketing strategies – undifferentiated, differentiated and concentrated – and relate these to Porter's generic strategies of cost leadership and differentiation.

✔ Describe the four major subsets of general management, and show how they differ from marketing management.

INTRODUCTION

If one is to conduct a reasoned analysis of the nature, scope and role of marketing strategy and management, then it is essential to establish precisely what one means by the terms 'marketing', 'management' and 'strategy'. In the process we will also look briefly at the debate about deliberate as opposed to emergent strategy. Even more important, one must also define what one means by marketing management and marketing strategy. This is the essential purpose of Chapter 3, which will be developed as follows.

First we propose to establish why marketing has assumed much greater visibility and importance in the past 50 years or so.

The second task will be to define the terms 'strategy' and 'management' in the business context, and to distinguish between strategy as the formulation of policies to be pursued by the organisation, and management as the process by which these policies are translated into action. Philosophically, our definition of marketing tends to claim that it is pervasive, and it will be necessary to examine the distinction between corporate strategy and marketing strategy, so as to test its validity.

Given a definition of strategy, it will then be argued that there is only a limited portfolio of basic alternatives open to the decision-maker. It follows that a primary task in devising a strategy is evaluation of these basic alternatives in the light of an organisation's ambitions, objectives and resources, which is the subject of extended treatment in later chapters.

THE DEVELOPMENT OF A MARKETING ORIENTATION

With rare and localised exceptions, the history of mankind has been one of scarcity. Not until recent times, and even now on only a limited scale, has it been possible to do much more than satisfy the basic physiological needs of people. Thus, the provision and acquisition of food, shelter and clothing has been the major preoccupation of the majority, with only a small and privileged minority able to develop and satisfy demands for higher order needs concerned with leisure, recreation, the arts, etc. In such circumstances the basic choice tends to rest between having and not having, rather than selecting between alternative means of satisfying different needs. In these circumstances the nature of demand tends to be simple and basic and the producer will maximise satisfaction by creating the largest possible output at the lowest possible unit cost.

Such an approach has been characterised as a production orientation and is immortalised in Henry Ford's dictum that 'you can have any colour of car so long as it is black'. In other words, Henry Ford recognised that the basic need which he was satisfying was for a cheap form of personal transportation. Only when this basic demand had been satisfied did consumers become more sophisticated and begin to look for ways of differentiating one motorcar from another, and so express a preference for differentiated motorcars, including the provision of different colours. Henry Ford has frequently been criticised as an arch example of the old-fashioned production orientation, in which the emphasis was laid upon product standardisation in order to achieve the lowest possible unit cost through pursuit of the economies of scale production. Such criticism tends to ignore the fact that when Henry Ford first produced the Model T, he was exactly in tune with the needs of his market, and that his failing, if such it was, was in not seeing that the basic demand for cars had become saturated and the demand needed to be stimulated through the provision of a differentiated product.

From the foregoing comments it is clear that consumer demand must not be regarded as a homogeneous and unchanging entity. In fact, it is just the reverse – it is heterogeneous and dynamic, and it is these factors which decree that one must not only establish the dimensions of consumer needs before setting out to satisfy them, but that one must also anticipate change and adjust one's output to respond to these changes. However, inertia or resistance to change is an endemic human condition. In the short run, inertia may appear to work, but in the long run it is inevitably doomed to failure, and retribution is invariably more immediate and final in the case of goods and services (as opposed to ideas, political systems, etc.), for consumers can easily switch or withhold the money votes on which suppliers depend for their existence. Herein, then, lies the essential difference between the marketing orientation with its emphasis upon the future, and the production and/or sales orientations with their emphasis upon the past and present, which result in attempts to mould demand to match the existing and often obsolescent supply. (Chapter 21 has an extended discussion on the major business orientations.)

If one accepts the proposition advanced by Lawrence Abbott that we quoted in Chapter 2, namely that satisfaction is particular to the individual, then it would seem fairly logical that if we wish to maximise consumer satisfaction we must first establish what it is that consumers want. It also seems fairly obvious that perhaps the easiest way to establish what it is that people want is to ask them. Hence, while basic demands may be so obvious as not to require specification, the recognition that all consumers are not alike demands that we try and classify the nature of similarities and differences between individuals in order that we may identify aggregations or segments of sufficient size to warrant the production of a specialised product. Thus it was that, in the 1920s and 30s, increasing attention was given to the development of one of the basic elements of the marketing function – marketing research. At the same time producers were also faced with the need to sell what they could make, and this led to a transitional period between the so-called production orientation and the present marketing orientation. In the transitional period, the emphasis has to be on sales and promotion, in order to enable the producer to dispose of the products that their existing capital investment was designed to produce. In the short term this is an operational necessity, for unless investors can capitalise their existing investment, they will be unable to generate funds to invest in the new plant and equipment designed to satisfy the new needs of customers, as identified by and through marketing research.

With increasing affluence, consumers spend less of their disposable income on basic goods and services, for which demand is fairly predictable, and are left with an increasing amount of discretionary purchasing power to spend (or save) in accordance with their own personal preferences. In consequence, we can discern two basic tendencies – on the part of producers an increased aware-

ness of the need to establish the precise nature of consumer preference, and on the part of the consumers a desire to satisfy higher order needs. Many of these higher order needs fall into the category of personal services, and so the two trends coalesce, with producers seeking to get closer to their customers in order to establish a closer personal relationship, while consumers seek to extend the satisfaction gained through the consumption of physical goods by increasing their consumption of services, which, by definition, require a high level of personal contact.

In the opinion of marketers, recognition of the need to establish closer contact with the customer predicates the adoption of a marketing approach, which may be summarised as consisting of the following basic steps:

1. Identification of a need which can be satisfied profitably within the constraints and opportunities represented by the potential supplier's portfolio of resources, and which is consistent with the organisation's declared objectives
2. Definition of a particular segment or segments of the total demand which offers the best match with the producer's supply capabilities (the target audience)
3. Development of a specific product or service tailored to the particular requirement of the target audience
4. Preparation of a marketing plan specifying the strategy to be followed in bringing the new offering to the attention of the target audience in a way which will differentiate it from competitive alternatives. (The main elements of such a plan will comprise pricing, promotion, selling and distribution policies)
5. Execution of the plan
6. Monitoring of the results and adjustment as necessary to achieve the predetermined objectives.

Collectively these activities constitute the objectives of marketing strategy, and encompass the responsibility of marketing management. All of them will be dealt with in greater detail in later chapters.

However, as noted earlier, many people would claim that, in defining the scope of marketing so broadly, we go beyond the province of a function of business and describe business itself. It will help, therefore, if we examine first the nature of corporate strategy as the basis for a comparison with marketing strategy.

CORPORATE STRATEGY

In recent years the term 'corporate strategy' has been widely adopted by management to describe the activities associated with the statement of an organisation's overall goals or objectives and the means by which they are to be achieved/fulfilled. It is this topic that constitutes the central theme of this section.

However, before embarking upon a discussion of the nature, scope and purpose of corporate strategy, it will be helpful to offer a more precise definition than that given in the preceding paragraph. It will also be helpful to clarify the relationship between business policy and corporate strategy, for management books and company statements use both terms in many different contexts and with many apparently different connotations.

POLICY AND STRATEGY

As Ansoff notes when addressing the issue of whether policy and strategy are different names for the same concept (1968), 'the term policy has long been a standard part of familiar business vocabulary'. However, he proceeds to distinguish two distinct connotations, only one of which corresponds with his own definition of strategy as 'a rule for making decisions'. Thus Ansoff argues that a policy is a contingent decision, in that the decision-maker has specified a particular response to a defined set of circumstances whose nature is well understood although their occurrence cannot be specified in advance, as, for example, would be the case in the event of an employee's sickness, or the interruption of work due to a power failure.

Conversely, a strategy is a statement of the action to be adopted under a state of partial ignorance, where all the alternatives cannot be recognised and stated in advance of the need for a decision. It follows, therefore, that under this definition the implementation of policy may be delegated, whereas the implementation of strategy cannot, as it depends upon the exercise of judge-

ment by the decision-maker, i.e. one cannot pre-define the situation, nor the response, in advance, with sufficient clarity to permit delegation.

Thus, under the Ansoff approach, types of decisions are characterised by reference to the decision-maker's level of ignorance in line with the definitions developed by mathematical decision theorists. Under conditions of certainty, one knows the outcome of the occurrence of a given set of events in advance, and for these circumstances one develops standard operating procedures. Under conditions of risk, one knows all the alternatives and the probability of their occurrence in advance, and so may specify the preferred response or policy. But, under conditions of uncertainty, while one knows the alternatives, one does not know the probability of their occurrence. In the latter situation one may assign a judgemental probability to the likelihood of events and by applying the Bayesian methodology, as developed by Raiffa (1968) and Schlaifer (1967), determine which of the possible alternatives is to be preferred in line with one's own judgement and chosen decision criterion. (A decision criterion is the basis selected for choosing between alternatives, e.g. price, profitability, ROI, etc.) Accordingly, under conditions of uncertainty, top management may well be prepared to delegate the authority to make decisions to persons whose judgement they trust, as they can specify:

■ the alternatives to be evaluated
■ the decision criterion to be applied.

Under Ansoff's classification such delegation would constitute a policy.

By contrast, with the situations of certainty, risk and uncertainty described above, a condition of partial ignorance predicates that one is unable to specify all the alternatives open to the decision-maker in advance. Clearly, a time must come when a decision has to be made, when one may still be unable to assert categorically that all possible outcomes have been defined. Although Ansoff is not explicit upon the point, one is entitled to infer that unperceived alternatives are ignored or, more likely, subsumed under a generic catch-all such as 'others', and assigned a conditional probability, whereafter one may proceed to make a decision as under conditions of uncertainty.

It is because of this latter possibility that the Ansoff mathematical school of decision theorists' distinctions between strategy and business policy can appear contrived. Given that many ideas that enjoy currency in discussions of corporate or business strategy have been derived from the writings of military strategists such as Sun Tzu and Clausewitz, consideration of these sources may help throw light on the subject. In turn, one of the best-known analysts of the subject is Liddell Hart.

In commenting on Clausewitz's definition of strategy, Liddell Hart (1967, p. 333) identifies two defects. First, it 'intrudes on the sphere of policy, or the higher conduct of the war, which must necessarily be the responsibility of the government and not of the military leaders it employs as its agents in the executive control of operations'. Second, it limits the word 'strategy' to battle, which implies this is the only means to the strategical end. As students of Sun Tzu know, battle is but one, and often the least preferred, means to the desired end.

Liddell Hart observes that the distinction between policy and strategy, would not matter much if a single person like Napoleon were responsible for both functions. However, as few political leaders actually get involved in 'the executive control of operations', policy is usually separate from strategy and superior to it, i.e. strategy is formulated within the stated policy and is confined to the use of the means made available to attain the desired objectives. Thus, Liddell Hart points out that political leaders may avoid direct confrontation with an enemy and pursue a strategy of 'limited aim' until the balance of power is more in their favour. In consequence, Liddell Hart proposes a shorter definition of strategy as: 'the art of distributing and applying military means to fulfil the ends of policy' (p. 335).

Liddell Hart also makes a distinction between strategy and *higher* or *grand strategy*. Grand strategy is practically synonymous with policy but brings out the sense of 'policy in execution'. In the business domain, these distinctions are reflected in the difference between corporate strategy and marketing strategy. Corporate strategy determines the implementation of policy across a number of SBUs, whereas marketing strategy defines the implementation of policy at the SBU level.

On the basis of his definitions, Liddell Hart returns to the original conception and sees strategy as 'the art of the general'. He continues: 'Strategy depends for success, first and most, on a sound *calculation and coordination of the end and the means*' (p. 336). Because of the intrinsic uncertainty of war (and competition), perfect solutions are impossible so that however much science is employed, execution will remain an art.

Certainly there seems to be much to recommend the less precise approach typified by the Harvard Business School Faculty, which has played such an instrumental and major role in developing the field of business policy. In fact, it has included courses in the subject of business policy for over 90 years now, although closer examination reveals that it uses the term 'business policy' as synonymous with 'strategy'. This is not to argue that differences between states of knowledge (or ignorance), as characterised by the mathematical theorists, are not important – they are – but to assert that no particularly useful purpose is to be served by attributing precise meanings to the terms 'business policy' and 'strategy' when practitioners appear to find no utility in such a distinction. However, both schools of thought use 'policy' with the connotation 'course of action', and it is this general meaning which is intended hereafter (Bell, 1966).[1] This view would seem to be supported by Liddell Hart who distinguishes strategy as being concerned with 'generalship' or the direction of military operations as distinct from policy which governs its employment.

DEFINING CORPORATE STRATEGY

How then are we to define corporate strategy? Our own preference is for the sense associated with military usage (from which so many apparently new business ideas have been borrowed with little or no acknowledgement), namely, the achievement of a stated purpose through the utilisation of available resources. In a business context we follow the definition proposed by Andrews (1971), namely:

> Corporate strategy is the pattern of major objectives, purposes, or goals, and essential policies and plans for achieving those goals, stated in such a way as to define what business the company is in or is to be in, and the kind of company it is or is to be.

Before leaving the question of how to define strategy, it will be helpful to distinguish between strategic and tactical decisions.

In their book *Strategic Marketing* Weitz and Wensley (1984) cite George Steiner and John Miner's (1977) set of eight dimensions, which we referred to in Chapter 1. They then distinguish between levels of strategic decision-making: 'Strategic decisions at the corporate level are concerned with acquisition, investments, and diversification', i.e. the management of a portfolio of businesses or SBUs.

At the business or SBU level, strategic decisions focus on how to compete in an industry or product–market. Business level strategy deals with achieving and maintaining a competitive advantage. Strategic decisions at the business level are concerned with selecting target market segments and determining the range of products to offer.

It is with these issues that this book is concerned.

Finally, before leaving the issue of definitions, we should note that Donald Melville (1983) provides a useful taxonomy, reproduced as Figure 3.1. As Melville points out, this is how he intends to use the terms in his work. The reader should be conscious that most authors/planners are not so considerate, and should be careful to make explicit the meaning they attach to these terms in formal communications originated by them. In practice, what matters is that one establishes clear definitions for use within a decision-making unit so that there is no ambiguity as to the intended meaning between its members.

THE CONCEPT OF THE FIRM'S BUSINESS

Andrews's definition of corporate strategy owes much to a pioneering article by Theodore Levitt

---

'Since the words "strategy", "objectives", "goals", "policy" and "programs" may have different meanings to individual readers or to various organizational cultures, I have tried to use certain definitions consistently throughout this article. For clarity – not pedantry – these are set forth below:

- A *strategy* is the pattern or plan that integrates an organization's major goals, policies, and action sequences into a cohesive whole. A well-formulated strategy helps marshal and allocate an organization's resources into a unique and viable posture based upon its relative internal competencies and shortcomings, anticipated changes in the environment, and contingent moves by intelligent opponents.

- *Goals (or objectives)* state what is to be achieved and when results are to be accomplished but they do not state how the results are to be achieved. All organizations have multiple goals existing in a complex hierarchy, from "value objectives", which express the broad value premises toward which the company is to strive, through "overall organizational objectives", which establish the intended nature of the enterprise and the directions in which it should move, to a series of less permanent goals which define targets for each organizational unit, its subunits, and finally all major program activities within each subunit. Major goals – those which

affect the entity's overall direction and viability – are strategic goals.

- *Policies* are rules or guidelines that express the limits within which action should occur. These rules often take the form of contingent decisions for resolving conflicts among specific objectives. For example: "Don't use nuclear weapons in war unless American cities suffer nuclear attack first" or "Don't exceed three months' inventory in any item without corporate approval". Like the objectives they support, policies also exist in a hierarchy throughout the organization. Major policies – those that guide the entity's overall direction and posture or determine its viability – are called strategic policies.

- *Programs* specify the step-by-step sequence of actions necessary to achieve major objectives. They express how objectives will be achieved within the limits set by policy. They insure that resources are committed to achieve goals, and they provide the dynamic track against which progress can be measured. Those major programs that determine the entity's overall thrust and viability are called strategic programs.

Strategic decisions are those that determine the overall direction of an enterprise and its ultimate viability in light of the predictable, the unpredictable, and the unknowable changes that may occur in its most important environments.'

FIGURE 3.1 A taxonomy of strategic decision-making

SOURCE: Melville, D. R. (1983) Top Management's Role in Strategic Planning, in R. A. Kerin and R. A. Peterson (eds) *Perspectives on Strategic Marketing Management* (2nd edn). Boston, MA: Allyn & Bacon

'Marketing myopia', which appeared first in the July–August 1960 issue of the *Harvard Business Review* and has been reprinted countless times since. Levitt's thesis is that declining or defunct industries got into such a situation due to their being product-oriented rather than customer- or marketing-oriented. As a result the concept of their business was defined too narrowly. Thus the rail-roads failed to perceive that they were and are in the transportation business, and so allowed new forms of transportation to woo their customers away from them. Similarly, the film industry suffered severe trauma with the advent of tele-vision, in that the new medium was viewed as a direct threat, although not a very serious one, to the traditional movie, as conceived of by the old movie moguls. Levitt contends that the film industry could have avoided all the problems which have beset it for many years had it defined its business in terms of customer needs and characterised itself as being in the entertainment business.

Levitt goes on to argue that 'the history of every dead and dying "growth" industry shows a self-deceiving cycle of bountiful expansion and unde-tected decay', and distinguishes four factors which make such a cycle almost inevitable.

1. A belief in growth as a natural consequence of an expanding and increasingly affluent population.
2. A belief that there is no competitive substitute for the industry's major product.
3. A pursuit of the economies of scale through mass production in the belief that lower unit cost will automatically lead to higher consump-tion and bigger overall profits.
4. Preoccupation with the potential of research and development per se, i.e. to the neglect of marketing.

The first of these assumptions is essentially reasonable and will remain valid so long as the population continues to expand and increase in affluence. However, since the 1960s there has developed an increasing awareness that the earth's resources are finite and there is a need to conserve and protect these resources, not least through population control (see for example, Hodson, 1972). Thus in China, where the popul-ation reached 1.3 billion in 2006, 50% of whom are under 22 years old, urban families are presently limited to one child and rural families may have a second child only if the first is a girl. While an extreme example, there is ample evidence to suggest that the rate of population growth is diminishing worldwide. On the other hand, a direct consequence of this is likely to be an increase in economic welfare so that continued growth in aggregate demand may be anticipated, although the composition of this demand is likely to vary considerably.

Similarly, there is substantial evidence to show that, for all but a few products, lower prices will lead to increased consumption, always accepting that ultimately there is a finite demand for every-thing so that consumption is never an automatic consequence of production.

With regard to the fourth proposition, Levitt goes on to argue that even in situations where companies claim to research their market, such research fails in that it only measures preferences between existing alternatives, and so fails to account for switches which may occur in such preferences with the introduction of a new sol-ution to the customer's basic problem or need. In the same vein he argues that much of this type of market research is designed to help companies improve what they are currently doing rather than probe into real needs which may require them to undertake a drastic change of policy.

There can be no doubt that Levitt exaggerates in order to make his point, for firms are certainly not as naive as he tends to infer. Also he falls into the same fault himself, in that his own projections of the changes which are likely to occur have turned out to be little better than those which he criticises. For example, his discussion of the oil companies ignores two fundamental changes which occurred in the 1960s, namely the concern with air pollution and the wish of developing countries to exercise greater control over their own resources.

Further, as Ansoff (1968) notes, Levitt's definit-ions of the firm's business are too broad to be taken literally and lacking in

> what the investment community calls a 'common thread' – a relationship between present and future product–markets which would enable outsiders to perceive where the firm is heading and the inside management to give it guidance.

TABLE 3.1 Alternative product life-cycle concepts

Concept	Definition	Typical length	Examples
Need	Basic underlying requirement	Indefinite	Transportation Calculating
Demand	Specific solution to a need	Very long	Car, Computer
Technology	Current state of the art	Short	Composite engine, 32-bit computer
Product	Product with specific technology	Shorter	4-wheel drive car 32-bit PC
Product form	Variant of product	Very short	Open-top 4-wheel drive 32-bit notepad PC
Brand	Manufacturer's offer	Long	Toyota Rav, IBM Thinkpad

SOURCE: Adapted from Doyle, P. (1999) Product life-cycle management, in M. J. Baker (ed.) *Encyclopedia of Marketing*. London: International Thomson Business Press, pp. 356–67

It is for this reason that authors such as Doyle (1995) have elaborated Levitt's definition of the firm's business in order to distinguish increasingly more refined expressions of a basic need (Table 3.1).

DEFINING THE FIRM'S BUSINESS

As discussed, the importance of defining the nature of the firm's business highlighted in Levitt's (1960) 'Marketing myopia' is that this proscribes the scope of an organisation's activities and so lies at the very root of all strategic planning. The importance of spelling out the scope of a firm's activities was highlighted during the late 1980s and early 1990s as the global economy went into recession and competition intensified. Against this background organisations were encouraged to define their core business and the competencies and skills associated with it that provided them with a source of competitive advantage. In turn, these pressures led many organisations to enter into partnering arrangements and strategic alliances to secure some degree of control over non-core aspects of their business. A very useful review of the issues involved is provided by McTavish (1995).

As McTavish points out, few organisations give frequent or explicit consideration to the scope of the firm's business. In part, this is because the organisation is locked into technology, products and markets so that its scope appears to be self-

evident and, in part, it is because other concepts such as 'vision', 'role', 'mission', 'focus', and 'strategic thrust' may all help to define the scope and nature of the firm's activities.

Another weakness of the Levitt approach of defining the business in terms of the needs served and the benefits offered by the firm's product or service is that it can give excessive attention to the customer. As we have seen when discussing the growing recognition of the importance of relationships, the essence of the marketing concept is a win–win outcome that is mutually beneficial to both seller and buyer. While it is incontrovertible that the firm can only succeed if it offers goods and services in demand by customers, it is also true that it can only survive if its revenues exceed its costs. Thus, while it may be true that in the long run all costs are variable, in the short run this is not the case. It follows that the primary responsibility of management is to make the best possible use of the resources it controls, and it is for this reason we have given such emphasis to the need for organisations to identify opportunities that allow them to deploy these resources to best advantage. As McTavish points out, this approach has been identified as the resource-based view of strategy outlined in Chapter 2. He comments:

Proponents of the resource-based approach view the successful firm as a bundle of somewhat unique resources and capabilities. If the firm's core capabilities are scarce, durable, defensible, or hard to imitate, and can be closely aligned with the key success factors of target markets, they can form the basis of sustainable competitive advantage and profit. The central focus of the approach is on developing those core capabilities that will be effective in various possible market segments and in several different possible futures.

This process of matching resources with opportunity comprises six basic steps:

1. Developing scenarios
2. Macro environmental analysis
3. Industry and competitor analysis
4. Customer analysis
5. Internal analysis
6. The development of strategic alternatives.

Taken together, these steps comprise what we call 'The Marketing Appreciation', following the use of the word 'appreciation' as used in planning military strategy where it embraces a comprehensive review of all the factors which may influence or impact upon the courses of action open to the decision-maker. This appreciation is the subject of Chapters 7 to 11.

McTavish cites a number of case studies where an appreciation of the kind advocated in this book has caused a radical redefinition of firms' scope. In the case of Xerox, its dominant position in the copying business was based upon light lens copiers and duplicators. However, this technology has been overtaken with the development of scanners that can digitise information and combine this with other functions such as editing and colour changes. In turn, this scanned information may be integrated with other digital information such as that created by computers enabling the generation of complex and sophisticated document systems. In order to play a part in this new technological environment, Xerox needed to redefine its business scope from the sale of stand-alone copying equipment to designing innovative business systems to improve customer productivity.

McTavish also cites the case of Nike as an instance where it is the customer's perception that defines the organisation's scope, which may be somewhat different from the organisation's own perception of itself. McTavish comments:

From the outset the marketing perception was: here is a running shoe, Nike is a running shoe company, and the brand name stands for excellence in track and field. However, the company did not immediately appreciate the limitations on its scope set by this perception. Faced with a slowing down of the running shoe market in the early 1980s, partly as a result of competition from Reebok, Nike entered the casual shoe market. The reasoning was that customers in any case use their Nike shoes for several purposes, and the company was good at producing shoes. But Nike failed badly.

As a result of this failure, Nike redefined its scope more narrowly as a sports and fitness company with beneficial results.

In defining the scope of the firm's business, most commentators follow the distinction made by Abell (1980) who identified the two main dimensions as the firm's products and services on the one hand and the served markets on the other. In turn, these two dimensions can be disaggregated into four key factors:

1. Customer functions
2. Technology
3. Customer segment served
4. The stage in the value chain.

Evidently, the inputs necessary to operationalise the definition of the firm's scope will be the outputs of the marketing appreciation.

GROWTH VECTOR ANALYSIS

At the time when Ansoff was criticising Levitt because his definition was too broad to be useful, he was prepared to accept that the common thread need not necessarily be strong, largely because there were a number of eminently successful conglomerate companies operating in the early and middle 1960s. Their fortunes have been more mixed since that time, because they were put together by managers particularly skilled in recognising underutilised assets who acquired them for far less than their true market value. By liquidating assets and ruthlessly disposing of plant and labour surplus to immediate requirements, the conglomerates expanded at an enormous pace.

However, by the mid-1960s cheap acquisitions were less easy to find and the growth of the conglomerates faltered and, in many instances, due to their short-term reorganisation policies, went into reverse. The more astute managements of conglomerates realised that their businesses possessed a common thread, but not in the product–market terms used by Levitt and Ansoff. Their common thread lay in their financial skills. Accordingly, the top managements of the still successful conglomerates have delegated the responsibility for the management of component parts to managers skilled in the various market interfaces in which they operate and have contented themselves with the allocation of resources between the member companies based upon their perception of their needs and prospects in much the same way as the board of a multidivisional company operates within an industry. It is our opinion, therefore, that there must be a strong common thread in the product–market sense for the purpose of developing a conventional corporate strategy – a view supported by the concept of the strategic business unit (SBU), which is discussed at length in the next chapter.

In the conglomerate form of organisation, the board of directors are in a position more akin to the management of an investing institution, in that they choose between the apparent merits and demerits of strategies proposed by a number of different companies and so influence the direction of development by either extending or withholding financial resources. In other words, the boards of conglomerate and diversified multidivisional companies influence the selection of strategy, but are rarely involved in its direct development. On the other hand, one might characterise their activity as grand strategy, in that their role and function is to coordinate a number of diverse strategies in order to achieve an overall objective. It is our belief, however, that, in most instances, if one were to try and specify the objectives of grand strategy, one would finish up with a generalisation of a very limited practical utility similar to Levitt's 'transportation' or 'entertainment' businesses.

However, we are in agreement with Ansoff when he points out that whereas Levitt's concepts of business may be too broad to be useful, the traditional identification of a firm with a particular industry has become too narrow. Essentially, this is so because many firms have acquired a diverse range of products through policies of vertical and horizontal integration in order to protect their existing markets and also, through new product development, undertaken to exploit technological innovation and to develop new markets with opportunities for growth.

While it is accepted that Western society at large is not as convinced today as it was, say, a few years ago that the undiluted pursuit of growth is automatically good, nonetheless it must be recognised that for the vast majority of companies the pursuit of growth is seen as an essential prerequisite of survival. Accordingly, it will be assumed hereafter that growth is a prime objective of most companies. If, therefore, we put together this proposition with that contained in the preceding paragraph, that strategy is evolved in terms of product–market interfaces, then we will find the matrix developed by Ansoff of considerable help in identifying basic alternative strategies open to the firm (Figure 3.2).

This matrix first appeared in the *Harvard Business Review* (1957) in an article entitled 'Strategies for diversification', in which Ansoff defined the alternative strategies as follows:

1. *Market penetration:* the company seeks increased sales for its present products in its present markets through more aggressive promotion and distribution.
2. *Market development:* the company seeks increased sales by taking its present products into new markets.
3. *Product development:* the company seeks increased sales by developing improved products for its present markets.
4. *Diversification:* the company seeks increased sales by developing new products for new markets.

In the original article Ansoff was concerned with what he termed 'intensive growth strategies' and so he did not dwell upon diversification, which could hardly be classified as such, although (in *Corporate Strategy*) he does discuss diversification strategies at some length.

At this juncture, however, it would probably be

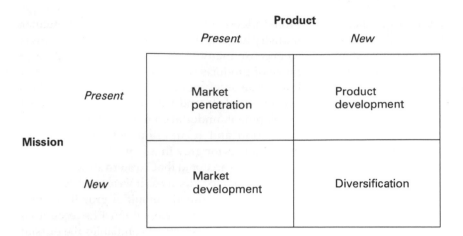

FIGURE 3.2 Growth vector components

SOURCE: Ansoff, I. (1965) *Corporate Strategy.* New York: McGraw-Hill; Ansoff, I. (1957) Strategies for diversification, *Harvard Business Review* (September–October)

more helpful to consider all the basic alternatives open to a company which I term, perhaps some-what grandiosely, the concept of limited strategic alternatives.

THE CONCEPT OF LIMITED STRATEGIC ALTERNATIVES

Many of the basic ideas relating to the formul-ation of strategy have been developed by the military; accordingly, a military analogy should not prove out of place in describing our concept. (After the debacle of Vietnam, military analogies found little favour with American managers or academics. Norman Schwarzkopf's success in the Gulf War of 1991 appeared to have radically changed the acceptability of such comparisons. However, this perception may have changed again following the invasion of Iraq in 2004, despite the fact that its failings were due more to a lack of a coherent strategy and strategic thinking than the principles that should have informed the action in the first place.)

In war the basic objective is to overcome the enemy's forces and secure control over the territory held by them. Conventionally, therefore, one is faced with a situation in which two armies face each other and each seeks to acquire control over the area occupied by the enemy. However, it is not necessary to consider the complexities faced by the commanders of armies in order to isolate the alternative strategies that are open to them. This may be achieved equally well by considering the alternatives open to a much smaller unit, say an infantry platoon.

Traditionally the problems posed to subunit commanders presume a growth strategy in that they emphasise attack and pay much less attention to more negative outcomes such as withdrawal and retreat. Further, as in most purposeful organisations, a strategy of doing nothing is not generally considered as a viable alternative. As a consequence, the usual problem posed is one represented by the simplistic diagram which appears as Figure 3.3 in which our decision-maker is required to advance from A to B overcoming the resistance offered by the enemy occupying stronghold B. Essentially, three solutions are offered to the subunit commander faced with this problem:

1. He may continue his advance on a direct line and attack the enemy head on
2. He may seek to outflank the enemy to either left or right
3. He may consider that he lacks the resources necessary to achieve his objective and call upon the next subunit up in size to assist him.

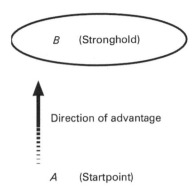

FIGURE 3.3 The 'attack' problem

In their training, most subunit commanders are encouraged to believe that the remedy is to be found in alternatives 1 and 2, as otherwise they would not be called upon to exercise their own initiative but would rely upon that of their superior.

It is this necessity to inculcate a positive frame of mind which minimises consideration of the fact that the enemy is rarely a fool and therefore unlikely to have exposed himself to easy defeat by the pursuit of alternatives 1 or 2, i.e. a head-on or flanking attack. Equally, little consideration is given to the possibility of withdrawal or, even worse, retreat. At higher command levels within the military such possibilities are considered and policies and procedures have been developed to cope with them. However, where two opposing forces are equally balanced in terms of resources available to them then it is very likely that a stalemate will develop as was the case during the First World War. Under these circumstances a solution is usually only to be found through what I term the 'bypass strategy'.

Fundamentally, the bypass strategy recognises that a stalemate exists due to limitations of current thinking and technology and thus seeks to get round this impasse through technological innovation. In the First World War the invention of the tank constituted such technological innovation although its potential was lost due to premature use. Similarly, much of the swing of fortunes during the Second World War may be attributed to innovations that enabled one adversary to change the rules. Thus, throughout the Cold War, neither of the world's basic ideologies possessed a sufficient competitive advantage for it to be able to impose its will upon the other by force. Under

such circumstances, we may identify a strategy of coexistence.

It is my contention that there is a direct parallel in the world of business in terms of the range of alternative strategies open to a company. Head-on attack may be likened to the economist's concept of price competition between undifferentiated products. Essentially, such a strategy is one of attrition in which the competitor with the greater resources must ultimately win, although only after squandering many of its resources in destroying its competitor. It may also be left vulnerable to attack by a third party. Finally, as a rule of thumb, one is only likely to succeed if one possesses at least three times as many resources as one's adversary.

The flanking attack may be compared with the strategy of indirect competition wherein the firm seeks to differentiate its output from that of its immediate competitors and pre-empt a segment or segments of the total market. Such differentiation may be objective and accomplished through the firm's product policy; it may be subjective and accomplished through its promotional policy, or it may combine elements of both arising from the firm's distribution policy.

Withdrawal and retreat have different connotations. The former suggests one extracts oneself from a situation on one's own terms, whereas the latter suggests that one is compelled to accept another's superiority. Further, withdrawal suggests that the setback may be only temporary and that one may wish to continue in competition after a period of reorganisation, whereas retreat tends to suggest a cessation of operations. In a business context there are many instances of both strategies. In terms of the Ansoff schemata reproduced as Figure 3.2, a strategy of direct competition may be allied to that of market penetration, while that of indirect competition corresponds closely to product development. Withdrawal suggests primarily market development, although it may also include product development. Cessation of operations is not covered in the matrix, but the diversification alternative bears a close resemblance to our own bypass strategy, in that the company seeks to develop completely new markets through innovation.

Finally, there is a strategy somewhat similar to coexistence, which basically is one of doing nothing. This strategy may prove particularly attractive to a company within an industry which is experiencing considerable competition from a new industry, as has happened, for example, between natural and synthetic fibres, and between glass and metal packaging materials and plastics. In many such situations the majority of companies decide that in order to survive they must diversify into the new industry and acquire the new technology. On the other hand, the 'do nothing' firm adopts a posture that the primary demand for the output of both the old and the new industry is sufficient to ensure a sufficient level of demand to provide an attractive market for it for a long time into the future. Such a firm may also believe that, as many of its competitors leave the old industry to adopt the new technology, so its own competitive standing in the old industry will be improved. Further, in that the 'do nothing' company is not required to make large investments in the new technology, it may well enjoy a period of above-average profitability.

A more elaborate statement of limited strategic alternatives is to be found in a recent book called *Strategy Moves* by Jorge A. Vasconcellos (2005), which identifies six options for attack, and eight defensive strategies. All 14 strategies are derived from military principles and may be applied in a business situation, although it is recognised that the latter may differ in a number of important ways. Among these are that in business the organisation is usually operating on many more different fronts than would be the case in war and business is continuous and there are no armistices. Further, while luck has a role to play, size does not really matter and it is the leader with the best grasp of strategy who will win the day.

The six offensive strategies are: guerrilla, bypass, flanking, frontal attack, differentiated and undifferentiated circle. In the case of defence, the eight strategies are signalling, creating entry barriers, global service, pre-emptive strike, blocking, counterattack, holding the ground and withdrawal. The first four are initiated before a competitor attacks and are designed to deter such an attack; blocking and counterattack are responses to an attack and holding and withdrawal are alternatives after an attack has occurred. All the strategies depend upon having superior knowledge about one's competitors and, as in warfare, it is usually easier to defend a position than to attack one.

If we are correct in our claim that there is a limited set of strategic alternatives open to any company, then it follows that a fundamental activity of the corporate strategist must be an evaluation of these various alternatives in relation to environmental trends and the company's own strengths and weaknesses. In our opinion, it is frequently overlooked in management texts dealing with strategy that the role of the decision-maker should be to reduce ignorance to the smallest possible proportions. In turn, this places a premium on the skills of problem definition, data acquisition and analysis, as a means of enabling the decision-maker to choose between the basic alternatives that confront him. We return to these topics in later chapters.

GUERRILLA MARKETING

As noted elsewhere, most discussions of strategy tend to assume that one is dealing with a large organisation operating in multiple markets in much the same way that military strategists focus mainly on conflict between armies. But, as the history of conflict over the past 60 years makes clear, many 'engagements' involve large, organised units seeking to deal with small, irregular guerrilla forces who adopt quite different tactics.

In a nutshell, the first principle of guerrilla warfare is 'Attack when the enemy retreats; retreat when the enemy attacks'. Indeed the objective of guerrilla warfare is never to get closely involved with the enemy but always to try and keep them off balance so that they will gradually squander their superior resources and become vulnerable to opportunistic attacks on them. In this way, the guerrillas conserve their more limited resources and use surprise and flexibility to win local advantages. As the Malaysian campaign against communism in Malaya in the 1950s and 60s showed, the only way to combat guerrillas effectively is to 'win the hearts and minds' of the indigent population and adopt the same flexible tactics as the guerrillas. By contrast, the failure of the Americans in Vietnam was that they thought overwhelming force using conventional weapons would overcome an army that refused to fight except on its own terms.

In a competitive market, much the same principles apply. Guerrilla marketers can use their speed and flexibility to win gains from the larger, established players who have more to lose by trying to retaliate than by suffering relatively minor losses to the attackers. For example, if a guerrilla marketer cuts the price to gain some volume, the firm losing share may do better to accept this than cut its own prices in retaliation and forego the margin on a much higher volume.

BUSINESS STRATEGY OR MARKETING STRATEGY?

We have already noted that a cynic might well regard the posturing of marketing men as a takeover bid for the general management function. Rarely, if ever, do we find the reverse. Thus, while general managers do not claim to be marketing managers, and corporate strategists do not claim to be marketing strategists, the marketer would often seem to want to usurp both of these functions. It is my belief that while general managers do not see themselves as marketing managers, they should be just that, in the sense that they ought to subscribe to the philosophy of business encapsulated in the marketing concept, as we have defined it. Similarly, corporate strategists must be marketing strategists, for without a market there is no purpose for the corporation and no role for a corporate strategist, which would not deny any claim that the corporate strategist takes a broader view than the firm's activity in the marketplace.

However, if we are forced to assess the relative importance of marketing within the corporation as a whole, then we would assert that it is of primary importance – it is a necessary, if not sufficient, condition of survival. As Levitt's analysis in 'Marketing myopia' makes clear, a firm must adopt a forward orientation and seek to anticipate change so that it can be ready to meet and exploit such change when it occurs. The general manager who loses sight of our simple proposition that supply must be the servant of demand is doomed to join eventually the ranks of the buggy-whip manufacturers, the railroad tycoons and the movie moguls in whatever Valhalla commercial dodos aspire to, for this is the inevitable consequence implicit in the product life-cycle (PLC) concept.

The PLC concept is familiar to students of marketing and draws an analogy between biological life-cycles as experienced by living organisms, and the pattern of sales growth shown by successful products ('successful' is an important but often forgotten qualification, for it is generally accepted that more new products fail than succeed).

Gerard J. Tellis and C. Merle Crawford (1981) draw an analogy between patterned change in biological evolution and product life-cycles. The five phases that characterise biological evolution are:

- *Cladogenesis* – the divergence of a new species from an evolutionary line, triggered by some environmental stimulus
- *Anagenesis* – a pattern of adaptation by a species to its environment characterised by increasing complexity and numbers of members of the species
- *Adaptive radiation* – a period of increasing variations among members of a particular species, leading to the formation of subspecies, each adapted to a particular niche in the environment
- *Stasigenesis* – a period of stability or stagnation when there is not much change in the members or variation of a species
- *Extinction* – the dying out of a species that can no longer cope with environmental change.

Clearly, each of these phases is mirrored by the phases of the PLC. Figure 3.4 distinguishes the four main phases of the PLC – introduction, growth, maturity and decay.

An extensive review (Baker, 1975) of the history of many successful products and ideas confirms that there is a remarkable consistency in the growth pattern they exhibit with regard to the first three phases. However, the comparison between product and biological life-cycles becomes strained in respect of the fourth, decay stage, for, while this is inevitable for living things, many would argue that it can be deferred if not postponed indefinitely for products. In fact, one of the managerial uses for the PLC is as a control device to monitor the onset of maturity, so that action can be taken to avoid decay. Such action may consist of product improvement and/or increased promotional action to extend the mature phase, or a rejuvenation strategy based on either product or market development, which may

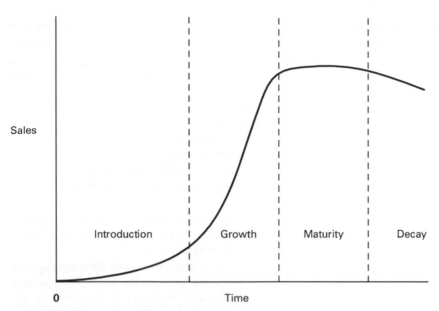

FIGURE 3.4 The product life-cycle

initiate a new growth phase. While medical science has yet to achieve a comparable level of success, there can be no doubt that it will, and we will have to redraw our life-cycles with much longer mature phases than at present. We shall return to the PLC in much greater detail in Chapter 5 when discussing analytical frameworks for strategic marketing planning.

But none of this denies the fact that decay will set in if action is not taken to prevent it. In a commercial context this means that we must monitor competitive activity, which may suggest new and better ways for consumers to satisfy their basic needs for mobility (cars rather than railways) for entertainment (TV rather than films) for convenience foods (frozen rather than canned or dried) and so on. We must also monitor changes in consumer demand which originate from changes in the structure and composition of the population, from their economic status, and in their taste and preferences due to social change. In other words, we must subscribe to a forward-looking approach, and embrace change if we are to survive – both factors are central to a marketing orientation. Further, while many external factors may impinge on and influence the corporation to change its policies and practices (e.g. health and safety at work, equal opportunities, price controls,

etc.), the firm can only conclude an exchange relationship if it has a product or service for which there is a demand, and this alone ensures that the product–market interface is the abiding and continuing focus of the firm's mission. For all these reasons we find it difficult to distinguish between corporate and marketing strategy in a meaningful way. While it is clear that within the overall strategy there will be a need to develop specific policies for each of the main functional areas of the business (R&D, production, personnel, finance and marketing), all of these will be subordinate to the strategy which specifies how the firm will approach its market.

According to Wensley (1999), there is a continuing debate as to whether 'strategy implies a formal and explicitly stated logic', whilst others have argued that a strategy can emerge from a set of decisions and need not be explicitly stated. Thus Henry Mintzberg, who first made the distinction between 'deliberate' and 'emergent' strategy (Mintzberg and Waters, 1985) continues to argue that it is vital to focus on issues of strategy implementation rather than formulation (Mintzberg, 1994).

According to Wensley (1999, p. 162):

The basic principles of marketing strategy are simply stated: to achieve persistent success in the marketplace over the competition. The firm needs to have the appropriate capabilities (broadly defined), it needs to respond to and indeed anticipate the current and changing nature of demand and finally to do so in a manner which is more effective and efficient than its competitors. The overall notion of sustainable competitive advantage (SCA) is often used to encapsulate this approach.

Wensley identifies three methods for building a sustainable competitive advantage: those relating to the firm as a whole; those advantages residing in the functional area such as R&D, production, purchasing or marketing; and those advantages based on relationships between the firms and external entities.

In a marketing context, pricing rarely offers a sustainable competitive advantage. Location frequently may but the two most important bases of SCA are customer brand loyalty and channel relationships.

BUSINESS STRATEGIES

A well-known typology developed by Miles and Snow (1978) identifies four kinds of business strategy:

- *Prospectors* are firms that take an aggressive and proactive approach to the market. With a strong emphasis on new product development, prospectors pursue market opportunities as they perceive them, often without detailed research and analysis. They see 'first mover advantages' as a means of charging high prices (skimming) and establishing a dominant position before the competition can react.
- *Defenders* take the opposite approach to prospectors. They believe in establishing a strong and stable position in the market, which they then defend from attack by offering value for money to loyal customers in a largely mature, replacement market.
- *Analysers* pursue an intermediate strategy, which combines both new product development and defence of their existing markets with a balanced portfolio of products at different stages of development. The majority of firms

seek to develop such strategies in conformance with the normative theory.

- *Reactors* are firms that, effectively, do not have a strategy as they only respond to moves made by their competitors.

EMERGENT STRATEGY

Whilst there is a large body of evidence to confirm that a formal structured analytical approach to strategic planning is reflected in better performance, there is an alternative school of thought which thinks that this approach has been overemphasised. Members of this latter school take the view that insight, creativity, human resource management skills and innovation – a learning organisation – is more important.

The prescriptive model of strategic marketing planning is enshrined in the subtitle of Philip Kotler's (1967) bestselling text *Marketing Management*, namely, *Analysis, Planning* and *Control*. This top-down view of strategic formulation and implementation is to be found in the majority of textbooks on the subject and underlies the practice of most major consultancies. It is also an approach favoured in this textbook. However, this is not to deny that in the real world the practice often departs significantly from the normative theory.

One of the first scholars to draw attention to the discrepancy between theory and practice was Rosemary Stewart in *The Reality of Management* (1963), although probably the best-known proponent of the alternative school of thought is Henry Mintzberg.

According to Mintzberg, managers are strongly oriented to action and dislike reflective activities. Further, his research among senior managers indicated that they had a strong preference for interactive personal communication rather than impersonal but formal communication.

In our view, effective strategic planning represents a compromise between these two alternative explanations. And it is perhaps this that Eisenhower had in mind when he said 'Planning is everything, the plan is nothing'. Further, while Mintzberg's concept of 'emergent strategy' is frequently presented as if it is an alternative to a formal and planned strategy, we consider this to be a misinterpretation. Indeed, in his original conceptualisation, which is summarised in Figure 3.5, Mintzberg actually identified five possible 'strategies'. As can be seen from Figure 3.5, the first of these is intended strategy, which is the product of the formal planning approach recommended in the textbooks. But, in seeking to implement this strategy, other events and decisions concerning them will occur and lead to modifications of the intended strategy. The consequence of this 'emergent strategy' is to modify the intended strategy,

part of which will be 'unrealised'. The remaining elements of the intended strategy (deliberate) then combine with the newly emerging strategy to form the realised strategy.

What is missing from Mintzberg's diagram is a formal reference to the overall objective of the intended strategy. In Figure 3.6 two possibilities are identified. Point A is a straightforward extrapolation of the intended strategy, while Point B is the outcome of the realised strategy. As a sailor,

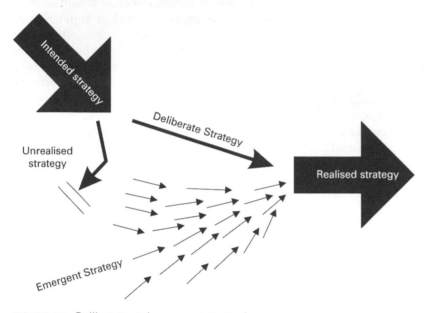

FIGURE 3.5 Deliberate and emergent strategies

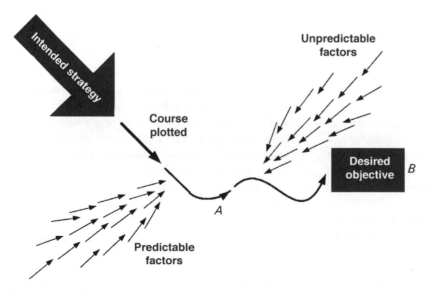

FIGURE 3.6 Adjusting to both predictable and unpredictable factors in achieving the desired objective

one of the reasons why I strongly support formal planning systems and the development of intended strategies is that, if my true objective is Point B and I have sufficient information about the wind, tides and currents that are likely to influence my course, then I may well set off aiming for Point A but knowing through careful calculation that by doing so I will arrive at my desired destination Point B. If this analogy is a reasonable one then, clearly, what I need to incorporate into my original intended strategy is the best possible forecast of those eventualities that will impact upon it as events unfold. As any sailor will tell you, the more distant the intended objective, then the more likely it is that less predictable or even unpredictable events will require you to modify your original plan. Thus, ocean currents and tidal streams are reasonably predictable on a long-term basis. However, their velocity will be influenced in the short term by wind speed and the speed and direction of winds are much less predictable than tides and currents. As a result, charting a course to one's desired destination is a continuing exercise in monitoring the environment, modifying one's assumption and adjusting one's action plan accordingly.

Earlier we cited the original title of Philip Kotler's standard text *Marketing Management*. It is not without significance that since the first edition, the subtitle has been changed from *Analysis Planning and Control* to *Analysis Planning, Implementation and Control*. The inclusion of 'implementation' recognises that the original formula was highly prescriptive and very strong on what to do. Such explanations, however, were usually silent on 'how' to put the advice into practice. It is for this reason that we consider it essential that one has a clear sense of direction and a goal to be achieved (the port of destination in our sailing analogy) and that in selecting this desired goal we have made the best possible use of available information in developing an intended strategy. Support for this point of view is implicit in Montaigne's epigram 'No wind blows in favour of the ship with no port of destination' which, in Ted Levitt's modern idiom may be translated as

'If you don't know where you're going, any road will take you there.' What we have seen in recent years, therefore, is the recognition of the need to integrate the theory of strategic marketing planning with its practice. This integration is sometimes termed incrementalism which implies the thoughtful incorporation of planned modifications in response to changes in the organisation's environment. Pursuing our sailing analogy further, while it may be the captain (CEO) who selects the desired destination and the direction to be followed, it is the watch keepers (middle managers) who make the operational adjustments necessary to implement the strategy.

In advocating the importance of developing a formal marketing strategy, Paul Fifield of the Winchester Marketing Strategy Group cites Seneca and Voltaire in support of this view:

> Our plans miscarry because they have no aim. When a man does not know what harbour he is making for, no wind is the right wind. (Seneca)
>
> Each player must accept the cards life deals him or her. But, once they are in hand, he or she alone must decide how to play the cards in order to win the game. (Voltaire)

According to Wikipedia (en.wikipedia.org/w/index.php?title=Strategic_planning&printable=yes) – the free online encyclopedia – the essence of an effective strategy is summarised clearly, and it should:

- Have the capability to obtain the desired objective
- Fit well with the external environment and an organisation's resources and core competencies – it should appear feasible and appropriate
- Have the capability of providing an organisation with a sustainable competitive advantage – ideally through uniqueness and sustainability
- Prove dynamic, flexible and able to adapt to changing situations
- Suffice on its own – specifically providing value or favourable outcomes without the need for cross-subsidisation.

Box 3.1   *Pepsi vs. Coke*

For decades the 'cola wars' and the attempts of Pepsi to dethrone Coca-Cola as the number 1 brand have been a classic case study in marketing strategy and tactics. In 1996 *Fortune* carried an article ridiculing Pepsi's efforts. Ten years on in 'The Pepsi Machine' (6/02/06), it reported how Pepsi had gained its revenge and outmanoeuvred Coke by looking beyond the cola wars and taking account of a changing marketplace. As a result, in December 2005, Pepsi outperformed Coke for the first time ever. Katrina Brooker's article summarises how this was achieved.

> Pepsi today is one of the best-run companies in the country. In the food and beverage business, there are no game-changing innovations – no iPods or Xboxes. It is a detail-driven industry, a long hard slog where gains are measured in fractions of a percent and a single percentage point in market share or margins is a big deal. This is a game Pepsi has mastered.

While some of Pepsi's success is attributable to mistakes by Coke, what few envisioned was that a changing environment would change the demand for carbonated beverages. Thus a preference for other soft drinks like water and sports drinks was reflected by a move towards a broadened soft drink and snack food market that was dominated by Pepsi. Pepsi moved into bottled water first and its Aquafina brand is number 1 in front of Coke's Dasani, while in sports drinks Pepsi's Gatorade has 80% of the market while Coke's Powerade has only 15%.

In addition to these drinks, Pepsi owns Frito-Lay, which controls 60% of the US snack food market. Formerly taking a back seat to the high-profile cola business, Frito-Lay has become at least an equal partner and a new coordinated marketing campaign, 'The Power of One', has been developed, linking snacks and beverages together. It is these moves that enabled Pepsi to overtake Coke for the first time in 2005.

BASIC MARKETING STRATEGIES

At a very simple level we can isolate three basic marketing strategies – undifferentiated, differentiated and concentrated.

An undifferentiated strategy exists when the supplier offers the same or undifferentiated product to all persons/organisations believed to have a demand for a product of that type. In light of our earlier comments concerning the individual nature of needs, such an approach might be seen as the antithesis of a marketing orientation, and a classic case of a production orientation. Our own view is that under certain circumstances a production orientation is synonymous with a marketing orientation and reflects a correct appreciation of the priorities – as we observed about Henry Ford – a cheap standard motorcar is preferable to no car at all.

Three sets of circumstances immediately suggest themselves as being suited to an *undifferentiated* strategy:

1. The introduction of an innovation

2. The mature/decay stage of the PLC
3. Commodity marketing where the conditions most closely approximate the economist's model of perfect competition.

When introducing a new product into the marketplace – especially a radically different product – several factors may predicate an undifferentiated strategy. For example, it is widely recognised that much of the risk attendant upon a new product launch is uncertainty as to the scope and nature of demand, which may result in a perceptual mismatch between supplier and potential user. Inertia and commitment to the known and safe product or process, not to mention the capital invested in the current technology, make it very difficult to forecast just what interpretation prospective users will make of the benefits offered by the innovation. Under such circumstances a broad approach may be preferable to an attempt to preidentify receptive customers – as many of the examples in Corey's (1956) book make clear, focusing on the 'obvious' customer often leads to considerable delay in gaining consumer acceptance.[2] While I have argued at length (Baker, 1983) that preidentification is desirable it may well be more cost-effective to pursue an undifferentiated approach when customers will select themselves. (In so far as they will then probably represent a subset or segment of a broader market, it could be argued that this amounts to a 'concentrated' strategy – it is not, for reasons which we discuss below.)

Assuming that a new product is successful and begins to grow rapidly, then an undifferentiated strategy may continue to prove the most suitable, for under these conditions production and distribution problems tend to dominate, with an emphasis upon cashing in on the rapidly expanding demand. However, as saturation begins to approach so suppliers will seek to differentiate their output from that of their competitors and adopt either a differentiated or concentrated strategy.

A *differentiated* strategy exists where the supplier seeks to supply a modified version of the basic product to each of the major subgroups which comprise the basic market. (Methods for segmenting markets are discussed at some length in Chapter 12.) In doing so he will develop a different marketing mix in terms of the product's characteristics, its price, promotion and distribution, although attempts will often be made to standardise on one or more of these factors in the interest of scale economies (usually distribution, e.g. car dealerships, consumer durables etc.). Such differentiation is only possible for very large firms that can achieve a sufficient volume in each of the segments to remain competitive.

For the smaller producer, a *concentrated* strategy may be the only realistic option. Under this option, the producer selects one of the major market segments and concentrates all their efforts upon it. It should be noted that this is different from the user self-selection that we described earlier in connection with an undifferentiated strategy for an innovation. In the latter case the subsets of the market are not clear – the supplier does not possess profiles of different market groupings – and so they cannot devise a targeted or concentrated strategy for matching their output to the needs of one segment. By contrast, in the mature stage of the PLC, the boundaries between different user groups have become apparent and become crystallised as different suppliers seek to pre-empt a segment or

segments through consciously devising a differentiated or concentrated marketing strategy.

As demand begins to decline due to competition from new or substitute goods, so the maintenance of a concentrated or differentiated strategy may become uneconomic, and suppliers may revert to an undifferentiated strategy. In this situation, the dying product is well known and understood by suppliers and users alike, and its marketing will be very similar to that of commodities.

Before leaving the view that there are three basic marketing strategies, it will be helpful to relate these to Michael Porter's well-known concept of 'generic strategies'. This concept is to be found in *The Competitive Advantage of Nations* (1990, p. 37) in which he writes:

> In addition to responding to and influencing industry structure, firms must choose a position within the industry. At the heart of positioning is competitive advantage. In the long run firms succeed relative to their competitors if they possess sustainable competitive advantage. There are two basic types of competitive advantage: lower cost and differentiation. Lower cost is the ability of a firm to design, produce, and market a comparable product more efficiently than its competitors. At prices at or near competitors, lower cost translates into superior returns … Differentiation is the ability to provide unique and superior value to the buyer in terms of product quality, special features, or after-sale service … Differentiation allows a firm to command a premium price, which leads to superior profitability provided costs are comparable to those of competitors.
>
> The other important variable in positioning is competitive scope, or the breadth of the firm's target within its industry. A firm must choose the range of product varieties it will produce, the distribution channels it will employ, the types of buyers it will serve, the geographic areas in which it will sell, and the array of related industries in which it will also compete (p. 38).

Porter proceeds to argue that the type of advantage and scope of advantage may be combined into his notion of generic strategies which offer different approaches to superior performances in an industry. By combining the concepts of competitive advantage and competitive scope Porter offers a simple 2 × 2 matrix as shown in Figure 3.7.

Competitive advantage

Lower cost   *Differentiation*

	Lower cost	Differentiation
Broad target	COST LEADERSHIP	DIFFERENTIATION
Narrow target	COST FOCUS	FOCUSED DIFFERENTIATION

Competitive scope

FIGURE 3.7 Generic strategies

SOURCE: M. E. Porter (1990) *The Competitive Advantage of Nations.* London: Macmillan – now Palgrave Macmillan

Clearly Porter's reformulation closely resembles that which has been used by marketers for the past 50 years or more. Cost leadership invariably depends upon standardisation and so is equivalent to an undifferentiated marketing strategy. Differentiation is identical in both models. Cost focus and focus differentiation are both variants of a concentrated marketing strategy and involve niche marketing of the kind discussed earlier.

In their standard text *Business Policy*, Learned et al. (1965) spelt out nine criteria for the evaluation of a strategy:

1. Is the strategy identifiable and has it been made clear either in words or practice?
2. Does the strategy exploit fully domestic and international environmental opportunity?
3. Is the strategy consistent with corporate competencies and resources, both present and projected?
4. Are the major provisions of the strategy and the program of major policies of which it is comprised internally consistent?
5. Is the chosen level of risk feasible in economic and personal terms?
6. Is the strategy appropriate to the personal values and aspirations of the key managers?
7. Is the strategy appropriate to the desired level of contribution to society?
8. Does the strategy constitute a clear stimulus to organisational effort and commitment?
9. Are there early indications of the responsiveness of markets and market segments to the strategy?

While more than 40 years old, these criteria are as relevant today as when they were first spelt out. They also confirm that current concerns with environmental and social factors and the importance of corporate competencies are not as novel as some recent writers imply.

HIDDEN FLAWS IN STRATEGY

In an article in the *McKinsey Quarterly* (2003), Charles Roxburgh explores the ways in which the human brain can lead senior executives to make serious mistakes when selecting and implementing a strategy.

While most people conceive of economics as a discipline founded on the concept of rationality, behavioural economists take a different view. According to them, the brain is not an objective, rational calculating machine but an organ that has evolved over time, developing 'shortcuts, simplifications, biases and basic bad habits' in the process. Based on the study of these, behavioural economics has been used widely to diagnose bad decisions, especially in financial services. However, the author claims that behavioural economics has not been used widely in the world of strategy formulation and draws on his experience in the financial services sector to identify a number of insights that help to explain bad strategic decisions.

The first flaw is that the brain is *overconfident*, particularly in its ability to make accurate estimates. The problem is that when asked to estimate something like the weight of a jumbo jet or the value of an antique, most people give a precise answer even though they have not been asked to do so, rather than suggesting a range within which the answer may fall. In other words, 'most of us prefer being precisely wrong rather than vaguely right'. Added to this, estimates tend to be overoptimistic and project higher values than are justified. To counter these flaws, it is recommended that one should test strategies under a wider range of scenarios, add 20–25% more downside to the most pessimistic scenario, and build more flexibility and options into the strategy so that one can adjust it as better information becomes available.

The second flaw was defined by Richard Thaler, a pioneer of behavioural economics, as an 'inclination to categorise and treat money differently depending on where it comes from, where it is kept, and how it is spent' – *mental accounting*. In essence, this means that company directors treat costs differently because of the way they are categorised, when in reality all represent real costs, e.g. capping expenditures on a core business while spending freely on start-ups, or creating new categories of spending such as 'strategic investment'. It is errors of this kind that led to the dot.com bubble that might have been avoided if every pound of investment had been treated equally when considering other alternatives.

The third flaw – identified as *status quo bias* – posits that people would rather leave things as they are. The risk of loss as a result of change outweighs the potential gains to be made. To avoid falling into this trap, it is recommended that one should regard all businesses in the portfolio as 'up for sale' and evaluate them as rigorously as all other investment options.

The phenomenon of *anchoring* constitutes the fourth flaw and describes the tendency of the brain to relate an estimate to one made previously. This is exemplified by the 'Genghis Khan date test'. First you ask someone for the last three digits of their phone number and then you ask them to estimate the date of Genghis Khan's death. Invariably, the numbers are correlated, with people assuming he lived in the first millennium and giving a three-digit estimate, when in fact he died in 1227. While one may use this phenomenon to advantage, such as suggesting a high sale price or citing evidence of strong past performance, becoming anchored to the past can be dangerous, especially in times of change. Roxburgh cites the example of returns on

equities where most people believe these offer high real returns over the long term. However, analysis shows that in the 1960s this was only an average 3.3%, falling to 0.4% in the 1970s. Indeed, over the past 13 decades, double-digit real returns have only been achieved four times. Accordingly, it is recommended that one needs to take a long-term perspective and it is here that some awareness of the Kondratieff cycle will be helpful (see Chapter 7).

Flaw five is the *sunk cost trap*, sometimes described as 'throwing good money after bad'. Here, the temptation to spend another £10 million on a failing £100 million project in an attempt to revive it is much greater than biting the bullet and writing off the £100 million as a loss. To overcome loss aversion, three solutions are recommended. First, do as the textbooks recommend and analyse incremental investments as rigorously as the original investment, while ignoring what has already been spent. Second, be prepared to kill strategic experiments early and, third, use 'gated funding', where the next tranche of investment is only released if the previous round has achieved its targets.

The sixth example of flawed behaviour is identified as the *herding instinct* – the desire to conform to the opinions and behaviour of others. Far better to fail together than fail alone. Given the importance of matching the competition, it is inevitable that firms should copy their competitors' behaviour to some degree, but 'me-too' strategies rarely confer any real advantage and it has been shown time and time again that innovation is the only real source of a sustainable competitive advantage.

Misestimating future hedonic states is identified as the seventh flaw. Put simply, this means that people are poor at estimating how much pleasure or pain they will feel if their circumstances change dramatically, for example in a takeover situation. Generally, both management and employees resist such change, despite the fact that there are countless examples to show that the vast majority benefit from such change. To counter this resistance to change, it is recommended that one should take a dispassionate and unemotional view and try to keep things in perspective.

The final example of behaviour influencing rational decision-making is known as *false consensus* – a tendency to overestimate the extent to which others share views, beliefs and experiences. Contributory causes are confirmation bias, selective recall, biased evaluation and groupthink. The greatest threat from false consensus is that it can lead strategists to overlook potential threats and persist with doomed strategies. To avoid this, it is important to create a climate in which options can be discussed and challenged freely as well as to establish a system of checks and balances to control the possible excesses of dominant individuals.

SUN TZU AND MARKETING STRATEGY

Despite the varying popularity of the military analogy when discussing business strategy, a significant number of publications have appeared that draw upon Sun Tzu's *The Art of War*. The essence of Sun Tzu's writing is that physical conflict is a last resort and that the job of the strategist is to outthink and outmanoeuvre their competitors. To this end, the three basic principles are know thyself, know the enemy and know the environment – all key factors in developing a business strategy.

A recent article by Macdonald and Neupert (2005) looks specifically at the latter factor – the environment – when they analyse Sun Tzu's advice on the importance of 'terrain and ground' as critical success factors. Sun Tzu's discussion of terrain and ground is focused on the physical geography/environment in which battles (competition) occur. In a marketing context, Macdonald and Neupert see this as involving the interaction between company, competitor and customer in the market.

Sun Tzu identifies six types of terrain and nine types of ground, each of which is described by Macdonald and Neupert, together with examples of their application relevance in a business context. Terrain may be described as accessible, entangling, indecisive, constricting, precipitous or distant.

In business terms, *accessible* markets are those with low barriers to entry and the key decision is whether to be a first mover or fast second. *Entangling* terrain describes markets that are relatively easy to enter because of the absence of a dominant firm(s). Whether one succeeds or becomes entangled is very much a matter of positioning and competitor reaction. If one has defined a gap in the market and fills it effectively, then you will win

share from the incumbents. On the other hand, if the incumbents react strongly and aggressively, you may not be able to attract sufficient customers to make the venture worthwhile.

Indecisive terrain is considered to be that which contains disadvantages for any entrant/competitor. Such a situation is typical of radical innovation when it is difficult to predict customer reaction and there is significant uncertainty as to how the market might develop. Under these conditions entrepreneurs/innovators may be willing to take the risk and experiment, while larger firms that control the current market adopt a 'wait and see' strategy.

Constricted terrain is the opposite of accessible terrain in that there are significant barriers to entry, which confer major advantages on the established players. If these advantages are particularly strong, the terrain may be described as *precipitous*. In the case of precipitous terrain, the dominant firm(s) may appear to have an impregnable position and all they have to do is defend it. However, as both history and business show, the Achilles heel of such dominance is complacency. Macdonald and Neupert cite Boeing as a classic example where it failed to match the improvements offered by Airbus and began to lose orders to it. Boeing then came out of its stronghold and began to take orders it knew it could not fill. This led to customer dissatisfaction, huge losses for Boeing and major gains for Airbus. However, one should never underestimate a sleeping giant, and in 2005 Boeing regained much of the ground it had lost.

As Macdonald and Neupert observe, having described six kinds of terrain, the discussion of nine types of ground might appear redundant. The authors argue that it is not, as they see Sun Tzu's analysis being to do with the 'psychology of the invading army' that is responsible for implementation of the strategy. Each of the nine 'grounds' is interpreted in a business context, and underlines the importance of the various factors that influence implementation – a subject that is more to do with tactics, motivation and leadership than with strategy formulation.

From the foregoing discussion it is clear that the firm's selection of a marketing strategy will influence and affect everything it does – to this extent marketing strategy and corporate strategy are inextricably interlinked. However, in the remainder of this book we will focus upon the marketing dimensions of strategy and will largely ignore issues of finance and control, production, research and development, and personnel, except where they impinge directly upon marketing. But before turning to this more detailed analysis, it will be useful to complete our review of definitions by considering the role of marketing management within the general management function.

GENERAL MANAGEMENT AND MARKETING MANAGEMENT

In essence, general management is the coordinating and integrative function, which both guides and controls the various functional areas of management to ensure that each maximises its contribution to the overall objectives of the firm. To this end the general manager's responsibilities may be subdivided into four major subsets:

1. Identifying opportunities
2. Specifying objectives and the basic policies for their achievement
3. Delegation of responsibility for performance of tasks necessary to accomplish the firm's mission
4. Evaluation and control of the tasks so delegated.

The first two areas are concerned with planning, and are the primary concern of the strategic function (corporate or 'marketing', according to your preference), while the second two areas are concerned with execution of the strategy. Execution is primarily a functional responsibility, and it is a relatively simple matter to distinguish between general management and marketing, or any other functional area of management, by contrast with the difficulty in differentiating between marketing and corporate strategy.

Kotler (1972) has defined marketing management as 'the analysis, planning, implementation, and control of programs designed to bring about desired exchanges with target audiences for the purpose of personal or mutual gain. It relies heavily on the adaptation and coordination of product, price, promotion, and place for achieving effective response.' More simply, it is concerned with the management of the marketing mix.

While Kotler makes reference to analysis and planning activities in his definition, this is not to contradict our earlier assertion that these are corporate responsibilities. The distinction rests in the level of the activity. At the general management level we are concerned with setting down the firm's product–market mission, and the broad strategy to be followed in achieving it. At the functional level we are concerned with the detailed analysis and planning within the guidelines or framework laid down in the corporate plan. The activities are tactical rather than strategic.

In other functional areas confusion of the two levels is much less likely to arise than is the case with marketing, for the same reason that, in a marketing-oriented company, the focus of both top management and marketing management is the product–market interface. While an interesting subject for debate, extended discussion of points of similarity and difference tends to be rather sterile, and for our purposes it will suffice if the distinction between general and marketing management is that the former embraces all the functional areas while the latter is concerned with only one. Thus while several aspects of marketing, such as identifying and measuring marketing opportunities, will overlap general management activities to a considerable degree, other dimensions of the latter, such as organisational structuring, will receive much less attention in this book.

CRM: MARKETING OR MANAGEMENT

It requires only a cursory review of the literature to establish that the acronym CRM has two meanings. The dominant usage appears to be concerned with customer relationship *management*, while the less frequent, but probably original definition was customer relationship *marketing*. Now, as we have argued strongly when distinguishing the 'marketing management' school of thought as a flawed interpretation of the marketing concept, management emphasises what firms seek to do *to* customers, while marketing emphasises what they do *for* customers.

Both terms share the words customer and relationship, so it would seem that, while at first sight they may appear to be synonymous, in fact they reflect almost diametrically opposite views of what is intended. Indeed, as I have argued else-where, 'relationship management' is not just an oxymoron, it is a contradiction in fact. While one may work at building satisfying relationships, seeking to exercise *control* over them through management practices is not the way to do this. It follows that we need to be very clear whether it is marketing or management that is intended when we come across the term CRM.

In an article 'CRM shifts the paradigm' (2005), Subhash Jain quickly makes it clear that it is marketing not management that he intends, and he cites Gronroos's (1990) definition as one of several to confirm this:

> CRM is a way 'to establish, maintain, enhance and commercialise customer relationships so that the objectives of the parties involved are met. This is done by a mutual exchange and fulfilment of promises.'

You will notice that this definition is very similar to the one we proposed for marketing in 1976, 30 years ago, namely 'Marketing is concerned with the creation and maintenance of mutually satisfying exchange relationships.'

Jain summarises a number of important benefits associated with CRM. Among these may be noted:

1. Close collaboration with customers drives innovation and increases profits.
2. It promotes a positive identity and leads to an attractive and distinctive corporate image.
3. In commoditised markets, a positive and distinctive image is a source of differentiation and competitive advantage.
4. Improved customer information enables firms to enhance their value proposition.
5. Enhanced value propositions improve cus-tomer retention which improves profitability.
6. The firm's customer relationship activities simplify buying decisions for customers and, by reducing choice considerations in decision-making, save time and possible dissonance.
7. Loyal customers benefit from price discounts and better service.

In light of these benefits, Jain observes:

> Considering the importance of customer relationship marketing, it is imperative that marketers incorporate

it in their decision-making … Relationship marketing should be made an integral part of the 4Ps frame-work. (p. 276)

But he then continues: 'In this way, customer relationship *management* (emphasis added) will become an essential part of the marketing discipline.'

So, confusion appears once again. But, bearing this in mind, at the time of writing (early 2006) Jain's is one of the most recent contributions to the debate and merits further review.

The benefits of customer relationship marketing are documented in some detail in Jain's wide-ranging literature review that identifies the current state of marketing knowledge, and gaps in thinking about the subject. The key features of this review are:

- CRM is not new – it was the essence of exchange relationships in the days before seller and buyer lost direct contact as a result of mass production and mass distribution.
- CRM is seen as originating with interest in 'relationship' marketing but this does not answer the question 'does CRM reinforce the emphasis on the customer or does it add a new dimension to customer focus?'
- A major concern of CRM is the benefits accruing to both suppliers and customers.
- 'Customer lifetime value or customer equity has emerged as the core of CRM. It is defined as the net present value of future revenue streams from a customer.' (p. 277)
- Establishing relationships and customer reten-tion are critical success factors.
- Causes of customer defection need to be under-stood and remedied.
- Not all customers are profitable. Unprofitable customers should be identified and dropped.
- 'Technology permits database marketing which makes CRM feasible.'

Jain maintains that CRM may start with data-base marketing but is much more than that. It comprises:

- Gathering and utilising data to anticipate chang-ing customer priorities and market dynamics

- Increasing the effectiveness of its contacts with its most valuable customers
- Driving revenue generation by cross-selling, up-selling and customer loyalty
- Increasing profitability by improving its time to channel effectiveness
- Using privacy as an avenue to customer loyalty and increased wallet sharing
- Monitoring and measuring business results. (p. 278)

In order to create a customer-centric organisation in an increasingly competitive environment, Jain believes that everyone in the organisation must focus on the customer and that marketing is the function to facilitate this. He then suggests that to achieve this kind of transformation 'a fifth "P" be added to the marketing mix framework; this may be called "profiling the customer".'

Jain then conceptualises the fifth P as involving:

1. Capturing the right customer information
2. Managing the quality customer data
3. Integrating channels to build relationships
4. Understanding customer value
5. Designing a revenue and customer-focused CRM strategy
6. Using privacy to enhance profitability
7. Deploying cross-departmental business processes

8. Measuring incremental CRM results.

The traditional marketing mix is seen as the means of making contact with buyers through transactions. The challenge is to convert these into relationships and it is here that the fifth P is seen as the basis of developing knowledge of the customer that can be used to create scenarios about their future needs and behaviour. In turn, this knowledge can be used to deliver superior value and build trust and commitment.

However, in order to achieve this, there is a need for more research into a number of issues, which Jain combines into nine topics and 26 specific propositions. He concludes by saying:

> While CRM is absolutely necessary to gain competitive advantage, most firms have failed in launching a successful CRM program because CRM has been practiced as a technical rather than as a marketing concern. The customer should be the focus of any CRM exercise.
>
> In my view this will only occur when we can escape from the old marketing management paradigm, realise that marketing need not be a zero sum game with winners and losers, and subscribe fully to the marketing concept, with its philosophy of 'mutually satisfying exchange relationships'. (Jain, 2005)

Chapter summary

In this chapter we have attempted to establish the nature and scope of both corporate and marketing strategy in order to highlight the similarities and differences between the two activities. Essentially our position is that in so far as the attainment of corporate objectives is a direct consequence of its success in managing the interface between its output (product or service) and its markets (customers), then corporate strategy is indistinguishable from marketing strategy. That said, it is also clear that the interests and responsibilities of the corporate strategist or general manager extend well beyond the functional interests and responsibilities of the marketing manager. The remaining chapters are concerned largely with clarifying these potentially contradictory propositions, and in Chapter 4 we start by examining in detail the precise nature of strategic marketing planning.

Recommended reading

Cravens, D. W. and Piercy, N. F. (2005) *Strategic Marketing* (8th edn). New York: McGraw-Hill Education.

Doyle, P. (2000) *Value-Based Marketing*. Chichester: John Wiley and Sons.

Kay, J. (1993) *Foundations of Corporate Success*. Oxford: Oxford University Press.

Wensley, R., The basics of marketing strategy in Baker, M. J. (ed.) (2003) *The Marketing Book* (5th edn). Oxford: Butterworth Heinemann.

REFERENCES

Abell, D. F. (1980) *Defining the Business*. Englewood Cliffs, NJ: Prentice Hall.

Andrews, K. R. (1971) *The Concept of Corporate Strategy*. Homewood, IL: Dow Jones-Irwin.

Ansoff, I. (1957) Strategies for diversification. *Harvard Business Review* (September/October).

Ansoff, I. (1965) *Corporate Strategy*. New York: McGraw-Hill

Ansoff, I. (1968) *Corporate Strategy*. Harmondsworth: Penguin.

Baker, M. J. (1975) *Marketing New Industrial Products*. London: Macmillan – now Palgrave Macmillan (especially Chapter 2).

Baker, M. J. (1976) *Marketing: Theory and Practice*. London: Macmillan – now Palgrave Macmillan.

Baker, M. J. (1983) *Market Development*. Harmondsworth: Penguin.

Bell, M. (1966) *Marketing Concepts and Strategy*. London: Macmillan – now Palgrave Macmillan.

Brooker, K. (2006) The Pepsi machine, *Fortune*, 2 June.

Corey, E. R. (1956) *The Development of Markets for New Materials*. Boston, MA: Harvard University Press.

Doyle, P. (1999) Product life-cycle management, in M. J. Baker (ed.) *Encyclopedia of Marketing*. London: International Thomson Business Press, pp. 356–67.

Hamel, G. and Prahalad, C. K. (1994) *Competing for the Future*. Boston, MA: Harvard Business School Press.

Hodson, H. V. (1972) *The Diseconomics of Growth*. London: Pan/Ballantyne.

Jain, S. C. (2005) CRM shifts the paradigm, *Journal of Strategic Marketing*, **13**(4): 275–291.

Kotler, P. (1967) *Marketing Management: Analysis, Planning, Implementation and Control*. Englewood Cliffs, NJ: Prentice Hall.

Kotler, P. (1972) *Marketing Management* (2nd edn). Englewood Cliffs, NJ: Prentice Hall.

Learned, E. P., Christensen, C. R., Andrews, K. R. and Guth, W. D. (1965) *Business Policy: Text and Cases*. Homewood, IL: Irwin.

Levitt, T. (1960) Marketing myopia, *Harvard Business Review* (July–August).

Liddell Hart, B. H. (1967) *Strategy: The Indirect Approach* (2nd edn). London: Faber & Faber.

Macdonald, J. and Neuport, K. (2005) Applying Sun Tzu's terrain and ground to the study of marketing strategy, *Journal of Strategic Marketing*, **13**(4): 293–304.

McTavish, R. (1995) One more time: what business are you in?, *Long Range Planning*, **28**(2).

Melville, D. (1983) Top management's role in strategic planning, in Kerin, R. A. and Peterson, R. A. (eds) *Perspectives on Strategic Marketing Management*. Boston, MA: Allyn & Bacon.

Miles, R. E., and Snow, C. (1978) *Organisational Strategy, Structure and Process*. New York: McGraw-Hill.

Mintzberg, H. (1994) *The Rise and Fall of Strategic Planning*. Hemel Hempstead: Prentice Hall.

Mintzberg, H. and Waters, J. A. (1985) Of strategies deliberate and emergent, *Strategic Management Journal*, **6**: 257–72.

Porter, M. E. (1990) *The Competitive Advantage of Nations*. Basingstoke: Macmillan – now Palgrave Macmillan.

Raiffa, H. (1968) *Decision Analysis*. Reading, MA: Addison-Wesley.

Schlaifer, R. O. (1967) *The Analysis of Decisions under Uncertainty*. New York: McGraw-Hill.

Steiner, G. and Miner, J. (1977) *Management Policy and Strategy: Text, Readings and Cases*. New York: Macmillan.

Stewart, R. (1963) *The Reality of Management*. London: Heinemann.

Tellis, G. J. and Crawford, C. M. (1981) An evolutionary approach to product growth theory, *Journal of Marketing*, **45**(4): 125–32.

Vasconcellos, J. e Sá, (2005) Strategy moves, in *UK Marketing Pocket Book*. World Advertising Research Centre, Henley: Financial Times/Prentice Hall.

Weitz, B. A. and Wensley, R. (1984) *Strategic Marketing*. Boston, MA: New-Publishing.

Wensley, R. (1999) Marketing strategies in M. J. Baker (ed.) *Encyclopedia of Marketing*. London: International Thompson Business Press.

NOTES

1   It is acknowledged that many authors still prefer to maintain a distinction between policy and strategy. Thus Martin Bell writes: 'Strategy is not the same as policy, and is always subordinate to it. Military strategy in the United States in planned within the framework of national defence policy. This policy is established by the President of the United States in line with the basic foreign relations objectives of his administration.' Clearly, Bell regards policy as superior to strategy, while Ansoff regards it as inferior, and most authors use the terms as if they were interchangeable. Our own view, as with the definition of marketing, is that semantics are less important than appreciation of the distinction between objectives and courses of action to achieve them.

2   For example, linoleum manufacturers did not see vinyl flooring as the logical development in the smooth floor-covering market; they regarded it as a suicidal means of highlighting the disadvantages of linoleum, thereby making their investment obsolete. The manufacturers of van trailers could see no benefit in substituting aluminium for timber and steel, with which they were familiar, as the potential increase in load capacity accrued to the operators. Only when the latter demanded the lighter van was the change made.

Principles of strategic marketing planning

If you don't know where you are going any road will take you there.

TED LEVITT

After reading Chapter 4 you will be able to:

✔ Justify the role and importance of strategic marketing planning (SMP).

✔ Explain the concepts of mission, vision and strategic intent.

✔ Trace the development of alternative approaches to SMP.

✔ Define SMP.

✔ Define the nature of objectives and show how these shape marketing strategies.

✔ Describe the cycle of SMP and the stages involved in it.

✔ Illustrate some key principles of SMP using a framework developed by Arthur D. Little.

✔ Identify and describe the three steps involved in formulating a corporate strategy.

✔ Spell out some of the criticisms of and obstacles to the adoption and implementation of SMP.

INTRODUCTION

In Chapter 3 we attempted to provide some answers to basic questions concerning the nature and scope of marketing and the distinction, if any, between corporate and marketing strategy. Underlying much of the discussion was an implicit recognition of the evolutionary progress of mankind and the inevitability of change in the economic and social environment in which individuals and the organisations to which they belong must live out their lives. While some fatalists might take the view that they can do little if anything to control these environmental forces for change, at the very least management believe that they should seek to anticipate change so that they and their organisation may be best placed to respond to this change when it occurs. However, most managers do not only wish to respond to their environment, they also wish to exercise some control over it through their own actions. It is for this reason that planning plays such an important role in the management task.

In this chapter we shall seek to establish a framework not only for strategic marketing planning (SMP), but also for the book as a whole in the sense that most if not all of the later chapters will seek to expound and clarify specific aspects of marketing planning. However, before looking at SMP as a process it will be helpful if we consider first some of the benefits claimed for formal planning as well as arguments against it. Next we shall establish a framework for SMP, and the chapter will conclude with a summary of some of the key principles of SMP and their relationship to the formulation of corporate strategy.

However, before proceeding to a detailed analysis of the nature of SMP, and the different approaches and techniques used in its implementation, it will be helpful to sketch in the stages in the evolution of management systems that have given rise to the current emphasis upon such planning. It is also important to stress that while this textbook is founded on the same basic assumption as most other textbooks – namely, that we are concerned with an established medium- to large-sized company with several products operating in a number of different markets, and with a fairly sophisticated management structure – the underlying principles of SMP are just as relevant to the small and newly established firm with a single product and a single market.

The choice of what type of organisational process is used to formulate strategy ranges from the 'back of an envelope' informality of the entrepreneur, to the 'muddling through' or adaptive approach, to the highly formalised systems of planning strategy typically applied by the large multinationals. The stage of development of the organisation is therefore one of the major factors influencing the degree of formality in the process (see Table 4.1).

TABLE 4.1 Factors influencing an organisation's planning system

Organisational factors	Informal (simple)	Formal (sophisticated)
Organisational size	small	very large
Organisational complexity	simple	complex
Magnitude of gap between present position and objectives	small	very large
Magnitude of change anticipated in the organisation's strategy	small	very large
Environmental factors		
Rate of change in the organisation's environment	little	rapid change
Degree of competition in the industry	little	rapid change
Length of time for which resources must be committed	short	very long
Process factors		
Need for internal consistency	little	great
Need for comprehensiveness	little	great

SOURCE: Hofer, C. W. (1977) *Conceptual Constructs for Formulating Corporate and Business Strategies*. Boston: Intercollegiate Case Clearing House, 9–378–754, p. 33

TABLE 4.2 Stages of corporate development

	1 Start-up	2 SME/SBU	3 Multidivisional	4 Multinational
Structure	Owner-manager	Single unit Teams of managers	Several units Management teams Corporate HQ	As for 3 but operating in several countries with both national and corporate HQ
Product–market relationship	Single product – one market, one distribution channel	Portfolio of related products Limited markets and distribution channels	Portfolio of products serving several categories Multiple markets and channels	Ditto but portfolio may be standardised (global) or adapted to each country
Top management	Single manager, specialist skills, e.g. accounting, outsourced	Several managers, with complementary functional skills	Ditto but with additional specialist functions to coordinate the SBUs	Ditto
Performance measures	Informal, personalised, not based on formal criteria	Operating budgets for each function. Broad-based financial measures like ROI	Ditto but with more detail and comparative measures	Ditto

SOURCE: Based on an idea by Salter, M. (1968), Harvard Business School class notes

Clearly the implicit assumption of the large complex organisation is necessary to justify consideration of marketing as a distinct function in its own right, but this does not deny the importance of a marketing orientation and the discipline of formal planning in organisations at an early stage of corporate development. In Table 4.2 we show a concise statement of the stages of corporate development based on an idea of Malcolm Salter of the Harvard Business School. While the following review will be largely concerned with firms in stages 3 and 4, firms in stages 1 and 2 will still benefit considerably from applying the principles discussed here – indeed firms at stages 1 and 2 correspond closely to the 'mini-businesses' or strategic business units which are the basic building blocks of most formal planning systems.

However, irrespective of the size of the business unit, Gunn (1991) suggests that strategic management implies a number of distinctive characteristics which may be summarised as:

1. Involves a proactive rather than reactive approach
2. Is a deliberate self-aware style of management in which managers 'plan to plan'
3. Is a style of management characterised by 'rationality'
4. Sees strategy as providing a framework within

which later policies and specific decisions will be made
5. Involves being able to ask (and answer) the questions: What are we trying to do? Why? How will we know when we've done it?
6. Requires managers who look further ahead, can see the broad picture, are more analytical and emphasise the need for choice
7. Emphasises the need for choice in terms of alternative futures, priorities between objectives and the generation of options
8. Requires close attention to the implementation and monitoring of innovative policies and courses of action
9. Involves an understanding of and sensitivity to trends in the larger environment.

All these characteristics will become evident in the chapters that follow.

THE EVOLUTION OF MANAGEMENT SYSTEMS[1]

In Chapter 3 we traced the development of management through a series of broad orientations from production through sales to marketing and concluded that a marketing orientation is the most satisfactory approach to solving the basic economic problem of maximising satisfaction from the consumption of scarce resources. But, while a marketing orientation has dominated practice for the past 50 years, a closer examination soon reveals a number of distinct phases in the evolution of the management systems used to translate philosophy into action:

1. *The 1950s:* During this decade post-war reconstruction and the reversion to a peacetime economy gave rise to a boom with full employment and significant growth in real incomes. Demand was buoyant and the major emphasis was upon production. However, competition was fierce and efficiency in manufacturing, distribution and sales were all at a premium leading to stress being placed upon professional management, decentralisation and management by objectives. Major car manufacturers (GM and Ford) were at the forefront of thinking and practice during the earlier parts of the decade with companies like General Electric and Pillsbury taking the lead in the later years.

2. *The 1960s:* Demand and supply were in near equilibrium and producers turned increasingly to marketing as a means of differentiating themselves in the eyes of consumers. Market segmentation and product diversification emerged as key strategies and gave rise to a focus on profit centres and the use of standardised systems of control in order to measure and direct the performance of these distinctive units. A belief developed that the key to continued success was to acquire a portfolio of businesses that complemented and reinforced one another, the 'conglomerate', of which International Telegraph and Telephone (ITT) and Lifetime Television (LTV) were prime examples. A salient feature of the conglomerate is that top management redeploys capital within the group on the basis of its expectations about future earnings related to the assets employed. With the benefit of hindsight, it is now clear that this mechanistic approach gives rise to an emphasis on the short term and those investments that offer the best opportunity for certain returns – a 'milking' strategy that gives insufficient attention to the inevitable cycle of growth, maturity and decay characterising the changing fortunes of every industry.

3. *The late 1960s:* Towards the end of the 1960s, the underlying dissatisfaction of critics of the materialistic society (Galbraith, Nader, Packard) surfaced as the consumerist movement and forced manufacturers to give even closer attention to products, markets and competition. This concern was sharpened by the intensification of international competition as domestic markets became saturated and firms looked elsewhere for new opportunities for growth.

4. *The 1970s:* The pressure exerted by better informed and more discriminating customers increases and is given even greater impetus by the oil crisis of 1973. The reverberations of the oil crisis create a climate of turbulence that lends even more force to a competitive, market-oriented focus, and a change from profit centres to businesses as the key factor in developing strategies for coping with a volatile environment. This trend continues throughout the 1970s.

5. *The 1980s:* Recession is now worldwide and the competition is global. Faced with an increasingly complex and often hostile environment, firms increase their efforts to develop new products and markets and so exaggerate the intensity of the competitive pressures they are seeking to escape. The publication of Hayes and Abernathy's pungent criticisms (1980), and Michael Porter's (1980) book emphasise the deficiencies of the milking approach favoured by professional managers with a short-term financial orientation. The need to adopt a more flexible and long-term financial orientation, which recognises the cyclical nature of competition, is acknowledged and puts a premium on strategic analysis and long-range planning.

6. *The 1990s:* Recessionary conditions prevail in the West, but rapid growth is maintained in the 'tiger' economies of Southeast Asia until the late 1990s when overheating leads to a near collapse in Indonesia, Malaysia and Thailand, and very difficult conditions in Hong Kong, Japan and South Korea. Global players concentrate on core competencies and strategic alliances and outsourcing are commonplace. Scenario planning assumes increasing importance with an emphasis on foresight and plotting the future.

In parallel with the evolution of management systems, there also evolved a series of different approaches to planning. My colleague at Strath-clyde University, Professor Lewis Gunn (1991), has produced an excellent summary of the types of strategic planning, which is reproduced as Table 4.3. As well as summarising the main approaches to strategic planning, Table 4.3 also reflects the chronology of the development of planning systems from the highly structured top-down systems planning of the 1960s and early 1970s to the more marketing-oriented approaches of the late 1970s and early 1980s. In turn, the formalised approaches began to give way to less formalised alternatives – strategic issues planning and logical incrementalism – in the mid-to-late 1980s. (Logical incrementalism has always been with us but enjoyed a revival at this time as a reaction against the perceived failures of overformalised planning approaches.) During the 1990s, the fashion swung towards the participative and cultural modes that recognise the need to involve multiple constituencies in the planning process and place particular emphasis upon the underlying value systems that bond people to organisations.

TABLE 4.3 Types of strategic planning

Systems planning:	Comprehensive 'corporate top down' 'Paralysis by analysis'?
SWOT:	Strengths and weaknesses Opportunities and threats
Marketing approaches:	Industry structure analysis Competitive strategy Portfolio analysis
Strategic issues planning:	Selective, focused key (make or break) Issues c.f. 'KRA' (key results areas)
Logical incrementalism:	Muddling through opportunism, side bets Tentative, experimental
Political/participative:	Pluralist, stakeholder model Consult, negotiate, bargain
Cultural ('excellence'):	Integrating corporate 'culture' 'Framework for innovation' Avoid 'paralysis by analysis'

SOURCE: Gunn, L. (1991) Teaching notes. University of Strathclyde

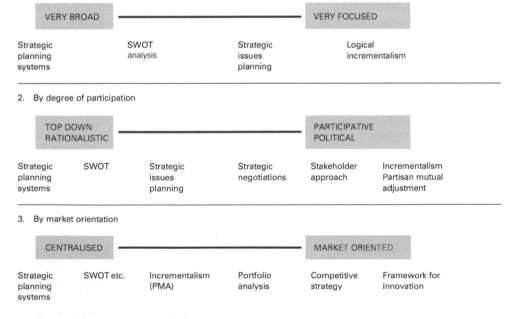

Along three dimensions . . .

1. By comprehensiveness of approach

VERY BROAD	————————		VERY FOCUSED
Strategic planning systems	SWOT analysis	Strategic issues planning	Logical incrementalism

2. By degree of participation

TOP DOWN RATIONALISTIC			PARTICIPATIVE POLITICAL	
Strategic planning systems	SWOT	Strategic issues planning	Strategic negotiations	Stakeholder approach	Incrementalism Partisan mutual adjustment

3. By market orientation

CENTRALISED	————————		MARKET ORIENTED
Strategic planning systems	SWOT etc.	Incrementalism (PMA)	Portfolio analysis	Competitive strategy	Framework for innovation

ALL TRENDS ARE TO RIGHT?

FIGURE 4.1 Trends in strategic planning

SOURCE: Gunn, L. (1991) Teaching notes. University of Strathclyde

Gunn categorises trends in strategic planning (Figure 4.1) along three dimensions in terms of their comprehensiveness of approach, degree of participation and emphasis upon the market (as opposed to the organisation itself) and poses the question as to whether all trends are towards the right. At the time of writing, this would seem to be the case.

McDonald (2003) cites Baillie and Johnston (1994) who identify six different approaches to the development of business strategies:

1. *A planning model.* Here, strategic decisions are reached by using a sequential planned search for optimum solutions to define problems. This process is highly rational and is fuelled by concrete data.
2. *An interpreted model.* Here, the organisation is regarded as a collection of associations, sharing similar values, beliefs and perceptions. These 'frames of reference' enable the stakeholders to interpret the organisation and the environment in which it operates. Information which does not fit with the dominant reference system is actively ignored or downgraded. The same could be said for people. In this way a particular culture emerges which encourages individuals to lend themselves to self-fulfilling organisational prophecies, uncontaminated by deviant behaviour or information. Strategy thus becomes the product, not of defined aims and objectives, but of the prevailing values, attitudes and ideas in the organisation.
3. *A political model.* Here, strategy is not chosen directly, but emerges through compromise, conflict and consensus seeking among interested stakeholders. Since the strategy is the outcome of negotiation, bargaining and confrontation, those with the most power have the greatest influence.
4. *A logical incremental model.* Here, strategies emerge from 'strategic subsystems', each concerned with a different type of strategic issue. Strategic goals are based on an awareness of needs, rather than the highly structured analytical process of the planning model. Often, due to a lack of necessary information, such goals can be vague, general and non-rigid in nature until such a time when events unfold and more information becomes known.
5. *An ecological model.* In this perspective, the environment impinges on the organisation in such a way that strategies are virtually prescribed and there is little or no free choice. In this model, the organisation which adapts most successfully to its environment will survive in a way which mirrors Darwin's natural selection.
6. *A visionary leadership model.* Strategy emerges as a result of the leader's vision, enforced by his/her commitment to it, his/her personal credibility, and how he/she articulates it to others.

There is a certain irony in the evolutionary process described above, for it is clear that over the past four decades we have seen a concept of long-range strategic planning turn into an increasingly short-term mechanical and specialised process which has led to its own self-destruction. Such a process is familiar to the student of evolution, for it is clear that while specialisation (i.e. adaptation to the prevailing conditions) may lead to above-average short-term rewards, it also puts you at greatest risk if you become so specialised that you cannot accommodate or adapt to a change in the environment. In that 'survival' is generally accepted as the primary object of all organisations it is clear that short-term gain is only to be pursued if it is consistent with the long-term goals of a firm and does not reduce the firm's ability to respond to turbulence in its environment. We are thus faced with the paradox that while 'planning' has fallen into disrepute for leading us into the present impasse it is also seen as offering the greatest potential for escaping from it.

TIME SPAN

Generally speaking strategic planning is considered to be planning for periods of more than three years into the future. For major investments such as construction projects like the Channel Tunnel or a new airport the expected life of the investment will span decades and the project itself may take many years to bring to completion. Planning for such infrastructural projects may well be associated with the use of long waves or Kondratieff cycles of the kind we describe in Chapter 7. Similarly, the time span for other kinds of strategic plans may cover time frames of 15–25 years (the building cycle), 7–11 years (the investment cycle) or 3–5 years (the business cycle).

Anything less than three years would normally be considered as short-term planning, which, together with budgeting, provides for adaptation of the long-range plan in the light of changing circumstances. Obviously, the more turbulent and changeable the environment, the greater the need for flexibility and short-term planning. In order to address specific and one-off changes, such as new government regulations, budgetary changes etc., ad hoc planning is necessary. However, recognising the dynamic and turbulent nature of the environment, there is a need for contingency planning that is often associated with the development of scenarios (see Chapter 5) where an organisation has identified a number of possible futures with varying degrees of likelihood of occurrence.

SOME DEFINITIONS

Earlier we alluded to the paradox that strategic or long-range planning has been criticised as a major contributor to the mechanistic and inflexible approach to management that underlay many of the economic problems of the late 1970s and the 1980s, while, at the same time, it is proposed as a palliative if not a cure for these self-same ills. To some degree, this misunderstanding would seem to arise from disagreement as to the precise nature of SMP. Accordingly, before conducting our own analysis of this concept and the techniques associated with it, it will be helpful to consider some definitions that indicate the salient features of this approach to management.

A review of SMP by Brownlie (1983) would seem to support the view that there is no single, universally accepted definition of SMP: he offers us the following seven definitions:

1. The answers to two questions were implicit to Drucker's early conceptualisation of an organisation's strategy: 'What is our business? And what should it be?'
2. Chandler defined strategy as 'the determination of the basic long-term goals and objectives of an enterprise, and the adoption of courses of action and the allocation of resources necessary for carrying out these goals'.
3. Andrews' definition of strategy combines the ideas of Drucker and Chandler: 'strategy is the pattern of objectives, purposes or goals and plans for achieving these goals, stated in such a way as to define what business the company is in or is to be in and the kind of company it is or is to be'.
4. Hofer and Schendel define an organisation's strategy as 'the fundamental pattern of present and planned resource deployments and environmental interactions that indicates how the organisation will achieve its objectives'.
5. According to Abell, strategic planning involves 'the management of any business unit in the dual tasks of anticipating and responding to changes which affect the marketplace for their products'.
6. In 1979, Derek Wynne-Jones, head of the planning and strategy division of P. A. Management Consultants, considered that strategic planning 'embraced the overall objective of an organisation in defining its strategy and preparing and subsequently implementing its detailed plans'.
7. Christopher Lorenz, late editor of the management page of the Financial Times, considered strategic planning to be 'the process by which top and senior executives decide, direct, delegate and control the generation and allocation of resources within a company'.

But, while these definitions may differ in the particular, there does appear to be a common thread, which is that SMP is concerned with establishing the goal or purpose of an organisation and the means chosen for achieving that goal. Perhaps, then, the differences of opinion revolve around how one defines an organisation or 'business'. We have already referred to the stages of corporate development and claimed that SMP is as relevant to complex multinational corporations like IBM as it is to any single-product owner-managed business. That said, we must recognise that differences of size, scale, diversity, complexity etc. will inevitably result in significant differences between 'firms' and make generalisations about them difficult if not impossible. To overcome or reduce this difficulty, most analysts now prefer to define the business in terms of its strategic functions rather than try to define businesses first and then discover that there are major discrepancies in strategic functions between them. As a conseq-uence, most discussions of SMP are now focused upon the concept of the strategic business unit (SBU), which has been defined succinctly by Arthur D. Little as:

> A Strategic Business Unit – or Strategy Centre – is a business area with an external marketplace for goods and services, for which management can determine objectives and execute strategies independent of other business areas. It is a business that could prob-ably stand alone if divested. Strategic Business Units are the 'natural' or homogeneous business of a corporation.

Abell and Hammond (1979) also subscribe to the view that SMP should be executed at the level of the 'business unit', which they regard as a 'reasonably autonomous profit centre' normally under the control of its own general manager. More precise definitions than this are seen as impossible due to the diversity encountered in practice, but the common features include a wide degree of independence and the existence of the basic functional departments such as R&D, man-ufacturing, sales etc.

Given this elaboration we can propose a definit-ion of strategic marketing planning as:

> The establishment of the goal or purpose of a strat-egic business unit and the means by which this is to be achieved.

If this definition is acceptable, then it would seem that the next logical step would be to look at the manner in which firms formulate objectives, and the process by which they seek to achieve them. This we seek to do in the following sections, but, first, it will be helpful to consider the concepts of mission, vision and strategic intent from which specific objectives are derived.

MISSION, VISION AND STRATEGIC INTENT

In the course of their two-year research project into the nature and importance of the concept of corporate mission, Andrew Campbell and Sally Yeung (1990) of the Ashridge Strategic Manage-ment Centre were frequently asked to define and

distinguish between the concepts of mission, vision, and strategic intent. In an article in the August 1991 issue of *Long Range Planning*, the authors offer their preferred definitions as well as their views of the position of mission in the strat-egic planning process.

Two broad definitions of mission prevail. For some organisations, mission is conceived of primar-ily as an intellectual discipline and a strategic tool which is fundamental to strategic management and addresses the key questions: 'What is our business, and what should it be?' For others, mission is regarded 'as the cultural "glue" which enables them to function as a collective unity'. Campbell and Yeung take the view that mission is about both culture and strategy, and state

> A mission exists when strategy and culture are mutu-ally supportive. An organisation has a mission when its culture fits with its strategy …
>
> Mission is an organisation's character, identity and reason for existence. It can be divided into four inter-relating parts: purpose, strategy, behaviour standards and values. Purpose addresses why an organisation is in being: for whose benefit is all this effort being put in? Strategy considers the nature of the business, the desired positioning vs other companies and the source of competitive advantage. Behaviour stan-dards are the norms and rules of 'the way we do things around here'. Values are the beliefs and moral principles that lie behind the behaviour standards, beliefs that have normally been formulated within the organisation by a founding dynasty or a dominant management team.

The Ashridge Mission model is depicted in Figure 4.2

In defining vision, Campbell and Yeung draw on the seminal work of Warren Bennis and Burt Nanus and their theory of leadership. In this theory, vision is seen as a necessary attribute of the leader who can articulate an attractive future for an organisation that will motivate its members to seek its achievement. Such visions may be vague or precise, but they give the organisation a sense of purpose and direction. Campbell and Yeung believe a vision and a mission 'can be one and the same', but suggest that the two concepts do not completely overlap one another in that visions refer to the future and may be achieved. When this

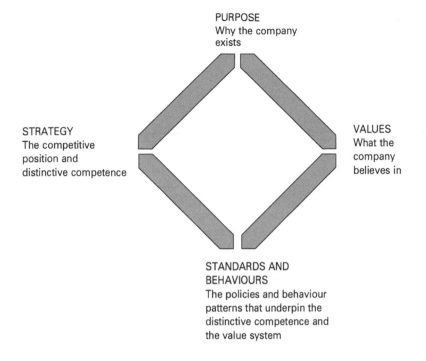

PURPOSE
Why the company exists

STRATEGY
The competitive position and distinctive competence

VALUES
What the company believes in

STANDARDS AND BEHAVIOURS
The policies and behaviour patterns that underpin the distinctive competence and the value system

FIGURE 4.2 The Ashridge Mission model

SOURCE: Campbell, A., Devine, M. and Yeung, D. (1990) *A Sense of Mission.* London: Hutchinson Business Books

occurs, a new vision will need to be articulated. By contrast, a mission is concerned with the present – what we are about, while remaining 'a timeless explanation of the organisation's identity and ambition'. In sum, 'A vision is, therefore, more associated with a goal whereas a mission is more associated with a way of behaving'.

The third concept that overlaps with those of mission and vision is strategic intent – a term popularised by Gary Hamel and C. K. Prahalad's article of that title in the *Harvard Business Review* (1989) Hamel and Prahalad stated that:

On the one hand strategic intent envisions a desired leadership position and establishes the criterion the organisation will use to chart its progress. Komatsu set out to 'encircle Caterpillar'. Canon sought to 'beat Xerox', Honda strove to become a second Ford, an automotive pioneer. All are expressions of strategic intent. At the same time strategic intent is more than just unfettered ambition. (Many companies possess an ambitious strategic intent yet fall short of their goals.) The concept also encompasses an active management process that includes: focussing the

organisation's attention on the essence of winning; motivating people by communicating the value of the target; leaving room for individual and team contributions; sustaining enthusiasm by providing new operational definitions as circumstances change; and using intent consistently to guide resource allocations.

Given this definition, Campbell and Yeung see it as a concept containing elements of both mission and vision – goals as an integral element of vision, and strategy of mission. Overall, however, intent is seen as suffering from the same deficiency as vision in that its achievement will call for restatement, whereas mission or purpose has the 'advantage of being everlasting'.

Campbell and Yeung's view on mission planning appears to be somewhat at odds with their repeated statements that 'mission is everlasting'. If mission is 'everlasting' and 'timeless' then it should not need tinkering with on a regular basis by linking it with formalised strategic planning. Clearly the difference between mission and strategy resides in the enduring quality of the mission, and the cultural norms and values it reflects and promotes. Strategy is the means whereby specific action plans (both short and long term) are measured against this benchmark to determine whether they conform to its requirements. Only in dire circumstances should one reformulate the mission – for, by doing so, it challenges the whole ethos of the corporate culture and 'the way we do things around here'. To achieve such a change requires great determination and courage on the part of top management, and will involve considerable investment in human resource development to accomplish.

In common with our earlier discussion in Chapter 3 concerning the definition of terms like 'policy' and 'strategy', the claimed similarities and differences implicit in attempts to classify concepts

like mission, vision and intent inevitably degenerate into a matter of semantics. What is important is
that one recognises the difference between the
fundamental essence of an organisation, which
attracts people to it and secures and sustains their
loyalty over time (its spirit), as distinct from its
modus operandi, or strategy, which represents its
best attempt to achieve its purpose according to
changing times and circumstances. In the next
section we look specifically at the nature of the
mission statement.

THE MISSION STATEMENT

During 1989 Mary Klemm, Stuart Sanderson and
George Luffman of the University of Bradford
Management Centre undertook a survey among
UK companies of the types of mission statement
issued by companies, their content, usage, and
value to managers. Their findings were reported in
the June 1991 issue of *Long Range Planning*, 'Selling
corporate values to employees'.

Klemm et al. indicate that there are two simple
views of the purpose of mission statements. The
first is that mission statements are primarily for
external public relations; the second is that they
are meant to motivate employees. Obviously, the
purposes are not mutually exclusive, but the question is: 'Which is the primary purpose?'

One of the earliest writers to refer to the
mission statement was Philip Selznick who, writing on leadership in 1957, saw its purpose as
defining the organisation's distinctive competence. However, Klemm et al. suggest that 'Current
thinking on mission statements could be said to
originate in the 1970s when Peter Drucker (1974)
focused on the need for a business to define its
purpose'. (Students of marketing would suggest
that it was Ted Levitt who first prompted this
concern in 1960 with the publication of 'Marketing myopia' in 1960.) Over time, this concern
with purpose has been expanded to embrace the
firm's philosophy as reflected in its culture
and value systems (see the Ashridge Model in
Figure 4.2).

In practice, Klemm et al. found that there is no
single definition of a mission statement, and that
companies use a variety of terms to embrace the
concept:

- Mission statement
- Corporate statement
- Aims and values
- Purpose
- Principles
- Objectives
- Goals
- Responsibilities and obligations.

The research also confirmed work in the USA
by David (1989) into the content of mission statements, which indicated nine elements: products or
services, customers, philosophy, self-concept,
public image, location, technology, employees and
concern for survival. However, the UK research
suggested that these elements were frequently
ordered into a hierarchy, which Klemm et al.
defined as follows:

- *Statement 1* The mission
A statement of the long-term purpose of the organisation reflecting deeply held corporate views

- *Statement 2* Strategic objectives
A statement of long-term strategic objectives
outlining desired direction and performance in
broad terms

- *Statement 3* Quantified planning targets
Objectives in the form of quantified planning
targets over a specific period

- *Statement 4* The business definition
A statement outlining the scope and activities of
the company in terms of industry and geographical spread.

While Klemm et al.'s survey comprised only 59
companies from the Times 1000, it showed that
while two-thirds of the respondents had both a
mission and strategic objectives statement, 80%
had a published business definition. Another
significant finding was that 70% of the respondents with mission statements had drawn them up
since 1985, and a number were in the process of
composing them at the time of the survey.

Writing in *Industrial Marketing Management* in
1997, Christopher K. Bart explored the content of
mission statements and whether any of these

made a difference in terms of firm performance. Based upon an extensive literature review, Bart identified 25 main components that he summarised under 12 headings:

1. Organisational purpose or raison d'être ('why do we exist?')
2. Statement of values/beliefs/philosophy
3. Distinctive competence/strength of the organisation
4. Desired competitive position
5. Competitive strategy ('how we compete?')
6. Relevant/critical stakeholders identified
7. Specific behaviour standards and policies to be observed
8. Statement of general corporate aims/goals
9. One clear and compelling goal
10. Specific financial performance targets/objectives
11. Specific non-financial performance targets/objectives
12. Definition of the business ('what business are we in?' or a very general statement of products and customers)
13. Specific customers/markets served
14. Specific products/services offered
15. Statement of self-concept/identity ('who are we?')
16. Statement of desired public image ('how do we want others to see us?')
17. Identification of the business location
18. Definition of technology
19. Concern for future/long-term survival
20. Concern for satisfying customers
21. Concern for employees and their welfare
22. Concern for suppliers
23. Concern for society
24. Concern for shareholders
25. Statement of vision.

Based upon a sample of 44 industrial firms' mission statements, 11 of the components were found to be used to a fairly high degree. Further analysis suggested that the relationship between the mission components and the four financial performance measures used was both tenuous and inconsistent. The area of greatest mission component impact was associated with influencing the behaviour of employees. This produced a consistently positive association with 11 of the mission component variables, which were therefore judged to 'make a difference'. They were:

- Purpose/raison d'être
- Value/philosophy
- General corporate goals
- Self-concept
- Desired public image
- Concern for customers
- Concern for employees
- Concern for suppliers
- Concern for society
- Concern for shareholders
- Vision statement.

Bart concludes: 'The benefits from mission are emotional and psychic.'

These findings support those of Klemm et al. (1991) who concluded that:

mission statements are seen by managers as more important internally than externally. They are more likely to be published to staff than outside the firm, more likely to be revised as a result of a change in senior management than a change in the external environment and seen as most valuable in giving leadership and motivating staff.

According to Wikipedia, http://en.wikipedia.org/w/index.php?title=Strategic_planning&printable=yes the features of an effective vision (mission) statement include:

- Clarity and lack of ambiguity
- A vivid and clear picture, not ambiguous
- Describing a bright future (hope)
- Memorable and engaging expression
- Realistic aspirations, achievable
- Alignment with organisational values and culture, rational
- Time-bound if it talks of achieving any goal or objective.

FORMULATING OBJECTIVES

While discussions of planning invariably contain some reference to the need to establish objectives as a prerequisite to formal planning, it is rare to find any explicit reference as to just how one

---

Box 4.1 — *Values*

At WHSmith our business goal is to rebuild our position as Britain's most popular stationer, bookseller and newsagent. We strive to be an outward facing, customer focused, store responsive organisation that delivers on our promises.

Living our four values is an important part of achieving this goal. These values are as follows:

Customer Focus
We will keep the customer at the heart of all that we do

Drive For Results
We will act with tenacity to deliver ambitious and competitive results

Accountability
We take personal responsibility and deliver what we say we will

Value Our People
At WHSmith our people are respected and valued in an honest, open environment

---

should set about formulating these objectives in the first place. As Malcolm McDonald (1982) observes:

> The literature on the subject [marketing planning] is, however, not very explicit, which is surprising when it is considered how vital the setting of marketing objectives is.
>
> An objective will ensure that a company knows what its strategies are expected to accomplish and when a particular strategy has accomplished its purpose. In other words, without objectives, strategy decisions and all that follow will take place in a vacuum.

In *Corporate Strategy* (1968), Igor Ansoff stresses the importance of objectives as the basis for appraisal, control and coordination and defines an objective as:

> A measure of the efficiency of the resource-conversion process. An objective contains three elements: the particular attribute that is chosen as a measure of efficiency, the yardstick, or scale, by which the attribute is measured, and the goal – the particular value on the scale which the firm seeks to attain.

In Chapter 3 we emphasised the critical importance of a clear statement of objectives as the basis for determining where the organisation is headed, the means for reaching that goal, and the basis for determining the progress that has been made. In particular, McKay (1972) suggests that it is possible to distinguish two categories of issues to be considered when setting objectives – the

general application to all businesses, and the specific that provides for a closer and more detailed examination.

GENERAL

1. Business scope, i.e. What business should we be in?
2. Business orientation, i.e. What is the orientation best suited to our business scope and to our continuing purposes of survival, growth and profit?
3. Business organisation, i.e. Does our present organisation – in style, structure and staff – fit the orientation chosen?
4. Public responsibility, i.e. Are our selections of business opportunities made in light of present and future social and economic needs of the public?
5. Performance evaluation, i.e. Does our appraisal system mesh properly with our planning system?

SPECIFIC

These concern more specific areas for deeper and more precise examination for each SBU, including:

1. Customer classes
2. Competitors
3. Markets and distribution
4. Technology and products
5. Production capability

6. Finance
7. Environment.

Taken together these issues provide the focus for the marketing appreciation, which we discuss in detail in Chapters 7 to 11, and form the basis for developing the short-term marketing plan based on a manipulation of the elements of the marketing mix.

McDonald cites extensive support for the view that in developing objectives one should move from the general to the particular, from the broad to the narrow, and from the long term to the short term. He also stresses the importance of viewing all these objectives as part of a hierarchy which must be internally consistent and mutually reinforcing. It follows then that marketing objectives constitute a subset of the overall corporate objective (which will also dictate the objectives for the other major business functions such as R&D and production), and in turn will determine the objectives of other marketing functions such as product development, advertising, selling and distribution.

In discussing marketing objectives, Peter Drucker (1968) identifies seven that he believes must be given explicit consideration in any company:

1. The desired standing of the existing products in their market in turnover and percentage share measured against direct and indirect competition
2. The desired standing of existing products in new markets measured as in 1
3. The existing products that should be phased out and ultimately abandoned, and the future product mix
4. The new products needed in existing markets, the number, their properties and the share targets
5. The new markets that new products will help to develop, in size and share
6. The distribution organisation needed to accomplish the marketing goals and the pricing policy appropriate to them
7. A service objective, measuring how well the customer should be supplied with what he considers value.

Implicit in this approach is the concept of a port-folio of products that may be at quite different stages in their life-cycle. We shall return to this concept when we examine the analytical framework proposed by the Boston Consulting Group in Chapter 5.

McKay (1972) identifies only three basic marketing objectives – to enlarge the market, to increase market share and to improve profitability – but then proceeds to spell out a number of distinct strategies for achieving these objectives:

1. **To enlarge the market**
(a) *By innovation or product development:*
   - Through improving existing products or lines to increase use
   - Through developing new products or lines
(b) *By innovation or market development:*
   - Through developing present end-use markets
   - Through discovering new end-use markets

2. **To increase market share**
(a) *By emphasising product development and product improvement for competitive advantage:*
   - Through product performance
   - Through product quality
   - Through product features
(b) *By emphasising persuasion effort for competitive advantage:*
   - Through sales and distribution
   - Through advertising and sales promotion
(c) *By emphasising customer-service activities for competitive advantage:*
   - Through ready availability, order handling and delivery service
   - Through credit and collection policies
   - Through after-sale product service

3. **To improve profitability**
(a) *By emphasising sales volume for profit leverage:*
   - Through strengthened sales and distribution effort
   - Through strengthened advertising and sales promotion effort
   - Through strengthened advertising effort
(b) *By emphasising elimination of unprofitable activities:*
   - Through pruning products and lines
   - Through pruning sales coverage and distribution

■ Through pruning customer services

(c) *By emphasising price improvement:*
■ Through leadership in initiating needed price increases
■ Through price improvement gained by differentiating products and services from those of competitors

(d) *By emphasising cost reduction:*
■ Through improved effectiveness of marketing tools and methods in product planning, in persuasion activities and in customer service activities.

McKay then proceeds to offer a series of guidelines for formulating objectives and strategies based upon his own extensive review of the literature. The majority of these have already been covered in the preceding discussion, but it is worth stressing the point made by McKay that 'Each strategy carries with it certain essential related commitments, which must be accepted when the strategy is selected.' This assertion is emphasised in Table 4.4, in which push and pull strategies are contrasted in terms of the 'must do', 'might do' and 'don't do' factors.

A useful acronym used when developing objectives is SMART, which stands for Specific, Measurable, Achievable, Relevant, Targeted and Timed.

A FRAMEWORK FOR STRATEGIC MARKETING PLANNING

In developing a framework for the execution of SMP, it will be helpful to conceive of it as a process consisting of a number of discrete steps and governed by a number of specific principles.

The actual number of steps proposed in the SMP process varies according to different authors who have analysed and described the sequential events. However, closer inspection of these alternative models reveals a high degree of consistency between them as will become evident in our review of some of the better known statements.

Box 4.2   *Objectives/priorities*

In 1996 the acting chief executive of Cable & Wireless plc stated: 'Our objective is to grow and protect shareholder value by providing telecommunications services and products to customers in our chosen market.' To this end, Cable & Wireless has five priorities. The five priorities stated were:

1. First, to deliver high-quality service and value to our customers at a competitive price.
2. Second, to provide customers and partners with creative and innovative telecommunications solutions.
3. A third area of focus is to deploy leading edge technology consistent with our objective of being the operator with the most competitive cost base.
4. To optimise our global presence and the opportunities that arise from working in many markets.
5. To develop and exploit our partnering skills.

In its annual statement for 1995, Yorkshire Water plc articulated its strategy as follows:

Achieving added value in a closely regulated utility business is a matter of balance. On the one hand, customers and regulators demand ever higher standards of quality from our products and services. On the other, investors demand that we improve efficiency and performance in order to build shareholder value. Yorkshire Water's strategy aims to reconcile these demands. Within our utility business we will meet, and aim to beat, regulatory standards and achieve value for money by controlling investment, by focusing resources and by the application of new technology. In parallel, we will develop new business ventures which offer the greatest growth potential, yet remain close to our core competencies. We will make a contribution to the community and to environmental improvement.

TABLE 4.4 Contrasting strategy requirements

Actions	Pull-through strategy	Push-through strategy
Objective	Seek competitive advantage through building brand acceptance and demand direct with customer	Seek competitive advantage by motivating distribution to carry and move your product
Must do	Use communication media to promote desirable image of product or brand, and maintain consistent image Keep improving effectiveness of messages to the customer Price to cover services rendered by distribution plus fair profit	Provide incentives in margins, bonuses and allowances to stimulate volume selling Strive for more and better outlets Maintain standards of distribution service and communications consistent with product and company identity
Might do	Force distribution through customer demand Provide maximum availability so customer stimulation can be promptly satisfied Use direct contacts to assist sales through distributor	Maintain superiority in training and selling assistance provided Encourage distribution commitment to your company and product objectives
Don't do	Continually offer special prices to distributors as incentive to load inventories in distribution channels Assist distributor sales through direct sales effort	Price so distributor has little or no profit Carry on extensive advertising and promotion

SOURCE: McKay, E. S. (1972) *The Marketing Mystique.* New York: American Management Association

The most broadly based models distinguish only three stages or 'cycles' in the process of SMP which may be summarised as:

- Evaluation
- Strategy formulation
- Detailed planning.

Abell and Hammond (1979) elaborate on this basic framework and state that a strategic market plan may be thought of as involving four sets of related decisions:

1. Defining the business, i.e. answering the question 'What business am I in?' The definition must state:
   - Product and market scope: in particular, which customers are to be served, which customer functions (needs) are to be satisfied and what ways ('technologies') are to be used to satisfy the functions
   - Product and market segmentation: in particular, whether and how the firm recognises differences among customers in terms of their needs and the ways they are satisfied.
2. Determining the mission (or role) of the business, i.e. the set of objectives to be pursued. These should be stated in terms of performance expectations with regard to 'sales growth, market-share, return on investment, net income and cash' for each distinct product/

market and must be based upon a full analysis of the firm's strengths and weaknesses, and the opportunities and threats which face it (i.e. a SWOT analysis).
3. Formulating functional strategies; including marketing, production, etc. Interaction with general management. The results of the strategy formulation process should be completed strategy statements which possess the following characteristics:
   - They should describe each of the major components of the organisation's strategy, i.e plan scope, distinctive competencies, growth vector, competitive advantage, intended synergy
   - Should indicate how the strategy will lead to the accomplishment of the organisation's objectives
   - The strategy should be described in functional rather than physical forms
   - It should be as precise as possible.
4. Budgeting, resource allocation decisions, sales forecasts.
   Levitt in 'Marketing myopia' (1960) makes the case for functional rather than physical statements of strategy. Drucker (1964) points out that Levitt's approach leads to broad impracticable working statements and counsels the use of both specific and precise strategy statements. A good strategy statement would thus appear in cell 3 of Figure 4.3.

	Broad	**Precise**
Functional terms	1 Transportation business	2 Long-distance transportation of low-value, low-density products
Physical terms	3 Railroad business	4 Long-haul, coal-carrying railroad

FIGURE 4.3 Characteristics of effective strategy statements

SOURCE: Hofer, C. W. and Schendel, D. E. (1978) *Strategy Formulation: Analytical Concepts.* St Paul, MN: West Publishing

TABLE 4.5 Checklist for strategic market planning

1 External environment

Social environment:
- social movements (for example, the consumer movement)
- sociocultural drift (for example, working wives, lifestyles)
- agents for change (for example, rising educational levels)
- demographic changes

Add for international markets:
- culture (values, beliefs, for example religious, social institutions)
- language
- form of government
- foreign policy

Economic environment:
- trends in GNP
- interest rates
- levels of discretionary income
- currency fluctuations
- inflation rates
- unemployment levels
- fiscal policies

Add for international markets:
- balance of payments
- wage/price controls

Technical environment:
- government and industry spending on R&D
- technological forecasts
- patent protection

Legal environment:
- government regulation and deregulation
- tax legislation
- trademark legislation
- international trade regulations
- employment laws

2 Market
- barriers to entry (threat of entry)
- rivalry
- substitutes from other industries
- power of buyers
- power of suppliers
- evolutionary stage
- growth rate
- demand fluctuations
- industry profitability
- market share trends

3 Customer
- different choice criteria
- shopping habits
- attitudes
- decision processes
- influences

4 Competition
- number of immediate rivals in served markets
- identity of and market shares of rivals
- strategies of competitors
- innovativeness and resourcefulness of competitors
- leadership in marketing, manufacture and technology
- relative costs
- erosion of patent protection/proprietary knowledge

5 Company
- trends in sales, net income and net cash flow
- thrust/core competencies
- share of served markets
- growth path
- innovativeness
- capacity utilisation
- cost trends

SOURCE: O'Shaughnessy, J. (1999) Strategic marketing planning, in Baker, M. J. (ed.) *Encyclopedia of Marketing.* London: International Thomson Business Press, p. 178

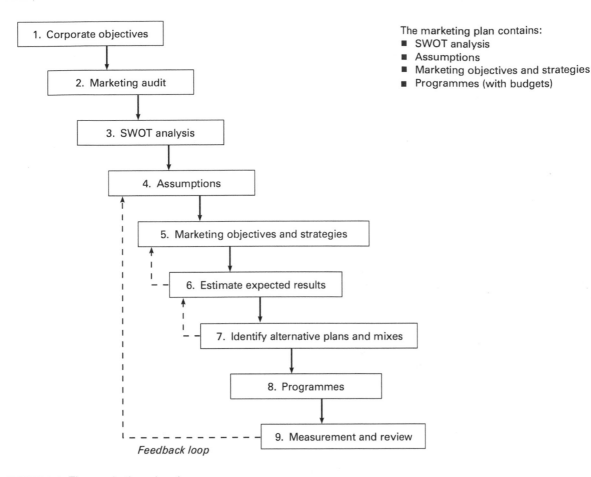

FIGURE 4.4 The marketing planning process
SOURCE: McDonald, M. H. B. (1984) *Marketing Plans*. London: Heinemann

Abell and Hammond also distinguished the SMP from a marketing plan (MP) by stressing that the latter is seen as dealing 'primarily with the delineation of target segments and the product, communication, channel and pricing policies for reaching and servicing those segments – the so-called marketing mix', while the former is 'a plan of all aspects of an organisation's strategy in the marketplace'. The essential difference is one of detail. The SMP is more disaggregated than the MP and is concerned with long-term issues. The SMP states clearly who does what, when and with what resources. We return to these distinctions in Chapters 14 and 22. An indication of the scope of strategic marketing planning is provided by the checklist in Table 4.5.

A number of other writers and commentators suggest that SMP, like corporate strategy formulation, should be the result of the answers to a self-examination catechism comprising seven questions. Taylor (1976) summarises these as follows:

1. What are the objectives to be achieved and how should we define the scope of our business?
2. What limits are set on these objectives by our personal values and social responsibilities?
3. On which strengths can we build and what are the weaknesses which need to be compensated for?
4. What opportunities are to be taken advantage of and what threats should be avoided?
5. What are the main decisions to be taken and to what major courses of action must we commit ourselves?
6. What resources will be required and where will these resources come from?
7. What are the risks in this strategy and what contingency plans are required?

McDonald (1984) also specifies a seven-step sequence as follows:

1. Defining the business
2. Situation audit and statement of assumptions
3. Establishing objectives
4. Identifying strategic alternatives
5. Selection of specific courses of action ('strategies')
6. Implementation
7. Measurement, feedback and control.

From the foregoing summaries it is clear that there is a high degree of consensus on the basic steps in the SMP process and that variations in the number of stages are largely the result of elaboration of that basic framework. Thus McDonald's final model is extended to nine steps as can be seen in Figure 4.4 and could easily be subdivided still further if it were felt that making a step explicit would improve the clarity of the process and plan.

In Figure 4.4 and much of the preceding discussion we have referred to 'steps' in the marketing planning process. In practice it is more realistic to think of SMP as a cyclical activity, as illustrated in Figure 4.5. Such a cycle recognises that the great majority of companies already exist and so may be at any point on the cycle, whereas flow diagrams imply a once and for all sequence of a new organisation, even when they possess feedback loops as in Figure 4.4.

So much for the process, what about the principles which are felt to govern it? Again one can find a number of different approaches set out in the literature of SMP, but one of the best developed and comprehensive schemes which has withstood the acid test of implementation is that discussed by Arthur D. Little (ADL). Accordingly, we shall use this as an exemplar of a proven approach that works in practice.

PRINCIPLES OF SMP

ADL's strategic planning process centres on five principles:

1. Strategic business units or 'strategy centres'
2. Planning is a data-based activity
3. Business is not random; it is shaped by competitive economics
4. There is a finite set of available strategies for each business unit
5. Strategy selection should be condition-driven not ambition-driven.

Much of this book is an elaboration of these principles with the exception of point 5. Nonetheless a summary of the explicit meaning attached to these principles will be a useful prelude to the detailed treatment of later chapters.

We have already adopted ADL's definition of an SBU or strategy centre and noted that all the major writers on the subject now use SBUs as the basic building block for SMP.

The second principle, that 'planning is a data-based activity', also enjoys universal acceptance although, as we shall see in Chapter 6 when dealing with marketing research, most agree that facts can only provide a basis for decision-making. Where facts are not available or uncertainty exists as to their accuracy, reliability or validity then it will be necessary to combine hard data with judgement. (We shall look more closely at this mode of decision-making later.) However, the principle is sound – one should always seek to establish and secure those facts that are available about the environment in general, about the industry in which the firm operates and about the SBU itself and analysis of data should correspond to these three levels. As ADL comment:

■ *At the market level:* an assessment of market size, growth and segmentation in light of macro-forces

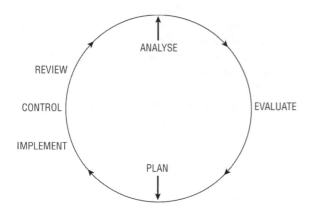

FIGURE 4.5 The cycle of SMP

- *At the industry level:* a strategic segmentation and competitive analysis as a function of industry structure and dynamics
- *At the business unit level:* an evaluation of operations, performance vs. past strategies, and the determination of key strategic issues.

To these we would add customer analysis, the subject of Chapter 9.

The third principle that 'Business is not random' predicates that there are discernible patterns to both competition and performance. Much of the discipline of economics is founded on an acceptance of the first proposition and in Chapter 2 we examined the insights which an understanding of market structure, conduct and performance can provide in the formulation and execution of marketing strategy. ADL argue that there are two key factors to examine in determining the strategic condition of a given business – industry maturity and competitive position. Industry maturity is specified in terms of an industry life-cycle as being in an embryonic, growth, mature or ageing state as determined 'by a number of factors including:

- Growth rate/potential
- Product line breadth/activity
- Competitor's number/structure
- Customer loyalty
- Market-share distribution/stability
- Ease of entry
- Technology focus/stability'.

It is claimed that, inter alia, industry maturity has implications for the natural strategies available, which lends support to McKay's view that once a basic strategy has been selected or determined there are things you must do, might do, and don't do if you are to maintain consistency. In addition this concept of stages in the life-cycle also has significant implications for likely performance and cash generation levels as well as for the most appropriate type of management system. We shall return to these points in Chapter 5 when looking at different approaches to or techniques for strategic planning.

A firm's competitive position is determined by the geographical scope of the industry and the strategic segments (i.e. specific product–market combinations) in which the SBU is competing. Competitive position is more than just market share and is determined by a combination of three factors:

- Market share = the result of past strengths and weaknesses
- Competitive economics
- Other factors usually reflecting present strengths and weaknesses, e.g. technology, what Hamel and Prahalad call 'competencies'.

The significance of market share as an indicator of a firm's competitive standing tends to increase with industry maturity and we shall return to this proposition when discussing the Boston Consulting Group's product portfolio approach and the Profit Implications of Market Strategy (PIMS) study in Chapter 5.

ADL have developed their own scheme for classifying a firm's competitive position and recognise five categories of positions:

1. *Dominant:* Very rare and usually the result of a quasi monopoly or from strongly protected technological leadership, e.g. De Beers in diamonds, Xerox (originally) in photocopying
2. *Strong:* Strong competitors can usually follow strategies of their choice, irrespective of their competitors' moves
3. *Favourable:* When industries are fragmented, with no competitor clearly standing out, the leaders tend to be in a favourable position
4. *Tenable:* Cases where profitability can be sustained through specialisation
5. *Weak:* Either too small to compete effectively or big and inefficient.

By combining maturity and competitive position one obtains a 'strategic condition' matrix, as depicted in Figure 4.6.

Once SBUs have been diagnosed they can be located on the matrix and one can evaluate appropriate strategies for them bearing in mind the fourth principle that 'there is a finite set of available strategies for each business unit'. ADL propose six generic strategy groups:

1. Market strategies (domestic and international)
2. Product strategies

3. Technology strategies
4. Operations strategies
5. Management and systems strategies
6. Retrenchment strategies.

With the exception of the last of these, it is clear that ADL are proposing a very different conceptual approach from that underlying the concept of limited strategic alternatives set out in Chapter 3. Clearly the latter are concerned more with the direction in which one is seeking to move, while the former are concerned with business functions or the means of moving the firm in a chosen direction – an interpretation consistent with ADL's definition of strategies as 'a series of coordinated actions which direct resources'.

In developing strategies the final principle proposed was that 'Strategy selection [should] be driven by the condition of the business, not the ambition of its Managers'. As stated, this is clearly a plea for realism in selecting strategies with the inference that one should not overreach oneself. But, towards the end of the chapter when we discuss the advantages and disadvantages of strategic planning, it will become evident that the lack of growth in the advanced Western economies in the late 1970s and early 1980s was as much due to a lack of ambition as to an excess of it. More recently (1998), ADL have recognised this and now exhort management to incorporate ambition into

their strategic planning. In doing so, however, it becomes even more important to plan how one is to bridge the potential gap between the present and the desired future – a theme which we return to in Chapter 11.

While firms at stages 1 and 2 of corporate development will only have one SBU, and so can move to detailed planning and implementation for that SBU, larger and more complex firms at stages 3 and 4 will have to undertake an additional step which is to ensure that the individual SBU strategies are internally consistent and mutually reinforcing and so conducive to that elusive phenomenon of synergy (the '2 + 2 = 5' concept) in an overall corporate strategy.

THE FORMULATION OF CORPORATE STRATEGY

According to ADL, the formulation of a corporate strategy involves three steps:

1. A reconciliation of various internal and external inputs with business unit plans and strategy alternatives, to select mutually consistent corporate strategies.
2. Assessment of the implications of the selected strategies in terms of new activities or businesses to be developed and acceptance or modification – we call it revectoring – of specific

Stages of industry maturity

	Embryonic	Growth	Mature	Ageing
Dominant				
Strong				
Favourable				
Tenable				
Weak				

Competitive position

FIGURE 4.6 The strategic condition matrix

SOURCE: Arthur D. Little, Inc. cited in Patel, P. and Younger, M. (1978) A frame of reference for strategy development, *Long Range Planning* (April): 6–12

business unit plans, prior to the preparation of a revised corporate plan.

3. Allocation of corporate resources.

In turn, these basic stages call for a formal and detailed assessment of:

- The external environment
- The internal environment
- The business portfolio
- New business opportunities
- The corporate risk portfolio
- Corporate human resources and requirements
- Corporate financial resources and obligations
- Corporate goals and objectives.

ADL's detailed review of each of these steps reveals a marked overlap with the analytical frameworks developed by other organisations. Thus the review of the internal and external environments comprises the marketing audit and SWOT analysis found in the normative approach to SMP. ADL extend these steps to develop what they term a 'strategic condition matrix', as depicted in Figure 4.6, which proposes four broad alternatives – natural development, selective development, turnaround and abandonment – and corresponds closely to Shell's directional policy matrix which we review in Chapter 5.

The third step in ADL's analysis reviews the SBUs in terms of their cash generation/absorption

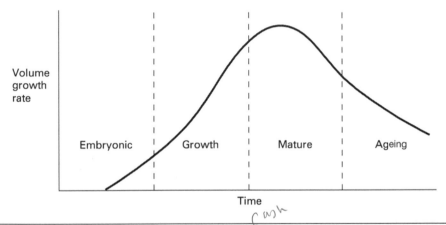

Market	High growth/low share	High growth/high share	Low growth/high share	Low growth/low share
Financial	Cash hungry Low reported earnings Good P/E High debt level	Self-financing, cash hungry. Good to low reported earnings High P/E. Low–moderate debt level	Cash rich High earnings Fair P/E No debt–high debt capacity	Fair cash flow Low earnings Low P/E Low debt capacity
Managerial	Entrepreneur	Sophisticated manager	Critical administrator	Opportunistic milker
Planning time frame	Long enough to draw tentative life-cycle	Long-range investment pay-out	Intermediate	Short range
Structure	Free form or task force	Semi-permanent task force, product or market division	Business division plus task force for renewal	Pared-down division
Compensation	High variable/low fixed, fluctuating with performance	Balanced variable and fixed, individual and group rewards	Low variable–high fixed, group rewards	Fixed only
Communication system	Informal/tailor made	Formal/tailor made	Formal/uniform	Little or none, command system
Measuring and reporting	Qualitative marketing, unwritten	Qualitative and quantitative early warning system, all functions	Qualitative, written, production orientated	Numerical, written, balance sheet oriented

FIGURE 4.7 A depiction of the strategy centres concept

Source: Arthur D. Little, Inc. cited in Patel, P. and Younger, M. (1978) A frame of reference for strategy development, *Long Range Planning* (April): 6–12

characteristics using a 'Ronagraph' which bears a striking resemblance to the so-called 'Boston Box' developed by the Boston Consulting Group (see Chapter 5). Once the potential of the existing businesses has been assessed the analysis is extended to explore possible external opportunities which are then compared with the internal opportunities. This comparison leads naturally to an evaluation of the corporate risk portfolio and eight factors are cited as affecting the risk of each SBU:

1. Industry maturity
2. Competitive position
3. Inherent industry risk
4. Unit objectives
5. Unit assumptions
6. Unit strategies
7. Past unit performance
8. Management record.

Once each has been assessed, the separate assessments can be combined into an overall corporate risk portfolio.

The same procedure is then repeated in terms of external uncertainties and the likelihood of their affecting each of the SBUs ('exposure'). These are then aggregated into a corporate risk profile, which ADL graphed on eight axes as illustrated in Figure 4.7.

Step 6 is the qualitative and quantitative evaluation of the corporate management resources, while step 7 embraces determination of the corporate financial resources and obligations. Finally, these analyses lead to an explicit statement of corporate goals and objectives and a timetable for their achievement. Emphasis upon making the process explicit is supported by all the proponents of SMP to ensure that all the key steps have been taken, that the issues considered have been duly recorded so that subsequent reference can be made to them, and to provide an action document for those responsible for implementing the plan. Thus, according to ADL, such a formal plan should cover all the following issues:

1. The key environmental assumptions
2. The corporate weaknesses requiring attention
3. The corporate values and objectives
4. The basic corporate strategic thrusts
5. Strategic mandates for functional units

6. Unit strategy revectoring process
7. New budgeting process.

In running through the process of strategic planning using Arthur D. Little as an exemplar frequent reference has been made to 'life-cycles' and in Chapter 5 we will review this concept in some detail as it is fundamental to all major frameworks for strategic marketing planning.

CRITICISMS OF AND OBSTACLES TO STRATEGIC PLANNING

In the aftermath of the recessions precipitated by the energy crises of the 1970s many commentators attributed lacklustre performance (particularly in the USA) to an overdependence upon formal strategic planning. This issue was the subject of an article by Daniel H. Gray entitled 'Uses and misuses of strategic planning' (1986), in which he argued that there was nothing wrong with the concept of strategic planning – it is faulty preparation and implementation which causes the problems.

Based upon a year-long research project, Gray concluded that a major problem with strategic planning was (and is) the tendency to regard it as a separate discipline or management function rather than as an instrument to support strategic management: in other words, a tendency for the system to assume a greater importance than its product as an input to the managerial formulation of strategy. With over 500 respondents Gray found a high level of commitment to the concept of formal planning but 87% reported feelings of disappointment and frustration with their systems. Of the sample, 58% attributed this to difficulties experienced in the implementation of plans while 67% of those from multibusinesses attributed implementation difficulties to faults in the design and management of their system.

More detailed analysis indicated that many of the claimed difficulties in implementation were really due to pre-implementation factors which could be summarised as:

1. Poor preparation of line managers
2. Faulty definition of business units
3. Vaguely formulated goals

4. Inadequate information bases for planning
5. Badly handled reviews of business unit plans
6. Inadequate linkage of strategic planning with other control systems.

Clearly, all these factors are amenable to correction and improvement (Gray provides his own detailed advice as to how to set about this).

In 1987 Michael Porter wrote in *The Economist:*

Strategic planning was born amid a flurry of optimism and industrial growth in the 1960s and early 70s. It quickly became a fad. Today strategic planning has fallen out of fashion. The criticism is well-deserved. Strategic planning in most companies has not contributed to strategic thinking. The answer is not to abandon planning. The need has never been greater. Instead strategic planning needs to be rethought.

That said, the sources of resistance to SMP remain much the same as those identified by Malcolm MacDonald (2000), namely:

1. The company has made good products without it
2. Planning is time consuming and prevents people from doing their real job
3. Plans are constraining, prevent initiative and create inflexibility to rapid change
4. Plans never come true, and valuable time is wasted writing them
5. Companies know their business well; there is no point writing down the obvious
6. No one reads the plan when it is written so it becomes a traditional annual ritual
7. Some industries are different and do not need plans
8. Long-range plans are full of meaningless numbers
9. Plans are based on unrealistic objectives and prepared without hard market information
10. Departments cannot agree amongst themselves so the plan is never finalised.

In broad terms, the failing enthusiasm for strategic planning may be diagnosed as a problem of trappings versus substance following Charles Ames' (1970) analysis of a similar disenchantment with the marketing concept in the 1960s. As suggested earlier, a contributory factor was that SP had become established as a separate specialist function in its own right and so 'detached' from senior management who were (are) its rightful owners. A further explanation of the 'disarray' in which strategic business planning finds itself is provided by an article by Thomas Marx (1991).

In Dr Marx's view SP has been seen to fail in delivering the promised benefits because of the numerous bureaucratic obstacles put in its path. The obstacles identified occur at each of the four phases of the development of strategic management identified by Gluck et al. (1982) and illustrated in Figure 4.8. Most companies proceed smoothly through phases 1 and 2 as competitive pressures and investment planning require them to look three to five years ahead. But, as Figure 4.8 indicates, there is a step function in both commitment and expenditure to progress from phase 2 to phase 3. Marx comments:

It is in phase 3 of the planning process that the difficult processes really begin. It is here that the company is organised, for planning purposes, into strategic business units (SBUs); extensive training is required; thorough analysis of competitors and the external environment and an inventory of internal strengths and weaknesses are undertaken; and formal business plans are written, reviewed and monitored for the first time. It is also here that the organisational changes are most severe, and that the planning process becomes most vulnerable to its natural enemies – inertia, entrenched interests, and risk aversity.

Unless the firm can overcome these difficulties, it is unlikely that it will achieve the transition from externally oriented planning (phase 3) to true strategic management (phase 4). Marx describes in some detail the kinds of obstacles which can be raised in phase 3 and contrasts these with the characteristics of phase 4 as illustrated in Table 4.6. From Table 4.6 it is clear that if one acquires the trappings of strategic planning (usually at considerable expense) the outcome is virtually antithetical to the intention of the substance of strategic management – dynamic, responsive, flexible, results-oriented and – above all – in the hands of those responsible for direction and implementation.

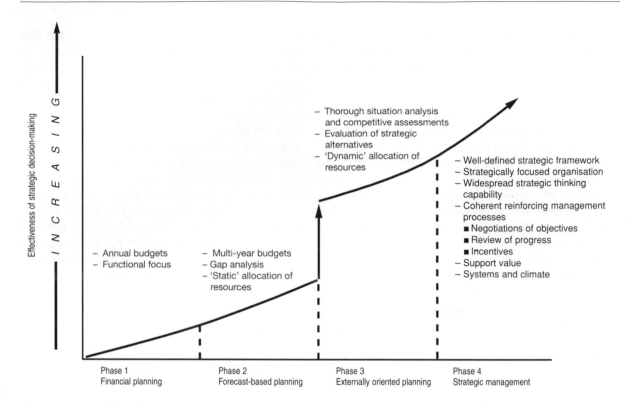

FIGURE 4.8 Phases in the development of strategic planning

SOURCE: Marx, T. G. (1991) Removing the obstacles to effective strategic planning, *Long Range Planning*, 24(4)

TABLE 4.6 Obstacles to effective strategic planning

Phase 3 Obstacles	Phase 4 Characteristics
PLANNING PROCESSES	
Uniform procedures	Flexible procedures
Regularly scheduled reviews	Scheduled as needed
Strict time limits on reviews	As much time as needed
Formal presentations	Informal presentations
Numerous observers	Decision-makers only
Massive paperwork	Ten-page plans
Restricted discussion	Open dialogue
No decisions	Decisions mandatory
Process emphasised	Results emphasised
CONTENT OF THE PLANS	
Data, numbers, facts	Business intelligence
Financial analysis	Strategic analysis
Short-term focus	Long-term focus
Generic strategies	Strategic action plans
MONITORING AND REWARD PROCESSES	
Random progress reviews	Regular progress reviews
Limited accountability	Strict accountability

SOURCE: Marx, T. G. (1991) Removing the obstacles to effective strategic planning, *Long Range Planning*, 24(4)

The obstacles encountered in phase 3 are attributed by Marx to one of four basic root causes:

1. Lack of top management commitment
2. Staff, rather than line management, control of process
3. Entrenched self-interest
4. A risk-averse corporate culture.

Marx describes and analyses each of these causal factors in some depth and concludes that successful companies which are able to overcome the obstacles progress from the bureaucratic parody of planning of phase 3 to the realities of strategic planning in phase 4. By its nature, hands-on strategic planning and management eschews the bureaucracy of its trappings and reduces the practice to its substance. Because of the contrast between trappings and substance some commentators mistakenly believe that phase 4 firms have dropped strategic planning and so may be compared with the Japanese who, the conventional wisdom would have us believe, 'don't plan at all'. Marx (1991) observes:

> It is the lack of the most obvious obstacles to effective strategic business planning in the Japanese systems which leads to this misperception. The elimination of formal presentations, large meetings, massive planning books, and regularly scheduled, annual reviews is not the abandonment of planning – it is the liberation of planning!

MARKETING PLANNING AND PRACTICE

During the late 1980s Baker et al. (1994) undertook two detailed surveys of British companies in order to establish the existence and nature of critical success factors. As part of these two studies (Project MACS and Profit by Design) respondents were asked what, in their opinion, goes wrong with marketing planning in practice. In the view of the executives interviewed failure was not due to a lack of scientific methodology but to a number of other factors which may be summarised as:

1. *Analysis instead of planning:* Executives frequently claimed that they saw planning as being bogged down with analytical techniques and models which were far removed from the reality they perceived and which failed to lead to actionable plans.

2. *Information instead of decision:* Many executives described planning as disintegrating into constant demands for information, and some were cynical enough to suggest that the reason for this was that it was easier than making decisions. This, too, is associated with considerable difficulty in producing an actionable plan from the planning process.

3. *Incrementalism:* At its simplest, executives described many situations where the primary determinant of a plan was the previous plan, or at least the previous budget. Thus, the planning task can easily deteriorate into negotiating minor departures from the previous year, rather than creating new strategies.

4. *Vested interests rule:* Executives suggest that the powerful exert undue influence over plans, to project budgets and head counts, to build empires, and so on.

5. *Organisational 'mindset':* Many executives suggested that conventional planning processes are inward looking and bounded by 'the way we do things here'.

6. *Resistance to marketing change:* Some executives suggested that strategic change emanating from the marketing department was seen as threatening – or even 'unreasonable' – and so is resisted by other departments and organisational interest groups.

7. *No 'ownership' or commitment:* It seems that in many cases plans are produced (often by staff planners) and accepted but, in the absence of champions determined to make them work, nothing ever happens as a result of the planning effort.

8. *No resourcing:* Executives cited many resource related pitfalls: the simple refusal by management to provide resources; the rejection of plans with the comment that they are unrealistic because it should have been known all along that resources would not be realised; and perhaps the most threatening being approval and acceptance of the plan but rejection of the accompanying resource request.

9. *No implementation:* Many respondents complained bitterly about situations where planning absorbed resources and management

time, and even created excitement and support for change, but led to nothing more than a report, which was never effectively acted on.

10. *Diminishing effort and interest:* Largely as a result of lack of resourcing and implementation. Executives pointed out that if planning was to be no more than an annual ritual and managers perceive this, then it is hardly surprising that efforts and interest diminish over time.

STRATEGIC PLANNING

Faced with the prospect of ever increasing competition, planning for the future assumes even greater importance. But it is clear that old methods involving highly formalised procedures are inappropriate to anticipate and capture the surprises and uncertainties in a rapidly changing environment. In Henkoff's (1990) view, 'At too many companies strategic planning has become overly bureaucratic, absurdly quantitative, and largely irrelevant'. Given the volatility of the marketplace, the strategic planning popularised in the stable 1960s needed to be replaced with a more responsive, hands-on approach in the 1990s – an activity increasingly referred to as 'strategic thinking'.

The key characteristics of strategic thinking are seen as focus and flexibility:

Focus means figuring out, and building on, what the company does best. It means identifying the evolving needs of your customers, then developing the key skills – often called core competencies – critical to serving them. It means setting a clear, realistic mission and then working tirelessly to make sure everyone – from the chairman to the middle managers to the hourly employee, understands it … Flexibility means sketching rough scenarios of the future – what General Electric [GE] Chairman Jack Welch calls bands of possibilities – then being ready to pounce on opportunities as they arise. (Henkoff, 1990)

As Henkoff observes:

GE was once the corporate citadel of quantitative forecasting. The 350-member planning staff churned out voluminous reports, meticulously detailed and exquisitely packaged. Now GE has but a score of full-time planners. Called business development special-

ists, they are there only to advise line managers, who have the prime responsibility for formulating strategy.

The heads of GE's 13 businesses each year develop five one-page 'charts', memos that alert them to possible opportunities and obstacles in their industries over the next 24 months. When Hungary opened its doors to foreign ownership in state-run companies, GE needed just 60 days to cut a deal for 50% of Tungsram, the country's leading lighting company. Tungsram had been on GE's chart for years.

As noted previously, the challenge of successful strategic thinking/planning is the ability to identify market opportunities and then deploy the organisation's resources to exploit them profitably. It is the ability to think conceptually in terms of the need served and then define this in terms of currently appropriate solutions; to be flexible but control and manage the pace of change so as to optimise present skills and investment while acquiring new skills and releasing capital for new investment. To do this effectively calls for a marketing orientation irrespective of whether one subscribes to the 'technology push' or 'market pull' theory of innovation and change. Market pull lends itself to incremental change, technology push to discontinuities and step changes in the way in which things are done. Market pull works back from existing customers and their consumption behaviour using conventional market research to document possibilities for enhancing current products and services. Technology push arises from insight, intuition and creativity and promises major gains in satisfaction. But, because it is radically different, it engenders resistance which becomes greater the greater the change proposed. Based on over 40 years of experience and research, I am convinced that successful innovation – defined as the commercialisation of invention – is highly dependent upon the innovator's ability to identify the most receptive market segment – something which depends centrally upon an understanding of markets and customer behaviour. As Henkoff observes, 'In a world awash with forecasts, opinions, theories, seminars, consultants, and concepts, many companies have come to the conclusion that the only oracles worth listening to are their customers.'

However, in 'listening to one's customers' it is important to make the distinction implicit in the previous paragraph when discussing the difference between technology push and market pull. Customers are both able and willing to tell suppliers what they like and dislike about current offerings, and it is this feedback which enables the continuous upgrading and improvement of such products where the benefits justify the costs involved. But customers are much less able and willing to speculate about radical change and such theorising and conjecture inevitably falls to the lot of the inventor and entrepreneur. As the record shows, the failures of would-be inventors and entrepreneurs greatly exceed the few well-documented success stories, and it is here that both academic and practitioner have a role to play in seeking to isolate and describe those activities and procedures that appear to enhance the potential for success. Formal strategic planning is an attempt to do just this and the fact that its usefulness has become compromised and open to question should not distract the professional manager from the potential contribution from the activity, provided it remains an aid to strategic thinking and not a substitute for it. Because strategic planning practice has degenerated into a form of detailed tactical documentation, more akin to the operational budget statement, does not mean that the concept of strategic planning is deficient, too. What is needed is a return to the broadly based speculation about alternative futures, which was the origin of techniques such as those developed by GE, Shell and the Boston Consulting Group.

In his *Fortune* article Henkoff reports that scenario planning has emerged as an approach which combines both focus and flexibility. Describing practice at California Edison, whose painstaking long-range plans had been rendered virtually useless by unanticipated events such as OPEC price-fixing, restrictions on sulphur emissions and accidents at Three Mile Island and Chernobyl, Henkoff (1991) comments:

> Looking ahead ten years, the utility came up with 12 possible versions of the future – incorporating an economic boom, a Middle East oil crisis, expanded environmentalism, and other developments. Each scenario carries implications for how much power Edison would need to generate, from 5,000 megawatts more to 5,000 megawatts less than the 15,000 megawatts it was producing in 1987.

To cope with such radical variations in demand, Edison has built flexibility into its system. It can repower or depower oil-and-gas generating plants, buy juice from other utilities and intensify or diminish its campaign to help customers use less electricity. Edison is stepping up conservation in response to new state regulations that reward utilities for encouraging reduced consumption.

Similarly, Royal Dutch/Shell, which had been doing scenario planning for many years and is widely regarded as the master of the craft, currently has two 20-year scenarios in place. The first, called 'Sustainable World', predicts increased concern about global warming trends and an expanded emphasis on conservation, recycling and emission controls. The second scenario, ominously entitled 'Mercantilist World', postulates an increase in protectionism, a slump in world growth, and a de-emphasis on environmentalism.

PAYOFF FROM STRATEGIC PLANNING

During the early 2000s, McKinsey & Co. undertook research to determine why many CEOs complain that their strategic planning process yields few new ideas and is often fraught with politics.

To begin with the researchers took an in-depth examination of the strategic planning process in 30 companies, both successful and less successful, from a variety of industries and representing a range of approaches. Some were analysed using insider information and interviews; others using published sources and interviews with persons with specialised knowledge of the company. Among the companies analysed were American Express, Boeing, BP, Coca-Cola, GE, IBM, Intel, Johnson & Johnson, Merrill Lynch, Monsanto, Rubbermaid, SmithKline Beecham and Unilever. The findings from this analysis were then tested in workshops and discussions in approximately 50 other companies around the world. Finally, these findings were synthesised with those drawn from many years' experience of studying and helping to implement strategic planning.

The authors of the report Eric D. Beinhocker and Sarah Kaplan (2002) indicate that the findings point to a dispiriting conclusion about the benefits of the process:

The annual strategy review frequently amounts to little more than a stage on which business unit leaders present warmed-over updates of last year's presentations, taking few risks in broaching new ideas, and strive above all to avoid embarrassment. Rather than preparing executives to face the strategic uncertainties ahead or serving as the focal point for creative thinking about a company's vision and direction, the planning process is like some primitive tribal ritual. There is a lot of dancing, waving of feathers, and beating of drums. No one is exactly sure why we do it, but there is an almost mystical hope that something good will come out of it.

Despite the views of critics like Henry Mintzberg who considers 'strategic planning' to be a contradiction and therefore an oxymoron, Beinhocker and Kaplan believe that a formal planning process can add value, provided it has two overarching goals. The first is the building of 'prepared minds' so that the decision-makers have a solid understanding of the business, its strategy and the assumptions underlying that strategy. Given such shared understanding, executives will be able to respond rapidly to new threats and opportunities as they emerge. The second goal is to increase the innovativeness of a company's strategies. Despite the reputation of the companies in their sample, none was found that was best at achieving both of these goals. While GE came close, companies tended to be better at one or the other of the two. Based on their analysis, the authors suggest a number of guidelines that represent a composite of best practice.

In terms of *preparing minds*, the recommendations are:

- Restrict involvement to the principal strategic decision-makers
- Limit the number of attendees to no more than 10
- Set aside sufficient time – 20–30 days
- Separate strategy reviews from discussions of budgets and financial targets
- Those executives who carry out strategy must make it
- Limit guidance to SBUs to basics such as analysis of customers, competitors and economics, and allow latitude to the actual decision-makers
- Culture and tone in the reviews are critical – all the participants should feel they are playing for the same side
- Disciplined follow-up is essential.

While these guidelines are useful in helping to develop a shared understanding that provides a basis for effective action, they do not automatically stimulate creativity. To encourage *creative accidents*, two mechanisms are proposed:

1. Encouraging bottom-up experiments
2. Driving top-down initiatives.

'Strategic experimentation occurs when a company pursues a variety of strategic options in parallel within a given business.' By contrast, top-down initiatives are set by the CEO who requires everyone to think through the implications of, say, implementing six sigma quality improvement.

Taken together the message is clear; strategic planning is not a mindless ritual designed to propitiate unknown forces – a sort of risk insurance; strategic planning is a conscious effort to achieve declared objectives to maximum effect.

Box 4.3 **Management tools 2005,** by Darrell Rigby, Bain & Company

In 1993 Bain & Company launched a multiyear research project to document the use of management tools, with the objective of helping managers to identify, select, implement and integrate tools that will improve bottom line results. The 2005 results, based on the responses of 960 managers, focused on the 25 most popular tools and techniques and built on a database that then exceeded 7,000 over the 12-year period. To qualify for inclusion, a tool had to be relevant to senior management, topical, as evidenced by coverage in the business press, and measurable.

Four major themes emerged from the survey:

1. Customer focus with a large and growing concern for CRM.
2. The innovation gap – a concern that more and more goods and services 'behave like commodities'. The answer? More emphasis on innovation and less concern for cost reduction.
3. Finding the money – cost reduction is still seen as vital, with outsourcing and off-shoring regarded as major ways of achieving this.
4. Extensive use of IT. CRM and knowledge management (KM) have become more sophisticated and extensive

use is made of computers in TQM, supply chain management, and scenario and contingency planning.

User satisfaction with the available tools is summarised below, based on a scale of 1–5. With an overall mean of 3.89, this is relatively high, with the top five being:

1. Strategic planning — 4.14
2. Supply chain management — 3.99
3. Benchmarking — 3.98
4. Core competencies — 3.97
5. Customer segmentation — 3.97

It is significant that, despite the doubts expressed about the value of strategic planning, it tops the list in terms of both satisfaction and usage, which suggests that managers find it a useful discipline with well-established tools and techniques to underpin it. On a regional basis, however, strategic planning does not come top in Asia.

Over the period since the first survey, the popularity/usage of different tools has changed and is summarised in a table of winners and losers contained in the report.

It is in this spirit of flexibility and broadbrush approaches to strategic planning that we have confined the discussion largely to what we have described as CUGs – currently useful generalisations. Such generalisations provide a framework for thinking about and analysis of strategic issues without dulling the mind and spirit with the pseudo-precision of the detailed formal planning systems beloved by the specialist. This is not to suggest that detail has no place in strategic planning but to emphasise that its place is subordinate and supportive – a fact long recognised in successful military organisations where the 'teeth arms' actually do the fighting and the staff and support services attend to the administration, logistics and communications. Accordingly, in Chapter 5 we look at some of the techniques and procedures that inform the detailed planning process, but without getting into the detail itself.

Chapter summary

In this chapter we have attempted to provide a framework for the remainder of the book by examining some of the principles of strategic marketing planning and thereby linking the key areas of marketing, strategy and planning into a single, coherent structure.

To introduce this structure we looked first at the concept of stages of corporate development and concluded that while the degree of detail called for would grow with the increased size and complexity of an organisation, the need for and discipline of strategic planning was appropriate to all forms and sizes of organisation. This conclusion was reinforced by a brief review of the evolution of management systems and

concomitant planning systems which lend considerable support to General Eisenhower's often quoted maxim, 'The plan is nothing; planning is everything.' In other words, the process is infinitely more important than any specific output from it.

Plans represent the translation of the organisation's aims into actions. Against this background we looked next at the origin of aims through a discussion of the ideas of mission, vision and strategic intent leading to formulation of specific objectives.

Next we looked at definitions of SMP. As with terms like 'strategy', 'marketing', and 'planning' so it is with their combination

into the description of a practice – we can easily agree on the general, it is the particularities which lead to the differences as to precisely what is involved. Accordingly, we proposed that SMP may be defined as:

The establishment of the goal or purpose of a strategic business unit and the means by which this is to be achieved.

If one has a goal or purpose, then it is reasonable to expect that one can specify this in the form of a specific objective or objectives. The formulation of objectives was the subject of the next section of the chapter and we drew on the writings of several experts to help spell out the kinds of objectives which satisfy our concern for CUGs. In turn, this led us to propose a framework for SMP itself, as either a sequence of 'steps' or, more likely, a continuous cycle of activity from analysis to evaluation to planning to implementation to review to analysis and so on. Underlying this cycle we can discern a number of key principles. While acknowledging the universality of these principles we chose to use the framework developed by Arthur D. Little

as our exemplar. That said, the frameworks of other leading consultancies such as the Boston Consulting Group or McKinsey's are just as useful (and very similar!) as a basis for helping decision-makers impose structure on the problems of strategy formulation and planning.

Next, we considered briefly some of the criticisms of, and obstacles to, the use of strategic marketing planning. In the main, the problems associated with SMP reflect the confusion of trappings with substance

and the lack of commitment in implementation. Finally, to cope with the uncertainty associated with competition and economic turbulence we looked briefly at scenario planning as a basis for defining possible futures and developing strategies to cope with them. These are recurring themes which we address fully in Part III of the book. Meantime we move on to survey some of the techniques and procedures which will help those committed to the principles of SMP to translate it into practice.

Recommended reading

Baker, M. J. (1998) *The Marketing Manual.* Oxford: Butterworth Heinemann.
Grant, R. M. (2004) *Contemporary Strategy Analysis.* Oxford: Blackwell Publishing.
Hooley, G. J., Saunders, J. A. and

Piercy, N. F. (2003) *Marketing Strategy and Competitive Positioning* (3rd edn). London: Prentice Hall Europe.
MacDonald, M. (2003) Strategic marketing planning: theory and practice, in Baker, M. J. (ed.) *The*

Marketing Book (5th edn). Oxford: Butterworth Heinemann.
O'Shaughnessy, J. (1999) Strategic marketing planning, in Baker, M. J. (ed.) *Encyclopedia of Marketing.* London: International Thomson Business Press.

REFERENCES

Abell, D. F. and Hammond, J. S. (1979) *Strategic Marketing Planning.* Englewood Cliffs, NJ: Prentice Hall.
Ames, B. C. (1970) Trappings versus substance in industrial marketing, *Harvard Business Review* (July–August).
Ansoff, I. (1968) *Corporate Strategy.* Harmondsworth: Penguin.
Arthur D. Little, Inc. cited in Patel, P. and Younger, M. (1978) A frame of reference for strategy development, *Long Range Planning* (April): 6–12.
Baillie, A. and Johnston, G. (1994) *The process of strategy development.* Cranfield School of Management Research Paper.
Baker, M. J., Black, C. D. and Hart, S. J. (1994) Competitive success in sunrise and sunset industries, Chapter 4 in Saunders, J. (ed.) *The Marketing Initiative.* Hemel Hempstead: Prentice Hall.

Bart, C. K. (1997) Industrial firms and the power of mission, *Industrial Marketing Management*, **26**: 371–83.
Beinhocker, E. D. and Kaplan, S. (2002) Tired of strategic planning?, McKinsey & Co.
Brownlie, D. (1983) Analytical frameworks for strategic marketing planning, Chapter 11 in Baker, M. J. et al. *Marketing: Theory and Practice* (2nd edn). London: Macmillan – now Palgrave Macmillan.
Campbell, A. and Yeung, S. (1991) Mission, vision and strategic intent, brief case in *Long Range Planning*, **24**(4).
Campbell, A., Devine, M. and Yeung, D. (1990) *A Sense of Mission.* London: Hutchinson Business Books.
David, F. R. (1989) How companies define their mission, *Long Range Planning*, **22**(February).
Drucker, P. (1964) The big power of little ideas, *Harvard Business Review* (May–June).

Drucker, P. (1968) *The Practice of Management.* London: Heinemann.
Drucker, P. F. (1974) *Management Tasks, Reponsibilities and Practices.* New York: Harper & Row.
Gluck, F., Kaufman, S. and Walleck, A. S. (1982) The four phases of strategic management, *Journal of Business Strategy* (winter).
Gray, D. H. (1986) Uses and misuses of strategic planning, *Harvard Business Review*, January–February.
Gunn, L. (1991) teaching notes, University of Strathclyde.
Hamel, G. and Prahalad, C. K. (1989) Strategic intent, *Harvard Business Review*, **67**(3): 63–76.
Hayes, R. H. and Abernathy, W. J, (1980) Managing our way to economic decline, *Harvard Business Review* (July–August).
Henkoff, R. (1990) How to Plan for 1995, *Fortune*, 31 December.
Hofer, C. W. (1977) *Conceptual Constructs for Formulating Corporate and Business Strategies.* Boston:

Intercollegiate Case Clearing House, 9–378–754, p. 33.

Klemm, M., Sanderson, S. and Luffman, G. (1991) Selling corporate values to employees, *Long Range Planning* (June).

Levitt, T. (1960) Marketing myopia, *Harvard Business Review* (July–August): 45.

McDonald, M. H. B. (1982) *The Theory and Practice of Marketing Planning for Industrial Goods in International Markets*. PhD dissertation. Cranfield Institute of Technology.

McDonald, M. H. B. (1984) *Marketing Plans*. London: Heinemann.

McDonald, M. (2003) Strategic marketing planning: theory and practice, Chapter 5 in Baker, M. J. (ed.)

The Marketing Book (5th edn). Oxford: Butterworth Heinemann.

McKay, E. S. (1972) *The Marketing Mystique*. New York: American Management Association.

Marx, T. G. (1991) Removing the obstacles to effective strategic planning, *Long Range Planning*, **24**(4).

O'Shaughnessy, J. (1999) Strategic marketing planning, in Baker, M. J. (ed.) *Encyclopedia of Marketing*. London: International Thomson Business Press.

Porter, M. E. (1980) *Competitive Strategy*. New York: Free Press.

Porter, M. E. (1987) The state of strategic thinking, *The Economist*, 23 May.

Selznick, P. (1957) Conclusion, in

Leadership in Administration. New York: Harper & Row.

Taylor, B. (1976) Managing the process of corporate development, *Long Range Planning* (June).

NOTES

1 This summary, and many of the key concepts and ideas discussed in this chapter, draw heavily upon the work of the Arthur D. Little consulting organisation, which has long been in the forefront of developments in this field of corporate planning and management.

2 This section borrows heavily from McDonald (1982), which was published as *Marketing Plans* (1984).

Analytical frameworks for strategic marketing planning

A problem defined is a problem solved. ANON.

After reading Chapter 5 you will be able to:

✔ Explain the application of demand curves to SMP.

✔ Describe the concept of the product life-cycle and justify its use as a basic input to formal planning.

✔ Spell out the strategy alternatives appropriate to each of the major stages of the PLC – introduction, growth, maturity, decline.

✔ Suggest how diffusion theory may be used to aid formal planning.

✔ Explain the nature of portfolio analysis and the key concepts it embraces – PLC, market share, experience effects and scale effects.

✔ Review and critique criticisms of portfolio analysis as an approach to SMP.

✔ Describe the analytical approaches developed by Shell and GEC as a basis for determining the strategic threats and opportunities facing them.

✔ Relate expectations to outcomes using Baker's Box.

✔ Describe and explain the techniques of gap and scenario analysis and the nature of SWOT analysis.

INTRODUCTION

In Chapter 4 we traced the evolution of management systems during the second half of the last century and described how formalised approaches to planning had developed to help professional managers cope better with an increasingly complex and turbulent environment. This review revealed the paradox that much 'planning' appears to have been short-term and responsible for the faltering growth of many Western economies – especially those of the UK and USA despite the fact that the normative theory of strategic planning is claimed to offer the best long-term solution to competitive success. However, more recent research in several countries seems to suggest that the problem with strategic planning is similar to that identified by B. Charles Ames regarding the implementation of the marketing concept.

Ames's (1970) article was prompted by a growing chorus of complaint from industrial companies that, while marketing might be all very well for fast moving consumer goods firms, it was of little help to them. Ames's analysis and diagnosis was that the reason 'marketing' wasn't working for these industrial companies was because they had mistaken the 'trappings' of the marketing function for the 'substance' of the marketing concept. Instead of identifying the full implications of becoming market-oriented and customer-driven companies, which usually required a change of both values and corporate culture, management looked for a 'quick fix' by increasing marketing expenditures on advertising and promotion, changing job titles, etc. The consequence, of course, was that little, if anything, happened. Indeed, the increased expenditures often worsened rather than improved corporate fortunes. The need clearly was for a much better understanding of the philosophy of marketing, and less emphasis upon its practice.

As with marketing, so with strategic planning. Accordingly, the remainder of Chapter 4 was concerned with seeking to establish the objectives, nature and purpose of SMP in order to communicate its substance. In this chapter we turn to issues of implementation and consider a number of analytical frameworks that have proved their worth in converting concept to practice.

Most of the frameworks presented in this chapter satisfy the definition of CUGs (currently useful generalisations) offered in Chapter 2 – they are simple, robust and known to work in practice. Their value lies in their ability to help impose structure on complex problems and curtail them to manageable proportions. Because they are simple, and often reduce problems to only two dimensions, they are frequently criticised or dismissed by theoreticians who can afford the luxury of simulating complex problems without any penalty for failure. Some reference will be made to the more important of these criticisms but, in general, they are rejected on the grounds that experience shows that the methods described in this chapter do help managers solve problems. However, it is important to recognise from the outset that they can offer assistance only in diagnosing, defining and solving problems. As with any other tool or technique, incorrectly selected and applied they will have little or no effect except, perhaps, a negative one. The skill of the professional manager lies in his or her ability to select the appropriate method from the repertoire available. To do so requires that the manager knows what is in the repertoire.

It is widely accepted that the average person can only cope with a limited number of ideas, concepts or bits of information simultaneously. If one attempts to increase the input to the short-term memory in which information processing is managed then overload is likely to occur. Research by Miller (1956) suggests that most individuals have a capacity of seven bits of information, plus or minus two, for immediate processing purposes. To overcome this limitation we use a number a personal strategies including chunking and selectivity.

Chunking is a form of data reduction by which we collapse information into more manageable pieces each of which contains considerable detail. This detail may be recalled if we wish by disaggregating the chunk. Brands and the country of origin are examples of chunks of information used by consumers to summarise knowledge, experience and attitudes into a simple summary construct.

Selectivity is a form of learnt behaviour that enables us to discriminate between relevant, less relevant, and irrelevant information or stimuli. The great majority of selectivity occurs at the subconscious level where the phenomenon of selective perception screens and either stores or discards incoming information. Very occasionally our subconscious perception will draw our attention to incoming information when it considers it should take precedence to or inform our conscious attention. You don't step off the pavement in the path of an approaching bus. You do notice information (including advertisements) that addresses problems you are grappling with.

Given the phenomena of chunking and selectivity, managers have resorted to a number of procedures and techniques to help simplify complex decisions. One such device is matrix analysis.

Matrix analysis is inevitably a compromise, and many would claim an oversimplification, in attempting to solve complex problems. It is a compromise in that it seeks to reduce the elements of an analysis into two dimensions which capture the essential nature of a relationship without delving into the multiplicity of factors represented by the dimensions. As such, matrix analysis should be regarded as a technique which enables the decision-maker to zero in on the real problem to be addressed by eliminating other possible problems or courses of action which may exist but are less relevant. Used in this way, matrix analysis has had a major impact on strategic thinking in recent years, notable examples being: Igor Ansoff's product–market matrix; the Boston Consulting Group's growth-share matrix or 'Boston Box' and Shell's directional policy matrix (DPM). In this chapter we will consider matrix analysis as an aid to strategic planning in some depth.

As will become apparent, perhaps the best known of all the planning matrices – the Boston Box – is based upon the concept of the product life-cycle (PLC). Accordingly, in this chapter, we will look first at three 'curves' which provide considerable insight into the operation of markets. First, we examine one of the best-known but probably least used ideas – the demand curve – which captures the fundamental relationship between supply and demand. Next, we look at the PLC and then the experience curve as dimensions of both are incorporated in the Boston Box. Our discussion of the PLC is extended as we believe its understanding is critical to effective strategic marketing planning. As will be seen this is not a universal view, but readers will have to decide for themselves whether to use this diagnostic tool or not.

The development of the Boston Box which combines elements of the PLC and experience curves is founded on portfolio theory and a discussion of this precedes our review of the 'Box' itself. Next we look at some criticisms of business portfolio analysis before examining some other planning matrices widely used in practice. In addition to these we have included a planning matrix of our own – Baker's Box – which has proved useful in selecting target positions within given markets.

The chapter then concludes with a short reprise of gap analysis and a discussion of scenario planning, which builds on the material introduced in the preceding chapter, and an introduction to the concept of SWOT analysis.

THE DEMAND CURVE

In Chapter 2 we used Michael Porter's model of competitive forces as a basis for identifying those factors which govern competition in an industry. One of these factors was barriers to entry. In identifying barriers to entry Porter was building upon pioneering work by Bain (1956) in which he identified four basic sources: absolute cost advantages of incumbents at any level of output; economies of scale; product differentiation and advantages of incumbents; and total capital requirements to set up a firm of minimum optimal size. To these Porter added: access to distribution channels and government policy.

The importance of the concept of barriers to entry lies in the fact that where there is complete freedom of entry and exit this is equivalent to a state of 'perfect competition' in which every firm faces a perfectly elastic (horizontal) demand curve. Under conditions of perfect competition firms have no discretion over pricing, prices will be set equal to marginal cost and no firm will earn more than normal profits. Clearly, given the absence of any control or influence over the market, perfect competition is a state to be avoided if at all possible. But, in all other types of market structure, a firm faces a downward sloping demand curve and has the possibility of earning super-normal profits. Put another way, active competition only exists in markets characterised by downward sloping demand curves.

Despite the attention given to demand analysis within the discipline of economics it receives comparatively little attention in the marketing management literature. In part, this is attributable to the difficulties involved in defining accurately any given demand curve and, in part, to the belief that every competitive firm enjoys a demand curve of its own. In our view, however, the concept of downward sloping demand curves provides an interesting and important insight into market behaviour.

The importance of the downward sloping demand curve, as illustrated in Figure 5.1, is that it reflects the law of demand that stipulates that the lower the price the greater the quantity demanded (and vice versa). Thus, the demand curve represents the aggregated demand of all those individuals or organisations which have a need for the product or service in question, and resources with which to acquire a supply. The shape of the curve is determined by the actual price intending buyers are prepared to pay which, in turn, depends on the salience or importance of the object to the purchaser, and to their available disposable income. Further consideration of the demand curve suggests only two basic alternative strategies – undifferentiated and differentiated marketing. Under conditions of undifferentiated marketing it is assumed that consumers cannot discriminate significantly between the competitive offerings available, with the result that they will buy from the lowest priced source. In turn, this means that the most efficient supplier will gain further economies of scale and experience thus consolidating their cost leadership position. But, in any industry only one (monopoly) or a small number of sellers (oligopoly) are able to achieve the economies of scale which enable them to exercise cost leadership. For the vast majority of competitors survival depends on differentiating their output in some meaningful way so that buyers will be willing to pay a higher price for the additional benefits offered. In other words, differentiated marketing enables the seller to create a micro-demand curve of their own.

In most industries the Pareto principle applies, whereby 80% of total output is accounted for by 20% or less of the firms involved while the remaining 20% is accounted for by a multiplicity of small and medium-sized enterprises (SMEs).

Economic progress and growth is largely the result of innovation through which new and better ways of satisfying basic needs are established. Consider, for example, the demise of the once dominant railroad industry which was the subject of Levitt's 'Marketing myopia' (1960). Levitt's diagnosis of the decline of the railroad industry was that its management became preoccupied with the supply side and complacent about the existence of competitive threats. As a result of defining their industry in terms of the product offered – railroads – rather than the need served – transportation – the railroad companies failed to identify the potential threat of the new automobile industry.

In the early twentieth century, the manufacture of motorcars was essentially a batch engineering process in which individual manufacturers assumed responsibility for most of the tasks involved in designing and constructing the motorcar. As a result of the fragmented nature of the industry and the absence of economies of scale, even the lowest priced cars cost around $1000 and were well beyond the reach of the average purchaser. Whether or not Henry Ford had a diagram of the downward sloping demand curve in front of him when he conceived of a plan to revolutionise the automobile industry, it is clear that he based his vision on the law of demand. Obviously, and without any need to draw a demand curve for the automobile industry, Ford knew that if he could drastically reduce the price

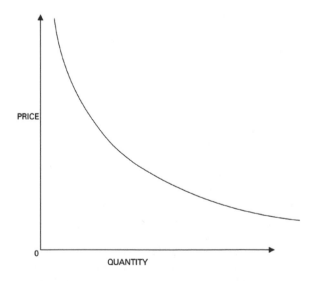

FIGURE 5.1 The downward sloping demand curve

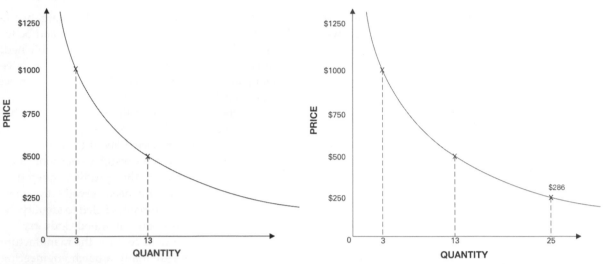

FIGURE 5.2 Impact of halving price

FIGURE 5.3 Market size for Ford's $286 Model T

of a car then he would sell a much larger volume. Accordingly, he set himself the target of halving the current cost of automobile production from $1000 to $500. As Figure 5.2 indicates, this resulted in the potential for a vast increase in demand.

In order to achieve his objective Ford 'invented' the concept of outsourcing and mass-assembly and achieved such massive economies of scale that, by 1916, the Ford Motor Company accounted for over 60% of all cars sold in the USA and was selling the Model T for $286.

Given the extent of his market power, it is not surprising that competitors could not see any way of competing with Ford on a cost/price basis. (After all, Ford could sell a car for less than his rivals could make them for). However, it is at this juncture that a different interpretation of the downward sloping demand curve suggests the opportunity for a way of avoiding head-on competition with a much larger competitor with a cost-leadership position.

If we look at Figure 5.3 two interpretations of Ford's dominant position are possible. First, we observe that his selling price is $286 and seek to find a way of undercutting this. Second, the shape of the demand curve tells us that every single customer to the left of the price point representing $286 is willing to pay more for the supply of a motorcar but, obviously, they would only be prepared to do so if they considered that the additional benefits offered by such a car exceeded the

additional cost. Whether it was this insight which prompted Alfred Sloan at General Motors to conceive of his product line policy, this was to become the strategy which enabled General Motors to displace Ford as the No.1 automobile manufacturer.

In essence Sloan's insight was to recognise the difference between price and value. Price is an objective amount but value is something subjective to the individual. While the price one can afford is limited by one's disposable income, the actual amount one is prepared to pay for a given object is a function of how much satisfaction the possession of that object will give, always taking into account what we have to forego by spending our money on one object rather than another (the idea of opportunity cost). As noted, the logic of the downward sloping demand curve is that added value will command a higher price so that the challenge is to establish what would be perceived as adding value by prospective car buyers. Sloane's answer was to develop a range or portfolio of products at different price-points catering for a spectrum of user needs. In addition General Motors developed the idea of the annual model change so that those buyers for whom cars had a particularly high salience would wish to trade-in their nearly new car for the latest model. GM facilitated this by offering generous trade-in allowances and so created a buoyant second-hand car market in which buyers could acquire a value-added GM model for less than the cost of the basic Model T. By doing so GM was able to neutralise GM's cost leadership of the car market.

THE PRODUCT LIFE-CYCLE (PLC)

In Chapter 3 we introduced the PLC concept in the context of a discussion of the inevitability of change, and of the need for the firm continuously to update its product offering in order to cater for the changing needs of its customers. In this section we shall examine the PLC in greater detail in terms of its value as an input to SMP.

The PLC concept enjoys wide currency in marketing circles and is probably the most widely known yet most misunderstood theoretical construct in marketing. While the supporters of the concept probably outnumber those who denounce it, it is important to make it clear from the start that many highly respected practitioners and academics have rejected the PLC as a useful weapon in the marketer's armoury. Foremost among the critics are Dhalla and Yuspeh (1976), whose article found considerable support for their contention that the PLC concept is without empirical support and has led managers to make incorrect decisions particularly concerning products in the mature phase of the cycle.

As a confirmed supporter of the validity of the PLC, I reject outright the claim that there is no empirical support for the concept (see, for example, Baker, 1975, especially pp. 24–47, and Baker, 1983, Chapter 2) and would argue that the fact that managers have made wrong decisions when seeking to apply the concept is due to their misinterpretation of it rather than an intrinsic deficiency in the concept itself. Such misinterpretation invariably arises from the mistaken belief that the PLC is a precise forecasting tool when, in reality, it is 'a generalised model of the sale trend for a product class or category over a period of time, and of related changes in competitive behaviour'. (Buzzell, 1966)

As such the PLC may be regarded as an important tool for planning at the strategic level, always recognising that it is not of itself deterministic and may be influenced significantly by environmental changes and/or marketing action. In this respect the PLC is remarkably similar to the biological life-cycles on which it is founded, for in favourable conditions species (and products) will proliferate while in adverse circumstances only the strongest and fittest will survive. Similarly, there is no finite length to any stage of the life-cycle and there will be marked differences between different species, albeit that some broad parameters may be distinguished for individual members of any given species. It is also important to remember that the PLC is usually presented in a very simplified form comprising only four phases and it would be surprising if such a broad division were able to accommodate detailed variations in action or behaviour. (It is significant that the consumer behaviour life-cycle popularised by Wells and Gubar, 1966, contains nine phases.) That said, experience shows that dividing a product's life into four distinct phases does enable one to make useful generalisations about the main characteristics of each phase, of the basic strategic alternatives available, and of the most appropriate marketing mix for the implementation of each basic strategic option. It will be useful, therefore, to review briefly each of these four phases.

INTRODUCTION STAGE OF THE PRODUCT LIFE-CYCLE

While it is obvious, many people overlook the fact that the classic PLC depicts the sales trend for a *successful* new product that survives the pangs of birth and the essentially hostile environment into which it is precipitated. Many new products are stillborn or suffer from basic deformities which severely limit their chances of survival and, while the statistics on new product success and failure are often impressive and contradictory, it is clear that 'infant mortality' is far greater than it should be.

There are numerous reasons why this should be so and many of these are discussed and illustrated in *Market Development* (Baker, 1983). Fundamentally, these reasons can be classified into half a dozen categories. Thus Buzzell (1966) attributes slow initial growth 'to some combination of four possible causes:

1. Delays in expansion of production capacity
2. Technical problems, i.e. "working out the bugs"
3. Delays in making the product available to

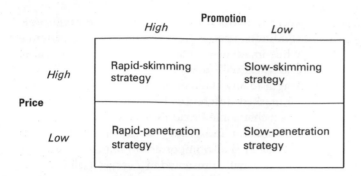

FIGURE 5.4 Four introductory marketing strategies

SOURCE: Kotler, P. (1980) *Marketing Management* (4th edn). Englewood Cliffs, NJ: Prentice-Hall

customers, especially in obtaining adequate distribution through retail outlets

4. Customer inertia, arising primarily from reluctance to change established behaviour patterns.'

Kotler (1980) adds two more possible causes 'in the case of expensive new products:

5. Small number of buyers who are attuned to innovation

6. High cost of the product inhibits purchase.'

Put even more simply, the success or failure of a new product depends on a number of technical factors and the prospective buyer's behavioural response to them. In my own research I have

usually adopted the simplifying assumption that technical factors such as product characteristics, cost-price, distribution and the like are well known to and under the control or influence of the seller and that, if we are to improve the likelihood of survival, we need to concentrate more attention on the behavioural response of potential users and concentrate our selling efforts on those with the greatest receptivity to innovation. Unfortunately, innovativeness tends to be situation specific and difficult to predict (see the case histories in Baker, 1983), which means that it is often simpler to use an undifferentiated strategy emphasising the price and promotion variables as a means to stimulate interest in and early sales of the product. This approach is advocated by Kotler (1980) who proposes four introductory marketing strategies as depicted in Figure 5.4.

Kotler then sets out the situations in which each of these strategies may be appropriate, which Firth (1980) has tabulated in Table 5.1.

GROWTH

Assuming that a product survives the introductory phase, then all the evidence points to a period

TABLE 5.1 Introductory marketing strategies and suitable situations

	TYPE OF STRATEGY			
	Rapid-skimming	**Slow-skimming**	**Rapid-penetration**	**Slow-penetration**
Suitable situations	1. Large part of the potential market is unaware of the product 2. Those who become aware of the product are eager to have it and are able to pay the asking price 3. The firm faces potential competition and wants to build up brand preference	1. The market is relatively limited in size 2. Most of the market is aware of the product 3. Those who want the product are prepared to pay a high price 4. There is little threat of potential competition	1. The market is large in size 2. The market is relatively unaware of the product 3. Most buyers are price sensitive 4. There is strong potential competition 5. The company's unit manufacturing costs fall with the scale of production and accumulated manufacturing experience	1. The market is large 2. The market is highly aware of the product 3. The market is price sensitive 4. There is some potential competition

SOURCE: Firth, C. (1980) New Approaches to Strategic Market Planning. Unpublished MBA dissertation. University of Bradford

of rapidly accelerating growth which is exponential in character and may be represented mathematically by some form of logistic curve. In many senses the take-up of a new product may be likened to the spread of an infectious disease, in that in the early stages there are large numbers of 'unaffected' consumers so that it is relatively easy to make contact with such a person. However, as progressively more and more persons buy the new thing, so the size of the potential market is reduced and new prospects become increasingly difficult to find until the market is saturated and sales stabilise at the replacement rate.

Critics of the PLC argue that in real life the growth curve seldom assumes the smooth symmetry depicted in the textbooks, nor do its parameters conform to the mathematical formulae that summarise diffusion processes in the physical and natural sciences. Given the number of intervening variables that can interfere with the process, it would be very surprising if sales did expand smoothly, and the fact that they don't should not be seen as invalidating the broad, underlying trend. Thus supply and/or distribution difficulties, seasonality, competitive reaction, a downturn in the economic climate, etc., could all act to slow down the process, while cheap money, tax changes, new suppliers, etc., could all serve to speed it up. It is also important to take into account the technical complexity of the product, the size and nature of the investment necessary to produce supplies of it and also the existence or not of patent protection. In the case of the latter a firm may well prefer to develop a market more slowly, consolidating its gains as it proceeds and financing further investment from its cash flow. Conversely, where a firm lacks patent protection and/or its product is easily imitated it may well wish to capitalise on its advantage of being first and seek to expand production as quickly as possible. By doing so the firm hopes to capitalise on the economies of both scale and experience, and secure cost and marketing advantages that will act as barriers to entry for would-be imitators.

Thus, in assessing the slope of the growth curve, it is important always to bear in mind what I have termed a marketing maxim, namely that 'Consumption is a function of availability'. This is not quite the same as Say's law, which asserts that supply creates demand, but a truism which stresses that the physical availability of an object is the ultimate constraint on its consumption. It follows that if producers can restrict supply without fear of direct competition, they will be able to exercise much greater control over the marketing mix and so earn above-average profits. In doing so they will ensure a shallow growth curve quite different from the classic PLC. On the other hand many so-called fad or fashion goods that exhibit almost vertical sales curves do so because there was a sufficient supply to meet all needs almost instantaneously. Indeed for products like hula-hoops, mini or maxi skirts, Rubik cubes, fashion colours, etc., the ease of creating a supply, and the absence of barriers to entry, will often result in excess supply and large unsold stocks. Further, the very nature of the fashion good dictates that it is unlikely to be repeat-purchased, with the result that once the market is saturated sales stop, resulting in the classic fashion good PLC shown in Figure 5.5.

However, the patent protected monopoly and the fashion good (which is usually found in markets approaching conditions of perfect competition) represent boundary states. The great majority of new products are introduced into markets which the economist would define as imperfect in the sense that while competition exists it is restricted to some extent by barriers to entry. In such market conditions (which were analysed in some detail in Chapter 2) we are most likely to find growth characteristics which mirror the traditional PLC as each firm seeks to maximise its share of the expanding market.

Because of the scale and experience effects mentioned earlier, profit margins tend to be great-

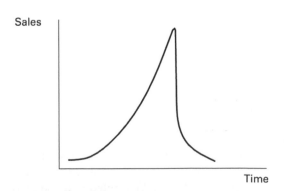

FIGURE 5.5 The classic fashion good PLC

est during the growth phase, but actual profits are often small as firms reinvest in new production facilities and in developing new markets through vigorous promotion and distribution policies.

MATURITY

As the market approaches saturation so the growth rate slows down until eventually it stabilises at a sales level equivalent to the replacement rate, together with any natural growth in market size due to demographic changes. Usually this is the longest single phase of the life-cycle and, normally, will be proportionate to the length of the gestation/introduction phase. That this should be so is logical in that the very forces which accelerate or delay the acceptance of a new product invariably hasten or sustain its decline. For example, consider the forces of resistance to change that slow down the market penetration of many new products. At a conference organised by Sperry Univac in France in 1979, one of the participants[1] argued that 'the future may be further away than people think' and cited the following potential sources of delay:

1. The inherent inertia of human society. (Baker, 1975, cites 12 reasons why individuals and organisations will resist change in the status quo.) In addition it has to be recognised that the majority of the world's population live in the underdeveloped countries and the potential for radical change in these countries is highly impractical.
2. Resistance to manipulation.
3. The existence of dissident minority. As technology displaces satisfying jobs so the number of dissidents resisting such change will increase. (Not borne out in the UK in the late 1970s and early 1980s, but see Point 4.)
4. The need to keep costs down – if technology destroys jobs wholesale then social security costs may exceed the savings from the new technology, e.g. North Sea oil revenues and the UK in the early 1980s.
5. Communications technology is not really needed, i.e. those who will use services like Ceefax and Oracle will be limited to those who used libraries in the past.

Conversely the more closely a new product approximates that for which it is a substitute, the more likely its speedy adoption, and the more likely that it will in turn be displaced by another incremental innovation.

Although profit margins usually decline through the maturity phase, products at this stage of their life-cycle almost invariably comprise the backbone of an established firm's business and generate most cash for reinvestment in the future. Firth cites seven reasons given by Rogers (1962) which account for declining profit margins:

1. Increasing numbers of competitive products leading to overcapacity and intensive competition
2. Market leaders are under growing pressure from smaller competitors
3. Strong increase in R&D to find better versions of the product
4. Cost economies are used up
5. Decline in product distinctiveness
6. Dealer apathy and disenchantment with a product with declining sales
7. Changing market composition where the loyalty of those first to adopt begins to waver.

In turn, and because of this profit erosion, the industry tends to stabilise as a set of well-entrenched competitors all seeking a competitive advantage. This they usually attempt to do by adopting one of four basic strategies which have been characterised as:

1. An offensive or 'take-off' strategy
2. A defensive strategy
3. A recycle strategy
4. A stretching and harvesting strategy.

An offensive strategy has as its objective a major extension of the PLC, and will often lead to one or more periods of renewed growth followed by stabilisation at an overall higher level of sales. Perhaps the best-known example of this strategy is that reported by Levitt (1960) for nylon in which four quite distinct approaches were used to extend the life-cycle:

1. Promoting more frequent usage among current users

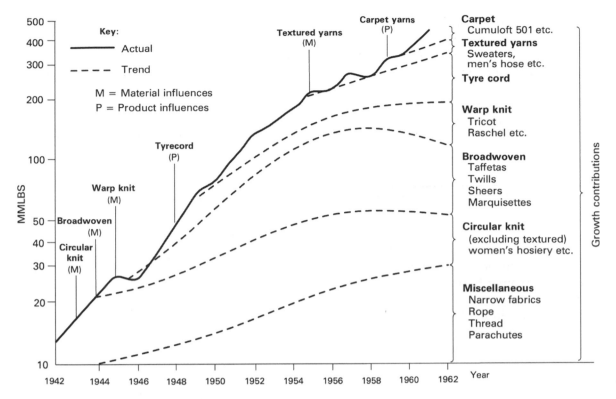

FIGURE 5.6 Innovation of new products postpones the time of total maturity – nylon industry

SOURCE: Yale, J. P. (1964) The strategy of nylon's growth: create new markets, *Modern Textiles Magazine*, February, p. 33

2. Promoting more varied usage among current users
3. Attracting new users
4. Developing new uses for the basic material.

The collective effect of these strategies is well illustrated in Figure 5.6, from which it can be seen that as usage of nylon for one group of end-products began to level off a new application initiated a fresh period of rapid growth.

Where it is not possible to develop new uses or markets for a product it becomes necessary to protect one's existing share of the market through a defensive strategy. This is often referred to as 'dynamic adaptation' and involves manipulation of the non-product elements of the marketing mix – price, distribution and promotion.

A recycling strategy is most often found in the markets for FMCG, but is also applicable to consumer durables and industrial products. Like a defensive strategy, recycling seeks to preserve a product's market share against erosion through a preplanned series of relaunches based upon one or

more elements of the mix, e.g. product improvements, repackaging, new advertising campaign, different channels, etc.

Stretching or harvesting strategies are most common for products with high market shares and little or no direct competition. Because of its dominant position such a product requires below average marketing support on a unit basis and so enjoys above-average profit margins. Products in this category are often described as 'cash cows' – a term first proposed by the Boston Consulting Group (BCG) – and their role is discussed more fully in the next section, which deals with the BCG's product portfolio approach to marketing management.

DECLINE

Despite the firm's best efforts to prolong the mature phase of the product's life-cycle, decline is ultimately inevitable and tends to mirror the growth phase in that it accelerates over time. Perhaps the major reason for product decline is technological innovation which results in new and improved ways of satisfying basic needs. Thus mechanical watches have been displaced by electronic watches and the Swiss watch industry was almost decimated until it reinvented itself with the development of Swatch; synthetic fibres have been extensively substituted for natural fibres such as cotton and wool; and the internal combustion engine has largely replaced the horse as motive power.

While technological innovation usually results in a substitute product, economic change often makes alternative sources of supply available at a lower cost and so changes the competitive standing of the different suppliers to a market. Lower prices for an equivalent or better product are immediately apparent to consumers and largely account for the success of the Japanese car makers in penetrating world markets to the discomfort and demise of many longer established producers.

Yet a third source of change which can lead to the decline of a product is boredom or dissatisfaction on the part of the consumer, which is frequently the result of suppliers becoming complacent and failing to sustain the perceived value of their offering through aggressive marketing.

Faced with a declining product, management has only three basic options open to it:

1. To delete it from the product line (retreat)
2. To phase it out over time (withdrawal)
3. To attempt to resuscitate it.

Option 3 is rarely a viable one for, if the product is already in decline before management tries to do anything about it, recovering lost ground is usually a forlorn hope. It is for this reason that I am such a strong proponent of using the PLC as a broad framework for strategy formulation, and as a basic diagnostic tool. If the stages of the life-cycle are inevitable, and are heralded by changes in the inflexion of the sales curve, then the onset of maturity is the time to consider rejuvenation strategies when the product is still in good health. Once it has gone into decline, it is much more costly, and sometimes impossible, to reverse or even stabilise such a trend.

Of the other two alternatives, a phased withdrawal is much to be preferred for, as we noted in Chapter 3, a withdrawal implies that one retains

control over the process while a retreat means that one is merely reacting to competitive pressures. One must also consider that in the case of durable products (consumer and industrial) one has an obligation to provide after-sales service, which means that a retreat could well become a rout or total defeat.

Until recently the elimination/withdrawal decision has received comparatively little attention, but, due to the pioneering work of Avlonitis (1983), its strategic importance is now much better appreciated and will be discussed at greater length in Chapter 15, which is concerned with product policy.

DIFFUSION THEORY

My own interest in product life-cycles and their relation to diffusion theory dates back to the period 1969–71 when I was pursuing research for my doctorate at the Harvard Business School. A product of this research was published as *Marketing New Industrial Products* (Baker, 1975).

The purpose of this research was to establish whether there is an observable pattern for the take-up of new products when introduced into a marketplace. Product life-cycle theory clearly suggests that there is, and in turn this theory may be related directly to a much longer established body of knowledge associated with the processes of diffusion and other exponential processes. The following discussion is based on *Marketing New Industrial Products*.

THE DIFFUSION PROCESS

New products are but one manifestation of innovation, just as the manner in which they penetrate and spread through a market is only one example of the process we call diffusion. It is now seven decades since Pemberton (1936) identified the tendency for diffusion of an innovation over time to approximate the parameters of the normal distribution such that if one plots the number of adopters of an innovation – assuming that it has fully diffused – against time of adoption since first introduction then the bell-shaped curve in Figure 5.7 results. Alternatively, if one plots the cumulative number of

FIGURE 5.7 Distribution of adopters over time

SOURCE: Baker, M. J. (1975) *Marketing New Industrial Products*. London: Macmillan – now Palgrave Macmillan

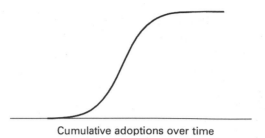

FIGURE 5.8 Cumulative adoptions over time

SOURCE: Baker, M. J. (1975) *Marketing New Industrial Products*. London: Macmillan – now Palgrave Macmillan

adopters against elapsed time since first introduction then an ogive, or S-shaped curve results similar to that depicted in Figure 5.8. Since Pemberton first focused attention on this relationship many researchers in a diversity of research traditions have observed a similar phenomenon.

Theoretically, once an exponential process has been initiated it will continue to infinity. In reality, however, the process is subject to limiting conditions which invariably result in the existence of an upper boundary, or at least to the presumption that such a boundary exists. A well-documented field is that of biological growth and a simple example drawn from this area will help to clarify these points.

Assume that we possess a simple organism that reproduces itself by cell division then, ceteris paribus, we may anticipate that the rate of increase of the population will follow the series 1, 2, 4, 8, 16, 32, 64.

Unfortunately for our simple cell it is not immortal, but can only reproduce itself twice before dying so that the population will in fact expand in a series which starts 1, 2, 3, 5, 8, 13, 21. Further, it is also apparent that there must be a finite limit to the resources on which the organism depends for its existence so that growth cannot continue indefinitely. The validity of this contention may easily be demonstrated by placing a simple cell which reproduces itself by division into a restricted environment such as a sealed test-tube. Growth may well continue to the point where the test-tube is visibly filled with cells which are invisible by themselves but, ultimately, the lack of space and necessary nutrients will stabilise growth at some upper limit. In fact, if some

factors are in fixed supply then their consumption will eventually lead to the decline and extinction of our population of cells.

However, one must be careful not to assume that decline and extinction will automatically occur for, as de Solla Price (1963) points out, the existence of a ceiling to exponential growth frequently gives rise to a strong reaction as that ceiling is approached.

De Solla Price describes a number of ways in which an exponentially growing phenomenon will seek to avoid a reduction in growth as it nears its ceiling. Two of these – 'escalation' and 'loss of definition' – are viewed as particularly important for they occur more frequently than the 'plain S-shaped ogive' (p. 25).

In the case of escalation, minor modification of the original phenomenon takes place at or near the point of inflection and 'a new logistic curve rises phoenix-like on the ashes of the old'. In a marketing context a close analogy of this is provided by the 'product rejuvenation strategy' whereby further modification of a product is undertaken to revitalise stagnant demand for it. (qv. the nylon life-cycle).

In many cases, however, it is not possible to raise the ceiling through modification and the phenomenon will fluctuate wildly in an attempt to avoid the inevitable. As a result of these oscillations the phenomenon may become so changed as to be unrecognisable (loss of definition), e.g. the cell described in our earlier example may mutate into a new species of cell suited to the conditions which were limiting the continued growth of the original cell. Alternatively, the phenomenon may accept the inevitable, smoothing out the oscillations and settling in equilibrium at a stable limit, or under different circumstances, slowly decline to nothing.

Recognising that there are several possible forms of S-shaped curve, the question arises 'Which variant should be accepted as typical of the diffusion process?' Dodd (1955) has shown that the precise form of the diffusion function may be summarised by a 'brief dimensional formula [Am]t' which he terms the 'power-moments' model. Once one knows how many attributes the innovation possesses, and the means by which these attributes spread among a relevant population, then one can predict whether diffusion will grow in a cumulative normal, exponential or logistic manner.

Addressing this same issue, Zvi Griliches (1957) comments that:

> The choice of a particular algebraic form for the trend function is somewhat arbitrary. As the data [diffusion of hybrid seed corn] are markedly S-shaped, several simple S-shaped functions were considered. The cumulative normal and the logistic are used most widely for such purposes. As there is almost no difference between the two over the usual range of data, the logistic was chosen because it is simpler to fit and in our context easier to interpret.

Although this tends to contradict Price's conclusion cited earlier that variants occur more often than the plain S-shaped ogive, there seems to be strong support for Griliches's view that the actual differences between specific functional forms are of minor consequence within the usual range of data. We conclude, therefore, that any of several variants of the S-shaped curve are equally acceptable and one should use the one that best fits the available data.

The above discussion of the properties of S-shaped curves was prompted by an implied acceptance of Pemberton's observation that such curves are descriptive of the diffusion process. Having described briefly some of the properties of S-shaped curves, it will be useful to present some evidence which supports the original inference.

THE PERVASIVE NATURE OF THE S-SHAPED DIFFUSION CURVE

Since Pemberton (1936) and Sorokin (1962) first focused attention on the fact that innovations tend to diffuse in a consistent manner, there has accumulated a growing body of evidence which confirms that if one plots the number of adopters of a given innovation against elapsed time since first introduction then an S-shaped curve will result. However, it must be noted that while Pemberton and Sorokin are generally credited with being the first researchers to test for the existence of an S-shaped diffusion curve, its existence had long been recognised. Thus Rogers (1962, p. 152) quotes Tarde's (1903) observation that an innovation 'shows slow advance in the beginning, followed by rapid and uniformly accelerated progress, followed again by progress that continues to slacken until it finally stops'.

In the rural sociology research tradition, the studies of Ryan and Gross (1943) and Griliches (1957) on the diffusion of hybrid seed corn convincingly demonstrated an S-shaped cumulative growth curve – a finding which has been confirmed time and time again in parallel studies in the subsequent literature.

Studies of the spread of three new business techniques – Gantt charts, statistical quality control, and critical path techniques – indicate that they diffused in a manner which approximates an S-shaped curve (Wattel, 1964).

Mansfield's (1968) studies of 12 innovations in four industries led him to conclude that 'the growth in the number of users of an innovation can be approximated by a logistic curve'. Subsequently, Ray (1969) commented, in presenting the preliminary findings of a multinational study of innovation, that, although there were insufficient data to specify the diffusion curves applicable to the innovations studied and so permit unconditional acceptance of Mansfield's logistic curve, nonetheless the data did suggest 'good cause for using another type of sigmoid or S-shaped curve'.

In the marketing literature, as we have already noted, the widely accepted product life-cycle concept stipulates that over time the sales of a product will exhibit cumulative growth initially, and then stabilise, until either competition results in a decline in sales volume, or further innovation results in renewed growth. In turn, this concept has been successfully applied to help explain some of the variance in the patterns of international investment and trade (see Freeman, 1963; Vernon, 1966; Wells, 1968). An OECD (1970) publication lends further support to these researchers' findings as analysis of the diffusion of four recent and significant innovations – man-made fibres, plastics, computers and nuclear power – reveal a consistent S-shaped curve in three distinct geographic regions – USA, Europe and Japan.

A similar exponential curve is also reported for numerically controlled machine tools (American Machinist, 1968) while Lynn's (1966) investigation of the commercial growth of a number of major technological innovations in several diverse fields lends additional substance to the pervasive nature of such diffusion curves.[2]

Taken together, these and many similar findings, predicate that S-shaped diffusion curves are so consistent that one may infer that diffusion is a natural process which obeys immutable laws.

In my view the evidence in support of the existence of a product life-cycle is incontrovertible. However, as we noted earlier, the PLC is 'not of itself deterministic and may be influenced significantly by environmental changes and/or marketing action'. How then can we use the theory to help us plan more effectively?

As we have seen, the most critical phase in a new product's life is its introduction to the marketplace. While it appears that more professional marketing has reduced the instance of new product failures in recent years, there can be no doubt that this continues to be a major source of significant losses for many companies. The question must be: how do you initiate a life-cycle and how do you sustain the new product in the difficult and dangerous introductory phase? This was the question we addressed directly in *Marketing New Industrial Products* (Baker, 1975) by using the distribution of adopters over time as the basis for seeking to determine whether there were any measurable characteristics which distinguished earlier from later adopters. The concept of adopter categories was first advanced by researchers at Iowa State University (Griliches, 1957) who observed that the distribution of adoption over time assumed the characteristics of the normal distribution. Accordingly, they proposed that one could use the parameters of such a distribution (mean and standard deviation) to define different categories of adopter. This they did, as illustrated

in Table 5.2. Obviously the question is what, if anything, distinguishes innovators from early adopters and early adopters from the early majority, etc.? Numerous studies have attempted to establish this but, as is often the case, the results are indeterminate.

TABLE 5.2 The classification of adopter categories

Classification	As % of persons adopting		Cumulative total (%)
Innovators	First	2.5	2.5
Early adopters	Next	13.5	16.0
Early majority	Next	34.0	50.0
Late majority	Next	34.0	84.0
Laggards	Last	16.0	100.0

As a result, many practitioners are tempted to dismiss this as yet another piece of academic theorising of no practical purpose. To do so would be to miss the point that if academic theorists could solve all the real world problems there would be no need for real world managers! The observation that there will always be innovators in any new market is tautologous. The practical payoff from the theory is that one accepts the existence of such a class of people, recognises that they are likely to differ from product to product, market to market and over time, but then uses one's own knowledge and experience of specific product market interfaces to define the most profitable prospective market segments. It is this issue which we consider in the next section which deals with using the PLC as a planning tool.

USING THE PLC AS A PLANNING TOOL

In our view the two most important insights offered by the PLC are:

1. It underlines the inevitability of change
2. It makes clear that change is an evolutionary and self-sustaining process with an underlying continuity.

Taken together these factors predicate that ultimately all single product firms are doomed to extinction unless, like the Phoenix, they can rejuvenate themselves. In the case of products based upon a robust core technology this life span may be considerable, but this does not change the fact that sooner or later it will be displaced by something new. Stone gave way to bronze, bronze gave way to iron, and iron to steel. Steel producers would do well to heed Levitt's warning in 'Marketing myopia' (1960):

> As a generalisation, the more a basic technology is refined and developed, and the closer a product becomes to a consumer convenience good, the shorter its life-cycle. Further, because of competitive pressures such life-cycles are becoming shorter. In the light of this it would seem reasonable to argue that firms should seek to protect their futures by reducing their dependence upon individual products and developing a portfolio of products, each of which may be at a different stage in its life-cycle, such that products in the growth stage are compensating for those in the decline phase.

In the next section we will look at the product portfolio concept more closely but, before considering the interaction between products at different stages in the life-cycle, it will be useful to recognise that each of the main phases calls for a rather different marketing strategy and mix and specify what these are. It will also be helpful to stress that, for multiproduct firms with products at different stages of development, it will be necessary to practise what I have termed '3-in-1 marketing'.

Three-in-1 marketing recognises that, in its most rudimentary form, SMP is concerned with providing answers to three basic questions:

1. Where are we now?
2. Where do we want to go?
3. How do we get there?

In other words we are concerned with the present, the future and the intervening or transitional period in between, and it would seem self-evident that the successful firm must give consideration to all three if it is to survive, let alone succeed. Thus, while past failings may rightly be attributed to an overemphasis upon the existing business (the production orientation), there is a very real danger that too much concentration upon the future (the marketing orientation) may result in a dangerous neglect of the existing resource base on which that

future must be founded. Similarly, stressing selling (a sales orientation) is an inadequate basis for long-term prosperity, but selling has a vital transitional role to play and deserves greater recognition than it has enjoyed since 'marketing' came on the scene.

Clearly what is required is a careful balance between present capabilities and future aspirations for, in a dynamic environment, one must possess both a sense of vision (where one wants to go), and a sense of continuity (how one is going to get there). There is no merit in adopting the attitude of the local resident asked for directions by a tourist who responded 'If I was trying to get there I wouldn't start from here', which epitomises so much academic writing – the assumption that we can ignore our pasts, are in possession of infinitely mobile resources and can start every project with a clean sheet of paper.

Essentially, then, the 3-in-1 approach recognises that the introduction and growth phases of the life-cycle require a future or marketing orientation, maturity a production orientation and decline a sales orientation. This is not to say that the firm requires three different sets of managers, for research by Axel Johne (1982) of The City of London Business School has provided the important finding that in successful firms the management are able to operate in different modes or roles. When required to develop plans for the future they adopt organic organisational practices, but the further they proceed towards the actual production and sale of a product the more structured and controlled is their approach so that it corresponds to the so-called mechanistic structure – a process Johne has aptly called 'the mechanistic shift'.

Clearly, a threefold division is a very basic one and is amenable to considerable refinement. As a minimum, most writers would argue for a different emphasis as between the introduction and growth phases of the PLC, and come up with a summary similar to that proposed by Dhalla and Yuspeh (1976) and reproduced as Table 5.3.

Similarly, the emphasis on particular mix elements will vary throughout the growth phase and, as we saw earlier when discussing the mature and decline phases, a number of quite different strategies are available here too. The important point to make is that decision-making is a sequential process and that the main thing is to refine one's focus through a series of choices between limited sets of alternatives. Ideally (as in computer programming) choice should be binary – yes/no, either 'a' or b' – but the intrinsic complexity and uncertainty of business decisions usually result in more than two basic options. The greater the number of options, the more difficult it becomes to balance the pros and cons of each, and the greater the potential for making incorrect decisions. It is for this reason that we advocate simple models and frameworks as the basis for making strategic decisions for, once these have been made correctly, adjustment and refinement may be achieved through the management process.

Finally, we are in sympathy with Firth's (1980) conclusion based upon his extensive review of the PLC literature when he states:

The evidence from this research shows that: (1) Most products do follow a broad life-cycle pattern and that competition affects profits as outlined for the various stages. (2) The average length of the PLC is shortening due to rapid economic, technological, social and political changes. (3) There is no common length of time of stages for products. (4) The PLC can be drastically altered by external factors.

TABLE 5.3 How PLC advocates view the implications of the cycle for marketing action

	Stages of the PLC			
Effects and response	**Introduction**	**Growth**	**Maturity**	**Decline**
Competition	None of importance	Some emulators	Many rivals competing for a small piece of the pie	Few in number with a rapid shake-out of weak members
Overall strategy	Market establishment; persuade early adopters to try the product	Market penetration; persuade mass market to prefer the brand	Defence of brand position; check the inroads of competition	Preparations for removal; milk the brand dry of all possible benefits
Profits	Negligible because of high production and marketing costs	Reach peak levels as a result of high prices and growing demand	Increasing competition cuts into profit margins and ultimately into total profits	Declining volume pushes costs up to levels that eliminate profits entirely
Retail prices	High, to recover some of the excessive costs of launching	High, to take advantage of heavy consumer demand	What the traffic will bear; need to avoid price wars	Low enough to permit quick liquidation of inventory
Distribution	Selective, as distribution is slowly built up	Intensive; employ small trade discounts since dealers are eager to store	Intensive; heavy trade allowances to retain shelf space	Selective; unprofitable outlets slowly phased out
Advertising strategy	Aim at the needs of early adopters	Make the mass market aware of brand benefits	Use advertising as a vehicle for differentiation among otherwise similar brands	Emphasise low price to reduce stock
Advertising emphasis	High, to generate awareness and interest among early adopters and persuade dealers to stock the brand	Moderate, to let sales rise on the sheer momentum of word-of-mouth recommendations	Moderate, since most buyers are aware of brand characteristics	Minimum expenditures required to phase out the product
Consumer sales and promotion expenditures	Heavy, to entice target groups with samples, coupons, and other inducements to try the brand	Moderate, to create brand preference (advertising is better suited to do this job)	Heavy, to encourage brand-switching, hoping to convert some buyers into loyal users	Minimal, to let the brand coast by itself

SOURCE: Dhalla, N. K. and Yuspeh, S. (1976) Forget the product life cycle concept!, *Harvard Business Review* (January–February), p. 104

PRODUCT PORTFOLIO ANALYSIS

In the preceding section it was suggested that a major implication of the PLC is that the firm should seek to develop more than one product so that as some mature and decline others are being developed to replace them. Of course, as soon as a company has more than one product it becomes necessary to allocate resources between them. An important tool for achieving this is provided by the growth-share matrix developed by the Boston Consulting Group (BCG).

The growth-share matrix combines elements of the PLC, which plots the growth and decline of sales, with findings concerning the cost and profit implications of varying market shares. With respect to the latter there is a widely held view that as size and market share increase costs will decline and profits will increase. In the early 1970s the Marketing Science Institute (MSI) published the preliminary findings of a study designed, inter alia, to explore this relationship, which it designated PIMS – an acronym for profit implications of market strategy. Early results from a study of 620 firms indicated that market share, investment intensity (ratio of total investment to sales) and product quality are the most important determinants of pretax returns on investment (out of 37 contributory factors). As a rough guide a market share of <40% yields an average pretax return on investment (ROI) of 30% which declines to 9.1% with a share of >10% (i.e. ROI declines at half the pace of market share). The PIMS study now has over 200 companies operating more than 2000 businesses who pool their experience in return for detailed analysis of their own position.

MARKET SHARE STRATEGIES

The importance attached to market share was prompted in the early 1970s as a result of a study carried out by the Marketing Science Institute and the Harvard Business School to determine the profit impact of market strategies (PIMS). In two articles published in the *Harvard Business Review*, Schoeffler et al. (1974) first demonstrated a clear link between strategic planning and profits and then Buzzell et al. (1975) demonstrated a positive correlation between market share and return on investment (ROI).

Having identified a strong and clear relationship between market share and pretax ROI, three possible explanations for this are suggested:

1. Economies of scale and the experience effect
2. Market power
3. The quality of management.

It should be noted that these explanations are not mutually exclusive.

In analysing the PIMS database to help explain the observed relationship between market share and ROI it is stressed that the PIMS sample includes a wide variety of both products and industries so that comparing businesses with market shares under 10% with those over 40% embraces a diversity of industries, types of products, kinds of customers, and so on. From their analysis of the data four important differences emerged:

1. As market share rises turnover investment rises only somewhat, but profit margins on sales increases sharply
2. The biggest single difference in costs, as related to market share, is in the purchases to sales ratio
3. As market share increases, there is some tendency for marketing costs, as a percentage of sales, to decline
4. Market leaders develop unique competitive strategies and have higher prices for their higher quality products than do smaller share businesses.

Since the publication of these findings in 1975, there has been much evidence, both empirical and anecdotal, to confirm their relevance. Put simply:

- Big companies with powerful brands can charge premium prices.
- Big companies with powerful brands exercise more power in the value chain. (In 1975 Buzzell et al. suggested that vertical integration and a smaller proportion of bought-in supplies might be one explanation of the purchases to sales ratio. Today, as firms concentrate on their core competencies, partnering and strategic alliances may be a more likely explanation.)

- With the erosion of technology lead times, and developments in manufacturing technology (CAD, CAM, flexible manufacturing systems, etc.), economies of scale in production have been largely displaced by economies of scale in marketing.
- Learning organisations with effective strategic planning outperform the 'amateurs'.

As we saw in Chapter 4, the relevance of market shares as a strategic objective has been challenged and subject to criticism. But, notwithstanding the difficulties of defining precisely what market share means, continuing analysis of an enlarged PIMS database confirms the existence of the relationship. It follows that the three market share strategies defined by Buzzell et al. remain relevant:

1. *Building strategies* based on active efforts to increase market share by means of new product introductions, new marketing programmes, and so on
2. *Holding strategies* aimed at maintaining the existing level of market share
3. *Harvesting strategies* designed to achieve high short-term earnings against the background of a declining market share.

BCG GROWTH-SHARE MATRIX

The Boston Consulting Group (BCG) growth-share matrix was developed by Bruce Henderson, founder of BCG, in the late 1960s and dominated thinking about strategy for over a decade. It still commands substantial support and is invariably included in texts, courses and seminars concerned with the development of marketing strategy. However, as we shall see, it has also been the subject of considerable criticism – especially, following the fragmentation of markets which has arisen with increased international competition, the acceleration of technological change and the impact of information technology. As a result, its continuing value is more as an analytical framework, which encourages structured analysis of the implications of the product life-cycle (PLC) for competitive strategy, than as a planning technique in its own right.

The matrix was developed from Henderson's

earlier work with experience curve effects which he applied as a purchasing agent at Westinghouse to help explain the link between increased experience and lower manufacturing costs. Although the phenomenon was not new it was Henderson who brought it to real prominence and demonstrated how it could be harnessed for purposes of strategic planning. In essence the experience curve – or learning curve as it was more widely known prior to Henderson's publication of *Perspectives on Experience* in 1968 has been known for centuries. As Winfred B. Hirschmann (1964) pointed out, it is encapsulated by the well-known aphorism 'Practice makes perfect'. With experience we learn how to perform tasks more efficiently and effectively giving rise to significant improvements in productivity. Of course, such gains are not automatic, nor will they necessarily lead to cost reduction unless these are consciously and assiduously pursued. When Henry Ford set out to make an affordable car, his original ambition was to produce one for $500 – less than half the prevailing price in the early twentieth century. In 1918, not 10 years after starting production at Baton Rouge, he had got the cost down to $286, a cost which no one else could hope to equal unless they were able to achieve the same economies of sourcing, production, selling and distribution as were enjoyed by Ford.

But experience effects are not just the product of scale economies or learning effects. For example, scale effects are independent of time. As one increases the scale of a project the cost of additional capacity or output will usually not grow proportionately with the increase in scale, but this relationship is not dependent upon time. Experience is. Similarly, learning effects are, strictly, concerned with the notion that productivity will grow with familiarity and repetition as a worker learns a job. By contrast, the idea of experience embraces a number of other dimensions. Schnarrs (1991) summarises these as:

- The learning curve
- Specialization of labour
- Process innovations
- New materials
- Product standardisation
- Product redesign.

Clearly, these dimensions are closely related to one another. With experience one discovers new and more efficient ways of completing the task in hand, including both product and process innovation.

In *Perspectives on Experience* (Henderson, 1968), the BCG propose two idealised experience curves

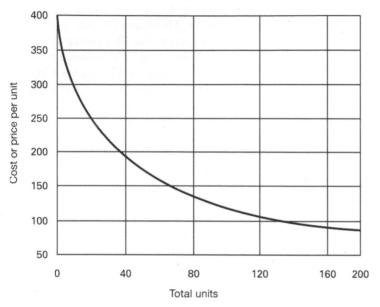

FIGURE 5.9 Idealised experience curve (linear scale)

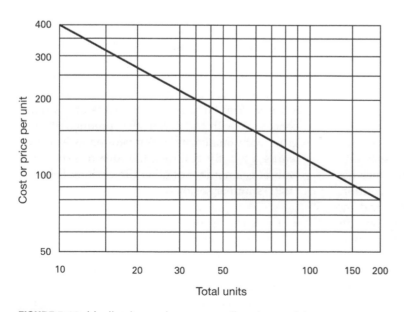

FIGURE 5.10 Idealised experience curve (log–log scale)

in which total units produced are plotted against cost or price per unit. On a linear scale the result is a smooth curve similar to that in Figure 5.9. However, when plotted using double logarithmic scales the result is a straight line similar to that in Figure 5.10. The latter is claimed to be the more useful as it demonstrates 'the unique property of showing percentage change as a constant distance, along either axis at any position on the grid' which can be read straight from the plot.

That said, it is the linear plot that demonstrates the properties of the experience effect most clearly – costs per unit decline as the volume produced increases, but increasingly slowly. The nature of the relationship varies by industry, but the usual range is a fall in costs of between 10 and 30% for each doubling of output, with 20% considered average. Perversely, however, experience curves are described in the opposite way so that a 90% experience curve implies that costs will fall by 10% for each doubling of output, 80% represents a 20% fall in costs, etc. It is important to emphasise that the experience curve measures the relationship between costs and volume. The firm's fortunes will depend on the prices it can obtain in the marketplace. The BCG analysis pays close attention to this and suggests that the relationship between price and cost will vary depending upon the overall competitive situation.

Irrespective of whether conditions are stable or unstable, costs tend to exceed prices when a product is first introduced into a market. With increasing experience, costs fall below prices and two distinct patterns emerge. In stable markets, increasing cost efficiencies are paralleled by price reductions. But, in unstable markets, demand outstrips supply in the growth phase, and sellers are able to command higher margins as it is not necessary to pass on cost efficiencies as price cuts. The result is much as economic theory would predict. The opportunity to earn above-average profits attracts new investment and an increase in supply. However, if demand continues to grow more quickly than supply, costs will tend to fall more quickly than prices. Inevitably, demand will cease to grow as the market approaches saturation and a shake-out will occur as suppliers cut prices to hold on to their share of the market. Only the fittest (most efficient) will survive but, once excess capacity has been removed, stability will return to the mature market and the remaining players will tend to avoid using price as a competitive weapon.

Given that the opportunity to earn above-average returns is greatest in unstable markets, exhibiting rapid growth in demand, it is unsurprising that these are intrinsically more attractive to capitalists and entrepreneurs. It is also clear, however, that if one is to succeed in such a market, one must be able to survive the shake-out when it comes and that, as competition will be based mainly on price in this stage, one will only be able to do so if one's costs are similar to those of other major competitors. In turn, it follows that this will only be the case if one is producing a similar volume of output and has a comparable experience function. Expressed another way: sales volume = market share. Hence the fascination with market share and the evolution of the BCG growth-share matrix.

If costs do decline with market share, clearly there are significant competitive advantages to be gained by using growth in market share as a basic corporate objective, particularly if such growth is faster than one's immediate competitors.

As noted earlier the growth-share matrix, or Boston Box, seeks to combine these two sets of relationships into an analytical framework which can provide both broad strategic guidelines as well as detailed monitoring of one's competitive status. In addition, the growth-share matrix is based on four assumptions (Firth, 1980, p. 43):

1. Margins and cash generated increase with relative market share, due to the experience and scale effects.
2. Sales growth requires cash to finance added capacity and working capital.
3. Increase in market share usually requires cash input to support increased advertising expen-

ditures, lower prices and other share gaining tactics. Alternatively, a decrease in share may make cash available.
4. Growth slows as the product reaches maturity and without losing market position cash generated can be reinvested in other products that are still growing.

If one has only one product, the growth-share matrix is only of academic interest. But, if one has a number of products/businesses, it is a powerful tool in helping diagnose how these products compare one with another, and determining the most effective strategy for their joint management. In its basic format the growth-share matrix comprises a 2 × 2 rectangular array as appears in Figure 5.11, with the two dimensions representing market growth and market share each dichotomised into high and low.

Each of the quadrants summarises a position in the life-cycle of a successful product to which the BCG attached a label:

- Quadrant 1 represents a product being introduced into a market which is perceived to have high growth potential. But, as it has yet to perform successfully and has only a low market share it is regarded as a *question mark*.
- Quadrant 2 represents a successful product with a high market share in a rapidly growing market. It is undoubtedly a *star*.
- Quadrant 3 represents an established player in a mature market. It has survived the shake out and is now benefiting from experience effects in a stable and not particularly aggressive market. It has become a *cash cow*.
- Quadrant 4 defines the product in the decline phase. There is little or no market growth and the product's low share means that it lacks the cost advantages enjoyed by cash cows. In the BCG nomenclature it is a *dog*. (Unfortunately the British regard dogs as pets and cherish them. In the USA this is true too but, in this context, American usage denotes something useless to be disposed of.)

Another important aspect of the matrix is that it indicates likely cash flows associated with each quadrant/stage of the life-cycle. As noted earlier, *new products* in both stable and unstable markets

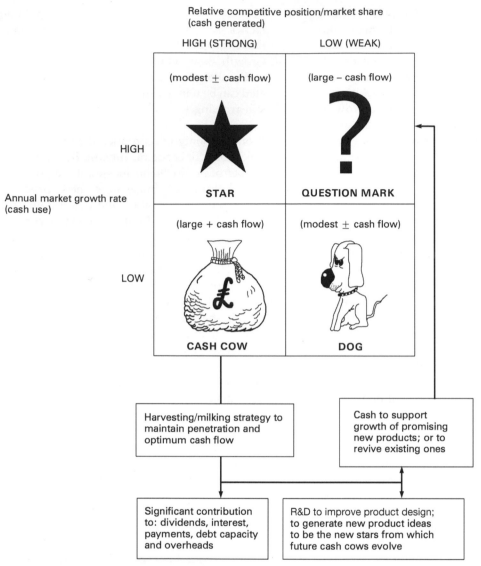

FIGURE 5.11 The growth-share matrix

tend to have a negative cash flow (costs exceed revenue) due to the high costs of promoting and distributing the product, and the absence of any significant experience effects. In the *rapid growth phase*, successful firms tend to plough their profits back into the business to both grow and protect their position. As a result cash flow tends to be marginally negative or neutral. In *maturity*, the benefits of experience and stability accrue, and cash flow is invariably positive and provides funding to support new products in the earlier stages of their life-cycle. Finally, products in *declining markets* are usually portrayed as being in balance or negative in

terms of cash flow. If negative, then the conventional wisdom is that they should be eliminated. However, as we shall see (particularly in Chapter 15) in recent years more attention has been given to managing products in the decline phase of the life-cycle, leading to the conclusion that dog products may also be cash positive if properly managed.

So far, so good. The matrix offers a useful analytical tool which allows planners to plot the position of all their products in an easily understood way. More than that, having classified where our products are in their life-cycle, we can identify the strategic options available by reference to a checklist such as that provided in Chapter 4. However, the BCG growth-share matrix depends upon the concept of relative market share and it is determining this which creates problems. In some markets comparative data are available so that one can establish which firm has the largest market share so that one can express one's own and other competitors' market shares as a proportion of this. It follows that if one firm has a larger share than any other (say 30%) then it will be classified as high (either a star or cash cow) whereas another large firm with a 25% share would be classified as 'low' and considered either a question mark or dog!

Numerous refinements have been proposed for both plotting and diagnosing the matrix. Size of market may be incorporated by plotting circles whose size reflects the importance of the product to the firm's overall sales or profits. Similarly, following a methodology proposed by Day (1977),

one can plot the direction in which products are expected (or intended) to move in the future thus introducing dynamism into an otherwise static analysis.

Based upon their original analysis, the Boston Consulting Group developed a number of strategic implications from the growth-share matrix which, in turn, underpin the evolution of explicit market-share strategies. Simplistically, the message of the Boston Box is that because of the inevitable progression of product life-cycles one needs a continuing stream of new products with the surpluses from cash cows being reinvested in question marks and stars to ensure their future success. In other words, one needs a balanced portfolio, and appropriate strategies for managing products at different stages of their life-cycle. In addition, it is important to recognise that particular advantages may accrue to first movers – they start to acquire

TABLE 5.4 Product portfolio sector: strategic guidelines

	Star	Problem children	Cash cow	Dog
Market characteristics	Rapid growth Market proving itself Competitors enter Increasing consumer awareness and trial Brand preferences start to emerge Product replacing old products		Growth slows and stops Market saturation Concentration – shake out Awareness at maximum, trials completed Loyalty established Beware new products satisfying needs Growing importance of repeat purchases	
Marketing objectives and strategy	Maintain or improve market share Market fortification (plug the gaps) Ensure availability	Improve market share by: (a) all-out push (b) segmentation Abandon if unlikely to achieve growth (harvest and out)	Hold market share Extend product life (a) Increase frequency of purchases (b) Encourage new product uses (c) Geographic expansion	(a) Harvest (b) Segment and find defensible niche (c) Divest (d) Delete
Product	Improve quality – stay ahead Product line extension (fill the gaps) Product differentiation	Improve quality – be better (a) Look for unfilled gaps (segments) (b) Buy competitors (a) and (b)	Ensure keeping up with technology but avoid costly revisions of product Cosmetic revisions	(a) No change (b) Position in selected segments
Price	Will be leader due to experience Ability to kill competition	Will be follower May be unable to compete on price (pay more attention to segmentation)	Cut only to kill competition or to protect share Now is the time to reap rewards	(a) No change or up (b) Depends on segment distinctiveness and price elasticity
Promotion	Heavy brand promotion Induce awareness and trial Create brand loyalty	Heavy brand promotion Direct at new market entrant and specific segments	Lower Reinforce brand loyalty Promote new uses 'new', 'improved'	(a) Low, zero (b) Aim at segment (c) Differentiate
Distribution	Secure channels Offer better margins through turnover advantage	As not selling so rapidly may need better margins Look for special innovative outlets	Maintain Look for new outlets for new uses	(a) Maintain (b) Aim at segment outlets

SOURCE: Hooley, G. J. (1979/80) *MBA Core Course Lecture Notes.* Bradford Management Centre

experience first – and to those with the largest market shares as they are likely to have the lowest cost base and so be best placed to resist price competition and/or earn above-average margins.

Most texts devote a chapter or chapters to market share strategies, with advice on gaining and holding share, i.e. the management of question marks and stars respectively, to harvesting cash cows and divestment of dog products in the decline stage (see Schnarrs, 1991, Chapter 4). Table 5.4 summarises well some strategic guidelines for managing products at different stages of their life.

The reader should consult one or more of these sources for advice on managing the product portfolio, a subject which is also dealt with in some detail in later chapters of this book. At this juncture we will conclude this section by reviewing some of the criticisms levelled against the Boston Box approach with its emphasis on market share.

As we have observed already, the weakness of the market share approach to developing a successful marketing strategy is that, ultimately, only one or a very small number of evenly matched competitors can prosper from adopting such an approach. The logic of the experience curve is that the firm with the largest share will always enjoy a cost advantage over smaller competitors. Whether it chooses to use this to build more share by pursuing a price leadership over extended periods reflects the weakness of management in exploiting this advantage itself. As the evidence shows, some firms are better than others at defending a leadership position, with the result that those seeking to displace them by seeking to build their own market share have often failed because their costs are higher and they run out of cash before they can achieve the same market share as the leader which would eliminate its cost advantage. It is for this reason that most firms, and especially those with low market shares, seek to compete through a strategy of *differentiation*. Differentiation leads to the fragmentation of markets and reduces the economies of scope and scale which comprise a major element in the experience effects which yield cost advantages in undifferentiated markets. This is not to say that cost and price are not important elements in determining competitive advantage in fragmented markets. They are, but the source of cost savings is more likely to arise from innovat-

ion, managerial efficiency and implementation, than from the size of the firm's market share.

Schnarrs cites 13 sources of criticism which have been levelled against the growth share matrix (1991, pp. 85–90). In our view they are all related to the fundamental distinction between strategies of cost leadership and differentiation and the fact that for the great majority of firms the latter is the only realistic option. That said, we believe the growth-share matrix is both valuable and important because:

1. It reinforces the inevitability of change implicit in the PLC concept
2. It underlines the importance of having a portfolio of products at different stages of development
3. It requires formal consideration of the competition and their relative standing
4. It is intuitively appealing and simple to implement conceptually despite the difficulty of operationalising it in practice.

Much the same advantages are seen to attach to other similar approaches and a brief review of these follows.

SHELL'S DIRECTIONAL POLICY MATRIX

As noted earlier, we do not consider the directional policy matrix (DPM), developed by corporate planners at Shell, strictly as a portfolio planning model. However, many other authors do, so, in the interests of completeness, it will be described here as representative of a number of similar models designed to inform strategic product/market decisions, such as General Electric (GE)'s stoplight strategy.

Shell's DPM (1975) is based upon two key parameters – the company's competitive capabilities and the prospects for sector profitability – each of which is divided into three categories as in shown in Figure 5.12.

The basic matrix may be used to plot the position of products in the company's portfolio, or it could be used for competitor analysis by plotting the position of all competitors in a particular business sector. In their original conceptualisation, Robinson et al. (1978) suggest a hypothetical portfolio of

Prospects for sector profitability

		Unattractive	Average	Attractive
Company's competitive capabilities	Weak	Disinvest 9	Phased withdrawal 6 Custodial	Double or quits 3
	Average	Phased withdrawal 8	Custodial 5 Growth	Try harder 2
	Strong	Cash generation 7	Growth 4 Leader	Leader 1

FIGURE 5.12 The directional policy matrix

SOURCE: *The Directional Policy Matrix: a New Aid to Corporate Planning* (1975). Shell International Chemical Co.

products for a chemical company as shown in Figure 5.13.

In order to use the DPM it is necessary to develop measures of the two parameters – business sector prospects and company competitive capabilities. In the context of a petroleum-based chemical business like Shell, four main criteria are suggested:

1. Market growth rate
2. Market quality
3. Industry feedback situation
4. Environmental aspects.

Obviously, these may vary by industry, although the first two will usually apply to any industry. Similarly, the precise values for assessing growth rate will vary both by product/industry and stage of the life-cycle, and the intention should be to establish an average growth rate – say 5–7% – so that greater or lesser rates may be classified as such in relation to the average.

With regard to market quality, Robinson et al. (1978) acknowledge that these are difficult to quantify but suggest that some of the more important questions to be answered might be:

■ Has the sector a record of high, stable profitability?

■ Can margins be maintained when manufacturing capacity exceeds demand?
■ Is the product resistant to commodity pricing behaviour?
■ Is the technology of production freely available or is it restricted to those who developed it?
■ Is the market supplied by relatively few producers?
■ Is the market free from domination by a small group of powerful customers?
■ Has the product high added-value when converted by the customer?
■ In the case of a new product, is the market destined to remain small enough not to attract too many producers?
■ Is the product one where the customer has to change his formulation or even his machinery if he changes supplier?
■ Is the product free from the risk of substitution by an alternative synthetic or natural product?

While these specific questions relate to an industrial chemicals company, it is clear that they embrace competitive forces, such as barriers to entry and exit, contained in Porter's five forces model.

With regard to a company's competitive capabilities, three basic criteria are identified:

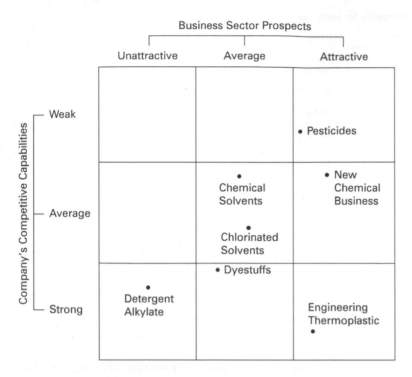

FIGURE 5.13 Positions of business sectors in a hypothetical company's portfolio

SOURCE: Robinson et al. (1978) The directional policy matrix, *Long Range Planning*, 11(June): 2–8

1. Market position
2. Production capability
3. Product research and development.

Market position is measured in terms of market share and the firm (or firms) is classified according to whether it is a leader, with a pre-eminent position, a major producer, i.e. one of several evenly matched competitors, etc. Production capability is a composite factor designed to encapsulate issues such as process economies, manufacturing capacity, sources of raw materials, etc., while product R&D embraces product range, product quality, record of successful NPD, service capability, etc. Table 5.5 provides a good summary of factors contributing to market attractiveness and business position.

Robinson et al. recommend that, once the definitions of factors and measurement criteria have been developed, ratings should be secured from a combination of functional specialists and non-specialists to provide both expertise and a degree of detachment. It is further suggested that while individual ratings should be encouraged initially

these should provide the basis for a group discussion to evolve a consensus view. Failing this some form of averaging may prove necessary. However, a process involving the participants likely to be affected by the outcome is seen to be preferable to more 'objective' methods based on sampling methods and computerised analysis. Once a 'score' has been agreed this may be weighted to reflect the factor's relative importance to the company. The outcome is then plotted on the matrix as shown earlier in Figure 5.12. For diagnostic purposes specific strategies are recommended for each position on the matrix as shown in Figure 5.12.

It should be stressed that the regularity implied in the rectangular format of a matrix rarely exists in real life, and the boundaries between one position and another are likely to be decidedly 'fuzzy' and call for considerable judgement in their interpretation. It should also be recognised that the 'recommended' strategy may be infeasible or inappropriate. For example, a version of the DPM was used to analyse the perceived standing and attractiveness of various subjects in a university.

TABLE 5.5 Factors contributing to market attractiveness and business position

	Attractiveness of your market	Status/position of your business

Market factors	Size (dollars, units or both)
	Size of key segments
	Growth rate per year:
	   Total
	   Segments
	Diversity of market
	Sensitivity to price, service features and external factors
	Cyclicality
	Seasonality
	Bargaining power of upstream suppliers
	Bargaining power of downstream suppliers
		Your share (in equivalent terms)
		Your share of key segments
		Your annual growth rate:
		   Total
		   Segments
		Diversity of your participation
		Your influence on the market
		Lags or leads in your sales
		
		Bargaining power of your suppliers
		Bargaining power of your customers

Competition	Types of competitors
	
	Degree of concentration
	Changes in type and mix
	Entries and exits
	Changes in share
	Substitution by new technology
	Degree and types of integration
		Where you fit, how you compare in terms of
		   products, marketing capability, service,
		   production strength, financial strength,
		   management
		Segments you have entered or left
		Your relative share change
		Your vulnerability to new technology
		Your own level of integration

Financial and economic factors	Contribution margins Leveraging factors, such as economies of scale and experience Barriers to entry or exit (both financial and non-financial) Capacity utilisation	Your margins Your scale and experience Barriers to your entry or exit (both financial and non-financial) Your capacity utilisation
Technological factors	Maturity and volatility Complexity Differentiation Patents and copyrights Manufacturing process technology required	Your ability to cope with change Depths of your skills Types of your technological skills Your patent protection Your manufacturing technology

Sociopolitical factors in your environment	Social attitudes and trends
	Laws and government agency regulations
	Influence with pressure groups and
	   government representatives
	Human factors such as unionisation and
	   community acceptance
		Your company's responsiveness and flexibility
		Your company's ability to cope
		Your company's aggressiveness
		
		Your company's relationships

SOURCE: Abell, D. F. and Hammond, J. S. (1979) *Strategic Market Planning.* Englewood Cliffs, NJ: Prentice Hall, p. 214

According to the analysis, physics and mathematics were located in the unattractive column and performance defined as weak to average. According to the proposed strategies the university should have started to get out of these subjects. Such a diagnosis was unacceptable. Physics and mathematics are core disciplines which underpin many others. In a university renowned for its engineering faculty quite the opposite strategy was necessary – at the very least physics and maths needed to be moved into the Strong category as subjects in their own right, through focused investment. Alternatively, if physics and maths were seen as essential components in subjects like electronic engineering and computer science they needed classifying under the attractive column. As the example makes clear models of this kind are useful as analytical frameworks – they can be useless, or positively danger-ous, if regarded as prescriptive planning devices.

Before leaving the DPM one final comment is called for. Both the DPM and BCG growth-share matrix have been reported here as they were orig-inally described by their 'inventors'. What would happen if we were to relabel the DPM as below?

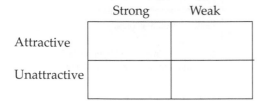

If we were to do this and incorporate the diagnosis from both GSM and DPM, we would find the sit-uation shown in Figure 5.14.

Much the same similarities are to be found in other strategic overview/portfolio planning mod-els. While this may not be immediately obvious it is unsurprising, given that all such models seek to capture the product or firm's standing vis-à-vis its rivals and the status/nature of competition which, in turn, is largely determined by the stage of the product/industry life-cycle. For example, General Electric's stoplight strategy (Figure 5.15), is remarkably similar to Shell's DPM (Figure 5.12). In GE's case the two axes are labelled 'business strengths' and 'industry attractiveness' and each is

categorised as high, medium, and low to yield a 3 × 3 matrix. However, instead of labelling each posit-ion, GE uses a simple 'traffic light' coding of red (danger, beware), amber (proceed with caution), and green (full steam ahead) for the groups with low, medium and high overall attractiveness.

As Wensley (1981) has pointed out, a salient difference between the growth-share matrix and other 'box classifications' is that the former is based upon univariate dimensions, while the DPM, A. D. Little and GE/McKinsey schemes are based on composite dimensions involving the subjective weighting of a number of factors The issue, there-fore, is which approach is to be preferred?

This issue was addressed by Wensley (1981) and we can do no better than quote his conclusions.

> In undertaking strategic marketing analysis of any particular investment option it is important to avoid the use of classificatory systems that deflect the analysis from the critical issue of why there is a potential sustainable competitive advantage for the corporation. The market growth/share portfolio approach advocated by BCG encourages the use of general rather than specific criteria as well as imply-ing assumptions about mechanisms of corporate financing and market behaviour that are either unnecessary or false. The DPM approach, on the other hand, appears to add little to a more specific project based form of analysis.
>
> Both classificatory schemes would be positively harmful if used to justify some form of cash budget-ing, since it is essential that any major project is assessed independent of its box classification. The financial basis of such an assessment should be an evaluation of the project's benefits against the appropriate discount rate related to the project's systematic risk or Beta. It is critical, however, that the financial analysis should not dominate a thorough evaluation of the competitive market assumptions upon which the project is based. Such a project based evaluation must focus not only on direct cost exper-ience effects but also on the degree to which the project can be effectively imitated by others if it proves to be successful, the extent to which the project's progress will be adequately monitored and suitable changes implemented at a later date, and the particular ways in which the project will (beyond its direct substantive benefits) also enhance the firm's ability to exploit further opportunities at a later stage.

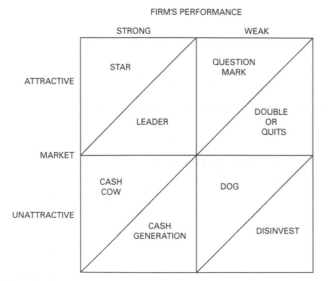

FIGURE 5.14 Firm's performance

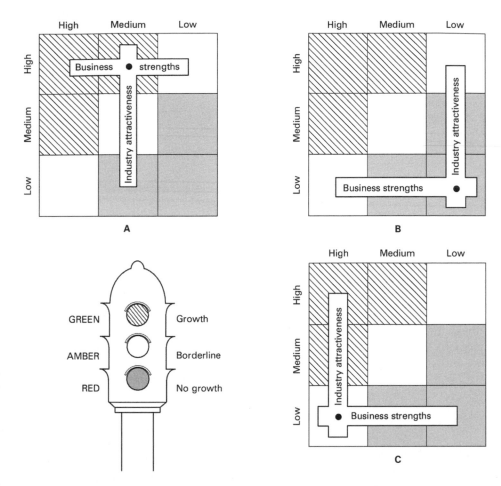

FIGURE 5.15 General Electric's 'stoplight strategy'

In other words, 'boxes' are a useful aid to analysis; to be operationalised they need to be associated with a rigorous financial analysis, but, in doing so, one must not lose sight of the competitive assumptions on which this is based and possible future changes in these.

Day's (1983) review of the various strategy analysis methods is strongly recommended for the perspective it provides upon their contribution to the overall strategic planning process, as well as the benefits of using the different methods in combination with one another. As he comments:

> There is a truism in planning circles that the process of strategic planning is more important than the plan. An effective process has broad management participation that encourages a shared understand-

ing of strategic issues and alternatives. The payoff is in subsequent commitment by these managers to the implementation of strategic decisions. Strategy analysis methods can improve this payoff by providing a common language and a logical structure that can be used to:

- Isolate areas where critical information is lacking
- Communicate judgements and assumptions about strategic issues
- Facilitate the generation of alternatives to be given detailed consideration
- Identify trade-offs involved in undertaking various strategic alternatives.

These benefits are primarily realised during the early stages of the planning process within a

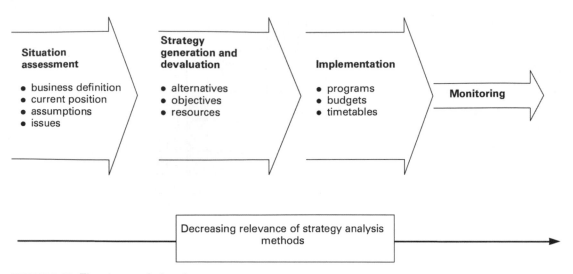

FIGURE 5.16 The stages of planning

SOURCE: Day, G. (1983) Gaining insights through strategy analysis, *Journal of Business Strategy*, 4(1)

division or strategic business unit. The strategy analysis methods have virtually no role in later stages of implementation and monitoring (see Figure 5.16).

BAKER'S BOX

It is against this background that we propose Baker's Box as a diagnostic tool for capturing executive opinion on competitive positioning within a market as the basis for developing more effective marketing strategies.

In developing a competitive strategy it is vital to establish the criteria used by customers in making purchase decisions. One must also determine how the competing players seek to differentiate themselves from one another while still meeting the customer's needs. In other words, how do competitors position themselves in the market? Perceptual mapping is a method which allows one to capture both a firm's perceived performance as well as its relationship to competitive offerings. Baker's Box is based on this method.

As originally conceived, perceptual mapping is a sophisticated quantitative procedure designed to overcome the problems of getting consumers to explain their evaluation and choice behaviour directly. A variety of research techniques may be used in perceptual mapping, of which the most popular is multidimensional scaling (MDS). Based upon respondents' rating of the degree of similar-

ity between alternatives two at a time using rating scales ranging from 'highly similar' to 'highly dissimilar' a computer-based program generates a two-dimensional map similar to that shown in Figure 5.17.

As generated, there are no labels on the axes and the analyst has to infer these based on the amount of variance explained by the ratings of different parameters. Usually the two parameters that emerge reflect cost–benefit or price–quality relationships, and in Figure 5.18 we have inserted these labels together with a line of best fit of the observations that we have designated the 'line of expectations'. We have also enclosed the space to create a 2 × 2 matrix.

THE BASIC 'BOX'

On the grounds that objects (products or services) that exceed expectations have added value, then those above the line will be preferred over those below the line which do not meet expectations. However, while price is essentially unidimensional, quality is multidimensional. It follows that in order to interpret and understand the positioning of the objects, and the basis of differentiation between them, one needs to know what factors constitute 'quality' in this market and their perceived salience. In mature markets with relatively stable market shares the identification and measurement of differentiating factors using tech-

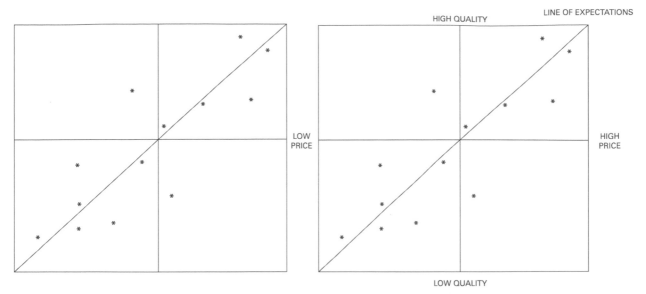

FIGURE 5.17 Two-dimensional perceptual map (a)   **FIGURE 5.18** Two-dimensional perceptual map (b)

niques such as MDS is usually feasible – but expensive! In emerging and growth markets, where competition is more dynamic, formal measurement may not be possible, or be of little value due to rapidly changing tactics.

Under the latter circumstances a judgemental approach drawing on the experience of those directly involved may be appropriate. If so then we need a basic matrix, similar to the DPM, in which the decision-makers can plot their judgement. The Basic Box illustrated in Figure 5.18 provides this. By introducing two further concepts of credibility and gullibility the diagnostic power may be significantly improved.

Credibility and gullibility are derivatives of knowledge, or expertise, allied to objectivity, and represent the boundaries of belief, with expectations lying between the two states. 'Expectation' reflects what the person with average knowledge/expertise would regard as likely – 'You get what you pay for'. Anything which exceeds this will have added value and be preferred – but only up to a point which represents the bounds of credibility. Beyond this point potential buyers will perceive a risk which they are unwilling to take – 'There must be a catch somewhere!' Hyundai experienced this effect in 1995 when their midrange saloon was priced at £4,000–£5,000 less than leading brands such as Toyota while claiming comparable quality and performance.

Persons with less than average knowledge and expertise, or who allow subjective factors to influence their judgement (I like the colour of Lada cars), exhibit a degree of gullibility. But, like credibility, there is a limit to most people's gullibility and beyond a certain point even disadvantaged consumers will refuse to buy.

In Figure 5.19 we have inserted lines parallel to expectations, representing credibility and gullibility, thus creating an octet of positions.

In our experience working with executives, most people find it relatively easy to visualise where they and their principal competitors fit in such a two-dimensional space. Following the procedure described earlier for operationalising the DPM, those responsible for developing and implementing product or brand strategy can quickly download and share their personal views. (Using transparent film and overlaying the individual plots enables one quickly to identify points of agreement and disagreement). Once one has defined the location of the various competitive brands relative to one another, the next step is to diagnose what factors underlie or contribute to these distinctive positions, i.e. what are the critical success factors which combine to deliver 'quality' or 'performance'? Once the individual factors have been identified separate perceptual maps can be drawn using each of these to represent the vertical axis.

To complete the diagnosis, in Figure 5.20 we

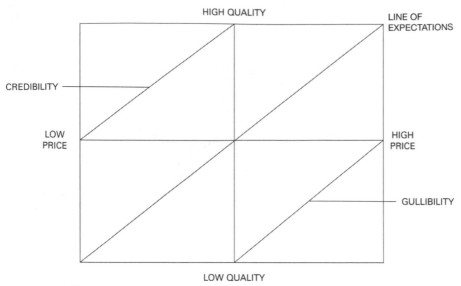

FIGURE 5.19 The zone of expectations

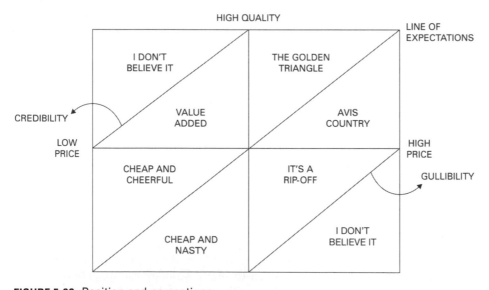

FIGURE 5.20 Position and perceptions

have inserted labels to describe each of the eight possible positions. These labels are self-explanatory and may help in making initial judgements as to where to place an object as well as deciding on the strategy to be followed to either sustain or improve one's position. The implications are obvious:

1. The basic proposition must be believable, otherwise you will find yourself outwith the purchase zone.

2. If you exceed expectations, you can anticipate growth and profitability and vice versa.

3. Cheap and cheerful, value added and the golden triangle are distinct segments, which reflect the logic of downward sloping demand curves in terms of salience and disposable income.

4. No position is permanent. Since the end of World War II, Japan has moved from cheap and nasty to cheap and cheerful to value added into the golden triangle. With increased price

competition, it may now be moving into Avis country as China assumes the 'cheap and cheerful' position.

In conclusion, Baker's Box is intended as a diagnostic tool to aid managerial thinking. Its objective is to help focus and structure your judgement as to where you and your competitors currently are. Once this has been established, and agreed on, it is possible to decide whether one is content with the current position and so wish to reinforce and hold it; sees advantage in attacking a new position or might want to consider withdrawal and a completely new approach. Given the strategic implications, one can then concentrate resources – time and money – in a more detailed analysis of the specific issues relevant to one's chosen strategy.

To familiarise decision-makers with using the technique, and so focus on process rather than opinion (and emotion), in the first instance it might be helpful to have a trial run using a product or service outwith the firm's current range. Publications of the Economist Intelligence Unit, Keynote, etc. will provide most of the factual data needed to initiate discussion on objects – cars,

instant coffee, beer – which are familiar to participants as consumers and about which they will have formed perceptions and attitudes. Once familiar with the technique and having agreed the ground rules a real-time analysis should yield worthwhile results.

GAP ANALYSIS

Gap analysis or 'identification' is a simple and widely used technique to help the firm establish to what extent its current strategies and product–market mix will enable it to achieve its goals. At the corporate level the analysis is best conducted using a single summary statistic (sales, profits, ROI or whatever) and plotting the desired level of performance against the forecasted level of performance. If a gap exits as shown in Figures 5.21 and 5.22 then clearly there is a need for some remedial action.

Where action is needed and what should be done will depend upon a careful analysis of each product in the portfolio using the techniques outlined earlier. The advantage of gap analysis is

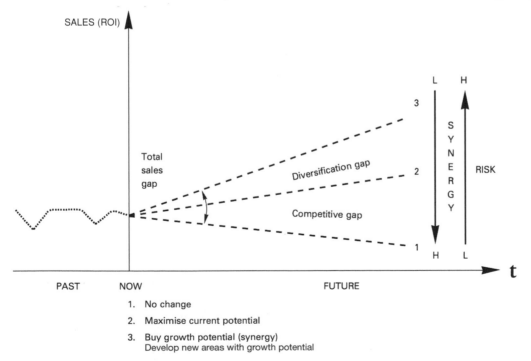

FIGURE 5.21 Ansoff's gap analysis chart

SOURCE: Ansoff, H. I. (1965) *Corporate Strategy*. New York: McGraw-Hill

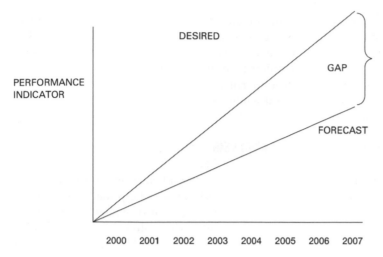

FIGURE 5.22 Gap analylsis

that it provides a synoptic overview of the corporation's overall position. It is, of course, no substitute for the detailed product by product, market by market analysis required when completing a Boston Box or similar portfolio analysis.

As with many concepts in the strategic planning repertoire, 'gap analysis' owes much to the original work of Igor Ansoff (1968, 1990).

Ansoff's chart (Figure 5.21) contains three projections for sales or ROI (the chosen performance indicator): 1 indicates what will occur if the firm continues with its present strategies and predicts a steady decline; 2 projects the potential opportunity for the firm if it redeploys its current resources more effectively; and 3 represents a possible scenario if the firm can diversify into new areas of activity.

Thus Ansoff perceives two kinds of gap, which he labels 'competitive' and 'diversification', and so provides a link with his growth vector components model introduced in Chapter 3 (see Figure 3.2). Where a competitive gap exists, the three strategies described in Chapter 3 – market penetration, market development and product development – are the ones to consider. But, if these are insufficient to close the gap between the firm's objectives and the projected outcomes, then it will need to have recourse to the fourth strategic option – diversification (see Figure 5.21).

Figure 5.22 reproduces Ansoff's gap analysis chart, which indicates how it may be used for planning purposes.

Gap analysis as described here should not be confused with the identification of gaps in the market itself. Such gaps, which represent possible market opportunities, may be identified using the segmentation or positioning techniques described in Chapters 12 and 13 respectively.

SCENARIO PLANNING

As noted already, recent years have seen a growing disenchantment with formal strategic planning due to the increasing mass of detail associated with it, and its inability to respond to the 'surprises' so characteristic of the turbulent environments faced today. One antidote to this dissatisfaction has been the use of scenarios as the basis for analysis and planning.

Scenario analysis is not new and was used successfully by Royal Dutch/Shell to anticipate the oil shortages of 1973–74 and 1979. Indeed in recent years a number of distinctive approaches to scenario planning have been developed and were the subject of a major review article by Huss and Horton in 1987. The following draws extensively on this source.

Huss and Horton observe that traditional forecasting techniques depend heavily on extrapolation which assumes that tomorrow will be very similar to today. Consequently, such forecasts fail when they are needed most – to help anticipate major change in the business environment. By contrast, scenario analysis encourages planners to think more broadly and creatively about the future and incorporate uncertainty into their projections. Huss and Horton identify three alternative approaches to scenario analysis, which they classify as:

1. Intuitive logics as practised by SRI International and Royal Dutch/Shell.
2. Trend-impact analysis as practised by the Futures Group.
3. Cross-impact analysis as practised by the Centre for Futures Research (INTERAX) and Battelle (BASICS).

The main features of these three approaches are discussed below.

INTUITIVE LOGICS

According to Huss and Horton:

> The intuitive logic approach assumes that business decisions are based on a complex set of relationships among economic, political, technological, social, resource and environmental factors. Most of these factors are external to the company but must be understood to provide insights and improve decisions relating to product development, new ventures, capacity expansion, new technologies and business strategies. Some of these variables are precise, quantitative and to some degree, predictable, such as demographics. But many other variables are imprecise, qualitative and less predictable, such as consumer attitudes, politics, financial structure, life style and product demand.

To cope with this complexity, SRI International see scenarios as 'devices for ordering one's perceptions about alternative environments in which one's decisions might be played out' and so enable one to evaluate risks, anticipate key changes and consider trade offs when developing strategy.

The SRI International method comprises eight steps:

1. Analysing the decisions and strategic concerns
2. Identifying the key decision factors
3. Identifying the key environmental forces
4. Analysing the environmental forces
5. Defining scenario logics
6. Elaborating the scenarios
7. Analysing implications for key decision factors
8. Analysing implications for decision and strategies.

Steps 1–4 are common to most strategic planning methodologies and it is steps 5 and 6 which lie at the heart of and distinguish the SRI International approach. As Huss and Horton explain: scenario logics are organising themes, principles, or assumptions that provide each scenario with a coherent, consistent and plausible logical underpinning. Scenario logics should encompass most of the conditions and uncertainties identified in preceding steps. Scenario logics need not cover every distinct possibility. Trial and error are usually necessary in arriving at useful scenario logics. Workshops are often effective settings for accomplishing this step.

These scenario logics are not simply optimistic/pessimistic or high, medium, low scenarios. Instead they describe alternative futures such as buyer's or seller's markets or a regulated or unregulated market. Each of these scenarios presents opportunities and threats to the user company. Therefore they cannot be considered exclusively optimistic or pessimistic.

In step 6 the scenarios are combined with the environmental analyses to provide a more focused and detailed picture for comparison with the key decision factors (step 7). Finally, the full implications of the scenarios are reviewed in the context of a number of specific questions, which Huss and Horton list as:

1. Does information about the future validate the original assumptions supporting strategies or proposed decisions?
2. What do the scenarios imply for the design and timing of particular strategies?
3. What threats and opportunities do the scenarios suggest?
4. What critical issues emerge from the scenarios?
5. What special cases deserve to be addressed by specific contingency plans?
6. What kinds of flexibility and resilience do the scenarios suggest are necessary from a company's planning perspective?
7. What factors and forces deserve monitoring in light of information from the scenarios?

The obvious strength of the SRI International method is its 'ability to develop flexible, internally consistent scenarios from an intuitive, logical perspective'. Its obvious weakness is that its subjective nature makes it liable to the dangers of selective perception/distortion and to undue influence by a dominant person or subgroup.

TREND-IMPACT ANALYSIS

Trend-impact analysis is a methodology which employs an independent forecast of the key dependent variable which is then modified to reflect the effect of other events impacting upon it. Its advantage is seen in its combination of formal forecasting techniques, such as time series analysis and econometrics, to establish trends which are then examined in terms of a series of impacting events which may be derived from a Delphi study, jury of executive opinion or similar well informed but judgemental source. The likelihood or probability of impacting events over time is estimated and used to modify the original independent trend forecast. Finally, narratives are developed for each of the scenarios. Its major disadvantage is that the technique does not explore the effect which the impacting events may have on each other and its focus on a single key decision or forecast variable.

CROSS-IMPACT ANALYSIS

Cross-impact analysis seeks to overcome the narrow focus of trend-impact analysis and was developed to help interrelate intuitive forecasts of future outcomes derived from methods such as brainstorming, Delphi studies, morphological analysis or even simple opinion surveys. Several companies have developed their own cross-impact methodologies of which two of the better known are INTERAX and BASICS.

INTERAX (interactive cross-impact simulation) was developed by the Centre for Futures Research in the University of Southern California Graduate School of Business Administration and is 'a forecasting procedure that uses both analytical models and human analysts to develop a better understanding of alternative future environments. It does this by generating scenarios one year at a time so that policy makers can interact with each scenario as it is being generated to experiment with policy options'. The early stages are similar to other methodologies in that one first must define the issue and time period of the analysis. Next one must define the primary variables or key indicators that one is seeking to forecast, and these are then projected using independent methods such as time series or econometric analysis. Step 4 seeks to identify impacting events as described for trend-impact analysis but also uses the INTERAX Delphi database derived from an ongoing study of 500 experts on future trends and events. In steps 5 and 6 the user develops an event probability distribution and then estimates the impact of each event on each indicator variable. In step 7 the cross-impacts of each event on each indicator variable are analysed and, finally, in step 8 the

computerised model is run until a series of scenarios have been generated.

INTERAX may be run interactively and produces path scenarios which unfold over time. It comes with a comprehensive database which is readily updated and produces 'excellent statistical distributions of outcomes around the average'. However, it has a high start-up cost, is perceived as difficult by many analysts because of its interactive features, and will generate outputs based on the input data irrespective of whether they make sense or not.

BASICS (Battelle scenario inputs to corporate strategies) was developed in 1977 as a cooperative venture between several laboratories of the Battelle Memorial Institute. 'The BASICS method differs from INTERAX in that it does not use Monte Carlo simulation, and it does not require an independent forecast of the key indicators or variables'. Otherwise BASICS is similar to the methodologies described earlier and the reader should consult Huss and Horton for a detailed description and comparison with these methods.

It was Dwight Eisenhower who observed: 'The plan is nothing, planning is everything'. As in so many things, the process is more important than a particular outcome at a specific point in time. Experience and personal prejudice predispose the writer to the less sophisticated approaches defined here as intuitive logics. While the power of the computer and formal econometric and statistical analysis may yield many more combinations and permutations than ordinary human analysis, they are often as likely to confuse as to inform. Further, the computer or other formal model is rarely able to discriminate between the quality of inputs, and so will process them as if all were of equal value. All the models described here have very similar structures – the possible problem is that trend and cross-impact analysis introduce complex analytic methods which may lull the undiscriminating analyst into a false and dangerous sense of security in the quality of the outputs when GIGO – garbage in, garbage out – will always prevail.

SWOT

As discussed in Chapter 4, SWOT is an acronym for strengths, weaknesses, opportunities and threats and defines the desired output from the formal analysis which must precede the selection of strategy and the formulation of plans to implement it.

Successful strategy formulation is essentially a 'marketing' process whereby an organisation seeks to deploy its values and resources in those areas where they will achieve the maximum return. In other words, firms seek to match their strengths with opportunities. In doing so they will be conscious of the need to avoid the threats of external environmental change and competitive activity, and also of the desirability of improving areas of possible weakness. It follows that, to do this effectively, organisations must have a good understanding of all four elements covered by the SWOT analysis – as in most things, effective prognosis depends upon accurate diagnosis. This being so each element of the SWOT analysis is given extended treatment.

In Chapter 7, it will be argued that to all intents and purposes the external environm 'market' constitutes the boundary con ___ within which firms must compete one with another, to determine who will succeed and who will fail. Thus, while national economies may seek to protect their own firms and industries from external competition (and this tendency is weakening with the growth of global competition) they will seek to encourage it between domestic suppliers to encourage the efficiency which such competition generates. As a very minimum, therefore, one must develop a clear understanding of the threats and opportunities which the current and future environment has to offer.

Subsequently, Chapters 8 to 11 explore industry and competitors, buyer behaviour and the organisation's own strengths and weaknesses before pulling these altogether in a discussion of matching, through which the firm chooses those courses of action that offer it the best opportunity for success.

Chapter summary

In this chapter we have been concerned with a number of organising frameworks, procedures and techniques designed to assist planners to impose structure upon the complex and multidimensional problems they wish to solve. In the course of this review we have sought to emphasise three things:

1. The selection is eclectic, not comprehensive. There are many more analytical and problem solving methods described, often at some length, in the literature. Our intention has been to present the better known approaches which appear to satisfy our definition of CUGs. Critics have dismissed some of these procedures for a variety of reasons and several of the major criticisms of the PLC and portfolio analysis were included to sensitise the reader that they do not enjoy universal support. The acid test, as always, must be 'does it help/work for me?' If it does, use it.
2. Simplicity is preferred to complexity.
3. The techniques are an aid to decision-making – not a substitute for it.

In this spirit we have given considerable attention to the concept of product life-cycles and the theory of diffusion which suggests how the phenomenon may be used in developing marketing strategies. This consideration leads naturally into discussion of portfolio models of the kind first developed by the Boston Consulting Group which use the phases of the PLC as the basis for analysing the performance of products over time. Portfolio analysis is now regarded as old hat by some critics and a summary of some of the major criticisms was reviewed. This review led to much the same conclusion as that made of the PLC itself – the concept provides help in structuring and analysing problems but, in and of itself, it cannot come up with precise solutions to specific problems. This is the responsibility of the decision-maker.

The next section was concerned with another aid to strategic decision-making – the two-dimensional overview of the kind developed by Shell and GE. These and similar strategic overviews are helpful devices for enabling planners perform a 'first-cut' analysis by classifying products and markets in terms of their intrinsic attractiveness and the firm's capabilities in serving these markets. Such analysis may range from a broad brush judgemental evaluation to one in which hard data on specific performance indicators are provided to give greater precision to the classification of particular products and markets. A further planning matrix that may be used for segmenting markets and targeting positions within them is introduced in Baker's Box.

The chapter concludes with brief descriptions of three other techniques designed to assist formal strategic planning – gap analysis, scenario analysis and SWOT. Gap analysis is a simple technique for identifying possible discrepancies between an organisation's declared objectives and likely outcomes if current practices are not modified to enable the firm to achieve them. Scenario analysis reflects the difficulty of extrapolating current trends (required by gap analysis) given the rate of change and turbulence in the competitive environment. Scenario analysis thus offers a variety of approaches to help planners capture and model experience and judgement in defining future outcomes.

Finally, SWOT was introduced as an acronym for the process of internal and external analysis through which the firm can establish which opportunities offer it the greatest likelihood of future success so that it can devise strategies and plans to achieve them. It is to these issues which we turn in succeeding chapters.

Recommended reading

Hooley, G. J., Saunders, J. A. and Piercy, N. F. (2003) *Marketing Strategy and Competitive Positioning* (3rd edn). London: Prentice Hall.

Kerin, R. A., Mahajan, V. and Varadarajan, P. R. (1990) *Contemporary Perspectives on Strategic Marketing Planning*. Boston, MA: Allyn & Bacon.

REFERENCES

Abell, D. F. and Hammond, J. S. (1979) *Strategic Market Planning*. Englewood Cliffs, NJ: Prentice Hall, p. 214.

American Machinist (1968) American Machinist's Tenth Inventory.

Ames, B. C. (1970) Trappings versus substance in industrial marketing, *Harvard Business Review* (July–August).

Ansoff, H. I. (1965) *Corporate Strategy*. New York: McGraw-Hill.

Ansoff, H. I. (1968) *Corporate Strategy* (2nd edn). Harmondsworth: Penguin.

Ansoff, H. I. (1990) *Implanting Strategic Management* (2nd edn). Englewood Cliffs, NJ: Prentice Hall.

Avlonitis, G. A. (1983) The product elimination decision and strategies, *Industrial Marketing Management*, **12**: 31–4.

Bain, J. S. (1956) *Barriers to New Competition*. Cambridge, MA: Harvard University Press.

Baker, M. J. (1975) *Marketing New Industrial Products*. London: Macmillan – now Palgrave Macmillan.

Baker, M. J. (1983) *Market Developement*. Harmondsworth: Penguin.

Buzzell, R. D. (1966) Competitive behaviour and the product life cycle, in J. S. Wright and J. L. Goldstrucker (eds) *New Ideas for Successful Marketing*, Proceedings of the 1966 World Congress. American Marketing Association.

Buzzell, R. D., Bradley, G. T. and Sultan, R. G. M. (1975) Market share – a key to profitability, *Harvard Business Review* (January/February): 97–106.

Day, G. (1977) Diagnosing the product portfolio, *Journal of Marketing* (April).

Day, G. (1983) Gaining insights through strategy analysis, *Journal of Business Strategy*, **4**(1).

de Solla Price, D. J. (1963) *Little Science, Big Science*. New York: Columbia University Press.

Dhalla, N. K. and Yuspeh, S. (1976) Forget the product life cycle concept!, *Harvard Business Review* (January–February).

Dodd, S. C. (1955) Diffuson is predictable: testing predictability models for laws of interaction, *American Sociological Review*, **10**: 392–401.

Firth, C. (1980) New approaches to strategic marketing planning, unpublished MBA dissertation, University of Bradford.

Freeman, C. (1963) The plastics industry: a comparative study of research and development, *National Institute Economic Review* (November): 22–62.

Griliches, Z. (1957) Hybrid corn: an exploration in the economies of technological change, *Econometrica*, **25**(October): 501–22.

Henderson, B. (1968) *Perspectives on Experience*. Boston, MA: Boston Consulting Group.

Hirschmann, W. B. (1964) Profit from the learning curve, *Harvard Business Review* (January/February): 125–39.

Hooley, G. J. (1979/80) *MBA Core Course Lecture Notes*. Bradford Management Centre.

Huss, W. R. and Horton, E. J. (1987) Scenario planning – what style should you use?, *Long Range Planning*, **20**(4): 21–9.

Johne, A. (1982) Innovation Organisation and the Marketing of High Technology Products, unpublished PhD dissertation, Strathclyde University.

Kotler, P. (1980) *Marketing Management* (4th edn). Englewood Cliffs, NJ: Prentice Hall.

Levitt, T. (1960) Marketing myopia, *Harvard Business Review* (July–August).

Lynn, F. (1966) An investigation of the rate of development and diffusion of technology in our modern industrial society, in *The Employment Impact of Technological Change*, Appendix Volume II, Technology Automation, and Economic Progress. Washington, DC: US Government Printing Office.

Mansfield, E. (1968) *Industrial Research and Technological Innovation*. New York: W. W. Norton.

Miller, G. A. (1956) The magical number seven, plus or minus two: some limits on our capacity for processing information, *Psychological Review*, **63**(March): 81–97.

OECD (1970) *Gaps in Technology*,

Comparisons between Member Countries in Education, Research and Development, Technological Innovation, International Economic Exchanges. Paris: OECD.

Pemberton, H. E. (1936) The curve of culture diffusion rate, *American Sociological Review*, **1**(August): 547–56.

Ray, G. F. (1969) The diffusion of new technology. A study of ten processes in nine industries, *National Institute Economic Review* (March): 40–83.

Robinson, S. J. Q., Hichens, R. E. and Wade, D. P. (1978) The directional policy matrix, *Long Range Planning*, **11**(June): 2–8.

Rogers, E. M. (1962) *Diffusion of Innovations*. New York: Free Press.

Ryan, B. and Gross, N. C. (1943) The diffusion of hybrid seed corn in two Iowa communities, *Rural Sociology*, **8**: 15–24.

Schnarrs, S. P. (1991) *Marketing Strategy* (2nd edn 1998). New York: Free Press.

Schoeffler, S., Buzzell, R. D. and Heaney, D. F. (1974) Impact of strategic planning on profit performance, *Harvard Business Review* (March/April).

Shell (1975) *The directional policy matrix: a new aid to corporate planning*. Shell International Chemical Co.

Sorokin, P. A. (1962) *Social and Cultural Dynamics*, 4 vols. Englewood Cliffs, NJ: Bedminster Press.

Tarde, G. (1903) *The Laws of Imitation* (trans. Elsie Clews Parsons). New York: Henry Holt.

Vernon, R. (1966) International investments and international trade in the product cycle, *Quarterly Journal of Economics*, **53**(2): 197–207.

Wattel, H. L. (ed.) (1964) *The Dissemination of New Business Techniques*, vol. 2. Hempstead, NY: Hofstra University.

Wells, L. T. Jr (1968) A product life cycle for international trade?, *Journal of Marketing*, **32**(3): 1–6.

Wells, W. D. and Gubar, G.(1966) Life cycle concepts in marketing research, *Journal of Marketing Research* (November): 355–63.

Wensley, R. (1981) Strategic marketing: betas, boxes or basics, *Journal of Marketing*, **45**(3): 173–82.

Yale, J. P. (1964) The strategy of nylon's growth: create new markets, *Modern Textiles Magazine*, February, p. 33.

NOTE

1. Heinz Wolff, reported in Is the future so frightening?, *International Management*, October 1979.

2. Research undertaken by the Federal Bank in Dallas (www.dallasfed.org) reported in *Fortune*, June 8, 1998, showed that the penetration rates of 15 major consumer products in US households all followed an S-shaped curve.

Research for marketing

Facts are stubborn, but statistics are more pliable. MARK TWAIN

After reading Chapter 6 you will be able to:

✔ Explain the importance of marketing research and its contribution to competitive success.

✔ Describe the differences between quantitative and qualitative research, when to use them and how they complement each other.

✔ Identify the role of secondary data sources as an input to market analysis.

✔ Define the nature of primary data and describe the methods by which it can be collected – observation, experimentation, simulation and sample survey.

✔ Suggest a checklist for assessing a market's worth.

✔ Explain the process for analysing sample data and drawing inferences from it.

✔ Discuss probabilistic approaches to decision-making under conditions of uncertainty, following the principles of Bayesian analysis.

✔ Show how to structure problems, identify alternatives, develop decision trees, select a decision criterion and solve problems by combining facts and judgement.

INTRODUCTION

In earlier editions the chapter dealing with marketing research was to be found in the section dealing with the management of the marketing function. The decision to locate it there was that in the original conceptualisation of the so-called 'marketing mix', Neil Borden (1975) included it along with what have now become the familiar 4Ps of marketing – product, price, place (distribution) and promotion. Taken together the elements of the marketing mix represent those aspects of marketing over which management exercises control in executing a specific marketing plan. In this book, however, we are concerned first with the development of strategy upon which operational plans are based. To develop strategy it is necessary to carry out a wide-ranging evaluation and analysis of all those factors which have a bearing upon the courses of action open to the decision-maker. As noted earlier, in the realms of military planning, this phase is identified as an appreciation and so we have decided to distinguish Part II of the book as *The Marketing Appreciation*.

Clearly, fact-finding and analysis call for specialist tools and techniques and these are the domain of the marketing research function. It is for this reason that we open this section with an overview of the topic. Surprisingly, most textbooks on strategic marketing planning make no explicit reference to marketing research, despite the fact that there is an implicit assumption that decision-makers are defining options and alternative courses of actions based upon consideration of relevant information. So where does this information come from if it is not captured and synthesised in some formal way?

As we shall see in this chapter, not all firms do take formal steps to gather, analyse and store market data. We shall also provide evidence that those that do so perform better than those that don't. A vital ingredient in this process is marketing research and the establishment of a marketing information system (MkIS) as an integral part of the firm's larger management information system (MIS).

In a broadly based book of this kind, one can provide only a limited introduction to what is a major subfield of the marketing discipline. Extended, detailed descriptions/analysis of the role and uses of marketing research can be found in many specialised texts, several of which are listed in the recommended readings at the end of the chapter, written specifically for users of research to illuminate and help solve marketing problems (as opposed to a book for practitioners emphasising technique and procedure). In this chapter, we will seek to establish why marketing research is so important, together with providing evidence of the reasons why it is believed to make such an important contribution to overall competitive success. We will also examine some of the criticisms of formal marketing research and distinguish the differences between quantitative and qualitative approaches.

Having established the nature and scope of marketing research we examine the distinction between secondary and primary data and review briefly the main methods of primary data collection. Next we provide a checklist for assessing market potential – the heart of marketing research – before discussing data reduction and analysis as a necessary discipline to reduce potential information overload to manageable proportions. Finally, we present an extended review of the Bayesian methodology, which enables decision-makers to combine facts and judgement and so make decisions under conditions of uncertainty – the primary activity of managers and the one which distinguishes their role from all others.

THE NEED FOR MARKETING RESEARCH

In their book *Marketing Decisions: a Bayesian Approach*, Enis and Broome (1973) identify three sets of factors that create particular difficulties in applying formal analytical procedures to marketing decisions:

> First, many marketing problems are more or less unique. A new product, for example, is offered to the market only once. There are no historical data from which long-run relative frequencies can be calculated for traditional statistical analysis. Consequently, past experience often provides only general guidelines for decision making. Secondly, marketing's interface with buyers results in problems not found in other areas of business, buyers can think for themselves. They may, therefore, change their mind, reorder their

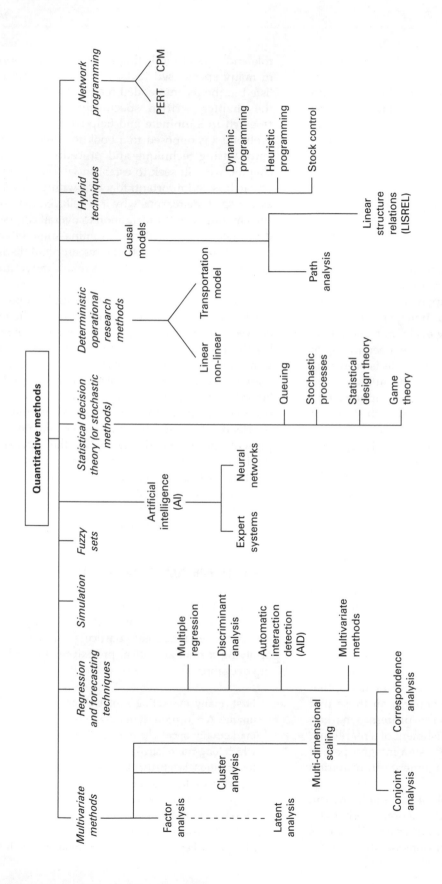

FIGURE 6.1 Quantitative techniques in marketing

SOURCE: Moutinho, L. and Meidan, A. (2003) in Baker, M. J. (ed.) *The Marketing Book*. Oxford: Butterworth Heinemann

priorities, or otherwise alter their behaviour patterns. By contrast, the production manager may feel reasonably confident that his raw materials will not refuse to become part of the product he is manufacturing.

A third barrier to formal analysis of marketing problems is the complexity of such problems.

It is because of these difficulties that many managers dismiss the relevance of the more formal decision-making procedures, which depend upon basic statistical laws such as the law of statistical regularity and the law of inertia of large numbers. Similarly, such managers have little patience with the techniques developed by operational researchers, even though many of these are eminently suitable for many classes of marketing problems as shown in Figure 6.1.

In part, rejection of these models and approaches is felt to arise from the intrinsic fear which a significant proportion of managers exhibit when faced with anything which calls for a quantitative analysis. (The prevalence of this fear is well established, but it is difficult to understand particularly when one considers the nature of the Graduate Test for Studies in Business, which seeks to measure performance in terms of both numeracy and verbal skills. Candidates are awarded a composite score which reflects their performance in terms of both these dimensions which many persons regard as mutually exclusive. Assuming the dimensions are equally weighted it is clear that to come in the top 10% of all performers if you gain full marks on one dimension then you must still score not less than 80% in the other – in other words high performers tend to be good on both verbal and quantitative tests.) Because of this fear there is a proclivity to stress judgemental approaches and emphasise the importance of 'experience' as a basis for informed decision-taking where there are genuine doubts about expected outcomes

Because of the novelty, complexity and dynamic nature of marketing problems referred to earlier, judgement and experience have a very important role to play in managerial decision-making, but it would be foolish to ignore the benefits which accrue if such skills are combined with a formal and structured approach to problem-solving. Similarly, it would be foolish to ignore the benefits associated with a formal and structured

approach to the collection and analysis of marketing information.

Naturally all managers seek to keep themselves informed of changes in the marketplace and their own organisation – it is an essential part of the manager's job and a vital input to strategic planning of the kind discussed in this first part of the book. The critical issue would seem to be at what point one should switch from informal to formal monitoring and analysis. In *Research for Marketing* (Baker, 1991) we argue that decision-making is the outcome of a process of 'successive focusing', which may be represented by a funnel similar to that shown in Figure 6.2.

This funnel corresponds closely to the hierarchy of effects models described in Chapter 9 and the sequence of decision-making in our model of buyer behaviour (Chapter 9). Of course, one may decide to break off the process at any stage or may short-circuit it when, say, undirected viewing such as passing a shop window reminds us of a need which we can satisfy by a purchase based upon a learned and routinised response.

Strictly speaking, market research is concerned with formal search which is triggered by recog-

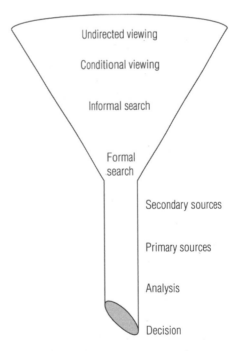

FIGURE 6.2 Successive focusing

SOURCE: Baker, M. J. (1991) *Research for Marketing*. London: Macmillan – now Palgrave Macmillan

nition of the need to find out more about an issue. The preceding stages in the model are taken from Aguilar's (1987) now classic work on *Scanning the Business Environment* in which he describes how managers become aware of and analyse issues. Thus undirected viewing may be thought of as general exposure to information where the viewer has no specific purpose in mind save the recognition that one needs to monitor the environment in case there is something of possible interest going on. In other words undirected viewing is a stage of general awareness. As a result of such undirected viewing, some cue or stimulus may attract the conscious attention of the scanner and lead them to a state of conditional viewing, i.e. they will examine the information that has attracted their attention to see if it is really of any interest. If the information is of interest then the viewer will move on to an informal search, which may be defined as a relatively limited and unstructured effort to obtain specific information or information for a specific purpose. This stage we may characterise as 'keeping an eye on things'. If this further stimulates the viewer's interest, then it is likely he or she will institute a formal search. In marketing, this is where marketing research will come into play. The danger, as we have hinted earlier, is that if managers believe they are rewarded for exercising judgement they may short-circuit the process without going to the effort (and cost) of a formal search.

As long ago as 1964 the National Industrial Conference Board (NICB) in the US published the results of a survey into the causes of product failure, which clearly showed that the major reason for such failure was an incomplete and/or inadequate understanding of market and competitive conditions, precisely the kind of information which marketing research could have provided. Numerous studies since have confirmed the view that expenditure on marketing research can easily be justified on the grounds of improved competitive performance. Thus, in 1984, Hooley et al. undertook a wide-ranging survey of the use of marketing research in the UK, from which they concluded there was 'a clear association between conducting marketing research and improved company performance both in terms of profit margin achieved and self-assessed performance'. They went on to say:

While the research cannot prove that the higher levels of usage have caused better performance the high level of association found does indicate that strong inferences can be drawn. The relationship between usage of marketing research and performance suggests that those companies with zero or low usage could significantly improve their performance by making better use of marketing research.

The findings of the survey by Baker and Hart (1989) led to precisely this conclusion. Indeed, out of over 60,000 possible relationships between marketing practices and improved performance, greater use of marketing research was one of the very few where a significant correlation was detected.

QUANTITATIVE OR QUALITATIVE RESEARCH?

Earlier we caricatured the reluctance of managers to use marketing research as arising from a fear of the mathematical/statistical techniques which seem to dominate the subject, reinforced by a preference for their own judgement based upon experience. This division between quantitative and qualitative approaches is also apparent within the practice of marketing research itself.

Baker (1991, pp. 32ff) presents a table that appears to suggest that quantitative and qualitative research may be regarded as polar and mutually exclusive alternatives, as can be seen from Table 6.1.

But, as our discussion then points out, more recently a more balanced approach has emerged in which both kinds of researcher admit the contribution of the other. In parallel with this trend (or perhaps because of it) there has developed a growing recognition amongst the users of research that qualitative research is essential to address questions of what, how (process) and why, while quantitative research is appropriate to answer questions of who, where, when and how (quantity).

In very broad terms one should use qualitative research:

1. To define the parameters of the market
2. To understand the nature of the decision-making process
3. To elicit attitudinal and motivational factors which influence behaviour

4. To help understand why people behave the way they do.

TABLE 6.1 Qualitative versus quantitative research

Qualitative	Quantitative
Soft	Hard
Dry	Wet
Flexible	Fixed
Grounded	Abstract
Descriptive/exploratory	Explanatory
Prescientific	Scientific
Subjective	Objective
Inductive	Deductive
Speculative/illustrative	Hypothesis testing
Political	Value free
Non-rigorous	Rigorous
Idiographic	Nomothetic
Holistic	Atomistic
Interpretivist	Positivist
Exposes actors' meanings	Imposes sociological theory
Phenomenological	Empiricist/behaviourist
Relativistic case study	Universalistic survey
Good	Bad
Bad	Good

SOURCE: Halfpenny, P. (1979) The analysis of qualitative data, *Sociological Review*, **27**(4)

Overall, qualitative research is best suited to areas calling for a flexible approach while quantitative research is necessary to define more precisely the issues identified through qualitative methods. According to Peter Sampson (1967), the areas calling for a flexible approach may be summarised as:

1. Concept identification and exploration
2. Identification of relevant behavioural attitudes
3. Establishing priority among and between categories of behaviour, attitudes, etc.
4. Defining problem areas more fully and formulating hypotheses for further investigation.

Wendy Gordon and Roy Langmaid (1988) have suggested that the most important areas for qualitative research are:

- Basic exploratory studies
- New product development
- Creative development
- Diagnostic studies
- Tactical research projects.

Exploratory studies are usually called for when seeking to identify market opportunities for new product development, to monitor changes in consumption patterns and behaviour, to help define the parameters and characteristics of newly emerging markets or when seeking to enter established markets of which one has no prior experience. Gordon and Langmaid (1988) indicate five specific types of information that may be obtained from studies of this kind, namely:

1. *To define consumer perceptions of the market or product field* in order to help understand the competitive relationships between different types of product and/or brand in any product category – from the consumer's point of view rather than the manufacturer's.
2. *To define consumer segmentations in relation to a product category or brand*, e.g. psychographics and lifestyle segmentations.
3. *To understand the dimensions that differentiate between brands*, specifically on the basis of rational criteria and emotional beliefs. Where objective differences can be developed between products, rationality will predispose consumers to select those which conform most closely with their own preferences or criteria. Unsurprisingly, objective differences are comparatively easy to emulate with the result that emotional beliefs have come to play an increasingly important part in purchase decisions – industrial as well as consumer.
4. *To understand the purchase decision-making process and/or usage patterns.*
5. *Hypothesis generation.*

Qualitative research then is particularly useful in gaining insight into behaviour and the 'reasons' underlying it. We put 'reasons' in quotes because an intrinsic weakness of all respondent-based research is that there is rarely if ever any compulsion to participate in a market research survey which means that those who agree to do so invariably want to help the interviewer. There is also often an implicit belief that there are 'right' and 'wrong' answers which predisposes respondents to give you the answer which they think you want. Even more problematical is the fact that consumers can rarely visualise radical product improvements such as microwave ovens and so would be highly unlikely to express a need for an oven that cooks without heat. It follows that 'listening to the voice of the market' will not automatically identify the best marketing opportunities. A striking example of this that is frequently cited is the case of the noiseless food blender. When asked what improvement users of food blenders would like, there was strong support for ones which were less noisy than current models. After much research and effort, a leading manufacturer launched a much quieter version only to have it rejected by potential users on the grounds that it lacked power! Technically this was not the case but, given that users equated noise with power, it proved impossible to convince them otherwise.

As a broad generalisation, then, qualitative research is an essential prerequisite to most quantitative research in that it will help clarify the issues to be addressed, the parameters to be defined and measured and the likely relationships between them.

The distinction between quantitative and qualitative research, and their mutual dependence, was illustrated by an article by Johansson and Nonaka

(1987) entitled 'Market research the Japanese way'. In this article, the authors report Japanese disdain for the volume of formal market research conducted in the USA. They point out that when Sony researched the market for a lightweight portable cassette player the results indicated that consumers would only buy one with a recording facility. Akio Morita ignored this finding and the Walkman is history. Citing examples such as Matsushita and Canon, the authors report how Japanese companies depend upon a combination of 'soft data' gathered by managers actually visiting customers and distributors and 'hard data' about shipments, inventory levels and retail sales. However, the authors also cite evidence of Japanese failures in American markets, which they attribute to a lack of understanding of the attitudes and opinions of American consumers that could have been established by the use of some of the survey techniques they have eschewed. The conclusion is that both kinds of research are called for. Clearly, with highly innovative and novel products it is unlikely that consumers could conceptualise the possibilities for a portable, personal entertainment system such as the Walkman. But, once the technological possibilities have become apparent, and markets begin to grow and mature, then the need to segment markets and position products will call for the kind of quantitative data that is unavailable when developing wholly new product concepts.

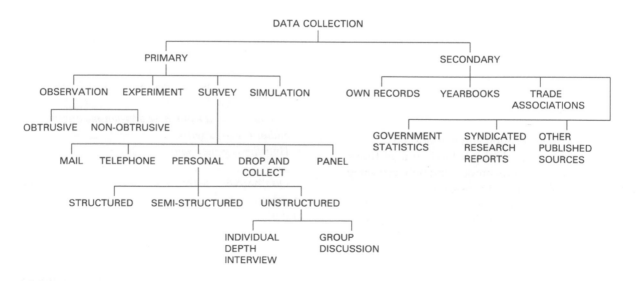

FIGURE 6.3 Methods of data collection

DATA COLLECTION

Given that one is persuaded of the desirability of conducting marketing research and setting up a MkIS, the obvious question is: how does one set about collecting the necessary data? A cursory examination of any basic textbook quickly reveals there is a wide range of techniques and procedures available. Discussion of these is well beyond the scope of a book of this kind but, in Figure 6.3, we have summarised the major approaches one is likely to encounter. A brief summary of the more important areas is also given but for a detailed explanation one should consult one of the recommended textbooks.

SECONDARY SOURCES OF DATA

Secondary sources consist of existing data and it is common sense to identify and consult these first. The starting point for research into these sources will evidently depend upon how novel the product and/or market are in relation to the firm's existing product range. Clearly, if one is considering modification to existing products or marketing practices then the firm's existing records will be a logical and fruitful place to start. On the other hand, if one is diversifying into a completely new market with a radically different product, one will need to look for other published sources of information when the initial difficulty is more likely to be the apparent wealth of information rather than the absence of it. We say 'apparent' advisedly for closer inspection often reveals that relatively little information bears directly upon one's problems. However, there is some truth in the cliche that there is nothing new under the sun for, in a basic sense, even major innovations are a substitute for a previous product for which data is available. Thus xerography or electronic scanning is but the latest in a long line of copying devices, the market for which was well documented at the time the Xerox process was introduced. Obviously, what was not known was the penetration that the new product would achieve, i.e. share of existing market, nor the effect it would have on the growth of the market. In the event, xerography revolutionised the copying business and both attracted demand from alternative methods of reproduction, e.g.

stencils and duplicators, while expanding total usage due to its simplicity and cleanliness of operation and the quality of the finished product. Of course, few products are as successful or so well protected by patents (which effectively limit direct competition), as Xerox was, but it is worth bearing in mind that radically new or improved products may lead to an increase in total demand by suggesting new uses and by converting latent demand into effective demand.

Broadly speaking, sources of published data fall into five categories:

1. Government publications – both domestic and foreign. Salient among the former are the various *Censuses of Population, Production and Distribution*, the *Monthly Digest of Statistics*, the *Annual Abstract of Statistics, Trade and Industry* and *Business Monitor*. Major foreign sources are the various publications of the European Union, the International Monetary Fund, the OECD, the UN, and, of course, the foreign governments and their agencies.
2. Trade associations and chambers of commerce. Trade associations tend to publish highly specific data about their own industry, chambers of commerce more generalised information about business opportunities.
3. Universities and non-profit research organisations, e.g. *Oxford Bulletin of Statistics*, Stanford Research Institute. This category also includes the various academic journals.
4. Commercial research organisations, e.g. Economist Intelligence Unit, Attwood Statistics, Keynote, Arthur D. Little, Booz, Allen & Hamilton, Gallup, etc.
5. The press, both general, e.g. *Financial Times*, and specific, e.g. *Fortune, Business Week*, etc.

From sources such as these, researchers should be able to build up a fair picture of the market for the product they are considering developing, at least in quantitative terms, e.g. total size, growth trends, seasonality, location, number of buyers, usage and replacement rates, etc. However, such parameters only serve to define past and current demand for other, albeit related products. While this may be sufficient to justify development of some products, e.g. where the risk is small or can be made so, as for example in a joint development with a prospective buyer, a very significant cost/price or quality/price advantage, etc., in many cases the developer will want to know much more about the operation of the market than is apparent in bare statistics. In order to obtain this information, and/or to fill the gaps in the published data, it is usually necessary to engage in field research to collect this original or primary data.

THE COLLECTION OF PRIMARY DATA

Primary or original data may be collected by one, or a combination of four methods – *observation*, *experimentation*, *sample survey* and *simulation*.

While observation of buying and usage behaviour may yield useful clues to consumer needs which may be incorporated in the product design, packaging, promotion policies, etc., it is not a particularly useful source of information on market size or potential. Much the same is true of both experimentation and simulation as techniques. Thus, by a process of elimination, the major source of primary data is the sample survey. In theory, of course, the ideal method of acquiring information about a 'population' (e.g. all potential purchasers of a new product) is to conduct a census of that population. In practice this is rarely feasible due to the size of the population, and the time and cost of establishing contact with it. In fact experience of censuses suggests that 100% response is impossible to achieve and that a figure nearer 90% is more realistic. Accordingly, because of the time and expense involved in attempting a census, the knowledge that 100% response is unattainable, and the delay and cost involved in processing the mass of information yielded by the census,[1] most researchers prefer to conduct a sample survey. The only exceptions are the few cases where the population is small, easily identified and accessible, e.g. buyers of steel-making plant in Europe.

Sample surveys, or, as they are popularly known, 'opinion polls', are a familiar part of our daily life and generally accepted as a fairly accurate reflection of opinion at large, despite occasional lapses in predicting the outcomes of elections. However, as the pollsters point out, in many elections a swing of 2–3% will give an opposite result from that predicted while in most commercial situations, a level of accuracy of 97–98% would be more than adequate for decision-making purposes. In fact, if greater precision is required this can usually be achieved by increasing the sample size, always bearing in mind that costs tend to increase geometrically and accuracy only arithmetically, making the expected value of the additional information a very real issue.

Fundamentally, sampling theory rests upon two statistical 'laws' – the 'law of statistical regularity' and the 'law of inertia of large numbers'. The first law states that any set of objects taken from a large group of such objects will tend to have the same characteristics as that larger group, while the second law holds that large groups are more stable than small groups because deviations about the mean tend to cancel each other out. Simplistically, therefore, if we can identify the members of a population in which we are interested (electors, buyers, etc.), then a given portion or sample of them should be representative of the whole, and the bigger the sample the more representative it will become. Sampling theory is now highly developed and the subject of many books in specialised fields such as operations research, production management, marketing research, etc. Reference should be made to these specialist treatments by those wishing to explore the subject further; for our purposes we must confine our comments to a brief description of the types of survey used in marketing research to establish market potential.

PROBABILITY SAMPLES

Broadly speaking, sample designs fall into two categories – those based on probability theory and those which are not. Samples based on probability theory tend to be better known and are essential if one wishes to use the results for predictive purposes. In a probability based sample the chance that any given unit will be selected may be assigned a definite, non-zero probability. Given this knowledge it is possible to state within determinate limits, or 'degree of confidence' how likely it is that the sample results are an accurate reflection of the population from which the sample has been drawn. Among the better known types of probability sample, four are used fairly often by market researchers:

1. *Random samples:* in which, theoretically, every member of the universe has an equal chance of being selected. In fact it may not be possible to preidentify every member of a population as is possible when sampling, say, units of output in a factory, but it is usually possible to draw a sample that can be treated as unbiased for all practical purposes.
2. *Systematic sample:* unlike the true random sample, where every unit is identified, allocated a number and selected by a random process (cf. Ernie and Premium Bonds), the systematic sample is drawn by selecting units at a predetermined interval from a chosen starting point, e.g. every eighth house, every third member on a list.
3. *Stratified samples:* the population is segmented into strata and random samples drawn from each stratum by either method (a) or (b).
4. *Area sampling:* an area, usually a country, is broken down into sub-areas. A sample of sub-areas is then drawn and these are then sampled using one of the three preceding methods. This approach is followed for most national surveys.

We have already noted one difficulty in using probability sampling in a marketing situation – that of preidentifying all members of the population. A second difficulty arises from the non-homogeneous nature of the units which comprise populations of interest to marketers. This lack of homogeneity is particularly marked in the case of usage or consumption patterns and is illustrated by what has been termed the 'heavy half' syndrome.

This phenomenon is apparent both in industrial and consumer markets where it can usually be shown that a relatively small proportion of all users account for a disproportionately large share of total consumption. Thus one may find that the two or three largest firms in an industry of several hundreds, or even thousands, account for half of the usage of a given product, while in consumer markets it is often contended that 20% of the users account for 80% of the consumption while the remaining 80% of consumers account for the balance of 20%. Clearly, from a marketing point of view we are primarily interested in the heavy users, while, from a sampling point of view, we are concerned that our sample should be representative. If, however, every unit has an equal chance of

being included, it also has an equal chance of being excluded such that, if we are faced with a population in which the parameter we wish to measure is not distributed normally, there is a strong likelihood that our sample will be unrepresentative. For example, it would be like Unipart, with thousands of customers, trying to forecast demand for a new electrical component having drawn a sample that excluded the major car manufacturers. It is because of this possibility that marketing researchers make extensive use of non-probabilistic sampling methods.

NON-PROBABILITY SAMPLES

Three types of non-probability sample are in common use. The most basic and the crudest method is the *convenience* sample in which one solicits information from any convenient group which may have views pertinent to the subject of inquiry, e.g. one could ask Saturday afternoon shoppers for their views on pedestrian-only precincts, off-street parking facilities, adequacy of public transportation services, etc. This method is usually only used in the design stage of a survey to obtain a cross-section of opinion. A slight refinement of the convenience sample is the *judgement* sample in which the interviewer deliberately sets out to pick out a representative cross-section of opinion. For example, one would anticipate somewhat different attitudes to banning cars from city centres from non-car owners, car owners who use them for pleasure purposes and car owners who use them for business. Accordingly, one would seek opinions from each of these categories.

Although both the foregoing methods provide a useful insight into opinions, attitudes and behaviour, one would be hesitant to extrapolate from such a survey. Under certain circumstances, however, one would be prepared to make market projections from the third type of non-probability sample – the *quota* sample. Quota sampling recognises that certain characteristics in which the researcher is interested are distributed through the population in a particular way and so draws a sample in which quotas are set that reflect this distribution. For example, in the case of our electrical component for a car, we might set our quotas so as to reflect past purchase patterns for a similar item and poll all the car manufacturers, most major retailers such as Halfords, a fair number of the major garage chains and car distributorships, and a very small proportion of all the independent garages that install and sell spare parts. Due to problems of bias arising from non-response in probability based samples it is quite possible that a well-designed and executed quota sample will yield equivalent if not better results.

It is clear that selection of a sample is a matter requiring both skill and judgement. The same attributes are equally necessary in selecting the method for establishing contact with respondents.

FIELD SURVEY METHODS

Once a firm has identified the nature of the information required (usually the points unanswered by desk research), and the identity of members of the population which can supply this information, it must be decided who it will approach (sample design) and how it will approach them.

Basically, there are three main methods of administering a questionnaire, by *post, email, telephone* and *personal interview*. Each method has its advantages and disadvantages, and these we consider briefly below.

The major advantage of the mail questionnaire is its ability to reach named individuals, household or business establishments anywhere in the country at very low cost. (Cost depends on the length of the questionnaire, number of follow-ups, etc., but normally is in the range of £2–£5 per completed interview.) Other advantages are that mail questionnaires can convey complex information for evaluation using pictures, diagrams, etc.; this gives the respondents time to reflect before answering, i.e. the respondent is not 'under pressure' when a 'don't know' might be given to difficult questions, and they are not subject to interviewer bias, i.e. the respondent is not influenced or led by the interviewer. However, set against these are a number of corresponding disadvantages. In the final analysis the relevant cost criterion is, 'How much per usable response?' Obviously if each questionnaire costs £2 to administer and the response rate is 10%, then the true cost is £20. Unfortunately, low response rates are

typical of mail surveys and 20%–30% would be considered good. Naturally, there are ways of increasing response rates, but these usually cost money and require simplification of the questionnaire itself to the point where its information yield is very small. If, therefore, only a limited proportion respond we must be immediately sensitive to the fact that perhaps people who answer mail questionnaires are different from those who do not – in other words the possibility of bias is very high and steps must be taken to check on reasons for non-response. In the absence of an interviewer to prompt, explain and generally maintain interest, questionnaires must be short and unambiguous – their value is correspondingly reduced.[2]

An alternative to the mail questionnaire that has been shown to achieve very high response rates at a reasonable cost is the 'drop and collect' survey. Using this method, an 'interviewer' physically delivers a structured questionnaire to intended respondents and asks them to complete it by a given date when the interviewer will call back.

Some of these difficulties may be overcome by using the telephone when the interviewer can interact with the respondent while, at the same time, executing interviews quickly and at low cost. Telephone interviewing is especially useful in the industrial market and increasingly so in consumer surveys where possession of a telephone is now estimated at over 90% of all households. Widespread ownership of mobile phones has also increased the use of telephone interviewing of individuals. Like postal questionnaires, telephone interviews are best kept short and explicit. Perhaps their greatest ability is a back-up to postal or personal interviews when the telephone may be used to locate respondents, to check-up on non-respondents and validate completed interviews. That said, the linking of telephones with computer databases through the use of computer-aided telephone interviewing (CATI) has become increasingly popular in recent years.

It is largely because of the deficiencies of postal and telephone surveys that researchers depend heavily upon personal, face-to-face interviews. In general, such interviews may be structured, semi-structured or open-ended. *Open-ended interviews* (also known as *unstructured* and/or *non-directive interviews*) fall into two broad categories. Superficially, both appear to be loose discussions about a theme, which is generally true in the exploratory stage of a research problem when one is seeking to define the scope and parameters of the problem. In these circumstances, both interviewer and respondent are unsure what the discussions will generate, which is rather different from the open-ended interview where interviewers are familiar with the ground they wish to cover with respondents, but are sufficiently skilful to do this in an apparently spontaneous manner, using one set of responses as a lead into the next series of questions. Open-ended discussions, particularly with a group of people (focus groups), are very helpful as both a source of ideas and for concept testing. As an interviewing technique, it is dependent upon the skill of the interviewer but, when executed properly, is usually the most fruitful due to the freedom given the interviewer to interact with the respondent.

At the other extreme from the open-ended interview is the *totally structured questionnaire* in which all the questions are set in advance. Not only is the content of the questions predetermined, so also is the precise wording and sequence of the questions. The interviewer is allowed no discretion in executing such an interview. As a result of this standardisation, structured questionnaires should elicit directly comparable data and be largely free of the bias which interviewers may create in less formal interviewing situations. These features make the structured questionnaire a virtual must in consumer research where very large samples are necessary, and less skilled interviewers have to be used because of the number of interviews involved.

However, because of its standardisation, the structured questionnaire lacks the flexibility to cope with many of the problems which arise in opinion research, e.g. defining what is meant where the form of words used is ambiguous or not understood, probing the reasons for a given response, etc. Accordingly, where the subject is complex, the numbers to be interviewed are not excessive, and trained interviewers are available, many researchers prefer the *semi-structured questionnaire*. These, too, vary in terms of the degree of standardisation followed from a set sequence of open-ended questions where the respondent's answers are noted verbatim and probed when necessary, to a mere aide-memoire or checklist of points to be covered with no restrictions as to wording or sequence.

Clearly, selection of a sample design and execution of a survey are matters demanding considerable skill. With the exception of the very largest organisations, few companies possess these skills 'in house' and, even where they do, they are likely to use the services of a specialised marketing research agency to supplement their own resources. The benefits of using an agency are considerable and include access to:

1. Specialist knowledge of methodology and techniques
2. Specialist skills, e.g. interviewers, psychologists
3. Specialist facilities, e.g. laboratories for product testing
4. An objective and fresh approach to one's problems
5. Experience in related, or even the same product area.

A further benefit of using an agency is that many of them produce regular reports on a syndicated or subscription basis. Much of this data is collected from panels of respondents (e.g. housewives, doctors, retail stores) who keep diaries of their purchase/sales activities and so allow the researcher to track buying and selling behaviour on a continuous basis.

However, if a firm is to derive the maximum benefit from the skills and resources available in a marketing research organisation then it is essential that it be able to specify its needs clearly and that it will be willing to take the agency into its full confidence. Thus, even in the firm without marketing research personnel of any kind it is important that an executive be nominated to liaise with the agency. It will be helpful, therefore, if we summarise the basic types of information which the company may need in order to decide whether a market is worth exploiting and as a basis for developing a research strategy.

MARKET ASSESSMENT, RESEARCH CHECKLIST

1. What are the possible uses for the proposed product?

The intent is to identify who might use the product, how, in what circumstances and under what conditions as a basis for specifying different end-use markets or market segments.

2. What are the salient characteristics of each of the markets/segments?

(i) *Size*
- Total volume $\begin{cases} \text{Domestic} \\ \text{Foreign} \end{cases}$

- Total value $\begin{cases} \text{Domestic} \\ \text{Foreign} \end{cases}$

- Volume and value of subdivisions within the market
  - by type of user
  - by size of user
  - by location
  - by preferred product characteristics (size, price, quality, grade)
- Size of markets for close substitutes
- Trends in each of the above last year, last five years

(ii) *Structure*   Number of suppliers
- Number of consumers/users
- Concentration ratios
- Changes in user and/or supplier industries likely to affect competitive structure

(iii) *Demand*
- Elastic or inelastic in terms of
  - price
  - quality
  - near substitutes
- Seasonality
- Cyclical characteristics
- By category of user
- Durability, that is, what is lifecycle of typical product?
- Trends in the above

(iv) *Competition*
- The nature of competition is implicit in many of the above factors, nonetheless an explicit statement should be made in terms of the basic policies followed by the major competitors in each market covering
  - price
  - packaging
  - promotion
  - distribution
  - selling
  - financing
  - service
  - reciprocity

(v) *Buying practices*
- Individual or group responsibility
- Frequency of purchase
- Size of purchase
- Inventory practices
- Criteria used (cf. demand conditioning factors)
- Conditions imposed – e.g. delivery, quality etc.

The above points serve only as an indication of the broad areas to be documented and analysed. For a more explicit and much lengthier checklist the reader is referred to Appendix A in Aubrey Wilson's book (1993). However, in the final analysis, and as indicated in the introduction to this chapter, the firm's decision ultimately depends upon its interpretation of the information at its disposal which is the subject of the next section.

DATA REDUCTION AND ANALYSIS

With the advent of the computer, the old complaint of 'insufficient information' has become less common and in some instances has been replaced by criticisms of 'too much information' – usually from overburdened executives whose desks are groaning under huge piles of computer printout. As with so many things, it is not the quantity of information which is so important as the quality, and in this section we review some of the techniques and methods that enable one both to reduce data into a useful and meaningful input to a decision, as well as to determine the value or importance to be attached to the data themselves.

In preceding sections, we have discussed the collection of data from both secondary or published sources and direct from respondents by means of some type of survey (primary research). In the case of secondary data, it was noted that such information may not have been collected for precisely the purpose with which the inquirer is concerned or that there may be uncertainty about the actual methods used which casts doubt on its accuracy, validity etc. Further, it is unlikely that the data will be published in a format that corresponds with the researcher's needs. While these problems should be much less in the case of primary data, on the grounds that they have been collected for a specific purpose, there still exist problems in arranging the raw data in a style suited to the needs of the decision-taker. Problems such as these are a subject in their own right and numerous books are available that deal with them. For readers wishing to explore the topic in more detail, there is a short bibliography at the end of the chapter, but for our immediate purposes we can do no better than quote from Green and Tull's (1966) standard work on marketing research.

The overall process of analysing sample data and drawing inferences from it can be considered as involving a number of separate and sequential steps:

1. *Ordering the data into appropriate categories* – organising the data into forms which give it meaning within the context of the problem at hand and the initial hypotheses to be examined.
2. *Summarising the categorised data* – using summarising measures to provide economy of description and so to facilitate understanding and manipulation of the data.
3. *Formulating additional working hypotheses* – arriving at tentative explanations of behaviour or relationships among variables that were not originally considered in the problem statement.
4. *Inferring whether meaningful differences exist among categories* – drawing inferences concerning whether observed differences among categories are the results of chance variation due to sampling process or reflect actual differences in the population being studied.
5. *Inferring relationships among variables* – arriving at conclusions concerning the nature and existence of underlying relationships among the variables involved.

Ideally, one establishes categories prior to data collection but this is not always possible, particularly when one is undertaking exploratory research using depth interviews, open-ended questions, projective techniques etc. However, whether one establishes categories ante or post hoc, it is generally agreed that they must satisfy four conditions:

1. Data within categories must be sufficiently similar as to be considered homogeneous.
2. Data between categories must be sufficiently different to merit a distinction being drawn between the categories.
3. Each category should be based upon only one relevant criterion.
4. The categories defined should be mutually exclusive and collectively exhaustive.

For example, when using age as a basis for classification one might well use the following categories:

- 0–4
- 5–15
- 16–24
- 25–45
- 46–64
- 65 and over.

These divisions are purely arbitrary but reflect the following descriptive labels (again largely arbitrary):

- Pre-school
- School age
- Young adult
- Family life
- Empty nest
- Senior citizen.

Categories such as these may be predetermined and there is a large number of such divisions that have become accepted through custom and practice, thus ensuring that data collected at different times can be easily compared without having to reorganise the basic classificatory system, e.g. social class groupings. On the other hand, when conducting primary research, one may prefer not to anticipate patterns in the data and so only establish categories when these appear of their own accord. Indeed the advent of the computer, and the ability to manipulate very large and complex databases, has led to a rather promiscuous approach to research in which everything is collected without prior justification, and order is imposed through processes such as factor analysis. This is not to decry the power of such techniques, but to advocate the perhaps old-fashioned scientific method which presumes that one is pursuing research with a particular purpose in mind and so has some working hypotheses against which to test one's observations.

The statement of categories permits one to organise the data in tabular form and relate different factors to each other through the process of cross-tabulation, e.g. using our age categories we could examine, say, the consumption of milk to determine if there is any pattern or apparent association between age and milk consumption. It also becomes possible to develop so-called summary statistics which provide a concise statement of the distribution of data within and between the different categories. Summary or descriptive statistics fall into two main groups – measures of central tendency and measures of dispersion. Measures of central tendency comprise the arithmetic mean, the median and the mode, while the measures of dispersion include the range, standard deviation, variance and coefficient of variation, definitions and descriptions of which are to be found in any statistics textbook.

The third step in formal analysis is the development of additional hypotheses – 'additional' because, as we argued earlier, research is intended to provide answers to questions (i.e. hypotheses) suggested by previously observed data. Clearly, if we had a sufficiently high prior probability concerning a particular hypothesis then the expected value of further information would probably be so low that it would preclude further research. Thus, most marketing research is 'designed to reduce areas of uncertainty surrounding business decisions' and it would be surprising if new information did not suggest new questions and solutions.

The final step in analysis is to establish whether any observed differences are real or are the result of chance, and, if real, draw conclusions concerning the relationship between the variables involved. Hypothesis testing traditionally involves four elements (see Tull and Albaum, 1973):

1. A probability distribution of the sample statistic to be tested
2. A null and alternate hypothesis which contains predictions of the population value against which the sample statistic is to be tested
3. A test statistic
4. A rejection region in the probability distribution.

Under this practice there is a tendency to prefer inaction to action by only rejecting the null hypothesis (i.e. no difference exists) given very high levels of certainty or significance (often as high as 0.95). But, in the managerial sciences in general and marketing in the particular, it is rare to find such high levels of certainty, and one must be prepared to reduce one's criterion. (Technically, one should consider Type II errors – the probability of rejecting a hypothesis when it is true in reality – more important than Type I errors, which is the opposite of the approach favoured by basic researchers – see Tull and Albaum, 1973, pp. 175–82 for a full discussion.)

Analysis of data is a subject in its own right, and dealt with at length in many texts on quantitative methods. A review of methods used in analysing marketing data is to be found in Green and Tull (1978, Chapter 9) and Tull and Albaum (1973, Chapter 9 particularly) and readers should refer to these for further information.

BAYESIAN ANALYSIS

INTRODUCTION

It will often happen that, even if it is possible to collect the complete facts on a situation, the cost of so doing would be so prohibitive that absolute certainty is not worthwhile, and the decision-maker will accept the risk involved in acting on only some of the facts. However, there are many situations in which even if the decision-maker so wished he would be unable to collect perfect information and so would be left with an irreducible element of uncertainty concerning the decision to be taken. Thus the decision-maker can be in one of three states.

1. *Certainty* – he has perfect information and

knows the outcome of a given combination of events with the result that he can predict these precisely – e.g. an eclipse of the sun, high water at Tower Bridge in a month's time, the behaviour of falling objects etc.

2. *Risk* – the decision-maker has extensive past experience (personal or vicarious) of similar events to the extent that he can predict the general outcome but not the specific result of any given event. For example, O level passes used to be based on the expectation that students in the top 40% of the ability range would be able to gain them. It follows that if I predict any given child will fail, I have a 60% chance of being right.

3. *Uncertainty* – as with risk there are several possible outcomes, but in this case one has little or no prior experience and so cannot assign an objective probability to the possible outcomes.

Of course an inability to assign an objective probability does not prevent us from developing subjective expectations as to the likelihood of a given event, and from acting upon our judgement. In the real world of decision-making this is normal everyday practice, but ordinary mortals should not be deluded into thinking it is as simple as it looks. If ever there were a case of natural selection then judgemental decision-making is it – those who are able to do it (intuitively or otherwise) succeed and those who can't fail and are not usually allowed to repeat the mistake – hence Napoleon's quest for 'lucky' generals. Fortunately, we can learn from those who appear to have an innate ability, and by following a similar approach learn to combine facts and judgement to arrive at a decision which is consistent with our overall attitude to risk. In essence, the key to successful decision-making would seem to lie in an ability to specify the alternatives, the likelihood of their occurrence, and the consequences associated with each. In the case of important decisions it is likely that we will seek to obtain evidence to test the validity of our expectations – in other words we will undertake marketing research – and then seek to synthesise the two pieces of information into a single composite 'decision'. To assist managers to improve their decision-making ability, a new school of decision theorists has developed in the past 40 years or so who, following the lead of Raiffa and Schlaifer at the

Harvard Business School in emphasising the role of probability in decision-making, have developed the concept of decision 'trees' and have resurrected Bayes' theorem as a means of combining prior estimates with new information to generate a set of revised or posterior probabilities. It is the particular power of this latter technique which has led to the generic term 'Bayesian' being applied to probabilistic approaches to problem-solving.

PROBLEM SPECIFICATION

It is often claimed that problem definition constitutes 90% of the difficulty in problem-solving. Experience shows this often to be the case in the sense that once decision-makers have clearly articulated their objectives it becomes possible to assess the factors which will hinder or encourage their achievement, and so determine the possible courses of action open to them. Depending upon the decision-maker's confidence in their ability to predict the likely outcome of each of the alternatives, they will either make their decision or defer it pending the acquisition of further information, up to the point where the marginal cost of further information is equal to its perceived value. This sequence of events is illustrated in Figure 6.4 from Enis and Broome (1973).

From Figure 6.4 it is clear that if the decision-maker is satisfied with their prior analysis then they will automatically select the alternative which appears optimal to them and implement this decision. But, if there is an element of doubt about the outcome, they may well reflect upon the advisability of spending resources (time and money) in improving the information available to them – in Bayesian terminology this is called preposterior analysis. If the likely cost exceeds the expected value, then the decision will be taken; but if it is thought the expected value exceeds the cost, then more information will be collected and analysed through a posterior analysis. The procedure will then recycle and a decision be made or deferred pending more data acquisition. Enis and Broome (1973) summarise this Bayesian approach as consisting of five elements, namely:

1. The decision-maker is involved in a situation in which there are at least two alternative ways of

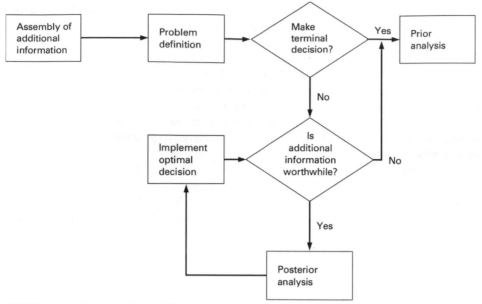

FIGURE 6.4 A Bayesian view of the decision process

SOURCE: Enis, B. M. and Broome, C. L. (1973) *Marketing Decisions: a Bayesian Approach.* Aylesbury: Intertext

reaching a specific objective(s), and has the power to decide among the alternatives.

2. The decision-maker is uncertain as to which decision alternative to select, because they do not know the set of environmental conditions (state of nature) which will actually prevail at the time the decision is implemented.

3. The decision-maker has some knowledge of the situation, e.g. relative payoffs of alternatives, and likelihood of occurrence of various events or states of nature which affect these payoffs.

4. The decision-maker is willing to use expected value as their decision criterion, i.e. accept the view that to optimise decision-making they will take the course of action with the highest expected value (utility).

5. The decision-maker may be able to obtain additional information (at some cost) which might change their assessment of the situation.

Thus, three concepts are central to the Bayesian methodology:

1. The identification of alternatives
2. The assignment of probabilistic expectations to the alternatives
3. The use of expected value (utility) as the decision criterion.

We shall now consider each of these concepts in turn.

THE IDENTIFICATION OF ALTERNATIVES

Diagnosing the Problem

Unless and until one has specified the possible courses of action open to the decision-maker, it is impossible to express a judgement on the likelihood of occurrence of any one of them, for the simple reason that the combined likelihood of an exhaustive set of alternatives must always add up to 1.00 where occurrence is mutually exclusive. Thus, even if one cannot specify fully all the possible alternatives, one should still be able to assign an expectation to the residual and unspecified alternatives that will express one's expectations about them vis-à-vis those of which one is aware.

In order to develop alternatives, one must first define and diagnose the nature of the problem itself. According to George P. Huber (1980) there are three tendencies that frequently interfere with adequate problem exploration:

1. The tendency to define the problem in terms of a proposed solution

2. The tendency to focus on narrow, lower order goals
3. The tendency to diagnose the problem in terms of its symptoms.

The first tendency is a widespread and pervasive phenomenon, which has sometimes been characterised as 'a solution searching for a problem'. The more 'expert' a person is, the greater the likelihood that they will fall victim of this fallacy and tend to recast or interpret the facts in terms of their own selective perception. Thus all problems become seen as a manifestation of the problem-solver's own expertise, and it is no accident that as top managers emerge from given disciplines and functions, they tend to view all the problems they encounter from that perspective and classify them as 'finance', 'marketing' or 'production' problems. (This tendency becomes even more dangerous when the decision-maker seeks to avoid 'guilt by association' and shifts the onus to another functional area solely to divert attention from their own possible culpability.) The greatest danger of this approach is that it provides a focus and so excludes consideration of other possibilities.

The second tendency is also commonplace among managers who seek to reduce problems to a comfortable order of magnitude which falls well within their existing experience and competence. Such managers will be happy with fine tuning the marketing mix, but will shy away from a radical programme of innovation and new product development which will lead them into new and unfamiliar markets.

The third tendency of diagnosing problems in terms of their symptoms is also familiar, but much less dangerous than the two previous diversions from the search for alternatives. Indeed in many circumstances, good diagnosis must be a sequential process in which you relate the symptoms to the most likely cause and prescribe accordingly. Most headaches are temporary and acute phenomena that may rise from any of a large number of causes which are equally temporary and acute. The need is to alleviate the symptoms and monitor their progression. If after 24 hours all is well, and the symptoms do not return, we will discount the cause as unimportant. But, if the symptoms persist, we will probe more deeply and try other remedies until, by a process of trial and error, we

discover the true cause. Such a procedure exemplifies well the concept of the expected value of information for, in the absence of highly distinctive and unmistakable symptoms, one does not admit to hospital for a brain scan every person who complains of a headache.

Huber argues that these tendencies are part of a defensive mechanism designed to reduce tension among problem-solvers by enabling them to move on to steps that help to alleviate the discomfort which problem recognition creates. Conversely, generating alternatives may only exacerbate the problem, and suggesting that a man with a headache may have a brain tumour is unlikely to be seen as a helpful suggestion. Clearly, a narrow path has to be trodden and experience suggests that the development of decision trees has much to commend it in that the creation of alternatives occurs sequentially in an ordered manner which is psychologically less stressful than less structured, open-ended listing and ordering techniques such as brainstorming.

DEVELOPING A DECISION TREE

One of the clearest and earliest explanations of the use of decision trees in problem-solving is to be found in John F. Magee's article (1964). This article has seldom been equalled and never bettered and provides the basis of this section.

Magee starts with a simple example to illustrate the salient characteristics of the decision-tree approach by posing the problem of what to do on an overcast Saturday afternoon when 75 people are coming round for cocktails. This he describes as follows:

> You and your wife feel it is time you returned some hospitality by holding a party. You have a pleasant garden and your house is not too large; so if the weather permits, you would like to set up the refreshments in the garden and have the party there. It would be more pleasant, and your guests would be more comfortable. On the other hand, if you set up the party for the garden and after all the guests are assembled it begins to rain, the refreshments will be ruined, your guests will be damp and you will heartily wish you had decided to have the party in the house ... What should you do? This particular

decision can be represented in the form of a 'pay-off' table:

Events and results

Choices	Rain	No rain
Outdoors	Disaster	Real comfort
Indoors	Mild discomfort, but happy	Mild discomfort, but regrets

In turn the information in the pay-off table can be represented pictorially by means of a decision tree (see Figure 6.5).

As Magee comments:

The tree is made up of a series of nodes and branches. At the first node on the left, the host has the choice of having the party inside or outside. Each branch represents an alternative course of action or decision. At the end of each branch or alternative course is another node representing a chance event – whether or not it will rain. Each subsequent alternative course to the right represents an alternative outcome of this chance event. Associated with each complete alternative course through the tree is a payoff, shown at the end of the rightmost or terminal branch of the course.

From this description, it is clear that a decision tree will always combine action choices with different possible events or outcomes that are subject to

some degree or other to chance (distinguished by different symbols for emphasis).

In the case of the relatively simple decision discussed so far, one probably needs neither a pay-off table nor a decision tree to help one come to a decision. But, given more complex decisions where several alternatives are available, it is easy to understand how the content of a pay-off table could confuse rather than illuminate, while a decision tree would help disaggregate the problem in a clear and meaningful way. Magee presents such a tree when he analyses the familiar marketing problem of whether or not to invest in product development. Although he does not pursue the analysis of this tree further in his article, its relevance to marketing is such that it is used as the basis for the discussion which follows.

The inevitability of change and the pressures that it creates for a continuing process of new product development have already been touched on in looking at the nature of competition, and are central to the theme of Chapter 15 which is concerned with product policy. Faced with the decision of whether or not to commit funds to the improvement or replacement of an existing product in order to maintain or improve market share, the marketing manager may well come up with a decision tree such as that in Figure 6.6. Clearly, this tree does not cover all possible eventualities. For example, if the development fails you may decide

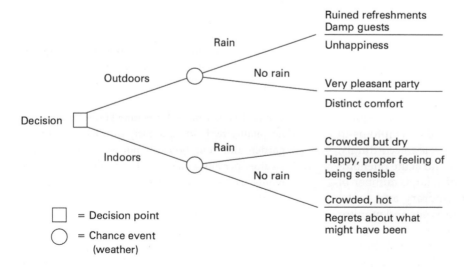

FIGURE 6.5 An exercise in decision-making, showing the possible results of a chance event

SOURCE: Magee, J. F. (1964) Decision trees for decision making, *Harvard Business Review* (July–August)

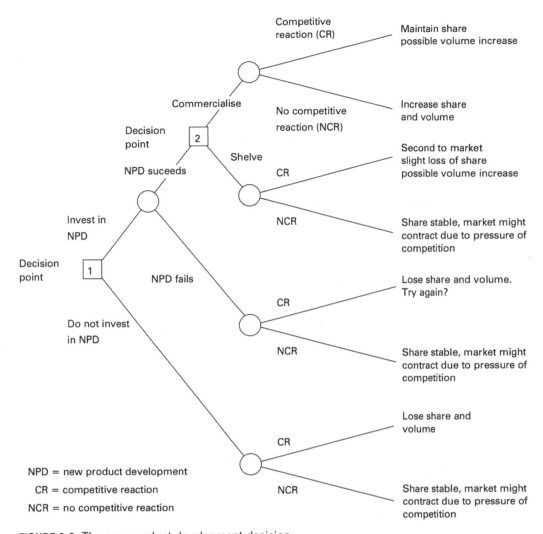

FIGURE 6.6 The new product development decision

that you cannot wait and see what your competitor does and so will immediately recycle to the initial decision point and commit additional funds to further development. However, it is sufficient to illustrate the application of the technique.

As it stands our decision tree has already served a useful purpose in making clear the alternatives open – it now remains to show how one can use the decision-maker's knowledge and expectations to reach a decision.

PROBABILITY

Earlier in the chapter we referred explicitly to the distinction between 'certainty', 'risk' and 'uncer-

tainty' and since then have used terms such as 'expectations', 'likelihood' and 'outcomes' in a rather loose way. In order to make our decision tree operational, and understand the application of Bayes' theorem, it is necessary now to review briefly the concept of probability.

In simple terms, probability reflects the likelihood of an event expressed on a scale which runs from certain to impossible to which, by convention, have been assigned the values 1.0 and 0.0 respectively. Intermediate points are assigned values that reflect the frequency with which they are expected to occur, and the critical issue is the basis upon which the expectation is founded. In his book Howard Thomas (1972) identifies three methods of assessing probability with which the manager should be familiar – a priori, relative frequency and subjective.

An *a priori probability* expresses the frequency with which an event may occur in terms of the total number of possible outcomes, so that the a priori probability of a head in coin tossing is ½ or 0.5; of a six on a single throw of a dice ⅙ or 0.166; of the ace of spades on a single draw from a pack of cards ¹⁄₅₂ or 0.019 and so on. However, as Thomas observes, 'This concept of probability, based on equally likely outcomes, has little application as a means of measuring probability other than in games of chance.'

The *relative frequency* method of assigning probabilities is much more useful and is the technique used when defining risk in the sense in which we defined it earlier. As the term suggests, probabilities of this kind are based upon knowledge concerning the frequency with which an event has occurred in the past, thus enabling one to express a view as to the likelihood of its reoccurrence in the future. This concept is central to the whole theory of sampling, which is a procedure used extensively in marketing research and reviewed briefly in an earlier section.

However, the use of relative frequencies depends upon the availability of objective information concerning previous occurrences of events identical to the one which we are trying to predict. But, as we saw when defining uncertainty, the dynamic and interactive nature of most marketing activities tends to militate against identical occurrences, and it is this which makes prediction of marketing events so difficult. For this reason we have to depend upon the skill and experience of the decision-maker, and use their *subjective* expectation of the occurrence of an event as the basis for an actual decision.

From Figure 6.4, illustrating the Bayesian view of the decision process and our new product development decision tree, it is clear that most decisions are not just simple 'either or' choices, but involve multiple, mutually exclusive but interdependent alternatives. It follows that we need some rules to explain how probabilities will interact given a compound decision of the kind most likely to be encountered in marketing. Statements of the rules of probability are to be found in most statistics textbooks and also in books on managerial decision-making (see, for example, Thomas,

1972) and are beyond the scope of this chapter. However, analysis of our decision tree will throw some light on the rules and demonstrate that in very simple terms probabilities may be added or multiplied, but their sum must always be unity. But, before we can solve our decision problem, we must first agree upon the criterion to be used, and show how one's expectations can be converted into probabilistic statements.

THE DECISION CRITERION

Although a number of possible decision criteria are available, theorists are unanimous in recommending that one should seek to 'maximise the expected utility' (MEU) flowing from a decision. Utility is usually thought of as an objective, economic concept, but, in reality, it is subjective and relative. In cases where decision-makers are acting solely on their own behalf, the distinction between objective and subjective is irrelevant, but when one is acting on behalf of an organisation, or in conjunction with a number of other decision-makers, it is important that all of them handle risk in a similar way.

One of the best and earliest discussions of the application of utility theory in decision-making was that contained in the *Harvard Business Review* by Ralph O. Swalm (1984). In this article Swalm focuses clearly on the issue of the decision criterion in his opening paragraphs:

> Suppose that you were lucky enough to be offered the following alternatives:
>
> (1) Accept the payment of a tax free gift of $1 million.
> (2) Toss a fair coin. If heads come up, you get nothing; if tails come up you get a tax free gift of $3 million.
>
> Which would you choose? Would it be the certain $1 million, or the 50–50 chance of $3 million or nothing.

When confronted with this choice, most people say they would choose the certain $1 million, even though the gamble has what is called an 'expected value' of $1.5 million. (The term 'expected value', often used in quantitative analysis, is the product of the hoped for gain and the probability of winning it $3,000,000 × 0.5 in this case.)

Swalm continues to speculate that most people

would probably continue to take the certain $1 million even if the odds were increased to $5 million if tails came up. Clearly, this is not the sort of objective behaviour you would expect of businessmen – or is it? According to two of the founding fathers of decision analysis, John von Neumann and Oskar Morgenstern, it is, and is defined by them as cardinal utility theory. Swalm comments: 'oversimplifying a bit, this concept proposes that each individual attempts to optimise the expected value of something which is defined as utility, and that for each individual a relationship between utility and dollars can be found.'

The remainder of Swalm's paper is concerned with a further explanation of cardinal utility theory, and the doubt which it casts on 'the classical notion of the American businessman as a risk taker and on the validity of many control systems set up to monitor manager behaviour'. Following a description of a methodology for developing an individual's utility function, Swalm reports the results of an experiment that illustrates vividly the wide variation in attitudes to risk which may be found among executives in the same corporation. Because of these discrepancies, Swalm (and numerous others since him) advocates the use of cardinal utility theory as a means of making explicit different decision-makers' attitude to risk, thereby providing a basis for reconciling such differences and encouraging a more objective and realistic attitude to risk.

Despite these exhortations, it is clear that much still remains to be done. Writing in 1980, Bob Hayes and Bill Abernathy attributed the lacklustre performance of the US economy since the Second World War to the short-term risk-avoiding tactics of most American managers. In that the same condition is to be found in most of the advanced industrial countries, it is small wonder that Hayes and Abernathy's diagnosis has received widespread support. To a large degree 'milking the investment' is encouraged by an emphasis upon short-term planning horizons and the accounting mentality which has come to afflict so much of professional management. If marketers are to avoid falling into the same trap, they must take a long-term view of success, and be prepared to adjust their own risk behaviour to bring it in line with the more objective approach that takes into account the expected value of alternative courses

of action. To this end we recommend the use of expected value as its decision criterion. (Because expected value is usually expressed in terms of money, it is usual to use the term EMV or 'expected monetary value').

ANALYSING THE DECISION TREE

We are now in a position to add some rational data to our new product development decision tree and describe the process known as 'rollback' to indicate what decision should be taken. In Figure 6.7 we have added the costs of new product development, our best expectations about likely events and the ultimate financial consequences to us of each end-position, as described earlier and shown in Figure 6.6. Because we are a successful firm, and good at NPD, we assess the likelihood of success as 0.8. However, past experience suggests that markets often change during the course of NPD, so we consider that having invested £500,000 in development, there is a 0.2 chance we will put our innovation 'on the shelf', leaving a 0.8 probability that we will commercialise it.

Given that we do launch our new product, we believe strongly (0.8) that our competitors will try to launch a 'me-too' product so that the net benefit would be approximately £1 million. On the other hand, if they do not, the rewards will be very considerable indeed (£5 million). Assuming that we have shelved a product because we think the time for a launch is unpropitious, we have a fairly high expectation (0.7) that no one else will do so, and it seems reasonable that, because the signs are unpropitious and there is no aggressive marketing action, the overall market will contract and our sales with it. Conversely, if we are mistaken and a competitor livens up the market with a new product launch, we will have ours ready in the wings and will be able to gain some benefit from the revitalisation of consumer interest.

Should we fail in developing our new product, then it could be that a competitor could take advantage of the opportunity which would have led us to launch a new product if we had one. We estimate this as a 50–50 chance, and the same applies if we had not attempted to develop a new product ourself in the first place although, in the latter case, we would have saved the £500,000 on

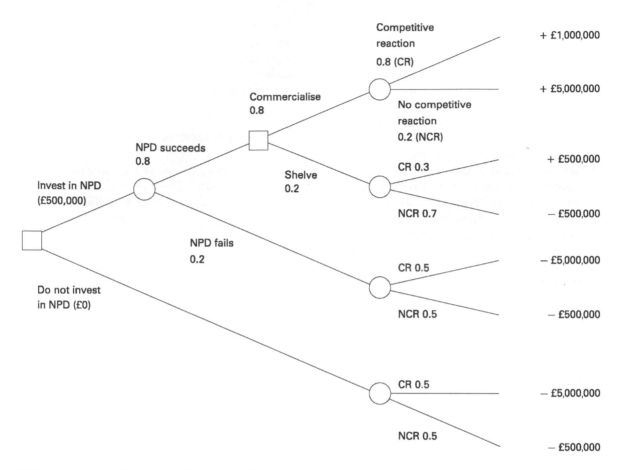

FIGURE 6.7 Expected outcomes for new product development

NPD. So what should we do? Figure 6.8 makes it quite clear that we must go ahead with new product development. If we do not, the expected outcome is a loss to us of £2,750,000, whereas if we go ahead the exercise will yield an expected value of £70,000 net of £500,000 development costs. These figures are arrived at by the simple process of computing the likelihood of any given outcome by multiplying the probabilities associated with it and relating them to the expected value of that outcome. We then 'roll back' the tree from the end-points to the decision-point, enabling us to assign a value to the basic choice of developing or not developing a new product in the first place.

This analysis also highlights the application of the concept of the expected value of information, for at the point where we have succeeded in developing a new product, we can decide whether to alter our original 80–20, produce or shelve decision, and whether or not it would be worth spending money on market research to firm up our expectations.

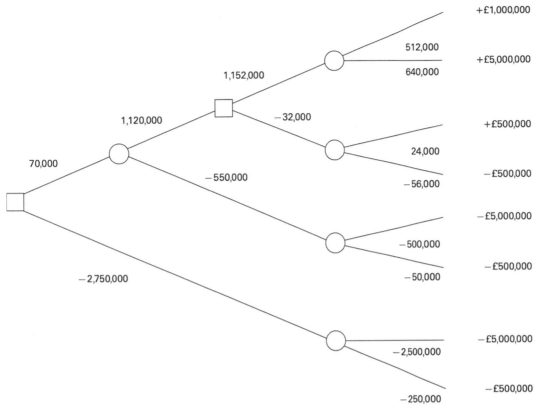

FIGURE 6.8 Decision for roll-back

The Bayesian approach to decision-making has widespread application to the type of problems which predominate in marketing, which Philip Kotler has described as having to be made 'in the context of insufficient information about processes that are dynamic, non-linear, lagged, stochastic, interactive, and downright difficult'. The treatment in this chapter can do no more than sketch in some of the salient features of the technique and the procedures associated with it, but the reader is strongly recommended to consult at least some of the sources cited.

In addition we have also attempted to provide an overview of the sources of data available to the manager (primary and secondary), and summarised the major methods of data collection – observation, experimentation and sample survey. The discussion of sample survey methodology

suggested that in most cases only the largest and most sophisticated companies are likely to have a marketing research function of their own, so that most work of this kind will be subcontracted to a specialist agency. (This is also true of large companies in the case of large-scale field surveys.) However, to ensure the maximum benefit from such contracted-out research it is important that the organisation should have a clear view of its research needs, and appoint someone to liaise directly with the market research agency.

Some consideration was also given to the problems of too much information and the means of classifying and categorising this in order to reduce it to meaningful and usable proportions. From this review it became clear that, despite the apparent information overload, decision-makers are often faced with situations where objective

data are not available and they need to combine the 'facts' with their own judgement to arrive at a decision. In doing so the construction of decision trees and Bayesian methods of analysis appear to offer a useful framework. That said, there is little evidence that firms avail themselves of the technique or, indeed, make extensive use of marketing research when taking strategic decisions that have major implications for the future of their businesses. Whether this is the consequence of ignorance or overconfidence, the outcome is still the same – more new products fail than succeed, the average life span of a company is 40 years or less and one-third of the Fortune 500 disappears every 10 years. Faced with these kinds of statistics there can be little doubt that intelligent marketing depends upon marketing intelligence. In the next section we suggest how this might be done.

Recommended reading

Diamantopoulos, A. and Schlegel-milch, B. (1997) *Taking the Fear out of Data Analysis*. London: International Thomson Business Press.

Webb, J. (1995) Marketing research, in Baker, M. J. (ed.) *Mar-keting: Theory and Practice* (3rd edn). Basingstoke: Macmillan – now Palgrave Macmillan.

West, C. (1999) Marketing research, in Baker, M. J. (ed.) *Encyclopedia of Marketing*. Lon-don: International Thomson Business Press.

Wilson, A. (2002) *Marketing Research: An Integrated Approach*. Harlow: FT Prentice Hall.

REFERENCES

Aguilar, F. J. (1987) *Scanning the Business Environment*. New York: Macmillan.

Baker, M. J. (1991) *Research for Marketing*. London: Macmillan – now Palgrave Macmillan.

Baker, M. J. and Hart, S. (1989) *Marketing and Competitive Success*. London: Philip Allen.

Borden, N. H. (1975) The concept of the marketing mix, in E. J. McCarthy et al., *Readings in Basic Marketing*. Homewood, IL: Irwin, pp. 72–82.

Enis, B. M. and Broome, C. L. (1973) *Marketing Decisions: A Bayesian Approach*. Aylesbury: Intertext.

Gordon, W. and Langmaid, R. (1988) *Qualitative Market Research: A Practitioner's and Buyer's Guide*. Aldershot: Gower.

Green, P. E. and Tull, D. S. (1966) *Research for Marketing Decisions*. Englewood Cliffs, NJ: Prentice Hall.

Green, P. E. and Tull, D. S. (1978) *Research for Marketing Decisions*, (4th edn). Englewood Cliffs, NJ: Prentice Hall.

Halfpenny, P. (1979) The analysis of qualitative data, *Sociological Review*, **27**(4)

Hayes, R. and Abernathy, W. (1980) Managing our way to economic decline, *Harvard Business Review* (July–August).

Hooley, G. J., Lynch, J. E. and West, C. J. (1984) *Marketing in the UK: A Survey of Current Practices and Performance*. The Institute of Marketing.

Huber, G. P. (1980) *Managerial Decision Making*. Glenview, IL: Scott, Foresman.

Johansson, J. K. and Nonaka, I. (1987) Market research the Japanese way, *Harvard Business Review* (May–June).

Magee, J. F. (1964) Decision trees for decision making, *Harvard Business Review* (July–August).

Moutinho, L. and Meidan, A. (2003) in Baker, M. J. (ed.) *The Marketing Book*. Oxford: Butterworth Heinemann.

National Industrial Conference Board (1964) *Why products fail*, Conference Board Record (October).

Sampson, P. (1967) Commonsense in qualitative research, *Commentary* **9**(1).

Swalm, R. O. (1984) Utility theory – insights into risk taking, *Harvard Business Review* (November–December).

Thomas, H. (1972) *Decision Theory and the Manager*. London: Pitman.

Tull, D. S. and Albaum, F. S. (1973) *Survey Research*. Aylesbury: Intertext.

Wilson, A. (1993) *The Industrial Marketing Researcher's Check List*. London: Department of Trade and Industry.

NOTES

1 Preliminary results from the Government Census of Population, Distribution, and so on normally take one or two years to prepare, the full report takes three or more years.

2 Similar issues exist with the use of the internet for data collection.

Part 2

THE MARKETING
APPRECIATION

Macro-environmental analysis[1]

*The only thing we know about the future is that it will
be different.*

PETER DRUCKER

After reading Chapter 7 you will be able to:

✔ Define and describe the impact of environmental forces on the firm's strategy.

✔ Review and describe the main environmental factors – demographic, economic, social, technological and political – and their influence upon strategic planning.

✔ Distinguish the underlying cyclical pattern of economic activity and its implications for strategic planning.

✔ Appreciate the impact of environmental change upon strategic marketing planning.

✔ Understand the need for and limitations of forecasting.

INTRODUCTION

In an article published in the Strategic Planning Society's Newsletter (*News*, January 1995) Raymond W. Smith, chairman and CEO of Bell Atlantic Corporation, reflected on the change which had occurred since he joined the Bell system in the 1960s.

> When I joined the Bell system in the 1960s, for example, every new manager learned that monopolies were forever; that employment was for life; that telephones were black.

On becoming independent from AT&T in 1985, business strategy and culture change have been central to Bell Atlantic's development.

> By the late 1980s, the competition we predicted would develop began to appear, challenging some of our traditional revenue streams. It also became clear that digital technology was causing a convergence of markets and industries – a phenomenon that ultimately would completely transform our business.
>
> 'Convergence' refers to the fact that advances in fibre optics, microprocessors and operating systems have expanded capacity, lowered processing costs and permitted the manipulation of huge amounts of data – meaning that transport systems could handle simultaneous transactions on a distributed basis.
>
> Convergence also means that the three principal consumer communications devices – computer, TV and telephone – are merging into one, and as they do, so too are the distinctions among once separate businesses.
>
> It is clear that before this industry transformation is through your computer will speak, your TV will listen, and your telephone will show you pictures. This convergence will transform the way we work, play and learn. We are entering an era that will put unprecedented choice, control and convenience in the hands of our customers.

Smith concluded:

> The hardest thing in management is to convince the great and powerful company that competitive advantage today doesn't mean competitive advantage tomorrow. Technology can be replicated, new products can be imitated, market share can be lost, franchises can be eroded – and all this can happen even

while management is continuing to do its job as efficiently as it has in the past. In fact, any study of world class companies operating in dynamic markets makes it clear that the only sustainable competitive advantage is the ability to innovate – which means, as one Japanese executive defines it, 'To recreate the world according to a particular vision or ideal' – and to do it faster than your competition.

A decade or more later, some of the changes predicted by Smith have come to pass, some are in process and yet others are in doubt. As we shall see, the notion of convergence has been challenged strongly but Smith's overall conclusion is as true now as when he made it – change is inevitable and firms must anticipate and adapt to it through innovation if they are to survive.

In Chapters 4 and 5 it was argued that significant benefits will accrue to the company that practises strategic marketing planning (SMP). Subsequently, a number of broad conceptual frameworks were reviewed and analysed, with particular emphasis upon the product life-cycle as a common factor underlying a continuous process of dynamic change to which the firm must respond. We also acknowledged that, in order to operationalise the concepts and approaches advocated, the firm must be able to define and measure the key factors contained in the various models, particularly market size and share, the state of competition or industry attractiveness, and the stage of the life-cycle in which product or industry is located. It is to these and related issues that we turn in this chapter.

To this end we shall look first at some of the reasons why environmental factors constitute the ultimate constraint upon the firm's strategy. Next we shall review some of the secular trends in the environment, with particular reference to the business cycle, the long wave or Kondratieff cycle and some of the factors accounting for the accelerating rate of change especially in the twentieth century. Based upon this analysis, we shall argue that the environment establishes the parameters within which firms must operate, but that ultimately their success will depend as much upon their interaction with each other as upon their interpretation of and adaptation to the general environment. Finally, we conclude the chapter with a synopsis of the main considerations to be taken into account in looking to the future influence of environmental change.

THE ENVIRONMENT AS THE ULTIMATE CONSTRAINT

Although the oil crisis of 1974 is now something of a distant memory, the reverberations of its impact are still being felt, rather like the aftershocks that follow an earthquake. Clearly, conditions are not going to return to the 1970s when most of today's most senior managers gained their first experience of management. Scientific and mechanistic approaches to management have been displaced by a concern for a more subjective and organic conceptualisation of business as a human activity, conducted by people on behalf of people. As a consequence, the shift in emphasis has moved from the factory to the marketplace, and the managerial orientation from production to marketing. Concomitant with this switch in emphasis has been a growing awareness of the accelerating rate of technological change, the finite nature of the world's resources, and the present generation's responsibility to husband these carefully for the benefit of future generations.

Taken together, all these trends demand that, if management is fulfilling its primary responsibility to ensure the survival and continued well-being of the organisation, it must carefully monitor the environment in which it carries out its business. Such monitoring and analysis are essential if the firm is to be able to anticipate change and turn it to its advantage as a marketing opportunity, rather than be surprised by it when it occurs and perceive it as a threat. This ability has certainly characterised the growth and success of firms that have prospered in the turbulent trading conditions of the past thirty years including three major recessions and a major shake-out of marginal performers everywhere. Firms which have succeeded in these difficult times possess many common factors including an adaptive and flexible managerial style, a balanced portfolio of products and a well-developed intelligence and information system designed to monitor and anticipate environmental change.

While most firms have probably always undertaken some form of environmental analysis. It is only in the past 30 years or so that attempts have been made to formalise and structure this process. In a 1983 review article, John Diffenbach identifies three distinct changes in the evolution of corporate environmental analysis. First, there was an *apprec-iation* stage stimulated by a number of books and articles, which advocated that one should look beyond short-term market conditions and consider the wider implications of the economic, technological, social and political factors which comprise the general business environment. Acceptance of this proposition leads naturally to the second phase of *analysis*, which 'involves finding reliable sources of environmental data, compiling and examining the data to discern trends, developments and key relationships. It also includes monitoring environmental developments and anticipating the future.' In turn this interest led to the publication of numerous books and articles on environmental scanning, scenarios, the Delphi technique, cross-impact and input–output analysis and sociotechnological and environmental forecasting. (Diffenbach, 1983, gives references for the more important of these works.) More recently this has given way to a preoccupation with foresight.

The third and current phase is that of *application* in which top management seeks to incorporate what are usually staff evaluations into strategies and action plans.

What then are the external environmental factors which the firm must take into account when formulating its strategy? Essentially they may be classified into five major categories:

1. Demographic
2. Social and cultural
3. Political
4. Economic
5. Technological.

An extended list comprising eight factors is given in Table 7.1.

Although it is immediately obvious that all the factors are interrelated and interdependent, and that some may be further subdivided e.g. 'Ethical' issues, for the purposes of analysis it will be useful to consider the key ones separately. Before doing so it must be stressed that, while firms may occasionally be able to influence these external factors to a limited degree, they can rarely, if ever, control them. It is in this sense that the macro-environment represents a common and ultimate constraint to all business activity. This being so, it is vital that firms develop the best possible understanding of what these macro-environmental

TABLE 7.1 A framework for environmental analysis

Cultural	Including the historical background, ideologies, values and norms of the society. Views on authority relationships, leadership patterns, interpersonal relationships, nationalism, science and technology
Technological	The level of scientific and technological advancement in society. Including the physical base (plant, equipment, facilities) and the knowledge base of technology. Degree to which the scientific and technological community is able to develop new knowledge and reapply it
Educational	The general political climate of society. The degree of concentration of political power. The nature of the political organisation (degree of decentralisation, diversity of functions etc.). The political party system
Legal	Constitutional considerations, nature of the legal system, jurisdictions of various governmental units. Specific laws concerning formation, taxation and control of organisations
Natural resources	The nature, quantity and availability of natural resources, including climatic and other conditions
Demographic	The nature of human resources available to the society; their number, distribution, age and sex. Concentration of urbanisation of population is a characteristic of industrialised societies
Sociological	Class structure and mobility. Definition of social roles. Nature of social organisation and development of social institutions
Economic	General economic framework, including the type of economic organisation – private versus public ownership; the centralisation or decentralisation of economic planning; the banking system, and fiscal policies. The level of investment in physical resources and consumption

SOURCE: Baker, M. J. (1994) adapted from F. E. Kast and J. E. Rosenweig (1974) *Organisation and Management: A Systems Approach* (2nd edn). Maidenhead: McGraw-Hill

factors are. To achieve this it is recommended that firms establish a formal environmental scanning system, the key attributes of which are summarised in Table 7.2.

TABLE 7.2 Attributes of a formal approach to environmental scanning

- Environmental trends, events and issues are regularly and systematically reviewed
- Explicit criteria have been developed that can in turn be used to evaluate the impact of environmental trends
- Scanning activities are guided by written procedures
- Responsibility for scanning activities has been clearly assigned
- Scanning reports, updates, forecasts and analyses are documented in a standardised format
- Such documentation is generated on a regular basis and disseminated to predetermined personnel according to a timetable
- The application of formal techniques such as Delphi studies and multiple scenarios

SOURCE: Baker, M. J. (ed.) (1995) *Companion Encyclopedia of Marketing*, London: Routledge

More recently, Douglas Brownlie (2000, p. 239) summarises the benefits of formal environmental scanning as follows:

1. Increased awareness by management of environmental changes

2. More effective strategic planning and decision making
3. Greater effectiveness in governmental and legislative matters
4. More informative and insightful industry and market analyses
5. Improved results in foreign businesses
6. Improvements in resource allocation
7. More effective representation of company policies in public fora.

DEMOGRAPHIC FACTORS

Ultimately, 'markets are people' in the sense that the demand for consumer goods depends directly upon the size of the population. In turn, consumer demand determines the demand for industrial and capital goods – hence 'derived demand' – as these goods possess value only in so far as they facilitate and satisfy the ultimate consumption needs of individual consumers. It follows that the size and structure of the population is of vital concern to the marketer. Indeed, the rediscovery of marketing was as much due to a slowing down of growth in demand in the advanced economies, in parallel with a slowing down of population growth, as it was due to an increase in supply as a result of technological change. That said, the subject of demographics has received comparatively little attention in the marketing literature until very recently. However, this neglect appears to be coming to an end as business publications such as *Marketing, Fortune, Business Week* etc. regularly include demographic projections in their editorial matter.

Derived from the Greek (*demos* = the populace, *graphein* = to write), demography is defined in the *Oxford Dictionary* as the 'study of statistics of births, deaths, disease, etc., as illustrating conditions of life in communities'. Every country in the world compiles such statistics and, while their reliability may vary, these data provide an essential foundation for any forecast about an area or region's potential level of marketing activity.

Of course demographic forecasts rest on assumptions and, like any other forecast, changes in these assumptions can lead to major changes in the actual outcome compared with the forecast. This is clearly illustrated in Figure 7.1 which summarises the UK Government Actuary's projections of the UK population at various dates together with the actual position determined by official censuses. In the case of demographic fore-

casts the key assumptions relate to births (fertility), mortality and migration, all of which are liable to significant change.

The twentieth century saw dramatic changes in life expectancy as a consequence of medical developments, public health improvements in water supply, sanitation and housing standards, dietary changes and advances in the preservation and distribution of food, health education etc. Thus, at the beginning of the century life expectancies in the UK were 48 for males and 52 for females. By the 1980s these had increased to 71 and 77 respectively – an improvement of almost 50%. With declining infant mortality (a major contributory factor to the extension of average life expectancies), and the greater certainty that children would survive to adulthood, so birth rates began to fall resulting in a dramatic slowing down of the overall rate of population growth and the emergence of an ageing population.

Given the basic relationship between age – or stage in the family life-cycle – and consumption patterns, it is variation in the composition of the population which is of most immediate interest to

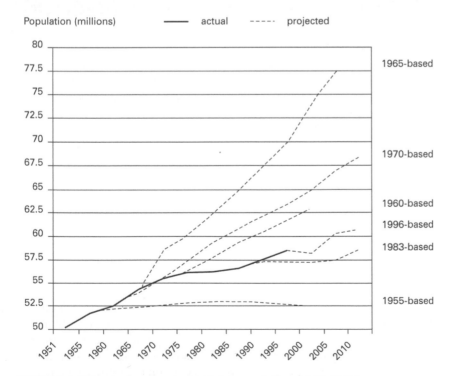

FIGURE 7.1 UK actual and projected total population, 1945–2010

SOURCE: Office of Population Censuses and Surveys, Government Actuary's Department

marketers seeking to project future patterns of demand. Clearly the precise relationship between the numbers in various age groups may alter significantly if there are major changes in birth rates (another baby boom like the 1950s and 1960s), mortality (AIDS or some other unforeseen disease) or migration (less likely given the present distribution of population). It has happened before and can clearly happen again. Nonetheless we possess sufficient information about the numbers in different age groups to essay broadly based scenarios of their implications for business. But, while the inferences drawn concerning the needs of different age groups are very similar, it is important to bear in mind that the position varies markedly from country to country. Europe as a whole has the slowest population growth in the world but countries in the south and east have much higher rates than those in the north. Similarly, while birth rates declined dramatically in the UK in the 1970s, they soared in Japan, with the result that there was a major increase in the 20–29 age group in the 1990s.

While the age of the population is a major determinant of its consumption behaviour, this will be mediated by a number of other factors – most importantly, education and income. Recognition of these multiple influences on consumption behaviour has led to the development of a variety of composite measures of which social grade, life-cycle and geodemographics are among the better known. These measures are widely used to segment markets and are discussed in more detail in Chapter 12.

In all advanced countries, and many developing ones too, hard data and expert comment of this kind are freely available in official publications, and the marketing planner can have no excuse for omitting such vital information from his environmental analysis.

But, while population data and projections may provide an essential starting-point for the assessment of future threats and opportunities in the external environment, it is clear that it is the interpretation of the implications of these data which is vital to SMP. For this interpretation we must look closely at all the other factors.

Box 7.1　*Demographics*

While analysts have long used age as a major segmentation variable, the predictability of this factor rarely seems to have been put to full use. Having moved into the new millennium, however, so the immediate post-war generation of 'baby boomers' have moved into their fifties, frequently identified as the 'third age'. An article in *Marketing Business* ('Vintage Crop', Robert Dwek, September 1995) offers some interesting insights into the implications of this change.

He comments:

The massive demographic changes caused by the increased birth rate between 1945 and 1964 should eventually result in the following startling fact: A 28% increase in the number of 50 to 74-year-olds over the period 1961–2021. That compares with an increase of just 17% for the 16 to 29 age group and 8% for the 30–49 age group. Youngsters, meanwhile, will be in short supply with a 10% decline in the number of 0–15-year-olds over the same period. (All figures from OPCS/MAPS).

He continues:

References to a new kind of older consumer have so far been restricted to the usual ragbag of buzz words – notably, 'the grey market' and 'empty nesters' – which may be an advance on 'wrinklies' and 'golden oldies' but still masks the enormity of the cultural shift taking place.

Given that 80% of the nation's wealth is held by those over 50, it seems clear that much greater effort needs to be given to understanding the nature of the sociological changes which have occurred and continue to occur. Citing Peter Laslett, a Cambridge historical sociologist, who is an acknowledged expert on the third age, Dwek argues that an obsession with youth is a complete denial of the third age and hence a waste of time when appealing to the older generation:

Instead, companies should seek out the more clearly defined character traits of older consumers, for example concentrating less on fashion than on quality or recognising that, ironic as it may seem, older people often have a greater sense of the future than their younger counterparts. Hence, their relatively high interest in long-term savings, investment products and in environmental issues.

That said, there is also a significant danger in the assumption that age will be an effective predictor of consumer behaviour. Rather, age should be regarded as a first order factor for segmenting a population following which more detailed analysis is required to capture the psychological and sociological components that shape individual behaviour. We return to this in Chapter 12.

SOCIAL AND CULTURAL FACTORS

One of the recurring themes of this book is the inevitability of change, while a second is that when innovation or change does occur it tends to be an exponential process which accelerates rapidly from slow beginnings.

The cumulative effects of change were vividly described by Karl Albrecht (1979):

The period from 1900 until the present stands apart from every other period in human history as a time of incredible change. Mankind, at least in the so-called 'developed' countries, has lost its innocence entirely. The great defining characteristics of this period – the first three-quarters of the twentieth century – have been change, impermanence, disruption, newness and obsolescence, and a sense of acceleration in almost every perceptible aspect of American society.

Philosophers, historians, scientists, and economists have given various names to this period. Management consultant Peter F. Drucker (1968) has called it the Age of Discontinuity. Economist John Kenneth Galbraith (1958) has called it the Age of Uncertainty. Media theorist Marshall MacLuhan (1964) called it the Age of the Global Village. Writer and philosopher Alvin Toffler (1970) called it the Age of Future Shock. Virtually all thoughtful observers of America, Americans, and American society have remarked with some alarm about the accelerating pace with which our life processes and our surrounds are changing within the span of a single generation. And this phenomenon is spreading all over the industrialized world. I call this the Age of Anxiety.

TABLE 7.3   Key international issues for the 1990s

Issues	Characteristics
Low economic growth	Political instability; rising energy costs; growing unemployment; growth in international capital flows; trends to international protectionism if GATT fails; decline of basic industries; rising inflation; shortages of basic materials; falling productivity; emergence of new market economies of Eastern Europe and Far East trading blocs; increasing national indebtedness and monetary growth; falling investment
Political uncertainty	Political fragmentation in Europe; expansion of EC; trend towards decentralising government; growth in terrorism and armed conflict; failure of foreign and international trade policy; rise of nationalism/tribalism; regional convergence on trade and investment policy; decline of liberal democratic values; urban conflict
Rise of the multi-locals	Large firms decentralise, downsize and form loose federations by devolving responsibility to autonomous units; growth in smaller enterprises; more cross-border networks/partnerships
Environmentalism	Growing influence of environmentalist lobby; worldwide enactment of legislation on pollution and product liability; closer scrutiny of firms' environmental track record; growth in environmental audit requirements
Lobby politics	Rising power and influence of lobby groups on issues such as gender, age, consumer protection, health, housing, pollution, materialism, consumer choice, representation, social responsibility, race, poverty, discrimination, access to education
Growth of government	Closer EC and NAFTA integration and convergence brings with it more bureaucracy and democratic institutions
Accountability and participation	Demands for greater accountability and transparency in the activities and decisions of government; greater access to local government and participation in it; greater access to information; more disclosure of information and scrutiny of decisions and activities.

SOURCE: Brownlie, D. (1995) Environmental analysis, in Baker M. J. (ed.) *Companion Encyclopedia of Marketing*. London: Routledge, pp. 238–50

Thirty years on the same trends continue remorselessly and are summarised in Table 7.3.

As a result of these changes, Albrecht identifies five significant areas of change in lifestyle:

1. From rural living to urban living
2. From stationary to mobile
3. From self-sufficient to consuming
4. From isolated to interconnected
5. From physically active to sedentary.

Albrecht reviews these factors in some detail, mainly to establish his thesis that such change has led to significant physiological and psychological effects and greatly increased the levels of stress among people which, in turn, has become a causal factor in influencing people's lifestyle.

However, it is also apparent that the writings of authors like Albrecht, Kinsey, Nader, Carson, Packard, Schumacher, Toffler, Meadowes and the Club of Rome etc., have made us much more aware of ourselves and our environment. Simultaneously, increased affluence in the advanced economies has allowed us to react to this awareness through further social and cultural change which has seen the emergence of consumerism, of concern for equal opportunities, of environmentalism etc.

At the time of writing the first edition in 1984, few could have anticipated that 'green' issues could have achieved the prominence they enjoy today. With the benefit of hindsight, of course, one can point out that the diffusion of this interest/concern follows the classic pattern of the diffusion/life-cycle curves discussed in Chapter 5. But, as we pointed out when discussing this phenomenon, the difficulty with using the PLC as a predictive device lies in knowing when takeoff will occur and what will trigger it. No doubt future historians will be able to chronicle the sequence of events that heightened the awareness in advanced countries of the weakening of the ozone layer, global warming, the destruction of non-renewable resources, and the threat of unrestricted population growth. The problem is being able to predict when such awareness stopped being the preoccupation of cranks and the creation of 'fad' products, and became of general concern and the rapid introduction of fashionable green products that accelerated the whole process by substituting these for environmentally unfriendly products.

In the final analysis such a matter must be one of judgement, and those able to make such judgements will, like Napoleon's 'lucky generals', succeed. One of the justifications for this book, however, is that 'luck' is the product of insight and experience, both of which can be increased significantly by knowledge transfer of the kind attempted in textbooks and formal education. 'Luck', in the context of predicting trends, is a matter of developing a sound understanding of the current position and the events leading up to it, of accepting the inevitability of change and of keeping one's mind open for cues or signals that change is indeed occurring. It follows that the marketer must be sensitive to these changes, and the effects they are likely to have on consumption patterns, and should make full use of the powerful techniques that have been developed for both monitoring and modelling lifestyle (see Chapter 12).

POLITICAL AND GOVERNMENTAL FACTORS

Once social groups attain a certain size, some form of political process becomes necessary to regulate the functioning of the group and the interaction of its members. In most countries, and certainly the great majority with a market economy, the political process leads to the election of a government with a mandate to undertake certain functions on behalf of the society as a whole. These functions are usually very wide-ranging and cover such areas as:

- Security and defence
- Education
- Transportation
- Social security and welfare
- Health
- Employment
- Foreign relations and trade.

Governments develop specific policies for all these areas and support them to varying degrees with investment and expenditure derived from direct and indirect taxation. Accordingly, the government will also have an economic policy, and this will have a significant influence upon the regulation of competition, upon permissible business practices, upon standards etc.

It requires little imagination or experience to recognise the extent of political influence on business activities and it is widely accepted that many of the UK's economic problems may be attributed to the radically different political philosophies of the two major parties that have governed the country since the Second World War. The Conservatives believe basically in a free-market economy, while the Socialists believe in a state-managed and more centrally controlled economy. Given that governments last a maximum of five years before they have to be re-elected, it is unsurprising that many businessmen are loath to consider long-term investment when an election may result in a complete U-turn in economic policy.

Today, however, it is clear that businessmen in the UK will be less able to plead short-termism as a consequence of political uncertainty than in the past. To a large degree the economic, and so political, fortunes of the UK have become influenced increasingly by membership of the European Community. While '1992' did not result in a step-function change, as is frequently implied by references to this particular date, the process of integration into the greatly enlarged European markets has surely and inevitably continued. If anything, it can only be accelerated by the union of Germany, the breakdown of the Soviet economy and its recognition of the importance of market forces, and the enlargement of the European Union. Closer to home, the Labour party has recognised that, despite growing dissatisfaction with many aspects of Conservative government, the majority of voters are motivated by self-interest rather than ideology and so prefer the more laissez-faire market-based philosophy. Labour has modified its policies accordingly, to the point that it is becoming increasingly difficult to distinguish them from those of the Conservatives – a factor that undoubtedly assisted in their landslide electoral success in 1997, and success in two subsequent elections.

In that government policies are invariably made mandatory through legislation, no firm can afford to lose touch with political events. However, once the government has published its programme, there is a very high probability that it will be enacted and firms may take action accordingly – the real problem lies in the longer term, and the possibilities of a change in the government and/or a change in relationships between the country and other countries. For the UK, with its dependence on international trade and its involvement in international business, such considerations are of vital importance to strategic planning.

ECONOMIC FACTORS

Changes in the size and structure of the population and in lifestyle and consumption patterns, together with the prevailing political philosophy, all have a significant influence upon economic factors. At their simplest, economies are concerned with the central problem of maximising satisfaction through the utilisation of scarce resources, which, in turn, may be classified as land, labour and capital. Land is the source of food and raw materials; labour is necessary to grow the food, extract the raw materials and transform them into consumable products; while capital, particularly in the shape of technology, plant, equipment, transportation etc., is vital to enhance the efficiency and productivity of this process. To some extent the factors of production may be substituted for one another, but such substitution takes time and can rarely be accomplished in the short to medium term. Thus any major disturbance in the balance between the three factors of production can result in a serious distortion of the economic system. Within a single, self-contained economy such distortion is easier to anticipate and control, but, in the modern world, few if any economies are self-contained as the theory of comparative advantage clearly shows that economic welfare will be optimised through international trade. It is because of the development of dependency upon international trade that the Arab increase in oil prices in 1974 had such wide-ranging repercussions upon so many national economies – not necessarily directly, but as a knock-on or domino effect. Thus the immediate effect was felt in the USA and Western Europe where price rises and inflation led to a decline in consumption and a lesser level of demand for imports from developing countries whose economies declined accordingly.

As noted earlier, given time one can adjust to such a radical distortion and a wide range of responses may be identified. First, most oil-dependent economies instituted energy-saving programmes to extract the maximum benefit and efficiency from the scarce resource. Second, many countries turned to other energy sources such as coal and oil shale which had been uneconomic when oil prices were low. Similarly, the high price of oil prompted the exploitation of many marginal oilfields and a stepping-up of exploration and development, especially of offshore deposits. Looking even further ahead, research into the potential of renewable sources of energy – wind, wave, solar and nuclear power – was promoted. The net result of these efforts was that in 1982 and 1983 the OPEC producers found it increasingly difficult to sustain a common supply and price policy and had cause to consider the inevitability of product life-cycles and Levitt's (1960) observation: 'Every declining industry was once a growth industry.'

In summarising reactions to a swingeing rise in the price of a vital raw material, it is apparent that these fell into two major categories – those prompted 'automatically' by market forces and those put into effect by those responsible for overall economic policy and management (governments). The 'automatic' or market response is that which economic theory predicts will occur if one changes the supply of or demand for a product.

The consequence (or cause) of such changes will be a change in the market price and the process that both prompts and reflects this process is competition. (In 1999, when preparing the last edition, oil was its lowest price for 20 years – less than $20 a barrel. At the beginning of 2006, it is selling for three times as much – a powerful example of the difficulty of predicting environmental changes!) Competition was discussed in Chapter 2 and will be returned to later in this chapter, while price is the concern of Chapter 17, and we shall discuss these topics more fully there. With regard to governmental response, we have already discussed this briefly and the point is returned to here solely to emphasise the interdependence and interaction between the environmental factors.

TECHNOLOGICAL FACTORS

As with the other factors, technology and technological change may be both the cause and effect of environmental change. The distinction is a simple one – between *technology push*, usually associated with a production orientation, and *market pull*, usually associated with a marketing orientation. As we saw in Chapter 4, firms would be ill-advised to depend solely upon either one or the other of these approaches and should seek a judicious balance between basic R&D in pursuit of radical innovation, and applied R&D intended to improve and sustain its current market share.

Earlier in this chapter reference was made to the accelerating rate of technological change and the social and cultural consequences of this.

Figure 7.2 summarises some of the major technological innovations of the twentieth century, many of which could have occurred within a single lifetime. Clearly, anticipating and predicting the possible impact of such innovations is a major challenge and calls for new approaches and methods, many of which have now been proven in practice. In Chapter 5 we discussed the use of scenarios as a means of seeking to capture future uncertainties and in Chapter 6 we described the Bayesian approach for incorporating uncertainty into decisions analysis. At a more prosaic level, we look later at sales forecasting as a basis for developing short- to medium-term extrapolations for use in tactical marketing plans.

In *Fortune* magazine, Nelson D. Schwartz (1999), identified 10 trends that he believed would dominate the infotech markets in the new millennium. Whilst most attention has been given to the potential of the internet to transform consumer retailing, Schwartz believes that the real action will be in business-to-business e-commerce. Central to this will be what have been termed 'infomediaries', which will be online exchanges linking buyers and sellers through the efficient distribution of market information. The key to success is seen as focus with different industries having different needs and industry exchanges have already appeared for steel, paper, research chemicals, hospital supplies, marine equipment, home equity loans and trucking. Schwartz observes:

> The appeal of an exchange is its ability to lower transaction costs, especially in fragmented markets where prices are difficult to compare. For instance, information on laboratory chemicals is so hard to find that a chemist can spend five hours a week thumbing through thick paper catalogues. The price

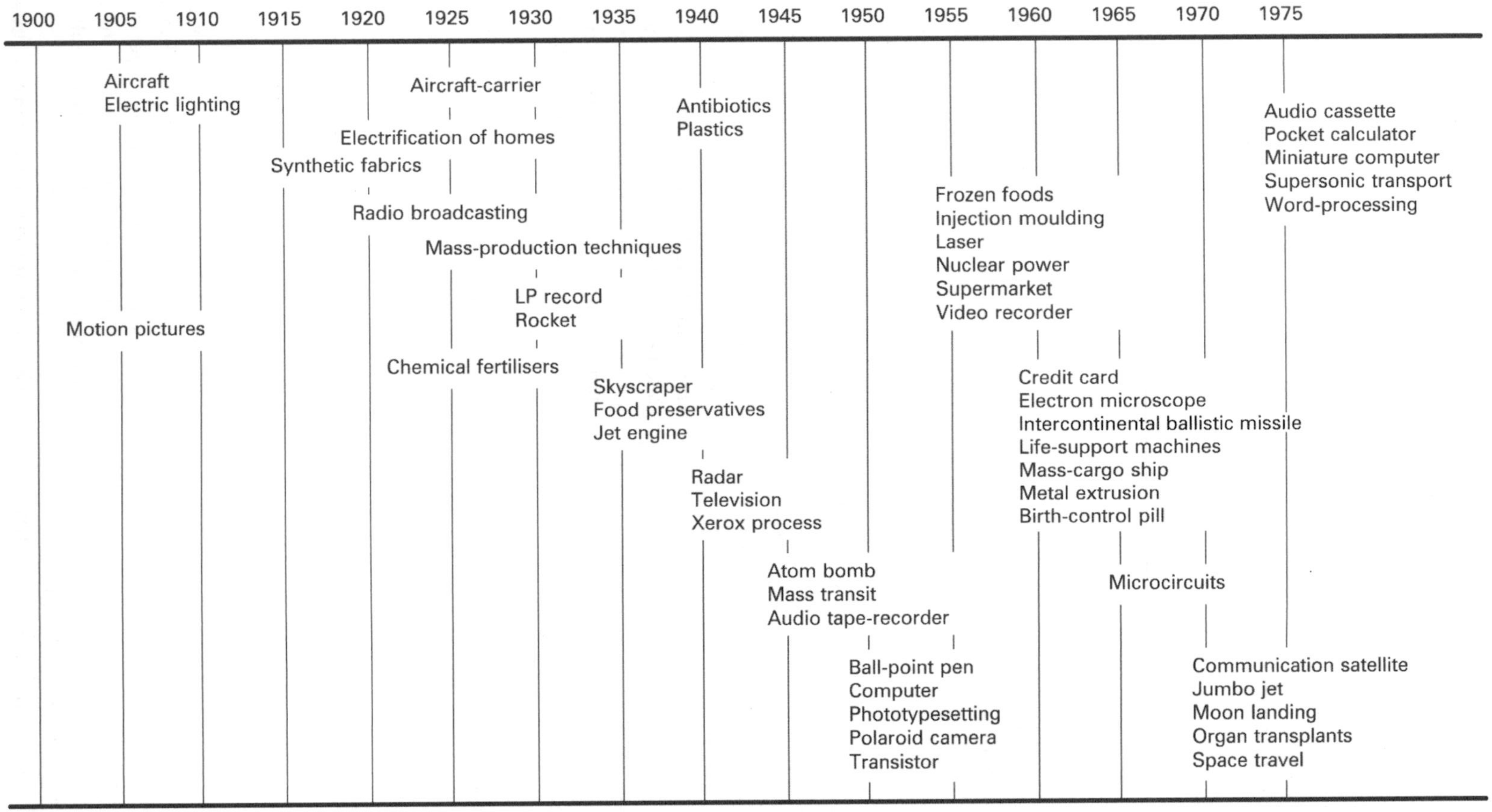

FIGURE 7.2 Significant technological events within a single lifetime

SOURCE: Albrecht, K. (1979) *Stress and the Manager.* Englewood Cliffs, NJ: Prentice Hall

of a single chemical can vary by more than 200%. Now pharmaceuticals-industry and university scientists can search electronically through multiple suppliers' products on chemdex.com and cut their research time to an hour a week.

A second major trend is the development of networks that speak the internet's language (internet protocol or IP for short). Employing digital technology IP can transmit vast quantities of data simultaneously thus greatly reducing the cost per message or call. The threat of this competition is encouraging telecom companies to invest in 'digital subscriber lines' (DSL), which employ special modems that can increase the capacity of copper wires twentyfold now and by up to a thousandfold with the development of broadband.

A third trend is the development of stand-alone devices that can work independently of a PC. Schwartz comments:

> Cutting the core to the PC is a burgeoning trend in digital devices. It's affecting the design of printers, scanners, and other peripherals. Dirt-cheap memory and inexpensive logic chips have opened the door to all kinds of simple appliances that each perform a single task extremely well. Some carry out their digital jobs so well that you might start to wonder whether you need a PC in your life at all ... This may signal the first time in the short history of widespread digital technology that the IQ of devices rises while the IQ needed to make them work declines.

A further prediction in the article is that, after free email and free internet access, the next wave of giveaways is likely to be free hardware. The underlying theory is that technology has always been 'a business of razors and razorblades'. 'In other words, give them a razor, and the blades will sell themselves. That was certainly true in wireless phone service, which took off when manufacturers started handing out cellphones. Personal computer makers may not be far behind.'

More recently, Paul Roberts and Jess Hill (2005) published a short *Survival Guide to the Near Future* (www.brandchannel.com/papers_review. asp?sp–id=677) in which they identify the three major changes that are converging to change our world – changes in human values, business structure and technology.

Starting with changes in human values the authors state: 'Everything you took for granted in the twentieth century has changed in the twenty-first. Children are acting like teenagers, adults are acting like kids, and men are wearing makeup.' While these are challengeable generalisations, they are symptomatic of the radical changes that have taken place in recent decades, in terms of the traditional roles of men and women, the abandonment of traditional life stages, the decline of the nuclear family and the growth of single-person households, and the increase in disposable time (in the 1920s, household chores averaged 55 hours per week; now it is four) and income. Together, these and many other changes mean that identifying and targeting market segments has become much more complex and difficult.

While the agrarian economy lasted for thousands of years and the industrial economy for 250 years, the information age is barely 20 years old and already beginning to morph into what futurists characterise as the bio-economy – an economy modelled on biological and natural systems. The information age has meant that via the internet global brands can be built in just three years – a tenth of the time it used to take in the industrial age. The internet has lowered barriers to entry, increased competition and consumer buying power and enabled small entrepreneurial companies to compete with even the largest corporations:

> In the Information Age, a new set of competencies determine success:
> 1. Entrepreneurship
> 2. Flexibility
> 3. Risk-Taking
> 4. Innovation
> 5. Passion
> 6. Relationship Building
> In the Industrial Age, businesses were defined by their products. In the Information Age, businesses are defined by the relationships they have with their customers, and the emotional experience they are providing when their customers interact with them. Forget factories – what you have to own is the customer relationship. (Roberts and Hill, 2005)

The onset of the bio-economy is already apparent in the appearance of genetically modified

(GM) foods and nanotechnology. While GM crops have been adopted enthusiastically in some countries, in the UK and Europe they have met with resistance. The same reaction is predicted for nanotechnology.

> Put simply, nano-technology identifies ways of manipulating matter at the level of atoms – 1/100,000th the width of a human hair. At this level we are able to change the order of molecules or insert different ones, which could turn a rose into a glass vase. This technology also enables us to make existing materials stronger, thinner, better, smaller. Effectively, nano-technology enables us to build the world the way we want it, atom by atom. (Roberts and Hill, 2005)

The bio-economy and nanotechnology both offer huge benefits for mankind. GM foods have the potential to eradicate hunger everywhere, while nanotechnology will enable us to develop new materials to replace non-renewable natural resources, reduce waste and pollution in manufacturing processes, and enable major breakthroughs in medical science and treatment.

Faced with evidence of this kind, one is reminded of the question posed previously concerning environmental change as a whole –

'Could we have anticipated it?' to which the answer must be an unequivocal 'Yes'. The inevitability and accelerating nature of change of this kind is the basic message of the product life-cycle and it is for this reason that we have placed so much emphasis upon the concept. In doing so we have dismissed the criticisms of those who question whether the PLC is a true reflection of reality, but we have been careful not to challenge the complaint that even if PLCs do exist in general, they are not very useful as a predictive device in the particular. This criticism is accepted and we must look elsewhere for methods and techniques for predicting particular future events for use in strategic planning, but – and this is the cause of my obsession with the PLC concept – if you don't accept the general implications of the concept first, it is unlikely that you would go to the time and trouble of setting up a formal technological forecasting system.

Because of increased awareness of the need to try and predict the future, considerable effort has been invested into developing techniques for doing this. In the next but one section we look more closely at some of the secular trends in economic levels of activity that are so heavily influenced by technological factors and of particular importance to long-term strategic planning.

Box 7.2   *Fuel of the Future*

A major article in *Fortune* (6 February, 2006), 'How to beat the high cost of gasoline – forever', encouraged the reader to

> stop dreaming about hydrogen. Ethanol is the answer to the energy dilemma. It's clean and green and runs in today's cars. And in a generation it could replace gas.

Chemically, ethanol is identical to grain alcohol and, traditionally, has come exclusively from corn or sugar cane. Now, however, a breakthrough in biotechnology means that it can be made from all kinds of agricultural waste. This new biomass fuel is cellulosic ethanol and reduces carbon dioxide emissions by 80% compared with gasoline, and eliminates completely the release of sulphur dioxide, which causes acid rain.

Ethanol itself is not new – Henry Ford's Model T ran on it – but what is not widely known is that there are more than 5 million ethanol-ready cars already on the roads in the USA and that 73% of new car sales in Brazil in 2005 can use either ethanol or gasoline. The ability to use either fuel and distribute it through current distribution channels is a major advantage when compared with hydrogen, as the latter would require new production and distribution systems and new fuel stations as well as new cars.

As of now, relatively few gas stations are equipped to handle the most common mixture of 85% ethanol and 15% gasoline (E85) and there would have to be a huge increase in capacity for it to become a serious challenge to gasoline. But, given its environmental credentials, and the West's dependency on imported oil, a gradual substitution of ethanol for gasoline seems likely. All the more so as production costs have fallen dramatically and further technological innovations indicate that ethanol can be price competitive – and likely to be even more so as demand from India and China keeps oil prices high.

UK COMPETITIVENESS

UK competitiveness was the subject of a report prepared by Michael Porter and Christian Ketels published in May 2003 and prepared at the invitation of the Department of Trade and Industry (DTI) and the Economic and Social Research Council (ESRC).

The objective of the review was 'to synthesise, interpret, and draw implications from the available evidence on the competitiveness of the UK, applying the Porter competitiveness framework and drawing on the learning from dozens of national competitiveness projects over the last decade'. While not considered to be a comprehensive study of UK competitiveness, it illustrates well the application of Porter's diamond framework and provides high-level guidance to policymakers on broad priorities.

The UK is seen as having achieved a remarkable success in halting the economy's protracted decline of the pre-1980 period as a result of major economic policy reforms that have changed fundamentally both the microeconomic and macroeconomic context for competition. Nonetheless 'pessimism and the lack of an overall strategic perspective characterise much of the public discussion about UK competitiveness'. The main sources of this pessimism appear to be the continuing productivity gap when compared with the US and other economies and recognition that the UK is 'moving from a location competing on relatively low costs of doing business to a location competing on unique value and innovation'. What is lacking is a consensus of how best to adapt to this changing environment.

Productivity is seen as the main source of competitiveness but the UK still lags behind many other advanced economies and will only improve with higher levels of skill, capital intensity and the application of technology. 'Productivity growth is underpinned by trade, foreign investment, and innovative activity ... the UK's export position is stable; its attractiveness for foreign direct investment is high but decreasing; its innovation performance is weak'. While the UK is seen as having a strong science base, it lags in patenting and commercialisation. Further, strength in the life sciences masks lower performance in other areas of science and technology. But, while investment in manufacturing is below the European average, it is greater for service companies.

Levels of productivity and innovation are the consequence of the macro- and microeconomic context in which firms compete. At the national level, a sound macroeconomic, political, legal and social context are necessary but not sufficient for the achievement of competitiveness. The existence of poverty and social deprivation are seen as weaknesses in the UK but it is seen as being stable on the other three dimensions. (In the longer term, eradication of poverty could create additional resources that would help improve productivity.)

With regard to the microeconomic context, Porter's 'diamond' identifies four interrelated factors that help determine competitiveness – factor conditions; firm strategy, structure and rivalry; demand conditions; and related and support industries – as shown in Figure 2.3. Analysis of the UK business environment identifies a number of competitive advantages and disadvantages that are summarised as follows.

Competitive advantages:
- Highly *open* to international trade and investment
- Very low *regulatory barriers* to competition at the national level
- Sophisticated *capital markets*, especially equity markets.

Competitive disadvantages:
- Weak and deteriorating *physical infrastructure*

- *Skill deficits* in the labour force despite favourable international rankings on educational achievement
- Constrained access to *debt capital*
- Low levels of *R&D* investment and *commercialisation* infrastructure despite strong science base
- Large *regional* differences in the quality of the business environment
- Limited presence/effectiveness of *institutions for collaboration*.

Clusters are defined as 'geographically proximate groups of interconnected companies, suppliers, service providers, and associated institutions in a particular field, linked by commonalities and complementaries'. Clusters affect competitiveness in three broad ways:

1. They increase the level of productivity as proximity reduces the need for stockholding, increases the speed of response between firms, which reduces cycle time
2. They increase the capacity for innovation and productivity
3. They stimulate and enable new business formation.

The UK does not rank high on measures of cluster development and lacks clear definitions permitting detailed analysis. It has a strong position in services, particularly financial and media. Exports are seen as a good surrogate for clusters and the UK has strong positions in defence, products for personal use, healthcare and telecommunications. Entertainment, semiconductors and computers, transportation and office products also perform well.

The lack of institutions for collaboration (IFCs) is cited as a weakness in improving competitiveness in the UK. IFCs are not firms, government agencies or universities but are intermediaries that 'organise and perform collective action and enable more effective collaboration between parts of a cluster'. Examples include chambers of commerce, industry associations, quality centre university alumni associations etc. The Australian wine industry is cited as an example of the way in which IFCs enhance competitiveness to the extent that Australia has doubled its wine exports over a five-year period.

Porter and Ketels (2003) were asked to pay special attention to the role of management in improving competitiveness. Their analysis of competitive advantages and disadvantages listed the following.

Competitive advantage:
- Sophisticated *marketing* and *branding*
- Strengths in *supply chain management, distribution* and *retailing*
- High level of *professional* versus family management and use of incentive compensation
- High level of *internationalisation*.

Competitive disadvantages:
- Low *capital stock*
- Low investment in *innovation*
- Compete less on *unique value* (versus cost) than advanced nation peers
- Some indications of low uptake of *modern management techniques*
- Some indications that *manufacturing* is lagging in the overall economy.

In conclusion, the review sees the UK economy in a transitional phase in which it needs to upgrade its competitiveness in order to maintain or improve its position as a major global economy:

> To achieve higher prosperity UK companies will need to upgrade their productivity by competing on more unique and more innovative products and services. This will require changes in management behaviour, but it will also require targeted investments in the business environment, and the development and strengthening of new types of institutions. It will no longer be sufficient to just increase the efficiency of the existing infrastructure, the educational institutions, and the science and technology.

CYCLES AND TRENDS

With the downturn in economic activity that accompanied the OPEC price increases of the early 1970s, many commentators remarked on the similarity between the period and that of the Great Depression of the 1930s. Such comparisons provoked considerable interest in the assertion as to whether there is an underlying long-term cycle in economic activity, with the obvious corollary that, if there is, can such a trend be used for predicting and controlling economies?

Research into long waves or Kondratieff cycles has become a major preoccupation of many economists, particularly in Europe, and there has been a substantial increase in publications dealing with this phenomenon. Much of this research was synthesised in a 1983 book by J. J. van Duijn and this section draws heavily on this source.

Cycles vary enormously in general although, in the particular, all exhibit a basic regularity comprising a number of distinct phases. It is the expectation of changes in direction and the reasons underlying them that are of central interest and concern. In the economic cycle, six phases are distinguished (compared with four in the standard PLC) and are shown in Figure 7.3.

While many different types of cycle have been distinguished, four enjoy particular support which van Duijn lists as:

1. The Kitchin or inventory cycle, with a length of 3–5 years (the 'business cycle')
2. The Juglar or investment cycle, with a length of 7–11 years
3. The Kuznets or building cycle, of 15–25 years' duration
4. The long wave or Kondratieff cycle, which is said to be of 45–60 years.

The shorter the cycle, the more predictable it is, which undoubtedly reinforces the emphasis upon short-term tactical moves to the neglect of long-term strategic planning. Thus it is much easier to adjust inventories to reflect the prevailing supply/demand conditions than to commit oneself to absolute increases or decreases in the level of investment.

As noted, the longer the periodicity of a cycle the more difficult it is to distinguish and define. Accordingly, there is by no means universal agreement upon the existence of long waves in economic activity with life spans of from 45 to 60 years. However, there is an extensive and growing body of evidence to support the proposition that such long waves do exist and that they may be used to forecast infrastructural change.

Views differ as to whether the four cycles are dependent or independent of each other. As van Duijn comments, it is very tempting but also very simplistic to propose that by juggling with the lengths of the various cycles, we can come up with an equation that states:

1 Kondratieff = 3 Kuznets = 6 Juglars = 12 Kitchins

Although it is unlikely that the relationship will ever be so neat, especially now that governments seek to manage their economies, it is equally

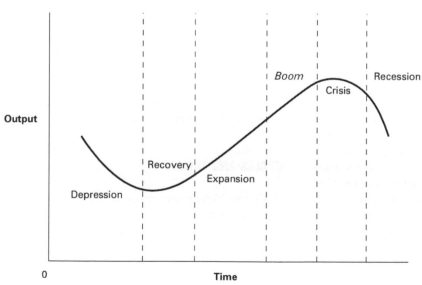

FIGURE 7.3 The phases of an economic cycle

SOURCE: van Duijn, J. J. (1983) *The Long Wave in Economic Life*. London: George Allen & Unwin

unlikely that there is no interdependence at all. Certainly, there is a common thread in the normal 'life expectancy' of the four basic types of investment – inventory, plant and equipment, buildings and major infrastructural investments such as railways, motorways, airports etc. (the Kondratieff cycle). That said, much of the argument in *Marketing New Industrial Products* (1975) and *Market Development* (1983) is concerned with the contribution of technical innovation to economic growth and change, and the role that behavioural factors play in delaying or accelerating such change. It is also apparent that while market pull innovation implies a reaction to express needs, technological push frequently ignores such forces and, if sufficiently attractive, may override a natural desire to capitalise fully on investment by depreciating it over its intended life span, i.e. the original investment criterion may be discarded in the light of new information on comparative cost benefits resulting from innovation.

For those seeking an explanation of the four types of cycle outlined above, van Duijn provides a clear and concise summary (pp. 8–19) and there is a wealth of literature describing the form and parameters of the inventory (business) and investment cycles, which is suited to short-to-medium-term economic forecasting. However, for the purposes of strategic planning, a longer term time horizon is desirable and it is here that van Duijn's analysis of long waves is seen as being of particular value. Fundamental to his analysis (and possibly the reason why it finds favour with this author) is recognition and acceptance of economic growth, as an S-shaped phenomenon based on many of the same arguments set out in Chapter 2 of *Marketing New Industrial Products* (1975).

Having established that economic growth, in terms of products, industries and even national industrial output over certain time periods, resembles closely the now familiar PLC pattern, van Duijn proceeds to inquire whether an S-shaped curve is also an adequate representation of the secular growth of an economy. Perhaps the best known of theories of secular economic growth is that put forward by Rostow (1962), in which he proposes six stages:

1. Traditional society
2. Preconditions for takeoff
3. Takeoff
4. The drive to technological maturity
5. The age of high mass consumption
6. The search for quality.

Evidently there are close parallels between Rostow's stages and the phases of the PLC, and van Duijn puts forward considerable evidence to support the existence of the stages and the fact that, like PLCs, growth in per capita GNP may be represented by an S-shaped curve. But, just as the stylised PLC is unable to provide a complete explanation of the real world, so the S-shaped secular growth hypothesis does not provide a complete explanation of the above-average growth rates in the period 1948–73. To answer this question, van Duijn cites the four explanatory factors proposed by Rostow, namely:

1. The post-war commitment of governments to maintain full employment, backed by a wide range of instruments for affecting the level of effective demand.
2. The backlog of technologies, ready for absorption by Western Europe and Japan; the added impetus of demand for capital goods in countries that had suffered physical war damage.
3. The efforts of the developing regions of Latin America, Africa, the Middle East and Asia to increase investment rates and absorb the backlog of unapplied technologies.
4. An environment of relatively falling energy prices and, from 1951 to 1972, relatively falling or low prices of foodstuffs and raw materials.

Van Duijn poses the question whether these were a one-off occurrence, or are they likely to be repeated. His own opinion inclines to the latter view and provides the justification for suggesting the existence of the long wave acting in conjunction with the secular trend identified by Rostow and others.

The remaining chapters of van Duijn's book are devoted to a review and analysis of a number of different long wave theories, of the empirical evidence underlying them and of the implications for economic policy particularly during a depression such as that being experienced almost universally during the early 1980s at the time he was writing. From a managerial (marketing) point of view, interest in long waves is largely derived from Schumpeter's contention that these reflect technological innovation rather than issues of fluctuations in prices and/or quantities which are the preoccupation of other schools of economic thought.

Put simply, the question for managers is 'Will an understanding of the processes of technological innovation (TI) enhance the likelihood of my developing an effective strategy for long-term survival and growth in a competitive marketplace?' It is this perspective which is seen as relevant to a consideration of product strategy and management.

While Kondratiev (cited in van Duijn, 1983) sees TI as a dependent variable responding to 'endogenous forces within capitalism', Schumpeter took the opposite view 'that long cycles are caused by, and are an incident of, the innovation process.'

Rosenberg and Frischtak (1984) argue that there is no precise evidence of the environmental changes which would precipitate the clusters (neighbourhoods) of TI that would initiate a long wave. However, their main criticism appears to be founded on the periodicity of the long wave, which is, in our view, the reason why life-cycles (long waves) cannot be used to forecast diffusion, although you can use them to predict the process.

Rosenberg and Frischtak cite a variety of factors which might slow down adoption and diffusion, including:

■ Primitive nature of new inventions
■ Very high initial costs
■ Absence of necessary production technology
■ Innovation/investment decisions are future oriented and so involve a high degree of uncertainty
■ Expectations (uncertainty) powerfully shape adoption and diffusion patterns
■ Substantial improvements in the threatened technology
■ Changes in factor costs
■ The availability of complementary inputs and/or a supporting infrastructure
■ The education and training of technologists may favour incremental development trajectories and discourage discontinuities.

Innovations may occur in clusters rather than a continuous stream because:

■ One innovation raises the economic payoff for another
■ Pressures to remove impediments to the exploitation of the first innovation
■ The first innovation 'provides a framework that makes it possible to conceptualise, design and work on a number of complementary and related technologies.' (Rosenberg and Frischtak, 1984, p. 32)
■ Investment in infrastructure, e.g. electric power distribution, creates opportunities for other innovations.

Rosenberg and Frischtak come to the 'tentative assessment' that one needs to combine both schools of thought if one is to come up with 'a convincing account of the generation of long waves':

Technologically driven long waves can be made to appear plausible only if macroeconomic factors can be shown to play a dominant role in shaping and disciplining the timing of the introduction of innovations. The beginning of an upswing would therefore be characterised by a sufficiently large stimulus from the 'M' clustering process upon the previously positioned 'T' cluster. In other words, at the initial phase of industry life-cycles, the state of the economy (or 'market conditions') regulates, to a large extent, the still incipient sectoral demands, so that the introduction of new products and processes tends not to occur unless the economic environment is conducive to increases in consumer expending and investment activity. (p. 33)

Rosenberg and Frischtak believe that, once initiated, the technology life-cycle will detach itself from short-run changes in demand and follow its own internal dynamics. (It is these which result in the consistent diffusion curve.) Specific reference is made to the substitution effect which is seen as a 'self-sustaining mechanism':

The economy-wide impact of technological innovations needs to be understood not only in terms of the direct impact of cost reductions and the release of resources to alternative uses, but of the strength of their backward and forward linkages. (p. 35)

Backward linkages are associated with expenditures on buildings, machinery, equipment and raw materials, i.e. *production* goods. This often leads to further process innovations that reinforce growth and enhance productivity in other sectors.

Forward linkages relate to *consumption* goods, i.e. reduced costs result in market growth and associated capital accumulation, output growth and technical progress. Similarly, the innovation, e.g. microchip, may spawn many new products and processes.

However, the complexity of the linkages and the interdependence of industries makes it difficult (impossible?) to isolate the relationships and 'prove' the existence or otherwise, of long waves.

Finally, Rosenberg and Frischtak explore the circumstances which might regularly 'trigger' new waves of innovation and business growth. They conclude Mensch's assertion that innovations bunch during periods of stagnation and depression is far from convincing. Overall, therefore, their analysis leads to a verdict of 'unproven'. That said, the discussion illuminates many of the underlying forces that underpin the regularity of economic/technological life-cycles, albeit they are unable to explain their periodicity.

(Other priorities preclude any further discussion of this important element in the forces that need to be taken into account when making an environmental analysis. However, it is hoped that this cursory commentary will serve to alert the reader to the wealth of insight available from other disciplines to help guide the formulation of basic assumptions that are the essential starting point for the development of long-term strategic plans. Certainly the environmental forces discussed in the preceding pages provide the framework within which firms must operate. As noted, these conditions are substantially the same for all firms, so that to a large degree their success and failure will depend upon their ability to cope with these while interacting with each other in a state of competition. We return to the subject of competition in the next chapter.

CHANGING TIMES = CHANGING VALUES

From our review it is clear that agreement on broad environmental changes is widespread. In attempts to manage their economies, governments will continue to experiment with diamet-rically opposed policies of regulation and deregulation, and in doing so are unlikely to improve business confidence as to the continuity of basic policy on competition. We may also look forward to a continuation of the rapid technological change precipitated by the microelectronics revolution. As a consequence of these three broad trends, one can already detect changes in both values and lifestyles.

In essence, the change in values and lifestyles is away from a Christian ethic of deferred gratification to a more hedonistic and short-term view of life that emphasises immediate gratification. The implications of this change were clearly demonstrated in research undertaken by Leathar into the promotion of non-smoking by the Scottish Health Education Group. The original campaign, which was highly thought of by advertising professionals and won several awards, cited a number of benefits of not smoking and stressed that non-smokers ran a much lower risk of contracting lung cancer and dying prematurely. In other words, don't smoke, and you may live longer. For the target audience of teenagers and young adults, the promise was both too uncertain (many smokers don't get lung cancer anyway) and too distant (60 is two lifetimes away when you're 20). Once this perception was distinguished, the theme was changed to one of more immediate payoffs, accenting that non-smokers are nicer to be near and more socially acceptable. Similarly, advertising on alcohol now underlines moderation in drinking behaviour rather than total abstinence.

Other examples of society rejecting the traditional values of hard work and thrift in the anticipation of a better future are legion. When inflation erodes or wipes out the value of hard-earned savings, and many in employment are visibly no better off than the unemployed, it is difficult to sustain a belief in the old order. Small wonder that those made redundant prefer to 'blow' their nest eggs on holidays or consumer durables that give immediate gratification rather than save up for the rainy day that is already here.

Returning to our earlier question as to whether such changes could have been anticipated, we believe that they could, through a combination of strategic planning and focused market research. But, as we suggested, the general climate of opinion rejected the possibility that one economic order was passing and another succeeding it. Given the events of the past few years, most are now persuaded that the future will be different and so are willing to consider a more professional approach to management than they were in the past.

FORECASTING DEMAND

A continuing problem faced by all types of organisation is that of projecting future demand for their goods and services, for it is upon such projections that policy and strategy must be based.

Although the actual time horizon will vary according to the nature of the firm's business it is convenient to think of forecasting for the short, medium and long term for which appropriate time horizons might be 1 to 2 years, 2 to 5 years and more than 5 years. Clearly, the further into the future one looks, the less certain one can be of the accuracy of one's projections. However long-range forecasting is an essential input to top management's thinking, for it provides a basis for deciding upon the direction in which an organisation is to go and so influences long-term capital investment decisions. It is also important to recognise that in this sense forecasting has a material effect upon future events – for example, if it takes 5 years to build an integrated steel plant with a life-expectancy of 15 years, then a decision taken today about the construction of such a plant will directly affect the availability of steel for a period 5 to 20 years from now. Similarly, our ability to sell products and services today is the consequence of past decisions to provide and sell such products and services.

It follows from the foregoing observation that an organisation's ability to change direction will be very limited in the short term, in that its alternatives will be constrained by its existing structure and product–service mix, while in the very long run its ability to change is almost infinite. For the purpose of this section we are concerned with the short to medium term in which an organisation is concerned with specific market opportunities open to it by virtue of its structure and skills, its product–service mix, its geographical scope etc. and will ignore the problems of long-range forecasting and policy formulation.

SOME DEFINITIONS ...

Forecasting:
    Forecasting is the systematic analysis of market data, the purpose of which is to make firm quantitative estimates of the size of consumer demand for a product at specified dates in the future. (John Treasure, personal correspondence)

    ... is a basic and inescapable responsibility of business management. The systematic marshalling of facts and judgement for gauging future company prospects is essential for sound decision-making, planning, and control. Most important of all in this process, for most firms, is the determination of future sales volume. (NICB, 1963)

Sales forecast:
    ... the basic planning document of the typical firm. (Koonz and O'Donnell, 1980)

Company sales forecast:
    ... is the expected level of company sales based on a chosen marketing plan and assumed environmental conditions. (Kotler, 1967)

Sales quota:
    ... the sales goal set for a product line, company division or company agent. It is primarily a managerial device for defining and stimulating sales effort. (Kotler, 1967)

Sales budget:
    ... is a conservative estimate of the expected volume of sales and is used primarily for making current purchasing, production, and cash flow decisions. (Kotler, 1967)

... AND AN EXPLANATION

These definitions of forecasting emphasise that the objective is the systematic preparation of a quantified statement of expected demand for a specified future time period. Second, they emphasise that the forecast is the basis for planning and thereby for control through the comparison of actual performance against projected performance. Third, forecasting requires the combination of facts and judgement.

In order to develop a forecast for a specific product or service, it is usually necessary first to make a broad forecast of the general business or economic climate, for the performance of any industry sector is closely tied to the performance of the economy as a whole. Similarly, an industry forecast is a necessary prerequisite for a company sales forecast, as individual suppliers can assess their own potential performance only in light of the total demand for products or services of the type they can supply and the competition from other suppliers for a share of this demand.

Once a company forecast has been prepared, management can assess what action will be necessary to permit its achievement and embody this in a plan for a specified future period. Within this plan the sales quota represents the target performance, while the sales budget spells out the financial implications of operating at this designated level.

PREPARING A SALES FORECAST

The NICB survey referred to among our definitions suggests the following 11 steps in the preparation of a sales forecast:

1. Determine purposes for which forecasts are to be used
2. Divide company products into homogeneous groups
3. Determine factors affecting sales of each product group and their relative importance
4. Choose forecasting method or methods best suited to job
5. Gather all available data
6. Analyse data
7. Check and cross-check deductions resulting from analysis

8. Make assumptions regarding effect of factors that cannot be measured or forecast
9. Convert deductions and assumptions into specific product and territorial forecasts and quotas
10. Apply these to company operation
11. Review performance and revise forecast periodically.

From this list it is apparent that steps 3 and 4 are of central importance. Among the many variables that must be taken into account (step 3) Buyers and Holmes (1959) suggest the following:

- The firm's own sales and those of its competitors area by area
- Whether its share of business is increasing or decreasing
- Seasonal fluctuations
- The effect of past or potential population movements
- Changing consumer tastes
- The effect of introducing new products by the concern itself or by competitors
- Increases or decreases to be made in the advertising budget
- The effect of sales promotion schemes planned by the firm itself or by its competitors (so far as is known)
- The effects of any planned improvement in existing products or of their discontinuation
- The possibility of selling in new territories or of discontinuing sales in existing ones.

It should be stressed that this checklist is suggestive not definitive, and items may be added or deleted by the forecaster, depending upon the particular requirements of their industry.

In turn, this decision will be heavily influenced by the method chosen for developing a forecast.

| Box 7.3 | *Anticipating trends* |

On 30 January, 2006, ACNielsen unveiled five predictions for the coming year in terms of retail trends based upon its detailed analyses of consumer behaviour.

The first trend predicted is that there will be a surge in demand for foods and beverages with a low glycemic index (GI). According to its research into health and wellness issues among American consumers, ACNielsen estimates that 50% are 'health neglectors' who care little about their weight and tend to be overweight. Given the size of this segment, it is clear that any new food trend will need to be taken up by at least some of these consumers if it is to take off. Between December 2004 and December 2005, sales of GI products increased by almost 150%, leading ACNielsen to predict the potential emergence of a blockbuster trend. Another major increase detected amongst 'health activists', who are highly educated and have more money to spend on expensive health foods, was a 52% growth in the demand for antioxidants, with liquid tea showing an increase of 1000% in dollar sales.

The second prediction is that the so-called 'dollar store' will increase the variety on offer, even though this will mean some products will exceed the one dollar price point, with a view to attracting sales away from the mass merchandisers on a value-based proposition

During 2005, beer sales, which constituted 54% of all alcohol sales, stalled. To counteract this downward trend, brewers are responding to consumers' desire for experimentation by launching new flavours, seasonal options and packaging innovations. Imported and craft beers are also expected to enhance the image of beer and win share from other beverages.

In 2006 the 'baby boomer' segment will see the oldest members turn 60. Given that 'boomers' have been regarded as a homogeneous segment for many years, it is anticipated that there could be a backlash from the younger members if marketers overemphasise the 'golden years' of retirement. The message is that you will need to tailor marketing campaigns to subsegments rather than treating all boomers in the same way.

The fifth prediction is that the grocery channels will continue to evolve to focus on service rather than convenience and so differentiate themselves from the category killers, mass merchandisers and supercenters.

SALES FORECASTING METHODS

Among the more common forecasting techniques are the following:

1. Jury of executive opinion (expert opinion)
2. Sales force composite
3. Buyers' intentions (users' expectations)
4. Time series analysis
5. Other mathematical techniques.

Jury of Executive Opinion
The 1963 NICB survey, *Forecasting Sales*, cites the following pros and cons of this method:

The process of combining and averaging or otherwise evaluating the opinion of top executives is one of the oldest methods of forecasting. It reflects a tendency to broaden the base of predicting. Any firm operating under such a system usually brings together executives from the sales, manufacturing, finance, purchasing, and administrative fields to secure a wide coverage of experience and opinion.

The advantages and disadvantages of this method are summarised by the NICB as follows.

Advantages:
1. Can provide forecasts easily and quickly
2. May not require the preparation of elaborate statistics
3. Brings a variety of specialised viewpoints together for a pooling of experience and judgement
4. May be the only feasible means of forecasting especially in the absence of adequate data.

Disadvantages:
1. Is inferior to a more factual basis of forecasting, since it is based too heavily on opinion
2. Requires costly executive time
3. Is not necessarily more accurate because opinion is averaged
4. Disperses responsibility for accurate forecasting
5. Presents difficulties in making breakdowns by products, time intervals, or markets for operating purposes.

Sales Force Composite
As the name suggests, this approach consists of pooling information from members of the sales force and modifying it in light of the judgement of successive levels of sales management (e.g. area, district, national) to arrive at an overall assess-

ment. A reversal of this procedure is then followed in setting quotas. The NICB assesses this method as follows.

Advantages:
1. Uses specialised knowledge of people closest to the market
2. Places responsibility for the forecast in the hands of those who must produce the results
3. Gives sales force greater confidence in quotas developed from forecasts
4. Tends to give results greater stability because of the magnitude of the sample
5. Lends itself to the easy development of product, territory, customer or salesmen breakdowns.

Disadvantages:
1. Salesmen are poor estimators, often being either more optimistic or more pessimistic than conditions warrant
2. If estimates are used as a basis for setting quotas, salesmen are inclined to understate the demand in order to make the goal easier to achieve
3. Salesmen are often unaware of the broad economic patterns shaping future sales and are thus incapable of forecasting trends for extended periods
4. Since sales forecasting is a subsidiary function of the sales force, sufficient time may not be made available for it
5. Requires an extensive expenditure of time by executives and sales force
6. Elaborate schemes are sometimes necessary to keep estimates realistic and free from bias.

Buyers' Intentions
Simplistically, this approach consists of asking customers, or a representative cross-section of them, what their buying intentions are for a future period.

The strengths and weaknesses of this technique are as follows.

Advantages:
1. Bases forecast on information obtained direct from product users, whose buying actions will actually determine sales
2. Gives forecaster a subjective feel of the market and of the thinking behind users' buying intentions

3. Bypasses published or other indirect sources, enabling the inquiring company to obtain its information in the form and detail required
4. Offers a possible way of making a forecast where other methods may be inadequate or impossible to use – e.g. forecasting demand for a new industrial product for which no previous sales record is available.

Disadvantages:
1. Is difficult to employ in markets where users are numerous or not easily located
2. Depends on the judgement and cooperation of product users, some of whom may be ill-informed or uncooperative
3. Bases forecast on expectations, which are subject to subsequent change
4. Requires considerable expenditure of time and manpower.

Time Series Analysis
The logic underlying time series analysis is that past results reflect a causal relationship between actions, e.g. buying, and trends in the environment which are likely to continue into the future. If, therefore, we can forecast changes in the underlying trends then we should be able to forecast the future behaviour of the action we are trying to predict.

Four factors are generally recognised as likely to affect sales on a month-by-month basis:

1. Secular trends – i.e. the long-term tendency of sales to increase or decrease as a result of changes in disposable income, population, etc.
2. Seasonal variations
3. Cyclical trends associated with the overall level of activity in the business cycle
4. Random, accidental or residual fluctuations – such as a strike of French aircraft controllers!

A battery of statistical techniques has been devised for adjusting data to allow for changes in these factors and a number of texts describe their use. Fundamentally, however, the final results are as good only as the data used in the calculations, so that the quality of the information used remains of critical importance.

Chapter summary

In this chapter we have explored the theme that environmental factors constitute the ultimate constraint upon an organisation's objectives and its ability to achieve them. Commencing with a review of the five basic environmental forces – demographic, social/cultural, political, economic and technological – we looked next at the broad cyclical and secular trends which result from their interaction.

Next we summarised some of the possible consequences of the environ-mental changes which we can see all around us at the present time. While it is probably true to say that man has always lived in a state of change, all the evidence suggests that the second half of the twentieth century was more dynamic and turbulent than most, with clear effects upon both values and lifestyles.

In order to cope with this turbulence, and the uncertainty that it engenders, it was proposed that organisations must undertake long-term strategic planning. An essential element of this strategic planning must be a highly developed information-gathering or early-warning system to pick up the first indications of environmental changes which may affect the organisation.

To end the chapter we looked briefly at sales forecasting as an essential input to the short-term action planning of the firm.

In the next chapter our focus will switch from the macro- to the microenvironment, with an examination of industry and competitor analysis.

Recommended reading

Aaker, D. A. (2004) *Strategic Market Management* (7th edn). Chichester: John Wiley and Sons.
Brownlie, D. (1999) Environmental analysis, in Baker, M. J. (ed.) *Encyclopedia of Marketing*. London: International Thomson Business Press.
Brownlie, D. (2003) Environmental scanning, in Baker, M. J. (ed.) *The Marketing Book* (5th edn). Oxford: Butterworth Heinemann.

REFERENCES

ACNielsen (2006) Year in Preview. Press release, 30 January, www.acnielsen.com.
Albrecht, K. (1979) *Stress and the Manager*. Englewood Cliffs, NJ: Prentice Hall.
Baker, M. J. (1975) *Marketing New Industrial Products*. London: Macmillan – now Palgrave Macmillan.
Baker, M. J. (1983) *Market Development*. Harmondsworth: Penguin.
Baker, M. J. (ed.) (1995) *Companion Encyclopedia of Marketing*, London: Routledge.
Brownlie, D. (1995) Environmental analysis, in Baker, M. J. (ed.) *Companion Encyclopedia of Marketing*. London: Routledge, pp. 238–50.
Buyers, C. I. and Holmes, G. A. (1959) *Principles of Cost Accountancy*. London: Cassell.
Diffenbach, J. (1983) Corporate environmental analysis in large US corporations, *Long Range Planning*, 16(3): 107–16.

Drucker, P. F. (1968) *The Practice of Management*. London: Heinemann.
Dwek, R. (1995) Vintage crop, *Marketing Business* (September).
Galbraith, J. K. (1958) *The Affluent Society*. Harmondsworth: Penguin.
Kast, F. E. and Rosenweig, J. E. (1974) *Organisation and Management: A Systems Approach* (2nd edn). Maidenhead: McGraw-Hill..
Koontz, H. and O'Donnell, C. (1980) *Essentials of Management*. New York: McGraw-Hill.
Kotler, P. (1967) *Marketing Management*. Englewood Cliffs, NJ: Prentice Hall.
Levitt, T. (1960) Marketing myopia, *Harvard Business Review* (July–August).
MacLuhan, M. (1964) *Understanding Media*. London: Kegan Paul.
NICB (1963) *Forecasting Sales*. New York, p. 109.
Porter, M. E. and Ketels, C. (2003) *UK Competitiveness: Moving to the Next Stage*. DTI (May).
Roberts, P. and Hill, J. (2005) *Survival Guide to the Near Future*.

www.brandchannel.com/papers_review.asp?sp–id=677.
Rosenberg, N. and Frischtak, C. R. (1984) Technological innovation and long waves, in Freeman, C. (ed.) *Design Innovation and Long Cycles in Economic Development*. London: Royal College of Art.
Rostow, W. W. (1962) *The Process of Economic Growth* (2nd edn). New York: W. W. Norton.
Schwartz, N. D. (1999) The tech boom will keep on rocking, *Fortune* (February).
Toffler, A. (1970) *Future Shock*. London: Bodley Head.
van Duijn, J. J. (1983) *The Long Wave in Economic Life*. London: George Allen & Unwin.

NOTE

1 Chapter 2 in Baker, M. J. (1996) *Marketing* (6th edn) Macmillan – now Palgrave Macmillan provides a broad overview of this topic.

Industry and competitor analysis

*Advance information about the enemy will enable a wise
sovereign or a good general to win more victories and achieve
greater success.*

SUN TZU

After reading Chapter 8 you will be able to:

✔ Discuss the nature of competition and explain why non-price competition has become
the dominant form.

✔ Justify, define and execute a competitor analysis.

✔ Describe the concept of the value chain and its use as a diagnostic tool.

✔ Define the nature of critical success factors and their role in developing a competitive
advantage.

✔ Understand the importance of skills and competencies to business success.

✔ Explain benchmarking as a process for evaluating competitor performance.

✔ Discuss the growth of strategic alliances as a response to competitive pressures.

INTRODUCTION

In conducting an external analysis one of the key areas for review is the competition. Despite this it often tends to be neglected or subjected to less formal analysis than other elements of the marketing appreciation. This view is implicit in a seminal article by William Rothschild (1979) entitled 'Competitor analysis'. In Rothchild's view far too little emphasis has been given to competitor analysis due to overconfidence about its importance, confusion as to how to set about it, and/or concern that such analysis might require them to do something unethical or illegal. As to what questions to ask, Rothschild suggests the following:

- Who is the competition now and who will it be in the future?
- What are the key competitors' strategies, objectives, and goals?
- How important is a specific market to the competitors and are they committed enough to continue to invest?
- What unique strengths do the competitors have?
- Do they have any weaknesses that make them vulnerable?
- What changes are likely in the competitors' future strategies?
- What are the implications of competitors' strategies on the market, the industry and one's own company?

As to whether one can obtain such information by legal and ethical means, the answer is unequivocally 'yes'. One only has to review financial analysts' reports or companies' own statements to appreciate how much they are willing to reveal of their broad intentions. Clearly, to determine who the competition is one needs to describe the product–market scope with varying degrees of specificity as discussed earlier – starting with brands and working back to Levitt's question 'What business are you in?', which requires one to consider all possible means of meeting the need served. Once competitors have been identified, then one should seek to answer Rothschild's questions in a formal and structured way using whatever sources of information one can.

From the discussion of competition in Chapter 2 and the subsequent discussion of competitive strategy in Chapter 3, it has become clear that the firm's ultimate success or failure depends upon its ability to position itself effectively vis-à-vis other firms seeking to serve the same end-use markets. It follows that a vital element in terms of the situation analysis prior to the formulation of a marketing plan is an assessment of the competition and their strengths and weaknesses.

In the new competitive environment that emerged in the second half of the twentieth century, leading to what we have identified as the 'rediscovery' of marketing, the sources of competitive advantage that had characterised competition from the time of the Industrial Revolution began to change. While technological innovation in both product and process development remains a *necessary* condition for competitiveness, it is no longer *sufficient*, save in a few industries such as pharmaceuticals where it is still possible to enforce intellectual property rights. Otherwise advantage based on technology is quickly eroded as firms benchmark their competitors and develop comparable products of their own. In this climate other sources of competitive advantage assume greater importance, many of which depend on relationships with suppliers and customers and recognition of the fact that firms do not exist in isolation but are part of a network or system represented by a *value chain*. Recognition of the existence of such a value chain focuses analysis on the organisations that comprise them and the nature and strength of the relationships between them. In turn such analysis has led to attempts to establish and define *critical success factors* and the role of *skills* and *competencies* as sources of advantage. To do so, benchmarking has become both important and fashionable and has led to recognition that success will often depend more on collaboration than competition leading to the formation of *partnerships* and *strategic alliances*. It is these issues that lie at the heart of competitor analysis and form the subject matter of this chapter.

COMPETITOR ANALYSIS

In an ideal world one would seek to document competitive firms in as much detail as possible following Rothschild's advice. However, the cost of acquiring and maintaining a database on competitive firms may far exceed the worth of the actual data and the cost of acquiring it. For example, in August 1991 the *Sunday Times* reported that ICI had spent over £10 million in documenting the activities of Hanson Trust as a basis for a defence against a possible takeover. In the view of some city analysts, such expenditures were regarded as at best misguided and at worse a misappropriation of shareholders' funds.

If, therefore, one is to undertake a reasonable assessment of one's competitors, one must first establish what are the most appropriate performance indicators, and then select those that can be documented most cost-effectively.

In John Stapleton's book (1987), it is suggested that the most appropriate means for assessing competition is in truly financial terms as this enables comparisons to be made and a standard to be developed against which the firm's own performance can be measured. To structure such an analysis Stapleton proposes nine different indicators. The first of these, which he calls 'financial performance', is a simple chart intended to highlight the profitability and growth of significant suppliers and compare their performance against each other. At a minimum, this requires recording of data for sales, net income, total assets, and number of ordinary shares together with net profit expressed as a percentage return on sales, total assets and ordinary shares. Superficially, it would appear very simple to obtain such data either from the company's own published accounts or else from companies such as Dun & Bradstreet, which specialise in the compilation of such information. Of course, the problem is that the more readily available such data is the more likely it becomes that the firm has multiple products on sale in multiple markets. But, as our discussion of strategy has indicated, the important criterion is the definition of market segments within which the firm has chosen to compete. Accordingly, unless the financial data relates to a single-product firm operating in only one market it will offer only the most generalised form of comparative data.

Much the same criticism applies to the second of Stapleton's analyses, which he calls 'standard comparison'. This comprises recording the entries one would find in a detailed profit and loss account for each main competitor.

A more broadly based summary is csontained in Table 8.1, and may be used at either the firm or at the specific product market level. As the headings suggest what is called for here is that appraisers seek to rate their own company's performance on a number of critical success factors and then perform the same analysis on the major competitive firms. Table 8.1 is included for illustrative purposes as the nature and number of critical success factors to be rated will depend very much upon the firm and industry to which it belongs. We return to these later in the chapter. The remaining documentation provided by Stapleton deals with price and market share relationships, geographical sales distribution, penetration of sales outlets, competitive pricing etc. While it may not be possible to get precise data on each of these factors, this is the kind of grassroots market data that one might reasonably expect the sales force to collect as part of its day-to-day activity.

Information of the kind discussed in the preceding paragraphs comprises an essential element of the firm's marketing information system (MkIS). The MkIS is itself a subset of the larger management information system (MIS), which will contain the firm's financial information system, production information system etc. Most MkISs will contain a number of separate modules dealing with sales, forecasting, product planning, market research, distribution, pricing, promotion and new product development. The objective of the MkIS is to synthesise and make readily available all the information which the firm possesses which is relevant to its marketing activities. To achieve this it is usual for a person (or persons) to be made responsible for collecting and collating the data and entering it into the database which is the heart of the system. Implicit in the previous paragraph is recognition that inputs to the MkIS may come from a number of different sources.

As we saw in Chapter 6, marketing data is usually classified as being either primary or secondary in origin. Secondary data is that which is available from published sources, while primary data is usually collected for a specific purpose, for example by using the sales force or commissioning professional marketing research. Some of these issues were discussed in Chapter 6 but readers requiring a more extensive coverage of the objectives and methods of collection should consult one of the recommended textbooks on market research.

TABLE 8.1 The role of marketing information in achieving critical success factors: some preliminary thoughts

Success factor	Studies citing importance	Operationalisation of success factors	Expected market information elements
Product advantage	Cooper, 1979; Cooper and Kleinschmidt, 1986, 1991	Strategic success factors Excellent relative product quality in comparison to competitive offerings; good value for money (perceived by the customer); excellence in meeting customer needs, inclusion of benefits perceived by the customer as useful; benefits which are obvious to the customer; superior price/performance characteristics; unique attributes	Customer perceptions of competitive offerings; technological dimensions of competitive offerings; customer perceptions of new product's attributes and benefits; feedback from customers after trial; feedback on customer understanding of the message; perceptual maps based on customer data; technical specifications; product design information; attributes and features specifications
Well-specified protocol	As above; Rothwell, 1977; Rothwell et al., 1974; Rubenstein et al., 1976	Firm's knowledge and understanding, prior to development, of the target market, customer needs, wants, preferences; the product concept; product specifications and requirements	Research information detailing market demographics/psychographics; customer needs, wants and preferences; technical specifications, product design information, attributes and features specifications (prior to development)
Market attractiveness	Maidique and Zirger, 1984; de Brentani, 1989	High growth rates, high market need for product type; stability of demand; relative price insensitivity; high trial of new products	Economic market data; economic trends; level of employment; income levels; inflation rates
Top management support	Ramanujam and Mensch, 1985; McDonough and Leifer, 1986	Levels of risk aversion; aspects of corporate culture	Risk involved; identification of product champions; power and influence distribution among managers
Synergy/ familiarity	Maidique and Zirger, 1984; Rothwell et al., 1974	Knowledge of technology; relevance to other projects; access to scientific institutes and laboratories	Extent of new knowledge involved; technology centres where knowledge resides; key scientists; technological networks of firms

SOURCE: Hart et al. (1999) The effectiveness of marketing information in enhancing new product success rates, *European Journal of Innovation Management* 2(1): 20–35

As Makens (1989) observes:

> The task of gathering and analysing competitive information is generally less difficult than knowing what to do with the acquired data. Managers within many industries find themselves flooded with competitive information, but seem to be baffled concerning what to do.

Makens accordingly suggests a number of key indicators to help distinguish the important from the unimportant.

First, Makens emphasises the importance of monitoring trends rather than responding to particular occurrences as and when they occur. Thus a lowering of price may be a temporary promotional device to move stock and help improve cash flows. However, a trend of consistently lowered prices may indicate that a firm is following an experience curve, production–pricing strategy, in an effort to gain market share and achieve new economies of scale. Of course an alternative interpretation of a firm consistently lowering its prices is that it is in deep competitive trouble in terms of its product performance and so can maintain sales only by giving away margins. In monitoring trends, therefore, one is seeking to establish consistency over time and also to be able to identify – and, hopefully, explain – variances from secular trends.

Other indicators Makens recommends one should monitor are shake-ups in management, as these frequently anticipate major changes in policy and strategy. Similarly stock market changes such as a change in share prices, in gearing or price–earnings ratios often reflect advanced knowledge of forthcoming changes in a firm's fortunes.

In sum, while it is important to monitor competitor activity, one has to be careful to avoid the trap of 'paralysis by analysis'. This phenomenon occurs when those responsible for creating and maintaining databases lose sight of the marginal value of information. When this occurs information overload is inevitable and analysts become paralysed by their inability to distinguish the important from the unimportant. While it may be tempting to squirrel away every little bit of information on one's market and competitors, a much more selective approach emphasising the number of key performance indicators that are regularly used, and are of proven relevance, is to be preferred.

According to West (1999):

A typical competitor information profile will cover:
- Ownership and organisational structure
- Financial history
- Financial resources
- Key decision-makers and their track records
- Staff resources
- Production resources and locations
- Product lines and portfolios
- Patents, licences and other unique assets
- Markets and segments serviced
- Distribution channels used
- Export activity and country supplied
- Sales and marketing activities.

The growing availability of computerised databases such as Textline, Dialog, Infoline and Nexis, which are available online for efficient and rapid searching, have greatly increased the potential of secondary research. West (1999) comments:

The depth and quality of information available varies considerably from market sector to market sector and from country to country but a diligent search can be expect to yield data on:
- Population size, structure into geodemographic groups and growth
- The structure of distribution and the importance of various channels
- Total sales, imports and exports of products
- Imports and exports by origin and destination
- Products available and their specifications
- New product launches
- Sources of supply
- New contracts and successful bidders for outstanding contracts
- List prices

- Advertising expenditure by product, industry sector and supplier
- New market entrants
- Staff movements
- Financial performance of suppliers. (pp. 259–60)

Clearly, each of the elements in these checklists may be disaggregated into numerous subfactors and documented in considerable detail. The earlier caveat on paralysis by analysis is repeated here. Further, in support of our view that simple summary diagrams are often much more illuminating than pages of statistics, we recommend the use of profiling diagrams or what John Saunders (1995) has called a 'competitor assessment grid'. Such a profile is given in Figure 8.1 and should be constructed using the critical success factors that are important in the industry/ market under consideration. We will return to these later in the chapter but first will revisit the subject of competition in general before introducing the idea of the value chain. Next we will look at critical success factors, which leads naturally into a discussion of skills and competencies. To conclude the chapter we discuss benchmarking as a procedure for appraising competitor performance and strategic alliances as a means of strengthening one's own position.

COMPETITION[1]

Although the concept of competition is central to both the study of economics and the practice of business, it is seldom that one finds economists attempting to define precisely what they mean by the term. It is equally rare for businessmen to consider the general nature of competition as a basis for making decisions about specific action. A recurring theme of this book is that while the dynamic nature of business means that one is rarely faced twice with exactly the same problem or decision, this is no justification for ignoring the potential contribution from past experience and the statement of theories based upon it.

In Chapter 2 we looked at competition in a generalised and abstract way and introduced the concept of market structure, conduct and performance as a framework within which to explore the role of marketing in the competitive process. As we

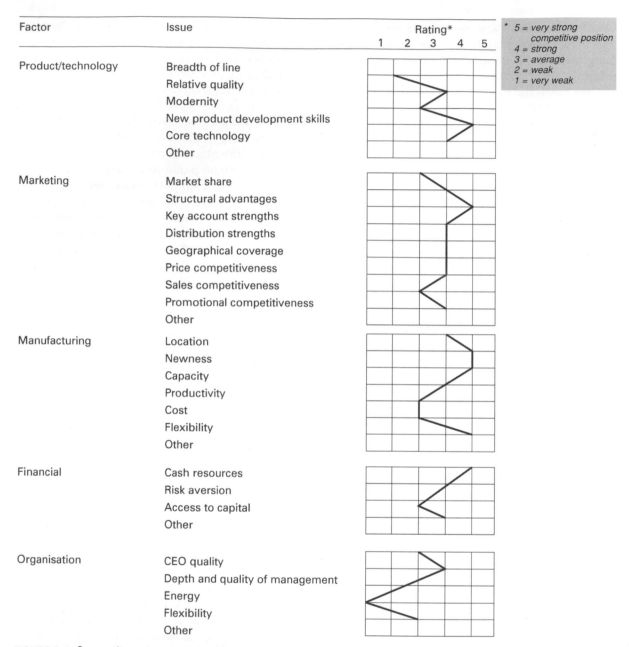

Factor	Issue	Rating*					* 5 = very strong competitive position 4 = strong 3 = average 2 = weak 1 = very weak
		1	2	3	4	5	

FIGURE 8.1 Competitor assessment grid

SOURCE: Saunders, J. (1995) Analysing the competition, in Thomas, M. J., *The Marketing Handbook* (4th edn). Aldershot: Gower

saw, this framework, developed by the school of industrial economists, provides the foundation for Michael Porter's analysis of competitive strategy and the basic options or generic strategies of cost leadership and differentiation. In turn this led to a broadly based discussion of the creation of competitive advantage and the contribution of marketing to competitive success. It is now time to examine these processes in more detail. Accordingly, in this section we shall seek to define competition and the different forms it can take, to provide some foundation for the subsequent discussion of the marketing mix and its component elements of product, price, promotion and place.

Lawrence Abbott (1995), a distinguished economist, suggests that outside the economic sphere, the word 'competition' means a type of activity that involves contestants who are pitted against each other, some common goal sought by them, efforts on the part of each to achieve superiority in attaining the goal, some methods of judging superiority, judges or judging mechanisms to do the judging, the selection of one or perhaps several of the contestants, and rejection of the others. Within the field of economics, precise definitions of this kind are less easy to come by, and usually finish up not by defining competition per se, but the conditions under which it exists, or its consequences. Among the exceptions to this generalisation is J. M. Clark (1961), who sees competition as the 'availability of alternatives', in which availability implies both the existence of alternatives and the ability of participants to choose freely between them.

Proponents of this school of thought approximate much more closely the businessman's view of competition than that of their more traditional professional colleagues, who assume product homogeneity as a basic prerequisite for the study of competition. As we saw in Chapter 2, it was the potential of excess supply for homogeneous products which motivated producers to differentiate their products in an attempt to create and sustain purchase loyalty, and precipitated a switch in orientation from production to selling and marketing. Thus Clark sees competition as a dynamic process, the central element of which is offering the other party a bargain good enough to induce them to deal with you in the face of their free option of dealing with others. Similarly, Abbott (1995) sees it as the effort of each producer to get, or to keep, patronage which might go to another. These efforts take the form of striving to make the offer more attractive to the buyers than the offers of competitors. This improved attractiveness of the offer may be a lower price, or it may be improved quality, a more attractive design, a more useful or attractive package, greater convenience of location of the point of sale, the assurance of dependability that comes from a long-established record (a 'brand'), improved after-sale services, such as repairs or adjustments, and many other features. By contrast, perhaps the ultimate irony is that the economists' so-called 'perfect competition' means the complete absence of all these activities.

According to the classical economist, under conditions of perfect competition the demand curve is horizontal, each supplier has a U-shaped cost curve, and produces a homogeneous product: there is a large number of buyers and sellers, all of whom have perfect knowledge; there is complete freedom of entry and exit from the industry, and the entrepreneurs' sole motivation is profit maximisation. The assumption of perfect knowledge eliminates both the need for, and the economic feasibility of sales promotion, while the assumption of product homogeneity eliminates the possibility of product differentiation, so quantity is the only variable of competitive behaviour, and the unique solution – what price and quantity – is the logical outcome of the assumed impersonal market force. Under these conditions, competition will result in a single price, for no one would buy from a supplier seeking a higher price than other sellers, and no seller would be willing to sell for less.

Such conditions describe a purely competitive market in equilibrium, which is the end result with which price theory is concerned. Before reaching equilibrium, price competition becomes more active when one seller creates a price differential and thus puts their rivals at a disadvantage, which forces them to adjust their own prices to meet competition until equilibrium is reached. At this point no further differential can be advantageous to anyone, and the price adjustment process stops. In other words, price competition does not occur under conditions of equilibrium, but is an institutional device for bringing about price movements towards equilibrium. Without competition a uniform price above equilibrium might persist, buyers would be exploited and resources would not be allocated in the most effective way. Thus, perfect competition represents an ideal situation, and any departure from it is considered to be imperfection in the market, which is undesirable.

The economists' strong emphasis on price relative to the other elements of a company's marketing strategy can be explained according to Philip Kotler (1972) by historical, technical and social reasons. The historical reason lies in the environment of the economy at the time when economists such as Adam Smith and Ricardo first began to develop systematic economic theory in conditions dominated by scarcity of resources, low consumer incomes, seller's markets and few economies of large scale. The typical nation's output consisted of raw materials and finished consumer goods, which were highly standardised, and little effort was made to differentiate them through branding, packaging or advertising. The major variable differentiating competitive offerings was price, and the low level of income emphasised the sensitivity of price as a marketing variable.

The technical reason is that price has more tractable properties for purposes of analysis, being quantitative, unambiguous and unidimensional, whereas product quality, product image, customer services, promotion and similar factors are qualitative, ambiguous and multidimensional. Similarly, for social purposes, the price mechanism provides an efficient and effective method to guide both sellers and buyers in maximising their satisfaction through the use of the scarce resources over which they have control.

Clearly there have been significant changes in the economic environment since Adam Smith's time. As Udell observed as long ago as 1972, the present economic environment is characterised by abundant resources, many wealthy consumers, a buyer's market and economies of large scale. As a consequence, competition can no longer be described in terms of a large number of firms offering homogeneous products to buyers with perfect knowledge, nor can a theory of competitive behaviour be restricted to pricing. Instead, today's theory must recognise the role of non-price factors, and it is these which are essentially the domain of marketing, and underlie its recent prominence as a business discipline.

NON-PRICE COMPETITION

Udell offers a satisfactory approach to distinguishing between price and non-price competition when he points out that the former implies that the firm accepts its demand curve as given, and manipulates its price to try to attain its objectives, while in non-price competition it seeks to change the location and shape of its demand curve.

The importance of non-price variables in influencing demand was first recognised in the early 1930s, when Joan Robinson (1933) and Edwin Chamberlin (1933) independently (but almost simultaneously) published their theories of imperfect competition. Chamberlin's theory introduced

the notion of product differentiation into the explanation of competitive behaviour when he argued that a general class of product is differentiated if any significant basis exists for distinguishing the goods or services of one seller from those of another. Such a basis may be real or fancied, as long as it is of any importance to buyers and leads to a preference for one variety of product over another. Where such differentiation exists, even though it be slight, buyers will be paired with sellers not by chance, as under competition, but according to their preferences. Chamberlin stated that differentiation may be based upon certain characteristics of the product itself, such as exclusive patented features, trade marks, trade names, peculiarities of the package or container, if any, or singularity in quality, design, colour or style. It may also exist with respect to the condition surrounding its sale, such as the seller's location in retail trade, the general tone of doing business, reputation for fair dealing, and all personal links which attach his customers either to himself or to his establishment.

Chamberlin's theory thus gives explicit recognition to three of marketing's four 'Ps' – product, price and place – and implicitly acknowledges the role of the fourth – promotion – when he refers to branding and personal links between the buyer and seller. These distinctions are also made and further developed in the work of economists such as Knight (1936), Stigler (1948) and Machlup (1953), and so provide a sound foundation for the evolution of a theory of competition which is central to the practice of marketing and enshrined in Borden's (1965) concept of the marketing mix (see Chapter 14). With four basic sets of variables to manipulate, it is clear that the marketer has many more degrees of freedom available to him in developing a unique selling strategy, and one which frees him from the tyranny of having to accept a market price set by impersonal forces outside his own control. As Udell (1964) points out, the use of non-price variables is preferable to only manipulating the price to get the customers' patronage for at least four fundamental reasons:

1. The relatively well-to-do customers of today are interested in more than just price. They are interested in product quality, distinctiveness,

style, and many other factors which lead to both physical and psychological satisfaction. From product differentiation and sales promotion, the consumer receives a great deal of psychological satisfaction and utility. Consequently, firms try to satisfy consumer desires and increase their sales by product differentiation and sales promotion.

2. The products of modern industry are fairly complex, and buyers often require a substantial amount of information in making purchase decisions. Marketing communications, in addition to being persuasive, are a major source of information about products, prices, and suppliers. Also important is the fact that many marketing communications help to reduce the amount of searching time required of buyers. Therefore, the informative value of sales efforts is important to buyers and sellers alike.

3. In today's competitive economy, supply or production capacity generally exceeds demand and, therefore, nearly all sellers are forced either to be highly competitive or almost collusive in their pricing. Because there may be little or no freedom for a company to deviate from the market price, pricing sometimes is not a meaningful parameter of competitive strategy as is readily apparent in the uniform prices of many consumer goods in the UK.

4. It is through successful product differentiation that a manufacturer may obtain some pricing freedom. Products known to be identical must be priced identically in the marketplace. However, if a product can be favourably differentiated in the eyes of consumers some degree of pricing freedom is usually achieved.

It would seem clear, therefore, that marketing is essentially about non-price competition, and that this concept is central to its theory and practice. In later chapters we shall examine the nature of the marketing mix and the development of specific policies for each of the major factors – product, price, promotion and place – in some detail and so will not elaborate on them here. In this chapter the emphasis will be on the sources of competitive advantage and will include a discussion of the value chain, critical success factors (CSF), skills and competencies, benchmarking and the role of strategic alliances.

THE VALUE CHAIN

Value chain analysis was developed first by McKinsey & Co. in the 1960s as a tool to evaluate competition based on the view that business is a system which links raw materials (supply) with customers (demand) and comprising six basic elements:

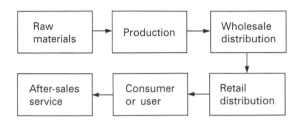

Starting with raw material extraction, the analysis proceeds by examining each major subsystem in turn in order to establish the interrelationship and interdependence between them in terms of:

1. *The degree of competition* within and between each subsystem; for example raw material extraction might be in the hands of only one or a few producers so that conditions are oligopolistic, while retail distribution could be characterised by thousands of small sellers, none of whom could influence the market. Clearly, the latter circumstances describe perfect competition, and both sets of conditions apply in the oil industry. Thus, in establishing the nature of competition one should measure:
   - the number of competitors
   - their profitability
   - their degree of integration
   - their cost structure
   - the existence and nature of any barriers to entry, for example technological, size of investment in production and/or marketing.
2. Where, in the total system, *value* is *added* by the activities of members of the production, distribution, or servicing subsystems. For example, a significant proportion of turnover in many consumer durable industries is accounted for by after-sales servicing and the efficiency of this sector may have a radical influence upon the market shares of individual suppliers, as well as on industry profitability.
3. *The location of economic leverage* in the system.

Does this arise from being a fully integrated producer, or can one exercise leverage by avoiding the extensive fixed investment implicit in vertical integration and concentrating on owning one subsystem?

4. Where is the system's *marketing leverage*? Usually this is associated with control of a scarce resource which might be an essential raw material, a patent or a process, control of a distribution channel, a brand name such as Intel or Elastoplast, or some other type of consumer franchise.

Once the analyst has established the major characteristics of the production, distribution and servicing subsystems, their next task must be a thorough

documentation of the consumer or user. Such documentation requires one to supply answers to the five basic questions which underlie all market research – who, what, where, when and how?

1. *Who* buys in terms of demographic and socioeconomic criteria such as age, sex, income, education, occupation, marital status etc. (for consumers), or status, authority, functional specialisation etc. (for users)? Who consumes? (Compare consumption and purchase of breakfast cereals, and hand tools in a factory and so forth).

2. *What* do people buy in terms of variety, design, quality, performance and price characteristics?

3. *Where* do people buy? In specialist outlets, in

Where in the system are company's measurable strengths and weaknesses
(How company compares with competition – today and future)

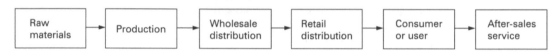

How does company compare in raw materials?
- Do they have advantage in supply?
- Degree of integration?

How does company compare in technology?
- What is their rate of product, process improvement?
- How good is process efficiency?
- Advantages in location of facilities?

How does company compare in cost and profit?
- Raw material costs?
- Processing costs?
- Profit?
- Return on investment?
- Access to capital?

How does company compare in channels?
- In which channels are company sales concentrated?
- Do products reach point of sale faster or more efficiently?

How does company compare in distributors?
- Have they more, larger, or more effective distributors?
- Share of channel's sales?

How does company compare in economics?
- Compensation of distributors?
- Distribution costs?
- Service costs?

How does company compare in products?
- Have they greater variety, better design or quality, lower prices, superior performance?
- Share of market?

How does company compare in customers?
- Who are core buyers; core customers?
- Do these customers buy more frequently in larger quantities or more consistently?
- How is company's product used?
- Who are core competitors?

How does company compare in service?
- Does company have a service advantage – type, quality, quantity?

How does company compare in pricing?
- Do they have price advantage (price/quality relationship)?
- Are they price leaders?

How does company compare in economics?
- Service costs?
- Cost of consumer marketing?

FIGURE 8.2 Company's measurable strengths and weaknesses

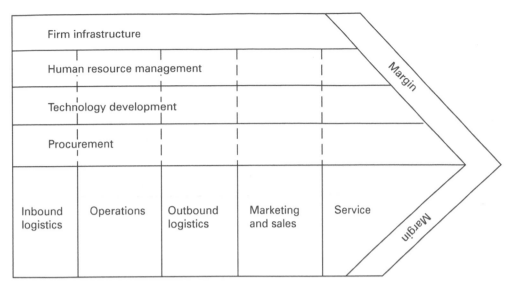

FIGURE 8.3 Porter's value chain

SOURCE: Porter, M. E. (1985) *Competitive Advantage: Creating and Sustaining Superior Performance.* New York: Free Press

general purpose outlets, by mail or telephone from a catalogue, in the home or on their premises, online via the internet; that is, how important is direct selling to representatives versus indirect selling via the media?

4. *When* do people buy? Are purchases seasonal, regular, irregular, associated with another activity etc.?

5. *How* do people buy? Impulsively, after considerable deliberation, in large quantities, small quantities, from multiple sources or a single source and so forth?

A sixth and equally important question is *why*? and like our other five questions one cannot usually supply a definitive and factual answer. However, when one considers that consumers (or users) do not buy products, as such, but rather the satisfactions yielded by the product, then even a partial understanding of the satisfactions looked for will go a long way towards explaining actual behaviour in the marketplace.

At this juncture one should have developed a good understanding of both the company and the environment in which it is operating. Given this information, it becomes possible to identify the company's particular strengths and weaknesses in terms of environmental opportunities along the lines indicated in Figure 8.2.

While it was McKinsey & Co. that introduced

the above analysis into the class 'creative marketing strategy' which the author was teaching at the Harvard Business School in 1970, it was Michael Porter who firmly established it as an important diagnostic technique in *Competitive Advantage* (1985). Porter's original conceptualisation is illustrated in Figure 8.3.

It should be appreciated that McKinsey and Porter's conceptualisations differ – the former is concerned with an industry and covers all the stages from the acquisition of the raw materials to be used in creating a product or service, and the value added by production, distribution (including sales and marketing activities) and after-sales services. As such it is concerned with the competitive activities in the industry/market and is similar to Porter's five forces model. By contrast, Porter's value chain is focused on the firm and is concerned with the primary activities involved in the creation of the product/service, and the support activities that enable and facilitate these primary activities. Most of the revenue earned by the firm is expended on these activities, with the margin representing the value added or surplus. Obviously, the more efficient the firm is in managing its primary and support activities, the larger the value added. Achieving the optimum balance between the nine activities will vary significantly according to the nature of the industry and its product, while within an industry, the individual firm's effectiveness will

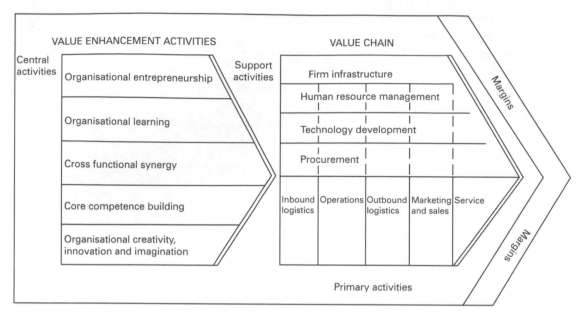

FIGURE 8.4 The composite value chain

SOURCE: Thomas, M. J. and Saxena, N. (1997) *The composite value system of the corporation.* University of Strathclyde Department of Marketing working paper

be a function of the success management has in developing a competitive advantage in one or more of the activities. In turn, this will call for detailed knowledge and understanding of both one's own and competitors' activities.

As originally conceived the value chain is concerned primarily with value creation and delivery and some aspects of value improvement. Since 1985, however, a number of other influential contributions by writers such as Hamel and Prahalad (1994), Bartlett and Ghoshal (1989) have elaborated further on value improving activities. These additional insights and Senge's (1990) work on the learning organisation led Normann and Ramirez (1993) to propose an expansion of the concept of the value chain into one of value constellation. They conclude that the 'value constellation' does not offer any breakthrough warranting replacement of the value chain concept, but it does lead them to the conclusion that the latter is capable of further enrichment by taking into account those activities that involve the entire organisation for value improvement. These they call *value enhancement activities*, which they categorise as comprising:

1. Organisational entrepreneurship
2. Organisational learning
3. Cross-functional synergy

4. Core competence building
5. Organisational creativity, innovation and imagination.

In the opinion of Thomas and Saxena (1997) the value enhancement activities need to be integrated with the value creation and value delivery activities to form a composite value system, as illustrated in Figure 8.4. They also express the view that one reason that Japanese companies outperform most Western companies is that they excel in the value enhancement activities where the West is still lagging.

VALUE ADDED AND BENCHMARKING

Recently, the Department of Trade and Industry (DTI) in the UK published the *Value Added Scoreboard* as a guide to the competitiveness of the most successful UK and European firms based on this criterion. For the purposes of the exercise value added (VA) is defined as:

Value added = Sales less the cost of bought-in goods and services

and is calculated based on 35 items of data taken

from the latest set of accounts available on 7 January of the 600 largest European companies and a separate ranking of the top 800 UK companies in terms of their VA.

The report explains:

This definition shows that there are three ways in which a company can maintain and increase its value added. The first is to develop and offer products and services that have much greater value to its customers than the cost of the materials, components and services used to make them. The second is to sell more of them, by developing new markets. The third way of increasing value added is to reduce the costs of bought-in items by more effective procurement and better use of bought-in material (e.g. minimising waste and reducing overuse).

In passing, it should be noted that the scoreboard is limited to UK and European companies as the accounts of American and Japanese companies do not contain sufficient information to calculate VA.

While the scoreboard is restricted to larger companies, the DTI point out that it is of value to smaller companies too because they can calculate their own VA and key value-added ratios and compare these with size-independent factors such as the rate of growth of value added, the way in which VA is used and the efficiency with which it is created. These measures can then be benchmarked with the best in class in their sector listed in the scoreboard. (The scoreboard contains full details on how to calculate VA and a calculator is provided on the scoreboard website.)

TABLE 8.2 Top 10 European and UK companies, 2005

European companies	(£billions)	UK companies	(£billions)
DaimlerChrysler	24.1	Shell	21.2
Siemens	22.5	BP	18.9
Deutsche Telekom	21.9	Vodaphone	17.6
France Telecom	21.6	HSBC	14.6
Shell	21.2	GlaxoSmithKline	12.5
BP	18.9	Royal Bank of Scotland	12.4
Vodaphone	17.6	BT	10.2
Total	17.2	Unilever	9.5
Volkswagen	17.0	Barclays	8.7
Allianz	15.8	Lloyds TSB	7.0

The scoreboard is published in two parts and is available free from the DTI. Part 1 contains commentary and analysis, while Part 2 contains detailed information on all 1400 companies included in the survey. The analysis covers the value added by different countries, by major sector and by individual companies.

There are 284 foreign-owned UK companies in the UK 800 accounting for £83bn of VA; the top ten of these companies contribute 20%.

The analysis also details the productivity and efficiency by sector. P1, or labour productivity, measures the value added per employee, while P2 is an efficiency measure calculated by dividing the value added by the sum of the cost of the employees plus depreciation (the equipment 'used up' during the year). Companies prefer P2 as a performance indicator since a high P2 means success and survival for the company. In recent years UK companies have scored much higher than European companies on P2 on all four scoreboards calculated by the DTI, details of which are contained in Part 1. Among the general conclusions drawn are:

1. Productivity and efficiency vary widely between the companies in any one sector in addition to the variation of their average values between sectors.
2. Successful companies grow their VA and do so efficiently.
3. In sectors where R&D and capex investment are important, investing a sufficiently high proportion of VA is necessary to sustain success. There is a clear link with performance.
4. In addition to adequate investment, successful companies:
   - Make good strategic choices
   - Exhibit operational excellence in terms of lean processes and attention to customers
   - Make wise and balanced investment in R&D, capex, brands and market development.

The *Value Added Scoreboard* is essential reading for anyone undertaking an analysis of industries and competitors in those industries.

CRITICAL SUCCESS FACTORS

A recurring theme of this book is that many currently fashionable topics in strategic thinking and analysis were first identified many years ago. The concept of critical or, as they are sometimes called, key success factors is a case in point, according to Klaus Grunert of the Aarhus School of Business, who is a leading authority on the subject.

According to Grunert and Ellegaard (1993):

> The idea that there are a few factors which are decisive for the success of the company, and that these factors can be ascertained, was first introduced by Daniel (1961) and later mainly elaborated by Rockart (1979); Bullen and Rockart (1981) in the context of designing management information systems. The identification of critical success factors was prompted by the observation that many senior managers did not make use of formal management information systems. In turn, this led to the conclusion that this was due to the fact that these systems were unnecessarily complex and should be structured around a smaller number of what they called *critical success factors*. According to Bullen and Rockart 'the limited number of areas in which satisfactory results will ensure successful competitive performance for the individual, department or organisation. Critical success factors are the few key areas where "things must go right" for the business to flourish and for the managers' goals to be attained.'

Grunert and Ellegaard believe that Rockart's (1979) concept of critical success factors was inspired by the issue of optimum match between environmental conditions and business characteristics. In other words, the core of business strategy. According to Rockart, there are five sources of critical success factors:

1. *The industry*, e.g. demand characteristics, technology employed, product characteristics etc. These can also affect all competitors within an industry, but their influence will vary according to the characteristics and sensitivity of individual industry segments.
2. *Competitive strategy and industry position* of the business in question, which is determined by the history and competitive positioning in the industry.
3. *Environmental factors* are the macroeconomic influences that affect all competitors within an industry, and over which the competitors have little or no influence, e.g. demographics, economic and government legislative policies etc.
4. *Temporal factors*, which are areas within a business causing a time-limited distress to the implementation of a chosen strategy, e.g. lack of managerial expertise or skilled workers.
5. *Managerial position*, i.e. the various functional managerial positions in a business each have their generic set of critical success factors.

However, Grunert and Ellegaard (1993) see Rockart's emphasis on the development of management information systems as only one of four different approaches to critical success factors, the others being:

1. As a unique characteristic of a company
2. As a heuristic tool for managers to sharpen their thinking
3. As a description of the major skills and resources required to perform successfully in a given market.

Based on these considerations, Grunert and Ellegaard defined a key success factor as:

> A skill or resource that a company can invest in, which, on the market the company is operating in, explains a major part of the observable differences in perceived value and/or costs.

According to their definition, key success factors possess the following characteristics:

1. A key success factor is a causal relationship. It expresses a relationship between the competitive advantage a company enjoys in a market, in terms of perceived value and relative costs, and the causes of that competitive advantage, in terms of certain skills and resources.
2. Since a key success factor is a skill or resource of the company, it is always actionable.
3. Key success factors are market-specific, but they transcend strategic groups in a market.
4. Key success factors are small in number. By definition, only a small number of factors can explain 'a major part' of the variance in perceived value and/or relative cost. This

implies that there may be markets where there are no key success factors, but only many small contributors to success.

5. Key success factors imply a causal relationship between a skill/resource and perceived value and/or relative cost. They are hence not directly related to performance measures like ROI.

As with many other management concepts, the logic is both compelling and attractive. The problem, however, is in operationalising the concept. In Chapter 2, reference was made to extensive research at Strathclyde University to establish a relationship between marketing, design and competitive success. Based upon the identification and classification of a very large number of factors that previous research had suggested were instrumental to success but, as was reported in Chapter 2 (under the heading Marketing and Competitive Success), 'Overall, it is possible to say that relatively few of the factors studied actually accounted for differences in performance.'

In a paper presented to the European Marketing Academy Conference in 1996, Grunert reported research in which he identified a number of key success factors in the market for seafood-based frozen ready meals, using a reverse laddering procedure that captured the relevant decision-makers' perceptions about how these factors determine the success of their companies. Based on his interviews, Grunert identified 11 potential *key success factors*, which were given names that were intended to be meaningful, unambiguous and expressing the contents of the factors that they represent. These are summarised in Table 8.3 below in which the factors are presented in accordance with the number of times they were mentioned.

Having identified the perceived success factors, the company with which Grunert was working used these as the basis for a competitor analysis. Having drawn up a list of the closest competitors, staff evaluated each of these relative to themselves in terms of each of the key success factors. Using a 7-point scale ranging from –3 (much weaker) to +3 (much stronger), each of the competitors was scored and those with a value of +1 were chosen for benchmarking. Table 8.3 summarises one competitor's position relative to the company, while Table 8.4 provides some possible explanations of the competitor's superior position.

TABLE 8.3 One competitor's position relative to own company

One competitor's position relative to own company (on a –3 to +3 scale)	Average	Min/max
1. Innovative product development	+1.9	0/+3
2. Systematic market analysis	+1.3	0/+2
3. Knowledge of consumers' quality/taste demands	+1.4	0/+2
4. Approved production facilities	+2.0	+1/+3
5. Supply consistent quality	+1.4	1/+2
6. Fast response to changes in customer/consumer demands	+1.3	0/+2
7. Respond to changes in supply of raw materials	+0.3	–1/+1
8. Image (primarily among consumers)	+0.5	0/+1
9. Supplier/customer relationship	+1.4	0/+2
10. Own production	+1.2	0/+2
11. Ability to offer competitive prices	+0.2	0/+1

TABLE 8.4 Possible explanations for the competitor's superior position

Ad 1: Competitor has close relationship with M & S: joint PD. Spillover from mother company
Ad 2: Competitor uses AGB market data
Ad 3: Competitor has many years experience, support by M & S
Ad 4: Production facilities are developed according to customer (M & S) specifications
Ad 5: Competitor has an excellent industry-wide reputation
Ad 6: Competitor has UK production unit works with M & S and others, experience
Ad 8: Competitor is private-label supplier to M & S/Tesco. These labels are well perceived by consumers
Ad 11: Competitor seems to have lost some products/customers (negative)

TABLE 8.5 Five critical factors leading to success

1. Customers	Understanding your customers' needs better than they do has to be the ultimate objective. This requires highly developed marketing skills and a customer-focused culture, supported by product innovation, operational flexibility and world-class customer service
2. Partners	Winning is not enough. You must choose the right partner who can supply complementary skills. Being 'grown up' enough to be able to cope with cooperating with a third party in one geography/segment and competing with them in another is extremely important
3. Cultural adaptability	This entails developing your organisation so it can understand, be sympathetic with and adapt to a wide range of social and political cultures. Using your local partners will help, as will careful selection and training of your own employees
4. Building a brand name	It is necessary to leverage that expensive brand-building money with governments, partners and customers. This will make the brand image remove the need for a hard sell
5. A focused strategy	It is important to establish a vision and strategy and work tirelessly to deliver it. With more markets liberalising, with improvements in communications and travel, opportunities for all sorts of companies abound

Given that one can identify a list of critical success factors and assemble enough data to make comparative judgements of competing firms in terms of these factors, this will provide decision-makers with a powerful diagnostic tool. As the seafood example quoted makes clear, many of these factors are highly specific to a given industry/market. That said, Table 8.5 summarises five generic factors identified by the executive chairman of Cable & Wireless in order to succeed in the global telecommunications market.

SKILLS AND COMPETENCIES

The notion of 'distinctive competence' first came into currency at the Harvard Business School in the business policy course. Selznick (1957) defined it as any factor at which a firm was uniquely good by comparison with its main competitors. Such distinctive competencies may exist in any key area, as suggested by Table 8.6.

Identifying distinctive competencies should be undertaken in conjunction with value chain analysis (see above).

The concept of distinctive competencies was further developed by Prahalad and Hamel (1990) in their analysis of factors underlying Japanese competitive success, in which they identified the acquisition and exploitation of distinctive, or what they called 'core' competencies, as a major course of competitive advantage. In Prahalad and Hamel's study a core competence was seen as a unique and difficult to replicate combination of a

TABLE 8.6 Distinctive competence in key areas

Key area	Dimensions
Product/market	Share of existing markets Range of products Position in product life-cycle Dependence upon key product for sales/profits/cash flow Distribution network Marketing and market research
Production	Number, size, location, age and capacity of plants Specialisation/versatility of equipment Production and cost levels Costs/availability of raw materials Production control systems
Finance	Present asset structure Present capital structure Access to additional equity and debt finance Pattern of cash flow Procedures for financial management
Technology	Currency of production methods and products R&D spending and effectiveness Organisation and human resources
Management style and succession	Staff development policies Management/labour force relationship Reward structures

SOURCE: Taken from Clarkson, A. (1996) Marketing Strategy. Notes prepared for the Masters in Technology Management Programme. Glasgow: Scottish Business School

number of distinctive competencies. Thus, while competitors might benchmark and match specific skills and competencies, it was the combination of these which conferred the *sustainable competitive advantage*. For example, Prahalad and Hamel see Coca-Cola's competitive advantage arising from a combination of brand strength, distribution network and geographic spread. For Benetton it is fast cycle times, computer-aided manufacture and just-in-time dyeing, while for Toyota it is just-in-time manufacturing, fast cycle times and economies of scale.

In some cases core competencies evolve or 'emerge' (Mintzberg and Waters, 1985), in others they are the outcome of deliberate strategic planning. For example, Prahalad and Hamel describe Canon's assault on the copier market as comprising an eight-step plan:

1. Establish the strategic intent to 'beat Xerox'
2. Identify Canon's existing core competencies
3. Understand Xerox's technology and patents to identify the necessary competencies
4. License the technology to gain market experience and develop the core competencies not already possessed
5. Invest in R&D to improve on the existing technology to acquire and start to exploit core competencies, primarily to achieve cost reductions, e.g. by standardisation of components, improving ease of maintenance and replenishment
6. License out own technology to fund further R&D and thus further consolidate the core competencies required to beat Xerox
7. Open challenge with 'business warfare', first by attacking markets where Xerox is weakest – Japan, then Europe
8. Finally, an innovative, rather than imitative, attack on markets where Xerox is strongest, e.g. by selling rather than leasing, distributing through office equipment retailers rather than direct, and focusing promotion on end-users rather than on corporate functional heads.

BENCHMARKING

Once one has identified the structure of the value chain, the critical success factors to succeed in an industry/market, the identity, skills and competencies of competitors, the next step in a competitor analysis is to benchmark those firms which are seen to possess some competitive advantage over one's own firm.

Traditionally, a benchmark was a survey mark or reference point used to determine altitude. In a business context this has now come to mean a reference point for the measurement of quality or excellence. The American Productivity and Quality Center's *The Benchmarking Management Guide* (1993) states:

> Benchmarking is the process of continuously comparing and measuring an organisation with business leaders anywhere in the world to gain information which will help the organisation to take action to improve performance.

Simply put: 'Benchmarking is the search for industry best practices that lead to superior performance' (David Kearns, Xerox).

Benchmarking, like environmental scanning, is an activity that most managers practice in an informal and unstructured way on a continuing basis. As with environmental scanning, the benefits from benchmarking are all about *organisational learning*, if it is undertaken in a structured and systematic way. Among the benefits identified from such formal benchmarking are:

- Improved understanding of internal systems and business practices
- Establishment of key success factors and true measures of productivity
- New ideas leading either to continuous improvement or breakthrough change
- Improvement in understanding and meeting the needs of customers
- A view of external conditions leading to the establishment of more relevant goals
- Becoming more competitive in the marketplace
- Becoming aware of and emulating industry best practices.

Modern benchmarking practice is often credited to Xerox Manufacturing Operations who, in 1979 compared its unit costs with Japanese competitors and found it was *selling products* for what it cost Xerox to make them. Methods were then devised to capture and apply best practice. Four kinds of benchmarking may be identified:

1. *Internal benchmarking* using comparisons with successful practice within the organisation

2. *Competitive benchmarking* using comparisons with successful practising firms with which one is competing directly
3. *Functional benchmarking* using comparisons with firms in any industry which have developed particularly effective processes and/or procedures for given functions, e.g. order processing, inventory control
4. *Generic benchmarking* using comparisons with firms in any industry to try and understand how they have achieved superior performance.

For benchmarking to be effective it needs to be undertaken at an appropriate level, that is, with firms of equivalent size and standing that are performing better. On the other hand, smaller firms operating in local markets will probably find that their immediate competitors are unlikely to be following 'best in world' practices and so may choose to benchmark larger and more successful firms in the same industry. An essential element of benchmarking is the identification of appropriate performance indicators such as margins, ROI, sales per employee etc. and the business processes that drive these performance indicators such as new product development or service levels.

A benchmarking exercise with which the author was directly involved was an analysis of graduate business schools and the delivery of MBA programmes. A review of this exercise in a context that is likely to be familiar to many readers of this book will illustrate how to apply the technique in practice.

To begin with it seems that there are three basic questions that business schools need to address:

1. What do business enterprises and their employees want from business schools?
2. What are the business schools doing to address these needs?
3. How can we tell if business schools are succeeding?

Then there seems to be a fairly wide measure of agreement that business graduates need three kinds of skills:

1. *Technical* – such skills are knowledge-based and may be both functional and inter-functional
2. *Interpersonal* – skills involved with teamwork, leadership, communications etc.

3. *Conceptual* – cognitive and thinking skills, creativity, analytical and problem-solving skills.

In addition to the acquisition of these skills that are fundamental to effective performance, it is also important to recognise that the nature of employment has changed significantly in recent years. Traditionally, individuals were employed by organisations in the anticipation that this would provide a lifelong career with increased responsibility and promotion as a reward for experience and performance. In the future, however, workers can expect to change jobs at least six times during their careers and these changes will involve major changes in their roles. It is also likely that many employees will work from home or temporary locations around the globe linked by communications technology. It is likely that there will be more job sharing and flexitime positions, and corporations will be structured more horizontally, with cross-functional teams given more responsibility to make decisions. There will be more diversity in organisations, with women and minorities making up a larger percentage of the workforce, and the growth in the job market will come from SMEs, not large corporations which will continue to shed middle management levels.

To meet these challenges, business needs graduates with:

- The ability to read, write and speak effectively
- The ability to think and reason
- The ability to work with others in teams
- The ability to solve problems
- Some knowledge of business principles
- The ability to perceive problems clearly
- The ability to discriminate between alternatives and make judgements about the best alternative
- The ability to comprehend and understand
- Reflective thinking and insight
- Value for society
- Creativity
- Confidence in decision-making
- Ability to improvise
- Ability to self-evaluate and make positive changes to behaviours
- Ability to continue learning
- Cross-functional skills and flexibility
- Integrity and honesty
- Mathematical or quantitative ability

- Computer literacy
- Self-motivation and autonomy.

From this long list of attributes, three conclusions may be drawn:

1. Functional skills are assumed in graduates
2. Computer literacy and quantitative skills are essential
3. It is the *soft skills* – getting things done – which matter.

In selecting a business school both employers and individuals will prefer those which can deliver on all three dimensions. In addition, a broadly based benchmarking exercise of leading business schools in a number of countries suggested the following critical success factors:

- Breadth, depth and relevance of the curriculum
- Completion rates
- Flexibility
- The learning environment
- Placement record
- The inclusion of a practical or project-related component
- The quality of other students
- The quality of teaching
- Staff–student ratios
- The availability of a wide range of electives.

Ultimately, however, it is the reputation of a business school which determines the final choice. In a report in *Time* magazine (7/4/1997) of competition between business schools, the reporter concluded:

In a world where there are as many qualifications, educational systems and standards as there are national currencies the quality assurance factor of an MBA from a good school, as much as the actual body of knowledge that comes with it, is uniquely attractive for recruiters on what has become a world-wide search for management talent.

From a benchmarking exercise of the kind described above, a number of benefits are likely to flow, including:

- An understanding of world-class performance in depth

- A stimulus for change and innovation
- Performance indicators and measurement tools for competitive analysis
- A practical tool for continuous improvement
- An opportunity to get 'outside the box'.

A publication by the DTI, *Closing the Gap* (1998), summarised some of the key findings from the UK Benchmarking Index (UKBI) on the performance of UK SMEs. The table relating to innovation (Table 8.7) is of particular interest in that it confirms the findings of the Baker and Hart (1991) study that more successful firms pursue strategies of penetration, product and market development simultaneously.

TABLE 8.7 UK SMEs' innovation performance

Measure	Lower quartile	Average	Upper quartile
Income from new geographies/ turnover (%)	0.0	0.0	3.4
Income from new market segments/turnover (%)	0.0	0.0	4.2
Income from new products/ turnover (%)	0.0	2.6	10.8
New customer/ total customer (%)	6.8	13.3	23.8
Total new income/ turnover (%)	0.3	6.2	19.0

SOURCE: DTI (1998) *Closing the Gap*. Report on the performance of SMEs

Interestingly, the transport manufacturing and electrical and electronics sectors spent the lowest proportion of their turnover on capital investment and most on R&D and marketing. These two sectors enjoy a growth performance significantly better than the chemical, metal products and general machinery sectors.

Across all sectors lower quartile companies can expect to receive 10 to 12 times the number of customer complaints compared with upper quartile companies. Overall the top 25% of UKBI companies achieve profit margins five times greater than those in the lower quartile. Data such as these clearly indicate the potential benefits that may flow from benchmarking performance both within and across sectors.

BEST PRACTICES

In 1998 the consulting firm Arthur Andersen published *Best Practices* (Hiebeler et al., 1998), which reported the results of over six years' research and an investment of $30m to understand how best practice companies focus on their customers, create growth, reduce costs, and increase profits. Based upon research in more than 40 companies, the perspective adopted is that best practices do not belong to any single company or industry but have universal application to companies large and small across all industries. In their efforts to define these, Hiebeler et al. adopt what they term 'a process view' of excellence in customer relationships. To begin with, they establish six first-level processes which they designate as:

1. Understanding markets and customers
2. Involving customers in the design of products and services
3. The marketing and selling of products and services
4. Involving customers in the delivery of products and services
5. The provision of customer service
6. The management of customer information.

In turn, each of these six major processes, which all businesses share, are broken down into a more detailed list of subprocesses.

As the sequence in which the processes are listed implies, everything begins with the development of an understanding of markets and customers. In turn, this activity is seen as consisting of three subprocesses:

1. Understanding the market environment
2. Understanding customers' wants and needs
3. Segmenting customers.

With regard to *understanding the market environment,* Andersen recommend a systematic analysis of the entire value chain as a basis for identifying both threats and opportunities. Such an analysis needs to go beyond merely identifying key players and should seek to *profile* them, 'specifying their relative size and growth rates, evaluating their strengths and weaknesses, and studying key events and alliances in their value chains.'

In terms of *understanding customers' wants and needs*, three key areas are identified:

1. Assessing 'value in use' benefits
2. Measuring critical incidents
3. Analysing customers' purchasing patterns that reflect expectations and responses.

Clearly, these two subprocesses are covered by what we have chosen to call 'the marketing appreciation'. Once complete this information may then be used in order to disaggregate the market into clearly defined market opportunities or segments. We return to this later in Chapter 12.

It is clear that the quantity and quality of the data gathered in the marketing appreciation phase will have a major bearing on all subsequent decisions. It is also clear that an effective research programme will operate at two levels. Macro-environmental and micro-environmental analysis will be broadly based and used as a coarse screen to identify the most attractive market segment. When market segments have been identified more sophisticated and in-depth research into buyer behaviour is an essential prerequisite to developing an effective marketing mix. Once determined it is essential to monitor the implementation of the chosen mix to ensure that it is delivering the intended benefits. In their book, Hiebeler et al. (1998) cite numerous cases of organisations such as Ritz, Carlton and American Express who have turned customer data into a sustainable competitive advantage that enables them to better anticipate and serve the needs of their customers, thereby achieving higher retention and repurchase rates than their competitors.

STRATEGIC ALLIANCES

Traditionally, management interest and its supporting business literature has largely focused on the concept of competition and its effects. Only recently has the focus begun to shift towards a consideration of collaboration and its potential benefits.

The growing interest in supplier partnerships and strategic alliances is a direct consequence of increased competition. As a result of this increased competition many of the traditional advantages enjoyed by firms such as cost, quality, speed of delivery and service have become necessary requirements to compete in the first place. To succeed, organisations need other competitive advantages that are unique and exclusive. It is against this background that higher order abilities such as partnering, learning and innovation abilities are more difficult to imitate. Thus, continued success has come to depend upon continuous development and renewal rather than increasing efficiency and effectiveness in old ways of doing things.

Globalisation has changed our perceptions of time and distance, and has steadily been chipping away at the forces that bind us to remain local. The integration of economies, regional agreements, monetary unions and converging consumer tastes and living standards makes firms that are merely reliant on geographically bound ideas, markets, products and facilities redundant. Firms that collaborate with suppliers, customers and even competitors across and within regions will have established a competitive position that will be hard to rival.

Of the strategic responses available to the firm, mergers and acquisitions tended to be the most popular despite the fact that mergers rarely, if ever, result in profitable long-term returns, while acquisitions are often less successful than anticipated due to the difficulties of finding appropriate partners at the right price. Against this, alliances and other forms of integration usually involve lower capital costs and offer greater flexibility than vertical integration. It is against this background that 'collaboration' is being promoted strongly as a basis for future success. In turn, this means that the ability to form and manage alliances is emerging as an important capability, and one that all firms need to develop and few can afford to ignore.

Companies cooperate in two broad ways and may either pool resources with a view to attaining mutually agreed objectives, or exchange resources in order to acquire complementary strengths. Among the goals and objectives may be included: access to hitherto unexplored markets and customers; introduction of new or better products; access to technology and know-how; reduction of costs and attendant risks; and productivity or efficiency gains. The real test of an alliance is whether it is of sufficient strategic importance for all the partners involved. The acid test is the marketplace and the judge and jury are the consumer or end user.

Strategic alliances lie along a continuum between operational market exchanges and mergers. The relationship between the partners is clearly a matter of degree and moves from one of 'association' to a more strategic perspective depending on the success of the intervening operational dimension. Elsewhere (Baker and Srivastav, 1997) it has been argued that successful alliances must evolve, and an association between partners should be a necessary precursor to a strategic alliance. This is necessary because strategic alliances involve commitments of a much higher order such as sharing technology, joint product development, substantial resource obligations etc. According to this view it could well be that the reason for the high failure rate of strategic alliances reported in the management literature may well be a consequence of the partners failing to get to know each other through a series of increasingly closer relationships. In turn, Oburai and Baker (1999) perceive strategic alliances as a precursor to higher forms of collaboration – networks, clusters, and mergers – that lead to total integration.

The concept of a boundaryless organisation with a network of connections is becoming increasingly visible in practice, contributing to a growth in alliances and a reliance on partner networks. Customer–supplier relations through alliances and partnerships are seen as an important source of various advantages that lead to competitive advantage.

The keys to success in alliances are complementary activities, well-matched functional strengths, and a solid business rationale rather than the self-improvement of partners. Cooperation increases interdependence and the need to share control, which may not be to the liking of all firms. But, to be successful, an alliance requires that one firm takes into consideration the needs and requirements of another in plotting its own future. As such, it is important to recognise that alliances are a trade-off between a need for resources and the control associated with ownership.

Bronder and Pritzl (1992) offer one of the most comprehensive classifications of the benefits of collaboration:

- *Time advantages* can arise from faster responses to changes in the environment. Implementing cooperative R&D programmes can substantially reduce development times.

FIGURE 8.5 Partnering in the value chain

- *Know-how advantages:* the complexity of product technology increases dramatically while products and other life-cycles become shorter. Mutual learning within a strategic alliance can help to overcome knowledge deficits due to these technological changes.
- *Access to markets* as an objective is getting more and more important due to increased global protectionism.
- *Cost advantages* from external synergy can arise through combining value chain activities.
- *System competence:* through strategic alliances, companies can achieve system competence in certain markets even though their own core competencies are focused on specialised areas.

Increasingly, modern business calls for a focus on core areas wherein competitive advantages may be developed (Prahalad and Hamel, 1990). The firm needs to invest its resources in its area of core operations. Non-core areas could easily be outsourced, or alliances with other firms could produce the desired results. Even within core areas of operation, there could exist avenues for cooperation when going alone may either take too long, or when internal resources are simply inadequate. To be first in the marketplace with new or improved products and services is an important advantage that firms cannot easily ignore. Focusing on core areas and collaborating with others who specialise in complementary fields allow a firm to simultaneously reap the benefits of economies of scale, and a differentiated or extended product range. Alliances and partnerships could free scarce resources for core functions to be performed within the organisation rendering a better focus on core areas. It is important to realise that others who have already built up expertise in that area could perform some functions better. Duplication of others' areas of expertise and reinventing the wheel are not likely to significantly contribute to a firm's growth and profitability.

All these potential benefits help to explain why supplier partnering is now receiving as much interest and attention as customer care and service. While value chains are almost invariably depicted as a series of arrows charting the addition

of value through the conversion of primary resources into final consumption and after-sales service, a more appropriate representation might be to show the flows operating in both directions simultaneously, as suggested in Figure 8.5.

According to Frankle et al. (1996), the following benefits accrue to alliances in general:

- Reduced cost through specialisation
- Improved synergistic performance
- Increased information to support joint planning
- Enhanced customer service
- Reduced risk and uncertainty
- Shared creativity
- Competitive advantage.

Traditionally, relationships between suppliers and buyers were largely adversarial and involved an exchange of goods for money and as little interaction as necessary. As opposed to the arm's-length transactional orientation, alliances are built on relational orientation with a view to maximising mutual benefits.

CUSTOMER–SUPPLIER ALLIANCES, PARTNERSHIPS AND NETWORKS

As the marketing discipline continues to evolve, the topics of relationship marketing, networks, partnerships and alliances have grown in importance. Research into these issues by Oburai and Baker (2006) have led us to propose what we have designated the '3 Rs of alliance strategy'.

As noted in Chapter 2, marketing literature (Turnbull et al., 1997; Hakansson et al., 2004; Narayandas and Rangan, 2004) in the past two decades has increasingly reflected the need for building bonds with suppliers, customers and other related constituents. Webster (1992) urges marketers to broaden the *agenda* of the marketing field, and suggests that:

Theory development must be accompanied by aggressive programs of empirical research ... survey research should be guided by strong theoretical frameworks from allied social science disciplines. Top priority should be given to analysis of the forces and factors that cause firms to move along the continuum from transactions to long-term relationships to strategic alliances and, perhaps, back again.

The main purpose of our research is to take a few cautious steps in moving towards building, or at least laying the foundations of a *theory* of strategic alliances. An extensive literature review covering a wide range of disciplines and fields of endeavour was undertaken in order to examine relevant views and integrate these into a coherent whole. In addition to the above processes of literature review and eliciting of views from marketing academics, views from practice were taken into account, based on a qualitative exploration of the purchasing practices of six organisations from diverse backgrounds and sectors. Evaluative summaries were made of a range of theories that together represent eight different schools of thought concerning strategic alliances and partnerships. A small survey was then undertaken to explore the processes of alliance formation in six different contexts, leading to the formulation of a routines–relationships–resources model to be identified as the 3Rs model.

REVIEW OF EIGHT MAJOR THEORETICAL STREAMS

A wide-ranging and thorough investigation of eight major strands of theories was undertaken to explore their foundations and implications for the current era in which strategic alliances and partnerships are increasingly adopted. It is argued that traditional notions of competitive advantage need to be supplemented with views from relational and resource-based theories. Sources of competitive advantage may well lie outside firms' boundaries. The fields of strategy, organisational theory and marketing have several distinct and interrelated explanations that were examined in Chapter 2 for their central orientations, assumptions and implications. The eight themes discussed are distinctive in some senses and overlapping in others. What may be needed is an integration of the different ideas to form a coherent and complete model that is workable.

Overall assessment

Table 8.8 summarises the main implications and criticisms of the eight theoretical explanations discussed. What is needed to view

TABLE 8.8 Summary and main implications of eight theoretical perspectives

Theories	Main implications	Criticisms
1. Transaction cost analysis	■ Safeguarding idiosyncratic investments ■ Reduction of transaction costs	■ Static nature of the model ■ Biased view of human behaviour ■ The cost-focused analysis neglects value considerations
2. Game theory	■ Enlarging the shadow of the future ■ Improve communication ■ Make unilateral commitments ■ Build reputation	■ Disembodied from context and ignores societal norms ■ Largel⁹y deals with two-party situations
3. Market power and industry structure theories	■ Industry structure is an important determinant of firm conduct and performance	■ Anchored in competition concepts ■ Insufficient attention to firm resources
4. Evolutionary theories	■ Firms evolve and adapt routines	■ Sticky routines limit the space for strategies
5. Resource-based theories	■ Unique resources underlie competences ■ Protect core resources	■ Excessively introspective ■ Uniqueness may preclude generalisation
6. Complexity theories	■ Order can emerge from self-organisation ■ Recurring patterns of interaction help predictions	■ In early stage and rely on computer models and binary logic ■ Reality cannot be captured through simple models
7. Interaction and network theories	■ A rich picture of mulitiple linkages and plurality of actors ■ Links enable as well as constrain	■ Empirical verification is difficult
8. Relational view	■ Integration of a variety of concepts in forming a coherent view of the rich contents that make up a relationship	■ The details that provide complementarity and connectivity lend the depictioin more reality but also make for complexity

Source: Oburai, P. and Baker, M. J. (2006) *Customer–Supplier Alliances, Partnerships and Networks: A Synthesis of Literature Review and empirical investigation Leading to 3Rs Framework*

holistically the cooperative yet, in many ways, simultaneously competitive nature of today's business is a more realistic portrayal. The concepts of power and structural interplay that play central roles in Porter's classic efforts are still relevant, even if less so today. Resource and innovation perspectives and costs of coordination are important. Much more so are the interaction, networks and relational views.

A SUMMARY OF KEY FACTORS OF SIX CASE STUDIES

A series of in-depth interviews were held with the senior purchasing executives of six organisations. The range of sectors represented and the varied nature of activities that these organisations are involved in lend to and serve to enhance the richness of both the context and firm-specific detail. Access was gained by making contact with the senior officials and office bearers of the local chapter of the Chartered Institute of Purchasing and Supply (CIPS). A semi-structured interview guide was employed for the purpose of gaining information. The approach adopted was to explore the processes of alliance and partnership formation and was exploratory in spirit in view of the main aim of theory-building. The objectives of the research were threefold:

1. To understand what processes and modes of alliance organisation lead to the creation of value
2. To explore the implications of customer–supplier alliances and partnerships and how these lead to performance improvements for partnering firms
3. To develop a theory of alliances.

A set of broad propositions was formulated to explore alliance/partnership formation motives, the value creation potential of collaboration, and process aspects. The interviews were designed to explore the strategies of organisations with respect to their suppliers and the relationships that these firms have with their key suppliers. In view of the sensitivity of information, the identity of the respondents has been disguised insofar as this is possible.

We studied the purchasing and partnership strategies of a leading university in Scotland, the government of Scotland, a computer and electronics multinational, a nuclear power generation firm, the IT operations of a utility, and a process engineering and consultancy services firm. The aim of this section is to explore and highlight *analytical dimensions* that are found in the rich and detailed description of the six cases. We explore relationships that link the varied organisations and also outline the distinct factors that embody the uniqueness of each of the firms studied.

University purchasing: An insight into the higher education sector's linkages

Joint purchasing at national, regional and local levels is an important influence on this institution's performance. Responsibilities for leading national and local-level agreements for different commodities are shared among universities. Edinburgh University is leading the consortium's efforts on buying copiers, Strathclyde on IT consumables, Dundee and Aberdeen on stationery and so on. *Convergence of practices* across educational bodies is an important manifestation of lateral cooperation. Public procurement laws and tendering procedures do place a level of *restriction* on the discretion of buyers to develop relationships with suppliers. This is overcome in the innovative way universities have found avenues for collaboration. In this sense universities are *relationship*-driven. The paucity of resources and environmental pressures on budgets appear to have been countered. Another element that could be seen at work is the changing of *routines*.

Scottish Office: Government purchasing is all about 'flux'

Diverse ranges of activities, customers and suppliers make public procurement relatively more complex than is the case with private procurement. The unique and non-recurring nature of demands in conjunction with the inherent intricacies of processes make the variety too complex to be subjected to task standardisation and control mechanisms. Legal directives and public scrutiny are other important issues to contend with. *Discontinuities* in the range and types of goods procured make it hard to gain any significant benefits of experience. The bargaining power that size offers may be more than offset by the inability of governments to accrue experiential knowledge and by the levels of *transaction costs* imposed by the need to have suppliers for a limited duration. Government purchasing may be best summarised by the characteristic, 'flux'. The avowed commitment to *market-based dealings* and the *nature of demands* severely limits the discretion on the part of the procurement staff. This is the impact that is induced by the rigidity of routines as described in the previous section. Routines are sticky when patterns are set, and limit manoeuvres and room for discretion.

Computer and electronics firm – I-comp: Global power and network dominance

I-comp manufactures all the servers and high-end computers. I-comp has outsourced a significant proportion of the assembly of lower end desktop computers. While no financial ties are in place, the extent of influence and control that I-comp has over its subcontractor is clear to see. Technology and processes that are employed by the prime subcontractor are determined by the firm, as are all the inputs. With inputs and conversion processes determined, the discretion of the subcontractor is greatly reduced. This is a paradox of outsourcing and network processes. Networks and alliances on the one hand allow division of labour, but on the other hand lead to asymmetric distribution of power and consequential dependencies. Networks do have informal hierarchies and command structures. To the extent that the firm shapes networks, it also establishes the pattern of *resource flows*, *relationships* and hence *routines*. These three elements are the pillars of strategy and form the *triad* of sources of distinctive skills and capabilities. The electronics and computer multinational has tremendous *resources* and consequent power.

Nuclear electricity major – NEC: A core of stability becoming responsive in a changing environment

NEC's growth and future prospects appear to be limited in view of the absence of any major plans aimed at augmenting the existing nuclear power generation capacity. The integrated, and to an extent self-contained, nature of the nuclear utility firm's operations only offers restricted scope to develop *relations* with external firms and draw on their *resources*. As a generator-supplier of energy that is fundamental to the economy, NEC adds tremendous value and contributes in many ways. However, this unique nature and the accompanying relative isolation tend to impose severe constraints on growth and further success. This is a case of existing *routines* imposing inertia. Routines, resources and relationships are interlinked and are of a mutually enhancing character. Internal and external linkages affect both the *stock* and *flow* of these vital ingredients that underpin the success and survival of firms. Absence of relationships could lead to resource gaps and limit the development of routines that aim at enhancing survival and success prospects.

Utilities – IT operation and outsourcing: Creating value outside the firm's boundaries

GP is a multinational firm with a portfolio of diversified businesses. GP has recently set up a joint venture (JV) with an American multinational firm. The JV will absorb all the ISD operations and staff and some equipment. Total outsourcing of all IT operations might have meant losing hard-won skills and insights, and would put GP at the total mercy of IT firms that are powerful and dominate the global field. A 50:50 JV is an ideal solution to many of the above-mentioned issues and a suitable vehicle for exploiting emerging market opportunities and leveraging resources. The JV allows linking up with the external environment and opportunities therein. In this sense the JV is a routine, a resource and above all a relational vehicle. This case also suggests a *progression from simple purchasing to outsourcing to adding value in the external sphere*. Buying in value is only a beginning. Adding value outside the boundaries of a firm may well be a paradigm shift in practice and business theories. Several parallels may be drawn from the case study examples discussed above. Universities are linking up with external parties, as are the electronic firms. While a JV involves financial equity, real value addition comes from the *accumulated competencies* and their application. The route that GP has taken is to build a *relationship* to rewrite industry rules and set patterns and routines of business.

Oil and gas industry – Process Engineering Consultancy services: Connecting growth and linkages

KSMS engineer, design, procure, construct and install onshore engineering projects. KSMS had nearly 2,000 suppliers two years ago. This has now grown to 3,000. This rise is driven by the firm's internationalisation of operation and consequent growth in the supply base that resulted from the inclusion of a number of non-EU vendors. KSMS is an *engineering expertise* and *know-how*-driven firm. While the uniqueness of its core skills and technology allow the firm great mobility and leverage, this also necessitates *pooling* suppliers' skills, equipment, and technology from other firms. Alliances and partnerships allow the company to combine resources and generate value. *Relationships* could well be argued to be the main *arteries* and *pathways* through which resources flow and let strategy routines be executed.

This section presented summaries of key factors in six organisations. The underlying idea was to explore each firm's supplier strategies, relationships and the impact of business context. It can be gathered that universities and the utilities firm (GP) are moving towards relying predominantly on *relationships*. KSMS is also attempting to build relationships with a few chosen firms. NEC and government purchasing are subject to regulations or constraints imposed by the nature of the business they are in. Observing these set ways of doing business leads us to infer that *routines* dictate their conduct. This may not always be desirable or to the liking of concerned managerial staff and may even be considered to be a handicap. I-comp is a multinational that has huge *resources* at its command and this is the element that drives their strategy.

Collaboration with other organisations is seen to be becoming increasingly important to firms as are the *organisational context* and *practices*. Three cores – resources, relationships and routines – that make up firms, industries and economic systems may be identified. Alliances, partnerships, networks and clusters are mechanisms that facilitate the building processes that generate and modify these three cores, and in turn are supported by these basic ingredients. In turn, management action is aimed at affecting the stock and flow of the 3Rs: routines–resources–relationships. The 3Rs framework is shown in Figure 8.6.

Contextual factors and managerial initiatives determine the *relative proportions* that make for a *recipe for competitive success*, which in turn determines outputs and outcomes of business strategies. The 3Rs framework also satisfies the key cumulativity criterion that all theory-building exercises and scientific endeavours are subject to. This constitutes a major and fundamental contribution of the thesis, in that it builds on and complements existing frameworks and theories in the subfields of marketing strategy and industrial and business-to-business marketing.

The 3Rs model is an independently derived framework and is a product of the *synthesis* of a wide-ranging number of theories from a number of related management disciplines. This model is analogous to the actors–activities–resources (A–A–R) model of industrial networks (Hakansson and Johansson, 1997). Network and business markets agenda and output are at the forefront of the process of challenging previously dominant notions of business strategy and offering alternatives (Hakansson and Snehota, 1997). The 3Rs framework is elaborate in its detail and recent conceptual and empirical developments are integrated. At the same time, the 3Rs model is parsimonious and has strong theoretical roots. This model also is an improvement on the architecture–innovation–reputation–strategic assets combination thought to underlie corporate success (Kay, 1993) and the seminal sources–positions–performance (SPP) framework forwarded by Day and Wensley (1988).

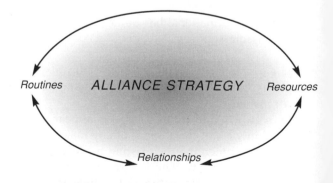

FIGURE 8.6 3Rs of alliance strategy

Routines–relationships–resources (3Rs) is a generic framework that could be employed at different levels. It is important to note the two-way influence that each of the three cores has on others in the triad. At its lowest level of usage, the 3Rs model could be employed as a *pedagogical tool* and a *descriptive mechanism*. At a higher level, managers and academics alike could utilise the framework as a *diagnostic* and *audit tool*. At a third and final level, the previous two levels of usage could be further incorporated into the strategy formulation and implementation aspects of organisations. Managers may assess the level of each of the three elements of the 3Rs model for the businesses they are concerned with, and may wish to modify one or more elements to gain rapid and sustainable competitive advantage. It is in this sense that the framework has *predictive* and *explanatory power*. Finally, the model is amenable to empirical verification and validation. As such, the 3Rs model is a key contribution to the theory-building process that aims at better understanding of strategic alliances, marketing relations, partnerships and networks. The practical significance and managerial implications referred to above make the framework useful.

Finally, the increased role of suppliers is illustrated by the fact that in developing its 7E7 Dreamliner, Boeing expects to reduce assembly time of 13–17 days to just 3 days by outsourcing 70% to its suppliers.

Chapter summary

In this chapter we have explored some of the issues involved in analysing competition at the micro-level. Building upon the earlier review of market structure, conduct and performance (Chapter 2) and Michael Porter's development of this, we looked at competitor analysis as an essential input to the development of competitive advantage. In achieving this it was argued that it is important to understand where one's own organisation lies within the value chain that converts resources and skills into products and services that compete with one another in the marketplace. In turn, such analysis should lead to the identification of critical success factors which are necessary conditions to be met if one is to compete effectively.

While the critical success factors are necessary to compete effectively, they are rarely sufficient – to outperform the competition something extra is required. The available evidence suggests that it is the skills and competencies that firms possess which determine performance relative to their competitors and we reviewed some of the intrinsic qualities of these. In identifying both critical success factors, and skills and competencies, the evaluation of one's competitors using benchmarking techniques has become a common practice and some discussion of the approach and methods used was given. This included a short reference to the notion of 'best practices' that emerge from benchmarking exercises.

Finally, we examined the nature of strategic alliances as a form of collaboration that many competing organisations have found to be necessary to enable them to survive in global markets subject to rapid and often discontinuous technological change.

In the next chapter we will turn our attention to the final element of the external analysis – the behaviour of customers.

Recommended reading

Aaker, D. A. (2004) *Strategic Market Management* (7th edn). Chichester: John Wiley & Sons.

Hooley, G. J., Saunders, J. A. and Piercy, N. F. (1998) *Marketing Strategy and Competitive Positioning* (2nd edn). London: Prentice Hall Europe.

REFERENCES

American Productivity and Quality Center (1993) *The Benchmarking Management Guide*. New York: Productivity Press.

Baker, M. J. (1991) *Research for Marketing*. Basingstoke: Macmillan – now Palgrave Macmillan.

Baker, M. J. and Srivastav, A. (1997) *Supplier partnering*. Working paper, University of Strathclyde.

Bartlett, C. A. and Ghoshal, S. (1989) *Managing Across Borders: The Transnational Solution*. London: Hutchinson.

Borden, N. (1965) The concept of the marketing mix, in G. Schwartz (ed.) *Science in Marketing*. New York: Wiley.

Bronder, C. and Pritzl, R. (1992) Developing strategic alliances: a conceptual framework for successful cooperation. *European Management Journal*, **10**: 412–21.

Chamberlin, E. J. (1933) *The Theory of Monopolistic Competition*. Cambridge, MA: Harvard University Press.

Clark, J. M. (1961) *Competition as a Dynamic Process*. Washington, DC: Brookings Institution.

Clarkson, A. (1996) Marketing strategy. Notes prepared for the Masters in Technology Management Programme. Glasgow: Scottish Business School.

DTI (1998) *Closing the Gap*. Report on the performance of SMEs.

Frankle, R., Whipple, J. S. and Frayer, D. J. (1996) Formal versus informal contracts: achieving alliance success, *International Journal of Physical Distribution and Logistics Management*, **26**: 47–63.

Grunert, K. G. and Ellegaard, C. (1993) The concept of key success factors: theory and method, in M. J. Baker (ed.) *Perspectives on Marketing Management*, Vol. 3. Chichester: John Wiley.

Hakansson, H. and Johansson, J. (1997) A model of industrial networks, in D. Ford (ed.) *Understanding Business Networks: Interaction, Relationships and Networks* (2nd edn). London: The Dryden Press, pp. 129–35.

Hakansson, H. and Snehota, I. (1997) *Developing Relationships in Business Networks*, London: ITP

Hakansson, H., Harrison, D. and Waluszewski, A. (2004) *Rethinking Marketing: Developing a New Understanding of Markets*. Chichester: John Wiley & Sons.

Hamel, G. and Prahalad, C. K. (1994) *Competing for the Future*. Boston, MA: Harvard Business School Press.

Hart, S., Tzokas, N. and Saren, N. (1999) The effectiveness of market information in enhancing new product success rates, *European Journal of Innovation Management* **2**(1): 20–35.

Hiebeler, R., Kelly, T. B. and Ketteman, C. (1998) *Best Practices*. New York: Simon & Schuster.

Kay, J. A. (1993) *Foundations of Corporate Success: How Business Strategies Add Value*. Oxford: Oxford University Press.

Knight, F. (1936) *Ethics of Competition* (2nd edn). London: George Allen & Unwin.

Kotler, P. (1972) *Marketing Management* (2nd edn). Englewood Cliffs, NJ: Prentice Hall.

Lawrence, A. (1955) *Quality and Competition*. New York: Columbia University Press.

Machlup, F. (1953) *The Economics of Sellers' Competition*. Baltimore, MD: Johns Hopkins University Press.

Makens, J. C. (1989) *The 12-Day Marketing Plan*. New York: Thorsons.

Mintzberg, H. and Waters, J. A. (1985) Of strategies deliberate and emergent, *Strategic Management Journal*, **6**: 257–72.

Narayandas, D. and Rangan, V. R. (2004) Building and sustaining buyer–seller relationships in mature industrial markets, *Journal of Marketing*, **68**(July): 63–77.

Normann, R. and Ramirez, R. (1993) From value chain to value constellation: designing interactive strategy, *Harvard Business Review*, **71**(4): 65–77.

Oburai, P. and Baker, M. J. (1999) Strategic alliances and supplier partnerships, in M. J. Baker (ed.) *Encyclopedia of Marketing*. London: International Thomson Business Press.

Oburai, P. and Baker, M. J. (2006) *Customer–Supplier Alliances, Partnerships and Networks: A Synthesis of Literature Review and Empirical Investigation Leading to 3Rs Framework*. A competitive paper submitted for presentation at the European Academy of Marketing 2006 Conference, May 23–26, Athens University of Economics and Business, Greece.

Porter, M. E. (1980) *Competitive Strategy: Techniques for Analyzing Industries and Competitors*, New York: Free Press

Porter, M. E. (1985) *Competitive Advantage: Creating and Sustaining Superior Performance*. New York: Free Press.

Prahalad, C. K. and Hamel, G. (1990) The core competence of the corporation, *Harvard Business Review*, **68**(3): 79–91.

Robinson, J. (1933) *The Economics of Imperfect Competition*. London: Macmillan – now Palgrave Macmillan.

Rockart, J. F. (1979) Chief executives define their own data needs,

Harvard Business Review (July/August).

Rothschild, W. (1979) Competitor analysis: the missing link in strategy, *Management Review* (July).

Saunders, J. (1995) Analysing the competition, Chapter 4 in Thomas, M. J., *The Marketing Handbook* (4th edn). Aldershot: Gower.

Selznick, P. (1957) *Leadership in Administration: A Sociological Interpretation*. Berkeley, CA: University of California Press.

Senge, P. M. (1990) *The Fifth Discipline: The Art and Practice of the Learning Organisation*. New York: Doubleday/Currency.

Stapleton, J. (1987) *How to Prepare a Marketing Plan* (4th edn). Aldershot: Gower.

Stigler, G. (1948) *Five Lectures on Economic Problems*. London: Longman.

Thomas, M. J. and Saxena, N. (1997) *The composite value system of the corporation*. University of Strathclyde Department of Marketing working paper.

Turnbull, P., Ford, D. and Cunningham, M. (1997) Interactions, relationships and networks in business markets: an evolving perspective, *Journal of Business and Industrial Marketing*, **11**(3/4): 44–62.

Udell, J. (1964) How important is price in competitive strategy?, *Journal of Marketing* (January).

Udell, J. (1972) *Successful Marketing Strategies in American Industries*. Madison, WI: Mirrer Publishers.

Webster, F. E. (1992) The changing role of marketing in the corporation, *Journal of Marketing*, **56**: 1–17.

West, C. (1999) Marketing Research, in M. J. Baker (ed.) *Encyclopedia of Marketing*. London: International Thomson Business Press, pp. 255–67.

NOTE

1 The discussion in this section draws heavily on the work of my former student Dr Hanaa Said: unpublished Ph.D dissertation, University of Strathclyde, 1986.

CHAPTER 9

Customer analysis

The consumer isn't a moron, she is your wife.   DAVID OGILVY

After reading Chapter 9 you will be able to:

✔ Describe and explain the major influences on choice behaviour.

✔ Define selective perception and distinguish its effect on the individual's interpretation of information.

✔ Illustrate the concept of a hierarchy of needs and its effect on consumer behaviour.

✔ Specify the stages through which buyers pass in making choice decisions.

✔ Propose a composite model of buyer behaviour which encompasses and reconciles the foregoing concepts and explains its application in practice.

✔ Devise a customer audit.

INTRODUCTION

The question of how people choose between alternatives is at the very heart of the social sciences and central to the great majority of the managerial disciplines. As a consequence, there is a plethora of textbooks dealing with choice behaviour, whether on the part of the individual or the organisation, as a subject in its own right. In a book of this sort, one can only scratch the surface and, at best, this chapter can only be an eclectic and perhaps idiosyncratic review of some of the major concepts and phenomena that appear to have a bearing upon this very important question.

Because of my view expressed earlier that it is divisive to make a distinction between consumer and industrial or business-to-business marketing, no distinction will be made between the manner in which individuals make choice decisions as opposed to organisations that comprise collections of individuals. Indeed, on the contrary, a brief discussion of group influence will seem to suggest that group behaviour is patterned on what is acceptable to the individuals comprising that group, so that both individuals and the group will act in a very similar way.

In this chapter we shall first review four different disciplinary explanations of choice behaviour, following a framework proposed by Philip Kotler. Next, we shall examine six key concepts that long experience in management education suggests are most helpful to practising managers to help them understand the multifarious influences affecting choice and, at the same time, provide them with some useful conceptual frameworks as a basis for organising their own knowledge and experience when taking decisions about buyer behaviour. Based on these ideas I shall propose a broadly based composite model of buying behaviour that seeks to synthesise the key concepts discussed in this chapter. Finally, we look at some of the issues one should take into account when conducting an audit of customers.

CHOICE AND THE SOCIAL SCIENCES

In his now classic textbook *Marketing Management*, Philip Kotler (1972) looks at four major motivation models that have been advanced by different social sciences. These are:

1. The Marshallian model, stressing economic motivations
2. The Pavlovian model, stressing learning
3. The Freudian model, stressing psychoanalytic motivations
4. The Veblenian model, stressing social psychological factors.

As Kotler comments:

> These models represent radically different conceptions of the mainsprings of human and consumer behaviour. Depending upon the product, different variables and behavioural mechanisms may assume particular importance. A psychoanalytic behavioural model might throw much light on the factors operating in cigarette demand, while an economic behavioural model may be useful in explaining the purchase of a home. Sometimes alternative models shed light on different demand aspects of the same product.

As a discipline, economists were the first to construct a specific theory of buyer behaviour, arguing that buying decisions are the result of rational and conscious economic calculations of the satisfaction or utility that will be derived from any given purchase decision. Overall, economic man seeks to maximise his total satisfaction by acquiring a collection of goods and services in which the marginal utility of each is in theory equivalent to the marginal utility of every other item in the collection. This economic view of buyer behaviour is firmly founded in the writings of Adam Smith, who argued that all economic activity is ultimately based upon man's self-interest, and Jeremy Bentham, who refined the idea by arguing that in pursuing his self-interest, man carefully calculates the advantages and disadvantages of any given purchase. It is significant that, as Kotler comments: 'Bentham's "felicific calculus" was not applied to consumer behaviour, as opposed to entrepreneurial behaviour, until the late nineteenth century.' It was at the end of the nineteenth century that a number of famous economists developed almost simultaneously the 'marginal utility' theory of value that underlay

Adam Smith's explanation but had not been developed by him. Foremost among these economists was Alfred Marshall, and it was for this reason that the economists' explanation of buyer behaviour is named after him.

It is an almost universal trait that when offered an explanation of something, we almost automatically compare this with our own experience or behaviour to see whether it is consistent. As we shall see later in this chapter, self-reference behaviour may be very misleading indeed. However, this does not prevent us from applying the test, and most individuals would probably claim that they wouldn't know a marginal utility if they saw one, let alone how to calculate such a statistic. For this reason most marketers would dismiss the concept of homo economicus as an inadequate explanation of much buyer behaviour. They would also be able to refer to many analyses of buyer behaviour in which conscious economic calculations have played little part. But, as Kotler (1972) points out, there are several ways in which the Marshallian model helps an understanding of buyer behaviour:

1. It is axiomatic that every buyer acts in the light of his own best interest. The question is whether an economist would describe these actions as 'rational' or not.
2. The model is normative in the sense that it provides a logical basis for purchase decisions, i.e. how one should decide, rather than being descriptive, i.e. how one actually decides.
3. The model suggests a number of useful behavioural hypotheses, e.g. the lower the price, the greater the sales; the lower the price of substitute products, the lower the sales of this product; the lower the price of complementary products, the higher the sales of this product; the higher the real income, the higher the sales of this product, provided that it is not an 'inferior' good; the higher the promotional expenditure, the higher the sales.

However, economics only provides a partial explanation of how buyers choose.

An alternative explanation of choice behaviour is that it is a form of learned behaviour in which one associates a given stimulus with particular outcomes and responds accordingly. This stimulus response theory is based very largely on the pioneering work of Ivan Pavlov, whose experiments with conditioning animals are well known to almost everybody. (One of the best known of his experiments was to present a dog with two stimuli simultaneously, food and the ringing of a bell, and subsequently remove one of the stimuli (the food) and observe the dog's behaviour. When presented with both stimuli, originally the dog's automatic response was to salivate in expectation of food. Subsequently, when the bell was rung by itself, the dog had learned that the ringing of the bell was associated with food and began to salivate in expectation of the food which was not present.)

The stimulus response model of behaviour has been developed extensively since Pavlov's original discovery and is based on four central concepts of *drive, cue, response* and *reinforcement*. Drives may be physiological or social in origin and constitute an internal stimulus impelling action. By contrast, 'cues are weaker stimuli in the environment and/or in the individual that determine when, where, and how the subject responds'. Thus, cues modify drives into a particular response, the nature of which will be influenced substantially by past experience. Depending upon the outcome of the response, the individual will learn from this experience, which will either reinforce and confirm earlier decisions of the same kind as being satisfactory or, if unsatisfactory, may create uncertainty as to whether to repeat the decision in future, or prefer an alternative choice when faced with the same drives and cues.

Clearly there are many applications of stimulus response theory of relevance to the marketer. For example, much branding and advertising is designed to act as a cue and stimulus to purchase at the point of sale. Thus, in a survey 'How and Why Shoppers Buy' reported in the 28 October 1981 issue of *Marketing*, Hugh Davidson reported research showing that 38% of housewives never made a list before going shopping and a further 36% made only a partial list, deciding on the rest of their purchases in the shop. Similarly, research has shown that repeat advertising has an important role to play, both in reminding potential purchasers of past satisfactions received, and also in reinforcing the rightness of their decision after the actual purchase event.

The Pavlovian explanation of behaviour is

clearly too mechanistic to be an exact replication of the real world. Whereas a great deal of human behaviour may be conditioned and therefore predictable, there are also many situations in which people appear to behave in an unpredictable and idiosyncratic way. One explanation of this unpredictability in human behaviour is provided by Freud's work on motivation. According to Freud, a man's psyche or inner spirit is comprised of three parts: the id, the ego and the super-ego. The id is concerned with the strong inherent drives and urges with which he was born, while the ego represents 'his conscious planning centre for finding outlets for his drives', and the super-ego 'channels his instinctive drives into socially approved outlets to avoid the pain of guilt or shame'.

During the 1940s and 50s, the findings of motivational research were used extensively in developing marketing strategy, particularly through the contributions of people such as Ernest Dichter (1960). However, the use of motivational research came under considerable criticism on the grounds that sellers were manipulating buyers and persuading them to act against their own better interests. Much of John Galbraith's (1958) criticism of the consumer society is based upon an implicit assumption that buyers can be persuaded to act against their better and, presumably, economic interests. The reaction against motivation research culminated in the publication of Vance Packard's book, *The Hidden Persuaders* (1957), one consequence of which was that this approach to marketing fell out of fashion, although there are now signs of a return of interest in this approach.

The fourth, broadly based model of buyer behaviour is that based upon social–psychological interpretations first proposed by Thorstein Veblen. Perhaps his best-known work is his *Theory of the Leisure Class*, first published in 1899, in which he argued that many purchases were not motivated by need as much as by concern for one's social standing and prestige. In this sense Veblen may be thought of as the originator of the mythical Joneses with whom the rest of society has to keep up. While Veblen's emphasis upon conspicuous consumption has now been greatly modified by subsequent research and analysis, his contribution in pointing out the importance of social relationships as an influence upon choice cannot be overstated. A basic concept which has had a pervasive

influence on marketing thought is that of social class – a concept which has been widely used as a basis for segmenting markets. Nowadays it is generally recognised that there is considerable mobility between social classes and that in some markets social class may be a very poor predictor of actual attitudes and behaviour. As a consequence newer methods based on lifestyle using techniques such as psychographics have been found to have much better discriminatory and predictive power. However, even these new techniques recognise the importance of social interaction between individuals and the groups of which they are a part.

In his analysis, Kotler (1972) includes anthropological concepts of culture and subculture within the Veblenian social psychological model. More correctly, the study of culture is the province of the discipline of anthropology and, as one would expect with any complex body of knowledge, is comprised of many different and sometimes conflicting theories and points of view.

In answer to the question 'What is the nature of culture', Bliss (1970) observes:

> For some, culture has to do with believing, feeling, and thinking. Are the peoples of a society materialistic or spiritualistic? Do they value tradition rather than innovation? Are they aggressive or passive? What aspirations are they striving towards? The questions imply different values, different cultures.
>
> For others, culture is behaviour – as evidenced in the widespread and persistent pattern of behaviour observable in one country as contrasted with another. In going about their daily activities, people react in a predictable manner, thus making communal life possible. Culture in this sense is behaviour which is taken for granted, which is expected.
>
> For still others, it is the interplay of values and behaviour that defines culture. The tendency to place undue, if not complete, emphasis on behaviour – i.e., the customs and mores of a society – is categorised by Bidney as the positivistic fallacy. On the other hand, to define culture in terms of norms and values and to ignore or minimise actual behaviour, is to commit the normative fallacy.

Thus, as a gross simplification, but nonetheless a generalisation with which most, if not all, anthropologists would agree, culture is a composite of underlying values and behavioural patterns which, in the words of Bliss, 'give meaning to the lives of its [society's] members and determine the overall climate of activity'.

A concept as powerful as culture must be treated with caution if one is to avoid the dangers of overgeneralisation – which leads to stereotyping – or overspecificity which ultimately could lead one to distinguish each individual as a culture in their own right. As with the concept of market segmentation, the practitioner must develop an operationally useful definition which permits an appropriate level of discrimination without falling into the trap of regarding, say, all Americans (or Japanese, or Jews) as being the same or, worse still, completely different from each other. Thus, within any distinct culture one would expect to find a number of subcultures each with its own distinctive features and different from other subcultures.

Perhaps the most important feature of social science explanations of choice behaviour is that none of them individually provides an adequate explanation of the real world. If we were forced to use one or other of the foregoing explanations then there can be no doubt that in most cases we would be able to classify any given choice decision as being influenced more by one model than another. Thus, if faced with a choice between two objectively similar products, one of which was priced lower than the other, economic man would probably prevail. However, if the two objectively similar products had a similar price then our choice would have to be based on other discriminating factors of a subjective kind. If we had previous experience of one product and knew it to be satisfactory, then the Pavlovian explanation might well apply and we would prefer the known to the unknown product. Alternatively, although both products might be objectively similar, one might appeal more strongly than the other to our subconscious motivations and a Freudian explanation would be appropriate. Finally, if one product were more 'visible' than the others then we might depend upon a Veblenian explanation to account for users preferring it.

In reality, what we need is a composite model incorporating dimensions of each of the separate and independent social science explanations derived from a particular discipline. We shall return to this later in the chapter but, at this junc-

ture, it will be useful to look at six key concepts which past experience has shown to be very useful in answering the basic question – How do buyers choose? These six key concepts are:

1. Selective perception
2. The hierarchy of needs
3. The hierarchy of effects
4. Post-purchase dissonance
5. Buy tasks and buy phases
6. The characteristics of goods.

We shall now consider each of these briefly in turn.

SELECTIVE PERCEPTION

One of the cardinal principles of marketing is that one should always seek to put oneself into the customer's position and analyse the selling proposition from their point of view. The importance of this principle lies in the fact that not only do individuals differ, one from another, they also change themselves over time. Now it is highly probable that there are other people in the world who have opinions and attitudes similar to our own and therefore are likely to behave in a manner similar to ourselves. Indeed, one of the factors which tends to distinguish successful from unsuccessful entrepreneurs is the former's ability to identify a latent need and then satisfy it. However, comparatively few people have this gift, and it is for this reason, if for no other, that so much time and money is now expended on formal management education, and on research to try and predict consumers' behaviour. Without research and information about prospective consumers, one is likely to fall into the self-reference trap alluded to earlier, and so assume that others will behave in the way in which we ourselves would behave under any given set of circumstances.

The intrinsic danger of making such an assumption can be easily tested by asking a supporter from each of two opposing football teams to describe an incident leading to a penalty being imposed upon one side. It was just such a situation that led to the classic example of selective perception first reported in a paper by Hastorf and Cantril (1954). Following a particularly acrimonious clash between the college football teams of

Dartmouth and Princeton, the two sociologists asked supporters from each team to give their views as to what had led to the incidents involved. While most uninvolved viewers felt that these were the joint responsibility of both teams, supporters of each side were almost unanimous in their view that all the trouble was of the other team's making. In other words, being a supporter of a team tends to make us extol its virtues and overlook its failings. Accordingly, if one of the players on our team is involved in a clash with a member of the opposing team, it is likely that we will interpret this as provocation by the other and justifiable retaliation by our own team member.

In addition to leading us to interpret the world in terms of our expectations of it, the phenomenon of selective perception also plays a very important role in protecting us from information overload. Thus it has been shown that, in the course of a normal day, most individuals are exposed to over 1,000 different messages concerning products or services sellers wish them to buy. Out of this enormous welter of information only six or seven of these messages will catch our conscious attention and lead us to reflect upon whether we wish to pursue our awareness of a new fact any further, or just discard it.

One of the most compelling examples of selective perception which I have come across in my own experience relates to some early anti-smoking advertising put out by the Scottish Health Education Unit (SHEU – now the Health Education Board for Scotland – HEBS). The basic principle behind the campaign was straightforward and firmly founded in behavioural research findings. In that young people learn from adults and particularly their parents, it was argued that parents act as exemplars for children. Thus, if adults are seen behaving in a particular way, it is likely that children will pattern their own behaviour on this. To this end the SHEU commissioned a series of advertisements in which adults were seen interacting with children in a number of situations. Two particular examples were as follows.

The first advertisement showed a small girl sitting up in bed cuddling a teddy bear, while next to the bed sat a well-dressed woman reading from a storybook. The woman is smoking. At the conclusion of the story the woman emphasises the moral and says, 'you see what I mean, dear?' The woman inhales on her cigarette and the little girl sucks her thumb and says, 'yes, mummy'.

The second domestic scene shows a man and a small boy sitting in what appears to be a kitchen with a bicycle upside down on the table. The man, who has a cigarette in his mouth, is adjusting part of the mechanism of the bike and saying to the boy, 'there, you see how it's done?', to which the boy, sucking on a screwdriver, replies, 'yes, I see'.

In order to test the effectiveness of these and other advertisements in the campaign it was decided to do a limited amount of qualitative research, using group depth interviews. Basically the respondents were divided into mixed groups of parents representing the upper and lower socioeconomic groupings. When shown the advertisements and asked to comment upon them, the results were surprising. In the first place none of the members of the groups picked out the smoking factor at all. When prompted, some respondents thought that the first advertisement in the bedroom was concerned with fire hazards and that the intended message was not to smoke in a bedroom. No associations were perceived in the second advertisement at all.

In fact the interpretations placed on the advertisements by the two groups seemed quite bizarre at first, but on reflection could be seen as quite reasonable in terms of the normal frame of reference of the respondents themselves. Thus, in the case of the mother reading a bedtime story, this scene was quite normal in the eyes of the upper social class respondents, who perceived the message as being that it was good for mothers to read to children and that it was part of normal family life. For the respondents from the lower socioeconomic groups, the scene was quite atypical and led to an interpretation which may be caricatured as follows: 'Her husband is on the nightshift at the factory and she's got a fancy man. That's why she's all dressed up. She's feeling guilty, that's why she's reading a story to the kid because she is going to leave it all alone. You should not leave children alone in a house unattended.' By contrast, in the boy-and-bike advertisement, members of the upper social classes spent most of their time commenting on the unhygienic behaviour of the lower classes who actually took bicycles into their kitchens. Members of the lower socioeconomic groupings saw this as a perfectly normal scene from family life and interpreted it as saying that it is important that fathers show sons how to make their bicycles safe so they don't get injured in an accident.

It is instructive that this particular campaign, which was singularly ineffective in communicating any of the objectives of the advertiser to its audience, was highly rated by other advertisers and advertising agents. Only by deliberately setting out to discover how the audience interpreted the advertising did it become clear that a completely different approach was required.

A second case history, which exemplifies the importance of understanding how selective perception may result in a very different interpretation of a product from that held by its producer, is provided by the marketing of super plastic aluminium. The full case history of this revolutionary material was reported by myself and Stephen Parkinson in an article entitled 'TI Superform's academic launch' (1978). Super plastic aluminium or Supral, as it was called, was the result of considerable research between Tube Investments and the British Aluminium Technological Centre. As a result of this research TI decided to set up a subsidiary (TI Superform) to market the new material. Supral offers significant benefits in the manufacture of complex shapes beyond the capabilities of rubber die pressing, and in quantities below 10,000 off where high tool costs would render multiple pressing or deep drawing of aluminium or steel uneconomic. Further, while Supral is not competitive with plastics on price alone, there are many applications where the high temperature capability of aluminium makes its use preferable. It also seemed possible that, with escalating oil prices, aluminium could become directly competitive with plastics on price alone, which would give it a significant overall advantage.

In light of the basic performance and cost characteristics, Superform identified eight basic market sectors as follows:

1. Aerospace
2. Specialist vehicles
3. Commercial vehicles
4. Case shells
5. Electrical/instrument housings
6. Gaming/vending machine cases
7. Architectural panels
8. Others.

With so many possible end-use markets, one of the problems Superform faced was how to focus its selling effort on those with the greatest promise of an early return. This question is one on which I have spent the great majority of my time, both as an industrial salesman and as an academic. While examination of a very large number of distinct cases has enabled me to develop some generalisations (Baker, 1983), perhaps the single, most important piece of advice is – put yourself in the shoes of the prospective purchaser and look at your selling proposition from their point of view. Obviously, in order to find out what the prospective purchaser's point of view is, one has to undertake some research among potential users. To focus our recommendations in the case of Supral, we undertook interviews with those companies which had decided to buy the product as well as those which had declined the offer. In addition to a number of general factors we shall return to when proposing our own composite model of buying behaviour, there was a significant number of situation-specific factors that appeared to have a major influence on the decision whether or not to buy Supral. Among these particular factors were:

1. The potential user's own press-shop/toolroom facilities. Where underutilised capacity exists manufacturers prefer to use their own facilities rather than buy in, even when buying in offers a piece price saving.
2. The amount of integration in the existing manufacturing process. The greater the integration, the greater the need for material compatibility. In other words, you don't mix steel with aluminium or plastic if you can avoid it.
3. The opportunity to buy in a completed 'bolt on' part will increase interest in cases where substantial hand finishing was necessary before.
4. When the prospective purchaser is developing a new product of their own then the low tooling costs on small runs would appear particularly attractive.
5. Single sourcing – a unique product is seen as much more risky than one available from a number of different competing sources.

Other incentives to early adoption included frequent design changes, the existence of formal value analysis programmes in user companies which substantiated the seller's claim of cost-effectiveness (unfortunately these were not very common), and familiarity with similar materials and/or manufacturing technology. Conversely, a number of distinct barriers to adoption were also identified, including:

- Product design/specifications set by a non-UK holding company
- Use of a performance specification to which all new materials must first conform, e.g. a British Standard (securing a rating often takes a long time for a unique new material)
- Commitment to the known and existing technology
- The costs of evaluating and testing the new material
- An existing commitment to suppliers through forward orders and/or investment in capital equipment
- Ineffective senior management (resistance to change).

While the foregoing factors were specific to a decision as to whether or not to buy Supral, a number of them are felt to have more general application. However, the main point we are trying to make here is that in any given buying decision it is not the facts themselves which are important but the potential buyer's perception of those facts. Because of selective perception, the potential benefits of a new product may look very different to the would-be buyer than from its committed seller's point of view. A simple example of this would be the case where a machine tool manufacturer had introduced Mark II and Mark III versions of a particular tool, each of which offered a 10% increment in capacity over the preceding model. It follows that Mark III offers an increment in capacity of rather better than 20% for owners of the Mark I model, but only 10% for owners of the Mark II model. Thus, the benefits to be gained from purchase of a Mark III model are relative to the capacity and performance of the existing model which one owns and it is this which is most likely to influence the would-be purchaser rather than the absolute capacity rating of the machine.

One concept which is helpful in assessing the likely saliency of a product to a potential user is to consider where it might be placed in that person's hierarchy of needs.

HIERARCHY OF NEEDS

Earlier in this chapter when discussing the Pavlovian and Freudian models of buying behaviour, we touched on the nature of drives and motives and their influence upon the individual's choice behaviour. Together, drives and motives are often called 'needs' and there is considerable evidence to support a theory put forward first by Abraham Maslow that needs can be classified into a simple five-step hierarchy as follows:

1. Physiological needs
2. Safety needs
3. Love needs
4. Esteem needs
5. Self-actualisation needs.

Usually people will seek to satisfy these needs in the order in which they appear in the hierarchy, such that physiological needs will normally take precedence over all others. For example, faced with death from hunger or thirst, the hunter would ignore safety needs and take extreme risks in order to kill an animal. However, once he has first satisfied his thirst and hunger, he would then become aware of possible danger from other animals and begin to look for a safe refuge from them. Once the basic physiological and safety needs have been satisfied, the individual seeks to satisfy their need for affection and the feeling of belonging to a group – the so-called social needs. Many consumer products are promoted as having attributes which will enhance one's acceptance with the group, or occasionally are sold on the basis that lack of possession could lead to ostracism or exclusion from the group. Similarly, esteem needs are fertile ground for the marketer as they are concerned with factors such as recognition, status, prestige etc., most of which can be inferred from an individual's possessions, mode of dress etc.

The highest level of needs are concerned with self-actualisation or, in the modern idiom, doing one's own thing. People who have achieved this stage are likely to be immune to marketing techniques and have a very clear view of what it is they want and want to do. Indeed, the reason why we qualified the fact that physiological needs override all others is that individuals who are able to self-actualise can override such physiological needs in pursuit of their own higher objectives, e.g. suicide bombers.

The value of this basic concept of a hierarchy of needs lies in the fact that it can be used as a first coarse screen for classifying buyer motivations and thus indicate the general kinds of marketing techniques and practices which are likely to be effective. But, to see how to use these we must turn to the third conceptual framework known as the hierarchy of effects.

HIERARCHY OF EFFECTS

The importance of studying buying behaviour is not so much for reasons of maintaining a historical record of what took place, but rather to obtain a better understanding of why such purchase decisions were made. Through such an analysis marketers hope that they will be able to determine some pointers which will enable them to predict how prospective buyers will act in future. Based upon past observation, most practitioners subscribe to the view that individuals pass through a number of stages in coming to a decision as to whether or not to buy an object. These stages are succinctly summarised in the salesman's mnemonic AIDA, which stands for the four distinct phases of awareness, interest, desire and action. In the jargon of the behavioural sciences, AIDA may be classified as a CAC model standing for cognitive, affective and conative or, in more general parlance, knowing, feeling and acting. Such models are also known as hierarchy of effects models in that they propose that a decision to act in a particular way is the consequence of a process which starts with recognition of a stimulus, evaluation of it and then a decision as to how to act upon that information. There are a considerable number of hierarchy of effects models and some of these are summarised in Table 9.1.

Table 9.1 is taken from my basic textbook, *Marketing* (2006), in which the reader will find a much fuller description of the role of hierarchy of

effects models. For our present purposes it is sufficient to emphasise that, depending upon one's definition of the various steps in the hierarchy, the model becomes tautological and self-fulfilling. Clearly, one cannot buy a product if one is unaware of its existence and interest can only follow awareness, while desire can only develop out of interest. That said, hierarchy of effects models have been subjected to much criticism on the grounds that awareness, interest and desire may reflect attitudes towards an object, but they do not necessarily imply action or behaviour with regard to those objects. Nonetheless, if we accept the statistic cited earlier that selective perception screens out the vast majority of all marketing stimuli to which the individual is exposed, it would seem reasonable to set marketing objectives in terms of moving people along the hierarchy of effects. Thus, one might set as an objective of an advertising campaign, the achievement of a predetermined level of awareness in the population to whom the advertising message is to be directed. Similarly, once one has achieved a given level of awareness, one could set objectives in terms of converting this awareness into interest in the sense that people could recall or play back claims made for the product in its advertising.

TABLE 9.1 Hierarchy of effects models

	Strong (AIDA)	Lavidge and Steiner	Rogers	Engel, Kollat and Blackwell
Conative (motive)	Action	Purchase Conviction	Adoption Trial	Purchase processes
Affective (emotion)	Desire Interest	Preference Liking	Evaluation Interest	Evaluation and search
Cognitive (thought)	Awareness	Knowledge Awareness	Awareness	Problem recognition
		Unawareness		

POST-PURCHASE DISSONANCE

A fourth general concept of particular value to sellers is that associated with the buyer's feelings after the purchase decision has been made. As we saw earlier when discussing the Pavlovian learning model of consumer behaviour, we identified four concepts of drive, cue, response and reinforcement. In a marketing context purchase is the desired response and the importance of the concept of dissonance is that it describes the purchaser's state of mind after the decision has been taken.

By definition dissonance is the opposite state to consonance, by which we understand the individual's effort to organise perceived stimuli into coherent and consistent patterns which are in accord with our knowledge, beliefs and attitudes. It follows that if when considering a particular choice/decision, one perceives stimuli which are not consistent with our view of the world, then we are likely to reject that object because it creates dissonance. The need to achieve consonancy between a product and its intended purchaser is so obvious as not to require further discussion here. However, the importance of work on dissonance following Leon Festinger's *Theory of Cognitive Dissonance* (1957) has been recognition of the fact that the act of purchase itself may create some uncertainty in the mind of the buyer, who will then seek reassurance that they have made the correct decision. Because of this uncertainty and the need to reinforce the buyer in their belief that they have made the correct decision, the importance of the role which after-sales service has to play is emphasised. Thus, research has shown that perception and readership of advertisements relating to products is highest among persons who have just purchased such a product, who would appear to be seeking reinforcement of the correctness of their original decision. Thus, in today's highly competitive markets it is vital that

marketers 'follow through' on every purchase and not regard the transaction as finished once the buyer has taken possession of the object.

BUY PHASES

A fifth concept of considerable practical utility to the marketer is the analytical framework proposed by Robinson et al. in their book *Industrial Buying and Creative Marketing* (1967). Although, as the title of the book suggests, this model was developed as a result of research into buying behaviour in industrial companies, it is felt that the framework is of equal value in analysing buying decisions by individuals or small groups.

The analytic framework developed by Robinson et al. is based upon two simple classificatory systems – buy phases and buy classes. As can be seen from Table 9.2, there are eight buy phases and three buy classes. The eight buy phases are a slightly extended version of the problem-solving sequence discussed earlier and do not merit any further explanation. Similarly, the buy classes' classification is self-explanatory and reflects the complexity and perceived risk experienced by the prospective buyer when considering a specific purchase. Thus, in the case of a new task, by definition the buyer has not previously evaluated the particular product in question and will have to be moved from a stage of unawareness through to a decision with careful attention to each of the phases, 1 to 6 shown in Table 9.2. In the case of a modified rebuy, it is assumed that buyers have

TABLE 9.2 The buy-grid analytic framework for industrial buying situations

Buy phases	BUY CLASSES		
	New task	Modified rebuy	Straight rebuy
1. Anticipation or recognition of a problem (need) and a general solution			
2. Determination of characteristics and quantity of needed item			
3. Description of characteristics and quantity of needed item			
4. Search for and qualification of potential sources			
5. Acquisition and analysis of proposals			
6. Evaluation of proposals and selection of supplier(s)			
7. Selection of an order routine			
8. Performance feedback and evaluation			

SOURCE: Redrawn from Robinson, P. J., Faris, C. W. and Wind, Y. (1967) *Industrial Buying and Creative Marketing*. Boston, MA: Allyn & Bacon, p. 14

previous experience of products of the general category which they are now considering but, whether because of dissatisfaction with a previous purchase, or recognition of improvement in the product since they last purchased it, they wish to re-evaluate what is available in the marketplace. In such a situation the first three buy phases may be skipped over and the process can really commence at phase 4. Finally, in the case of a straight rebuy, purchasers have direct knowledge of the product in question which they have purchased previously from a given source of supply with which they are satisfied. Accordingly, only phases 1 and 7 of the buy phases may be required when placing a reorder for that product.

A major factor influencing the amount of time and effort which will be put into evaluating a potential purchase will depend very much upon the nature of the product itself. Bearing in mind that prospective purchasers will be likely to perceive products differently, i.e. one person's convenience good may be another's shopping or specialty good, it will be helpful to isolate some attributes which will help us to classify how potential purchasers may see a given product.

CHARACTERISTICS OF GOODS

While many writers have proposed schemata for classifying goods, one of the most well known is that put forward by Leo Aspinwall in 1958, in which he suggested that five product characteristics be used to help decide on the most effective marketing strategy for a product. These are:

1. *Replacement rate:* the rate at which a good is purchased and consumed by users in order to provide the satisfaction a consumer expects from the product.
2. *Gross margin:* the difference between the paid in cost and the final realised sales price.
3. *Adjustment:* the amount of services applied to goods in order to meet the exact needs of the consumer.
4. *Time of consumption:* the measured time of consumption during which the goods give up the utilities desired.
5. *Searching time:* the measure of average time and distance from the retail store.

As the last item indicates, Aspinwall was primarily concerned with consumer goods, but it is believed that the general approach is equally relevant to industrial goods.

Aspinwall went on to propose that one could develop a scoring system for each of the five product characteristics and so classify them into broad categories. In his own analysis Aspinwall used three colours to designate three categories of goods, red, orange and yellow:

- Red goods: goods with a high replacement rate and a low gross margin adjustment, time of consumption, and searching time.
- Orange goods: goods with a medium score on all five characteristics.
- Yellow goods: goods with a low replacement rate and high gross margin, adjustment, time of consumption, and searching time.

Clearly these three definitions correspond very closely to the distinction between convenience goods, shopping goods and specialty goods in the consumer behaviour literature (Copeland, 1923), and straight rebuy, modified rebuy and new task categories proposed by Robinson et al. (1967).

BUYER BEHAVIOUR AND THE DECISION-MAKER

The foregoing review of four generalised models of buyer behaviour and six key concepts has made it abundantly clear that there is no single simple and easy way in which to predict how potential buyers will act in any given situation. In fact, quite the opposite impression may have been given, namely that buying decisions are complex, dynamic, based upon multiple factors and downright messy to the extent that the theorising of academics merely serves to add to the confusion rather than clarify it. It would be a great pity if this was seen to be the case. As we noted at the beginning of this chapter, its content is eclectic and reflects the idiosyncrasies of the author. Thus, our purpose has not been to present a comprehensive review of buyer behaviour as this goes far beyond the scope of a book of this type. Rather, our objective has been to select a sample of ideas from the literature which seem to provide useful pointers to the ways in which decision-makers can structure their own analysis and thereby arrive at better decisions more frequently.

At least two more things need to be stressed. First, the great majority of theoretical work reported here is based on empirical research into the way in which people behave in the real world. If there is bad theory then it is likely that it reflects bad practice, although occasionally it may result from misinterpretation by the researcher. Similarly, if researchers propose what they see as good theory based upon the observed procedures and practices in successful organisations, then failure to conform with such practices and procedures can only be justified after the most thorough of examinations, and the identification of unique factors which distinguish the normative recommendation from the reality facing a particular individual or company.

The second important observation to be made upon this chapter is that it is to be hoped that it has indicated to the reader the enormous wealth of ideas and insights available to practitioners to enable them to perform their task better. In exploring this literature one must beware of the trap of only using those ideas which confirm one's own existing prejudices (selective perception is rearing its ugly head again!). Some models and generalisations are more robust than others and should only be set aside after very careful consideration by the decision-maker. Conversely, there are fads and fashions in management thinking as in any other area of activity, and equal care must be taken in accepting fashionable new ideas in the absence of strong evidence to support their suitability.

In the final analysis, every decision-maker has to work out the modus operandi best suited to them. Experimentation is to be encouraged, and practitioners should not leave all the theorising to the academics. Rather, they should seek to develop their own CUGs as a basis for practice. To this end, I present my own so-called model of buyer behaviour. In doing so I am conscious of the fact that some of my fellow academics do not consider this to satisfy the criteria which theorists require of a model. That said, I, and a fairly extensive number of companies – large, medium and small, in growing and declining industries, with high, medium and low technologies – have found this model to be very helpful in organising their thinking about how buyers do choose, and how they may develop effective marketing strategies to reflect this behaviour.

THE BAKER COMPOSITE MODEL

The current version of the model may be expressed notationally as follows:

P = fS[SP(FN, EC, IS, CBA, BR) PPE]
In the model:
P = a Purchase
f = a function (unspecified)
S = a stimulus or stimuli
SP = selective perception
FN = felt need (*Awareness*)
EC = enabling conditions
IS = information search (*Interest*)
CBA = cost–benefit analysis (*Desire*)
BR = behavioural response (*Action*)
PPE = post-purchase evaluation

In the Pavlovian or learning model of buyer behaviour, reference is made to the need for some cue or stimulus to activate a drive and initiate action. In our model, this factor is placed at the beginning of the equation, on the basis that we are all constantly surrounded by *external stimuli* as well as being subject to our own *internal stimuli*. As described earlier, these stimuli are screened selectively through the process of selective perception. Those recognised and consciously attended to are defined as FN or *felt need*.

Once the need has been identified, the next step is to establish whether or not there is a means of satisfying this need. This we have identified in our model as *enabling conditions* or EC. Enabling conditions embrace all those factors which make it possible for a prospective purchaser to benefit from satisfying a felt need. The television is of no use if you have no electricity, nor a gas oven if you have no gas. Similarly, as noted earlier, many manufacturers try to avoid mixing materials such as steel, aluminium and plastics, since each requires different skills and techniques in use and increases the investment necessary in both plant and labour. In other words, the object being considered for purchase must be compatible with the user's current status and, in many cases, also with their self-image. In the absence of such enabling conditions, interest is likely to be short-lived and unlikely to proceed to an evaluation.

Having identified the need, and established that this appears to be compatible with one's existing status, the next step will be to verify and validate this by collecting and evaluating further information – IS or *information search*. Clearly, the nature and extent of this search will depend greatly upon a number of factors, including the novelty of the object under consideration, the risk perceived in the decision, and the number and availability of means of satisfying the need. In the case of complex innovations with which one has no prior experience, one is likely to engage in extended information-gathering, especially where high prices are involved. Conversely, faced with a new brand of low-cost convenience good, it is unlikely one will spend much time in seeking additional information beyond that available at the point of sale.

While the next element, *cost–benefit analysis* (CBA), is placed after information search in the model, in many cases this analysis will proceed in parallel with the gathering of information and be used to determine whether to consider or reject it. The inclusion of this factor is explicit recognition of the economic or rational school of buyer behaviour that views purchase decisions as the outcome of a careful comparison of the performance factors associated with a purchase and the price asked for any given combination of attributes.

As we have noted earlier, in the case of individual buyer behaviour, decisions are frequently made *without* the extended and careful consideration implicit in the Marshallian or 'economic' model. On the other hand, where more than one person is involved, or where an individual is acting on behalf of others, the evidence suggests that more attention will be given to spelling out performance factors and assessing their cost–benefit. Even so, it is important to recognise that cost–benefit, like selective perception, introduces significant subjectivity into the analysis. Thus the weighting given to individual performance factors or features in determining the benefit to be gained will vary from one individual to another. Further, as the concept of diminishing marginal returns makes clear, our perception of benefit will change as we acquire more of something, and also over time. It is for these reasons that no single function can capture or reflect the interaction between the variables in the model. Similarly, in order to apply the model, one has to examine every decision in its own context.

In the case of an organisation considering the acquisition of a major piece of capital equipment, it is likely that considerable effort will be given to drawing up a detailed specification of the attributes or performance factors looked for. This specification will then be used to compare competitive offerings and the overall cost–benefit calculated with apparently great precision. On the other hand, people buy cars and houses, which proportionately represent a much higher risk, with little formal evaluation of more than a small number of key attributes that matter to them.

Initially, most people tend to think of performance factors in terms of *objective* or tangible criteria but, as the burgeoning literature on service quality shows, the term also embraces *subjective* or intangible factors. A recent article by Woodall (2001) indicates how both dimensions are considered in purchase decisions.

Woodall cites Gronroos (1984) who, in turn, follows the suggestion of Swan and Comb that service *products* have both 'instrumental' and 'expressive' outcomes. This leads Gronroos to state that a 'satisfactory performance' in terms of the instrumental outcomes 'is a prerequisite for a satisfied customer'. According to Woodall, Gronroos's deconstruction of service quality led him to conclude that its principal components were technical quality, functional quality, and corporate image – the latter primarily determined by both conventional and emergent marketing techniques, but also substantially dependent upon both expectations and perceptions regarding the first two.

The penultimate variable in our model is *behavioural response*. At its simplest, this is the action taken after completing the cost–benefit analysis – to buy, defer the decision, or to reject the offer. However, our behavioural response may also require us to reconsider all the preceding stages in the process. This is likely to occur when our evaluation has not identified an option that is clearly to be preferred to all others. In most competitive markets this is a common occurrence as sellers seek to ensure that their offers at least match those of the competition in terms of price and performance factors. Indeed, choice in a competitive market means just that – the availability of more than one closely matched alternative. Of course the practices of segmentation, targeting and positioning are intended to resolve this problem by preidentifying differences between potential customers, and then adapting the object to the specific needs of the targeted buyer. Where successful, this will have influenced the perception of benefits, and the buyer's response. Where unsuccessful, the potential buyer will be left with a choice between two apparently identical objects, and so need to reconsider the earlier stages in order to reach a decision.

Finally, we have included another new variable in the current model – *post-purchase evaluation* or PPE. By doing so we acknowledge the importance of experiential learning which, in turn, will either reinforce or modify our attitudes, beliefs and values and through them our selective perception and future behaviour. In other words, as the current concern for customer relationship management makes clear, buying must be conceived of as a circular process with feedback loops. Despite this, it is still believed that the linear process model provides a helpful conceptual and analytical framework to help marketers understand better how buyers choose.

Thus, this is a sequential process model very similar to the buying decision process model introduced earlier.

Having described the general model, some elaboration of the variables will indicate what sort of factors one would need to take into account to use it.

In the Pavlovian learning model of buyer

behaviour, reference is made to the need for some cue – what is it that would make a buyer consider a change in the status quo? Clearly, dissatisfaction with existing alternatives constitutes a marketing opportunity, and is one type of precipitating factor. The need to replace or renew a piece of capital equipment or consumer durable is another opportunity, whether the need is caused by breakdown, loss, destruction or a planned replacement policy. Knowing which customers might be in this state would enable the firm to focus its marketing effort to much greater effect, both in terms of the information to be conveyed and the means of conveying it. Similarly, being able to satisfy a known need – we have a faster computer, a more economical car and so forth – is a claim likely to precipitate active consideration of a new purchase.

As noted earlier, 'enabling conditions' embrace all those factors that make it possible for a prospective purchaser to benefit from the new product. In other words, a new product must be compatible with the user's current status and, in many cases, also with their self-image. In the absence of such enabling conditions, interest is likely to be short-lived and unlikely to proceed further to an evaluation. You must have the wherewithal to pay for the purchase!

The economics or cost–benefit of a purchase are at the very heart of the Marshallian and 'rational' schools of buying behaviour models – CBA in our model. Ideally one should specify the advantages and disadvantages separately, partly because people do weigh up the pros and cons of courses of action, and partly because, if one is going to use the model, then one should specify as fully as possible what the merits and demerits are, weight these if necessary and only then come up with an overall judgement as to how the new product measures up against the competition.

Some broad guidelines as to the relative importance of different features that go to make up an effective selling proposition in industrial markets generally are shown for machine tools in Figure 9.1. But, while these offer an indication of the relative importance of groups of features, it must always be remembered that the majority of buying decisions turn on highly specific characteristics – another reason why a general model cannot possibly accommodate all conceivable sets of circumstances.

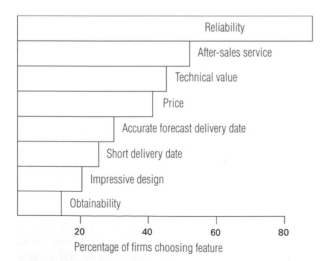

FIGURE 9.1 Features of a machine tool considered one of the three most important

We have already stipulated that the importance of behavioural response will depend heavily upon the objective evaluation of the available facts (albeit that these are perceived subjectively), and 'build a better product at an equivalent price or an equivalent product at a lower price' is clearly the best advice to management. But, in most competitive markets, there is often little to choose objectively between alternative offerings, and the buyer will have to make deliberate recourse to subjective value judgements to assist in distinguishing between the various items available. Because housewives do this daily when preferring Daz to Persil, Sunblest to Mother's Pride etc, they are often characterised as choosing irrationally. Nothing could be further from the truth. The important objective decisions about a shopping basket relate to its overall mix and composition vis-à-vis the available budget – the choice decision is which detergent, which bread and so on. It would be a fatal mistake to imagine that the industrial buyer doesn't have just the same problems when deciding between Scania, Mercedes or Leyland for his lorries, or Cincinnati or Kearney and Trecker for his machine tools.

USING THE MODEL

Much of *Market Development* (Baker, 1983) is taken up with the discussion of actual case histories of the launch and market development of new products and their subsequent success or failure. Where appropriate, the cases are followed by a brief analysis pointing out how the model provides an analytical framework which helps to explain the eventual outcome on the premise that, if this is possible a posteriori, then use of the model a priori is likely to improve overall success rates in new product development. However, it will be helpful here to provide a broad statement of how to apply the model.

At the outset it must be recognised that in no way does the model contradict the normative approach to market research and market segmentation described fully in almost every basic marketing text. Rather it should be seen as reinforcing and amplifying standardised techniques for the identification and measurement of potential demand – indeed, it would not be too extrav-

agant a claim to assert that our analytical framework seeks to emphasise the marketing dimensions of marketing research, in that it attempts to address the problem from the perspective of prospective buyers rather than from the standpoint of the seller. That said, it should be clear from our brief statement of the nature of enabling conditions (EC) that this factor seeks to establish a prima facie case of primary demand such that EC will describe the maximum potential market for any new product. Thus the existence of EC will define all those individuals or organisations which could conceivably have a use for our new product, more often than not by a process of exclusion rather than of inclusion. Thus, for example, our primary demand specification for baby products would be likely to use the birth rate as a basic parameter in establishing potential market size – being or having a baby constituting a basic qualifying criterion for the existence of EC. (Of course, as we all now know from the example of Johnson & Johnson, to confine the use of baby products to babies actually constrains the potential market since items such as powder and shampoo are widely used by adults. But, if one is launching a new baby product such as nappy liners, it would seem sensible, at least until the product has become established, to regard babies as the primary demand for the product.)

Thus EC is a necessary but not sufficient condition for defining the potential market for a product and constitutes the first crude cut at isolating a group of potential users for a more detailed analysis – for example, the use of two-digit SIC codes. Yet, as we have argued earlier, such a basic definition of a target market leaves a great deal to be desired, for it lacks focus and would undoubtedly lead to the dissipation and waste of a great deal of marketing effort. The whole thrust of our approach is to try and identify the most receptive subset or segment within the potential market as the target for our initial marketing development work.

To provide a more selective focus, we suggest that one should seek to isolate some cue or stimulus, which would have the effect of converting an essentially latent primary demand into an active recognition of the possible means of satisfying a felt need (FN). For firms already operating in a market, for whom a new product frequently represents a product line extension, such identification of a precipitating circumstance, or FN, should present much less difficulty than is the case with a firm which has no previous experience of or contact with a potential market. Nonetheless, there is considerable evidence to suggest that sellers frequently make inadequate or no use of information available to them through their continuing relationship with present customers, and/or frequently misinterpret such information as is available to them – the age of the existing stock or holding of a product, for example, which the innovation seeks to replace or substitute for. Perhaps the most obvious yet most frequently committed error, however, is to concentrate early marketing efforts upon the largest potential customers, presumably following the logic that they have most to gain and that by securing orders from them one will stand the best chance of achieving one's initial sales targets. They also have most to lose! There is considerable evidence, some of it recorded in cases reported in *Market Development*, to suggest that the alternative hypothesis, that small companies are most likely to adopt first, has much to commend it.

In discussing this 'strategy of the indirect approach' in my earlier analysis, I advanced the following arguments in favour of this proposition.

On the assumption that any new product which aspires to success must possess advantages over that which it seeks to replace, then it seems to me that this advantage is potentially of much greater significance to the small rather than the large user. For the large firm, the incentive to increase its share of market is limited. First, there is the possibility that an increase in market share might attract the unwelcome attentions of the Competition Commission or its foreign equivalent. Secondly, as any marked increase in market share must be at the expense of major competitors, there is a strong likelihood that any effort to achieve such an increase would result in aggressive retaliation by these competitors, probably to the detriment of all concerned. Thirdly, there may be strong grounds for adopting a 'wait and see' attitude ('anticipatory retardation' in Fellner's (1951) terminology), owing to the belief that the present innovation may itself soon be made obsolete by further improvements. Fourthly, there is a marked trend to pursue the 'strategy of the fast second' as described, inter alia, by Levitt in his 'innovative

imitation'. For these reasons alone, many large firms may well adopt a 'don't rock the boat' attitude towards those markets in which they already have a major share, on the grounds that, by disturbing the existing equilibrium, they are much more likely to lose than gain.

For the small firm, with a market share measured as a fraction of 1%, the situation is very different. Assume that such a firm were offered a new raw material with superior properties and a lower or equivalent cost to one of its major inputs. By adopting this new material, the small firm could, in turn, offer end users a superior product at a lower or equivalent price to the inferior substitute which it seeks to replace. Other things being equal, economic rationality predicates that end users will prefer the new product and transfer their demand to its supplier, thereby increasing the latter's market share. If it is assumed that the small firm originally had a 0.25% market share, then it is clear that, even were it to increase this fourfold to 1%, it could only reduce a major supplier's share by 0.75% of the total market. The significance of such a reduction would vary dependent upon the loser's prior market share as indicated in Table 9.3. Of course, the smaller the large firm's present market share, the less likely it becomes that the small firm's gain would be entirely at its expense.

TABLE 9.3 Impact of loss of 0.75% of total market share on various levels of existing market share

Present market share	Reduction in sales volume occasioned by loss of 0.75% of total market
10	− 7.50
15	− 5.00
20	− 3.75
25	− 3.00
30	− 2.50

If the foregoing assumptions are correct, then it follows that the small firm has a much greater incentive to adopt than does the large firm. Ignoring for the present the question of variation between small firms in terms of their receptivity to innovation, it has already been established that time to first adoption is a critical determinant of the speed and extent of the overall diffusion process. Once innovators have secured a successful first adoption, they may use this fact to substantiate their claims as to the value of the innovation in a far more convincing manner than is possible with purely theoretical or 'trial' data. Even though the small firm's increased share of the market may be insufficient to stimulate the market leaders to adopt the innovation, it may nonetheless be impressive enough to encourage other small firms to emulate its achievement, giving rise to the so-called 'bandwagon' or 'contagion' effect which underlies exponential growth. Clearly, if this occurs, the cumulative effect of several small firms securing an increased share of market will eventually result in the market leaders suffering a sufficient loss to prompt retaliatory action and so accelerate adoption even further.

Of course, in most markets one is still faced with large numbers of prospective customers, and it is here that the evaluation of the perceived benefits of adoption (technical and economic) will lay considerable weight upon careful and thorough analysis of both the status and needs of likely users. Any standard text on market research will provide a comprehensive review of the techniques available to accomplish this, and only two comments seem appropriate here.

The first is to emphasise yet again that the important, indeed critical thing is to try and look at the 'facts' from the standpoint of the possible buyer; and the second is to underline the value of actually asking the prospective customer for their views. Many sellers appear to be reluctant to attempt a direct approach to customers under the misguided impression that they will not cooperate. My own experience as a salesman, market researcher and consultant is directly contrary to this view since I have always found that buyers are just as anxious to secure information about possible sources of supply as sellers about sources of demand. I have also found that people and companies which have considered purchasing a new product and rejected the idea are very willing to tell you why, and are usually much more objective than are actual purchasers seeking to rationalise their behaviour in terms of what they think you want to hear. The message is quite clear: a direct, personal approach to potential customers is

likely to pay handsome dividends in defining precisely what they want.

Finally, we return to the influence of behavioural response, which may best be described as conscious selective perception, for whereas selective perception will have conditioned the prospective buyer's view of all the preceding variables, factual or not, its influence will have been largely subconscious, and behavioural response (BR) only assumes any importance when an 'objective' techno-economic analysis still leaves more than one alternative from which to choose. In these circumstances, the would-be buyer recognizes that subjective and qualitative factors have a contribution to make and consciously invokes them. It is for this reason that we argue that marketing has a double role to play, for not only can it influence perception in terms of creating attention, stimulating interest and helping to determine what 'facts' are evaluated, but, in a multiple choice situation, it can prove to be the determinant factor which results in a decision to buy rather than reject or defer purchase.

Ways in which marketing can achieve this discriminating role are manifold and often highly situation-specific, but a few examples will help make the point.

Consider the husband and wife trying to select a consumer durable such as a cooker, fridge or DVD player – the retail outlet has a wide variety on offer and those of comparable size/performance tend to have very similar prices. It is here that personal influence can help to tip the balance, but how many manufacturers offer to help train retail store assistants or otherwise influence them to put their weight behind their particular product? Similarly, how many manufacturers provide an adequate after-sales service to ensure satisfaction and predispose the buyer to repeat purchase when the need comes to replace a durable; or, equally important, try to communicate that, while you shouldn't need service and hope not to collect on your fire or health insurance, if you do it will be forthcoming willingly, speedily and without hassle?

In business-to-business markets, as we have already suggested, small firms are more often quicker to adopt than large, and because such innovation decisions are proportionately more important to them than is a similar decision in a large firm, where a first purchase may be no more than a trial, they are also more likely to commit themselves fully to making the innovation succeed. But, for many small firms, cash and technical expertise contribute major barriers to innovation, and it would seem reasonable to propose that sellers should seek to 'normalise' the financial implications by offering a package that makes it possible for the small customer to invest in innovation – after all, if it is going to improve their performance as significantly as you claim, should you not be willing to defer or spread payment until these cash flows are forthcoming? Similarly, technical advice both prior to sale and after installation will enable the seller to ensure that their product is used as intended, will provide information on performance in normal working environments (as opposed to prototypes in laboratories) which may be used for modification and improvement, and give the necessary reassurance to the buyer who might otherwise be put off by the sophistication of the technology. Training operatives also helps to achieve these objectives. In other words, marketing can help to reduce or 'eliminate' key factors in the decision process.

Marketing is essentially a dynamic and creative activity, and it is for these reasons that it is often difficult to prescribe appropriate courses of action. Each situation calls for its own analysis and for an original solution, albeit that the latter may be heavily influenced by either direct or vicarious (reading a book?) experience. It is in this spirit that the model is offered as a framework for structuring one's own analysis and decision-making.

CONDUCTING A CUSTOMER AUDIT

In Chapter 6 we suggested that marketing research is concerned with finding answers to six basic questions – who, what, when, where, how and why? For the purposes of conducting a customer audit then the following more specific questions will provide a useful basis. Obviously, this is a checklist to which one can add or subtract questions depending on how important an understanding of customer buyer behaviour is to the formulation of one's marketing strategy.

- *Who buys?* That is, what are the characteristics of the buyer in terms of:

  - Numbers – actual and potential
  - Age
  - Income
  - Occupation
  - Education
  - Sex
  - Marital status
  - Family size
  - Stage in the life-cycle
  - Whether buying for own or other's consumption

- *What do they buy?*
  - Quantity
  - Quality
  - Branded or unbranded goods

- *When do they buy?*
  - Time of day, week, month, season, year
  - How often?

- *Where do they buy?*
  - Retail outlet – type and location
  - Wholesaler or distributor
  - Manufacturer
  - Mail order
  - By phone
  - Internet

- *How do they buy?*
  - On impulse
  - On a planned basis
  - By description
  - By specification
  - By inspection
  - For cash
  - On credit

- *Why do they buy?*
  - Need to be satisfied
  - Benefits looked for
  - Attitudes, beliefs and motivations
  - High or low involvement

Although the emphasis in this checklist is on the individual consumer, many of the question are equally relevant to the business or industrial buyer.

Box 9.1

Customer analysis

Until recently, few companies undertook a detailed analysis of customer profitability. Conventionally, under the contribution approach, every sale makes a contribution to costs and so must be worthwhile. Further, the available information technology lacked the ability to calculate just how profitable individual customers might be. Nowadays, however, the information technology is sufficiently sophisticated to make this possible and companies are able to calculate just what an individual customer is worth to them.

According to an article in *Fortune* by Larry Selden and Geoffrey Colvin (2002):

Believe it or not, it's entirely typical to find that just 20% of a company's customers generate a huge portion of its share price – in some cases all of it. The trouble is, the worst 20% may destroy a ton of value, with the middle 60% making up the difference. Until a company starts managing its highly diverse customer portfolio, it can't hope to maximise shareholder value.

While infotech is important it isn't the key and many companies have spent large amounts on ERP (enterprise resource planning) and CRM (customer relationship management) without showing any noticeable benefit. The main reason for this is that to succeed requires a change in the corporate mindset so that the customer portfolio becomes the basis of how companies get organised, measured and managed.

Selden and Colvin cite the case of Fidelity Investments, the world's largest mutual fund company, as one that has achieved this successfully. It was recognised that some of their customers who did limited business with the company were taking up too much of the sales reps' time. To reduce this the reps began teaching such customers how to use the company's lowest cost channels – its automated phone lines and its website and made the latter friendlier and easier to use. These customers could still contact a rep but their incoming call was identified and put on hold until more profitable customers has been dealt with.

Fidelity couldn't lose. If the unprofitable customers switched to lower-cost channels, they became profitable. If they didn't like the new experience and left, Fidelity became more profitable without them. But Fidelity found that 96% of those customers stayed, about the same retention rate as in the industry overall, and most of them switched to lower-cost channels. Over time, customer satisfaction actually increased for the smaller customers as they learned how to save time and get faster service through the lower-cost channels, increasing Fidelity's operating profit within 12 months.

At the same time, the more profitable customers also got better service, making it a win–win outcome.

Similar benefits were gained by the Royal Bank of Canada when it recognised that the estates of many of its wealthy customers passed to heirs who were not customers or were transferring the assets to other institutions. By offering advice on the settlement of estates, Royal Bank was able to increase retention of assets from 30% to 50% and attracted new assets equal to another 25%. Overall, the programme translated into $1.5 billion of net new balances.

Using credit and loyalty card data, retailers can also make informed decisions on who are their most profitable customers. For example, one retailer found that the customers who spent most with them were only buying items on special offers and also made the most returns. Sending these 'special' customers information about offers was not improving profitability at all. Similarly, one needs to think carefully about retaining product categories in the belief that a full assortment is necessary for customer retention. But if your best customers for one product purchase other, complementary products elsewhere, e.g. shoes and dresses, then one needs to evaluate carefully the full costs associated with each product category to decide if both are really profitable.

Selden and Colvin cite two especially dangerous 'traps' – the illusion of growth, and the illusion of averages. The illusion of growth occurs when management spends money to attract new customers but the cost of acquisition exceeds the lifetime value of the customer – a frequent occurrence but one that can only become apparent through detailed analysis. Similarly, in the case of the Royal Bank of Canada where average profitability appeared satisfactory, closer scrutiny showed that 93% of all profits were earned from just 17% of customers!

It is clear that customer analysis of this kind is critical to effective marketing planning.

Chapter summary

This chapter comprised an eclectic review of some of the major factors influencing buyer behaviour. The reader should be aware that there are many textbooks dealing with this subject and most of these make a distinction between consumer behaviour (i.e. how individuals make choice decisions) and organisational buyer behaviour (OBB). However, based upon a review of the major influences that bear upon choice decisions, we have chosen to propose that all such decisions contain the same elements and follow the same sequence.

Central to our composite model is the view that some cue or stimulus is needed to make a buyer (individual or corporate) aware of a need and so initiate consideration of possible means of satisfying that need. In the process, the information considered will be interpreted in the light of the reviewer's own knowledge and experience, and the attitudes which have developed out of them. For this reason sellers must seek to establish the precise nature of their intended customers' needs so that they can devise products and/or services which will match these as closely as possible and, also, to enable them to communicate this information effectively to their intended audience.

To achieve this matching process, intending sellers need guidance to help them pre-identify those potential buyers who may be prepared to consider their offering. We return to these issues in Chapters 12 and 13 when we consider some of the techniques and procedures which have been devised to help disaggregate demand into meaningful market segments and enable the seller to position his product so that it will, at least, attract the intended buyer's attention. Before doing so we look next at the third element of the marketing appreciation – the internal audit of the organisation itself.

Recommended reading

Aaker, D. A. (2004) *Strategic Market Management* (7th edn). Chichester: John Wiley & Sons.

Blackwell, R. D., Miniard, P. W. and Engel, J. F. (2001) *Consumer Behaviour* (9th edn). Orlando, FL: Harcourt College Publishers.

Foxall, G. R. (2003) Consumer decision making; process, involvement and style, in Baker, M. J. (ed.) *The Marketing Book* (5th edn). Oxford: Butterworth Heinemann.

Lawson, R. W. (1999) Consumer behaviour, in Baker, M. J. (ed.) *Encyclopedia of Marketing*. London: International Thomson Business Press.

McGregor, L. (1995) Consumer behaviour, in Baker, M. J. (ed.) *Marketing: Theory and Practice* (3rd edn). Basingstoke: Macmillan – now Palgrave Macmillan.

Parkinson, S. (1999) Organisational buying behaviour, in Baker, M. J. (ed.) *Encyclopedia of Marketing*. London: International Thomson Business Press.

Rajagopal, S. (1995) Organisational buying behaviour, in Baker, M. J. (ed.) *Marketing: Theory and Practice* (3rd edn). Basingstoke: Macmillan – now Palgrave Macmillan.

Wilson, D. (1999) *Organizational Marketing*. London: International Thomson Business Press.

Zaltman, J. (2003) *How Customers Think: Essential Insights into the Mind of the Market*. Boston, MA: Harvard Business School Press.

REFERENCES

Aspinwall, L. (1958) The characteristics of good theory, in Lazer, W. and Kelley, E. (eds) *Managerial Marketing* (rev. edn). Homewood, IL: Richard D. Irwin.

Baker, M. J. (1983) *Market Development*. Harmondsworth: Penguin.

Baker, M. J. (2006) *Marketing* (7th edn) Helensburgh: Westburn.

Baker, M. J. and Parkinson, S. (1978) TI Superform's academic launch, *Marketing* (October).

Bliss, P. (1970) *Marketing Management and the Behavioural Environment*. Englewood Cliffs, NJ: Prentice Hall.

Copeland, M. T. (1923) Relation of consumers' buying habits to marketing methods, *Harvard Business Review* (April).

Davidson, H. (1981) How and why shoppers buy, *Marketing*, 28 October.

Dichter, E. (1960) *The Strategy of Desire*. New York: Doubleday.

Fellner, W. (1951) The influence of market structure on technological progress, *Quarterly Journal of Economics*, **65**(November).

Festinger, L. (1957) *Theory of Cognitive Dissonance*. New York: Row & Peterson.

Galbraith, J. K. (1958) *The Affluent Society*. Harmondsworth: Penguin.

Hastorf, A. M. and Cantril, H. (1954) They saw a game: a case history, *Journal of Abnormal and Social Psychology*, **49**.

King, S. (1991) Brand-building in the 1990s, *Journal of Marketing Management*, **7**(1).

Kotler, P. (1972) *Marketing Management* (2nd edn). Englewood Cliffs, NJ: Prentice Hall.

Packard, V. (1957) *The Hidden Persuaders*. Harmondsworth: Penguin Books.

Robinson, P., Faris, C. and Wind, Y. (1967) *Industrial Buying and Creative Marketing*. Boston, MA: Allyn & Bacon.

Selden, L. and Colvin, G. (2002) Will this customer sink your stock?, *Fortune*, 30 September.

Veblen, T. (1899) *Theory of the Leisure Class*. New York: Macmillan.

Woodhall, T. (2001) Six sigma and service quality: Christian Grönroos revisited, *Journal of Marketing Management*, **17**: 595–607.

Internal (self-)analysis

Know thyself. TEMPLE OF APOLLO, DELPHI

After reading Chapter 10 you will be able to:

✔ Define a marketing audit.

✔ Spell out the scope and major elements of a marketing audit.

✔ Assess the relevance of 'core competencies'.

✔ Explain some of the reasons why companies fail.

✔ Describe the role and importance of internal marketing.

✔ Identify some of the key issues associated with knowledge management.

INTRODUCTION

Up to this point in the book we have been concerned primarily with developing a conceptual understanding of the nature of marketing strategy and the forces external to the firm which influence and shape the strategic options available to it. In Chapter 10 we mark the transition from strategy to management by exploring how the firm can assess its own competitive standing in relation to its external environment and the current state of competition in the markets in which it intends to compete.

The discussion thus far has focused upon developing the theme that strategic marketing planning (SMP) is a prerequisite for success. We have examined a number of analytical frameworks, theories and techniques which provide a foundation for developing an SMP system. It is clear, however, that while diagnosis and prognosis are essential to the formulation of strategic plans it is the quality of the implementation which determines the degree of success enjoyed by the firm. As we pointed out in Chapter 8, when considering the relative importance of environmental analysis vis-à-vis an analysis of industry structure, all firms face a common external environment and it is their interaction with each other which determines their actual degree of success.

As has become evident from the discussion of the external environment, competition exists between firms which offer close substitutes at similar prices to one another. If one firm could clearly outperform all others on price and performance, then it would assume total control of the market as a monopolist. That this rarely occurs is due to the fact that consumers differ in their precise needs – Apple, Pepsi and Avis will always have their loyal supporters because they offer them products or services more closely attuned to their needs than do IBM, Coca-Cola or Hertz. It is these factors which underlie the downward sloping demand curve discussed in Chapter 5.

While objective differences will always play an important role in competition, the difficulty of maintaining an advantage on such factors has given rise to the emphasis on more subjective factors as implied by the model of buyer behaviour presented in Chapter 9. In the current competitive climate, the source of sustainable competitive advantage (SCA) increasingly depends on firms' human resources, the skills and competencies they display in managing organisations' physical assets and resources, and their relationships with suppliers and customers.

Implementation is the responsibility of the firm's management, and there is clear evidence that in our present turbulent environment a careful analysis of the firm's strengths and weaknesses in relation to the external opportunities and threats is a necessary, albeit not sufficient, condition for long-run competitive success. Some of the underlying forces which influence the external environment were explored in Chapter 7. In this chapter we concentrate primarily upon the assessment and measurement of the firm's internal strengths and weaknesses which comprise the other 'half' of a technique usually referred to as the marketing audit.

In this chapter we look first at the firm's assets and resources as they tend to be reflected in its balance sheet. However, such statements rarely give sufficient attention to the less tangible sources of what is sometimes called 'goodwill'. The existence of this is reflected in the market value of companies greatly exceeding the value of their physical assets, and resides in the customer franchise built up by a company through its brands and special relationships. In turn, these depend upon knowledge, skills and competencies which combine to create a learning organisation.

In order to tap the potential of a learning organisation its members must understand the synergy which arises from effective collaboration and integration – the consequence of what has become known as 'internal marketing'. But, as has been demonstrated frequently, knowledge is one thing, implementation another. To ensure resources are deployed effectively and efficiently one must be concerned with the *process* of management, and it is this which has given rise to the interest in *business process re-engineering*.

Based upon a review of these factors which form the subject matter of this chapter one can complete the internal audit by compiling a list of strengths and weaknesses which may then be combined with the output of the external audit to complete the marketing appreciation (the subject of Chapter 11).

MARKETING AUDITS

A marketing audit is a systematic and thorough examination of a company's marketing position. (Bell, 1972)

A marketing audit is a systematic, critical, and impartial review and appraisal of the total marketing operation: of the basic objectives and policies and the assumptions which underlie them as well as the methods, procedures, personnel, and organisation employed to implement the policies and achieve the objectives. (Shuchman, 1959)

Kotler (1972) offers a similar but more extensive definition:

A marketing audit is an independent examination of the entire marketing effort of a company, or some specific marketing activity, covering objectives,

programme, implementation, and organisation, for the triple purpose of determining what is being done, appraising what is being done, and recommending what should be done in the future.

Marketing audits are necessary to monitor changes in the environment in which the organisation conducts its business, and should take into account both the external and internal situation. In addition to evaluating both past performance and present practices the marketing audit should also help identify future threats and opportunities and so provide a basis for policy formulation and planning. Thus the marketing audit should be regarded as an input to the overall corporate planning function, and the foundation of the detailed marketing plan. An excellent tabulation of the scope and components of the marketing audit is provided by Kotler et al. (1977) and is reproduced as Table 10.1.

TABLE 10.1 The marketing audit

MARKETING ENVIRONMENT AUDIT

I. Macro-environment
Economic-demographic
1. What does the company expect in the way of inflation, material shortages, unemployment, and credit availability in the short run, intermediate run, and long run?
2. What effect will forecasted trends in the size, age distribution, and regional distribution of population have on the business?

Technology
1. What major changes are occurring in product technology? In process technology?
2. What are the major generic substitutes that might replace this product?

Political-legal
1. What laws are being proposed that may affect marketing strategy and tactics?
2. What federal, state, and local agency actions should be watched? What is happening in the areas of pollution control, equal employment opportunity, product safety, advertising, price control, etc. that is relevant to marketing planning?

Social-cultural
1. What attitude is the public taking toward business and toward products such as those produced by the company?
2. What changes are occurring in consumer life styles and values that have a bearing on the company's target markets and marketing methods?

II. Task environment
Markets
1. What is happening to market size, growth, geographical distribution, and profits?
2. What are the major market segments? What are their expected rates of growth? Which are high opportunity and low opportunity segments?

Customers
1. How do current customers and prospects rate the company and its competitors, particularly with respect to reputation, product quality, service, sales force, and price?
2. How do different classes of customers make their buying decisions?
3. What are the evolving needs and satisfactions being sought by the buyers in this market?

Competitors
1. Who are the major competitors? What are the objectives and strategy of each major competitor? What are their strengths and weaknesses? What are the sizes and trends in market shares?
2. What trends can be foreseen in future competition and substitutes for this product?

Distribution and dealers
1. What are the main trade channels bringing products to customers?
2. What are the efficiency levels and growth potentials of the different trade channels?

Suppliers
1. What is the outlook for the availability of different key resources used in production?
2. What trends are occurring among suppliers in their pattern of selling?

Facilitators
1. What is the outlook for the cost and availability of transportation services?

2. What is the outlook for the cost and availability of warehousing facilities?
3. What is the outlook for the cost and availability of financial resources?
4. How effectively is the advertising agency performing? What trends are occurring in advertising agency services?

MARKETING STRATEGY AUDIT

Marketing objectives
1. Are the corporate objectives clearly stated and do they lead logically to the marketing objectives?
2. Are the marketing objectives stated in a clear form to guide marketing planning and subsequent performance measurement?
3. Are the marketing objectives appropriate, given the company's competitive position, resources, and opportunities? Is the appropriate strategic objective to build, hold, harvest, or terminate this business?

Strategy
1. What is the core marketing strategy for achieving the objectives? Is it a sound marketing strategy?
2. Are enough resources (or too many resources) budgeted to accomplish the marketing objectives?
3. Are the marketing resources allocated optimally to prime market segments, territories, and products of the organisation?
4. Are the marketing resources allocated optimally to the major elements of the marketing mix, i.e. product quality, service, sales force, advertising, promotion, and distribution?

MARKETING ORGANISATION AUDIT

Formal structure
1. Is there a high-level marketing officer with adequate authority and responsibility over those company activities that affect the customer's satisfaction?
2. Are the marketing responsibilities optimally structured along functional product, end user, and territorial lines?

Functional efficiency
1. Are there good communication and working relations between marketing and sales?

2. Is the product management system working effectively? Are the product managers able to plan profits or only sales volume?
3. Are there any groups in marketing that need more training, motivation, supervision, or evaluation?

Interface efficiency
1. Are there any problems between marketing and manufacturing that need attention?
2. What about marketing and R&D?
3. What about marketing and financial management?
4. What about marketing and purchasing?

MARKETING SYSTEMS AUDIT

Marketing information system
1. Is the marketing intelligence system producing accurate, sufficient, and timely information about developments in the marketplace?
2. Is marketing research being adequately used by company decision-makers?

Marketing planning system
1. Is the marketing planning system well conceived and effective?
2. Is sales forecasting and market potential measurement soundly carried out?
3. Are sales quotas set on a proper basis?

Marketing control system
1. Are the control procedures (monthly, quarterly, etc.) adequate to ensure that the annual plan objectives are being achieved?
2. Is provision made to analyse periodically the profitability of different products, markets, territories, and channels of distribution?
3. Is provision made to examine and validate periodically various marketing costs?

New product development system
1. Is the company well organised to gather, generate, and screen new product ideas?
2. Does the company do adequate concept research and business analysis before investing heavily in a new idea?
3. Does the company carry out adequate product and market testing before launching a new product?

MARKETING PRODUCTIVITY AUDIT

Profitability analysis
1. What is the profitability of the company's different products, served markets, territories, and channels of distribution?
2. Should the company enter, expand, contract, or withdraw from any business segments and what would be the short- and long-run profit consequences?

Cost-effectiveness analysis
1. Do any marketing activities seem to have excessive costs? Are these costs valid? Can cost-reducing steps be taken?

MARKETING FUNCTION AUDIT

Products
1. What are the product line objectives? Are these objectives sound? Is the current product line meeting these objectives?
2. Are there particular products that should be phased out?
3. Are there new products that are worth adding?
4. Are any products able to benefit from quality, feature, or style improvements?

Price
1. What are the pricing objectives, policies, strategies, and procedures? To what extent are prices set on sound cost, demand, and competitive criteria?
3. Does the company use price promotions effectively?

Distribution
1. What are the distribution objectives and strategies?
2. Is there adequate market coverage and service?
3. Should the company consider changing its degree of reliance on distributors, sales reps, and direct selling?

Sales force
1. What are the organisation's sales force objectives?

2. Is the sales force large enough to accomplish the company's objectives?
3. Is the sales force organised along the proper principle(s) of specialisation (territory, market, product)?
4. Does the sales force show high morale, ability, and effort? Are they sufficiently trained and incentivised?
5. Are the procedures adequate for setting quotas and evaluating performances?
6. How is the company's sales force perceived in relation to competitors' sales forces?

Advertising, promotion, and publicity
1. What are the organisation's advertising objectives? Are they sound?
2. Is the right amount being spent on advertising? How is the budget determined?
3. Are the ad themes and copy effective? What do customers and the public think about the advertising?
4. Are the advertising media well chosen?
5. Is sales promotion used effectively?
6. Is there a well conceived publicity program?

SOURCE: Kotler, P., Gregor, W. and Rogers, W. (1977) The MA comes of age, *Sloan Management Review*, 18(1)

Despite its comprehensiveness, the checklist contained in Table 10.1 is illustrative only. While it covers the broad scope of a marketing audit, it is lacking in the detail which would be necessary in gathering the appropriate level of information for the preparation of a marketing plan. However, there are numerous books which provide such checklists and offer the level of detail required. For example Makens (1989) and Stapleton (1989) provide extensive examples of documentation to be used in undertaking a marketing audit. Table 10.2, from Stapleton's book, deals with the specific issue of a consumption audit and is but one of a large number of tables designed to ensure a comprehensive analysis.

It should also be noted that Table 10.1 dates back to the 1970s and so does not include a specific reference to service under the final marketing function audit, which it certainly would do if it were being prepared today.

The frequency with which marketing audits are undertaken is a function of several variables, including the firm's planning frame (monthly, annual, biennial etc.), the nature of its business, and the rate of change in the environment. The optimum approach is probably to undertake standardised audits at regular intervals and supplement these with special ad hoc surveys as conditions dictate. Similarly, the scope of the audit may be varied, with certain key areas being assessed with a high frequency, and more detailed, in-depth analysis being undertaken less often. Such detailed inquiry into specific topics, e.g. pricing policy, may well be amenable to some form of rota, so that all areas will be covered within the duration of a planning cycle. For example, if the firm normally operates on an annual cycle, then it may be convenient to monitor key indicators such as sales, prices, market share etc., on a monthly basis and the 'mix' elements on a bimonthly rota, e.g.:

TABLE 10.2 Consumption audit

1.	Is the total market in decline?	J	What price differentials are possible among market segments?
2.	Is the brand share in decline?	K	Is the buying derived from some other purchase?
3.	In what position does the brand rank?	L	Is the buying on impulse or predetermined?
4.	Will brand share increase if promoted?	M	Is the demand likely to be elastic?
5.	Can retail selling price bear an increase?	N	Is the brand likely to be price sensitive?
6.	Can production economies be achieved?	O	Is the demand going to be dependent on merchandising?
7.	Can range be reduced?	P	What factors are likely to limit demand?
8.	What other markets are possible?	Q	What is the effect of fashion/technological changes?
9.	What is the profit contribution	R	What seasonal factors are apparent?
10.	What is the break-even point?	S	What is likely to be the average rate of consumption?
11.	Can the brand be revitalised?	T	What factors are likely to affect the consumption rate?
12.	Can the brand be sold off?	U	What emotive/psychological factors need to be taken into account?
A	Who are the potential buyers?	V	What current legislation exists: safety, packaging, labelling, weights?
B	What is the size and scope of the potential market?	W	How are problems related to pre-sales and after-sales?
C	What is the distribution of the potential market?	X	What additional credit/financing is likely to be required?
D	What are the needs, habits, and buying motives of the potential market?	Y	What guarantees/warranties are appropriate?
E	What related products will/do people buy?	Z	What are market preferences for choice of outlet?
F	What is the expected buying frequency?		
G	What is the likely buying quantity		
H	Who is the purchasing agent in the target audience family?		
I	Who influences brand choice decisions?		

SOURCE: Stapleton, J. (1989) *How to Prepare a Marketing Plan* (4th edn). London: Gower

- Month 2   Pricing
- Month 4   Packaging
- Month 6   Promotion
- Month 8   Distribution
- Month 10   Sales
- Month 12   Market research.

Crisp (1959) suggests six alternative sources of audit:

1. Self-audit
2. Audit-from-across – persons in related activities on the same functional level audit each other
3. Audit-from-above
4. Company auditing office
5. Company task-force audit – a team is appointed on an ad hoc basis from within the company's staff
6. Outside audit.

While Crisp prefers the last option on the grounds of greater objectivity and freedom from internal operating pressures, there would seem to be merit in a composite approach involving more than one option, for example, the appointment of an external auditor to validate and integrate self-audit by managers with functional and/or departmental responsibility. Such a composite approach could well permit the benefits of external objectivity with the greater detail and frequency of data collection possible with internal systems.

Grashof (1975) suggests that a marketing audit falls into three phases – information assembly, information analysis and the formulation of recommendations – and that these central phases will be preceded by a planning stage (pre-audit activities) and followed by an implementation phase (post-audit activities). Phase I (information assembly) consists of the identification and acquisition of information bearing upon the

TABLE 10.3 Steps in a marketing audit

		Key elements develop:
Step One:	Define the market	1. Statement of purpose in terms of benefits 2. Product scope 3. Size, growth rate, maturity state, need for primary versus selective strategies 4. Requirements for success 5. Divergent definitions of the above by competitors 6. Definition to be used by the company
Step Two:	Determine performance differentials	1. Evaluate industry performance and company differences 2. Determine differences in products, applications, geography, and distribution channels 3. Determine differences by customer set
Step Three:	Determine differences in competitive programmes	Identify and evaluate individual companies for their: 1. Market development strategies 2. Product development strategies 3. Financing and administrative strategies and support
Step Four:	Profile the strategies of competitors	1. Profile each significant competitor and/or distinct type of competitive strategy 2. Compare own and competitive strategies
Step Five:	Determine strategic planning structure	When size and complexity are adequate: 1. Establish planning units or cells and designate prime and subordinate strategies 2. Make organisational assignments to product managers, industry managers, and others

SOURCE: Cannon, J. T. (1968) *Business Strategy and Policy.* New York: Harcourt Brace and World

major areas that affect a firm's marketing programme, including:

1. The industry
2. The firm
3. The market
4. The product
5. Distribution
6. Promotion
7. Pricing.

A similar approach is proposed by Cannon (1968), and recognises five steps, shown in Table 10.3.

In the view of Douglas Brownlie of Stirling University, there is a danger that the growing emphasis being given to external environmental factors may distract management from undertaking an equally rigorous review of their internal environment. This danger may well be exaggerated by the assumption that of course everyone knows what is going on inside the firm and so takes less care to document this thoroughly. In his article in the *Journal of Marketing Management*

(1989), Brownlie offers a wide-ranging review of the execution of an internal appraisal and its role in the overall strategic management of the firm. The paper also introduces a conceptual framework that integrates the tasks of defining, identifying and evaluating the firm's strengths and weaknesses. In doing so it also looks at functional areas of the firm, and gives examples of the strengths and weaknesses to be found in each. The paper contains extensive references, and so is an ideal starting point for readers wishing to explore this topic in greater detail.

CORE COMPETENCIES

We have already expressed the view on a number of occasions that, in the final analysis, the thing which distinguishes between superior and average or inferior performance is the quality of implementation. Obviously, organisations lacking basic assets and resources will be at a clear disadvantage and cannot expect to be winners in the marketplace. It follows that the first responsibility of management is to ensure that it does have the necessary assets to compete effectively as established by the macro- and microenvironmental reviews. It is a primary function of the marketing audit to ensure this. However, there is a danger that in completing an audit of the kind proposed in the preceding section this may degenerate into mechanical listing compromised by wishful thinking.

To avoid the first danger one should adopt the same procedures recommended for analysing the competition, namely benchmarking and the specification of best practices. One must also pay particular attention to the identification and specification of distinctive skills and competencies which underlie the existence of a sustainable competitive advantage. As was made clear in our model of buyer behaviour in the last chapter, buyers often have difficulty in discriminating between the objective characteristics of closely competitive products (and services in the sense that one 747 jumbo jet leaving Heathrow for Singapore at 11.00am is very much the same as another leaving 10 minutes later). Under these circumstances less tangible qualities such as reputation and trust come into play, and these tend to arise from the skills and competencies of past and present employees of the selling organisation.

The notion of skills and competencies were discussed at some length in Chapter 8 but a short reprise will be helpful here.

SKILLS AND COMPETENCIES

Writing in the 1997 *McKinsey Quarterly*, Coyne et al. revisit Hamel and Prahalad's concept of the core competence. Based on their consulting experience, the authors find that, like many managerial panaceas, it is widely known and referred to but apparently seldom used in practice.

> We are left with a conundrum. Core competence is clearly an important concept, and some companies seem to be able to make it work. But for most, it is like a mirage: something that from a distance appears to offer hope in a hostile environment, but then turns to sand when approached. (p. 42)

In an attempt to solve this conundrum, the authors reviewed the literature, assessed individuals' experience, and conducted case studies of companies that had attempted to develop a core competence. Their research led to four important findings:

1. Core competence is an umbrella phrase covering two distinct bases of advantage.
2. Certain tests can help predict whether a competence-led strategy will be successful.
3. There are three distinct paths to developing a competence.
4. Sustaining a core competence requires as much rigour as developing one in the first place.

To begin with the authors set out to define precisely what a core competence is. While Hamel and Prahalad's original conceptualisation focused primarily on knowledge of one or more technologies, the term now seems to be applied to cover almost any resource or activity. Accordingly, Coyne et al. (1997, p. 43) propose a simple definition:

> A core competence is a combination of complementary skills and knowledge bases embedded in a group or team that results in the ability to execute one or more critical processes to a world class standard.

Adoption of this definition allows core competencies to be defined into two categories:

1. Insight/foresight competencies which enable a company to discover or learn facts or patterns that create first mover advantages.
2. Frontline execution competencies which reflect a unique ability to deliver products and services that are consistently nearly equal in quality to what the best craftsman would have produced under ideal circumstances.

Given their definition, the authors consider that 'successful core competencies are rarer than many imagine' (p. 45). In order to establish whether a core competence truly exists, four key questions need to be addressed:

1. Are our skills truly superior?
2. How sustainable is the superiority?
3. How much value can the competence generate in comparison to other economic levers?

4. Is the competence integral to our value proposition?

If a perceived competence fails to satisfy these four questions, then the issue would seem to be whether the organisation could create one for itself. To do so, Coyne et al. believe that two fundamental principles must be adhered to: 'First, a world class competence must *steer the power structure* in a company' (p. 48). In other words, once the core competence has been identified, then it must drive all other functions of the business.

'Secondly, a core competence strategy must be *chosen by the CEO*, not by department heads acting independently' (p. 49). The authors continue:

> There seem to be three distinct routes to developing a core competence: *Evolution*, where a company attempts to build a skill at the same time as the individuals involved perform their usual jobs; *Incubation*, where a separate group is formed to focus exclusively on the chosen competence; and *Acquisition* where one company purchases another to obtain the skills it seeks'. (p. 49)

Each of these alternatives has its strengths and weaknesses and much will depend upon the prevailing climate within the organisation.

Assuming that an organisation has or can create a core competence, then the challenge is to sustain and increase its value. However, experience suggests that inattention may cause erosion of the core competence. Coyne et al. identify two common causes of this. First, skilled staff can gradually drift away, but their loss may not be noticed until a crisis occurs. And, second, where too many managers are empowered to initiate change, they can dilute and diffuse the source of the core competence.

COMPANY STRENGTHS AS A SOURCE OF SUSTAINABLE COMPETITIVE ADVANTAGE (SCA)

While all an organisation's functions may contibute to its strengths (or its weaknesses!), the major sources are technology, operations and marketing.

Technology:
- Inimitable R&D skills: patents, implicit knowledge, know-how

- Successful innovation i.e. the ability to convert *ideas* or *inventions* into commercial, *processes*, *products* or *services*.

Operations:
- Patent protection of processes and/or products
- Unique/superior process know-how
- Unique/superior manufacturing systems
- Unique/superior capital equipment
- Unique/superior procurement/sources of supply.

Marketing:
- Dominant market share
- Dominant brand(s)
- Control of distribution channels
- Unique/superior services
- Record of successful new product development.

Although procurement is included under operations, increasingly it is being recognised as a strategic function in its own right alongside human resource management (HRM) and finance. The role of HRM is a particularly important source of SCA in an information-led, knowledge-based society, while an efficient and effective finance function is essential for the control of costs and securing a competitive cost of capital for investment purposes.

WHY COMPANIES FAIL

It has been estimated that the *average* life span of a Fortune 500 company is 40 years. We emphasise average because, clearly, there are many companies that have been household names for far longer. Nevertheless, many organisations that have been eminently successful and leaders in their industry are no longer with us. Consider the following list drawn up by Lester Thurow, a former dean of the Sloan School of Management at MIT. List A shows the 10 largest US corporations in the USA in 1900, and List B the industries likely to dominate the twenty-first century. List A are all resource-based; List B are all knowledge-based, capable of being located almost anywhere.

LIST A
American Cotton Oil Co
American Steel Co

American Sugar Refining
Continental Tobacco
Federal Steel
General Electric
National Lead
Pacific Mail
People's Gas
Tennessee Coal and Iron
US Leather
US Rubber

LIST B
Microelectronics
Biotechnology
New materials
Telecommunications
Civilian aviation manufacturing
Machine tools plus robotics
Computers plus software

Consider, also, Ted Levitt's seminal 'Marketing myopia' (1960) which we have cited many times already. It opens with the observation that every declining industry was once a growth industry. But, organisations tend to focus on the products they make and the technologies underpinning them. Inevitably, as time passes, products decline and technologies become superseded by new and better ways of servicing the needs of customers and providing the benefits they look for. The importance of defining one's business in terms of the need serviced and the benefits looked for has been accepted wisdom for decades now, but still companies fail.

The heading of this section 'Why companies fail' was the title of an article by Kenneth Labich in *Fortune* (14 November, 1994). Prompted by the rapid increase in failed companies in the late 1980s and early 1990s, Labich consulted a number of corporate executives, management consultants, venture capitalists, investment bankers, turn-around specialists, equity analysts and portfolio managers and came to the conclusion that there are six basic causes of failure.

The first cause of failure is what Labich labels 'identity crisis'. Identity crises occur when those responsible for the direction of the organisation lose sight of or fail to realise what it was that made the firm successful in the first place. Such executives lack a sense of corporate history but, worse

still, they fail to understand what were the essential skills and competencies on which earlier success was founded. Labich cites the case of Jostens, a Minnesota firm with a record of 34 years consistent increase in sales and profits from its range of class rings, yearbooks and other college-related products. In the late 1980s they diversified into computer systems and by 1993 were reporting a $12 million annual loss. The lack of the common thread between the two activities appears obvious to the outsider. Why didn't corporate management see it? Well, in addition to a sense of history, new generations of managers appear to believe in change for change's sake and are seduced by the latest management fads and fashions. 'Management by walking around is followed by quality circles, which are followed by matrix management, TQM, and several rounds of re-engineering'. The result: 'change fatigue' and a demotivated workforce. Invariably those with the most to offer are among the first to leave.

Diversification is often the Achilles heel which brings corporations to their knees, especially when it is achieved through acquisition rather than organic growth through a combination of product and market development strategies. Labich cites some classic examples. Eastman Kodak moved into pharmaceuticals and consumer health products with very poor results. Subaru, a major supplier of inexpensive four-wheel drive vehicles in the late 1970s and early 1980s decided to produce a line of mid-size family saloon cars – just what everyone else had. In the process it let others into the niche it dominated and lost at least $300 million in market share before abandoning the saloons to concentrate on 4WDs. Honeywell in computers and aerospace, and IBM's neglect of personal computers are other classic examples. The difference in the case of these four companies, however, was that they realised the error of their ways and got back on course before it was too late.

But, as we have seen, it is not only important to understand the nature and source of your current strengths and success, it is also important to have a clear view of where you want to go. Thus 'failures of vision' are Labich's second category. Most of the examples he cites are of organisations like Levitt's buggy whip manufacturer who failed to appreciate that technological change and horseless carriages had made the industry obsolete. On the other hand, Mulliners who had handcrafted horse-drawn carriages for generations was able to transfer its skills and reputation into crafting the most expensive of car bodies. Similarly, while some publishers embrace electronic distribution and link it to traditional methods, others avoid or ignore it and fail to see where the real growth in the information market lies.

The third cause of failure is what Labich calls 'the big squeeze'. This occurs when firms increase their indebtedness in the pursuit of growth, often through acquisitions, but lack the cash flow to fund this when the economic cycle turns down as it so frequently does. Remember ADL's caution about strategy being condition- not ambition-driven.

Ironically, Labich's fourth cause of failure is an exaggerated case of the solution to the first – 'living in the past'. While a loss of identity may result from a lack of understanding of the sources of an organisation's success, an undue preoccupation with it can lead to complacency, and the lack of vision cited as the second cause of failure. Complacency is a threat to any firm but it can be especially dangerous for the very large organisation when it leads to a culture that is resistant to change, and bureaucratic structures and procedures that stifle initiative and change. IBM, GM, Digital Equipment, Honeywell and many others experienced such problems in the 1970s and 80s when faced with accelerating technological change and increasingly competitive global markets. What distinguishes them is that they were able to shake off this complacency, usually through the appointment of a new, visionary CEO with strong leadership skills able to motivate the employees and liberate their suppressed skills and competencies.

The fifth cause of failure is losing touch with one's customers:

> IBM was still pushing giant mainframes, which required hordes of white-jacketed technicians to keep them humming, when the whole world was cutting costs with desktops. Sears tried modest discounts to capture middle-class shoppers who had become beady-eyed bargain hunters at the likes of Wal-Mart. A. T. Cross, the penmaker, continued to turn out skinny little writing instruments and lost hefty market share to Montblanc's fashionably chunky offerings.

Given the subject of this book, we need say no

more about the importance of listening to the voice of the market!

Finally, the sixth source of failure comes from 'enemies within', employees who are not committed to the organisation. While a great deal has been done through modern HRM practices to reduce the traditional adversarial relationship between management and labour, there is still much to be done. Indeed 'internal marketing' is now seen to be just as important as external marketing.

INTERNAL MARKETING

According to Grönroos and Voima (1999), the term internal marketing was first used in the late 1970s. Initially associated with the development of interest in the marketing of services, the idea of internal marketing, based upon the concept of internal customers, has now diffused widely into the fields of service management, industrial marketing and relationship marketing. In turn, the concept of an internal customer is seen as a means of increasing the awareness of external customers amongst employees. Over time, however, the focus has moved away from emphasising the importance of motivating employees to become service oriented, to a view of organisations comprising internal markets with internal customers and suppliers. The natural development of this latter view is linked to both internal and external markets within the wider concept of relationships.

Traditionally, business schools have stressed the management of labour and capital, with less emphasis on 'land' as the third resource element to which value was added through the deployment of the first two. More recently, attention has been focused on ways and means of improving the efficiency and effectiveness of the value-adding process such as business process re-engineering (BPR), organisational design and value chain optimisation. Less attention has been given to ideas, skills, competencies and knowledge until recently when these 'soft' assets have resulted in far higher valuations for companies which possess them by comparison with firms based on 'hard' assets (multiples of 20, 30 or 40 compared with 5–10). Human capital in the shape of competencies, ideas, brands, relationships and networks, strategic alliances and the like are based on knowledge and it is recognition of this which has given rise to the current interest in knowledge management. 'Knowledge, after all, is the only resource that increases through use.'

> A learning organisation is one skilled in acquiring, creating, transferring, and retaining knowledge – as well as transforming that knowledge into improved performance or innovative products and services. (Probst, 1998)

Knowledge may be either explicit or tacit. Explicit knowledge is the kind which may be communicated formally through traditional educational processes. Tacit knowledge is more difficult to capture and resides in the skills and practices of individuals or groups who are demonstrably superior in performance of given tasks. An essential element of knowledge management is the conversion of tacit knowledge into explicit knowledge which can be learnt (and applied) without the direct involvement usually called for in the experiential learning.

ADL (Probst, 1998) find it useful to think about knowledge management in terms of four integrated dimensions: content, culture, process and infrastructure.

With regard to *content* it is important to be selective and identify those aspects of knowledge which are strategically relevant and avoid information overload by collecting everything which might possibly be relevant. A knowledge audit is a useful means of mapping an organisation's knowledge base and determining what it knows and, more importantly, what it needs to know.

Culture has been shown by research to be the principal determinant of success in knowledge management but it is also the most neglected aspect. Two aphorisms – 'Knowledge is power' and 'Ignorance is bliss' sum up the fundamental reasons why people hoard knowledge and refuse to share it or resist its acquisition for fear it will require them to change, making earlier knowledge and skills redundant and obsolete. It follows that knowledge transfer and management is inextricably tied in with change management.

ADL propose a 5-step knowledge management *process*:

1. Define knowledge objectives

- Define organisational core knowledge
- Describe future knowledge needs
2. Identify available knowledge
3. Save knowledge
4. Disseminate knowledge
5. Use knowledge.

The golden rule concerning the *infrastructure* to support knowledge management is that it must be adapted to the company's needs and not vice versa. It needs to be accessible, flexible and up to date and contain the strategically relevant information identified through the knowledge audit.

Probst (1998) described a knowledge management model that has five basic dimensions/aspects:

1. Compatibility – with existing processes and procedures
2. Problem orientation
3. Comprehensibility
4. Action orientation
5. Appropriate instruments.

Based on these criteria, Probst proposes a model containing eight building blocks (these offer little if anything, over the ADL model), with the key factor being the maintenance of a cycle linking the blocks.

Ultimately, the objective of knowledge management is to encourage and enhance innovation. Research by ADL (Probst, 1998) indicates that 'at least half the competencies that will determine their firms' competitive position will come from outside the company.' It follows that one needs to define precisely what knowledge and skills the firm has, what it needs, and how to fill the 'gap' from external sources. According to ADL's 1997 Global Innovation Survey, getting such information is the biggest obstacle to effective innovation:

> Any competence that will be relevant to your business in the next five years already exists. If you don't have it now, you can't 'invent' it in time. You have to find it wherever it currently resides, acquire it, and integrate it into your business.

Auditing and benchmarking are key.

A good starting checklist in knowledge management includes these eight practices:

- Map knowledge management directly to the business strategy and support it clearly with the technology strategy.
- Develop processes for continuously linking major decisions with the knowledge management system.
- As with any other major initiative, get senior management's commitment (including that of the CEO).
- Build an intelligence system by first focusing on a few intelligence topics and achieving short-term successes. This allows processes to be refined, generates momentum, and provides lessons for subsequent efforts.
- Establish legal and ethical guidelines for your intelligence activity early. The bounds of behaviour must be understood by everyone.
- Remember the 'soft skills' that enable innovation – the ability to negotiate a win–win deal

with an outside firm to obtain a piece of intellectual capital is just as important as the skills to develop a technology internally.

- Get human resources involved early, often, and actively in understanding the knowledge needs of the organization and striving, through training and recruiting, to maintain and enhance them.
- Develop and use performance metrics to evaluate both the results (examples: incremental earnings from new or first-to-market products introduced over the previous five years that stemmed from new technology knowledge, or number of plants that adopt a new technology and the time it takes them to implement it in production) and the process itself (example: number of queries to database and percentage that can be associated with technical and/or commercial successes).

Chapter summary

In this chapter we have reviewed a number of issues associated with the evaluation of the assets, resources, skills and competencies which go to make up an organisation.

To begin with we looked at the concept of the 'marketing audit' and provided a comprehensive checklist that also included some aspect of the external audits discussed in the preceding three chapters.

Next we revisited the idea of core competencies and some of the difficulties that have been experienced in translating a compelling and intuitively attractive idea into practice. In turn, this led naturally to an examination of some reasons why companies fail. Among the causes a lack of vision, complacency and demotivated employees were identified as major factors.

To overcome these failings firms need to empower their employees through a process of internal marketing and the development of a learning organisation.

In the next chapter we will explore how the various elements of the marketing appreciation may be pulled together.

Recommended reading

Aaker, D. A. (2004) *Strategic Market Management* (7th edn). Chichester: John Wiley & Sons.
Hooley, G. J., Saunders, J. A. and Piercy, N. F. (2003) *Marketing*

Strategy and Competitive Positioning (3rd edn). London: Prentice Hall Europe.
Wilson, A. (1999) The marketing audit, in Baker, M. J. (ed.) *Ency-*

clopedia of Marketing. London: International Thomson Business Press.

REFERENCES

Bell, M. L. (1972) *Marketing: Concepts and Strategies* (2nd edn). Boston, MA: Houghton-Mifflin, p. 428.
Brownlie, D. T. (1989) Scanning the environment: impossible precept or neglected art?, *Journal of Marketing Management*, **4**(3).
Cannon, J. T. (1968) *Business Strategy*

and Policy. New York: Harcourt, Brace and World.
Coyne, K. P., Hall, S. J. D. and Clifford, P. G. (1997) Is your core competence a mirage?, *McKinsey Quarterly*, **1**: 40–54.
Crisp, R. D. (1959) Auditing the functional elements of a marketing operation, *American Management Association Report*, **32**.

Grashof, J. F. (1975) Conducting and using a marketing audit, in McCarthy, E. J., Grashof, J. F. and Brogowicz, A. A. (eds) *Readings in Basic Marketing*. Homewood, IL: Irwin.
Grönroos, C. and Voima, P. (1999) Internal marketing – a relationship perspective, in Baker, M. J. (ed.) *Encyclopedia of Marketing*.

London: International Thomson Business Press, pp. 747–51.

Kotler, P. (1972) *Marketing Management* (2nd edn). Englewood Cliffs, NJ: Prentice Hall.

Kotler, P., Gregor, W. and Rogers, W. (1977) The MA comes of age, *Sloan Management Review*, **18**(1).

Labich, K. (1994) Why companies fail, *Fortune* (November).

Levitt, T. (1960) Marketing myopia, *Harvard Business Review* (July–August).

Makens, J. C. (1989) *The 12-Day Marketing Plan*. New York: Thorsons.

Probst, G. J. B. (1998) Practical knowledge management: a model that works, *Prism* (2).

Shuchman, A. (1959) The marketing audit: its nature, purposes and problems, *Analysing and Improving Market Performance*, Report 32. New York: American Management Association, p. 13.

Stapleton, J. (1989) *How to Prepare a Marketing Plan* (4th edn). London: Gower.

Matching – putting it all together

[strategy is] the match an organisation makes between its internal resources and skills … and the opportunities and risks created by its external environment.
C. W. HOFER AND D. E. SCHENDEL

After reading Chapter 11 you will be able to:

✔ Explain the need to match an organisation's strengths with market opportunities.

✔ Know why it is the organisation's assets, skills and resources that determine the courses of action open to management.

✔ Understand how to combine the products of the external and internal analyses (the marketing 'appreciation') into a simple summary analysis.

INTRODUCTION

In the preceding four chapters we have covered the key elements of the marketing appreciation. These consist of an evaluation of the macro-environmental conditions which define the boundaries within which competition takes place. Next we looked at competition at the industry level, building upon the discussion of market structure, conduct and performance introduced in Chapter 2. Incorporated with this was a review of competitor analysis as a basis for understanding the sources of competitive advantage in the market, and the development of a unique strategy of one's own. Chapter 9 completed the survey of factors external to the organisation with an examination of some of the key factors influencing buyer behaviour, culminating with the proposal of a composite model which included many of these key factors. Finally, in Chapter 10 we explored the internal environment as a basis for establishing the firms' strengths and weaknesses. In this short chapter, we will seek to pull these elements together through a process we call 'matching', usually accomplished by means of a SWOT analysis that is introduced briefly.

MATCHING

In the Prologue we touched on the problem facing writers of textbooks – the need to give a comprehensive treatment of the subject matter even though this means incorporating much material which is of limited relevance to much of the intended audience. Thus the textbook takes the perspective of the multidivisional, multinational mega-corporation likely to be included in the Fortune 500. While such firms dominate global competition, they are the exception rather than the rule, as it is estimated that over 90% of all people work in organisations employing less than 200 workers. So most people work in small firms with a single or limited portfolio of closely related products that they are selling into a local or regional market. In fact they represent what in the larger organisation would be considered a strategic business unit or SBU, albeit on a small scale. Thus many of the tools, techniques and procedures that may be necessary if not essential in the larger, more complex business unit may represent 'overkill' or irrelevancy in the small firm. It follows that management must choose for themselves what is appropriate in the context of the specific problems they are called upon to resolve.

However, irrespective of the size of a firm, survival, let alone success, depends upon management's skill in managing the resources they control both efficiently and effectively.

Efficiency and effectiveness are closely related concepts but they are not the same. Paraphrasing Peter Drucker: 'Efficiency is doing things right, effectiveness is doing the right things'. From this definition it follows that strategic thinking and planning is all about effectiveness. It involves the identification of market opportunities and the optimum use of resources to take advantage of the most promising opportunities available. And this is where efficiency comes in – ensuring that resources are used to optimum effect. Thus successful management is all about achieving a balance between the present and the future, making the best use of what we currently have while ensuring that we are adjusting both the composition and development of our resources and skills to ensure they will continue to be effective in the future. It is this activity that we call 'matching'.

With the 'rediscovery' of the marketing concept in the 1950s, and the evolution of the American 'marketing management' model which accompanied it, the importance of 'marketing' was frequently overstated. In part this was due to the evangelical zeal of the early disciples who wished to convert others to their belief but, in the process, it frequently led to criticism of other managerial disciplines and approaches. This negative treatment is epitomised by the 'three eras' description of the evolution of the Pillsbury Company by McKitterick (1957). According to this analysis, the company came into existence in the nineteenth century as a clear response to the growing need for flour-based products. To succeed in this market, production efficiency was essential to keep costs down for what was basically a commodity – hence the 'production era'. As the market grew and matured, Pillsbury began to look for ways of adding value to their products as a means to differentiating them from their competitors' offerings. While these changes were production-led, they also involved greater emphasis on selling and promotion – hence the 'sales era'. By the 1950s, however, competition had increased significantly, but demand was slowing down. To succeed in this new environment called for a different strategy in which much greater attention was given to establishing customers needs, and then developing new products to match them – the 'marketing era' was born!

While the three eras model is useful in highlighting the dominant focus of the company in adjusting its strategy to changing environmental conditions, many have mistaken a change in emphasis for a wholesale change in the management of the business as a whole. As we have seen, marketing is both a philosophy of business and a business function. As a business philosophy, we would argue that successful organisations have always been marketing-oriented in the sense that they have met the needs of the market better than their less successful competitors i.e. they have been more effective than the competition. In other words they were practising marketing irrespective of how they described their activities. What changed was that while accelerating technological change greatly increased both the volume and variety of goods and services, the demand for them slowed with a declining birth rate. For probably the first time in history, supply outstripped demand in a significant way. In order to cope with these changed conditions much greater attention had to be given to establishing the precise nature of consumer demand, to developing products that met these demands as closely as possible, to making them available as widely as possible at attractive prices, and to communicating their advantages to the prospective buyer. It is these activities that comprise the marketing function. But, the increased importance of this function does not mean it is better or superior to all the other business functions that have to be integrated in the management of a successful company. Unfortunately, many marketers mistakenly believed that it did, and so exaggerated the needs of the customer over the needs of the business. In reality what is called for is a balance between the two to achieve the mutually satisfying win–win relationship which we believe to be the epitome of real marketing.

Even if we agree with the proposition that it is marketing which is best suited to charting the future direction of the company, and selecting the best strategies and tactics to achieve the desired future, we should not lose sight of the fact that in the fullness of time that future will become the present. Thus, at any given point in time, the position in which an organisation finds itself is the consequence of past decisions. It follows that if marketing recommended the strategy then it must bear at least some responsibility for the current position too. While 'making what we can sell' is the objective of marketing, 'selling what we can make' may be a necessity for an organisation committed to a particular technology and market at a given point in time. Only by selling what it can make will the firm be able to capitalise its current assets with a view to redeploying them more effectively in future. It is for this reason that in Chapter 3 we argued that effective strategies combine both deliberate and emergent elements – the deliberate strategy is our best guess as to what will be most effective, our emergent strategy is what will be most efficient as events unfold.

Perhaps the strongest support for the view that effective management is concerned with 'matching' is to be found in the resource-based theory of the firm. Passing reference was made to this earlier in Chapter 8 when it was contrasted with what has been the more dominant model in recent years – Michael Porter's competitiveness analysis based upon the industrial economists' 'structure/conduct/performance' model. A fuller review of the resource-based view will help justify our opinion.

RESOURCE-BASED THEORY

While it has probably always been recognised that strategy formulation is concerned with the application of resources to the solution of problems and the achievement of desired objectives, the emphasis between resources (internal) and problems/opportunities (external) has fluctuated widely. For many years the idea of the market as the 'invisible hand' that determined competitive outcomes enjoyed supremacy, and in fact it is deeply embedded in some interpretations of the marketing concept which argue supply must be subservient to demand. Clearly, such an interpretation encourages a greater emphasis on external rather than internal factors. On the other hand, management is all about seeking to exercise at least a degree of control over the environment, which suggests that some weight should be given to an organisation's ability to react

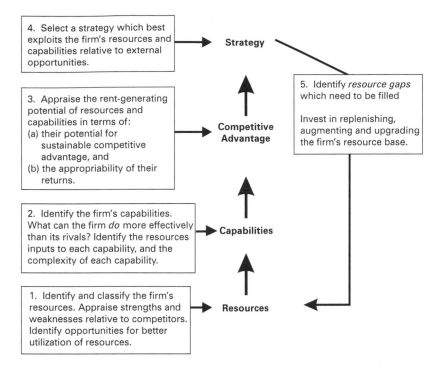

FIGURE 11.1 A resource-based approach to strategy analysis

SOURCE: Grant, R. M. (1991) The resource-based theory of competitive advantage: implications for strategy formulation, *California Management Review* (spring): 114–35

to and possibly control its environment. Indeed, one might argue that the principal objective of the organisation should be to try and identify situations where it *can* exercise at least a degree of control. It is this perspective which predisposes us to talk of 'matching'.

Like most ideas in the social sciences this is not an original one. In one of the earlier and more influential papers on the subject of 'resource-based theory', Robert M. Grant (1991) reminds the reader that in 1978 Hofer and Schendel defined strategy as 'the match an organisation makes between its internal resources and skills … and the opportunities and risks created by its external environment'. Unfortunately for Hofer and Schendel, their views were advanced when the ideas underlying industrial organisation theory were in the ascendancy due to the writings of Michael Porter (1980) who had restated them in a manner accessible to practising managers. As we have described in some detail (Chapter 2), the market structure, conduct and performance model at the heart of this theory stresses the need for the organisation to work within the constraints imposed by the external

environment. By contrast, resource-based theory, which can trace its origins back to the writings of David Ricardo (1817) in the nineteenth century, stresses the importance of the resources controlled by the firm. As Grant notes:

> At the corporate strategy level, theoretical interest in economies of scope and transaction costs have focussed attention on the role of corporate resources in determining the industrial and geographical boundaries of the firm's activities. At the business strategy level, explorations of the relationships between resources, competition, and profitability include the analysis of competitive imitation, the appropriability of returns to innovations, the role of imperfect information in creating profitability differences between competing firms, and the means by which the process of resource accumulation can sustain competitive advantage. (1991, pp. 114–15)

At the time he was writing, Grant claimed that while these ideas constituted the resource-based theory of the firm, this had not been articulated clearly, nor had its implications been spelt out for practising managers. It is this which he set out to do in his paper, starting with the framework reproduced as Figure 11.1.

As can be seen from Figure 11.1, the start point is an audit of the firm's resources, strengths and weaknesses, which enables it to define its capabilities, or what Hamel and Prahalad term 'skills and competencies'. Analysis of these indicates where the organisation is most likely to achieve the highest rate of return (rent-generation), which determines the strategy to be adopted. Implementation of the strategy is likely to identify gaps in the firm's resources, and management's role is to make good these gaps. In developing his model Grant embraces many of the concepts that have been discussed in detail in earlier chapters. However, the important point to be made is the change of emphasis in the analysis that sees the firm as proactive rather than reactive, which tends to be the case when pursuing the industrial organisation perspective dominating Porterian analysis.

A recurrent theme in the strategy literature is the importance of developing *sustainable competitive advantage* which cannot be easily eroded or replicated by one's competitors. On this theme, Grant points out that there are four characteristics of resources that are important determinants of the sustainability of competitive advantage: durability, transparency, transferability, and replicability:

- *Durability* reflects the rate at which resources/capabilities depreciate or become obsolete. In the face of accelerating technological change and shortening product life-cycles physical resources are often less durable than intangible assets such as reputation, brands and relationships.
- *Transparency* is a measure of the degree of difficulty others experience in determining the source of a competitor's advantage. The less transparent an advantage the more difficult it is to imitate it.
- *Transferability* represents the ability to acquire a source of advantage once it has been identified which, in turn, may be hampered by geographical immobility, imperfect information, firm-specific resources and/or the immobility of capabilities.
- *Replicability* mirrors the extent to which a competitor can reproduce the source of advan-

tage, assuming it can define it and acquire the necessary resources. As Grant observes, 'the firm's most important resources and capabilities are those which are durable, difficult to identify and understand, imperfectly transferable, not easily replicated, and in which the firm possesses clear ownership and control These are the firm's "crown jewels" and need to be protected; and they play a pivotal role in the competitive strategy which the firm pursues.' (1991, p. 129)

Of course protection is not enough – resources need constantly to be improved and upgraded – a central theme in Porter's analysis of the competitive advantage of nations and his work on clusters.

Two years after Grant's paper appeared, Margaret A. Peterhaf published 'The cornerstones of competitive advantage: a resource-based view' in *Strategic Management Journal* (1993). While on a very similar theme to Grant (1991), surprisingly she makes no reference to his work. Peterhaf's purpose is 'to develop a general model of resources and firm performance which at once integrates the various strands of research'. In doing so she proposes four theoretical conditions which underlie competitive advantage – *resource heterogeneity*, *ex post limits to competition*, *imperfect resource mobility*, and *ex ante limits to competition*.

Heterogeneity is important because it implies that firms of varying capabilities can compete with one another and at least break even. The more superior the resources the greater the potential to earn 'rents' a term used rather than 'profits' where the existence of such a surplus does not induce new competition. The assumption here is that the superior resources which give rise to rents cannot easily be replicated, otherwise one assumes the existence of surpluses would attract in new competition. Here, in essence is Andrews' (1971) idea of the 'distinctive competence' subsequently elaborated by Hamel and Prahalad (1994).

Ex post limits to competition mean that after the existence of rents becomes apparent there are limits which prevent other firms entering the market. The most frequently cited are imperfect imitability and imperfect substitutability which, inevitably, mean that heterogeneity can be maintained. The relationship with Bain's (1956) concept of 'entry barriers' is obvious. Peterhaf refers to the work of Dierickx and Cool (1989) as being particularly important because

> it focuses precisely on those kinds of resources and capabilities which are of central concern to resource-based theory; nontradeable assets which develop and accumulate within the firm. Such assets tend to defy imitation because they have a strong tacit dimension and are socially complex. They are born of organisational skill and corporate learning. Their development is 'path dependent' in the sense that it is contingent upon preceding levels of learning, investment, asset stocks, and development activity. For such assets, history matters. Would-be imitators are thwarted by the difficulty of discovering and repeating the developmental process and by the considerable lag involved. Importantly, assets of this nature are also immobile and thus bound to the firm. Factor immobility, or imperfect mobility is another key requirement for sustainable advantage. (Peterhaf, 1993, p. 183)

The final factor, *ex ante* limits to competitions, is related to uncertainty in the sense that if several potential competitors recognised the potential of a resource in advance, then they could compete that advantage away in attempting to gain control over it, i.e. success accrues to the firm that identifies opportunities not apparent to others.

Peterhaf contends that a major contribution of the resource-based model is that 'it explains long-lived differences in firm profitability that cannot be attributed to industry conditions' (p. 186). In other words, it should help managers to identify sources of sustainable competitive advantage.

As she also points out, the model, and its diagnostic potential, is freely available to all – its strategic implications will ultimately depend upon the firm's specific resource endowment. In turn, this underlines the importance of the marketing appreciation and, particularly, the internal audit as a means of identifying and measuring just what strengths and weaknesses an organisation has. Such an analysis is an essential first step in determining how to deploy one's assets and resources most efficiently in the short term and how to shape and redeploy them in the longer term to maintain and increase effectiveness. Before examining the SWOT analysis in more detail, we will look first at one more discussion of resource-based theory by Hunt and Morgan (1996).

In fact Hunt and Morgan have made two important contributions to what they call 'resource-advantage' (R-A) theory in the *Journal of Marketing* (1995, 1996), the later article being a response to comments on their first paper by Peter Dickson (1996) who had himself written on the subject in 1992. In essence, Dickson raised several questions about Hunt and Morgan's model that reflected specific concerns about its explanatory power. In their response, the authors gave particular attention to the issues of competitive dynamics, innovation and organisational learning. While the reader will have to refer to the original for the detailed arguments, Hunt and Morgan claim that R-A theory is able to accommodate the criticisms made of it and is a genuinely dynamic theory reflecting the reality of competition in the marketplace. Competition is seen as a force that seeks to create disequilibrium as firms struggle to secure a comparative advantage over their rivals reflected in superior financial performance:

> Competitive processes are significantly influenced by five environmental factors: the societal resources on which firms draw, the societal institutions that frame the 'rules of the game', the actions of competitors, the behaviours of consumers, and public policy decisions. (p. 109)

Hence the importance of the marketing appreciation!

In seeking to establish a comparative advantage, firms emphasise proactive innovation and depend upon superior organisational learning, both of which increase dynamism in the market.

Hunt and Morgan also address the question of 'path dependency', which seeks to explain why changes may occur in economic systems due to chance and/or remote events rather than more predictable systematic factors. While it is accepted that firms embark on courses of action based upon feedback from their environment, the evidence that this leads to less efficient market outcomes is seen to be largely 'mythical'. On balance the Scottish verdict of 'not proven' would seem to apply. That said, Hunt and Morgan claim the R-A theory can fully accommodate path dependencies because 'it is an evolutionary, non-consummatory theory of competition' (p. 111). This conclusion is congruent with the approach taken by the author as should be apparent from my endorsement of life-cycle theory and the inevitability of change as fundamental reasons supporting the need for strategic thinking and strategy formulation to ensure survival, let alone success.

The above discussion cannot do justice to the ideas deployed both for and against resource-based theories of competition. But, as with many other concepts and ideas introduced throughout the text, the purpose is to alert the reader that there is an extensive body of knowledge which provides insights into the options available to managers in developing courses of action. That there is no single *right* answer is readily apparent in the debate between opposing schools of thought. It follows, as has been stated frequently, that some options may appear better than others, but outcomes invariably depend upon context, timing and implementation.

Successful management is a process of continual adjustment to a changing environment. What we need to do is establish what our distinctive skills and competencies are through our internal analysis and then match these with best opportunities as revealed by our external analysis. Simultaneously, we must be sensitive to potential threats in our external environment and seek to avoid them as well as being conscious of potential weaknesses that need to be rectified. This is the purpose of the SWOT analysis which is the subject of the next section.

SWOT ANALYSIS

The acronym SWOT reflects well the thrust of this chapter in that it suggests we look first at the organisation and then seek to position it to best

effect within the external environment. As to whether one should undertake the internal or external audit first is very much a matter of choice, although the presentation here might suggest that one should work from the outside in rather than the other way around. While good arguments can be found for this, including the fact that the external evaluation is likely to be more comprehensive than it might be if one only looked at the environment from a company point of view, it might also be argued that it is more efficient to restrict the scope of the external analysis to those areas of most direct relevance to the firm. Either way, having completed the data gathering and preliminary analysis, we need a technique to reduce the available information to manageable proportions and it is here that the SWOT analysis comes into its own.

Essentially, the technique requires the decision-maker to distil the available information down into a series of summary statements that can be recorded on the equivalent of a single sheet of paper. By doing this it is possible to keep the key factors under review simultaneously, which greatly reduces the possibility of necessary information being overlooked. As we shall see in Chapter 13, there are severe limits to the amount of information humans can process simultaneously, so it is vital to reduce the output of our appreciation to the bare essentials. Obviously, this will require the exercise of judgement, and it will usually be necessary to prioritise the relative importance of the factors under consideration. This may be done by either verbal – extremely important/very important/important/not very important/unimportant – or numerical scaling, with only the critical factors being included in the final analysis. An example of such an analysis is given in Table 11.1.

TABLE 11.1 A factor rating table

Factor	Weighting	Firm A	Firm B	Firm C	Firm D	Firm E
Price	6	8	5	7	7	4
Performance	8	7	8	6	7	9
Reliability	10	7	8	7	6	9
Service	9	7	9	8	6	9
Delivery	5	8	7	7	8	6
Score		277	290	267	252	297
Ranking		3	2	4	5	1

Piercy (1997) is a strong proponent of SWOT analysis and recognises, like ourselves, that SWOT analysis has been criticised as an oversimplified and potentially misleading approach to strategic analysis due to a failure to follow a few simple guidelines as to its implementation.

To begin with, too many organisations follow a broadbrush and overgeneralised approach to SWOT analysis when what is required is a *focused* methodology. In Piercy's view this involves defining the elements of the marketing mix – product, price, place, promotion – as well as the chosen segment and likely competitors in precise terms.

Second, SWOT analysis is most valuable when used as a technique for getting managers to articulate their personal views and then share them with their peers with a view to achieving a consensus. Clearly, the greater the consensus between managers the greater the likelihood that they will work together to achieve implementation.

The third thing necessary to improve the diagnostic power of a SWOT analysis is to define the elements from a customer perspective rather than the organisational point of view. By doing so, what the organisation may well perceive as particular strengths may be seen as quite the opposite by their customers, so that strengths such as 'long-established' or 'trustworthy' may be seen by customers as meaning 'old fashioned'. Thus, while strengths and weaknesses are intended to define the organisation as a basis for determining how best to position and deploy these attributes, the diagnosis is only likely to be effective when the internal view is confirmed by external sources.

By the same token, opportunities and threats are external to the organisation and exist independently of the firm's internal strengths and weaknesses. As we observed earlier, the value of SWOT analysis for strategic marketing planning is that by defining the component elements objectively, one will be best placed to match strengths with opportunities, remedy weaknesses either by improving performance or eliminating the source of weakness, and avoid threats by taking purposive action.

The importance of defining corporate strengths and weaknesses precisely was the subject of an article by Stevenson in the *Sloan Management Review* (1976). Stevenson reported the views of managers in six manufacturing companies as to their own organisation's strengths and weaknesses. Based on 191 responses, Stevenson reported:

The results of the study brought into serious question the value of formal assessment approaches. It was found that an individual's cognitive perceptions of the strengths and weaknesses of his organisation were strongly influenced by factors associated with the individual and not only by the organisation's attributes. Position in the organisation, perceived role, and type of responsibility so strongly influenced the assessment that the objective reality of the situation tended to be overwhelmed. In addition, there were wide variations among standards of measurement and criteria for judgement employed.

Stevenson analyses his data in some detail but, while finding differences in the particular, returns to the general conclusion above. He then offers the following advice to improve managerial definitions of strengths and weaknesses:

The manager should:

- Recognise that the process of defining strengths and weaknesses is primarily an aid to the individual manager in the accomplishment of his task
- Develop lists of critical areas for examination which are tailored to the responsibility and authority of each individual manager
- Make the measures and criteria to be used in evaluation of strengths and weaknesses explicit so that managers can make their evaluations against a common framework
- Recognise the important strategic role of defining attributes as opposed to efficiency or effectiveness
- Understand the differences in the use of identified strengths and identified weaknesses.

Wensley (1999) identifies some potentially major flaws with the use of SWOT or TOWS analyses:

1. To a considerable extent the internal–external and positive–negative divisions are reflections of each other so any particular factor can be located in any box within reason (it is merely a question of how it is 'presented').
2. The link between individual factors and proposed strategic action is often naïve and merely semantic. In actual practice a more effective approach is to

redefine the competitive domain so that negative aspects become marginalised (or indeed positive).

3. There is a tendency to treat individual factors as distinct and uncorrelated, when they are merely

elements in a more general construct such as, say, market position. This applies not only between the boxes (see 1 above) but also within individual boxes. (p. 167)

Chapter summary

In this chapter we have put forward the view that a critical part of the manager's job is 'matching' organisational strengths with market opportunities in order to optimise the efficiency and effectiveness of the firm's assets, resources, skills and competencies. In support of this view, we looked at some of the more recent literature dealing with the resource-value-based approach to strategic analysis, which emphasises the importance of the firm's portfolio of resources over the constraints and opportunities existing in the external environment. As we have seen, this is a quite different emphasis to that taken by industrial economists, as epito-

mised by Michael Porter (see Chapter 2), who see the market structure as the force determining the strategic options available to the individual firm. As we have observed on a number of occasions, the truth probably lies somewhere in between, and the successful strategist needs to carefully balance both internal and external factors in crafting an effective strategy. To do this we recommend the use of the SWOT analysis in which the decision-maker is required to reduce all the possible factors that constitute strengths, weaknesses, opportunities and threats to a maximum of, say, five of each so that they may all be considered

simultaneously. In doing so we must be conscious of the dangers of selective perception introduced in Chapter 9 when discussing buyer behaviour, and take active steps along the lines suggested by Stevenson to ensure comparability in the judgements of those contributing to the analysis.

In the next two chapters we look at the subjects of market segmentation and positioning which are approaches developed by marketers to enable them to translate plans into action. As such these two chapters represent the beginning of the transition from strategic thinking into marketing management.

REFERENCES

Andrews, K. R. (1971) *The Concept of Corporate Strategy*. Homewood, IL: Irwin.

Bain, J. S. (1956) *Barriers to New Competition*. Cambridge, MA: Harvard University Press.

Dickson, P. R. (1992) Toward a general theory of competitive rationality, *Journal of Marketing*, 56(January): 69–83.

Dickson, P. R. (1996) The static and dynamic mechanics of competition: a comment on Hunt and Morgan's comparative advantage theory, *Journal of Marketing*, 60(October): 102–6.

Dierickx, I. and Cool, K. (1989) Asset shock accumulation and sustainability of competitive advantage, *Management Science*, 35(December): 1504–11.

Grant, R. M. (1991) The resource-based theory of competitive advantage: implications for strategy formulation, *California Management Review* (spring): 114–35.

Hamel, G. and Prahalad, C. K. (1994) *Competing for the Future*. Boston, MA: Harvard Business School Press.

Hofer, C. W. and Schendel, D. E. (1978) *Strategy Formulation: Analytical Concepts*. St Paul, MI: West Publishing.

Hunt, S. D. and Morgan, R. M. (1995) The resource-advantage theory of competition: dynamics, path dependencies, and evolutionary dimensions, *Journal of Marketing*, 60(October): 107–14.

Hunt, S. D. and Morgan, R. M. (1996) The comparative advantage theory of competition, *Journal of Marketing*, 59(April): 1–15.

McKitterick, J. B. (1957) What is the marketing management concept?,

in Bass, F. M. (ed.) *The Frontiers of Marketing Thought and Science*. Chicago, IL: American Marketing Association, pp. 71–81.

Peterhaf, M. A. (1993) The cornerstones of competitive advantage: a resource-based view, *Strategic Management Journal*, 14: 179–91.

Piercy, N. (1997) *Market-led Strategic Change: Transforming the Process of Going to Market*. Oxford: Butterworth Heinemann.

Porter, M. E. (1980) *Competitive Strategy: Techniques for Analysing Industries and Competitors*. New York: Free Press.

Stevenson, H. H. (1976) Defining strengths and weaknesses, *Sloan Management Review*, 17: 51–68.

Wensley, R. (1999) Marketing strategy, in Baker, M. J. (ed.) *Encyclopedia of Marketing*, London: International Thomson Business Press.

CHAPTER 12

Product differentiation and market segmentation

Diversity or heterogeneity are the exception rather than the rule.

WENDELL SMITH

After reading Chapter 12 you will be able to:

✔ Distinguish between product differentiation and market segmentation as alternative strategies.

✔ Suggest appropriate ways for segmenting markets.

✔ Define and describe four basic approaches – a priori, clustering, flexible and componential.

✔ Discuss the major segmentation variables grouped into four major categories:

■ Demographic

■ Geographic or location

■ Psychographic

■ Behaviouristic – usage, benefit.

✔ Describe factors to be taken into account when segmenting industrial markets.

✔ Indicate when it is appropriate to segment markets.

INTRODUCTION

Earlier chapters have been concerned largely with establishing a broadly based strategic overview of marketing, and with setting out some of the features which distinguish individual (consumer) and collective (market) behaviour, in order to provide the framework within which specific marketing decisions may be made. It is timely now to turn from such a comprehensive, and some would argue overgeneralised, perspective and begin to narrow the focus on these marketing decisions per se. A central and fundamental concept of marketing which provides a bridge between the general and particular, the theoretical and the real world is the notion of segmentation.

In Chapter 12 we look, first, at the difference between product differentiation and market segmentation as alternative competitive strategies by which the producer seeks to establish dominance over a subset or subsets of the total market. Next we review a number of different approaches to segmentation each of which would seem to offer particular benefits under given conditions and circumstances.

Such a review leads naturally to consideration of the procedures to be followed in segmenting markets and the various methods available. Here the treatment is concerned with the 'what' and the 'why' rather than 'how', and is intended to provide the decision-maker with an overview of the policy implications of market segmentation, rather than a technical description of how to execute a segmentation study which is a subject in its own right.

DEFINING THE MARKET

The precise definition of markets is elusive if not impossible and, as Day et al. (1979) have observed, 'ultimately all product–market boundaries are arbitrary'. That said, definition of a market is essential in that it identifies the characteristics of both customers and competitors that were the subject of extended discussion in earlier chapters. To resolve this problem, Day et al. recommend 'customer-oriented approaches to identifying product–markets' as the most productive method and suggest the adoption of two premises. First, that customers seek benefits and, second, they

'consider the available alternatives from the vantage point of the usage contexts of which they have experience and the specific applications they are considering.' They continue:

> From these two premises, we can define a product–market as the *set of products* judged to be substitutes, within those usage situations in which similar patterns of benefits are sought, and the *customers* for whom such usages are relevant.

Such an approach is clearly diametrically opposed to one which takes a supply orientation and defines markets in terms of the characteristics of the goods or the processes used to make them. This, however, is the 'normal' approach as enshrined in industry classifications such as the standard industrial classification (SIC) (or NTIC in US) codes. On the other hand, industry classification does provide a starting point in that it defines the *generic* products within which one will find a variety of substitutes. Lunn (1974) has distinguished a hierarchy of products comprising *product types* or subclasses, *product variants* and brands.

Product types are subclasses of products and satisfy major differences in demand, e.g. hot or cold breakfast cereals, carbonated or still mineral water. For each product type there may be a number of variants, and for each variant a number of brands. In the long run product types may serve as substitutes for one another while there is a greater likelihood of substitution between variants. In economic terms brands are perfect substitutes; in marketing terms the whole purpose of branding is to differentiate strongly in the hope of developing brand loyalty with a significant subset of customers. In Day et al.'s view these submarkets comprise part of a *strategic market segment* in the sense that there exist significant strategic barriers for competitors to overcome between them but not within them. They further argue that the test of strategic relevance is whether the segments require substantially different marketing mixes.

In distinguishing segments, usage data is the best guide to current behaviour under the prevailing competitive conditions, and are the better guide to tactical planning. By contrast, judgemental data gathered by AIO (attitudes, interests and opinions) research is usually a better guide to behaviour under changed circumstances, and so provides better inputs to strategic planning. Day et al. describe three different measures of usage behaviour, and four main approaches to the measurement of customer judgements. These are more the province of the specialist text and lead to a number of general conclusions which may be summarised as:

1. Boundaries between markets are, inevitably, arbitrary and not clear-cut.
2. 'The suitability of different empirical methods is strongly influenced by the character of the market environment' – in other words 'you pay your money and take your choice!'
3. The most useful methods are those which recognise a variety of usage situations.
4. Most methods, and particularly those using behavioural measures, are static and have difficulty in accommodating changes in the market.
5. 'The most persistent problem is the lack of defensible criteria for recognising boundaries.'
   In other words, and as so often is the case in marketing, the concept is powerful but its operationalisation is very difficult. In the remainder of this chapter we will examine some ways in which we may achieve this. To begin with, however, it will be useful to spell out the essential difference between the alternative strategies of product differentiation and market segmentation.

PRODUCT DIFFERENTIATION VS. MARKET SEGMENTATION

As we have seen, dissatisfaction with the classical economists' explanations of the interaction of supply and demand in the marketplace led to the formulation of the theory of imperfect competition in the early 1930s by Joan Robinson (1933) and Edwin Chamberlin (1933). It was this theory which was to provide the necessary underpinnings for the statement of the concept of market segmentation by Wendell Smith in 1956 in which he noted that 'diversity or heterogeneity had come to be the rule rather than the exception'. It was recognition of the existence of this heterogeneity in the demand for goods and services which led to the disaggregation of the traditional single demand schedule

and acceptance in its place of several separate demand schedules, each of which offers the opportunity to develop products specifically for that submarket or segment. This is not to suggest that suppliers had not previously appreciated the potential of product differentiation, as of course they had. Indeed, the development of imperfect competition is largely attributable to the attempts of the supply side of the market to avoid or minimise the competitive straitjacket implicit in the production and sale of homogeneous products. The distinction between product differentiation and market segmentation, first made by Smith, is that while the former is supply led (a production orientation) the latter is demand led and so constitutes a marketing orientation, i.e. the product is developed in full recognition and knowledge of the prospective users' needs.

Ultimately each individual consumer might properly be regarded as a distinct market segment in his or her own right, but, with very rare exceptions, such an approach is unrealistic as the costs involved would undoubtedly exceed the potential users' willingness or ability to pay. Thus, market segmentation offers a useful compromise between the extreme approach of both the economist and the behavioural scientist which is readily apparent in Figure 12.1.

This diagram is particularly useful in clarifying the two 'prototypical research patterns' of real-world segmentation studies distinguished by Wind (1978) in a masterly review of the subject, namely:

1. An *a priori segmentation* design in which management decides on a basis for segmentation such as product purchase, loyalty, customer type, or other factor. The survey results show the segments' estimated size and their demographic, socioeconomic, psychographic and other relevant characteristics.
2. A *clustering-based segmentation* design in which segments are determined on the basis of a clustering of respondents on a set of 'relevant' variables. Benefit, need, and attitude segmentation are examples of this type of approach. As in a priori segmentation studies, the size and other characteristics (demographic, socioeconomic, purchase and the like) of the segments are estimated.

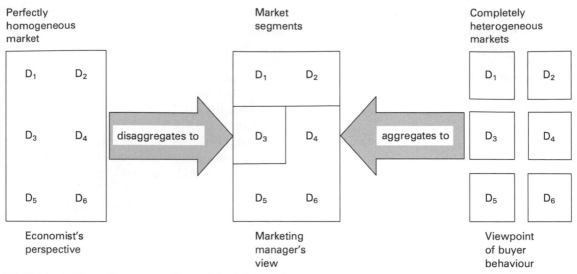

FIGURE 12.1 Alternative perspectives of the total market

SOURCE: Enis, B. M. (1977) *Marketing Priniciples* (3rd edn). Santa Monica, CA: Goodyear

Figure 12.1 also makes it clear that the central viewpoint is that of the marketing manager, and it is their responsibility to select the most appropriate basis for defining the target market or markets. Only if this is accomplished effectively will it be possible to design a marketing plan which will maximise the firm's potential. Much of the remainder of this chapter is concerned with examining ways and means of achieving this desired result. However, before looking at some of the bases for segmenting markets, and describing some of the available procedures and techniques, it is important to acknowledge that while the majority of marketers are in favour of segmentation, there is still a minority who are against it to some extent.

Bliss (1980) believes that much dissatisfaction with segmentation as a concept is due to the fact that it is inapplicable in many markets and also because too much emphasis is given to techniques to the neglect of the market itself and the competitive situation within it. Similarly, Resnik et al. (1979) argue that the soaring costs of products and services, changing values and lifestyles call for the opposite approach which they designate 'counter-segmentation'. In that Resnik et al. appear to have been arguing for larger segments rather than total homogeneity, their criticisms may be seen largely as a reaction to the difficult economic climate of the late 1970s and early 1980s, with its consequent

sharpening of a concern for value for money. A concern that continued into the 1990s.

It is also important to recognise that market segmentation is really only a viable strategy when a product–market actually exists. In the case of a radical innovation such as the microwave oven, cellular phones or computers one can only speculate as to who might be the most likely to perceive the benefits they offer and be among the first to adopt them. Only when the product is available in the market will it be possible to profile users, identify applications etc. In these circumstances then product differentiation leads the way.

Another change that has also called into question the value of a market segmentation is the impact of technological innovations such as CAD-CAM (computer-aided design/computer-aided manufacturing) and flexible manufacturing systems backed up by developments in information technology (IT) that have made 'mass customisation' possible. Examples of mass customisation are commonplace. In the auto industry it has been estimated that Ford Europe has the potential to create two million 'different' models by combining and permutating all the options it offers to potential buyers. Similarly, Dell has become one of the world's largest suppliers of computers by inviting buyers to specify exactly what configuration they require and then assembling to order.

Overall however, segmentation seems to offer

more benefits than disadvantages and, in that it can be undertaken to almost any degree of refinement and sophistication, is appropriate to theorist and pragmatist alike.

BASES FOR SEGMENTATION

As Wind (1978) notes, the development of a segmentation model requires one to specify a dependent variable which is the basis for segmentation, e.g. usage or time of adoption, and a set of independent variables or 'descriptors' which define the specific segments, e.g. age, occupation, etc. He continues to observe that 'over the years almost all variables have been used as bases for market segmentation' and any superficial review of segmentation studies would readily confirm this to be so. To a large extent the plethora of factors used to define market segments reflects the difficulty of putting the normative theory of marketing segmentation into practice, i.e. the normative theory as proposed by Smith is proactive in that one should use knowledge of consumer characteristics to develop a marketing strategy. In practice, however, most marketing managers who use segmentation studies do so reactively in that they seek to determine the response of different market segments to their marketing strategy. Obviously such information will be used to modify and improve the proposed strategy, but a purist would argue that the managerial approach is more closely akin to product differentiation than a normative approach to marketing segmentation.

Perhaps the real difference lies in the time horizon with which the manager is concerned. As we noted earlier (and doubtless will comment on again), a fully fledged theory of marketing needs to recognise the very real constraints which the firm faces in the short term which may be insignificant or unimportant when one takes a long-term view. The difference is perfectly reflected in the cost accountant's distinction between variable and fixed costs, and the recognition that in the long term all costs are variable, i.e. one can modify one's asset base and change the objectives and direction of the organisation. Thus, in the short term one must sell what one can make, and the best way to increase effectiveness and improve performance is to ensure that the product is targeted at those prospective users who can be identified as having a need profile most consistent with the product's performance.

In an ideal world, however, all new product development would stem from a clear identification of a market need. But, as any practising marketing manager would quickly tell you, the major difficulty with following such a counsel of perfection is that few consumers or users are able to specify precisely, and in advance, just what it is they would like, although they usually have an unerring facility to reject what they don't like once they have seen it. Given such a state of affairs, it may often prove more economical to pursue a trial-and-error approach to new product development, especially where this is of an incremental kind, and let consumers identify themselves though usage rather than expend large amounts on ineffective research. Wind (1978) appears to recognise this dilemma when he comments:

> In contrast to the theory of segmentation that implies that there is a single best way of segmenting a market, the range and variety of marketing decisions suggest that any attempt to use a single basis for segmentation (such as psychographic, brand preference, or product usage) for all marketing decisions may result in incorrect marketing decisions as well as a waste of resources.

So what should the manager do? Wind provides an excellent guide when he tabulates his own preferred bases for segmentation as follows:

For general understanding of a market:
- Benefits sought (in industrial markets, the criterion used is purchase decision)
- Product purchase and usage patterns
- Needs
- Brand loyalty and switching pattern
- A hybrid of the variables above.

For positioning studies:
- Product usage
- Product preference
- Benefits sought
- A hybrid of the variables above.

For new product concepts (and new product introduction):

- Reaction to new concepts (intention to buy, preference over current brand etc.)
- Benefits sought.

For pricing decisions:
- Price sensitivity
- Deal proneness
- Price sensitivity by purchase/usage patterns.

For advertising decisions:
- Benefits sought
- Media usage
- Psychographic/lifestyle
- A hybrid (of the variables above and/or purchase/usage patterns).

For distribution decisions:
- Store loyalty and patronage
- Benefits sought in store selection.

The common thread which links all these bases for segmentation is that they focus on the prospective buyer's response to marketing stimuli, which is precisely what the manager needs to know when formulating an action plan.

Unfortunately, as hinted earlier, there is no similar consensus about which descriptors will be most useful in helping to define segments in a particular market using one or other of these bases. Wind cites four reasons for this state of affairs which, in my own view, characterise most research in marketing, and explain much of the

suspicion which exists between academic and practitioner. These four factors are:

1. Lack of a systematic effort (by both academicians and practitioners) to build a cumulative body of substantive findings about consumer behaviour.
2. Lack of specific models which link behaviour (and other bases for segmentation) to description variables and thus predict which description variables should be used.
3. The non-representative nature of most of the academic studies with respect to sample design (e.g. small, convenient samples), type of respondents (e.g. students) and tasks (e.g. non-marketing-related tasks). Even many of the real-world segmentation studies are based on relatively small and non-representative samples.
4. Lack of comparable conceptual and operational definitions of variables across studies.

Due to these limitations, Wind argues that one should regard the literature as a source of hypotheses concerning which variables might be more appropriate in any given situation, and provides a useful listing of such hypotheses.

Much of my own research has been concerned with attempting to define innovators for new products on the perhaps simplistic assumption that the diffusion or acceptance of an innovation is functionally related to the speed of the first adoption, such that if one can pre-identify early adop-

---

Box 12.1   *To be or not to be in the global hotel industry*

As is the case in almost every industry nowadays, competition in the hotel industry is increasing as a result of economic crisis along with hostilities and terrorism around the world, which in turn reduce tourism and business travel. Thus, hotel chains are struggling to boost their bed occupancy rates. As a result of competitive pressures, hotel chains are developing more sophisticated marketing strategies. Companies are designing their marketing mix elements according to needs of unique target groups such as differentiating price, services, and product offerings. For example, Holiday Inn that once had a single brand and product concept, undertook a major business restructuring in order to better respond to changes in the market. Now, there are four distinct Holiday Inn brands operating around the world: Holiday Inn Plaza offering top-notch fac-ilities within cities; Holiday Inn providing good value for money around the world; Holiday Inn Garden, small 3-star hotels located around the cities of Europe; and, Holiday Inn Express offering comfortable rooms with limited catering and leisure facilities. It comes as no surprise that hotel chains are rediscovering the importance of segmentation in the heightened competitive environment.

SOURCE: Zafer Erdogan, personal communication

tors one will accelerate the acceptance of the new product or process and thereby enhance its prospects of success (or reduce the expense of failure by recognising it sooner!). This research has now covered a period of almost 40 years and, while I agree with Wind's four factors, I am more optimistic than he appears to be in that I think it possible to provide operationally useful models, such as that relating to buyer behaviour in Chapter 9, in which certain key variables will have general application, although fine-tuning the model to a particular product–market situation will require the use of situation-specific variables. Further, while I think the literature might provide a useful 'prompt' for the practitioner I consider that the most fruitful source of situation-specific descriptor variables is likely to be the decision-maker's own experience. An excellent example of this is provided for the UK car market where the Society of Motor Manufacturers and Traders (SMMT) has developed a comprehensive classification. Commenting on this, the Economist Intelligence Unit (EIU) observed:

The main criteria in delineating the segments have been the size of the vehicle and its type and use. Price has not been a determinant, so there can be wide variations within each segment. The size of the vehicle has used two main considerations – its length and its engine size – but general agreement was reached that all vehicles in a range would fall into the same class. For example, hatchback, saloon and estate versions of a vehicle would all be in the same segment and, similarly, 'sporty' versions of standard cars would be classed as standard and not as sports.

Even now there are some areas which are contentious, particularly the specialist sports classification, but the categorisation is systematic and gives an excellent basis for comparing product ranges and national markets. Manufacturing trends will make the process more difficult because of the trend towards using a single platform for a wide range of models, but that is for the future – for the present this analysis has conformed to the SMMT definitions.

The SMMT definitions are:

A segment – mini
- Normally less than 1000cc
- Miniature body style
- Normally 2-door
- Length normally not exceeding 3,050 mm (10 ft)
- Typical examples are the Rover Mini and the Fiat Cinquecento.

B segment – small
- Normally 1000cc to 1500cc
- Larger body style than mini
- Length not exceeding 3,745 mm (12.5 ft)
- Performance greater than mini
- More variety of trims
- Typical examples are the Renault Clio and the Nissan Micra.

C segment – lower-medium
- Normally 1300cc to 2000cc
- Length of saloon version not exceeding 4,230 mm (14 ft)
- Typical examples are the Volkswagen Golf and the Toyota Corolla.

D segment – upper-medium
- Normally 1.6–2.8 litres
- Length of saloon version not exceeding 4,470 mm
- Typical examples are the Ford Mondeo and the Opel Vectra.

E segment – executive
- Normally 2–3.5 litres
- Body generally bigger than upper-medium
- Normally 4-doors
- Length of saloon not exceeding 4,800 mm
- More luxuriously appointed
- Typical examples are the Volvo 800 Series and Mercedes C-class.

F segment – luxury
- Normally over 3.5 litres
- Most luxurious available
- Typical examples would be Mercedes S-class and Jaguar saloons.

G segment – specialist sports
- Sports saloons
- Sports coupes
- Sports roadsters
  But all must be separate developments, not a modification of a standard range. The Rover MGF is a typical roadster, but the segment also covers cars such as Ferrari and the Jaguar XJS.

H segment – dual-purpose
- 4WD with off-road capability
- Typical examples are Land Rover Discovery and Toyota RAV4

With the increasing popularity of smaller, lighter and less rugged vehicles, the term 'sports utility vehicle' (SUV) is becoming increasingly used.

I segment – multipurpose vehicle (MPV)
- 2WD or 4WD estates with a seating capacity of up to eight people. Often characterised by a much higher driving position than in a standard vehicle
- Typical examples are the Renault Espace and the Peugeot 806.

The EIU comments:

This classification is excellent as far as it goes but the market is changing rapidly. It is mature and, in consequence, the manufacturers are developing specific models aimed at niches in the market. Some of these segments are quite distinctive, such as the G, H or I segments outlined above, but variations are being developed within the more conventional segments, particularly the B and C segments which both take about 30% of the market.

Consequently a more detailed classification is needed to take account of this market fragmentation and to map out the changes that are taking place in people's tastes and preferences. Ideally this should be carried out by an industry body in order to obtain general agreement but, as one of the users of this information, we feel entitled to make some suggestions.

At present the categories are based on either size or function, with A to E based mainly on size and F to I describing function. The size categories are a useful first stage in classification, but the function needs to be examined in considerably more detail in order to explain why people are buying cars of one type and not another. We would propose a two-part categorisation with the first part defining the size of the vehicle and the second part defining the function. This would incorporate such important distinctions as saloon, hatchback or estate and 2-door or 4-door. However, there could be a case for bringing price into the equation. Volvo has been making C segment cars for some years and selling them at a premium price because of a claimed higher level of construction and

fittings. Audi is now following the same route with its A3 and both BMW and Mercedes-Benz are also moving into smaller segments.

The EIU report continues to suggest that 'design flair' is another dimension that could be incorporated into the analysis and points to the Renault Twingo and Ford Ka as examples. These cars reflect the way the market is evolving and so need, in the opinion of the EIU, to be included in the segmentation analysis. The EIU analysis points out that the B – small car – and C – medium-size car – account for about 30% each, followed by the upper medium category with about 20%. Executive cars account for under 10% with all the remaining segments being worth between 1 and 2% each. However, when it is appreciated that 1% is equivalent to over 100,000 cars per annum one can understand why these niche markets are so attractive and subject to so much competition.

The case of the European car market is an excellent example of segmentation in practice. In the next section we look at some approaches to this practice.

PROCEDURE AND METHODS

We have already noted two basic procedures for segmenting markets, namely a priori and clustering, to which Wind adds two other procedures which he describes as flexible and componential. A brief description of these procedures will be given prior to a review of the major segmentation methods which are found in common use.

It would be difficult to improve on Wind's (1978) definition of *a priori segmentation*, which is a model of clarity and brevity, namely:

A priori segmentation models have had as a dependent variable (the basis for segmentation) either product specific variables (e.g. product usage, loyalty) or general customer characteristics (e.g. demographic factors). The typical research design for an a priori segmentation model involves seven stages:
1. Selection of the (a priori) basis for segmentation.
2. Selection of a set of segment descriptors (including hypotheses on the possible link between these descriptors and the basis for segmentation).

3. Sample design – mostly stratified and occasionally a quota sample according to the various classes of the dependent variable.
4. Data collection.
5. Formation of the segments on a sorting of respondents into categories.
6. Establishment of the (conditional) profile of the segments using multiple discriminant analysis, multiple regression analysis, or some other appropriate analytical procedure.
7. Translation of the findings about the segments' estimated size and profile into specific marketing strategies, including the selection of target segments and the design or modification of a specific marketing strategy.

In practice, market segmentation addresses three technical market research problems:

1. To construct a spatial representation of consumers' perceptions of products or brands in a category
2. To position consumers' ideal points in the same space and so estimate consumer demand for a product located at any particular point
3. To construct a model which predicts preferences of groups of customers towards new or modified products.

Frequently, it will prove helpful to plot product offerings and/or consumers' perceptions of them on a perceptual map as discussed earlier when describing 'Baker's Box' in Chapter 5. Another example of this approach is shown in Figure 12.2,

which illustrates the needs of different end-users for hi-fi equipment in terms of two key dimensions – performance and economy. From such a map it becomes possible to identify the appropriate product configuration and marketing mix for each segment, as well as the possible existence of 'gaps' in the market.

Definitions of these segments are as follows:

- *Segment 1:* The buffs. Persons who are enthusiastic and very knowledgeable about the products. They are primarily concerned with quality and technical features.
- *Segment 2:* The singles. Persons who live alone. Although they are less technically competent than the buffs, they demand good performance from a product they may use more than the average consumer.
- *Segment 3:* The professionals. Persons who have a higher level of education and high incomes. They tend to be more independent of their occupation and to engage in many social activities. Their purchase of the product is partially motivated by social status needs.
- *Segment 4:* The high earners. Persons who have high incomes but do not possess the higher level of education or occupational independence of the individuals in Segment 3.
- *Segment 5:* Others. Persons who do not belong to the above groups. This segment represents the largest proportion of the population.

In the case of clustering, or *post hoc segmentation*, the only significant difference is that the segments

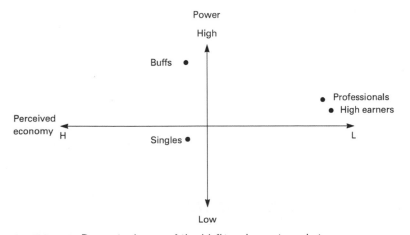

FIGURE 12.2 Perceptual map of the hi-fi equipment market

are determined after the data have been collected on the basis of perceived groupings or clusters within the data. Frequently such clusters will be determined through the use of factor analysis, whereby variables will be grouped on the basis of their correlation with each other (and their lack of correlation with variables included in other factors) and the amount of variance in the dependent variable which they are able to 'explain'.

Flexible segmentation is a dynamic procedure in which conjoint analysis (see conjoint measurement below) is combined with a simulation model to allow managers to explore a large number of alternative approaches to segmenting a particular market.

Finally, the *componential* procedure developed by Green et al. (1977) is an extension of conjoint analysis and 'shifts the emphasis of the segmentation model from the partitioning of a market to a prediction of which person type (described by a particular set of demographic and other psychographic attribute levels) will be most responsive to what type of product feature' (as Wind argues – see above).

Although Wind reports that Green et al. have used this technique successfully in a commercial application, there is little doubt that many managers regard such procedures with more than a little scepticism. This problem was highlighted in an article by Hooley (1980) in which he suggested that three factors encourage practitioners to steer clear of multivariate techniques.

1. Techniques are presented as a panacea for virtually all managerial ills.
2. An overemphasis upon techniques for their own sake – the 'have technique, will travel' syndrome – in which the merits are highlighted and the limitations glossed over.
3. A general lack of communication between the researcher and the practitioner.

In an attempt to overcome these deficiencies, Hooley provides a useful review of multivariate techniques, which he dichotomises as being either predictive or descriptive in nature. Among the more common predictive techniques may be numbered:

1. *Multiple regression* – seeks to develop a model of the relationship between a dependent variable

such as sales and two or more independent variables such as price, promotional expenditure etc., so that variations in the former may be explained and predicted in terms of changes in the latter.
2. *Multiple discriminant analysis (MDA)* – like regression, MDA uses a set of independent variables to predict one or more dependent variables. The technique is particularly useful in marketing as a means of discriminating between market segments in terms of member characteristics.
3. *Conjoint measurement* – seeks to identify the relative importance of each product attribute in creating an overall desirability for the product, i.e. you ask respondents to rank order a product in terms of each of the attributes which you consider might be important to potential buyers such as price, ease of use, taste etc.
4. *Automatic interaction detector (AID)* – develops a tree-type diagram in which the factors which help to explain the variance in the dependent variable are successively 'split' into their component parts (independent variables).

Two of the three major descriptive techniques – factor analysis and cluster analysis – have already been mentioned, the third being *multidimensional scaling* (MDS). MDS is frequently used to develop representations of the relationships between perceived brand images and the individual's product requirements as well as for defining market segments. Hooley notes that MDS possesses the disadvantages that its results are not always clear cut, the segments may be indistinct and may not be applicable to all markets, and that it presents a static rather than a dynamic picture and so requires continuous updating.

Although Hooley designates cluster analysis as a descriptive technique, in fact it is used for predictive purposes also. Indeed, cluster analysis is often used as a generic term within which are subsumed an enormous variety of specific techniques and a short review of these will be helpful to indicate to the practitioner just what is available.

CLUSTER ANALYSIS[1]

The marketer's interest in segmentation is a particular example of a general problem faced by analysts and decision-makers in virtually all areas of activity, namely: 'Given a sample of N objects or individuals, each of which is measured on each of p variables, devise a classification scheme for grouping the objects into g classes. The number of classes and the characteristics of the classes to be determined.' (Everitt, 1974, p. 1.)

Everitt continues:

> These techniques have been variously referred to as techniques of cluster analysis, Q-analysis, typology, grouping, clumping, classification, numerical taxonomy and unsupervised pattern recognition. The variety of the nomenclature may be due to the importance of the methods in such diverse fields as psychology, zoology, biology, botany, sociology, artificial intelligence and information retrieval.

In addition to the many fields of study in which different approaches to clustering have been developed, it is also important to recognise that such methods can be used for a number of different purposes. Thus Everitt cites Ball's (1971) list of seven possible uses of clustering techniques as follows:

1. Finding a true typology
2. Model fitting
3. Prediction based on groups
4. Hypothesis testing
5. Data exploration
6. Hypothesis generating
7. Data reduction.

In market segmentation studies, each of these different objectives may be appropriate.

Ideally clusters should be self-evident and capable of identification simply by reviewing a set of data and distinguishing natural groupings within it, e.g. classifying people as male or female. However, for most purposes decision-makers require a much finer discrimination than is possible using the two or three dimensions, which is the maximum which most of us can conceptualise simultaneously. Because of this need for greater sophistication, there has been a proliferation of techniques, which Everitt (1974) classifies into five types:

1. Hierarchical
2. Optimisation – partitioning

3. Density or mode-seeking
4. Clumping
5. Others.

Hierarchical clustering techniques may be either agglomerative or divisive in nature. Under the former procedure one would start from the stance of the behavioural scientist in our earlier description of approaches to market segmentation and regard each individual as a potential market in his or her own right. In most cases such an assumption would be unrealistic in economic terms so one would begin to combine individuals into groups. Conversely, the economists' undifferentiated demand schedule would be the logical starting-point for a divisive approach to segmentation. Everitt (1974) observes: 'Both types of hierarchical technique may be viewed as attempts to find the most efficient step in some defined sense, at each stage in the progressive subdivision or synthesis of the population.'

Partitioning techniques differ from hierarchical techniques in that they allow for adjustment of the original clusters, created on the basis of a predetermined criterion, through a process of reallocation. Thus, if one's a priori expectations as to the optimum way to segment a market lead to groupings which look less than ideal or do not perform as expected, one can relocate individuals until an optimum segmentation is achieved.

Density search techniques are, as the name suggests, methods which seek to emulate the human observer's ability to distinguish clusters of higher density surrounded by spaces with a lower density.

The fourth main type of technique, *clumping*, is seen as necessary where overlapping clusters are desirable. The case cited by Everitt is language where, because words tend to have several meanings, they may belong in several places. Finally, there are a number of other techniques such as 'Q' factor analysis, latent structure analysis etc., which do not conform to any of the previous categories. These techniques, and many more from the other categories, are described at some length in Chapter 2 of Everitt's (1974) book.

The existence of so many different clustering techniques is itself evidence of the fact that there is no clear 'best' method and that one can anticipate arguments for and against any given approach.

Everitt provides a useful summary of problems associated with cluster analysis, per se, and then in the context of the fivefold analysis discussed above. General problems include those of the precise definition of a cluster, the choice of variables, the measurement of similarity and distance and deciding the number of clusters present. These are technical matters beyond the scope of a book of this kind, but Everitt (1974) points out that there are various intuitively reasonable ways for validating clusters, namely:

> Firstly, several clustering techniques, based on different assumptions, could be used on the same set of data, and only clusters produced by all or by the majority of methods accepted. Secondly, the data could be randomly divided into two and each half clustered independently. Membership assignment in the partitioned samples should be similar to that of the entire sample, if the clusters are stable. A third method of establishing the underlying stability of groups produced by a clustering program is to make predictions about the effect which the omission of some of the variables would have on the group structure and then to check that the predictions are verified.

The final word should also be given to Everitt (1974), who reinforces the adage that any interpretation of data is only as good as the person making it, when he comments that:

> Cluster-analysis is potentially a very useful technique, but it requires care in its application, because of the many associated problems. In many of the applications of the methods that have been reported in the literature the authors have either ignored or been unaware of these problems, and consequently few results of lasting value can be pointed to. Hopefully future users of these techniques will adopt a more cautious approach, and in addition remember that, along with most other statistical techniques, classification procedures are essentially descriptive techniques for multivariate data, and *solutions given should lead to a proper re-examination of the data matrix rather than a mere acceptance of the clusters produced.* [emphasis added]

Having looked at the variety of clustering methods available to analysts who wish to classify

members of a population, we turn now to some of the methods in common usage by marketers.

Market segmentation is an important subfield of marketing and usually receives detailed treatment in introductory textbooks and courses. There are also numerous textbooks and monographs dealing with the subject in some depth. The following is only a brief overview of the topic.

MAJOR SEGMENTATION METHODS

There is widespread agreement in the marketing literature that for a segment to merit specific marketing attention, it must satisfy at least seven conditions. It must be:

1. Identifiable
2. Measurable
3. Accessible
4. Substantial
5. Unique in its response
6. Stable, i.e. can its behaviour be predicted in the future?
7. Viable, i.e. likely to respond positively to a • marketing mix developed specifically for it.

In addition to applying to the segment as a whole, it is clear that these conditions must also apply to the variables used in defining the segment itself. There are numerous lists of such variables and that shown in Table 12.1 is taken from Thomas (1980).

In this listing Thomas follows Kotler and others in grouping the variables into four major categories:

1. Demographic
2. Geographic
3. Psychographic
4. Behaviouristic.

DEMOGRAPHIC SEGMENTATION

The first question to be answered in developing a marketing strategy is, invariably, 'Who?' That is, who is the intended customer? The most straightforward and simplest answer to this question when profiling individual customers is to use

TABLE 12.1 Major segmentation variables

Geographic		Psychographic	– Producing psychological profiles or types
Region		Lifestyle	Straights, swingers, long-hairs
County size		Personality	Compulsive, gregarious, ambitious, introverted, passive, authoritarian
City			
Density – Urban, suburban, rural			
Climate		**Behaviouristic**	– **Effective marketing must address the needs normal consumers attempt to gratify**
Demographic		Purchase occasion	Should we segment people *or* their consumption occasions?
Age		Benefits sought	Economy, convenience, prestige
Sex		User status	Non-user, ex-user, potential user, first-time user, regular user
Family size			
Family life-cycle		Usage rate	Light, medium, heavy users
Income		Loyalty status	None, medium, strong, absolute
Occupation		Readiness stage	Unaware, aware, informed, interested, desirous, intending to buy
Education			
Religion		Marketing factor	Sensitivity quality, price, service, advertising, sales promotion
Race			
Nationality			
Social class			

SOURCE: Thomas, M. (1980) Market segmentation, *Quarterly Review of Marketing*, 6(1): 28

demographic factors such as age, sex, marital status and so on. When profiling organisational customers, then characteristics such as standard industrial classification (SIC) code, turnover, number of employees will be used. The great advantage of demographic factors is that they are usually easy to establish/identify and provide the basis for a great deal of data collection by governments, public sector bodies and marketing research agencies.

Given that so much consumption is closely correlated with demography, and that so much data is available, it is surprising that greater use is not made of demographics both for analysing current behaviour and, even more importantly, for forecasting and predicting future behaviour. For example, the consumption of basic social services such as health and education is closely age-related, yet public sector authorities seem to be singularly inept in projecting future demand. Given the number of live births in a given year, one would think it would be a simple matter to forecast the demand for postnatal care, preventive care (innoculations etc), nursery education, primary school-

ing, secondary and tertiary education and so forth. Given this information, some of which gives a lead time of 17+ years, it is difficult to understand why the necessary infrastructure is not available to meet demand. Similarly, if we know that people are living longer, and that the proportion of the population over retirement age is increasing, then it should not be difficult to predict the likely demand for sheltered housing, age-related medical care etc.

Commercial organisations are much more adept at using age as a predictor variable and developing specific products targeted directly at closely defined age groupings. For example, in the USA the 46 million people in the age group 29–40 have been defined as generation X (sometimes called Xers or baby busters in contrast with their parents, many of whom were baby boomers and now comprise the new 'grey' market). With an effective demand in excess of $125 billion, this age grouping represents a major market opportunity for the providers of goods and services.

Gender is another variable that is easy to establish and is closely associated with certain consumption behaviours. However, one needs to be careful not to fall into the trap of outdated role stereotyping, with males seen as the primary earner/breadwinner and females as household managers. Within such stereotypes, products such as tyres, car batteries, power tools, home maintenance equipment and so on would be regarded as 'male' products, and clothing, food stuffs and household remedies/medicines as 'female' products. No longer! That said, one would anticipate that older men and women might still conform somewhat to these stereotypes whereas their children would not. The important point here is that in developing a marketing segment, one will need to use more than one criterion to describe it precisely and accurately.

Other demographic variables frequently used in segmentation studies include education, occupation and income, and composite measures such as socioeconomic grouping or social class. Similarly, family/household status, life-cycle stage and so on provide a useful first set at segmenting a market, and a great deal of detail on these factors is to be found in *The Marketing Pocket Book (2005)*.

Age is one of the most basic criteria used when describing market segments and analysing buyer behaviour. In the case of American consumers, one of the most important groupings that has dominated marketing practice for the past 50 years are the so-called 'baby boomers' – persons born between 1946 and 1964 – who number 77 million and comprise 27.5% of the US population. Half these people are now aged 50 or over – an age when, traditionally, marketers lose interest in them, in the mistaken belief that by this age their consumption behaviour has become fixed. But, research into the attitudes and behaviour of baby boomers shows this not to be the case and points to the need for careful analysis to target them effectively.

> As a group, people aged 50 to 60 are flush, with more than $1 trillion of spending power a year, about double that of today's 60 to 70-years-olds. They are likely to be vigorous consumers, take on new jobs, relocate, support children they had in their 40s, go back to school, start a second or third career, remarry, inherit money from their savings-minded parents, pursue new hobbies, and tackle the health issues of aging. (*Business Week*, 24 October, 2005)

In the same *Business Week* article, marketers are advised to develop marketing strategies that recognise that the baby boomer generation are not set in their ways, with 52% saying they are willing to switch brands – the same proportion as for the total population. They are not obsessed with youth and react more positively to advertisements featuring people of their own age group rather than persons 20 years younger. They are not counting the days to retirement and many plan to continue working beyond 60. They also plan to stay healthy and focus on wellness rather than on remedies to treat the aches and pains of ageing. They want benefits stated clearly and eschew vague claims such as 'fortified with vitamins' or 'fast pain relief'.

In recent years demographic factors have been combined with geographic/locational data to provide very powerful segmentation tools.

LOCATION AS A BASIS FOR SEGMENTATION

The observation that 'birds of a feather flock together' owes much to the fact that people with similar social, economic and lifestyle characteristics have a tendency to congregate and settle close to one another in particular neighbourhoods. In that this behaviour has been apparent for thousands of years it is surprising that it was not until 1973 that any serious attempt was made to devise a formal methodology for utilising this knowledge as a basis for market segmentation. It was in this year that Richard Webber found that the application of cluster-analysis techniques to official statistics for Liverpool enabled him to define a number of distinctive neighbourhood types. Subsequently, and with the help of the Census Office, Webber found that the same approach on a national scale led to the isolation of thirty-six separate neighbourhood types, 'each of them different in terms of their population, housing and socioeconomic characteristics'.

Clark (1982) continues:

> The next step came as a result of a seminar at the Centre for Environmental Studies, when one statistician, Ken Baker, associate director of the British Market Research Bureau, promptly saw the system's value as a tool for controlling the field-work of the Bureau's Target Group Index. Baker

decided to categorise all the 24,000 respondents in the TGI consumer survey geographically according to Webber's neighbourhood groups. The result seemed to show without doubt that respondents in different neighbourhood groups displayed significantly different propensities to buy specific products and services.

Having established the potential for his technique, now designated ACORN (A Classification of Residential Neighbourhoods), Webber joined Consolidated Analysis Centers Inc. (CACI) in 1979 and set about improving the method to enable a finer discrimination to be achieved.

The following material is taken directly from the ACORN User Guide with the permission of CACI, www.caci.co.uk.

ACORN is the most powerful consumer targeting tool available on the market today. It combines geography with demographics and lifestyle information – places where people live with their underlying characteristics and behaviour – to create a tool for understanding the different types of people in different areas throughout the country.

It enables marketers to understand fully the kind of people buying their goods, using their services or shopping in their stores. Geodemographic targeting also helps marketers pinpoint the people who are most likely to need their products or services – and avoid those who are not.

ACORN groups the entire UK population into 5 categories, 17 groups and 56 types [Figure 12.3]. By analysing significant social factors and consumer behaviour, it provides precise information and an in-depth understanding of the different types of consumers in every part of the country.

Developed by CACI over 25 years ago, ACORN was the first geodemographic classification in the country. Since then we have built consumer classifications both for the UK and globally, introducing new innovative techniques for targeting consumers. ACORN remains the most respected and reliable consumer classification.

ACORN can be used to understand customers, identify profitable prospects, evaluate local markets and plan public resources.

By adding ACORN codes to a customer database, you can increase knowledge of your customers' behaviour and lifestyle. ACORN profiling will give you new insights into your customers and allow you to identify prospects who most resemble your best customers.

ACORN can be used to drive effective customer communication strategies including targeted direct mail, leaflet distribution and local newspaper advertising.

For local market planning, ACORN can be used to define and analyse the purchasing preferences and lifestyle characteristics of different areas through the UK. This results in a more effective estimation of the demand for your products and services and a more effective location planning strategy.

Once retailers and suppliers have understood the characteristics and make-up of a neighbourhood, by using ACORN they can make strategic decisions on the format of their branch or store and the range of goods carried.

- Where should I open, close or locate my next store?
- Which products will suit the area?
- How should I allocate my resources?
- What factors can influence my store performance?

As a result of this range of applications, ACORN is widely used in many sectors of business.

Financial Organisations use ACORN to understand their customers, cross-sell their product range, set branch targets, predict loyal customers, and plan their network strategy.

Retailers use ACORN to locate stores, plan product ranges, assess refurbishments, and target local marketing for stores.

Media Owners use ACORN to support advertising sales, evaluate sales potential, and develop new markets.

In FMCG ACORN is used to drive customer communication, in-store marketing, ranging and product distribution.

The *Public Sector* uses ACORN to target services to areas of need, and inform policy decisions.

CACI started planning the development of the new ACORN several years before the 2001 census was available. We had already successfully used a range of additional data sources, including lifestyle surveys, to update the previous version of ACORN. We now wanted to ensure we built the new ACORN using the most robust data from the best available sources [Figure 12.3]. In particular, we wanted to identify additional sources of data that would complement the Census.

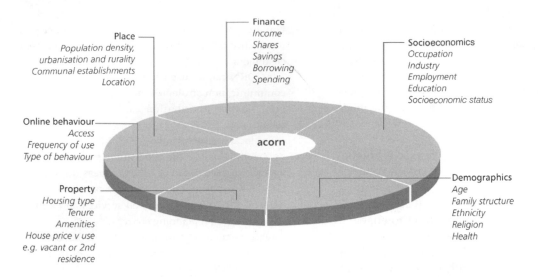

Category	% UK Pop		Group	% UK Pop
Wealthy Achievers **1**	**26.6%**	A	Wealthy Executives	8.6
		B	Affluent Greys	7.7
		C	Flourishing Families	8.8
Urban Prosperity **2**	**10.7%**	D	Prosperous Professionals	2.2
		E	Educated Urbanites	4.6
		F	Aspiring Singles	3.9
Comfortably Off **3**	**26.6%**	G	Starting Out	2.5
		H	Secure Families	15.5
		I	Settled Suburbia	6
		J	Prudent Pensioners	2.6
Moderate Means **4**	**14.5%**	K	Asian Communities	1.6
		L	Post-Industrial Families	4.8
		M	Blue-collar Roots	8
Hard-Pressed **5**	**22.4%**	N	Struggling Families	14.1
		O	Burdened Singles	4.5
		P	High-rise Hardship	1.6
		Q	Inner City Adversity	2.1
		U	Unclassified	0.3

FIGURE 12.3 The ACORN family of consumer classification

Over 400 variables were used to build ACORN and describe the different ACORN types. Of these variables, 30% were sourced from the 2001 Census. The remainder were derived from CACI's consumer lifestyle databases, which cover all of the UK's 46 million adults and 23 million households.

The unique two-stage method
CACI employed an innovative two-stage approach to creating the new ACORN. As a first stage CACI classified postcodes in the traditional manner, using a mixture of the Census and our other data sources.

The data inputs to the classification were carefully selected. This included a process of testing each variable's contribution to the power of the classification. We considered the effect of each variable individually, and their use in combination with other variables. This exhaustive testing ensured the ACORN classification was built using data that provided the greatest discrimination and targeting power.

But we didn't stop there. We then took advantage of the fact that, for the first time, the Census office attempted to publish data by geographic areas it believed contained the same kind of households.

We developed a unique second stage which selectively focused on any postcodes where ACORN might be improved. We used our substantial consumer lifestyle databases to check for subtle differences in areas which the Census office said contained the same kind of people. We then tested whether the postcodes in these areas were truly identical. When all our data sources agreed with the Census we were confident that we had the most accurate possible ACORN code.

When we identified postcodes that were not identical, we used all our additional data and a special set of decision algorithms to refine their ACORN codes. This unique methodology produced an ACORN classification that gives better discrimination. It also allows ACORN to be updated annually more easily than ever before, maintaining our picture of UK consumers' behaviour as it changes over time.

Understanding ACORN further

To help you understand ACORN further and give you in-depth and up-to-date information, CACI maintain a dedicated ACORN website. The site provides you with an extensive library of product purchasing and consumer behaviour profiles, with a pen portrait illustrating each type.

There is also a detailed explanation of the methodology behind ACORN, and, for our long-standing clients, matrices to help convert their old ACORN information into the new types. Visit www.caci. co.uk / ACORN.

PSYCHOGRAPHIC AND BEHAVIOURISTIC SEGMENTATION

Dissatisfaction with demographic criteria alone undoubtedly explains the development of psychographic and behaviouristic approaches. Segmentation by 'social character' or psychographics owes

much to the pioneering work of Riesman et al. (1950) and their three segment divisions of social character:

1. Tradition-directed behaviour – things are done 'as in the past' – i.e. behaviour is easy to predict and use for segmentation purposes.
2. Other-directedness – the individual seeks to conform with the current way of doing things as exhibited in the behaviour of his contemporaries or peer group, i.e. success means blending in with the environment.
3. Inner-directedness – one is indifferent to the behaviour of one's peers and contemporaries – the marketer's bête-noire!

While this fairly basic approach to classification has been subject to considerable criticism, it possesses the considerable benefit for the practitioner that it is simple, it is robust and best of all, it actually works. Thus a study by McCrohan (1980) on automobile purchase showed that other-directed segments bought more prestigious cars to 'fit in' with society while those not concerned to 'fit in' purchased less prestigious cars. While the results are unsurprising in themselves and are intuitively appealing, they are contrary to normal industry practice where size of car is the basic segmentation criterion not prestige. Now one may argue that size is a surrogate for prestige, but in a climate where 'small is beautiful', the outstanding performance of the new mini suggests this 'ain't necessarily so' and points up one of the basic rules of marketing which is that the act of consumption changes the consumer and one must continuously monitor and react to these changes if one is to remain successful.

The measurement of lifestyle (another name for psychographics) has progressed a long way since Riesman et al.'s major contribution and was the subject of a major review article by William D. Wells (1975). In this article Wells proposes an operational definition of psychographic research as 'Qualitative research intended to place consumers on psychological – as distinguished from demographic – dimensions', a definition which emphasises the distinctive features of the area – it has a quantitative rather than a qualitative orientation and goes beyond demographics. (An extensive review of the method is to be found in my basic textbook *Marketing*, 2006).

SEGMENTATION BY SOCIAL CHARACTER

Segmentation by social character usually involves a combination of lifestyle characteristics with psychographic information of the kind mentioned briefly in Chapter 9. As with the other techniques outlined already, the basic objective is to develop a *profile* of the intended customer in order to develop products and communication strategies that will zero in on their specific needs and wants. By exploring buyers' attitudes, beliefs, emotions and values, it is possible to build up a more detailed picture and, as with VALS (the marketing and consulting tool), many organisations have come up with classifications of their own.

For example, the Canadian-based Environics Research Group has more than 20 years' experience measuring, tracking and interpreting the social values/psychographics of new car buyers in Canada, the USA, and around the world. Rather than replace their clients' existing segmentation methods, they seek to add depth to them by analysing the beliefs, attitudes and emotions that trigger the vehicle choices they make. From their studies they have identified up to 105 values that may be associated with the purchase of a particular brand of car and combined these to define buyers according to their shared values and outlook on life, so providing marketing managers with segments that are more actionable because they are readily identifiable in the real world (http://erg.environics.net/automotive_research/05/08/2005).

PROFILING

Recognising that people do not necessarily behave in the same way because they share the same demographics, since the 1950s increasing attention has been given to profiling people in terms of their needs and motivations.

While Maslow's 'hierarchy of human needs' was not put forward as a tool for marketing research, it was soon adopted for this purpose – notably by Ernst Dichter (1960). It was Dichter's success in explaining why consumers frequently behaved in ways that differed significantly from their declared intentions, as revealed by conventional market research, that prompted Vance Packard to publish *The Hidden Persuaders* (1957) which claimed that advertisers and marketers were manipulating the consumers' subconscious to encourage them to buy their wares. Packard identified a number of 'hidden' needs that consumers have, including emotional security, ego gratification, a need to express our creative instincts, and reassurance of our worth. It is these needs that are targeted when advertisers seek to gain attention and build interest.

Following the publication of *The Hidden Persuaders*, motivation research fell into some disrepute, at least overtly, but this did not discourage market researchers from developing other approaches to classifying consumers. In the 1970s, Young and Rubicam proposed a classification of cross-cultural consumer characteristics based on individual aspirations that identified four 'types':

- *Mainstreamers* – seek security in conformity
- *Aspirers* – seek status
- *Succeeders* – concerned with maintaining their position
- *Reformers* – want to make the world a better place.

During the 1980s and 90s, segmentation based on motivation and behaviour became even more detailed, with the identification of niche markets with distinctive acronyms:

- OPALS – older people with active lifestyles
- YUPPIES – young, upwardly mobile professionals
- DINKYS – double income, no kids yet
- WOOPIES – well off older people
- SKI'ers – spending the kids inheritance (based on material from www.trinity.cumbria.sch.uk).

In the new millennium, with new electronic channels of communication, and increased use of direct advertising, even more precise targeting has become possible. The search for unique emotional and behavioural characteristics continues.

One outcome of this is that many marketers now look beyond the idea of target groups to the concept of a 'community' paralleling the transition from value-added product/service to the notion of 'satisfying experience'. Communities define themselves through shared experiences associated with a particular product e.g. Harley-Davidson owners' club, Starbucks coffee etc.

In order to understand the nature of 'satisfying experiences', interest in motivational research has enjoyed a resurgence of interest. One example of this is the Brand Strategy Research (BSR®) model developed by the SmartAgent®Company. The issue addressed is whether it is possible to develop instruments to operationalise the concept of emotion as a basis for segmentation, targeting and positioning:

> BSR® focuses on the individual needs and how these are translated into choices of specific products, brands and actual buying behaviour. Each individual will develop his own strategy in order to satisfy his needs, depending on his general personality and life history. However, in each market we can identify workable segments containing consumers with similar needs and motives. In combination with 'classical' descriptive customer information, motivational segmentation provides a valuable and stable input for target group selection, positioning of brands or products, and developing marketing strategies.

Thus the BSR model seeks to penetrate the demographic, behavioural and attitudinal layer to reach the motivational layer and the influences that have most impact on human beings: beliefs, values and fears. Only by digging deeper beyond the attitudinal layer concerned with lifestyles, loyalty and concepts is it possible to identify what finally determines consumer preference and behaviour.

> The BSR® framework consists of a strategic map, constructed by the three dimensions of the social sciences:

> - Sociological (ego versus group)
> - Psychological (introvert versus extrovert)
> - Anthropological (normative versus a-normative)

> In each study the 'sociological' axis is found to be the most important and explanatory dimension … Depending on the market, the second axis represents either the 'psychological' dimension … or the 'normative' dimension.

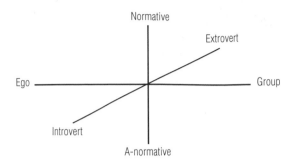

To position an individual on the map, they are required to respond to about 140 key words that cause emotional reactions. Words have been found more effective than statements or questions, as the latter 'cloud' basic emotional reactions by prompting rational feelings. By plotting answers on a two-dimensional matrix – ego – group and one of the other two dimensions, people can be assigned to one or other of four quadrants:

Extrovert

VITAL	HARMONY
CONTROL	PROTECTION

Introvert

The defining characteristics of each group are summarised in the diagram. Each group has similar demographic/income attributes but responds differently to communications, products and services. The application of the technique is illustrated by reference to the market for houses. (www.smartagent.nl/download/definetief%20Moscow%20en%20basis.pdf)

The final category we distinguished earlier is behaviouristic under which Kotler lists such variables as purchase occasion, benefits sought, user status, usage rate, loyalty status, readiness stage and marketing factor sensitivity. Most of these variables are self-evident and in any case are described more than adequately in most textbooks. However, two – usage and benefit – deserve some further explanation here.

USAGE SEGMENTATION

The application of Pareto's law, that a small proportion of all the observations related to a phenomenon contain the majority of the information about it – the so-called 80–20 principle – has wide application in marketing. Nowhere is this more so than in the case of usage patterns for products and services where it is commonly referred to as the theory of the 'heavy half'.

The relevance of this theory to the practice of market segmentation was encapsulated in an article by Dik Warren Twedt, first published in 1964, which has become a marketing classic in its own right. Given this status it seems more appropriate to reproduce the opening paragraphs rather than summarise them:

It's certainly no news that some people buy more gasoline, drink more bourbon, use more paper napkins, eat more candy, chew more gum and even use their credit cards more than other people. But what was news to us, when we began comparing purchase concentration for many different categories of products and services, was the extreme skewness, and the marked similarity of slope, of all these curves [see Figure 12.4]. Incidentally, the following discussion is limited to relatively mature product categories – it seems unlikely that the same rules would hold for new products.

One first step in the analysis was to eliminate the non-purchasers. Arraying the purchasers by amount consumed, and cumulating the percentage of total

volume accounted for by purchasing deciles, it became apparent that for a very wide range of products 'the heavy half' of purchasers – those above the median of usage – account for 80% to 90% of total volume [see Figure 12.4]. This relationship appears so consistently that it may be more appropriate to think of it as a marketing law rather than a theory to be proved.

The evidence for the next five propositions is not quite so well established as the heavy-half relationship, simply because the detailed analyses have not yet been made on all the product categories studied. They are, however, sufficiently well-founded so that I urge each of you to apply the theory to those product categories in which you are most interested. The five propositions are these:

1. In general, demographic characteristics (age, education, income, race, etc.) are such poor predictors of heavy usage that it is usually much more efficient to measure consumption directly, and then cross-tabulate by measures of consumer preference or by advertising vehicle exposure.
2. Heavy usage of different product categories is relatively independent – the fact that a household uses a lot of aluminium foil tells us nothing about how much canned dog food the family will buy. In

TABLE 12.2 Purchase concentration deciles

	% buying	10	20	30	40	50	60	70	80	90	100
Concentrated fruit juice	72	39	58	72	82	89	94	97	99	99	100
Beer (Dec)	33	42	62	74	82	88	92	95	97	99	100
Margarine	89	31	50	64	75	83	90	94	97	99	100
Dog food	31	34	55	69	80	88	93	97	99	99	100
Cake mixes	75	32	52	67	77	85	90	94	97	99	100
Hair tonics	48	42	60	72	81	87	91	95	98	99	100
RTE cereals	96	36	57	70	80	87	92	96	98	99	100
Soaps and detergents	98	28	46	61	72	81	88	93	97	99	100
Toilet tissue	98	24	40	53	64	74	82	89	94	98	100
Canned hash	32	40	58	70	79	86	90	94	96	98	100
Cola beverages (May–Aug)	78	44	65	77	84	90	93	96	98	99	100
Lemon-lime	58	56	72	81	86	91	94	96	98	99	100
Hair fixatives	46	52	68	76	83	88	92	95	98	99	100
Shampoo	82	32	50	63	73	81	87	92	96	98	100
Bourbon	41	48	66	76	84	89	91	92	95	98	100

SOURCE: *Chicago Tribune* Consumer Panel, special analyses of 1962 data

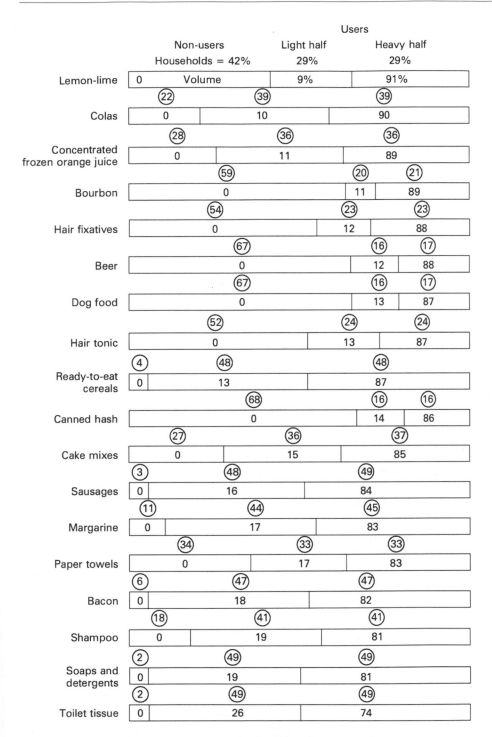

FIGURE 12.4 Annual purchase concentration in 18 product categories

SOURCE: Twedt, D. W. (1964) How important to marketing strategy is the 'heavy user'?, *Journal of Marketing* (January)

a study completed last month, intercorrelations of 26 product categories by heavy-half usage were all quite low. The highest relationship was found between bacon and wieners, but even here the phi coefficient was only 37. These low relationships are not surprising when we remember that the more we spend for one product category, the less we have to spend for others.

3. Among the heavy users, there seems to be less, rather than more, brand loyalty. Not only do they buy more – they buy more often, and they buy more different brands.

4. The heavy users are not price buyers. They pay as much, or even a bit more, for a unit of purchase, than do the light users.

5. Although there are changes in consumption patterns as the family's position in the life-cycle advances, these changes are usually not so abrupt or so pronounced as to impair the utility of direct consumption measures

In the period since this article was published, there has emerged considerable evidence to support Twedt's five propositions and little to refute them, and usage segmentation must be regarded as a robust method, particularly in mature and established markets.

It should be recognised that in such markets, defending one's existing market share depends on increasing and sustaining brand loyalty, while opportunities for growth or market penetration consist of encouraging light users to use more, and trying to convert non-users to users. In all cases, being able to identify consumers in terms of their usage pattern and then classify them in terms of other relevant segmentation criteria is vital when developing an effective strategy. Data gathered at the supermarket checkout is particularly valuable in achieving this.

BENEFIT SEGMENTATION

Much the same status as attaches to Twedt's work is also accorded to the seminal contribution of Russell I. Haley 'Benefit segmentation: a decision-oriented research tool'. Writing in 1968, Haley identified three segmentation approaches that enjoyed widespread support – geographic, demographic and volume or heavy half – but went on to propose that in and of themselves none of these was sufficiently selective. Specifically, Haley pointed out that while heavy consumers are the most valuable segment, they are not 'usually available to the same brand – because they are not all seeking the same kind of benefits from a product'.

In addition, Haley pointed out that all three extant approaches to segmentation were handicapped because:

All are based on an ex-post facto analysis of the kinds of people who make up various segments of a market. They rely on descriptive factors rather than causal factors. For this reason they are not efficient predictors of future buying behaviour, and it is future buying behaviour that is of central interest to marketers.

To overcome this deficiency, Haley argued that one should seek to establish the benefits which consumers are looking for in a product as these determine their behaviour much more accurately than do demographics or volume of consumption. In his words:

The benefit segmentation approach is based upon being able to measure consumer value systems in detail, together with what the consumer thinks about various brands in the product category of interest. While this concept seems simple enough, operationally it is very complex. There is no simple straightforward way of handling the volumes of data that have to be generated. Computers and sophisticated multivariate attitude measurement techniques are a necessity.

Several such techniques have been described in the preceding pages, but it will be helpful to reproduce Haley's segmentation of the toothpaste market to exemplify the potential output from a study following this approach (Table 12.3).

Given such an analysis, the marketer is in a much better position to develop the most effective mix in terms of pricing, product development, packaging, distribution, copy platform, media selection and so on. Indeed, such studies frequently identify gaps or niches in the marketplace and allow the producer to develop both a new product and a new strategy.

A useful summary of product benefits for which a consumer might pay is reproduced as Table 12.4.

TABLE 12.3 Toothpaste market segment description

Segment name:	The sensory segment	The sociables	The worriers	The independent segment
Principal benefit sought	Flavour, product appearance	Brightness of teeth	Decay prevention	Price
Demographic strengths	Children	Teens, young people	Large families	Men
Special behavioural characteristics	Users of spearmint-flavoured toothpaste	Smokers	Heavy users	Heavy users
Brands disproportionately favoured	Colgate, Stripe	Macleans, Plus White, Ultra Brite	Crest	Brands on sale
Personality characteristics	High self-involvement	High sociability	High hypochondriasis	High autonomy
Lifestyle characteristics	Hedonistic	Active	Conservative	Value orientated

SOURCE: Haley, R. I. (1968) Benefit segmentation: a decision-oriented research tool, *Journal of Marketing*, **32**(July)

TABLE 12.4 A summary of product benefits

1. Perceived objective performance rendered by the physical aspects of the product
2. Perceived social benefits represented by the consumption, use, or mere possession of the product
3. Psychological benefits derived from an association of the product with otherwise irrelevant attributes (for example virility, maturity)
4. Objective benefits confirmed by the location, manner and timing of purchase availability
5. Subjective satisfactions derived from the purchase location and manner of sale
6. Instructional, informational and technical services furnished by the seller in promoting the product
7. The assurance of dependability and quality imparted by brand or source
8. An assortment benefit, in the sense of variety of merchandise available or preferred

SOURCE: Wasson, C. R. et al. (1968) *Competition and Human Behaviour.* New York: Appleton-Century-Crofts, pp. 12–13 (cited in Stern, L. W. and Grabner, Jr, J. R. (1970) *Competition in the Market Place.* Glenview, IL: Scott, Foresman)

Box 12.2   *Marketing malpractices: the cause and the cure*

In an article with the above title in the *Harvard Business Review* (2005), Christensen et al. state:

Thirty thousand new consumer products are launched each year. But over 90% of them fail – and that's after marketing professionals have spent massive amounts of money trying to understand what their customers want.

In the authors' view, products fail because marketers are not applying fundamental ideas about market segmentation, brand-building and understanding customers. In the case of market segmentation, marketers appear to lose sight of the fact that customers buy a product because they need to get something done. To illustrate their point, they cite Levitt's observation 'A man goes into a hardware store to buy a ¼ inch drill – he needs a ¼ inch hole.' If the need doesn't exist, then neither does the market. As a result of ignoring this aphorism, much market segmentation solves the wrong problem 'improving products in ways that are irrelevant to their customers needs'.

'With few exceptions, every job people need or want to do has a social, a functional, and emotional dimension.' It follows that it is necessary to understand all three dimensions if one is to design a successful product.

It is also important to recognise that some products can do many jobs and Arm & Hammer Baking Soda is cited as a classic example. Originally used only for baking you can now buy:

- Arm & Hammer Complete Care Toothpaste
- Arm & Hammer Fridge-n-Freezer Baking Soda
- Arm & Hammer Ultra Max Deodorant
- Arm & Hammer Vacuum-Free Carpet Deodoriser

- Arm & Hammer Super Scoop Cat Litter
- Arm & Hammer Laundry Detergent.

Each of these is a 'purpose brand' that does a specific job and together they now account for 90% of consumer revenues.

It is argued that strong brands start with one product doing one job and that the name can then be applied to many products doing one job like the Sony Walkman. Alternatively, the purpose brand may evolve into an 'endorser brand' that can be used to develop new purpose brands, i.e. one brand, many jobs, such as Marriot and Holiday Inns which offer different types of hotel catering for quite different segments. In every case, however, a brand must be associated with a product that means something to the customers if it is to be successful: 'Focusing a product and its brand on a job creates differentiation'.

SEGMENTING INDUSTRIAL (BUSINESS-TO-BUSINESS) MARKETS

Although it is a recurring theme of this book that strategically marketing is marketing and the distinction of variants (consumer, industrial, service, not-for-profit, social, etc.) is counterproductive, it is also acknowledged that in the particular and at the tactical level one must be sensitive to situation-specific factors which underlie the wish to regard bank marketing as different from consumer goods marketing and so on. Clearly, the selection of a segmentation method is an area where tactical considerations are paramount and it might be helpful to indicate some of the factors which need to be taken into account when segmenting industrial markets to point up the similarities and differences with consumer markets.

While Choffray and Lilien (1978) claim that 'most segmentation analysis has been aimed mainly at consumer markets', there is ample evidence that industrial marketers have long used a variety of techniques to help them subdivide markets into meaningful segments. Thus the standard industrial classification (SIC) (now known as the NTIC) in the USA provides a closely defined methodology for specifying an organisation's type of activity in broad terms (2-digit code, e.g. 23 = apparel), in precise terms (3-digit code, e.g. 232 = men's, youths' and boys' furnishings etc.), and pinpoint terms (4-digit codes, e.g. 2322 = underwear). Although 4-digit codes are not available for every industry in every geographical location, SIC provides an excellent first cut at dividing up a market into meaningful subgroups.

Current thinking on industrial market segmentation is summarised well in an article by Cardozo (1980) in which he identifies four dimensions which may be used separately or in combination to classify organisational buying situations:

1. *Familiarity with the buying task:* this dimension is based upon the work of Robinson et al. (1967) in which they identify three different types of buying task – new task, modified rebuy and straight rebuy. Clearly each of these situations will call for a different approach to segmentation.
2. *Product type:* in this case one could segment on the basis of product use in terms of components, material and equipment required which, in turn, may be related to the 'degree of standardisation':
   - Custom – a unique design for a particular customer
   - Modular – a unique combination of standard components or materials
   - Standard – a combination of ingredients that has been offered previously.
3. *Importance of the purchase* to the buying organisation.
4. *Type of uncertainty* in the purchase situation.

The latter two factors are of special interest because they reflect the fact that buyers do try and segment the set of potential suppliers by developing criteria on which to assess them and setting up formal vendor rating schemes. Johnson and Flodhammer (1980) support the view that understanding the buyers' needs is as important in industrial as consumer markets when they assert 'Unless there is knowledge of the industrial users' needs the manufactured product usually has the lowest common denominator – price. Quality and service are unknown quantities.'

Key account management

A recent article by Wengler et al. (2006) in *Industrial Marketing Management* reported a survey of German sales engineers to determine the nature and extent of key account management (KAM) practices, factors influencing the decision to implement KAM, and what is involved in implementing the process. Prior to this study by Wengler et al., the last reported empirical study of the status of KAM was by Conlon et al. in 1997.

KAM is a well-established concept in marketing management that originated in the USA during the 1970s and early 1980s, and is

perceived as a supplier's relationship marketing program focusing on a single customer. Its implementation is the result of a strategic marketing management decision with considerable internal organisational consequences.

Based on a questionnaire mailed to 550 participants, 91 usable replies were received indicating that 54% had a KAM program, 30% were planning to set one up and 16% had no plans to do so. Of the reasons given for implementing KAM, the most important was an increase in the customer orientation of the supplier (over 80%), followed by increasing internationalisation of customers (approx. 75%). Next, in descending order of importance, were: hope to improve internal coordination (40%), customer segmentation (35%), increasing customer requirements (32%) and customer induced relationship intensity (29%).

WHEN TO SEGMENT

In the preceding pages we have considered several important aspects of market segmentation without addressing directly the key question of under what circumstances a segment will merit the development of a differentiated marketing strategy and mix. Frank et al. (1972) propose eight criteria for determining whether there is a prima facie case for segmentation, namely:

1. *Size* – is the segment, actual or potential, of sufficient size to justify the development of a differentiated marketing strategy?
2. *Incremental cost* – what additional costs will be incurred in seeking to satisfy a particular segment and will these be recovered with additional profit over that which could be anticipated if the market were not segmented in the first place?
3. *Size of intersegment differences* – the greater these are the more the justification for segmentation and for treating the segments as separate markets.
4. *Durability of differences* – the longer lasting the differences between segments the greater the justification for distinguishing them. A particular case which runs counter to this point is that

of new products where one may invest considerable effort to identify innovators and seek to reach them with a distinctive strategy in the knowledge that if the product is successful the segment will, by definition, be eliminated.
5. *Cyclical volatility* – the more stable a segment the better.
6. *Compatibility with other segments* – should seek to define segments which are mutually reinforcing rather than in opposition to one another, i.e. one must be careful not to 'cannibalise' one's own markets.
7. *Degree of 'fit'* – the company should seek to build upon its strengths.
8. *Degree of competition* – the best segments are those in which there is an absence of direct competition, i.e. one should seek to serve a gap in the market rather than select segments in which there are several existing contenders.

Assessment of these criteria comprise the first step in the four-stage procedure recommended by Worcester and Downham (1978), which may be summarised as:

- First stage: background clarification.
- Second stage: qualitative exploration. 'Having identified the main behavioural patterns in the

market, it is then important to explore the various factors determining or influencing these patterns.'

- Third stage: developing measuring instruments. Segments are defined according to a base or basis, and further description of target segments is included in terms of other variables or descriptors.
- Fourth stage: developing effective marketing programmes.

It is worth noting that many critics of segmentation who claim that it is all very well in theory but not very effective in practice, fall into the trap of paying insufficient attention to the first two stages.

As Young et al. (1978) comment:

Unfortunately the results of these [segmentation] studies often have been disappointing because the segments derived from the study have not been actionable from a marketing standpoint. A common reason for this lack of applicability is preoccupation with the techniques and method of segmentation such as whether to use generic benefits, problems, lifestyles, psychographics, or preferences and the type of factor or cluster analysis to be performed. In too many instances, marketing researchers have failed to analyse the marketing environment and competitive structure before applying their favourite methodological approach [cf. Hooley].

According to Young et al. there are many situations where a segmented approach is not even useful and the market should be analysed in its entirety. Specific examples are:

1. The market is so small that marketing to a portion of it is not profitable.
2. Heavy users make up such a large proportion of the sales volume that they are the only relevant target.
3. The brand's the dominant brand in the market.

Young et al. (1978) then provide three case histories to show how a successful segmentation study should be executed and the first of these is reproduced in the box below, both as an example of how to conduct and use a segmentation analysis and also of the technical jargon which is so off-putting for most managers.

BARRIERS TO SEGMENTATION

While the benefits of market segmentation and its use in strategic marketing planning are well known, less attention has been given to the barriers that firms may encounter in seeking to implement a segmentation strategy. These issues were the subject of an article in *The Marketing Review* (2005) by Sally Dibb, a leading UK authority on the subject.

Such research as has been undertaken into implementation is seen by Dibb as 'reactive', i.e. you encounter a problem and then seek to solve it. Her view is that one should be more proactive and pre-identify the barriers so that one can develop strategies to avoid or overcome them.

To begin with, Dibb identifies barriers described in the marketing literature and classifies these into two categories:

1. *Hard* – more tangible issues related to data, financial, personnel and time resources.
2. *Soft* – intangible issues linked to corporate culture, interfunctional coordination and leadership style.

In practice, the segmentation process may be impeded during planning (infrastructure), while segmenting (process), and when implementing (implementation). The nature of the barriers is summarised in Table 12.5 which may be used as a checklist when devising a market segmentation initiative. The application of the checklist is explained and illustrated in the article.

TABLE 12.5 Infrastructure, process and implementation barriers

Infrastructure

Hard 'Resource-Based' Issues

DATA:

Poor data availability

No Marketing Information System (MIS) in place

EXPERTISE:

Lack of general marketing expertise

Small or no marketing function

Low level of segmentation knowledge

RESOURCE ALLOCATION:

No financial or personnel provision for data collection and/or segmentation analysis

Few resources devoted to strategic thinking

Soft 'Culture/Structural' Issues

CULTURE:

No culture of data collection

Company inflexible and resistant to new ideas

Lack of customer focus

STRUCTURAL:

Inadequate senior management involvement or buy-in to marketing initiatives

Weak channels of inter/intra-functional communication

Process

Hard 'Resource-Based' Issues

DATA:

Poor data availability for identifying segmentation bases

No suitable software capability

EXPERTISE:

Lack of suitably skilled marketing personnel

Poor understanding/misuse of the basic segmentation process

Poor appreciation of fit with corporate strategic planning

Low level of analytical marketing skills

RESOURCE ALLOCATION:

Inadequate budget for undertaking required data collection and/or analysis

Dearth of personnel devoted to the segmentation process

Insufficient time devoted to the process

Soft 'Culture/Structural' Issues

CULTURE:

Poor commitment to sharing of data and ideas

Inadequate inter-functional/site buy-in

Weak leadership

STRUCTURAL:

Inadequate senior management involvement or buy-in to marketing initiatives

Weak channels of inter/intra-functional communication

Implementation

Hard 'Resource-Based' Issues

DATA:

Poor data availability for measuring performance

EXPERTISE:

Insufficient conviction or skills to operationalise the segmentation scheme

Poor fit between tactical marketing programmes and segment solution

No expertise in planning for implementation

RESOURCE ALLOCATION:

Inadequate or poor alignment of budgeting/resourcing for implementation

Insufficient time allowed to roll out the segment solution

Soft 'Culture/Structural' Issues

CULTURE:

Ineffective internal/external communication of segment solution

Product focus rather than customer focus in the distribution system

STRUCTURAL:

Inadequate senior managerial involvement in segment roll-out

Unclear demarcation of responsibility for implementation

Resistance to modifying organisational culture/structure/distribution

Resistance by senior personnel to modify their remit

Distribution system inflexible to change

SOURCE: Dibb, S. (2005) Market segmentation implementation barriers and how to overcome them, *The Marketing Review*, 5(1): 13–30.

Box 12.4 *Segmentation on generic benefits*

The Canadian Government Office of Tourism decided to conduct a marketing segmentation study of the US travel market to obtain a comprehensive picture of Americans who are potential vacation travellers to Canada. Because Canada is a large, diverse country with many different aspects, it truly can be many things to many people. Therefore, a segmentation approach was deemed desirable to ascertain the different groups of potential vacation travellers to Canada and which aspects of Canadian vacations could address their needs and desires. Once the segments had been identified and described, they could be evaluated in terms of the Canadian vacation business potential they offered, and those segments deemed attractive enough to cultivate then could be addressed through advertising and promotion campaigns portraying the advantages for a Canadian vacation of the specific type desired by the target segment(s).

However, because of the complexity of the travel and vacation business, certain conceptual problems and issues had to be resolved in planning and executing the study.

Though most segmentation studies will not be as complicated as this one, it demonstrates the process the researcher must follow to resolve three critical issues before designing the questionnaire and fielding the study: (1) who should be interviewed, (2) the frame of reference for questioning and (3) alternative methods of segmentation.

Who should be interviewed? This critical consideration must be addressed in all studies.

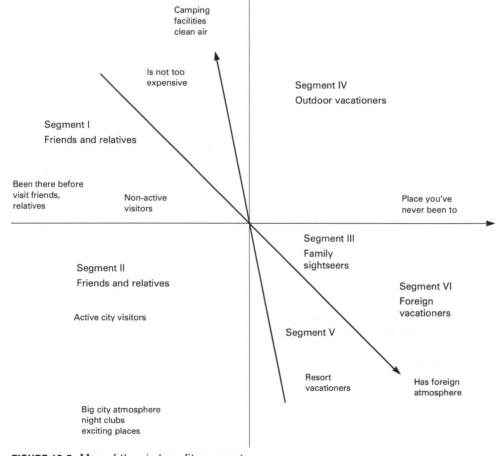

FIGURE 12.5 Map of the six benefit segments

Because the purpose of the travel study was to expand the number of Canadian vacations taken by US travellers, it was insufficient to include only those persons who had been to Canada because they accounted for only 5% of the US population. Instead, it was necessary to define relevant prospect groups to obtain new visitors to Canada.

Consideration of the profitability of various types of tourists to Canada dictated a decision to interview only those who had taken a vacation of at least a week's duration in the past, and the vacation decision-maker was the specific person to be questioned. Furthermore, the key analytical decision was dictated by the knowledge that the distance people have travelled on past vacations is a strong indicator of how far they would be willing to travel on future vacations. Therefore, the sample was designed to cover only those persons who had travelled the requisite distance for a Canadian vacation – defined in the study as three quarters of the distance to Canada.

Frame of reference for questioning. This factor was a particularly difficult problem for this study because most individuals were potential prospects for more than one type of vacation. To question about vacations in general was not relevant as needs and desires would vary by type of vacation. Also, asking about the ideal vacation would likely yield fantasised wishes that would have no relationship to the type of vacation a person would or could take. This problem was overcome by asking the respon-

dent to anchor all responses in terms of the last vacation taken. In this way, responses were based on the reality of a specific vacation experience for which behavioural and attitudinal information were obtained.

Alternative methods of market segmentation. As in most segmentation studies, this was the most critical issue. Because the best way to segment or group US travellers for developing marketing programmes was far from obvious, the following alternative methods were investigated.

1. By segmenting consumers on favourability toward Canada as a vacation area, US travellers could be grouped on the basis of their attitudes toward Canada. This approach could be most appropriate if Canada were a single entity and if attitudes toward vacationing in Canada were polarised. However, these possibilities did not appear to represent reality.
2. By segmenting on geographic area, or proximity to selected areas of Canada, respondents would be assigned by their US locality. This approach would be reasonable as an independent segmentation alternative if travellers' vacation behaviour and desires varied dramatically by region in the US, but they do not.
3. By segmenting consumers on desires sought in their last vacation, respondents could be segmented on what they were seeking in a vacation of the last type taken.

A pilot study consisting of 200 interviews was developed to test

the meaningfulness of each approach. The last approach (desires sought in the last vacation) was found to be most meaningful in terms of marketing and was the approach used in the major study.

Results
The major study consisted of 1,750 interviews with eligible respondents, i.e., those responsible for making a decision about an extended vacation of at least three-fourths the distance to Canada during the last three years. A national probability sample was used with one callback on the household and one on the eligible respondent.

A benefit segmentation was obtained for those desires sought in planning the most recent vacation meeting the eligibility criteria. The technique of segmentation was a Q-factor analysis. This approach consists of normalising the profile of the respondents across all benefits to obtain groups of homogeneous respondents through principal components extraction of eigenvalues and their associated eigenvectors, which subsequently are rotated by the varimax procedure [2–4, 8, 9, 12]. To facilitate the analysis and description of the marketing segments, a perceptual map derived by the multiple discriminant analysis technique is shown in Figure 12.5 [4, 10, 11].

The discriminant analysis was performed by a stepwise computer program to select those benefit items that can best predict group membership [5]. After the items had been selected, their relationship to the Q groups was shown in a two-dimensional space. The procedure was [10, 11]: (1) the eigenvalues and their associated canonical coefficients were computed through the principal components method for those variables that were selected as the best discriminators, (2) each individual then was scored on his first two canonical dimensions and the group means were computed, (3) the canonical scores were correlated with the original items which were plotted as vectors in two-dimensional space to show the relationship of the benefit items to each group.

Segment I. Friends and relatives – nonactive visitor (29%). These vacationers seek familiar surroundings where they can visit friends and relatives. They are not very inclined to participate in any activity.

Segment II. Friends and relatives – active city visitor (12%). These vacationers also seek familiar surroundings where they can visit friends and relatives, but they are more inclined to participate in activities – especially sightseeing, shopping, and cultural and other entertainment.

Segment III. Family sightseers (6%). These vacationers are looking for a new vacation place which would be a treat for the children and an enriching experience.

Segment IV. Outdoor vacationer (19%). These vacationers seek clean air, rest and quiet, and beautiful scenery. Many are campers and availability of recreation facilities is important. Children are also an important factor.

Segment V. Resort vacationer (19%). These vacationers are most interested in water-sports (e.g. swimming) and good weather. They prefer a popular place with a big-city atmosphere.

Segment VI. Foreign vacationer (26%). These vacationers look for vacations in a place they have never been before with a foreign atmosphere and beautiful scenery. Money is not of major concern but good accommodation and service are. They want an exciting, enriching experience.

Because of their relatively low vacation expenditures, segments I and II offered less attractive business potential than was offered by the other segments. Moreover, Canadian vacations could not provide an opportunity to visit with friends and relatives.

The other segments had vacation needs and desires that could be delivered by various areas of Canada through different types of vacations. For each of these segments, data from the questionnaire were used to determine a profile in terms of behaviour, psychographics, travel incentives, and image of a Canadian vacation.

Implementation

Unlike a commercial firm, the Canadian Office of Tourism had special problems in implementing the results of the study. It had to rely on an extensive program to inform the many elements of the travel industry of the study findings through meetings, seminars, and publications. As a result of these efforts, improvements were made in the following areas.

1. *Advertising execution.* The tonality or style of the advertising was made more compatible with the personality traits and lifestyles of the target groups. Creatively, the advertising message stressed the specific benefits sought by each segment, reinforced the positive images of Canada that each group already had, and corrected any undesirable impressions they may have held.

2. *Media considerations.* The study facilitated the selection of vehicles compatible with the lifestyle, demographic features, and personality of target groups. The study was not designed to measure individual media habits, but the results allowed a closer look at the media available and comparison of editorial environment of US consumer magazines with the unique audience profiles and desires for each segment. Television commercials were changed in mood, tempo, and emphasis to attract travellers in the most promising segment.

3. *Merchandising and promotional efforts.* Promotional brochures and specific types of vacation 'tours' or packages were developed along the lines suggested by the findings.

4. *Provincial tourist offices.* The results were passed on to the provinces so they could

adopt a segmented promotional effort, and to those areas that could deliver the benefits sought by one or more of the target groups.

In addition to providing marketing guidance, the study findings were useful in the planning of new hotels, accommodation, and tourist facilities by the

Canadian government and private groups (an updated version of this study with a larger sample can be found at: www.tourism.gov.on.ca).

SOURCE: Young et al. (1978) Some practical considerations in market segmentation, *Journal of Marketing Research*, 15(August): 405–12

Finally, in his review, Wind (1978) addresses the issues of translating segmentation findings into strategy and a quotation from this will provide a useful bridge between the broadly based issues which have been the subject of this and previous chapters and Chapter 13 in which we turn to look at the specific case of positioning. Wind observes:

> The most difficult aspect of any segmentation project is the translation of the study results into marketing strategy. No rules can be offered to assure a successful translation and, in fact, little is known (in the published literature) on how this translation occurs.

Informal discussions with and observation of 'successful' and 'unsuccessful' translations suggest a few generalisable conclusions aside from the obvious ones such as:

1. Involving all the relevant users (e.g. product managers, new product developers, advertising personnel, etc.) in the problem definition, research design, and data interpretation stages.
2. Viewing segmentation data as one input to a total marketing information system and combining them with sales and other relevant data.
3. Using the segmentation data on a continuous basis. The reported study results should be

viewed only as the beginning of a utilisation programme.

Finally, and as a postscript to a chapter which has largely advocated the merits of differentiated or concentrated marketing strategies through the use of segmentation techniques, we should not lose sight of the fact that many firms still prefer to pursue an undifferentiated approach. A classic example of this is provided by the world-famous Finnish textile firm Marimekko whose marketing policy is expressed as follows:

> We make things for ourselves and sell them to people who think like us.
>
> This is only slightly exaggerated. People are behind every stage in production at Marimekko and the users are also people.
>
> The Marimekko story would indeed have been short had there not been sufficient customers thinking like us. Thank goodness there were and in such abundance that Marimekko can build its future around a steady growth.
>
> Marimekko is no colossus able to penetrate the consciousness of people around the world through a massive advertising campaign. It has been compelled to build its marketing around its products and place its faith in them.

Chapter summary

In this chapter we started by considering the definition of product markets and then the basic differences between product differentiation and market segmentation as competitive strategies. Essentially the difference resides in the fact that product differentiation originates with the producer while market segmentation has its origins in the marketplace. Product differentiation thus

reflects the producer's perception of variations in the product which will appeal to different subgroups of consumers. By contrast, market segmentation starts from the observation that different subgroups or segments of a market exhibit different consumption preferences and then seeks to develop products or services which will match the needs of these segments.

In order to segment markets (the demand for specific products) one needs an appropriate indicator(s). Accordingly, we reviewed a number of different bases for segmentation and the contexts in which each would be appropriate. Four basic procedures – a priori, clustering, flexible and componential – were discussed and some of the available techniques outlined with a particular emphasis upon cluster analysis.

The characteristics of a viable segment were defined – it must be measurable, accessible, substantial, unique and stable in its response – as were the major segmentation methods. Each of the latter – demographic, geographic, psychographic and behaviouristic – was then reviewed to demonstrate its application in practice while two approaches – usage and benefit segmentation – were described in some detail.

Of course, it is not always appropriate to segment a market and Chapter 12 concluded with a discussion of the circumstances under which a segment will merit the development of a differentiated market-ing strategy. A case history conducted by the Canadian Government Office of Tourism of the US travel market exemplifies and reinforces the points made.

In Chapter 13, Positioning and Branding, we take a closer look at how firms seek to compete with one another within market segments.

Recommended reading

Evans, M. (2003) Market segment-ation, in Baker, M. J. (ed.) *The Marketing Book* (5th edn). Oxford: Butterworth Heinemann.

Hooley, G. J., Saunders, J. A. and

Piercy, N. F. (2003) *Marketing Strategy and Competitive Positioning* (3rd edn). London: Prentice Hall Europe.

Wind, Y. (1999) Market segment-

ation, in Baker, M. J. (ed.) *Encyclopedia of Marketing*. London: International Thomson Business Press.

REFERENCES

Baker, M. J. (2006) *Marketing* (7th edn) Helensburgh: Westburn.

Ball, G. H. (1971) *Classification Analysis*. Stanford, CA: Stanford Research Institute.

Bliss, M. (1980) Market Segmentation and Environmental Analysis, unpublished M.Sc thesis, University of Strathclyde.

Cardozo, R. N. (1980) Situational segmentation of industrial markets, *European Journal of Marketing*, **14**(5/6): 264–76.

Chamberlin, E. J. (1933) *The Theory of Monopolistic Competition*. Cambridge, MA: Harvard University Press.

Choffray, J. and Lilien, G. L. (1978) A new approach to industrial market segmentation, *Sloan Management Review*, **19**(3): 17–29.

Christensen, C. M., Cook, S. and Hall, T. (2005) Marketing malpractices: the cause and the cure, *Harvard Business Review* (December).

Clark, E. (1982) Acorn finds new friends, *Marketing* (16 December).

Colon, G., Napolitano, L. and Pusateri, M. A. (1997) *Unlocking Profits: The Strategic Advantage of Key Account Management*, National Account Management Association.

Day, G. S., Shocker, A. D. and Srivastava, R. K. (1979) Customer oriented approaches to identifying product boundaries, *Journal of Marketing*, **43**(4): 8–19.

Dibb, S. (2005) Market segmentation implementation barriers and how to overcome them, *The Marketing Review*, **5**(1): 13–30.

Dichter, E. (1960) *The Strategy of Desire*. New York: Doubleday.

Enis, B. M. (1977) *Marketing Principles* (3rd edn). Santa Monica, CA: Goodyear.

Everitt, B. (1974) *Cluster Analysis*. London: Heinemann.

Frank, R. R., Massey, R. and Wind, Y. (1972) *Market Segmentation*. Englewood Cliffs, NJ: Prentice Hall.

Green, P. E., Carroll, J. D. and Carmone, F. J. (1977) Design consideration in attitude measurement, in Wind, Y. and Greenberg, M. (eds) *Moving Ahead with Attitude Research*. Chicago, IL: American Management Association, pp. 9–18.

Haley, R. I. (1968) Benefit segmentation: a decision-oriented research tool, *Journal of Marketing*, **32**(July): 30–5.

Hooley, G. J. (1980) The multivariate jungle: the academic's playground but the manager's mine-field, *European Journal of Marketing*, **14**(7): 379–86.

Johnson, H. G. and Flodhammer, A. (1980) Industrial customer segmentation, *Industrial Marketing Management*, July: 201–5.

Lunn, J. A. (1974) Consumer decision process models, in Sheth, J. N. *Models of Buyer Behaviour*. New York: Harper & Row, pp. 34–69.

McCrohan, K. F. (1980) An application of the social character construct in market segmentation, *Journal of the Market Research Society*, **22**(4): 263–7.

Packard, V. (1957) *The Hidden Persuaders*. Harmondsworth: Penguin Books.

Resnik, A. J., Turney, P. B. B. and Mason, J. B. (1979) Marketers turn to counter segmentation, *Harvard Business Review* (September–October): 100–6.

Riesman, D., Glazer, N. and Dinny, R. (1950) *The Lonely Crowd*. New Haven, CT: Yale University Press.

Robinson, J. (1933) *The Economics of Imperfect Competition*. London: Macmillan – now Palgrave Macmillan.

Robinson, P., Faris, C. and Wind, Y. (1967) *Industrial Buying and Creative Marketing*. Boston, MA: Allyn & Bacon.

Smith, W. (1956) Product differentiation and market segmentation as alternative marketing strategies, *Journal of Marketing*, **21**(July): 3–8.

Thomas, M. (1980) Market segmentation, *Quarterly Review of Marketing*, **6**(1): 28.

Twedt, D. W. (1964) How important to marketing strategy is the 'heavy user'?, *Journal of Marketing* (January).

Wasson, C. R., Sturdivant, F. D. and McConaughy, D. H. (1968) *Competition and Human Behaviour*. New York: Appleton-Century-Crofts, pp. 12–13 (cited in Stern, L. W. and Grabner, Jr, J. R. (1970) *Competition in the Market Place*. Glenview, IL: Scott, Foresman).

Wells, W. D. (1975) Psychographics: a critical review, *Journal of Marketing Research*, **12**.

Wengler, S., Ehret, M. and Saab, S. (2006) Implementation of key account management: who, why, and how? An exploratory study on the current implementation of key account management programs, *Industrial Marketing Management*, **35**(1): 103–12 .

Wind, Y. (1978) Issues and advances in segmentation research, *Journal of Marketing Research*, **15**(August): 317–37.

Worcester, R. M. and Downham, J. (eds) (1978) *Consumer Market Research Handbook* (2nd edn). New York: Reinhold.

Young, S., Ott, L. and Feigin, B. (1978) Some practical considerations in market segmentation, *Journal of Marketing Research*, **15**(August): 405–12.

NOTE

1   The discussion in this section draws heavily on Everitt (1974).

CHAPTER 13

Positioning and branding

Positioning is an organised system for finding windows in the mind. It is based on the concept that communication can only take place at the right time and under the right circumstances.

AL RIES AND JACK TROUT

After reading Chapter 13 you will be able to:

✔ Define and describe key concepts such as:
- Positioning
- Branding
- Perceptual mapping
- Niche marketing
- Augmented product.

✔ Explain the importance of these factors in developing a sustainable competitive advantage.

✔ Spell out what is involved in developing successful brands.

✔ Understand why the rapid erosion of objective advantages has led to increased emphasis upon less tangible and subjective benefits.

✔ Discuss the trend towards marketing companies as brands and the factors likely to reinforce this development.

INTRODUCTION

In Chapter 12 we explored the concept of market segmentation as a bridge between broad generalisations about competition and buyer behaviour and the identification of specific markets. In Chapter 13 we take this process further by considering how firms compete with each other within market segments – a procedure which in recent years has come to be known as 'positioning'.

As the Westburn *Dictionary of Marketing and Advertising* (www.westburn.co.uk) explains:

> The term [positioning] has a simple meaning and a more complicated one. As typically used, it defines what is accurately called product positioning – that is, defining the location of a product (or service) relative to others in the same marketplace and then promoting it in such a way as to reinforce or change its 'position'. This is easier said than done, however. The process of defining a 'position' requires dimensions along which the competing products can be compared, and the resulting definition must be comparative if it is to be any use as the basis for positioning strategy.

The establishment and measuring of criteria which permit one to distinguish between similar products competing in the same market segment is the province of perceptual mapping, and this will be described in some detail below.

So much for the simple definition. What about the complex one? According to Al Ries and Jack Trout (2001):

> Positioning starts with a product. A piece of merchandise, a service, a company, an institution, or even a person. Perhaps yourself. But positioning is not what you do to a product. Positioning is what you do in the mind of the prospect. That is, you position the product in the mind of the prospect.

As the *Dictionary of Marketing and Advertising* points out, the 'collective mind is likely, inconveniently, to be already made up on the subject of products that already exist'. How then does one change peoples' minds? According to Ries and Trout, by using simple rather than complex and sophisticated messages – a proposition we look at in greater detail later in this chapter.

In order to position products, services and even companies it is essential to invest them with a distinctive 'personality' or 'brand'. The final part of the chapter examines the nature of branding and demonstrates how, increasingly, it is often the only real basis for differentiating between competitors.

PERCEPTUAL MAPPING

In the composite model of buyer behaviour (Chapter 9), it was suggested that consumers make choice decisions primarily on the basis of performance factors (i.e. how well the product meets the precise needs of the intending consumer) related to the cost of acquiring a given supply. However, it was also recognised that these objective characteristics would be 'interpreted' by the prospective purchaser in terms of their precise needs, the context in which the decision was being made and prior knowledge and experience, through the process of selective perception. Finally, it was noted that in many competitive markets consumers are faced with a wide choice of offerings which are near-perfect substitutes for each other in terms of performance and cost–benefit factors and so have to resort to other factors to enable them to choose between them. We termed this 'behavioural response' and so endorsed the view that perception influences decision-making at both the subconscious and the conscious level. At the subconscious level selective perception determines what information we will admit to our conscious mind, while at the conscious level it determines how we interpret and use that information. This being the case it is clearly very important that we are able to capture and measure consumer perceptions of competing products. As Urban and Star (1991) observed:

> If we are to make good positioning decisions, we need to know: (1) What dimensions do consumers use to evaluate competitive marketing programs – how many are there, and what should they be named? (2) How important is each of these dimensions in the decision process? (3) How do we and the competition compare on these dimensions? (4) How do consumers make choices on the basis of this information?

In Chapter 12, we cited a number of benefits that consumers typically look for when evaluating a product and also showed how these factors could be combined into two primary dimensions to yield a 'perceptual map' (Figure 12.2). First, however, one must identify just what the relevant factors are which prospective users will take into account when evaluating a product. Table 13.1 provides a list of 16 attributes or 'critical success factors' culled from an extensive review of the literature as part of the survey undertaken by Susan Hart and myself into the sources of competitive success (1989). (Critical success factors were discussed in detail in Chapter 8.) In our survey, we collected data from six different industries and used this to construct a rank ordering of the importance of these factors as shown in Table 13.2. Readers should not be surprised to learn that while it is quite simple to aggregate data in this way it can also be very misleading as there are significant differences between industries. For example, for the six industries we surveyed, design was ranked as the least important of the 16 factors – in a subsequent review of the market for household textiles it was ranked most important! That said, the 16 factors cover most of the attributes considered important in industrial or business markets and so provide a good basis for beginning to construct a perceptual map.

TABLE 13.1 Critical success factors

- Sale price
- Style/fashion (design)
- Durability
- Flexibility and adaptability in use
- Parts availability
- Attractive appearance/shape
- Technical sophistication
- Performance in operation
- Easy to use
- Safe to use
- Reliability
- Easy to maintain
- Quality of after-sales service
- Efficient delivery
- Advertising and promotion
- Operator comfort

SOURCE: Baker, M. J. and Hart, S. J. (1989) *Marketing and Competitive Success.* London: Philip Allan

TABLE 13.2 Critical success factors: product factors influencing competitiveness (in rank order)

1. Performance in operation
2. Reliability
3. Sale price
4. Efficient delivery
5. Technical sophistication
6. Quality of after-sales service
7. Durability
8. Ease of use
9. Safety in use
10. Ease of maintenance
11. Parts availability and cost
12. Attractive appearance/shape
13. Flexibility and adaptability in use
14. Advertising and promotion
15. Operator comfort
16. Design

SOURCE: Baker, M. J. and Hart, S. J. (1989) *Marketing and Competitive Success.* London: Philip Allan

A well-documented example of the use of perceptual mapping is to be found in Gary Davies and Janice Brooks' (1989) book *Positioning Strategy in Retailing*. In Chapter 6, the authors explain how to use multidimensional scaling (MDS) to produce maps for different kinds of retail markets and the following draws heavily on this source.

As noted above, the first problem in measuring the perception or 'image' of a store is to develop a list of criteria which are relevant and unambiguous. Based upon an extensive review of the literature, J. D. Lindquist (1974) developed a list of nine major attributes from 32 different elements, as shown in Table 13.3.

Davies and Brooks (1989) suggest that researchers should collect data on as many of these key attributes as possible, but counsel that in doing so one must allow for differences in perception between different groups of the population and also concentrate on specific factors that can be converted into strategic action.

The usual sources of information for identifying appropriate criteria are group discussions, word association tests and analysis of the retailer's own advertising. Such research is likely to generate many more criteria than MDS can cope with (most

TABLE 13.3 Lindquist's nine store image attributes

Attribute	Contributing factors/components
Merchandise	Quality; selection/assortment; styling/fashion; guarantees; pricing
Service	Service general; sales clerk service; self-service; ease of merchandise return; delivery service; credit policies
Clientele	Social class appeal; self-image congruency; store personnel
Physical facilities	Physical facilities, e.g. air-conditioning, washroom, store layout; shopping ease, e.g. width of aisles, architecture
Convenience	Convenience general; locational convenience; parking
Promotion	Sales promotions; advertising; displays; trading stamps; symbols and colour
Store atmosphere	Atmosphere congeniality, i.e. feelings of warmth and acceptance
Institutional factors	Conservative vs. modern projection of store; reputation and reliability
Post-transaction satisfaction	Merchandise in use; returns; adjustments

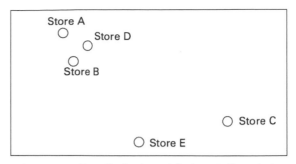

FIGURE 13.1 Hypothetical model of a retail market

SOURCE: Davies, G. and Brooks, J. (1989) *Positioning Strategy in Retailing.* London: Paul Chapman

perceptual maps have only two dimensions) and some means must be found of reducing these to manageable proportions – usually through the use of factor or cluster analysis as described in Chapter 12. Having decided on the attributes to be used, Davies and Brooks (1989) compare all the chosen retailers and all the chosen concepts in a market research survey structured to represent the known characteristics of the marketplace. Typically, respondents to the survey are asked to compare two retailers, two concepts or a concept and a retailer, and to rate their similarity. The gradings given are averaged for all respondents to produce a semi-matrix, which is the final market research data. The MDS analysis that follows is designed only to represent those data in such a way that the hidden structure in the data, the market structure, can be seen more easily. The map or model produced is not a theoretical model but a representation of data in a form that can be used to describe and predict consumer behaviour.

The output of an MDS programme (of which there are several variants) is a two-dimensional map in which the distance between two points reflects the similarity between them – the smaller the distance the more similar they are and vice

versa. Thus the output from an MDS analysis of the survey data might yield a map like that in Figure 13.1, which enables one to make statements that stores A, B and D are quite similar and C and E quite distinctive. However, in order to interpret the map and use it for decision-making purposes, a reference point is needed, and in Figure 13.2 this is provided by plotting the 'ideal store' based upon the opinion of the shoppers surveyed. Davies and Brooks interpret the map as follows:

> Store C now seems the only really well-placed store in that it is not only differentiated but, because it is placed close if not closest to the ideal, it has the widest appeal. Store C has adopted the best possible positioning strategy. Store D is also fairly well-placed; being close to the ideal store it has broad appeal. However, stores A and B compete with store D for the particular shopping experience associated by the shopper with all three stores. Stores A and B are

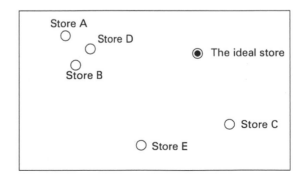

FIGURE 13.2 Hypothetical model of a retail market, including the position of the 'ideal' store

SOURCE: Davies, G. and Brooks, J. (1989) *Positioning Strategy in Retailing.* London: Paul Chapman

worse off in that they appear to be second choices to store D. All things being equal, the shopper will visit store D first and will be better disposed to buying similar merchandise there rather than at store A or B. Store E is clearly out on a limb.

In Figure 13.3 the authors include the concepts generated and screened in the market research, which enables one to interpret the positions much more effectively and decide whether and how to reposition oneself. From Figure 13.3 it is apparent that store E is a price leader and, being out on its own, is of greatest appeal to price-conscious shoppers.

Davies and Brooks (1989) concede that it is not possible to assess the statistical validity of the market maps produced by this technique. That said, their research shows the method is both robust and stable over time and so of considerable benefit to decision-makers. Certainly the technique, and the book describing its use, merit careful study by all those responsible for formulating retail strategies. Similarly, Chapter 8 'Product Positioning' in Urban and Star (1991) will be of value to those seeking a broadly based description of the use of multivariate techniques to help determine how products are perceived in the marketplace.

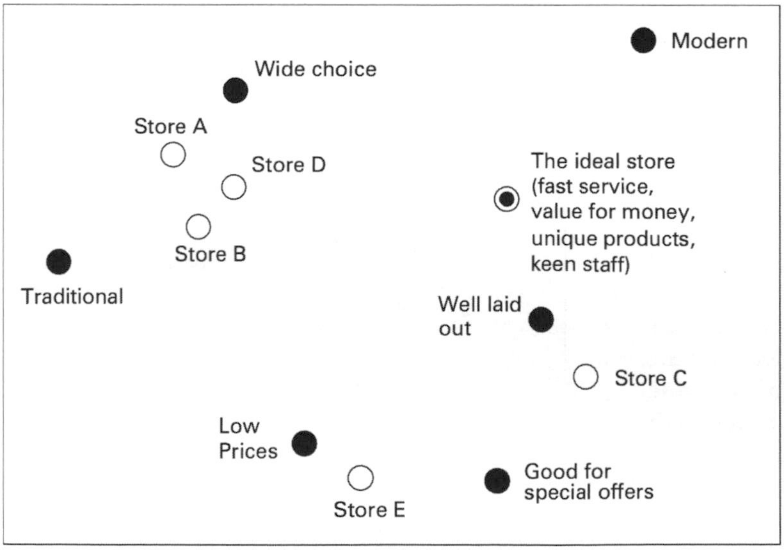

POSITIONING IN THE MIND

Mapping methods of the kind described in the previous section help establish how different competitors are seen in the market, both in relation to each other and to the ideal product. But, as noted in the introduction to this chapter, while this information is valuable the key issue is how to defend or improve/change one's position in the market. To achieve this, one must either reinforce or modify people's perceptions, and it is this second aspect of 'positioning' that was addressed in Ries and Trout's book (2001).

According to Ries and Trout 'positioning got started in 1972 when we wrote a series of articles entitled "The Positioning Era" for the trade paper *Advertising Age*'. Ries and Trout are primarily concerned with the impact of advertising in what they describe as 'an overcommunicated society'. They make their point vividly by explaining that (in 2001) the per capita consumption of advertising in America was $376.62 per year, so that if you have an advertising budget of $1 million per year, this is equivalent to less than half a cent spread over 365 days for the average consumer. More importantly, the other advertisers are spending $376.615 to divert his attention from you – odds of over 75,000:1! Ries and Trout comment :

In the communication jungle out there, the only hope to score big is to be selective, to concentrate on narrow targets, to practice segmentation. In a word, 'positioning'.

The mind, as a defence against the volume of today's communications, screens and rejects much of the information offered it. In general, the mind accepts only that which matches prior knowledge or experience. Millions of dollars have been wasted trying to change minds with advertising. Once a mind is made up, it's almost impossible to change it. Certainly, not with a weak force like advertising.

So what is one to do? According to Ries and Trout 'the best approach in our overcommun-

FIGURE 13.3 Hypothetical model of a retail market, including the 'ideal' store and concepts

SOURCE: Davies, G. and Brooks, J. (1989) *Positioning Strategy in Retailing*. London: Paul Chapman

icated society is the oversimplified message'. But even an oversimplified message will be effective only if communicated at the right time. Hence, 'Positioning is an organised system for finding a window in the mind. It is based on the concept that communication can only take place at the right time and under the right circumstances.'

Ries and Trout cite Harvard psychologist George Miller in support of the view that the human mind has a very limited ready-use capacity – usually, only seven bits or units of information. Hence the popularity of seven-unit lists which have to be remembered – seven-digit phone numbers, seven wonders of the world, Snow White and the seven dwarfs, seven deadly sins etc. With very important high-involvement topics, one may increase the number of units – the Ten Commandments – but with low interest/low involvement topics like product or supplier identities the number may fall to as low as two or three. Further, in the case of product identities, users tend to rank order these in a 'ladder' (hence, ladders in the mind) with the preferred or most important on the top rung. 'A competitor that wants to increase its share of the business must either dislodge the brand above (a task that is usually impossible) or somehow relate its brand to the other company's position' (Ries and Trout, 2001, p. 32).

Similarly, with a new kind of product one must build a new ladder and will be most likely to succeed if one can relate it to an existing ladder. This may often be done most effectively by defining what it is not, rather than what is, e.g. a horseless carriage, lead-free petrol, sugar-free diet foods etc.

Ries and Trout provide numerous examples to support their advice for successful positioning. To become a leader one should 'be firstest with the mostest', on the principle that while people can usually recall who was number 1 to achieve something they usually have difficulty in recalling number 2. On the other hand, if you can't be first then relating yourself to number 1 helps link your name with theirs as an alternative choice – remember 'Avis is No. 2 – and we try harder'.

However, the real benefit of positioning lies in identifying the gap or hole in the marketplace, and then filling it. Of course, to do this one must establish the relevant criteria and then plot the existing alternatives in the same way as the store positioning maps illustrated in Figure 13.3. A theoretical map taken from Baker and Hart (2007) is presented as Figure 13.4 and indicates a poten-

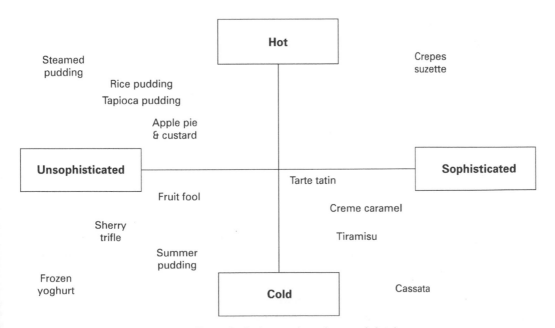

FIGURE 13.4 The dessert market (hypothetical – not based on real data)

SOURCE: Baker, M. J. and Hart, S. J. (2007) *Product Strategy and Management* (2nd edn). Hemel Hempstead: Pearson

tially large 'gap' in the market for hot, sophisticated desserts. Similarly, the discussion of Baker's
Box in Chapter 5 illustrated how the idea behind
positioning can be operationalised without access
to detailed quantitative data.

In some cases the axes of a perceptual map such
as that in Figure 12.2 may appear to be opposed to
one another (i.e. performance and price). But, as
the Japanese have shown in market after market,
they are adept at providing high performance at a
comparatively low price and so give the greatest
value for money – a much more meaningful
concept to the consumer than either price or
performance on their own. In other cases, however,
price may be used to convey images of quality and
value, particularly when consumers have difficulty
in evaluating more objective performance criteria.

All these tactics may be summarised within the
concept of 'niche marketing'. As noted in Chapter
3, niche strategies tend to be adopted by 'follower'
firms with a limited product portfolio that lack the
resources to attack on more than one front at the
same time. To pursue such a strategy successfully,
one must identify niches which are :

1. Of sufficient size and purchasing power to be
   profitable
2. Growing or having the potential to do so
3. Neglected by major companies
4. Ones in which the firm has superior competencies looked for by the customers
5. Capable of being defended through the establishment of a customer franchise.

Kotler (1991) asserts that specialisation is the
key to successful niche strategies and suggests 10
specialist roles open to the market nicher, namely:

1. *End-use specialist:* This firm decides to
   specialise in serving one type of end-use
   customer. For example, a law firm can decide
   to specialise in the criminal, civil, or business
   law markets.
2. *Vertical-level specialist:* This firm specialises at
   some vertical level of the production–
   distribution cycle. For example, a copper firm
   may concentrate on the production of raw
   copper, copper components, or finished
   copper products.
3. *Customer-size specialist:* This firm concentrates

on selling to either small, medium, or large-
size customers. Many nichers specialise in
serving small customers because they are
neglected by the majors.
4. *Specific-customers specialist:* This firm limits its
   selling to one (or a few) major customers.
   Many firms sell their entire output to a single
   company such as Sears or General Motors.
5. *Geographic specialist:* This firm focuses on the
   needs of a certain locality, region or area of the
   world.
6. *Product or product-line specialist:* This firm
   produces only one product line or product.
   Within the laboratory equipment industry are
   firms that produce only microscopes, or even
   more narrowly, only lenses for microscopes.
7. *Product-feature specialist:* This firm specialises
   in producing a certain type of product or
   product-feature. Rent-a-Junk, for example, is a
   California car rental agency that rents only
   'beat-up' cars.
8. *Job-shop specialist:* This firm stands ready to
   make customised products as ordered by the
   customer.
9. *Quality/price specialist:* This firm chooses to
   operate at the low or high end of the market.
10. *Service specialist:* This firm offers or excels in
    one or more services not readily available from
    other firms. An example would be a bank that
    takes loan requests over the phone or
    dispatches an officer to deliver the money at
    the client's home or office.

But what happens if one cannot identify a
niche? Ries and Trout (2001) counsel that in such
circumstances 'The basic underlying marketing
strategy has got to be "reposition the competition".' To do this one must change the perception
of consumers of the status quo – a straightforward
recommendation that is notoriously difficult to
implement. Copernicus showed that the earth
revolved round the sun, Columbus proved the
earth is not flat and the Wright brothers that we
could fly. How does one provide such proof?
Usually by supplying evidence which people can
easily verify for themselves or, alternatively,
reducing the credibility/acceptance of the
received wisdom so that people will look for
something else to replace it. Ries and Trout explain
how Tylenol 'burst the aspirin bubble' by promot-

ing the negative side effects of aspirin and then claiming that Tylenol avoided all these. Similarly, Stolichnaya vodka produced and bottled in Russia successfully broke into the US market against established brands like Samovar, Smirnoff, Popov etc. by simply saying 'Most American vodkas seem Russian' then listing where they were made, followed by the statement 'Stolichnaya is different. It is Russian.' Ries and Trout offer numerous other examples to support their argument, and point out that since the mid-1970s comparative advertising in which one comments adversely on competing brands has been legal in the US and UK and so a perfectly acceptable form of competition (always provided the statements are true!).

Ries and Trout continue: 'In the positioning era, the single most important marketing decision you can make is what to name the product.' In recent years the subject of 'branding' has become one of the most widely discussed in the marketing domain. Its importance deserves separate treatment.

BRANDING

One of the most successful and succinct discussions of the nature and role of branding is to be found in the chapter entitled 'Branding' in *The Marketing Book* (Baker, 1999). A version of this chapter by the late Professor Peter Doyle first appeared in the summer 1989 issue of the *Journal of Marketing Management* and was prompted by a major debate as to whether brands should be valued and included in the balance sheet. At the time a major takeover was being mounted against Rank Hovis McDougall (RHM). In fighting off the bid RHM management successfully persuaded their shareholders that the bid grossly undervalued the real worth of the company if one took into account the value of the international brands such as Cerebos, Hovis, Rank etc. in its product portfolio. The point was well made as Nestle's subsequent acquisition of Rowntree Mackintosh took full account of world class brands like Smarties, KitKat and Yorkie.

According to Doyle, a positive or successful brand can be defined as follows:

A successful brand is a name, symbol, design, or some combination which identifies the 'product' of a

particular organisation as having a sustainable differential advantage.

Several points are important about this definition. First, successful brands are positive. In 1990 British Telecom spent over £70 million in redesigning and repositioning its corporate identity or 'brand' in order to try and overcome the negative association of its reputation for poor service. (This sum covered the total costs of changing the company's visual identity and was not, of course, solely for design and promotion.) Second, brands can take many forms – not just names. Third, the 'product' can just as easily be a service, an organisation or even an aspiration. Brands are owned by organisations/people and they confer a sustainable differential/competitive advantage. Doyle defines 'differential advantage' as meaning that customers have a reason for preferring that brand to competitor's brands, while 'sustainable' means an advantage that is not easily copied by competitors and so represents a barrier to entry in the market segment in which the brand competes. Only if a brand has a sustainable differential advantage (SDA) should it appear on the balance sheet. Thus neutral or negative brands earn profits through property or distribution efforts (however much is spent on promotion) and so, like short-lived fashion brands, should not be considered as assets in the same way as brands with SDA. Like other assets, brands require continued investment if they are to maintain their value. In the short term it may be possible to increase profits by cutting back on brand investment (i.e. by 'milking' the brand). If this is done, then competition will gradually erode the brand's standing and lead to its depreciation.

The importance of brands for consumers is that they help simplify decision-making. The brand is a form of mental shorthand that neatly summarises the output of the complex process described in our model of choice behaviour in Chapter 9. When introduced to a new product or service we have to execute an evaluation in which we relate performance characteristics to our felt needs and determine whether consumption of the new offering will increase our overall satisfaction compared with our current pattern of behaviour. We have also seen that with low-involvement goods the easiest way to resolve this problem is through trial or experience rather than the kind of extended and complex evaluation which will precede even trial of a high-involvement (high perceived risk) object. Once we have learnt a pattern of behaviour, we will tend to repeat that behaviour in future until some event suggests that by breaking this habit we may increase our satisfaction in some way. Thus, as Ries and Trout point out, we form 'short-lists' of known solutions to possible consumption problems and find it convenient to rank order these in terms of expected outcomes. Brands enable us to identify acceptable solutions without having to remember or recall all the factors that led to our original choice.

But, as Doyle points out, successful brands with SDA do not depend solely on actual experience in use for their reputations. Indeed a great deal of a brand's reputation may be based upon perceptions that have built up over time. In his words 'Such preferences or brand images are based upon cultural, social and personality factors, as well as commercial stimuli like advertising, public relations and prominence of distribution.' As such we can form favourable or unfavourable attitudes towards brands even if we have no actual experience of them. One can like the Marlboro ads and not smoke and think well of Pedigree Chum and not own a dog. Undoubtedly, the 'owners' of such brands value this support from non-users not just

because if they become users they will have an immediate preference for the brand, but because this favourable opinion reinforces the actual users' attitude concerning the wisdom of their choice.

Of course, usage or consumption of the brand is the primary objective of the marketer – there being a well-established relationship between profitability and market share. Doyle cites the well-known PIMS (profit implications of market strategy) findings (Buzzell and Gale, 1987), which showed that brands with a market share of 40% generated three times the profit or return on investment of those with a market share of 10%, which increased to four times when the ratio was increased to 60:10, as shown in Figure 13.5.

These findings have been supported by research in many other countries and explain the sellers' concern to build successful brands with large market shares. A note of caution is appropriate. During the late 1980s research into the actual performance of companies seeking to build or improve market share showed that many of them became less profitable (or even unprofitable) than they had been with their original market share. This observation suggests that when you enjoy a large market share you are likely to be the most profitable player in that market, but if you are seeking to win market share from established brands the costs of doing so will very probably eliminate the profits anticipated from the increased volume. Clearly, this finding reinforces Ries and Trout's advice to be the 'firstest with the mostest', or the more general observation that much marketing expenditure should be regarded as an investment rather than an expense on the basis that the benefits are likely to be distant and long term rather than immediate and short term. Indeed it has been estimated that, as a working rule of thumb, it costs six times as much money to win a new customer as to retain an existing customer's loyalty (Peters, 1988). With odds like these, winning the brand share war against a strongly entrenched and preferred competitor is bound to prove very expensive and to be undertaken only if one has considerable confidence that the market is likely to survive well

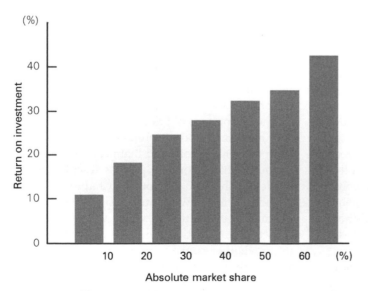

FIGURE 13.5 The relationship between market share and profitability

SOURCE: Buzzell, R. D. and Gale, B. T. (1987) *The PIMS Principles: Linking Strategy to Performance.* London: Collier-Macmillan

into the future. Most evidence suggests that such markets are most often found in the realm of consumer goods where the brand leaders have sustained a dominant position for decades. (Research in 1975 showed that 19 out of 25 leading brands in the USA were the same as in 1925, fifty years earlier! Many of these brands still occupy this position today.)

Long-term brand leadership of this kind is most usual where product differentiation opportunities are less available, i.e. where it is difficult to reposition a product through technological innovation without actually changing the nature of the product/market. This is not to say that product improvement will not occur, but the markets for carbonated beverages like Coca Cola, for breakfast cereals like corn flakes, or for soap products have been characterised by evolutionary rather than revolutionary change, mainly led by the companies with the dominant market shares. In markets where revolutionary change is possible through technological innovation the incidence of long-lived 'brand leaders' is much less. One reason for this is undoubtedly the 'marketing myopia' diagnosed by Ted Levitt (1960), which arises from too close involvement with a past or present way of doing things and an unwillingness to accept the displacement of such established ways with new ways. The irony of this is that all experience points to the fact that the perceived credibility and standing of a market leader offers the greatest likelihood of success in launching a new product, i.e. the 'halo' effect of a house brand like IBM or Marks & Spencer will help reduce much of the risk which a potential user would perceive if invited to try the same new product launched by an unknown company without such an established reputation. How then should one set about building a brand reputation?

BUILDING A BRAND REPUTATION

Before addressing the issue of how to build a brand reputation it will be useful to expand the simple definition of a brand given by Doyle. Writing in the July 1998 issue of the *Journal of Marketing Management*, Leslie de Chernatony and Francesca Dall'Olmo Riley explored the nature of branding in some detail and concluded that there are at least twelve different ways of thinking about brands.

These are summarised in Table 13.4 and spell out the key features or *antecedents* of each brand definition and the implications or *consequences* of adopting each definition.

Implicit in our model of choice behaviour is the belief that a rational person or organisation will always prefer objective and tangible evidence to subjective and intangible evidence in selecting between competing offerings. This belief is not equivalent to the proposal of a mechanistic process in which a third party could automatically determine another's preferred choice (as suggested in economic theory) for, as we have seen, the selection and interpretation of both objective and subjective data is mediated by the attitudes, opinions, beliefs and experience (habit) of the chooser. Nonetheless, the model does allow us to identify some necessary conditions, albeit that they may not be sufficient to predict brand choice. Further, we can see that choice is the outcome of a sequential process which may be aborted at any stage between awareness of a need and the adoption/rejection of a specific solution. These ideas are encapsulated in a modified version of Levitt's concept of the brand (1983), and illustrated in Figure 13.6.

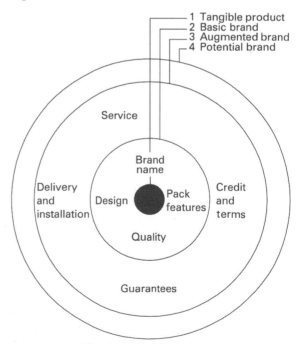

FIGURE 13.6 What is a brand?

SOURCE: Adapted by the author from T. Levitt (1983) *The Marketing Imagination.* London: Collier-Macmillan

TABLE 13.4 Antecedents and consequences to the brand construct

Brand definition	Antecedents	Consequences
1. Legal instrument	Mark of ownership. Name, logo, design. Trademark.	Prosecute infringers.
2. Logo	Name, term, sign, symbol, design. Product characteristics.	Identify/differentiate through visual identity and name. Quality assurance.
3. Company	Recognisable corporate name and image. Culture, people, programmes of organisation define corporate personality. CEO is brand manager.	Evaluate over long time horizon. Product lines benefit from corporate personality. Convey consistent message to stakeholders. Differentiation: proposition, relationship.
4. Shorthand	Firm stresses quality not quantity of information.	Rapidly recognise brand association. Facilitate information-processing, speed decisions
5. Risk reducer	Confidence that expectations are being fulfilled.	Brand as a contract.
6. Identity system	More than just a name. Holistic, structured with 6 integrated facets, including brand's personality.	Clarity, direction, meaning, strategic positioning. Protective barrier. Communicate essence to stakeholders.
7. Image	Consumer centred. Image in consumers' mind is brand 'reality'.	Firm's input activities managed using feedback of image to change identity. Market research important. Manage brand concept over time.
8. Value system	Consumer relevant values imbue the brand.	Brand values match relevant consumer values.
9. Personality	Psychological values, communicated through advertising and packaging define brand's personality.	Differentiation from symbolism: human values projected. Stress added values beyond functional.
10. Relationship	Consumer has attitude to brand. Brand as person has attitude to consumer.	Recognition and respect for personality. Develop relationship.
11. Adding value	Non-functional extras. Value satisfier. Consumers imbue brand with subjective meaning they value enough to buy. Aesthetics. Enhanced through design, manufacturer, distribution.	Differentiate through layers of meaning. Charge price premium. Consumer experience. Perception of users. Belief in performance.
12. Evolving entity	Change by stage of development.	

SOURCE: de Chernatony, L. and Dall'Olmo Riley, F. (1998) Defining a 'brand': beyond the literature with experts' interpretations, *Journal of Marketing Management*, 14(5): 417–43

At the heart of the product are the essential characteristics which enable users to identify it as a possible solution to their consumption need. This essential or 'core' product/service is largely defined by its performance characteristics, i.e. what it will do for the owner. For the industrial or organisational buyer seeking to purchase a complex offering it will be defined in detail in the formal specification, whether it be for the building of an offshore rig or the supply of a catering service in a new residential management centre. Associated with the core product will be a cluster of other attributes such as its design, appearance, packaging and identification (the brand) which enable potential users to differentiate between the offerings of competing suppliers. Without such attributes the product would become a commodity like wool, wheat, iron ore etc. where the only rational basis for purchase is cost–benefit: i.e. how much in time and space will I secure for any given expenditure? While attributes such as design,

packaging and quality will all assist the potential buyer to discriminate between products at the point of purchase, increasing competition and a concern for the user's needs has led to the development of what Levitt terms the 'augmented' product.

Augmented products reflect the seller's concern for the actual performance of the product and offer additional benefits to the intending buyer. Many of these benefits, such as guarantees and the provision of after-sales service, help to reduce the perceived risk which the buyer experiences in selecting a durable product or service whose benefits will be enjoyed over a period of time, like a piece of machinery, or else are intended to mature if a particular event such as damage, loss or theft occurs (insurance). Similarly, delivery, assistance with installation and the provision of credit are all additional incentives that add value and enable buyers to discriminate between objectively similar products.

Finally, the 'outer shell' of the product is the

'potential brand' which Doyle (1999) defines as 'anything that conceivably could be done to build customer preference and loyalty'. Despite Ries and Trout's assertion quoted earlier that advertising is a weak force and incapable of achieving major change in buying behaviour, there can be no doubt that advertising and promotion have a great deal to do with creating the just noticeable difference (JND) factor which mediates the decision-maker's final behavioural response (BR in our model of buyer behaviour in Chapter 9). Advertising and promotion are important at the beginning of the purchase decision because they attract our attention and help move us from a state of subconscious readiness to one of conscious awareness, i.e. they make us aware of a possible need. Having secured our attention, advertising and promotion can then provide information that can prompt us to further action – information search for high-involvement products and even purchase for low-involvement goods.

Advertising also helps reinforce our existing patterns of behaviour and provides reassurance that such behaviour is to our greatest benefit. All these attributes add value to the brand. In many instances, they create and sustain subjective associations which are the very essence of actual preference. In our model of buyer behaviour these are often the factors which enable buyers to tip the balance between augmented brands where competing suppliers have matched each other exactly in terms of all the performance factors and service attributes. Naturally, these marginal distinctions, which are usually highly specific to the individual decision-makers, will come into play only where alternatives appear identical in every other respect. Because the subjective associations created by advertising have this ability to influence the final choice, critics claim that advertising is manipulative. Such claims are clearly specious and do a grave disservice to the buyer who has performed a careful comparative assessment of the merits of available alternatives and, being unable to distinguish between them, instead of tossing the statistician's coin selects the offering in which he or she has the greatest confidence.

In suggesting that a brand has a core and up to three 'skins', we are reflecting the view that decision-making is a sequential process in which one uses increasingly selective criteria in order to make a final choice. It is clear that if the core product is sufficiently distinctive, then would-be buyers will not need to have recourse to second, third or even fourth order factors to position their offerings in the mind of prospective consumers. But, given the increase in global competition referred to in Chapter 2 and the turbulent and rapidly changing environment discussed in Chapter 7, it is obvious that more and more suppliers in all types of business must give careful attention to all aspects of the brand.

That said, some dimensions are more important than others and Doyle (1999) proposes that these are:

1. Quality
2. Superior service
3. Get there first
4. Look for differentiation.

In the case of quality, Doyle cites Buzzell and Gale's (1987) analysis of the PIMS data, which showed a similar relationship between perceived quality and return on sales and investment as that noted earlier for market share (see Figure 13.7).

Because products can be copied so readily Doyle argues that 'service is perhaps the most sustainable differential advantage'. Service is, of course, an intrinsic element of the exchange process and thus much more difficult to replicate

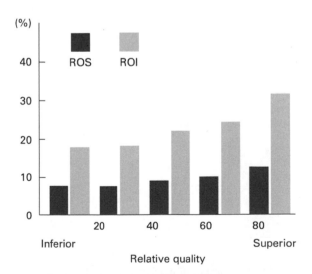

FIGURE 13.7 Quality and profitability

SOURCE: Buzzell, R. D. and Gale, B. T. (1987) *The PIMS Principles: Linking Strategy to Performance.* London: Collier-Macmillan

than physical features or attributes like delivery, credit terms etc. As we noted in Chapter 2, when discussing the contribution of marketing to competitive success, in the final analysis 'It ain't what you do, it's the way that you do it.' In Chapter 20 we discuss the role of service in the particular and in Chapter 21 we examine how successful organisations develop cultures that create added value for themselves and their customers. 'Get there first' was Ries and Trout's primary recommendation and Doyle quotes Clifford and Cavanagh's (1985) study which provides formal evidence to support this advice (see Figure 13.8). Doyle also suggests that there are at least five ways of getting there first:

1. Exploiting new technology (e.g. Xerox, IBM)
2. New positioning concepts (e.g. The Body Shop, Fosters Lager)
3. New distribution channels (e.g. Amazon, eBay)
4. New market segments (e.g. Dell)
5. Exploiting gaps created by sudden environmental changes (e.g. egg substitutes – a reference to a scare about infected eggs in the UK in 1990).

Doyle's fourth element – differentiation – is, of course, what branding is all about. As John Murphy (1991) observed, a brand is the product or service of a particular supplier that is differentiated by its name and presentation. Thus any manufacturer can produce a cola drink but only the Coca-Cola Company can produce Coke. Indeed, the only feature that a determined and well-resourced competitor would be unable convincingly to replicate is the brand itself. A brand is therefore more than the actual product, it is the unique product of a specific owner that has been developed over time to embrace a set of values, both tangible and intangible, meaningfully and appropriately to differentiate products which may otherwise be very similar.

In a survey undertaken by Landor Associates of the strength of major corporate, service and consumer brand names across international markets and industry categories, the world's 'Top Ten' brands are as shown in Figure 13.9. For the UK, the top five brands are shown in Figure 13.10.

As implied by Murphy's comments, branding has been considered primarily at the level of the individual product or service. However, the distinguished marketing practitioner Stephen King (1991) argued cogently that in the 1990s it would be more important to consider the actual

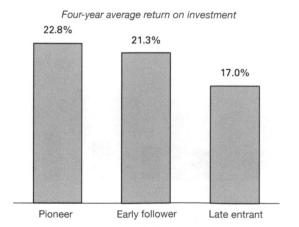

FIGURE 13.8 Timing of market entry and business

SOURCE: Clifford, D. K. and Cavanagh, R. E. (1985) *The Winning Performance: How America's High Growth Midsize Companies Succeed.* London: Sidgwick & Jackson

FIGURE 13.9 Top 10 global brands

SOURCE: *Business Week*, August, 2005

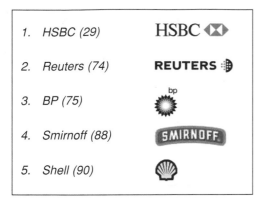

1. *HSBC (29)*	HSBC ◂✕▸
2. *Reuters (74)*	**REUTERS** ⬦
3. *BP (75)*	✹ bp
4. *Smirnoff (88)*	SMIRNOFF
5. *Shell (90)*	🐚

FIGURE 13.10 The top five UK brands (rank in Global 100)

SOURCE: *Business Week*, August, 2005

company as a brand. King's views were clearly highly prophetic and have been confirmed by the burgeoning literature on the subject. In view of its relevance and importance, a summary is reproduced below.

THE COMPANY AS A BRAND

Stephen King (1991) identified six areas of change that were exerting pressure on companies and which were likely to intensify over the next few years:

- More confident consumers
- New concepts of quality
- Shortage of skills
- Tightening of the competitive screw
- The side effects of new technology
- Restructuring.

As the 1990s showed, all these trends continue to have a significant impact on a firm's strategy.

In respect of consumers King points out they have become more confident, readier to experiment and trust their own judgement, have more disposable income and are more worldly wise. They have a greater understanding of 'marketing' in all its activities and this understanding will help ensure customers in business-to-business marketing become more demanding too.

Consumers have strong views on what gives them satisfaction and are less tolerant of goods and services that don't live up to their expect-

ations. Finally, and probably as a consequence of the preceding changes, they have become more independent and closer to the highest level of Maslow's hierarchy of needs – self-actualisation. The world may be a global market, but its tribes and their members still have a need to distinguish themselves from one another to express their growing individualism. Nowhere is this more the case than in consumers' increasing demand for quality and a quality founded on real values which go together to make up 'the good life', such as green products rather than products which consume non-replaceable resources, pollute the atmosphere or cause pain or suffering to other species.

Satisfying the needs of these 'new' consumers will call for radical changes on the supply side but here skills shortages, due to declining birth rates, and insufficient education and training, pose a threat to our ability to make these changes. However, international competition looks certain to intensify and will become even more acute as the leading players seek to secure the necessary labour inputs.

While it has become a cliché to talk of accelerating technological change, the trend persists. As King observes: 'Constant innovation will be a necessary part of normal commercial life, but few companies will be able to rely on having any demonstrable product or service advantage for more than a few months.' In the absence of objective criteria to guide the choice decisions, the relationship between seller and buyer will assume even greater importance. In consumer markets King believes this will reinforce the retailer's position as the consumer's friend at the expense of the manufacturer.

Faced with changes of the kind discussed above, producers will continue to restructure in an effort to secure economies of scale in manufacturing and marketing. In many cases this will involve mergers and takeovers, in others the striking of strategic alliances. Inevitably it will result in still greater concentration of market power in the hands of a small number of global players in the majority of industries. In order to survive, King, amongst others, is of the opinion that success will depend critically on brand-building, which he defines as:

using all the company's particular assets to create unique entities that certain consumers really want;

entities which have a lasting personality, based on a special combination of physical, functional and psychological values; and which have competitive advantage in at least one area of marketing (raw materials/sourcing, product/design/patents, production systems, supply/sales/service networks, depth of understanding of consumers, style/fashion, and so on).

Only through brand building will it be possible to:

- Build stable, long-term demand
- Add value looked for by customers
- Develop a sound base for future growth and expansion
- Recruit the growing power of intermediaries
- Become recognised as a company with a reputation and going places that people will want to work with and for.

However, King believed that brand-building in the 1990s would be quite different from that of the past which led to the emergence and dominance of classic single-line brands like Coke, Pepsi, Marlboro, Persil, Oxo, Kit-Kat and Andrex. As King points out, in 1969, 19 of the 25 top spending brands in the UK were repeat purchase packaged goods; in 1989 it was just 1. Now the trend is to the company brand, in which it is the subjective,

difficult-to-define aspects of service and reputation associated with a company which will position it in the consumer's mind and the marketplace:

> In essence, brand-building in the 1990s will involve designing and controlling all aspects of a company, leading people and activities well beyond the traditional skill of the marketing department and the agencies that it employs. It will be a lot closer to the marketing of services (such as airlines, hotels, retailers, building societies) than to the brand-building of the classic brands.

But such brand-building will have to be very different from most managers' current perception of 'brands' as fmcg or possibly the company's logo and corporate identity programme. In future the company 'brand' will have to encapsulate and communicate what an organisation is and what it stands for – its mission, culture and aspirations. In doing so it will be as important for the internal marketing of the firm as it is for its efforts to win a distinguished and distinctive place in the perception of its actual and prospective customers. To achieve this will require organisations to be market-oriented and customer-driven in a manner which embraces all members and functions of the organisation.

Box 13.1   **The Virgin umbrella**

In 1970, the Virgin Group was started as a mail-order business by Richard Branson and based in London. In 36 years, the group has become a global business empire operating in a wide number of industries such as airlines, the beverages market (both alcoholic and soft drinks), financial services, rail travel, entertainment and bridal wear. One of the factors affecting the group's remarkable success is its branding strategy; the use of the Virgin brand name on all companies. This strategy is termed 'umbrella branding' in which each product or company uses the main brand name as a family name. This strategy has not only resulted in massive brand recognition, but has also furnished every company with a distinct personality, linked with Richard Branson as a person, which has generated an enviable base of consumer loyalty. The branding approach used by the Virgin Group remains founded upon the Japanese model according to Branson (1998). The Japanese maxim of *small is beautiful* compels companies to create an increasingly complex web of companies in a bid to retain autonomy and individual con-

trol. This umbrella branding strategy functions by each individual company using the Virgin brand name and logo, whilst adding an additional name to ensure easy identification, e.g. Virgin Vodka, Virgin Direct, Virgin Atlantic, Virgin Radio, Virgin Brides. The result of this strategy has been almost global recognition of the Virgin brand name. Indeed, a recent survey found that 96% of British consumers had heard of Virgin and 96% can correctly name Richard Branson as its founder (Dearlove, 1998).

SOURCE: Zafer Erdogan, personal communication

Clearly, many companies heeded this advice and have developed positioning statements that seek to encapsulate the values the company subscribes to and offers its customers. Examples include:

- 'Access your flexible friend'
- 'It's you we answer to' (British Telecom)
- 'We won't make a drama out of a crisis' (Commercial Union)
- 'Everything we do is driven by you' (Ford)
- 'Helping you control your world' (Honeywell).

A striking example of a company branding strategy reinforced by highly focused targeting and positioning is Nike. The subject of an article in *Marketing Business,* Nike is seen as a classic exemplar of brand marketing, summarised by Seth (1998) as 'purpose, performance and price'.

To begin with, Nike set out to build a better product differentiated by its 'waffle' sole 'coupled with better cushioning, attractive design and constant, churning, Japanese level innovation, Nike was able to bring more than 300 new shoe designs to market each year.'

To reinforce the superiority of its brand Nike charges premium prices. At the same time it has sourced its footwear in the lowest cost countries in the world and has been widely criticised for exploiting sweated labour in countries such as Indonesia and China. In Seth's opinion this emphasis on cost leadership is essential, not to offer low prices but to provide the margins with which to build the brand and achieve its ambition of becoming the world's best sports goods company. It is creating and sustaining this perception which calls for enormous marketing investment.

Central to Nike's marketing strategy has been the use of celebrity endorsement. Seth (1998) comments:

> The external messages are consistent. The heroes are given high visibility, and what heroes they are: Michael Jordan, a vibrant model for US teenagers (few Europeans can comprehend his hold on black urban youth); Tiger Woods, a breakthrough golfing performer at 21; John McEnroe, brilliance, wit and rebellion all in one; Magic Johnson; Lennox Lewis; Pete Sampras; Eric Cantona; Ian Wright; and a panoply of Brazilian footballers … The list goes on, but these sponsors give the Nike brand more than

just weight and dominance. These figures have great self-belief and spontaneity. They transmit coherence, reputation and awareness. The familiar 'tick' neatly summarises the attitude with its 'here we go again, as you would expect' ubiquitousness. And with an annual $1 billion advertising and sponsorship spend, the target market sees a lot of them.

Despite the negative criticism directed at Nike in 1997 and 1998, Seth believes that Nike's focus and commitment will enable it to exploit a major potential in apparel followed by a range of leisure goods opportunities all with long-term growth prospects. It is this ability to innovate relevantly by thinking about its markets, brand and consumers that Seth believes will ensure Nike's long-term success.

In an article entitled 'Evolution', Alan Mitchell (1996) used Coca-Cola and McDonald's as the basis for developing 'ten tips for the top':

> Coca-Cola and McDonald's are extraordinary marketers. But what makes them extraordinary is not the size of their budgets or the brilliance of their communication. It is their thinking. They have what McKinsey would call 'a total system perspective'.

Central to this perspective is their use of a corporate brand through which they 'effectively stamp their brand on their entire supply chain'. In pursuit of this strategy Mitchell identifies 10 characteristics that underpin the success of global brands such as Coke. These may be summarised as:

1. Never fall in love with the line extension, i.e. don't compromise the core brand by seeing it as a product category.
2. Be resolutely global in outlook.
3. Think differently about market share. While Coca Cola's share of the global soft drinks market is 47% and as high as 80% in some regional markets, Coke points out that it accounts for less than 2% of the world's 5.7 billion people's daily fluid requirements. Clearly, the potential is enormous.
4. Use your new view of market share to transform your company's outlook.
5. Don't milk the brand by stretching its price/value relationship, i.e. keep prices low but profitable.

6. Never stop investing.
7. Have a fanatical eye for detail, i.e. think global, act local.
8. Build partnerships, e.g. through franchises.
9. Ensure the widest possible availability.
10. Exploit the distribution channel to communicate the brand.

In the 2000s, more and more organisations may be expected to take this advice and see the entire company as a brand that will represent the essence of the benefits customers will receive if they enter into a relationship with it. We return to this theme in Chapter 20.

Box 13.2 — **Private label brands**

Sales of many major consumer branded goods have been declining over the past two years in Europe, for example Unilever, Nescafé (including bottled waters such as Perrier and Vittel, down 8.4%), Danone and L'Oreal, as a result of competition from private label brands offered by major retail chains. In the UK private labels accounted for approximately 38% of all sales of food and other FMCGs, 30% in Germany, 25% in Spain, 22% in France and around 16% in the USA.

The growth of private labels has been driven by the need for the longer established groups like Carrefour to meet competition from discounters such as Aldi Group (Germany) and Leader Price (France), which are almost entirely private label, selling for 20–40% less than manufacturer's brands. Given that it is widely known that firms like Nestlé, Cadbury Schweppes and Heinz already sell private label versions of their products, many consumers are at least willing to try the lower cost alternatives. Where they find them satisfactory, the attraction of much lower prices is a strong incentive to switch.

For major manufacturers the options seem to be either to flex their muscles and discount heavily, as P&G has done with its Pampers brand of disposable nappies, or do a deal with the major discounters to get shelf space in their outlets and maintain or increase volume. Either way, given the growing power of the retailer, it seems clear that the manufacturers will have to be even more innovative and creative in their marketing if they are to resist the challenge of the growing number of specialist suppliers catering for the private label market.

SOURCE: *Business Week*, 21 March, 2005

Chapter summary

In this chapter we have looked at the need for firms to position themselves in the marketplace. Positioning is the development of a distinctive and unique selling proposition (USP), which enables sellers to differentiate themselves from all other sellers who are seeking to serve the same market segment.

The need for positioning has arisen due to increased international (and domestic) competition and the erosion of the ability to develop objectively different products based upon technological innovation. Given the proliferation of available solutions to the firm's/individual's consumption needs, and the intensity of the competitive effort clamouring for attention, it is unsurprising that buyers have developed decision rules to simplify the complexity of the situation. In such an environment the brand – product, service, and especially the company – has become a convenient shorthand to summarise a multiplicity of both objective and subjective attributes that have to be considered when making choice decisions. The nature and importance of these diverse attributes have been reviewed, as have techniques such as perceptual mapping which enable sellers to capture and analyse this complexity as the basis for developing differentiated marketing strategies.

Recommended reading

Aaker, D. A. (2002) *Building Strong Brands*. New York: Simon & Schuster.

de Chernatony, L. and McDonald, M. (2003) *Creating Powerful Brands* (3rd edn). Elsevier/Butterworth Heinemann.

Doyle, P. (2003) Branding, in Baker, M. J. (ed.) *The Marketing Book* (5th edn). Oxford: Butterworth Heinemann.

Hooley, G. J. (1999) Positioning, in Baker, M. J. (ed.) *Encyclopedia of Marketing*. London: International Thomson Business Press.

Ries, A. and Trout, J. (2001) *Positioning: The Battle for Your Mind*. New York: McGraw-Hill Education.

Sengupta, S. (2004) *Brand Positioning: Strategies for Competitive Advantage* (2nd edn). New York: McGraw-Hill.

Sherrington, M. (1999) Branding and Brand Management, in Baker, M. J. (ed.) *Encyclopedia of Marketing*. London: International Thomson Business Press.

REFERENCES

Baker, M. J. and Hart, S. J. (1989) *Marketing and Competitive Success*. London: Philip Allan.

Baker, M. J. and Hart, S. J. (2007) *Product Strategy and Management* (2nd edn). Hemel Hempstead: Pearson.

Buzzell, R. D. and Gale, B. T. (1987) *The PIMS Principles: Linking Strategy to Performance*. London: Collier-Macmillan.

Clifford, D. K. and Cavanagh, R. E. (1985) *The Winning Performance: How America's High Growth Midsize Companies Succeed*. London: Sidgwick & Jackson.

Davies, G. and Brooks, J. (1989) *Positioning Strategy in Retailing*. London: Paul Chapman.

de Chernatony, L. and Dall'Olmo Riley, F. (1998) Defining a 'brand': beyond the literature with experts' interpretations, *Journal of Marketing Management*, **14**(5): 417–43.

Doyle, P. (1999) Branding, in Baker, M. J. (ed.) *The Marketing Book* (4th edn). Oxford: Butterworth Heinemann.

King, S. (1991) The company as a brand, *Journal of Marketing Management*, **7**(1).

Kotler, P. (1991) *Marketing Management: Analysis, Planning and Control* (8th edn). Englewood Cliffs, NJ: Prentice Hall.

Levitt, T. (1960) Marketing myopia, *Harvard Business Review* (July–August): 45.

Levitt, T. (1983) *The Marketing Imagination*. London: Collier-Macmillan.

Lindquist, J. D. (1974) Meaning of image, *Journal of Retailing*, **50**.

Mitchell, A. (1996) Evolution, *Marketing Business* (May).

Murphy, J. (1991) *Marketing Business* (July–August).

Peters, T. (1988) *Thriving on Chaos*. London: Macmillan – now Palgrave Macmillan.

Ries, A. and Trout, J. (2001) *Positioning: the Battle for your Mind*. New York: McGraw-Hill.

Seth, A. (1998) Just doing it, *Marketing Business* (February).

Urban, G. L. and Star, S. H. (1991) *Advanced Marketing Strategy: Phenomena, Analysis and Decisions*. Englewood Cliffs, NJ: Prentice Hall.

Part 3

MANAGING THE MARKETING MIX

The marketing mix

A recipe should be a tune to which you can sing your own song.

RICK STEIN, MASTER CHEF

After reading Chapter 14 you will be able to:

✔ Explain the concept of the marketing mix.

✔ Describe the elements or ingredients which make up the marketing mix and critique some of the different classificatory schemes.

✔ Discuss the factors which influence the relative importance of mix elements and their selection and use.

✔ Suggest some possible mix patterns according to industry type and stage of the product life-cycle.

✔ Identify some criticisms of the mix concept.

INTRODUCTION

In common with many other professions, the practice of marketing is often made complex and difficult due to the sheer diversity of the problems with which it is confronted. To a large degree this diversity is because the principal actors in exchange processes are people, or organisations comprised of people, and so exhibit the dynamic and interactive behaviour associated with human beings. If human beings rarely became unwell and then only from a small range of causes, we would have need for many fewer doctors than at present. Similarly, if disagreements between parties leading to litigation were limited in their origins, then we would have a need for many fewer lawyers. However, like marketing, these two professions have to deal with an enormous variety of factors that might give rise to a need for medical care or litigation. Accordingly, professions all have a need for diagnostic frameworks that help them to isolate the most likely causes of the problem to be solved, so that these may become the focus of detailed examination.

In marketing, one such conceptual framework, particularly useful in helping practitioners to structure their thinking about marketing problems, is the so-called 'marketing mix'. To devise a product or service that will be seen as different in the eyes of prospective customers, to the point where they will prefer it to all competing substitutes, is obviously the ultimate objective of the marketer. In devising this unique selling proposition (USP) or bundle of benefits, marketers have four basic ingredients they can combine in an almost infinite number of ways to achieve different end results. These four basic ingredients are frequently referred to as the 4 'Ps' of marketing following the classification first proposed by McCarthy (1978). These 4 Ps – product, price, place (or distribution) and promotion are the subject of separate treatment in later chapters. Here our primary aim is to review how they may be combined to create a distinctive marketing mix.

According to John O'Shaughnessey (1984, p. 54):

Product, price, promotion and distribution are factors that, within limits, are capable of being influenced or controlled. Marketing strategy can be viewed as reflecting a marketing mix of these four elements. Every market has its own logic whereby excellence on one element of the mix, whether product, price, promotion or distribution, is often a necessary condition for success ... Knowing the key factor in the marketing mix is crucial in drawing up a marketing strategy since it means knowing what to emphasise.

THE EVOLUTION OF THE MARKETING MIX CONCEPT

Although marketers have always experimented with different combinations of product, price, place and promotion, it is only comparatively recently that serious attempts have been made to see if any particular combinations give better or worse results than others. Clearly, if this is the case, then such combinations are to be preferred or avoided as the case may be. One of the earliest studies of this kind was undertaken by the Harvard Business School Bureau of Business Research in 1929 which sought to determine if there were any common relationships to be found in the expenses on various marketing functions of a sample of food manufacturing companies. Almost two decades later James Culliton (1948) set out to discover whether a bigger sample and more careful classification of companies would yield a different result from that found in the earlier study (in the 1929 study, no common figures had been found which could be used for predictive purposes). Despite Culliton's more rigorous and larger scale investigation, the results were the same, and it was this which led Culliton to describe the business executive as a 'decider', 'an artist' – a 'mixer of ingredients who sometimes follows a recipe to the ingredients immediately available, and sometimes experiments with or invents ingredients no-one else has tried'. This description of a marketing executive as a mixer of ingredients appealed greatly to his fellow Harvard Professor, Neil Borden (1975), who began to use the term 'marketing mix' to describe the results. Borden wrote that

Culliton's description ... appealed to me as an apt and easily understandable phrase, far better than my previous references to the marketing man as an empiricist seeking in any situation, to devise a profitable 'pattern' or 'formula' of marketing operations from among the many procedures and policies that were open to him. If he was a 'mixer of ingredients', what he designed was a 'marketing mix'!

Given this idea of a marketing mix, it follows that the next step is to identify and classify the various ingredients available to the marketer and the uses to which they may be put.

IDENTIFYING THE INGREDIENTS OF THE MARKETING MIX

A search of the available literature concerned with the marketing mix components reveals that there is a wide diversity among marketers on what elements compose the marketing mix.

Many checklists and guides featuring different elements of the marketing mix have been proposed since the concept first came into being. These checklists, as Borden indicates, can be long or short, depending on how far one wishes to go on in the classification and subclassification of the marketing procedures and policies with which marketing managements deal when devising marketing programmes.

However, a brief review of the literature suggests that there are many classifications of the marketing mix elements ranging from the narrow classification (e.g. two-way classification) to the broadest one (the twelve-way classification).

Albert Frey (1961), uses two dimensions: the offering (product, package etc. and the tools (e.g. advertising and personal selling etc.).

Lazer and Kelley (1975) and Lazer et al. (1973) use a threefold classification:

1. The product and service mix, which includes many factors such as the number of product lines carried, as well as the product planning, product development, size, colour, price, packaging, warranties and guarantees, branding, labelling and the service of each individual's product.
2. The distribution mix, which comprises two components, the channels of distribution, and the activities of physical distribution.
3. The communication mix, which pertains to the strategic combination of advertising, personal selling, sales promotion and other promotional

tools used in communicating with the market-place.

McCarthy (1978), Stanton (1967) and Lipson and Darling (1971) among others, have used a four-way classification, namely, product, price, place and promotion.

Lipson and Darling, for example, divide the marketing mix elements into four components, namely, product component mix, terms of sale component mix, communications component mix, and distribution component mix. Figure 14.1 indicates these submixes. Each of the major components may consist of four dimensions or major variables, which are directed at a particular market segment.

By contrast, John Martin (1978) argues that the purpose of the marketing mix is to communicate with targeted buyers or buying groups whom he places at the centre of his conceptualisation of the marketing mix, as shown in Figure 14.2.

In the broadest terms, Borden (1975) lists the important elements or ingredients that make up marketing programmes. He distinguishes twelve subdivisions:

1. *Merchandising – product planning:*
   - Determination of product (or service to be sold – qualities, design etc.). To whom, when, where and in what quantities?
   - Determination of new product programme – research and development, merger
   - Determination of marketing research programme
2. *Pricing:*
   - Determination of level of prices
   - Determination of psychological aspects of price, e.g. odd or even
   - Determination of pricing policy, e.g. one price or varying price, use of price maintenance etc.
   - Determination of margins: freedom in setting?
3. *Branding:*
   - Determination of brand policy, e.g. individual brand or family brand
4. *Channels of distribution:*
   - Determination of channels to use – direct sale to user, direct sale to retailers or user, sources of purchase, e.g. supply houses

Product component mix

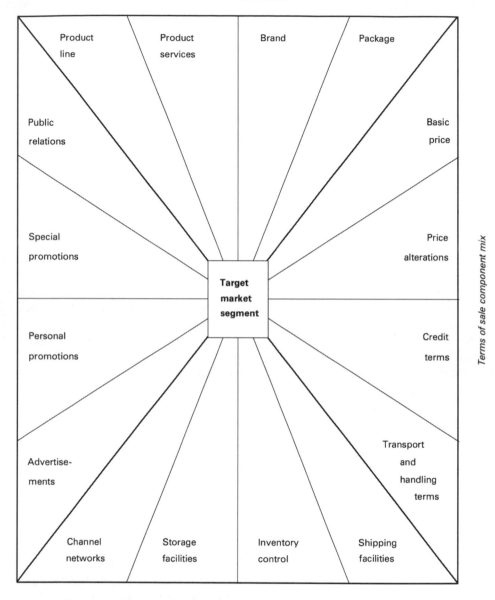

FIGURE 14.1 Model of the customer market offering dimensions of the marketing mix

SOURCE: Lipson, H. A. and Darling, J. R. (1971) *Introduction to Marketing: An Administrative Approach.* New York: John Wiley & Sons

- Determination of degree of selectivity among dealers
- Devising of programmes to secure channel cooperation

5. *Personal selling:*
   - Determination of burden to be placed on personal selling and methods to be employed:

- for manufacturer's organisation
- for wholesalers
- for retailers

- Organisation, selection, training and guidance of sales force at various levels of distribution

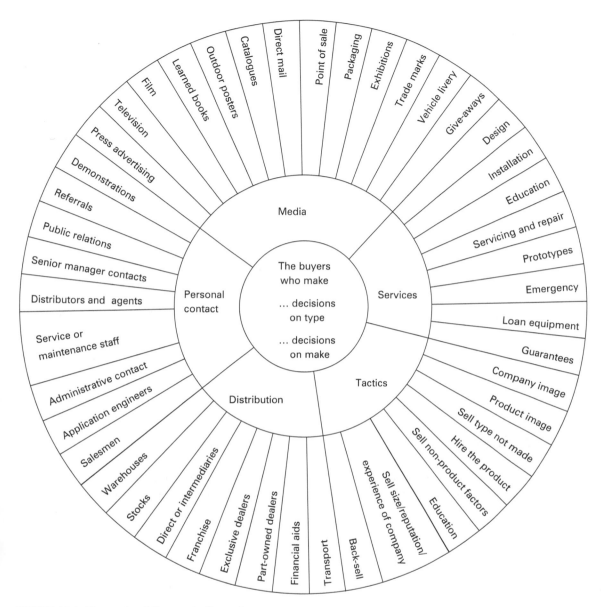

FIGURE 14.2 Elements of the marketing mix

SOURCE: Martin, J. (1978) The best practice of business, in *Marketing Planning*, vol. 5. London: John Martin Publishing

6. *Advertising:*
   - Determination of appropriation burden to be placed on advertising
   - Determination of copy policy
   - Determination of mix of advertising:
     - to trade
     - to consumers
   - Determination of media
7. *Promotions:*
   - Determination of burden to place on special selling plans or devices and formulation of promotions:
     - to trade
     - to consumers
8. *Packaging:*
   - Determination of importance of packaging and formulation of packages
9. *Display:*
   - Determination of importance and devising of procedures

10. *Servicing:*
    – Determination of importance of service and devising of procedures to meet consumer needs and desires
11. *Physical handling:* warehousing – transport-ation – stock policy
12. *Fact-finding and analysis:* marketing research.

With regard to the marketing forces bearing upon the marketing mix, Borden divides them into four categories, namely, consumer attitudes and habits, trade attitudes and methods, competition and government control, all of which govern the blending of the marketing elements.

From the above review of the different approaches to the marketing mix components, it can be argued that there is no widely accepted list that can be used by marketers. Some of them talk of the marketing mix in terms of the 4 Ps, i.e. prod-uct, price, place and promotion. Some others add a fifth element, i.e. after-sales service, while some marketers talk about 7 Ps and one A – price, promotion, packaging, personal selling, publicity, physical distribution and advertising.

SELECTING THE RIGHT MIX

These ingredients of the mix are valid in most situations. Nonetheless, there are environments in which the mix ingredients must be adapted to the specific needs of the marketplace. For a cosmetic manufacturer, packaging and advertising may be so important that they deserve classification as separate marketing activities, while storage may be so unimportant as not to deserve separate clas-sification. Each marketer should set up their own classification of marketing activities, emphasising those important to the operation's success, de-emphasising others.

Simon Majaro (1982) identifies three of the factors that help the marketer to make a decision as to whether a specific ingredient deserves a separate existence in the mix.

1. *The level of expenditure spent on a given ingredient:* Every ingredient involving a significant expen-diture would normally earn its separate iden-tity. Basically, it is a question of resources allocated to each ingredient which matters.

Thus, a firm that spends an insignificant amount of money on packaging would not bother to give this ingredient a separate exis-tence, but will attach it to the product or the 'promotional' mix, whichever appears more appropriate in the circumstances.

2. *The perceived level of elasticity and consumer responsiveness:* Where the marketer knows that a change in the level of expenditure (up or down) of a given ingredient will affect results, it must be treated as a separate tool in the mix. For example, if the marketer is able to alter the supply–demand relationship through price changes, this element deserves a separate place in the mix. On the other hand, for a firm enjoy-ing a monopoly or where the price is fixed by government edict, the price will be less impor-tant or may be removed from the mix.

3. *Allocation of responsibilities:* A well-defined and well-structured marketing mix reflects a clear-cut allocation of responsibilities. Thus, where the firm requires the services of a specialist to help to develop or design new packaging, as in the case of cosmetics firms, it is perfectly proper to say that 'packaging' is an important and integral part of the mix and deserves a separate existence therein.

So while the ingredients of the mix described above are valid in most situations, the mix elements and their relative importance may differ from industry to industry, from company to company and quite often during the life of the product itself. Furthermore, the marketing mix must take full cognisance of the major environ-mental dimensions that prevail in the market-place. This latter point adds a dynamic flavour to the marketing mix in so far as it has to be changed from time to time in response to new factors in the marketing scene.

Generally, in striving to maintain or improve his profit position, the marketer is an empiricist trying changes in the several procedures and policies which make up what we call a 'marketing programme'. Success depends to a large extent on understanding the forces of the market that bear upon any product or product line and skill in devising a 'mix' of marketing methods that conforms and adjusts to these forces in ways that produce a satisfactory net profit figure.

A study of the marketing programmes or mixes that have been evolved under this empirical approach shows a tremendous variation in their patterns. This variation is reflected in the operating statements of manufacturers, e.g. profit and loss accounts and balance sheets. As Culliton (1948) found, among such statements there is little uniformity, even among manufacturers in the same industry. There are no common figures of expense that have much meaning as standards, as holds true for many retail and wholesale trades, where the methods of operation tend to greater uniformity. Instead, the ratios of sales devoted to the various functions of marketing are widely diverse. This diversity in methods and in expenditures by categories, even within an industry, is accounted for largely by the fact that products, the volume of sales, the market covered, and the other facts that govern operations of each company tend to be unique and not conducive to uniformity with the operational methods of other companies, although there are tendencies towards uniformity among companies whose product lines are subject to the same market forces. As noted, in any category of expenses the percentage of sales spent may cover wide ranges. For instance, the advertising expense figure, which reflects the burden placed upon advertising in the marketing programme, will be found to vary among manufacturers from almost 0% to over 50%. Similarly, the percentages of sales devoted to personal selling will cover a wide range among different businesses.

To illustrate, proprietary medicine manufacturers often have no sales force at all. Advertising is used to sell the product to consumers and advertising literally 'pulls' the product through the channels of distribution. At the retail level, little or no effort is made to secure selling support. In contrast, manufacturers of other types of products, e.g. heavy machinery, often put relatively little of the burden of selling upon advertising and rely primarily on the 'push' of personal selling by either sales force or the sales force of distributors.

The part played in the marketing programme by the distributive trades varies markedly. Sometimes the trade plays a considerable part in the sales programme and the close support and cooperation of the trade is sought, as has generally been true with heavy appliances. In other instances the part played by the trade is not highly important and little effort is devoted to securing trade support, as is true among the proprietary medicine companies cited above. Likewise, the employment of sales promotional devices and of point of purchase effort in marketing programmes varies widely.

In the matter of pricing and pricing policy, wide variation is likely to be found. In some instances competition is carried out largely on price and margins are narrow. In other instances prices are set with wide margins and competition is carried out on non-price bases, such as product quality or services or advertising. In some instances resale prices are maintained; in others they are not.

It is possible to go on citing wide differences in the practices of branding, packaging and servicing that have been evolved.

In short, the elements of marketing programmes can be combined in many ways. Or, stated another way, the 'marketing mixes' for different types of products vary widely, and even for the same class of product competing companies may employ different mixes. In the course of time a company may change its marketing mix for a product, for in a dynamic world the marketer must adjust to the changing forces of the market. The goal of business in any instance is to find a mix that will prove profitable. To attain this end, the various elements have to be combined in a logically integrated programme to conform to market forces bearing on the individual product. Guptara (1990) provides a useful summary of variation in the marketing mix, as illustrated in Figure 14.3.

To summarise, the concept of the marketing mix is a schematic plan to guide analysis of marketing problems through utilisation of:

- A list of the important forces emanating from the market that bear upon the marketing operations of an enterprise
- A list of the elements (procedures and policies) of marketing programmes.

The marketing mix thus refers to the apportionment of effort, the combination, the designing, and the integration of the elements of marketing into a programme or 'mix' which, on the basis of an appraisal of the market forces, will best achieve the objectives of an enterprise at a given time.

In his original conceptualisation, Borden (1975)

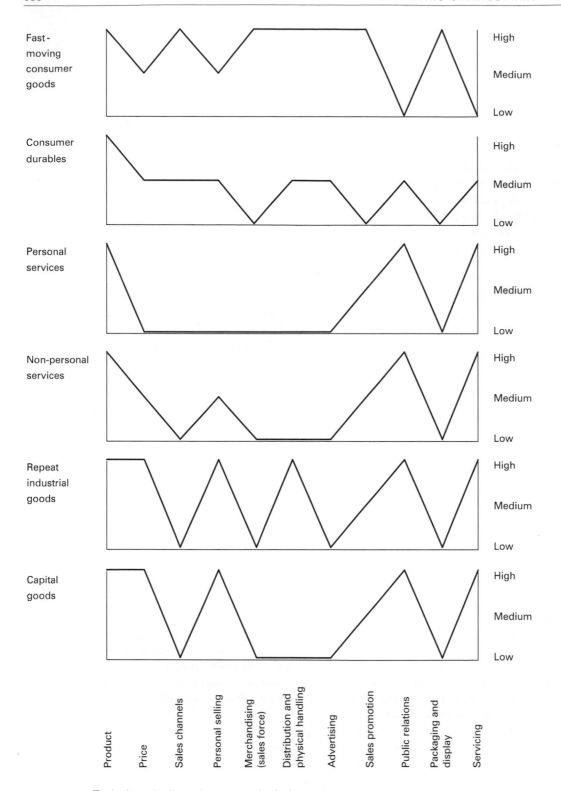

FIGURE 14.3 Typical marketing mix patterns by industry type

SOURCE: Guptara, P. (1990) *The Basic Arts of Marketing*. London: Hutchinson

suggested the following list of market forces bearing upon the marketing mix:

1. Consumer attitudes and habits:
   - Motivation of users
   - Buying habits and attitudes
   - Important trends bearing on living habits and attitudes
2. Trade attitudes and methods:
   - Motivation of trade
   - Trade structure
   - Trade practices and attitudes
   - Trends in trade procedures, methods, attitudes.
3. Competition:
   - Is competition on a price or non-price basis?
   - What are the choices afforded consumers:
     - in product?
     - in price?
     - in service?
   - What is the relation of supply to demand?
   - What is your position in the market – size and strength relative to competitors, number of firms, degree of concentration?
   - What indirect competition vs. direct competition?
   - Competitors' plans – what new developments in products, pricing, or selling plans are impending?
   - What moves will competition be likely to make to actions taken by your firm?
4. Governmental controls:
   - Over product
   - Over pricing
   - Over competitive practices
   - Over advertising and promotion.

It follows that the actual design and management of the marketing mix will depend upon the firm's own perception of its strengths and weaknesses vis-à-vis the threats and opportunities in the markets and environment in which it is to compete. In forming judgements as to the tactical deployment of the mix elements, management will need to undertake a closer analysis of demand and supply than that provided by the environmental review discussed in Chapter 7 or the broad discussion of buyer behaviour in Chapter 9. Two key inputs to detailed marketing planning within the framework of SMP are sales forecasting and

the execution of a marketing audit, as discussed in Chapter 10.

MANAGING THE MIX

Professor Peter Doyle (1999) provides a clear exposition of the key issues involved in managing the marketing mix. As he points out:

> There are two key decisions which are central to marketing management: the selection of target markets which determine where the firm will compete and the design of the marketing mix (product, price, promotion, and distribution method) which will determine its success in these markets.

Up to this point, the emphasis has been upon defining the context within which exchange or marketing occurs; of the forces – economic, behavioural, technological, political and legal – which shape and influence the exchange process; and of procedures for analysing and interpreting all these factors as a basis for developing a coherent and viable strategy. But, as we have seen, strategy identifies future objectives to which the firm aspires and which are likely to be modified due to changing circumstances. Thus strategy charts a direction to be followed to achieve a destination that will probably be changed as we approach it. However, to ensure that we remain on course, we will set a series of sub-objectives which represent points along the way from where we are to where we want to be. Given the convention of reporting financial performance on an annual basis, it has also become conventional to set performance targets on an annual basis and develop short-term plans for their achievement. In turn, short-term (one-year) plans are usually a subset of a medium-term (three- to five-year) plan equivalent to the Kitchin or inventory cycle described in Chapter 7.

Short-term plans and, to a lesser extent, medium-term plans, are clearly the domain of operational management. It is this operational management which is responsible for translating the strategy into plans and for devising marketing mixes for their realisation. Where a firm is practising undifferentiated or concentrated marketing, it will have only a single marketing mix but, where it is practising differentiated marketing, it will have

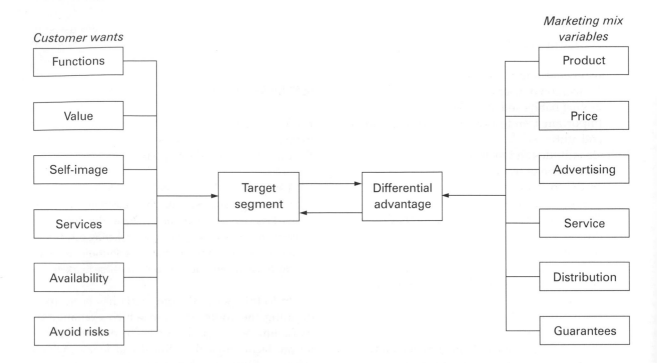

FIGURE 14.4 The marketing mix and differential advantage: matching customer service wants

SOURCE: Doyle, P. (1999) Managing the marketing mix, in Baker, M. J. (ed.) *The Marketing Book* (4th edn). London: Butterworth Heinemann

several. Irrespective of whether it has one or several mixes, the objective is the same – to develop and maintain a sustainable differential advantage (SDA). In order to do this it is necessary to undertake the kinds of analysis described in earlier chapters.

Simply analysing problems is not enough – as we have observed on several occasions it is a necessary, but not sufficient, condition for success. Marshalling evidence is a precondition for analysis but it does not follow that all decision-makers will draw the same conclusion from a given data set (selective perception strikes again!). What matters is the quality of the plan devised by managers based upon their analysis and the quality of the implementation. Central to all this is the understanding and deployment of the mix elements. Doyle (1999) provides a useful diagram to illustrate the nature of the matching process, which ensures that the marketing mix is consistent with the needs of customers in the target market (see Figure 14.4).

Similarly, Chester Wasson (1974) provided an excellent summary of the use of the various mix

elements in accordance with the phases of the PLC, as illustrated in Table 14.1.

SOME CRITICISMS OF THE MARKETING MIX

While the marketing mix has become one of the best-known models in marketing, described in detail in every basic marketing text and widely used in practice, the concept is not without its critics. Writing in the *Encyclopedia of Marketing*, van Waterschoot (1999) identifies a number of deficiencies in the concept, which may be summarised as:

1. It focuses on what marketers do *to* customers rather than *for* them
2. It is externally directed and ignores the internal market
3. It says nothing about interactions between the mix variables
4. It takes a mechanistic view about markets
5. It assumes a transactional exchange rather than a relationship.

In a nutshell, these five criticisms may all be seen to be dimensions of the same failing – a neglect of the people factor. It would seem appropriate, therefore, that we should extend and modify the 4 Ps model of marketing to include a fifth P – people.

Putting people into marketing is essential for many reasons. Within the limits of a short chapter of this kind we may only consider three of the more important ones.

First, marketing is a professional practice – it is something which people do. While it is perfectly feasible to theorise about marketing in the abstract, like many other academic disciplines, the main reason people study the subject is to provide a basis for success, for practice. Like medicine, engineering and architecture, marketing is what we have described as a synthetic discipline. Not 'synthetic' in the pejorative sense of 'a poor substitute for the real thing' but synthetic in the sense defined by the *Concise Oxford Dictionary* as 'the process or result of building up separate elements, especially ideas, into a connected whole, especially into a theory or system'. Thus, in marketing, we incorporate and integrate the best insight, and ideas from core disciplines such as economics, psychology and sociology and synthesise them into implementable practices. Market segmentation, targeting and positioning are examples of how marketing reconciles the economist's assumptions of homogeneous demand with the psychologist's perception of every individual differing from every other in some degree, and provides a practical solution of creating choice at an affordable cost. Marketing is something done for people by people.

A second reason for putting people into the marketing mix is that increasingly it is the people who provide the basis of differentiation between competing suppliers on which buyers make their choices. Traditionally, differentiation between competing suppliers has tended to rest upon the creation of objective differences through technological innovation. Nowadays, such objective differences are rapidly eroded by competition (it is relatively easy to benchmark your competitors' product to see how he's improved it) or else overtaken by the ever quickening pace of new product development. It is this trend that has led to the recognition that long-term competitive success depends on building relationships rather than seeing marketing management as responsible for ensuring that the seller gets the better of the buyer in a series of independent transactions each of which must be profitable to the seller. In turn, this recognition has highlighted the importance of internal marketing and the fact that in an increasingly knowledge-based society, people (human capital) are the organisation's greatest asset.

Finally, a third reason for putting people into the marketing mix is because it is not only people who plan and devise marketing mixes, it is people who implement such plans. Further, a great deal of research into competitiveness in recent years has confirmed beyond doubt that in the final analysis it is the quality of implementation that distinguishes between success and failure. In *Marketing and Competitive Success* (Baker and Hart, 1989), a rigorous survey into a matched sample of successful and less successful firms in six industries indicated that very few of the so-called critical success factors were present in successful firms and absent from unsuccessful firms, i.e. you could infer they were related to improved performance. On reflection, the reasons are not hard to find.

To begin with, nobody wants to fail. Accordingly, management staff in less successful organisations are just as ambitious as their opposite members in successful firms in studying for professional qualifications, reading management books, attending seminars and seeking advice from experts. In other words *they know what to do.* It follows that if they are less successful it is due to the quality of execution and, possibly, a little luck. The view conforms with Napoleon's expressed wish for lucky generals. Other things being equal, we must assume that the military commanders who become generals must both understand the principles of warfare and have demonstrated skill in their practice or they would not have been promoted to command an army. In warfare, however, we have the extreme form of competition as a zero-sum game with a winner and a loser, so what determines the outcome? People! In the words of the song, 'It ain't what you do, it's the way that you do it.'

But, even with the addition of 'people' many still believe the mix concept has outlived its usefulness. Among the more recent, best-documented and certainly most readable criticisms is an article

TABLE 14.1 Wasson's hypotheses about appropriate strategies over the product life-cycle

DYNAMIC COMPETITIVE STRATEGY AND THE MARKET LIFE-CYCLE

	MARKET DEVELOPMENT (Introductory period for high-learning products only)	RAPID GROWTH (Normal introductory pattern for a very low-learning product)	COMPETITIVE TURBULENCE	SATURATION (Maturity)	DECLINE
Strategy objective	Minimise learning requirements, locate and remedy offering defects quickly, develop widespread awareness of benefits, and gain trial by early adopters	To establish a strong brand market and distribution niche as quickly as possible	To maintain and strengthen the market niche achieved through dealer and consumer loyalty	To defend brand position against competing brands and product category against other potential products, through constant attention to product improvement opportunities and fresh promotional and distribution approaches	To milk the offering dry of all possible profit
Outlook for competition	None is likely to be attracted in the early, unprofitable stages	Early entrance of numerous aggressive emulators	Price and distribution squeezes on the industry, shaking out the weaker entrants	Competition stabilised, with few or no new entrants and market shares not subject to substantial change in the absence of a substantial perceived improvement in some brands	Similar competition declining and dropping out because of decrease in consumer interest
Product design objectives	Limited number of models with physical product and offering designs both focused on minimising learning requirements. Designs cost- and use-engineered to appeal to most receptive segment. Utmost attention to quality control and quick elimination of market revealed defects in design	Modular design to facilitate flexible addition of variants to appeal to every new segment and new use system as fast as discovered	Intensified attention to product improvement, tighten up line to eliminate unnecessary specialities with little market appeal	A constant alert for market pyramiding opportunities through either bold cost and price penetration of new markets or major product changes. Introduction of flanker products. Constant attention to possibilities for product improvement and cost-cutting. Re-examination of necessity of design compromises	Constant pruning of line to eliminate any items not returning a direct profit

Pricing objective	To impose the minimum of value perception learning and to match the value reference perception of the most receptive segments. High trade discounts and sampling advisable	A price line for every taste, from low-end to premium models. Customary trade discounts. Aggressive promotional pricing, with prices cut as fast as costs decline due to accumulated production experience	Increased attention to market-broadening and promotional pricing opportunities	Defensive pricing to preserve product category franchise. Search for incremental pricing opportunities, including private label contracts, to boost volume and gain in experience	Maintenance of profit level pricing with complete disregard for any effect on market share
Promotional guidelines Communications objectives	(a) Create widespread awareness and understanding of offering benefits (b) Gain trial by early adopters	Create and strengthen brand preference among trade and final users. Stimulate general trial	Maintain consumer franchise and strengthen dealer ties	Maintain consumer and trade loyalty, with strong emphasis on dealers and distributors. Promotion of greater use frequency	Phase out, keeping just enough to maintain profitable distribution
Most valuble media mix	In order of value: Publicity Personal sales Mass communications	Mass media. Personal sales. Sales promotions, including sampling. Publicity	Mass media. Dealer promotions. Personal selling to dealers. Sales promotion. Publicity	Mass media. Dealer-oriented promotions	Cut down all media to the bone – use no sales promotions of any kind
Distribution policy	Exclusive or selective, with distributor margins high enough to justify heavy promotional spending	Intensive and extensive, with dealer margins just high enough to keep them interested. Close attention to rapid resupply of distributor stocks and heavy inventories at all levels	Intensive and extensive, and a strong emphasis on keeping dealer well supplied, but with minimum inventory cost to him	Intensive and extensive, with strong emphasis on keeping dealer well supplied, but at minimum inventory cost to him	Phase out outlets as they become marginal
Intelligence focus	To identify actual development use systems and to uncover any product weakness	Detailed attention to brand position, to gaps in model and market coverage, and to opportunities for market segmentation	Close attention to product improvement needs, to market-broadening chances, and to possible fresh promotion themes	Intensified attention to possible product improvements. Sharp alert for potential new inter-product competition and for signs of beginning of production decline	Information helping to identify the point at which the product should be phased out

Note: Strictly speaking, this is the cycle of the category market, and only a high-learning introduction passes through all phases indicated above. The term, product life-cycle is sometimes applied indiscriminately to both brand cycles and category cycles. Most new brands are only emulative of other products already on the market, have a much shorter life than the product category, and must follow a strategy similar to any low-learning product.

SOURCE: Kerin, R. A. (1980) *Perspectives on Strategic Marketing Management* (2nd edn). Cambridge: MA: Allyn & Bacon

by Lisa O'Malley and Maurice Patterson (1998). Taking the view that theory development is an evolutionary process and one of displacement where new ideas supersede the old, O'Malley and Patterson utilise a road metaphor in the guise of a road movie to trace the origins and development of the marketing mix concept to support their view that it should now be left behind as we move towards more attractive destinations.

In tracing the evolution of marketing theory and practice it is pointed out that the 'mid-life crisis of marketing' identified by McKinsey in 1993 is not the first time that the discipline has reached a crossroads where it has had to determine the direction it has to take in future. As noted by O'Malley and Patterson (1998): 'The philosophical position of early marketing scholars was heavily influenced by the historical approach to economics and was more concerned with pressing social issues than business practice.' The catalyst for shifting emphasis to the managerial implications of marketing 'can no doubt be attributed to an expansion of large scale enterprise, an increase in the number of affluent buyers (Benton, 1987) and widespread employment of marketing techniques in industrialised societies (Fullerton, 1988).' As we saw in Chapter 1, the marketing management approach evolved during the 1950s in the US when the economic system was in danger of collapse as supply rapidly began to overtake demand. A similar imbalance had precipitated the Great Depression of the late 1920s and early 1930s and, as we have seen, an emphasis upon high-pressure selling had been insufficient to overcome this imbalance. Clearly, a more sophisticated approach was called for which, in turn, resulted in a demand for marketing education and a change in focus to 'The extension, refinement and evaluation of marketing as an organisational or management technology rather than on macro-level social issues, concerns, and problems' (Benton, 1987, p. 240, cited in O'Malley and Patterson). As O'Malley and Patterson note, 'This shift in philosophical position is encapsulated in the mix management paradigm'.

Underlying criticism of the marketing mix mode, in our opinion, is the mistaken view that it was ever intended as a 'theory' of marketing rather than a CUG or helpful learning and teaching tool. Certainly, Borden in his original conceptualisation

which, as we have seen, contains 12 variables, did not regard this as either a comprehensive or exhaustive list. It is equally certain than when McCarthy reduced the 12 mix elements to four – product, price, place and promotion – he, too, was more concerned with memorability than completeness.

Given that at least two generations of professional marketers have survived, and indeed prospered, believing in the marketing mix as a useful approach to the management of the marketing function, we should not now reject this approach on the grounds that its interpretation and implementation are flawed in terms of the philosophical intentions of the marketing concept itself. This point is highlighted by O'Malley and Patterson (1998), when they write:

> In terms of customer orientation, 'the marketing concept … calls for most of the effort to be spent on discovering the wants of a target audience and then creating goods and services to satisfy them' (Kotler and Zaltman, 1971, p. 5). However, far from being concerned with a customer's interests, the view implicit in the 4 P's approach implies that the customer is somebody *to* whom something is done rather than somebody *for* whom something is done (Dickson and Blois, 1983). The managerial approach to marketing, therefore, concentrates on the seller, and subordinates the customer to a passive as opposed to a pivotal role (Grönroos, 1994). Rather than the function of marketing being dynamic and market-oriented, it is instead a rather clinical, production-oriented approach (Grönroos, 1994; Laylock, 1983).

As a result of the emphasis upon manipulation of the 4 Ps, the marketing management function became dominant, resulting in the establishment of formal marketing departments. As we now know, this concentration of responsibility for marketing within a single department was a mistake as the essence of marketing was defined in Drucker's (1954) original statement that: 'Concern and responsibility for marketing must permeate all areas of the enterprise.' This is certainly the view that prevails today and is reflected in the disestablishment of formal marketing departments, the growth of internal marketing and the recognition that all members of a successful business organisation need to be marketing-oriented.

Other failings associated with the marketing mix concept include:

1. The inherent assumption that the firm is independent of its environment (Anderson and Soderlund, 1988)
2. The view that the seller is active and the buyer passive (Grönroos, 1994)
3. The assumption that markets are homogeneous and amenable to the application of a standardised marketing mix
4. The emphasis on marketing as a transaction which sees buyers and sellers as separate entities.

To accommodate these criticisms, many authors have increased the number of Ps, as we have ourselves, by suggesting the inclusion of people. Of course, by doing this they may just increase the complexity of the basic model and thereby reduce its memorability.

Fundamentally, however, the essential criticism of the marketing mix model by marketing scholars is that it is positivistic and prescriptive and so communicates an overly simplistic view of a complex reality. This issue was touched on in passing in our introductory chapter when we commented on the structure and content of standard textbooks. The fact that this chapter and several which have preceded it and will follow it contain discussions of alternative hypotheses and criticisms of prevailing models, should be sufficient to convince the reader that while the author may have his own view as to how things are or ought to be, the reader is perfectly entitled to form an alternative viewpoint.

While debate on the application of the marketing mix model is to be welcomed, one should be careful not to discard it prematurely because of perceived weaknesses in it. In line with our own preferred definition of marketing as being concerned with 'mutually satisfying exchange relationships', we must be careful not to tip the balance too much in favour of the buyer. The relationship between seller and buyer can only be mutually satisfying if both parties receive the benefit or satisfaction they looked for in entering into the relationship in the first place. In the case of the seller, this invariably means that income received exceeds the costs involved, so that the selling organisation can survive, prosper and deliver benefits to the stakeholders who depend upon it. It follows that those responsible for the management of the selling organisation must have a clear view as to how they can manage the resources under their control to achieve this outcome. It further follows that they need to have a view on what to do when entering into relationships with customers. If we also take the view that customers know what they are doing when they enter into a relationship with a seller, then perhaps we can also assume that they are not as easily manipulated as critics of the marketing mix paradigm would have us believe. Thus, while we willingly accept that many of the conditions that prevailed when the marketing mix model was first formulated – mass marketing practised by large divisionalised, hierarchical and functional organisations – have declined in importance, marketing is still concerned with time, place and consumption utilities and these are still very much determined by product, price, place and promotion.

Although O'Malley and Patterson (1998) claim that 'the marketing mix is a myth', the reader will have to decide for themselves if this is the case. (You should read the article in full before coming to any conclusions). For our part, we can only point out that, since time immemorial, people have believed in myths and this has and continues to have a significant impact on the way they lead their lives. Given that this text is as much about the practice of marketing as the theory which underpins it, the author's view is that the 4 Ps model is a useful simplifying device to enable marketing managers to impose some structure and direction on the tasks they must perform. It is in this belief that succeeding chapters deal with the key policies associated with the 4 Ps of product, price, place and promotion.

Chapter summary

Chapter 14 marks the transition from the strategic aspects of marketing planning to their application in practice. In this chapter we have been concerned with a conceptual framework that has proved to be particularly helpful in assisting practitioners to do this – the idea of the marketing mix. This idea is essentially simple and practical and proposes that, in seeking to develop a differentiated and competitive product, marketing managers will have recourse to a variety of 'ingredients' they can 'mix' together to create a unique 'recipe' or marketing plan.

Having traced the origins of the concept, we looked at a variety of different approaches to classifying the ingredients of the marketing mix. Our review identified very simple models containing only two factors – the offering and the tools – through McCarthy's well-known 4 Ps to Borden's original conceptualisation of 12 factors. Clearly, there is no single or definitive statement of the mix elements and practitioners must select the elements that are most important to the product–market situation with which they are concerned. Advice on how to do this was considered, together with a discussion of the factors which impact on this decision.

Next we took a brief look at the actual management of the marketing mix in terms of ensuring that it matches the needs of the intended target markets, and over the life-cycle of the product itself, before concluding with a look at some of the criticisms that have been made of the mix concept.

In the chapters which follow in Part III, we examine each of the mix elements in some detail. We would remind readers, however, that it is assumed that they have read a basic textbook or have practical experience of marketing. Accordingly, we have not discussed the descriptive aspects of the subject but have concentrated on the policy and management issues that need to be borne in mind when considering deployment and use of the individual mix variables.

Recommended reading

Constantinides, E. (2006) The marketing mix revisited: towards the 21st century marketing, *Journal of Marketing Management*, **22**(3/4): 407–38.

Doyle, P. (2003) Managing the marketing mix, in Baker, M. J. (ed.) *The Marketing Book* (5th edn). Oxford: Butterworth Heinemann.

Moller, K. (2006) Commentary, *Journal of Marketing Management*, **22**:(3/4).

van Waterschoot, W. (1999) The marketing mix, in Baker, M. J. (ed.) *Encyclopedia of Marketing*. London: International Thomson Business Press.

REFERENCES

Baker, M. J. and Hart, S. J. (1989) *Marketing and Competitive Success*. London: Philip Allen.

Borden, N. H. (1975) The concept of the marketing mix, in McCarthy, E. J. et al., *Readings in Basic Marketing*. Homewood, IL: Irwin, pp. 72–82.

Culliton, J. W. (1948) *The Management of Marketing Costs*. Boston, MA: Harvard University Press.

Doyle, P. (1999) Managing the marketing mix, in Baker, M. J. (ed.) *The Marketing Book* (4th edn). Oxford: Butterworth Heinemann.

Drucker, P. (1954) *The Practice of Management*. New York: Harper & Row.

Frey, A. W. (1961) *Advertising* (3rd edn). New York: Ronald Press, p. 30.

Guptara, P. (1990) *The Basic Arts of Marketing*. London: Hutchinson.

Kerin, R. A. (1980) *Perspectives on Strategic Marketing Management* (2nd edn). Cambridge: MA: Allyn & Bacon.

Lazer, W. and Kelley, E. J. (1975) *Managerial Marketing Perspectives and Viewpoints*. Homewood, IL: Irwin, pp. 72–82.

Lazer, W., Culley, J. D. and Staudt, T. (1973) The concept of the marketing mix, in Britt, S. H. (ed.) *Marketing Manager's Handbook*. Chicago, IL: Dartnell Corporation, pp. 77–89.

Lipson, H. A. and Darling, J. R. (1971) *Introduction to Marketing: An Administrative Approach*. New York: John Wiley & Sons.

McCarthy, E. J. (1978) *Basic Marketing: A Managerial Approach* (6th edn). Homewood, IL: Irwin, pp. 7–8.

Majaro, S. (1982) *Marketing in Perspective*. London: George Allen & Unwin, pp. 20–1.

Martin, J. (1978) The best practice of business, in *Marketing Planning*, vol. 5. London: John Martin Publishing.

O'Malley, L. and Patterson, M. (1998) Vanishing point: the mix management paradigm revisited, *Journal of Marketing Management*, **14**(November).

O'Shaughnessey, J. (1984) *Competitive Marketing: A Strategic Approach*. Winchester, MA: Allen & Unwin.

Stanton, W. (1967) *Fundamentals of Marketing* (2nd edn). New York: McGraw-Hill.

van Waterschoot, W. (1999) The marketing mix, in Baker, M. J. (ed.) *Encyclopedia of Marketing*. London: International Thomson Business Press, pp. 319–30.

Wasson, C. R. (1974) *Dynamic Competitive Strategy & Product Life Cycles*. St Charles, IL: Challenge Books.

Product policy and management

A market is never saturated with a good product, but it is very
quickly saturated with a bad one.   HENRY FORD

After reading Chapter 15 you will able to:

✔ Explain the central role played by products in the development of marketing strategy.

✔ Define the major terms associated with product management.

✔ Summarise some of the distinguishing characteristics of services.

✔ Identify the four basic growth strategies proposed by Ansoff, and their implications for product policy and management.

✔ Describe and illustrate the normative theory of new product development.

✔ Outline the concept of the product portfolio.

✔ Specify the actions most appropriate to the management of products at different stages of their life-cycles.

✔ Suggest procedures for monitoring product performance.

INTRODUCTION

According to the marketing concept – and in an ideal world – the primary focus of economic activity should be the market, for it is the market which mirrors demand and it is demand which reflects human needs. Thus textbook writers – and even some entrepreneurs – can start with the proposition that identification and selection of market opportunities should be the starting point for business activity. But, in the real world, things are very different. Most resources, or factors of production, are already committed to the creation of specific goods and services and a comparatively small surplus exists at any point in time which is available for new investment. Of course, in deciding the best use to which this surplus may be put, the normative theory of market planning will be of inestimable value in identifying market opportunities and selecting between them. Even so, choices will be severely proscribed, for existing organisations will usually seek to retain contact with one or other major dimension of their current operation (products or customers) and retain a common thread. Similarly, entrepreneurs rarely undertake a formal analysis of market opportunities and respond to a demand pull – usually they are implementing a strong drive to make and/or sell something for which they believe there is a need.

As a consequence of all these forces, the primary concern of most organisations is product policy and management rather than market policy and management. Once a firm has committed itself to a given market, all else flows from it and the decision is difficult if not impossible to reverse. As Corey (1975) has pointed out, choice of market 'builds a set of relationships with customers that are at once a major source of strength and a major commitment. The commitment carries with it the responsibility to serve customers well, to stay in the technical and product development race, and to grow in pace with growing market demand.'

Given the central role played by the product as the focus of the exchange process, it is clear that a single chapter in a book can only introduce some of the more important ideas and suggest where the reader may find more detailed information and explanation. To this end the chapter will open with a discussion of the role of the product in marketing and build upon earlier analyses of buyer behaviour and product portfolio planning. An attempt will also be made to define some of the terms used in the literature of product management.

Although we have argued that existing firms may be preoccupied with, or even locked into, certain products, the inexorable pressures of change will require them to determine how they can best position themselves to meet future needs. In turn, this will invariably require them to modify, update and even replace existing products with new ones and so will focus attention upon product development as a key strategic function. Our own analysis of product development will first look at it in the abstract as a process and will then seek to show how product policy and management will vary according to the different stages of the life-cycle – introduction, growth, maturity and decline. Finally in this chapter we will look at methods for monitoring product performance.

(For the purposes of this chapter 'services' will be considered to be synonymous with 'products'. While this may appear a heroic assumption, given that services account for more than 70% of all consumption in advanced economies when compared with physical products, it is our contention that in terms of marketing management, the differences are a matter of *degree* not *kind*. A brief description of some of the more important differences is included in this chapter and, in Chapter 20 we elaborate the point that most, if not all, physical products require services to enable them to be consumed, just as services need physical products to facilitate their creation and consumption. That said, if you are concerned with the marketing of services rather than products, you would be well advised to consult a specialised services marketing book for advice.)

THE ROLE OF THE PRODUCT IN MARKETING

For many years before the birth of the electronic watch, a classic case study in the armoury of any business school teacher offering a course in business policy, general management or marketing strategy was 'Hamilton Watch'. Almost without exception the first question posed on this case study was 'What is a watch?' and the answer would encompass a wide range from 'a scientific instrument for measuring time' through 'a gift' to 'a status symbol', thus allowing the instructor to make the basic point about any product, namely, it is a bundle of attributes and it is the need and perception of the consumer or user that will determine which of these definitions is most apposite in any given set of circumstances. Such an insight is fundamental to the marketing concept, underlies the reason why product differentiation became the basic competitive strategy in the 1920s, and explains why market segmentation has assumed such importance in the mature and saturated markets of the advanced industrialised economies.

As we attempted to show in Chapter 9, when addressing the question of how buyers select between alternatives, choice behaviour is conditioned by both objective and subjective factors. In recent years recognition that the objective factors which are intrinsic to the product (performance and price) are relatively easy to copy has led to much greater emphasis upon the qualitative and subjective dimensions which will become determinant when objective parity is perceived to exist. We say 'perceived' advisedly, for our analysis has shown that people have difficulty in distinguishing very small differences, to the extent that in business a useful working rule of thumb is that a difference must be at least 10% between the objects being compared if it is to become 'noticeable', i.e. 10% bigger, smaller, faster, more efficient etc. Two consequences flow from this:

1. Producers wrongly assume that small differentiating features will be perceived when they won't, with the result that
2. Greater emphasis is given to creating subjective differences between competitive products through service and promotional efforts.

The net outcome of these trends is that the recent literature on marketing has tended to give little specific attention to product characteristics and product differentiation and has concentrated more upon user characteristics and market segmentation. Such a change in emphasis is believed to have gone too far, for the simple reason that objective differences are easier to develop, control and sustain than subjective differences and, if they exist, will largely eliminate the need to try and create such subjective differences.

As Thompson (1962) observed:

You can change products: it is a comparatively simple matter of decision and cost. You can't change people – but you can influence them – but seldom if ever cheaply. It is far easier – and thus far more economical – to find out what people want and to supply it than it is to influence them to want what you make.

A sentiment echoing those of Ries and Trout (2001) in Chapter 13.

Support for the view that too much attention has been given to market 'need' as opposed to product content is to be found in a forceful article by Bennett and Cooper (1982). Citing the automobile industry as a microcosm of the American economy, Bennett and Cooper claim that lower cost and better fuel economy are simplistic explanations of the 30% market share secured by Japanese and European imports. In their view:

The Europeans and Japanese car makers have simply been better competitors; they anticipated market needs; they built a better product – one that is more reliable, has better workmanship, and is better engineered; and they did it effectively. In short, these manufacturers delivered better value to the American consumer.

Several similar instances (TV tubes, motorcycles etc.) are cited and lead to the conclusion that:

The failure to deliver product value to the customer is the prime reason for this lack of competitiveness. Twenty years of adherence to the marketing concept may have taken its toll of an American enterprise. The marketing concept has diverted our attention from the product and its manufacture; instead we have focused our strategy on responses to market wants and have become preoccupied with advertising, selling, and promotion. And in the process, product value has suffered.

Similarly, it is a truism to state that consumers will always prefer a better product at the same price or the same product at a lower price, but both observations underline the importance of trying to create objective product differences before resorting to the intangible and subjective elements.

Satisfaction is the end, but the product or service is the means by which it is achieved. As Lawrence Abbott (1955) has pointed out:

> What people really desire are not the products but satisfying experiences, [but] experiences are attained through activities. In order that activities may be carried out physical objects or the services of human beings are usually needed. Here lies the connecting-link between man's inner world and the outer world of economic activity. People want products because they want the experience-bringing services which they hope the products will render.

USER NEEDS AND PRODUCT CHARACTERISTICS

Ultimately it seems to me to be irrelevant whether one first identifies user needs and develops product characteristics to match them or, alternatively, creates a product and then seeks out customers whose needs match these characteristics. In the final analysis, the process is circular and subject to continuous adjustment. That said, there will be clear benefits if one can spell out some of the basic dimensions of user needs as this will make it that much easier to develop the appropriate product characteristics. A very helpful approach to this process is to be found in a monograph by Rothwell et al. (1983) published by the Design Council, which provides a framework for this section.

Rothwell et al. argue that user needs can be thought of as having four dimensions, which they define as follows:

1. *Need elements:* An indication of the overall price and specific performance characteristics required by customers
2. *Need intensity:* A measure of the degree of importance given to each need element by potential users
3. *Need stability:* A measure of the degree to which the need remains unchanged over time
4. *Need diffusion:* A measure of how widely felt the need is. This defines the size of the potential market.

Thus 'need elements' define the properties a product must contain and/or deliver, while 'need intensity' specifies the relative importance that

consumers will attach to any given element. As we have seen when analysing how buyers choose, many properties are assumed to exist as they are intrinsic to the product and it would not qualify for consideration at all if it didn't possess them. Further, buyers will often use a single performance or benefit criterion as a surrogate for a large number of individual product characteristics when assessing suitability or fitness for purpose, e.g. few buyers of machine tools will evaluate the metallurgical analysis of the materials used or the precise tolerances used in constructing the tool – they will assess its suitability in terms of its output potential. By the same token the purchaser of a TV set rarely inquires into the nature of the electronic gadgetry contained in the 'box'; they are concerned with the quality of the sound and picture which these components deliver. Of course there will always be exceptions to these generalisations, and it is for this reason that it is felt more attention should be given to spelling out the product's characteristics, for only by cataloguing them fully will we be able to establish whether our product possesses features others don't and, if so, whether these features will have appeal to a sufficient number of potential customers to constitute a viable market segment.

In Table 15.1 an attempt has been made to provide a consolidated listing of product characteristics or attributes to act as a checklist for assessing existing or proposed new products. Several sources have been used in an attempt to make the listing suitable for all categories of products.

In Figure 15.1 we reproduce a simple bar chart, which illustrates well how need elements and need intensity can be combined to give a quick visualisation of the product configuration desired by a particular market segment. Such pictograms should be constructed for each market segment and, when combined with an evaluation of the need stability and need diffusion, will enable planners to decide which offer the best opportunities in terms of their own aspirations and supply capabilities.

While physical attributes are a necessary condition for purchase they are not usually sufficient, particularly where there is little to distinguish one physical product from another.[1] In these circumstances our model of buyer behaviour predicates that subjective/behavioural influences will become determinant in enabling the individual to

TABLE 15.1 Product characteristics

TECHNICAL	ECONOMIC	
	Non-price	**Price**
Size	Servicing costs	List price
Shape	Availability of parts and service	Sale price
Weight	Running costs	Net price after trade-in allowance
Consistency	Breakdown costs	Financing or leasing arrangements
Materials used in construction	Depreciation	Discounts
Complexity	User training facilities	Sale or return
Power source	Instructions	Special offers
Power output	Delivery	
Speed/production rate		
Reliability		
Flexibility/adaptability		
Ease of use		
Ease of maintenance		
Safety		
Appearance/design features		
Smell		
Taste		

SOURCES: Rothwell, R. et al. (1983) *Design and the Economy.* London: The Design Council; Evans, J. R. and Berman, B. (1982) *Marketing.* New York: Macmillan

discriminate between competitive offerings. As we noted earlier, the creation of subjective perceived differences is likely to prove more difficult and more costly than the creation of objective differences, but the likelihood of being able to achieve this will be greatly enhanced if one adopts a

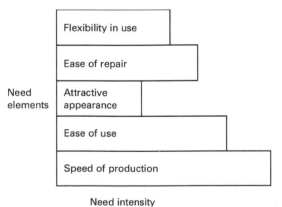

FIGURE 15.1 Bar chart showing need elements and need intensity

SOURCE: Rothwell, R. et al. (1983) *Design and the Economy.* London: The Design Council

marketing approach and defines one's product in terms of the benefit/satisfaction it provides rather than the function it performs. Levitt first propounded this philosophy in 'Marketing myopia' (1960), but elaborated on it in a subsequent contribution (1976b), when he wrote: 'One million quarter-inch drills were sold not because people wanted quarter-inch drills, but because they wanted quarter-inch holes.' Levitt also quoted the president of Melville Shoes as saying:

> People no longer buy shoes to keep their feet warm and dry. They buy them because of the way the shoes make them feel – masculine, feminine, rugged, different, sophisticated, young, glamorous, in. Buying shoes has become an emotional experience. *Our business now is selling excitement rather than shoes* (emphasis added).

This, of course, is an extreme statement and not to be taken too seriously. Clearly, people still do buy shoes to keep their feet warm and dry and have quite clear expectations as to the functions shoes must perform. But, the point is well made that different images and associations may well encourage people to buy more shoes, to suit different moods and situations, than are required for the sole purpose of protecting one's feet.

PRODUCT CLASSIFICATION AND MARKETING STRATEGY

Experience suggests that it is possible to classify types of products in terms of the relative emphasis that should be, or is, accorded to their objective and subjective characteristics and the manner in which they are bought. If this is so, then such classification will provide a useful basis for specifying the appropriate strategy to be used in the markets into which the different classes of goods are sold.

Perhaps the simplest and most obvious approach to product classification are the dichotomies industrial goods vs. consumer goods, and durable vs. non-durable goods. However, as Avlonitis (1980) has pointed out, these are at best approximations and a more sophisticated classificatory system is necessary to enable rational marketing strategy decisions to be made. He then reviews the three best-known schemata in the following terms:

> Historically, one of the most widely accepted classifications of products has been proposed by Copeland (1923). He proposed a trichotomy: convenience goods, shopping goods and specialty goods based on consumer buying habits. Although his concern was with consumer goods his scheme may be easily generalised to include industrial goods as well.

> Although this classification yields some anomalies and is not altogether satisfactory, it tends to be quite useful in guiding the development of marketing strategy. For instance convenience goods tend to require relatively heavy advertising and competitive pricing to achieve product differentiation and large distributive and selling organisations to deal with the need for widespread points of sale. Shopping goods that are of a higher unit value than convenience goods, and are purchased less frequently after deliberate comparison of alternatives, suggest more personal selling, selective distribution and quality conscious pricing. Speciality goods, because they are 'unique' in some regard so that special effort is required for their acquisition, suggest restricted promotion, exclusive

distribution, perhaps to the point of exclusive franchises and conformable pricing.

An alternative product classification scheme was introduced by Aspinwall (1958).[2] He proposed a trichotomy: pure Red goods (roughly parallel to convenience goods), pure Yellow goods (roughly parallel to shopping goods) and Orange goods (lying between the Red and Yellow goods) based on such characteristics as the replacement rate, gross margin, adjustment (services applied to goods in order to meet the exact needs of the consumer), time of consumption (durability) and searching time (time and distance from source of supply).

Aspinwall's scheme is useful for relating products to promotion and distribution strategy. For instance, the Red goods, because of the high replacement rate and low searching time required for their acquisition, suggest an intensive distribution system with long channels and mass advertising to pull products through the extensive channel network. The Yellow goods because of the adjustments required and the low replacement rates suggest more selective outlets. Also because customers desire to search out and compare alternative Yellow goods, personal selling becomes a better communication vehicle for this type of goods.

Aspinwall's work was revised and extended by Miracle (1969), who delineates five product groups instead of three by specifying nine product characteristics instead of five. The nine product partitioning characteristics are:

1. Unit value
2. Significance of each individual purchase to the customer
3. Time and effort spent purchasing by customers
4. Rate of technological change including fashion change
5. Technical complexity
6. Customer need for service before, during and after the sale
7. Frequency of purchase
8. Rapidity of consumption
9. Extent of usage or variety of ways in which the product provides utility.

When products are rated from very high to very low for each of these characteristics, certain combinations of rating occur together regularly for specific groups of products. On this basis, Miracle suggests that five product groups can be established. Having established product groups and their characteristics he then proceeds to recommend a marketing strategy for each group including the product variable (Degree of product variety) the price variable (Degree of control and variation in price) the distribution variable (Degree of distribution intensiveness) and promotion variable (Degree of emphasis between advertising and personal selling).

For Group I (cigarettes, candy bars, razor blades and soft drinks) little effort on product development, considerable effort on advertising with little or no personal selling, intensive distribution and little effort to control and adjust prices is required. At the other extreme, for Group V, the mix would consist of a custom-designed product sold directly from manufacturer to user, promoted through personal selling and transacted on the basis of an individually negotiated price. This Group includes electronic office equipment, steam turbines and specialised machine tools.

Marketing mix strategies for products in Groups II (groceries and small hardware items), III (radio and television sets) and IV (automobiles, high-quality household furniture) would reflect modifications of the mixes in Groups I and V.

Avlonitis proceeds to review some marginal refinements to Miracle's work, but these add little to the basic approach and can be ignored for our purposes.

While classifying products in this way will provide a useful first cut at selecting a marketing strategy, it is clear that other important considerations must also be borne in mind. Foremost among these is the stage of the product life-cycle and much of the remainder of this chapter will be concerned with identifying the influence and effect this will have on product policy and management. However, before turning to this subject, it will be helpful to define some of the terms in common currency in the product management literature and then review the broad policy alternatives which are available.

SOME DEFINITIONS OF THE 'PRODUCT'

From the foregoing review of product characteristics it is clear that there can be no simple or single definition of such a complex phenomenon as 'a product'. Indeed a central concern of our discussion to date has been an avoidance of such simple unidimensional definitions on the grounds that by adopting a particular slant we may exclude equally important alternatives. That said, the word 'product' is used quite specifically in a number of contexts in the marketing literature and it will be helpful to summarise and define these according to the common usage of the terms:

- *A product* is a combination of objective (tangible) and subjective (intangible) properties designed or intended to provide need-satisfying experiences to consumers
- *A product line* consists of a group of products with similar physical characteristics and/or similar end-use applications, e.g. lubricating oils, lathes, detergents, cosmetics
- *The product mix* comprises all the product lines of an organisation. With the emergence of the strategic business unit (SBU) as the basic planning unit, definition of the product mix is usually confined to the SBU. The product mix is usually assessed in terms of three dimensions – width, depth and consistency
- *Width* is defined in terms of the number of different product lines
- *Depth* measures the number of distinct products within a product line
- *Consistency* reflects the degree to which the various product lines enjoy similar end-uses and marketing mixes.

For the sake of convenience, products may be distinguished as industrial or consumer. Industrial products are usually classified as falling into one of four basic categories:

1. *Raw materials:* Those industrial materials which in part or in whole become a portion of the physical product but which have undergone no more processing than is required for convenience, protection, economy in storing, transportation or handling. Threshed grain, natural rubber and crushed ore fall into this category.
2. *Equipment:* Those industrial goods which do not become part of the physical product and which are exhausted only after repeated use, such as major installations or installations equipment, and auxiliary accessories or auxiliary equip-

ment. Installations equipment includes such items as boilers, presses, power lathes, bank vaults, etc., while auxiliary equipment includes trucks, office furniture, hand tools and the like.

3. *Fabricated materials:* Those industrial goods which become a part of the finished product and which have undergone processing beyond that required for raw materials, but not so much as finished parts. Steel, plastic moulding powders, cement and flour fit this description.

4. *Supplies:* Those industrial goods which do not become a part of the physical product or which are continually exhausted in facilitating the operation of an enterprise. Examples of supplies include fuel, stationery and cleaning materials.

Consumer goods, as we saw earlier, may be classified in several ways. The most common distinction is between consumption goods that are consumed at the time or soon after purchase, and durable goods that may be used repeatedly like industrial equipment, e.g. cars, TVs, washing machines.

Up to this point we have argued that in principle there are no major differences in the marketing of goods and services, and that the terms 'product' and 'service' are essentially interchangeable. Indeed much of the discussion so far has shown that even the most undifferentiated and tangible of products require some degree of service to make them available for sale and consumption, while the creation and delivery of a service invariably involves tangible products. That said, it has to be recognised that as services have come to play an increasingly important role in advanced societies, so they have become the subject of specialised and often separate treatment. Accordingly, we have included a short section that reviews some of the main characteristics of services which may require special attention when crafting a marketing strategy.

ARE SERVICES REALLY DIFFERENT?

One of the most striking features of the past three decades has been the enormous growth in the service sector within the world's advanced industrial economies. In part this growth has been due to the relentless acceleration in the pace of technological change that has resulted in significant improvements in productivity. In part it is due to the fact that the slowing down of population growth in these countries has reduced the expansion of demand for physical goods. Taken together, these trends have seen a marked shift in employment from the secondary or manufacturing sector to the tertiary services sector, accompanied by a similar shift in expenditure patterns from goods to services. In this section we will first review the nature and extent of this growth in services before examining the factors or characteristics that are seen as differentiating services from physical products – intangibility, inseparability, heterogeneity, and perishability and fluctuating demand.

Examination of these distinguishing characteristics leads naturally into a discussion of whether the marketing of services is similar to or different from the marketing of physical goods. As one might expect, two schools of thought exist: those who claim they are the same and those who claim they are different! Our analysis will suggest a

---

Box 15.1   ***Products vs. 'solutions'***

When Lou Gerstner became CEO of IBM in 1993, the emphasis was on selling hardware and software. Gerstner believed their customers had little interest in these per se – what they wanted were solutions to problems. To meet this need, Gerstner transformed a subsidiary unit of IBM's sales force, called Integrated Systems Services Corporation, into IBM Global Services with the objective of delivering integrated IT services to customers. Global services was the basis of the turnaround at IBM and contributed 80% of total revenue growth during Gerstner's period in office.

The need for solutions is driven by the complexity of much technological change, i.e. the user does not need/want to know what is in the 'black box', they want to know what they can get out of it.

compromise and argue that, while the basic principles are equally applicable to both, the distinctive nature of services calls for an extended marketing mix comprising seven elements, with process, physical evidence and people being added to McCarthy's familiar four Ps of product, place, price and promotion. Each of these is explored in some detail and points to the potential for applying marketing principles and ideas to the whole range of economic activity, including the service sector.

However, in the same manner that it is necessary to adjust the nature of the marketing mix to suit the nature of the product and the market which it serves, so it is with services. In the case of services this need is emphasised because, as Shostack (1982) has observed:

> The difference between products and services is more than semantic. Products are tangible objects that exist in both time and space; services consist solely of acts or process(es), and exist in time only.

TABLE 15.2 Some typical differences between manufacturing and service industries

Manufacturing	Service
The product is generally concrete	The service is immaterial
Ownership is transferred when a purchase is made	Ownership is not generally transferred
The product can be resold	The service cannot be resold
The product can be demonstrated before purchase	The service cannot usually be effectively demonstrated (it does not exist before purchase)
The product can be stored by sellers and buyers	The product cannot be stored
Consumption is preceded by production	Production and consumption generally coincide
Production, selling and consumption are locally differentiated	Production, consumption and often even selling are spatially united
The product can be transported	The service cannot be transported (though 'producers' often can)
The seller produces	The buyer/client takes part directly in the production
Indirect contact is possible between company and client	In most cases direct contact is necessary
The product can be exported	The service cannot normally be exported, but the service delivery system can

She believes that:

> The basic distinction between 'things' and 'processes' is the starting point for a focused investigation of services. Services are rendered; products are possessed. Services cannot be possessed; they can only be experienced, created or participated in.

Table 15.2 summarises some typical differences between manufacturing and service industries.

GROWTH OF SERVICES

Service industries are playing an increasingly important role in developed economies, and now account for over 70% of employment in many of them. The reasons for the growth in services can be attributed to the following:

- *Impact of technology:* The major technological breakthroughs achieved in recent years have been one reason for the growth in services. Technology has had a significant impact on the volume and quality of products now available, and it has been suggested in Markin (1982) that more goods or products often lead indirectly to an increased demand for services (the 'knock-on' or 'multiplier' effect).
- *Deregulation and increased competition:* In certain industries there have been changes governing the market entry requirements for firms which has resulted in greater opportunities for service companies to offer more services to customers more easily. For example, this has been a prominent feature of the financial sector in Australia, where credit unions can now offer cheque accounts, and have created a competitive advantage over the banks by offering interest on these accounts which the banks have had to match.
- *Customer sophistication:* As society becomes wealthier and people have more time available compared with 30–40 years ago, the basic needs in life such as housing and food are more easily satisfied and people begin to spend more of their income on wants, rather than needs. In this respect, they do not need more cars, refrigerators or clothing, but increasingly use their income to follow other, more leisure-based

activities, such as holidays, eating out or taking up new hobbies.

Intangibility is probably the single most important factor in distinguishing services from goods. While it is possible to describe the nature and performance of physical products using objective criteria, this is only possible to a limited extent in the case of services. Intangibility has two dimensions (Bateson, 1977): the physical inability to touch an item and the mental difficulty in accepting an idea. While it may be possible to elicit opinions or attitudes from friends or colleagues about a service before purchase is made, these characteristics have important implications for marketing planning. The evaluation of competition is more difficult vis-à-vis goods purchasing since the customer can touch most products to evaluate them, whereas the customer has to search for tangible clues of the service in order to evaluate it.

TYPES OF SERVICE

Services may be mainly professional or consumer-oriented. Professional service firms may serve the business-to-business market, the private individual or may serve both market segments. Professional services are often characterised by the following: advisory and problem-solving; provided by qualified professionals known for their specialty; include an assignment requested by the client; provided by a professional who is independent and not connected with other suppliers; supervised by professional associations which attempt to define the nature of the profession, to lay down requirements of competence, to control the practice of the profession and to enforce a code of ethics (Gardner, 1986). These would include services like financial advice, advertising, business and management consultancy, engineering, architectural and interior design, legal and medical (Gardner, 1986) to which may be added other agencies and brokers, such as estate agents, stock and insurance brokers, and market research agencies (Yorke, 1990). Those firms that tend to be non-professional again may either be in the business-to-business market, or be consumer oriented. Those services which may be included in the former category can include office catering and cleaning services, or offer cash transference services such as Armagard. Those service firms which may be in the latter category are the ones which the consumer is more acquainted with, such as holiday tour companies (for example, Contiki), fast-food outlets (for example, Pizza-Hut, McDonald's) or entertainment companies (for example, Roadshow).

Another important aspect of the intangibility factor is the ease with which services can be imitated and the lack of formal patent protection – which leaves service organisations the problem of distinguishing themselves from their competitors. Shostack (1982) states that, 'while "that which is marketed" may still be a simple product or unadorned service, it is often a more complex combination of products and services'. She illustrates her point in Figure 15.2.

However, some marketers regard the physical nature of a product as secondary in the sense that buyers are primarily concerned with the 'bundle of satisfactions' which flow from the product, rather than the product itself – for example, the technical specification of a television set is rarely considered by the user, who will probably judge it on the basis of picture and sound quality as they appear to them. Further, as it has been pointed out (Wickham et al. 1975), for many products tangibility does not permit physical evaluation in any meaningful way, so that such products tend to be selected on the basis of reputation, advice and experience rather than on the basis of physical examination. If this is the case, a consideration of ascertaining the benefits that consumers want or expect would be a more powerful means of developing effective marketing strategies.

THE NATURE AND CHARACTERISTICS OF SERVICES

The characteristics of services have been classified under four main headings, namely: intangibility, inseparability, heterogeneity, and perishability and fluctuating demand (Stanton, 1981).

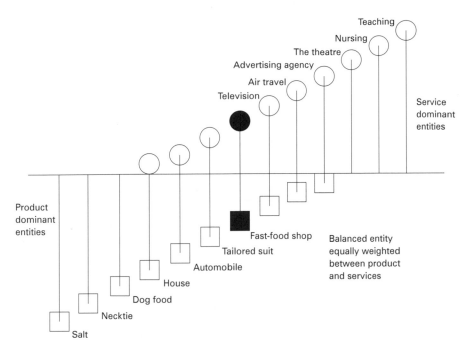

FIGURE 15.2 Scale of elemental dominance

SOURCE: Shostack, G.L. (1982) How to design a service, *European Journal of Marketing*, **16**(1)

INSEPARABILITY

The second differentiating factor of services is inseparability – that is, there is no distinction between *delivery* and *use* due to many services being produced and consumed simultaneously. Unlike manufacturing firms, the sale of the service must be made before production and consumption occur, and the customer receives the 'product' they are buying at the same time as it is being supplied. For example, you must be physically present at the dentist to receive dental treatment or at the hair dressers to have your hair cut. In this way, therefore, a retail outlet may encounter problems with unobliging staff, a restaurant may have a poor chef, or a businessman may be unhappy with the bank teller's attitude on a Monday morning. Alternatively, the service company also must realise the significance of customer participation in the process. For example, customers may not have the ideal knowledge for filling out an application form for a mortgage or bank loan, or know how a self-service petrol pump works. This then breaks down the production/consumption interface because the customer is behaving in a difficult way for the firm. Therefore, service firms need to control the

production side of the service as much as possible through the use of internal marketing as customers' perceptions of the service can be badly affected by the quality of the input as well as making the service easier to use for customers. The company must remember that some customers may not complain to the service firm directly about the poor-quality service they received, but would rather show their dissatisfaction by taking their custom elsewhere or spreading the news around their friends or colleagues about the poor treatment they received.

HETEROGENEITY

The third characteristic which distinguishes services from goods is the ability to be uniform or standard. Services are heterogeneous – that is, variable – while goods are usually uniform. One would usually know what to expect when one buys a car, but it is difficult to predict whether a rock band will give the same quality of performance at a concert on the opening night of their tour versus the final night performance – or, for that matter, whether the same performance would be appropriate for their fans anyway. This problem of expecting people to perform in an identical way each time is hampered by the high level of contact between 'producer' and consumer – for example, how would you feel if a customer was aggressive towards you or if a sales assistant was too impatient to answer your queries? Therefore it is difficult to forecast and ensure provision of the same quality of a service over time, when the quality itself can be affected by both the performance of the provider of the service, at the time it is provided, and the behaviour of the consumer. Due to this inseparability, it is difficult, if not impossible, for the service organisation to standardise output and gain economies of scale in the same way as a manufacturing organisation.

PERISHABILITY AND FLUCTUATING DEMAND

The fourth major dimension which distinguishes services from goods is that services cannot be stored or inventoried in the same way as physical goods. This inability to store services means that unused service capacity and revenue is lost forever. For example, empty seats in theatres, unsold air tickets and unbooked rooms in hotels illustrate the risk inherent in service perishability. This problem of large fluctuation in demand is often overcome, in service industries such as tourism and communications, by service firms encouraging the ordinary consumer to take a weekend break at a quiet time of year or to use the telephone at off-peak times. Demand management in services is far more subtle than it is for products, and it would be much more constructive to think in terms of capacity availability, that is, one can only consume what is available, yet this point is frequently ignored in developing marketing strategies for services.

MANAGING SERVICES MARKETING

Many marketing scholars have been preoccupied with discussing whether the marketing of services is similar to or different from the marketing of physical goods. There are two schools of thought with regard to the applicability of product-marketing concepts and techniques to services

marketing – that is, product-based versus service-based approaches. One school of thought believes that services are not different from physical goods, and that therefore the same concepts and techniques used in goods marketing can be directly translated to services marketing. Most of the arguments suggested by the adopters of this view centre round the following two points:

1. The claimed differences between goods and services are exaggerated and provide little insight to understanding either of them. In addition, the preoccupation with such a simple service–product classification is myopic and likely to be unsuitable. Instead more multi-dimensional classifications are needed in which the marketing strategy of the firm is a function of offer characteristics, market characteristics and characteristics of the exchange process (Wickham et al., 1975; Goodfellow, 1983).
2. The most important criterion to be considered when marketing any product (including physical goods, services, ideas etc) is buyers' expectations. Many commentators argue that consumers are not buying goods or services, but rather the value satisfaction of the offering. So it is suggested that the process of marketing strategy formulation should start with a product concept which recognises the bundle of benefits, often including both tangible and intangible aspects as it is perceived by the potential buyer (Levitt, 1974; Donnelly and George, 1981).

Dissatisfaction with this approach leads many authors to take their thinking to the other extreme and call for a theory for marketing services. According to the service-based approach, it is argued that services possess certain distinguishing features which make them fundamentally different from physical goods. Therefore, the suggestion advanced is that service marketers must develop a unique process of marketing strategy formulation for services which differs from the traditional one.

The development of a service marketing theory as a frame of reference that guides the marketer's thinking deals with either the service area (that is, its organisational aspects (Blois, 1982), consumer behaviour (Blois, 1982), marketing mix activities

(Shostack, 1982; Donnelly and George, 1981) or a specific aspect of it, for example professional services (Gummesson, 1979).

According to this approach, it is argued that the marketing of services is more complex than the marketing of goods due to fundamental difference in the end products and the simultaneous production and consumption processes. As such it is suggested that service marketers need new tools, strategies and organisation structures to carry out the process of marketing services effectively.

PRODUCT POLICY

In the preceding sections we have attempted to strike a balance between emphasising the physical characteristics of products and the needs they satisfy to show that in reality they are two faces of the same coin. It follows that undue emphasis upon one to the neglect of the other may well be counterproductive. However, in seeking to achieve balance, one must be careful that one does not end up 'sitting on the fence' and taking no positive action to shape the direction of the organisation through a clear statement of policy.

In Chapter 3 we adopted the assumption that growth is a prime objective of most companies on the basis that the opposite condition – contraction – is essentially inimical to the most fundamental corporate objective of all – survival. (Given

the rate of change in the [...] considered too risky an ob[...] assumption we then introd[...] famous growth vector ma[...] upon joint consideration o[...] change in the product (tech[...] market, as perhaps the simp[...] statement of the strategic altern[...] ...open to the firm. It will be recalled that the matrix appeared as in Figure 15.3, and that the four basic strategies were defined as:

1. *Market penetration:* the company seeks increased sales for its present products in its present markets through more aggressive promotion and distribution.
2. *Market development:* the company seeks increased sales by taking its present products into new markets (a market segmentation approach).
3. *Product development:* the company seeks increased sales by developing improved products for its present markets (a product differentiation approach).
4. *Diversification:* the company seeks increased sales by developing new products for new markets (a composite strategy).

The first three of these strategies hold constant one or both of the core strategic variables – product and market – and so sustain the common thread of the business. But, by definition, the fourth alternative of diversification breaks the thread and projects the firm into a totally new situation where it has experience of neither technology nor user needs.

Ansoff's (1968) definition of a 'common thread' is based upon three factors:

1. *The product–market scope,* which specifies the particular industries to which the company confines its product–market position
2. *The growth vector,* which indicates the direction in

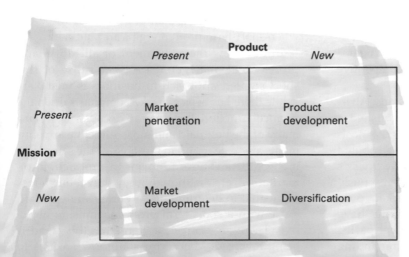

FIGURE 15.3 Ansoff's growth vector matrix

SOURCES: Ansoff, H. I. (1965) *Corporate Strategy.* New York: McGraw-Hill; Ansoff, H. I. (1957) Strategies for diversification, *Harvard Business Review* (September–October)

the company is moving with respect to current product–market position

. *The competitive advantage*, which seeks to identify particular properties of individual product markets that will give the company a strong competitive position.

Once again there is a tendency to project maintenance of a common thread as a straight 'either/or' proposition, when in reality what is needed is a judicious blend of both. A recurring theme of this book is that the firm must develop a portfolio of products, these products should ideally be at different stages of their individual PLCs to provide a balance between new and declining products with their varying cash needs and profit potential, and the firm should pursue distinctly different strategies for new, mature and declining products (what we term '3-in-1 marketing'). Frequent reference has also been made to the radical changes that took place in the environment in the 1970s and early 1980s, one consequence of which was a significant shift in managerial attitudes to corporate risk. Perhaps the most influential statement concerning this shift in attitudes is that published by Hayes and Abernathy (1980). The essential thesis of this article is that, as more and more firms come under the control of professional managers as opposed to entrepreneurs, there is a marked tendency to avoid uncertainty by concentrating on short-term projects with low risk and known pay offs. As a consequence, less and less effort is devoted to basic and applied research and more and more is concentrated on the development of existing products. Much of the latter investment is seen as trivial and gives rise to minor competitive advantages which are quickly eroded.

Almost simultaneously with Hayes and Abernathy's article, Peter Riesz (1980) published a similar view but was more specific in his diagnosis of the causes of these changes, which he attributed to a marketing orientation. Specifically, Riesz's argument is that by moving from a 'science push' (production orientation) to a 'market pull' (marketing orientation), American firms have sacrificed much creativity, technological parity, thoughtful product strategy and commanding market positions, particularly to countries like Japan which have been stepping up their R&D effort. In support of his argument Riesz states:

During the past decade, more than half of the 30% of research and development budgets previously spent on major innovation has shifted toward more conservative, shorter-term, less uncertain projects. Of an estimated $38.2 billion in research and development expenditures in 1976, 61% was for development, 27% was for applied research, while the remaining 12% was allocated to basic research.

Much of today's research and development is focused on the existing product, market, or process base rather than on the development of new ventures or technologies. Firms are increasingly reluctant to make new commitments that require complex technologies, heavy start-up costs, or previously untried marketing concepts. Rather research and development activity seems much more committed to building on what is called the 'common thread' of business.

Like Hayes and Abernathy, Reisz attributes much of this trend to the 'MBA syndrome', which 'is alleged to have produced super cautious managers who are unwilling to gamble on anything but a sure thing'. Other deterrents to innovation include low incentives to entrepreneurs, consumerism, government interference and regulation and the greater uncertainty which is associated with current environmental turbulence. Even more serious is the widespread tendency to regard R&D expenditure solely as a cost centre, with the result that, like investment in advertising where benefits are often long-term, future streams of earnings, such expenditures are among the first to be cut when short-term profit margins are squeezed.

In our view the indictment of all MBAs and professional managers as a basic cause of this short-sighted approach to business is mistaken. While there has been a marked emphasis upon the finance function for several decades now and many of the best paid and most attractive appointments are to be found in this area, at the same time many MBAs choose to major in production, or, marketing etc., although they have been less influential in determining corporate strategy than those with a short-term profit-maximising objective. There are now clear signs that this trend is being reversed. Many MBAs are now anxious to work in small business and set up on their own account. In addition there is a much clearer appreciation that most accounting conventions are just that and arbitrary as well. Hopefully, this realisation will help reverse the decision of the USA Financial Accounting Standards Board, which ruled that R&D expenditures could no longer be treated in the balance sheet but must be accounted for as direct profit or loss items in the year spent.

However the main thrust of Riesz's argument is that whereas a marketing orientation appears to be desirable and logical in that it focuses upon satisfying felt needs, such a 'shift from "science push" to "market pull" can have negative effects both on the firm and on public policy'. According to Riesz, the deficiencies in a market-pull orientation arise from at least three sources.

First, there are the well-known weaknesses in research methodology centring on issues such as sampling, survey design and response bias. However, in our view the fact that these weaknesses are known means that they can be anticipated and allowed for.

Second, the average customer is usually unable to articulate significant improvements in ways of satisfying their felt needs and is even less likely to be able to specify vaguely felt latent needs. This is more true of consumers than it is of organisational buyers.

The third weakness in the marketing orientation is the potential risk that failure to undertake basic R&D will result in the firm losing contact with and access to the scientific and technological community. In turn this increases the probability that the firm will be unaware of likely changes in the market due to technological innovation and so be bypassed by innovator firms.

Collectively, Riesz (1980) believes that these weaknesses will lead to a diminution in marketing's contribution to corporate strategy because: 'Among strategic variables which enable the firm to adjust to an ever-changing external environment, product policy is almost always identified as being crucial to the long-term survival and development of the firm.'

Riesz's views find strong support in the analysis of Bennett and Cooper referred to earlier. In developing their claim that adoption of a marketing orientation has led many firms to neglect product value, Bennett and Cooper (1982) tend to polarise the issues into an 'either/or' situation.

Box 15.2   ***Torment your customers***

In an article in the *Harvard Business Review* (2001) with the above title, Ulster University professor Stephen Brown promoted the provocative view that firms should *not* research customers' declared needs.

The truth is, customers don't know what they want. They never have. They never will. The wretches don't even know what they *don't* want, as the success of countless rejected-by-focus-group products, from the Chrysler minivan to the Sony Walkman, readily attests. A mindless devotion to customers means me-too products, copycat advertising campaigns, and marketplace stagnation.

The solution is what Brown terms 'retromarketing'. Instead of making life simple for the consumer by making goods readily available at a price people are prepared to pay:

By contrast, retromarketing makes 'em work for it, by limiting availability, by delaying gratification, by heightening expectations, by fostering an enigmatic air of unattainability. It doesn't serve demand; it creates it.

Brown claims that retromarketing, a desire for old products and the good old snake oil salesman's pitch of yesteryear is founded on five basic principles:

1. *Exclusivity* – make buyers wait for supplies
2. *Secrecy* – keep back information, e.g. Harry Potter books
3. *Amplify* – create a buzz
4. *Entertain*
5. *Tricksterism*.

This is not an acronym – unless you reverse it! TEASE!

Retromarketing is not suited to all occasions, 'But, then the modern marketing concept of caring, sharing, all hold hands is not always the right approach either.'

This is particularly the case in their discussion of market pull and technological push as opposing models of technological innovation ('The market-pull model is the antithesis of the technology-push approach'). Bennett and Cooper provide an excellent cameo of the market-pull model (reproduced as Table 15.3), which is contrasted with technology push where 'scientific discovery or the availability of new technology leads to the development of a product'. Ideas come from scientists and engineers, not from consumers.

TABLE 15.3 The market-pull model

The market-pull model has been perfected by the packaged goods industry. They search the market for clues and examine people's needs exhaustively. The result is usually a carefully focused product that is moderately successful. As an example, consider the market-pull model for the development of a new breakfast food by a hypothetical company:

Step 1 Do extensive market research to identify an unsatisfied need, segment, or niche in the marketplace. Using sophisticated market research tools if necessary (multidimensional scaling, tradeoff analysis etc), determine the ideal product's attributes. Let the market 'design' the product, e.g., a semi-sweet, easily prepared, baked breakfast product, with attributes somewhere between toast and a sweet roll.

Step 2 Ask the R&D group to develop a product that meets these market specifications exactly. No technological breakthroughs or inventions are necessary – just give the market what it says it wants. In our example, the result might be a waffle-like product, frozen, suitable for a toaster, with a sweet filling.

Step 3 Refine the product design (including consumer preference taste tests) and verify the financial attractiveness of the project (test marketing, for example).

Step 4 Launch the product. Position it in people's minds as a great-tasting, 'fun' breakfast food that is easy to prepare (hot from your toaster). Give it a name to reflect its position: 'Pop-Toasties'. Package it attractively and saturation advertise on television.

SOURCE: Bennett, R. C. and Cooper, R. G. (1982) The misuse of marketing: an American tragedy, *McKinsey Quarterly* (autumn): 55

But as we have argued earlier, firms with a portfolio of products at different stages of their lifecycles will require a combination of both market pull to ensure that developing products remain competitive and to rejuvenate mature lines, while more basic research and technology push will be pursued in the hope of achieving a significant breakthrough which will allow the firm to bypass its rivals. It is also important to recognise that even apparently superficial changes in a product form of the kind implied in Bennett and Cooper's 'market-pull model' depend upon significant advances in food technology, in packaging and in distribution – freeze-dried products like coffee may seem little different from instant coffee but the technology is radically different.

During the 1990s, Roy Rothwell of the Science Policy Research Unit at Sussex University advanced a more sophisticated model of innovation than the simple 'push-pull' one described above. According to Rothwell (1995), it is possible to identify five different models of innovation, namely:

1. Technology push
2. Market or need pull
3. Push and pull
4. Integration of suppliers and parallel development
5. Technological accumulation
   Strategic networking
   Time to market
   Integration of product and manufacturing strategies
   Flexibility and adaptability
   Quality and performance
   Regulatory responses, e.g. environmentalism

Thus while it is quite true to assert that 'A market-oriented R&D strategy necessarily leads to low-risk product modifications, extensions and style changes', it is also true that 'understanding user needs' and the 'customer-active' model of new product development (NPD) have been conclusively shown to be associated with successful innovation, whereas a much higher proportion of technology-push products fail. Successful management of a product portfolio demands that we balance the risks and, as the Boston Box clearly shows, 'question marks' and, to a lesser extent, 'stars' depend on the cash-generating 'cows' to sustain them. Clearly the longer we can prolong the useful life of the 'cash cows', the greater the opportunity to underwrite more radical R&D.

Thus, the essence of our argument is that market penetration, market development, product development and diversification are not mutually exclusive options from which the firm must select one. Rather they are interdependent and mutually

	New use	Market extension	Diversification
New market	Re-merchandise	Improved product	Product line extension
Extended market	Present position	Re-formulation	Replacement
No change	No change	Improved technology	New technology

Increasing market newness

Increasing technological newness

FIGURE 15.4 The technology market matrix

SOURCE: Adapted from Johnson, S. C. and Jones, C. (1957) How to organize for new products, *Harvard Business Review* (May–June)

reinforcing alternatives and the management task lies in achieving the optimum balance between them. To this end the approach proposed by Samuel C. Johnson and Conrad Jones (1957) probably offers more to the practising manager as it recognises an intermediate state between old and new – namely the 'improved' product and the 'strengthened' market. Johnson and Jones's model is reproduced as Figure 15.4 and is considered to be self-explanatory. (In passing it is interesting to note that this schemata antedates Ansoff by four months in the same publication.) The model also makes it clear that some form of product development is intrinsic to most positive strategies.

PRODUCT DEVELOPMENT

While much product development is an ongoing process which involves modifications and adjustments to existing products, most textbooks concentrate on describing the full cycle of events in bringing a new product to the marketplace. Such an approach has much to recommend it, for it establishes both a chronology and a procedure for developing new products from scratch as well as distinguishing discrete stages which may also be involved in product modification and improvement. Accordingly, this section will trace the normative theory of NPD as a statement of how it should be done.

If, as we have claimed, product differentiation

has become a basic competitive strategy, then two direct and immediate consequences become apparent:

1. It increases the relevance and importance of the product development function
2. It is likely to lead to more rapid product obsolescence and a shortening of product life-cycles.

While data and projections such as these provide impressive evidence of the contribution that NPD makes to the growth and success of firms, it is important to bear in mind that the net contribution is much greater for, in the absence of continuous product development, the forces of competition and the inevitability of the PLC would result in a contraction in the firm's market share and a corresponding decline in its profitability. Guiltinan and Paul (1982) suggest that, taking into account corporate strategy, portfolio analysis and product life-cycle analysis, managers can have at least five other objectives in addition to market share growth, namely:

- Market share maintenance
- Cash flow maximisation
- Sustaining profitability
- Harvesting
- Establishing an initial market position.

The suitability and relevance of these objectives will become clear when we review the manage-

of the product over its life-cycle later in the
pter. However, before doing so it will be useful
describe the concept of the product portfolio.

THE CONCEPT OF THE PRODUCT PORTFOLIO

The desirability of a portfolio or range of different
products is implicit in the concept of the product
life-cycle, which emphasises that, ultimately, all
products and the technologies which underlie
them will change. Thus human progress and
economic growth are the consequence of new and
improved ways of doing things being substituted
for old methods and approaches. It follows that as
a result of technological innovation, even the most
successful of products will become obsolescent
and displaced by new and better ways of serving a
particular need. For example, for centuries passen-
ger transport by sea was the only available option
for persons wishing to travel between Europe and
North America. It is now almost impossible to
arrange a transatlantic sea crossing and such as are
available are hardly likely to meet the convenience
or cost needs of persons wishing to travel. And so
it is with most other products and technologies.
Indeed, as we have seen in earlier chapters, given
that both generic strategies of cost leadership and
differentiation depend on innovation, new product and process development have become the
basis for competitive activity in all kinds of
markets. In turn this has led to an acceleration in
the substitution of new products for old and a
shortening of product life-cycles.

Faced with such a scenario it is clear that the
firm must take active steps to ensure that it does
not become a victim of market myopia. In Chapter
5 we introduced Ansoff's growth vector matrix as a
simple summary statement of the strategic options
available. In order to survive, let alone grow, the
firm needs to pursue simultaneously the strategies
of market penetration, (selling more of the existing
product to existing users) market development,
(finding new customers in new geographic regions
with similar needs to one's existing customers) and
product development (improving and changing
the product both to keep up with the changing
wants of one's existing customers and to attract
new customers whose needs were not satisfied by
the original product). The fourth option of divers-

ification was considered to be risky in that, unlike
the other options, it involves changing both product and market together, whereas the other three
options retained contact with one or both of the key
dimensions of the exchange process – products
and/or customers. That said, it was noted that a
product development could also result in a market
development by attracting new customers, while
market development might suggest new opportunities for product development. Thus both kinds
of development might lead to diversification – new
products in new markets – but by a less risky route.

The key lesson to be learned is that in order to
survive firms need to be constantly looking for
new products and new customers. However, there
is a working rule of thumb in marketing which
states that it costs five to six times as much money
to create a customer as it does to keep one. It is for
this reason that in recent years the emphasis in
marketing has moved away from the transaction
to the relationship. The tendency for customers –
individual and organisational – to prefer to repeat
purchase from a known and proven source of
supply may amount to satisficing behaviour but
that is the way most of us behave. In the absence of
any compelling evidence to the contrary, why
would one want to change one's behaviour provided that it yields satisfactory results? It is also a
well-known fact that many of the best ideas for
new products are generated by customers who
identify means of improving or changing existing
products so that they will perform better.

Given these facts, it seems reasonable to assert
that the first priority is to maintain and grow one's
customer franchise. From this it follows that one
must accept that, ultimately, our customers' first
loyalty is to themselves, their families and organisations so that if someone else can offer them better
value for money (greater satisfaction) then they
will switch to the new source of supply. To avoid
this one must anticipate the customers' needs and
to do so requires that one develop a range or portfolio of products designed to match changing
needs and situations.

The idea of the product portfolio is, of course,
borrowed from that of investment management, in
which investors seek to acquire a selection of
stocks and shares which will meet their needs.
Usually these needs will embrace a desire for
current income balanced by a desire for capital

growth. In turn, investment management theory is derived from the broader field of economics, in which the portfolio may comprise any kind of asset and the purpose of portfolio analysis is to determine the composition of the ideal or optimum portfolio taking into account basic preferences for fixed or variable yields, short- or long-term returns etc. It follows that the construction of a product portfolio will depend very much upon the overall objectives of an organisation and its attitude towards the basic trade-off between risk and return. Once these have been established, it becomes possible to determine what kinds of product are needed to achieve the desired balance.

One of the earlier contributions to the idea of developing a portfolio of products was Peter Drucker's (1963) article in which he proposed products could be classified as falling into one of six categories – 'breadwinners' (today's, tomorrow's and yesterday's), also-rans, failures and in-betweens (i.e. capable of becoming successful given appropriate action). Drucker's classification was based on the contribution of the product to overall profitability. Once diagnosed, the prescription was simple – support today's and tomorrow's breadwinners, 'milk' yesterday's breadwinners, make up your mind on the in-betweens and drop the also-rans and failures. Given that one is able to measure the criterion value (others use profitability, growth, market share etc. as criteria), then classification is relatively simple. The difficult decision is balancing the portfolio to achieve the overall objective(s). Wind and Mahajan (1982, p. 110) suggest the following questions need to be answered to make this decision:

1. What dimensions should be used in constructing a product portfolio?
2. What are the current approaches to portfolio management, and how do they differ from each other?
3. How can the portfolio management approach be used to develop guidelines to product marketing decisions?

However, before seeking to answer these questions, Wind and Mahajan suggest one must first decide the desired level of business analysis, the level of the market and the time dimension of analysis.

With regard to the level of business analysis, this will depend very much upon the extent of the firm's existing portfolio. For many small organisations there will only be a single line, albeit that there may be variants within it at different stages of their life-cycle conforming with Drucker's six-way classification. Larger firms may have two or more distinct lines, while the largest strategic business units will have multiple product lines. Irrespective of the number of product lines, the individual product line constitutes the basic unit of analysis and a clear understanding of each is fundamental to any higher order level of comparative strategic analysis.

With regard to the 'level' of market, Wind and Mahajan have in mind the degree of aggregation or, rather, disaggregation to be used in analysis. Given that it is users' perceptions that underlie consumption behaviour, the advice here is that one should disaggregate the market into profitable segments and then analyse the characteristics of the customers who comprise the distinct segments. However, it is also important to bear in mind that even brand loyal customers may switch to competing brands from time to time and also their choice is often influenced by a wider product assortment. Thus, in addition to analysing micro-segmentation variables, one should also keep in mind macro-segmentation factors and even different markets, which may be more attractive than existing markets but accessible to the firm given its assets and resources. For example, a packaging manufacturer specialising in metal containers could use its customer franchise to move into, say, plastic or glass packaging.

As to the time factor, Wind and Mahajan observe that most analyses of products relate to their current rather than their future position. Given the implications of the PLC, it is obvious that one should also take into account future trends and try to forecast the direction in which the product is moving – up, stable, or down – as this will have a major bearing on one's strategy and planning.

FACTORS INFLUENCING THE PRODUCT PORTFOLIO

As noted, the purpose behind developing a product portfolio is to allocate the firm's resources so as to optimise its long-term growth and profitability.

It follows that to do this effectively one must select measures for assessing the actual or potential contribution of individual products to the portfolio. Such measures may be objective, such as sales, profitability or market share, or they may be more subjective, such as competitive strength, perceived risk or stage in the product life-cycle. As was seen (Chapter 5) when discussing some of the standardised approaches to portfolio analysis, such as those developed by the Boston Consulting Group (BCG) or Shell, it has become conventional to plot the performance of individual products on a two-dimensional matrix, from which it follows that only two measures are to be used, albeit that one or both may act as a summary or surrogate for others. A review of the measures available will be useful.

Perhaps the most obvious and most frequently used measure is sales, if for no other reason than that actual or potential sales determine the firm's revenue and it is the timing and volume of revenue related to expenditure that determine whether the firm will succeed or fail. Measures of sales are also involved in computing profitability and/or market share either of which may be used as a surrogate for actual sales when constructing a portfolio matrix.

For purposes of analysis, several distinct sales measures are required. Obviously, the firm will know its actual sales at any given point in time but this information will be of limited value unless it can be compared with the total sales of the product class and those of other major competitors. Such information is essential to calculate market share, but this information will also be of limited value unless it summarises past sales trends and projects these into the future. In other words, one needs to establish whether sales of the product class are growing, stable or declining and how one's own product is performing when measured against these industry trends. By plotting both industry and firm's sales, it should be possible to establish the stage of both the industry life-cycle and that of the firm's own offering and, from this, project future sales for both.

Conventionally, sales are recorded in terms of volume, or units sold, and value. Ideally both should be measured as this will enable the analyst to form a view about the shape of the demand curve and price elasticity, both of which are important inputs when devising a compet-itive strategy or planning new product developments. When measuring sales, it is necessary to ensure one is comparing like with like and avoid mixing manufacturer, wholesalers and retailers' prices as well as making sure that data cover the same time period.

Comparative sales data are an essential input to the computation of market share, which is one of the primary dimensions of the Boston Consulting Group's growth/share matrix. Market share is widely cited as an important measure of competitive performance particularly since the publication of the PIMS (profit implications of market strategy) study in which it was found that there was a strong association between market share and profitability. However, one must be careful not to exaggerate the importance of market share comparisons, if for no other reason than they are difficult to compute on a consistent and meaningful basis, added to which market share may be a meaningless statistic for the great majority of competitors in a market.

Difficulty in accurately calculating a market share largely arises from problems of definition. One, extreme, view is that every firm has 100% market share whatever the value of its sales. This perspective is based on the proposition that a firm's customers must regard its product as distinctive in some way otherwise they would not prefer it to other close substitutes. The more conventional view is that we can define markets for a class or product, like carbonated beverages, detergents, petrol etc; calculate the total sales value of these products and then derive the individual seller's market share by dividing their sales by total sales to obtain a percentage. Of course calculations of this kind for a product class may disguise significant variations in the performance of individual brands within a firm's product line in terms of, say, colas versus fruit flavours, diet and non-diet versions etc. In the case of major markets of this kind, with significant and distinctive segments, it is likely that major suppliers will analyse market share at both the product class (industry) and brand level. But, such calculations would be meaningless for a small producer of a given product serving a local market. On the other hand, it might be meaningful to calculate the small firm's penetration or market share of its narrowly defined geographical market area, provided that the value of knowing this statistic was greater than the cost of establishing it.

This is not a trivial issue for, as we have pointed out earlier, the great majority of firms are small and the cost of performing analyses which may be useful or even necessary for large firms may greatly exceed any tangible benefit. As Wind and Mahajan (1982, p. 114) note, defining a brand's market share 'requires the explication of several concepts: the unit of measurement; the product definition; the boundaries of the market and competitors; the time horizon involved; and the nature of the denominator in the share calculation.' Wind and Mahajan then devote four pages to a discussion of these factors. It is doubtful if such an exercise in definition and measurement would be worthwhile for most small firms. For such firms a more subjective, judgemental approach would seem to be more appropriate. Whether such mainly judgemental methods constitute a product portfolio analysis or a more broadly based strategic overview is a matter of opinion.

THE NEW PRODUCT DEVELOPMENT (NPD) CYCLE

The development of a new product is seen as a sequential process normally containing six distinct phases. While some models contain additional subphases and may employ slightly different terminology, the most widely accepted sequence proposed by Booz, Allen & Hamilton, based on their experience with several hundred companies, is:

exploration → screening → business analysis → development → testing → commercialisation

This sequence may be represented diagramatically as in Figure 15.5

Like the PLC concept, the NPD model is of greatest value when regarded as a framework or structure to guide one's own approach. Clearly no single, simple process model can allow for all the complications and problems likely to be encountered by the firm that sets out to manage NPD, nor is such a model appropriate to many radical

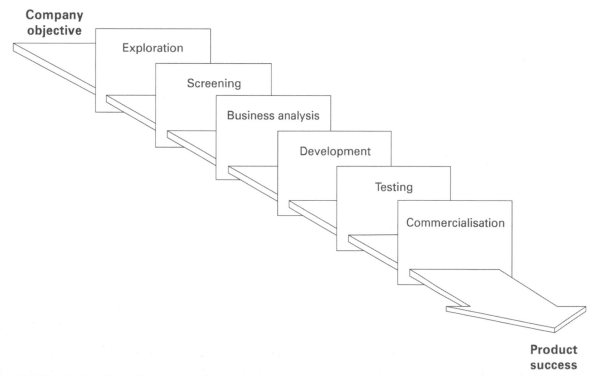

FIGURE 15.5 The Booz, Allen & Hamilton model of new product development. Overview of the stages of the new product development process

SOURCE: Baker, M. J. and Hart, S. J. (2007) *Product Strategy and Management* (2nd edn). London: Financial Times Press

innovations or to situations where technology 'push' is dominant. That said, however, all phases are recommended and are usually found to be present in case histories of NPD. Hence a brief review of each will be helpful.

The *exploration phase*, sometimes termed 'idea generation', may be structured, unstructured or serendipitous. A structured procedure for new product ideas may rest upon continuous market research into consumer reactions, both to one's own product and to those of one's competitors in order to give early warning of failing interest or dissatisfaction or, more positively, to suggest areas for improvement which will enhance the product's standing with its target audience.

Monitoring competitive activity has assumed increasing importance in recent years with the growing popularity of what is termed 'the strategy of the fast second' whereby firms depend more on their ability to copy or improve upon a new product and cash in on the market as it moves into the growth phase than on being the first to market with a new product. The Japanese are past masters of this strategy, and are imitative innovators of the first order across almost all classes of goods, depending upon an enhanced product, competitive prices and excellent distribution and after-sales service to ensure a dominant position in almost all the world's growth markets. Significantly, the Japanese have been responsible for no major technological innovations themselves.

A specific example of the strategy of the fast second is to be found in the competition between Seagram and Showering in the UK market for sparkling wines. Seagram pursued a classic NPD strategy in that they realised the need to broaden their product line as a means of achieving wider distribution for their range of spirits, and commissioned research to try and find a gap in the market which they might fill. The research suggested that females in the age range 18–25 would appreciate a drink which was less alcoholic than spirits, more glamorous than beer and more exciting than wine. Showering already marketed a product which met this specification – a champagne perry called Babycham – but the research indicated that the target group regarded this as an old-fashioned product more appropriate for their mothers than themselves.

Seagram went through the exploration phase

armed with a clear picture of the sort of product characteristics desired by the market segment they wished to reach and, after screening a number of possibilities, settled upon a sparkling white wine. Research had also underlined the importance of packaging and branding to products of this nature to convey the necessary associations of glamour and excitement, and after extensive testing the company settled upon a green, single-portion size bottle with a foil cap and named the product Crocodilo.

Equipped with their new, tested product, Seagram moved into the recommended test-market phase in which the product is marketed on a regional basis with the sort of support it would receive if launched nationally. The test market in East Anglia proved very successful and encouraged Seagram to 'go national' in late 1980.

Within two weeks of the announcement, Showering introduced a directly competitive product 'Green Dragon', and put it into widespread distribution through the holding company's (Allied Breweries) tied outlets and elsewhere as Babycham's 'little sister'. Showering's strategy is not hard to appreciate. If they (unilaterally) had launched a new sparkling wine drink, they would only have competed with themselves and could well have cannibalised sales of the existing product. But faced with a competitive threat on a regional basis the obvious thing to do is monitor the success or otherwise of the newcomer and plan accordingly. This Showering did very effectively, for they came up with a sparkling wine that was clearly preferred in blind-taste tests, which gave them a better product, in addition to the other advantages they already enjoyed as an established supplier of drinks of this type with effective national distribution. One can only speculate that all Seagram's promotional efforts only served to build primary demand for a new product on which the 'fast second' capitalised.

Unstructured idea generation tends to be more typical of firms with a single product or small range of products experiencing a decline in their current profitability – that is, the firm does not have a formal NPD function, but operates on an ad hoc basis. Brainstorming is a frequently used technique in these circumstances in which the second phase of screening or sifting the ideas assumes particular importance. An unstructured approach is also often associated with serendipity when an idea for a new product occurs by chance – as a by-product of research into something else, for example, or as the result of an approach by a prospective user asking if you could make something to meet a specific need.

Once the firm has generated a portfolio of ideas for new products, it is essential that these be *screened* to ensure that only the most promising are subjected to thorough analysis, if for no other reason than that the further one proceeds with any given idea the greater the expense involved, as shown in Figure 15.6. Screening is an essentially subjective procedure in which managers use their knowledge and experience to weed out the obvious non-starters. Beyond doubt, managers are most confident when applying their knowledge of internal constraints and will eliminate many ideas as being inconsistent with the firm's product policies and objectives, with the existing skills and

resources etc. In the same way, ideas that are incompatible with the firm's existing markets and its knowledge of its current users and customers are likely to be screened out at this phase as the firm seeks to build upon its existing strengths. The screening phase also includes *concept development* when ideas are tested with potential customers (see Baker and Hart, 2007).

Given a shortlist of 'possible' ideas, the next step is to subject these to a more formal *business analysis* – a task which will be greatly improved if an explicit checklist is developed, setting out the criteria and their relative importance one to another. In general this evaluation should assess each of the ideas in terms of its technology and its 'fit' with the production system, its marketability and its competitiveness, and finally in terms of the financial implications of proceeding with it further.

Assuming that evaluation indicates that development of the product appears feasible, that fore-

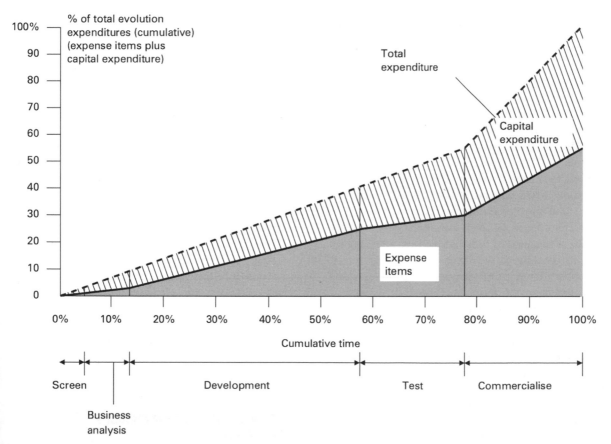

FIGURE 15.6 New product development costs

SOURCE: Management Research Department, Booz, Allen & Hamilton Inc.

casted sales and budgeted costs promise a satisfactory return on investment, and that the company is satisfied it can gain access to the target market, then the next phase in the process is *technical development*. At this juncture, the objective is to establish if it is physically possible to produce an object with the desired performance characteristics within the cost constraints indicated by the forecast demand schedule. Usually this phase is the longest in the whole process, and it is vitally important that, throughout development, the innovator should continue critically to observe events and changes in the proposed target market. In the case of one of the classic new product failures – the Edsel – its downfall arose, not from an incorrect assessment of a market opportunity, but because the market need changed during the course of the development of the car (for a full description, see Baker, 1983).

In addition to updating the product concept to reflect changes in the market, the development phase should also provide for testing the product under real-world usage conditions to ensure that it will deliver the promised satisfactions. The more complex the product, and the more radical the behavioural change required of the end user, the more important this phase becomes. Indeed, with many capital, material and consumer durable innovations, the development phase frequently continues well into the market launch stage on the grounds that deficiencies and defects in the final product will only become apparent once it is exposed to a broad spectrum of usage situations. For example, in the case of the JCB 110, the relocation of the engine behind the operator resulted in numerous engine failures caused by severe overheating. The cause of this overheating was the fact that, in confined working conditions, many drivers reversed until stopped by piles of spoil excavated from the foundations etc, on which the machine was working. By reversing into this spoil, the ventilator grilles became blocked, leading to overheating and engine seizure. Once the problem was known, a fairly simple redesign was all that was required to rectify it, but, as is so often the case, extensive usage was necessary to sensitise the makers to the intrinsic design fault.

With complex products, the development phase may well proceed in parallel with physical and market testing, but in other cases, such as that of Crocodilo considered earlier, the *test phase* may be a

discrete activity in its own right. Obviously testing is a risk-reduction strategy as the firm's commitment is limited and a final go/no-go decision can be deferred pending the test results. With a major and complex new product, marketing on a small scale to iron out the bugs has much to commend it, but, with less sophisticated products such as Crocodilo, test marketing can give the game away to one's competitors and allow them to counter your full-scale launch with a strong competitive reaction. Indeed, with many consumer goods test marketing can be a complete waste of effort as competitors create abnormal trading conditions in the test area so that little or no reliance can be placed on the results.

The final phase of the NPD process is *commercialisation* when the product is launched in the market, thus initiating its life-cycle. As can be seen from Figure 15.6 above, commercialisation increases the firm's financial commitment by several orders of magnitude. Capacity must be installed to cater for the anticipated demand; inventory must be built up to ensure that supplies can be made available to the distribution channel; intensive selling-in must take place to ensure widespread availability at the point of sale or to canvass orders from prospective buyers; maintenance and servicing facilities may be necessary and a large promotional investment will be needed to create awareness of the new product's existence. Given the importance of this phase, one might reasonably expect discussions of it to dominate texts dealing with the subject, but it only requires a cursory examination to reveal that this stage rarely receives equal treatment with the preceding phases and attracts comparatively little attention.

The problems involved in introducing new products into the marketplace is a major theme of *Product Strategy and Management* (Baker and Hart, 2007), which also seeks to provide empirical support for the composite model of buying behaviour introduced in Chapter 9, and persons interested in these topics are recommended to consult this source.

ORGANISATION FOR NEW PRODUCT DEVELOPMENT

If the firm is to practise 3-in-1 marketing, then it

will require a different organisational style to cope with the three distinct time horizons. Evidence from research by Axel Johne (1982) shows that successful firms appear to be able to operate in different modes and that managers can 'change gear' from an organic to a mechanistic style and back again. Other evidence and experience would seem to suggest that such transitions will be facilitated by certain organisational devices and in this section we shall look briefly at four of them:

1. New product committees
2. Venture teams
3. New product departments
4. Product managers.

A new product committee probably represents the lowest level of recognition that conventional organisational structures of a functional kind are not best suited to the task of NPD. Such committees are usually, but not always, ad hoc and are established to evaluate specific product development proposals. Members with relevant expertise will be drawn from the various functional areas and their brief will usually be to reach conclusions on proposed courses of action and then ensure that action is coordinated and integrated between the departments involved. Such an arrangement may well be adequate for firms with small product portfolios operating in markets where change is slow and life-cycles are prolonged. Where the rate of change is faster and/or the product line is bigger, then such a committee may be established on a standing basis. This arrangement may also suit a multidivisional firm where the top management requires advice on the comparative merits of proposals from divisions operating in radically different markets.

Venture teams are similar to new product committees in the sense that they are usually composed of experts drawn from different areas of the organisation and that they are formed for a specific purpose. However, while the new product committee's role is solely advisory, the new venture team assumes responsibility for the execution of the proposal too. Thus members will have to be seconded from their normal duties for the life of the project and the approach may best be thought of as establishing a new business in its own right.

New product departments are usually found

only in large organisations with big product lines subject to frequent change. The advantages of setting up a department with sole responsibilities for developing new products right up to the commercialisation phase when they can be handed over to the operating divisions are obvious. However, the efficiencies which may be expected to accompany task specialisation may well be diluted or completely negated unless communication between the partners is first class. Where it is not, an 'us and them' mentality may well arise and there is considerable evidence to suggest that new products succeed best where they are the responsibility of a single product champion who will see them through all the way from conceptualisation to commercialisation and beyond.

In recognition of this evidence many multiproduct firms have chosen to give full responsibility for the management of discrete products and product lines to a single product or brand manager. Such a manager will be responsible both for introducing new products and for managing them throughout their life-cycle. There is a very large literature which deals with the advantages and disadvantages of the product manager system, particularly as compared with the alternative of organising around markets as the common factor (see, for example, Baker and McTavish, 1976). From this literature it is clear that there are many different kinds of product management and that there is considerable difference of opinion as to the merits and demerits of the system. Many of the problems are a direct consequence of the difficulty in assigning product managers sufficient authority commensurate with their responsibility. A great deal certainly depends upon the calibre of the persons appointed to this position and many firms regard the product manager's job as a proving ground for aspirant general managers, which is hardly surprising given the seven roles Luck and Ferrell (1979) suggest they must play:

1. A coordinator of the various functions and department operations, so that they synchronise relative to the particular product(s) and programmes.
2. An entrepreneur or profit centre within the corporation who develops and is responsible for an area of the business, the assigned product(s).

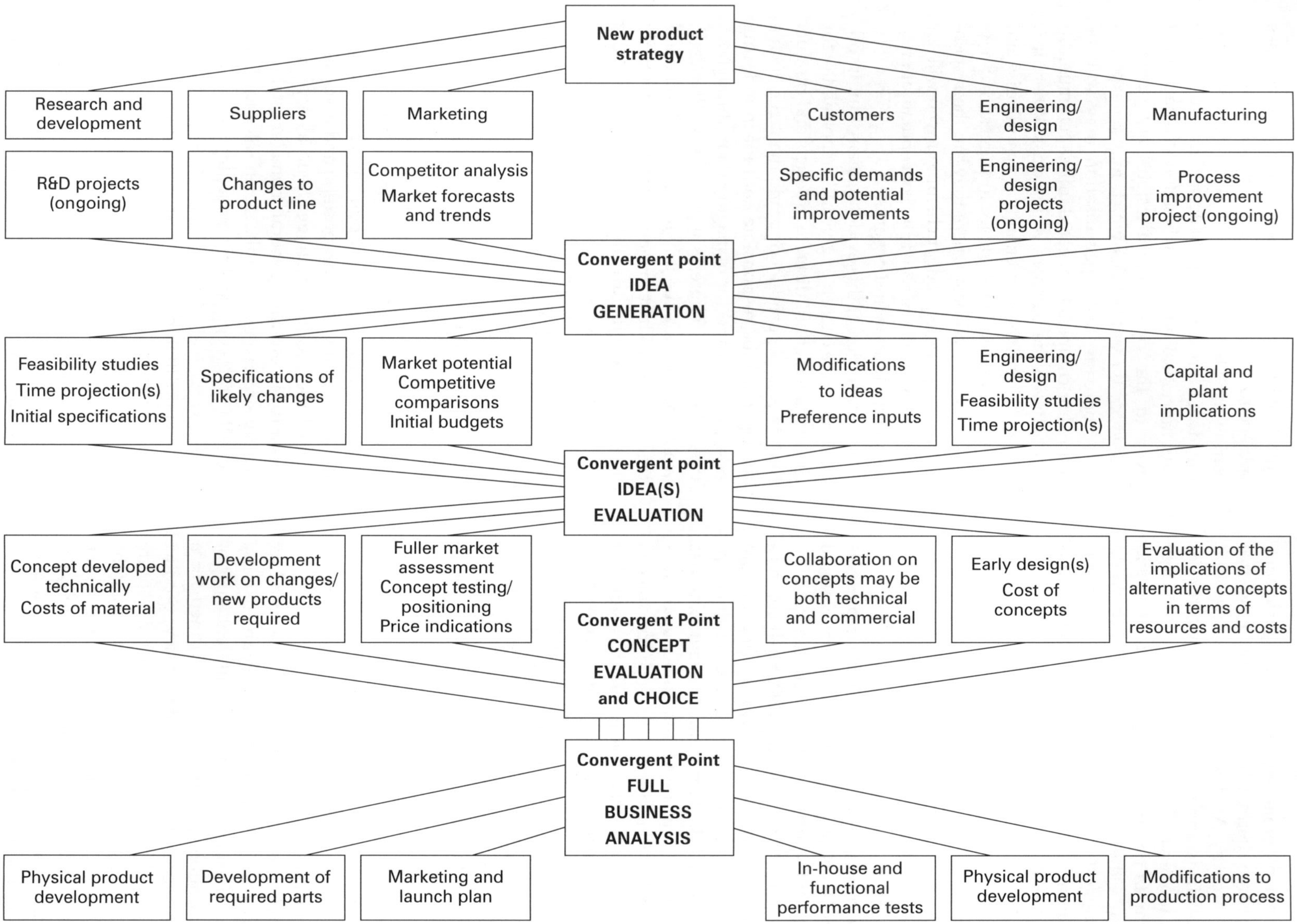

FIGURE 15.7 The multiple convergent process

SOURCE: Baker, M. J. and Hart, S. J. (2007) *Product Strategy and Management* (2nd edn). Financial Times Press

3. An expediter who sees that tasks get done, products are distributed, crises are met etc., relative to the product(s).
4. An expert information centre who is most knowledgeable about his or her products and their markets, serving as advisor and source of information about them.
5. A forecaster who studies the markets, competition etc., and projects the likely effects of plans, expenditure, and demand changes on the product(s).
6. An innovator who finds or creates new ideas regarding the product(s), their marketing etc.
7. An integrator who brings together the ideas, plans and viewpoints of others into a systematic product plan.

Ultimately the decision as to the most appropriate organisational form must represent a judicious balance between the frequency and importance of NPD, the homogeneity/diversity of the products and markets involved and the personal preferences of those with overall responsibility. In *Product Strategy and Management* (Baker and Hart, 2007), we discuss these issues in some depth and the reader should consult this source if they want more information. Overall, however, the trends point towards a project-based approach in which all the functions and stakeholders are involved in what we have called the 'multiple convergent process' as illustrated in Figure 15.7. Owing to the size of the page, only the first stages of the process can be shown, but the figure indicates that the core or spine of the process is the sequence of events proscribed by the normative theory of new product development and summarised in Figure 15.5. These steps become the convergent points when all those involved in the process come together to clear the development to progress to the next stage. By adopting this structure it is possible for those involved to act both simultaneously and in parallel rather than in the classic pass-the-parcel approach which characterised the functional 'box' mentality of earlier models.

MANAGING THE PRODUCT LIFE-CYCLE

Just as it was helpful to consider NPD as a process, so it will assist understanding of the most appropriate strategy for product management if we trace the product through its life-cycle. Some reference has already been made to the application of major mix elements as the product moves from introduction through growth and maturity to senility, but in this and succeeding 'mix' chapters we shall analyse the appropriate tactics in rather greater depth. By doing so we run the risk of giving the impression that one can manipulate a particular mix element while holding the others constant, which is rarely the case. On the other hand, by concentrating upon one element at a time we hope to isolate the major options so that we can then determine how combination with the other elements may affect the relevance in any given set of circumstances.

MARKET INTRODUCTION

Over the years a great deal of my own interest and research has been concentrated upon the problems of introducing new products into the marketplace. As we saw in earlier chapters, this interest is founded upon the proposition that product life-cycles represent an underlying process whereby innovations diffuse or spread through a population of adopters, from which it follows that there is a functional relationship between the time to first acceptance and full diffusion. Hence the more quickly one can achieve initial penetration, the more rapidly sales will build up, the greater the opportunity to establish a commanding position before imitators can climb on the bandwagon, and the more quickly one can recoup one's initial investment and move into profitability. In order to achieve this more rapid penetration, it was argued that one should pay particular attention to the manner in which selective perception might result in a mismatch between the seller's view of the benefits offered by his new product and the prospective purchaser's interpretation of them, so that one can concentrate the launch effort on those potential users most likely to see 'eye to eye' with the seller.

An explicit assumption throughout this work is that the marketer has a problem in penetrating the market and it would be as well at this juncture to make it equally plain that this is by no means always the case. As Chester Wasson (1974) has shown so clearly, many products proceed almost instantaneously from introduction to rapid growth and so present the seller with quite different problems from those associated with slow penetration. Wasson differentiates between products with a protracted introduction phase and those with almost no introduction phase in terms of the amount of consumer learning which is necessary to comprehend the benefits offered by the new product – high learning and low learning introductions respectively. It follows that the first step in devising a new product launch strategy is to decide whether the product requires high or low learning by the consumer.

In seeking to make such a distinction, one has to be careful to avoid circular reasoning, and it is not much help to suggest that something which it is easy to understand will require less learning than something which it is hard to understand! Notwithstanding this difficulty, Everett Rogers (1983), one of the most distinguished writers on innovation, offers us five product characteristics that have been found to determine whether or not a new product will require much consumer learning. These five factors are:

1. Relative advantage
2. Compatibility
3. Complexity
4. Divisibility
5. Communicability.

With the possible exception of divisibility, all these factors are comparative rather than absolute in value, in that they depend upon the potential user's existing status. From this it can be deduced that the more closely a new product approximates the existing status, the less learning will be required and the faster the prospect's reaction to the new product.

Based upon our earlier discussion of the 'just noticeable difference', it should also be apparent

that new products which are very similar to old ones may not be seen as different at all and certainly not as sufficiently different to merit the switching costs and possible dissonance which a change of purchasing behaviour may occasion. Slow sales build-up for low learning products obviously has quite different implications than it has for radically new innovations with high learning requirements.

Depending upon one's assessment of the learning requirements for the new product, one can evaluate the relative merits of an undifferentiated, differentiated or concentrated marketing strategy with the logical relationship being that depicted in Figure 15.8.

Of course other factors will also have to be taken into account, not least of which is the firm's existing competitive strength for this will strongly influence the investment in launch inventory, the physical distribution that can be achieved and the promotional effort possible. Another consideration is the novelty of the technology, for if this is difficult to replicate and/or enjoys patent protection then the innovator may wish to control the speed of the product launch to optimise their investment and cash flows. (A radically new technology does not necessarily imply that consumers will need a lot of learning to appreciate it – given availability and a low price, products such as TVs, VCRs, and pocket calculators could have diffused almost instantaneously!)

To sum up, the greater the product differentiation and the stronger the marketer's proprietorial rights in the differentiating factor, the greater the control they can exercise over their introductory marketing strategy. From this observation it follows that only very large and well-established firms can hope to survive on a policy of trivial incremental product innovation by depending upon economies of scale in volume (cost/price), in distribution and in promotion. Conversely, the only hope for the small firm to break such an

STRATEGY	Undifferentiated	Differentiated	Concentrated
Amount of learning required	LOW	MODERATE	HIGH

FIGURE 15.8 Marketing strategy: relationships

established market leadership is to 'bypass' the competition through radical product innovation.

GROWTH

Assuming that a product survives the introductory phase, the PLC concept predicts that it will enter upon a period of accelerating growth, which will be signalled by a distinct upward inflexion on the sales curve. In determining when a product has 'taken off', it is important to differentiate between low and high learning products, for in the case of the former the introductory phase may be very short or non-existent. For example, in *Market Development* (Baker, 1983), the case histories show that the benefits of needled woven polypropylene, coaxial tomography (the body scanner) and Ambush (an insecticide) were so obvious that almost the only constraint on take-up was physical availability. Conversely, superplastic aluminium, the JCB 110, and vinyl floor products required more learning and sales only built up slowly.

It is also important to consider the replacement rate because, where this is short as in the case of most consumer goods, one is liable to find extensive sampling of new products on a trial basis. (Short replacement cycles are almost always associated with low unit costs and/or a high rating in the consumer's overall scale of preferences.) It follows that it would be premature to assess the sales performance of such new products until the repeat purchasing behaviour of the early buyers becomes apparent.

A third important consideration when determining the appropriate product strategy during the growth phase is to bear in mind that the actual rate of growth is the outcome of both demand and supply factors – of both a contagion and a bandwagon effect. Contagion results from the increased physical visibility of the product in the hands of consumers (the 'new car at the kerbside' effect) and from the word-of-mouth activities of early buyers who seek to reduce possible post-purchase dissonance by telling their contacts of the benefits they are experiencing from ownership of the new thing. Bandwagon effects are the consequence of new suppliers entering the market and increasing the physical availability of the new product for purchase. Often this increased availability is accompanied by price cutting/discounting/sales promotion as the different suppliers seek to build up their individual market shares.

Of course the ability of new suppliers to enter the market will depend very much upon the existence or otherwise of barriers to entry (see Chapter 2 for a summary of these) and the precise nature of these barriers. As a simple rule of thumb, ease of entry is inversely related to the degree of product differentiation, from which it follows that the product strategy alternatives are:

1. Differentiate the product and create a monopoly for it
2. Accept that differentiation is difficult and concentrate on manufacturing and distribution efficiencies in order to keep costs down so that one can use price and dealer margins to build up market share and secure the benefits of the scale and experience effects (see Chapter 5).

Where a firm does have a monopoly of a new product or process, it is likely that it will have adopted a concentrated or skimming strategy on introduction and used price to restrict demand and enhance profit margins. To deter competition and/or avoid investigation by regulatory agencies, the firm will not want to be seen to exploit its monopoly for too long by earning excessive profit margins and so will seek to increase total profits by taking a smaller margin on an increased volume – usually by cutting price and 'sliding down the demand curve'. In order to make such price reductions acceptable to the early buyers who paid the full price, the seller would be well advised to modify the product and offer an economy model or perhaps introduce a new deluxe model so that the original can be seen as marginally out of date and so deserving of a lower price. Obviously this latter approach has the double advantage that it may encourage the original buyers to trade-up and so maintain their feelings of exclusivity and innovativeness.

Overall, however, the product variable may be expected to be fairly low key during the growth phase as the rapidly expanding demand suggests buyers are seeking to satisfy primary needs. Thus they may well find the claims of competing models on points of detail are more a source of confusion than clarification and emphasise availability, price and promotion rather than minor product features when making a choice.

MATURITY

Once sales level off and stabilise the product is considered to have reached the mature stage of its life-cycle. However, before coming to this conclusion it is important to determine whether there are any other geographic areas which are as yet unexploited and/or whether there may be alternative uses to which the product may be put. Thus by simply increasing the geographical availability of a product one may stimulate renewed sales growth and defer the onset of maturity. Alternatively, as we saw in Chapter 5, when discussing the PLC for nylon, it may be possible to find complete new uses for a product and so expand the total demand for it.

In most texts extending coverage and/or finding new uses are discussed as strategies for the mature phase of the life-cycle. In our opinion this is wrong, for if such possibilities exist they should have been pre-identified and constitute approaches for extending the growth phase. Only when these alternatives have been fully exploited and sales have levelled off should we consider the product to have reached full maturity. Of course, this is a counsel for perfection and in the real world most individuals and organisations appear to expect growth to continue unchecked indefinitely. So, it is only when growth stops that much effort is given to finding out why and what may be done about it. As a result of such inquiry new markets and new uses may be found that result in a renewal of growth but, by definition, they don't require a product change. For example, the frequently quoted case of Johnson's Baby Powder

shows how sales were increased substantially by promoting its use to adults, but with no change in the product, its price, distribution or packaging.

Another similar case with an interesting twist is Church & Dwight's Arm & Hammer brand of baking soda which has been on sale in the USA for well over 100 years. The makers knew that baking soda will absorb food odours in refrigerators, but their initial attempts to establish whether there would be interest in this use indicated there was no interest. Essentially the problem was that housewives were asked if they had an odour problem in their refrigerator and, not surprisingly, they said 'No'. Accordingly, the use was not promoted until the company decided to ignore the early research and put out an ad suggesting the use. The response was immediate and very large – as an insurance policy or a cure it was a very inexpensive and simple solution.

Once a product has truly reached the mature stage then clearly the prime objectives are to sustain this for as long as possible and to secure as large a share as possible of the available market. Both ends will be served through a policy of continuous product improvement which may involve an actual change in the product itself or in the services associated with its delivery and/or consumption.

Examples of improvements in mature products are not difficult to come by as can be seen by scanning almost any newspaper or magazine. Design and style changes may encourage people to replace products more quickly and maintain interest in them while discouraging competitors from seeking to develop radically different means of satisfying the consumer's basic need. However, despite their best efforts to sustain mature products, sooner or later new and improved products will appear, initiating a decline in sales.

| Box 15.3 | Extending the PLC | |

If a brand is not revitalised, it will disappear before it achieves its full potential regardless of whether it is the leader in its product category. One of the best examples of extending a brand's life span is the case of Lucozade.

Lucozade was originally launched by a chemist in Newcastle in 1927. Lucozade as a product is a carbonated glucose drink with a citric flavour. The glucose content is a highly concentrated source of energy that is

quickly absorbed into the blood. For years, the product was perceived as a convalescence drink. In the mid-1970s sales figures went down to 3 million bottles a year, from 5 million bottles a year in the 1950s, as a result of such factors as decline in the sickness level in 1970s, changing consumer attitudes, inflation and of course increasing competition. When, in 1977, sales decline was 12%, the company management decided to take action. It commissioned a usage and attitude survey, which found that while the majority of purchasers were buying for convalescent children, they only accounted for 30% of the sales volume. The rest of the sales volume came from healthy adults consuming the product for refreshment. This suggested that the product had a large potential in the refreshment market. But, if the product were to be reposit-

ioned as a strictly refreshing drink, the sales volume coming from child convalescence usage would have been lost. Thus, company executives decided to implement an extension strategy with new intrusive execution which would widen the product's usage without alienating its applications to illness. An advertising campaign named 'Ups and Downs' which mainly focused on recovery from feeling tired during the course of the day was developed. After a year, the sales volume was up 13% and people's perception of the product was changed from exclusive use in sickness to use in health. Then, the company

executives thought that the brand may benefit from being depicted as being especially refreshing and an appropriate accompaniment to hard physical activity. The company decided to use a sports personality, Daley Thomson, the decathlon world record holder at that time. The sales volume skyrocketed. Since then, the company has used several sports personalities such as John Barnes and Linford Christie to endorse the product. Without the measures taken by the company management Lucozade would have been among the brands that have been long forgotten.

SOURCE: Zafer Erdogan, based on Broadbent (1984)

DECLINE

Given that most new products are substitutes for existing products – hence the popularity of the 'what business are we in' approach to long-term strategic planning – one should not be surprised if cumulative sales curves are reasonably symmetrical. In other words all the factors which may delay or accelerate a new product's acceptance are just as likely to work for or against it when a substitute for it is subsequently introduced to the market. However, whether or not one anticipates that the decline phase of the life-cycle will be gradual or sudden one must have a clear policy for dealing with the ailing product.

Until recently comparatively little interest has been shown in the decline phase and at the time of the first edition (1985) there were only about five articles that dealt with the subject in any depth and most of these were rather dated and failed to address adequately the practical problems of implementation. However in the early 1980s, my former colleague George Avlonitis published a number of articles on the topic, dealing with both the theoretical considerations and the practicalities, using extensive research into the UK engineering

industry as an empirical foundation and launched a renewed interest in the topic. This has been continued by another colleague, Susan Hart, and in *Product Strategy and Management* (2007) she is largely responsible for Part 4 (Chapters 17–19), which deal with product elimination in great detail. Table 15.4 sums up the potential aims of product deletion.

While most writers on product elimination see it as a straight choice between phasing it out slowly – variously referred to as milking, harvesting, run-out and product petrification – and immediate withdrawal, Avlonitis (1983) identified two further alternatives:

1. Drop from the standard range and reintroduce as a 'special'
2. Sell out to another manufacturer ('divert').

Avlonitis believes that the ability to reintroduce a product as a special is probably unique to the industrial market, but otherwise the strategies would seem to be equally appropriate to both consumer and industrial products. That said, such evidence as there is points to a tendency for industrial goods to be phased out gradually, while consumer goods are more prone to immediate withdrawal.

TABLE 15.4 A wider view of the potential aims of product deletion

Implications of carrying excess products	Aims of deletion
Excessive burden on company resources:	
■ Physical	Create warehousing space for quick delivery of key lines
■ Financial	Transfer promotional funds from several slow-moving lines to fewer, buoyant lines
■ Managerial	Simplify product positioning
'Immeasurable costs'	Streamline selling procedures, cut the costs of distributing small orders
Opportunity costs	Create physical, financial and managerial resources to exploit a new product opportunity
Resources are spread too thinly	Simplify production planning
Old products are damaging to market image	Initiate the development of new products

SOURCE: Baker, M. J. and Hart, S. J. (2007) *Product Strategy and Management* (2nd edn). Financial Times Press

TABLE 15.5 Review criteria for identifying deletion candidates

Sales related criteria
■ Past sales volume
■ The product's percentage of overall company sales
■ Future sales volume

Market related criteria
■ Market growth
■ Market share
■ The stage of the product on its PLC curve
■ Customer acceptance of the product
■ Competitive activity in the marketplace

Profit related criteria
■ The product's profit contribution
■ Price trends
■ Sales generated versus resources used in generating sales

Operating criteria
■ Stock inventory levels
■ Service levels
■ Batch sizes
■ Operational problems

SOURCE: Baker, M. J. and Hart, S. J. (2007) *Product Strategy and Management* (2nd edn). Financial Times Press

Of course much will depend on whether the seller's production equipment is specific or non-specific and the extent to which it has been depreciated. Where the production equipment can be put to other uses or is near the end of its useful life an immediate drop decision is much more likely than a slow phase-out and vice versa. Further, in the case of durable goods the seller will have to give careful attention to service and maintenance obligations and the provision of spare parts and components. For such products, Baker and Hart (2007) provide a very helpful summary of factors to be considered in Table 15.5.

Once it has been decided to phase a product out, then the guiding principle must be to extract the maximum benefit at the minimum cost, and Luck (1972, pp. 75–6) provides an excellent set of strategic steps for accomplishing this:

1. Simplify the product line to the best selling items and, if workable, those that yield the higher gross profit margins.
2. Dress up the product with relatively inexpensive styling and feature changes that create a fresh impression.
3. Bring all marketing efforts into a narrower focus by determining which portions of the market are the heavier and more loyal users or are best served by the existing product. Make limited resources go further in concentrated markets, including selectivity in advertising media and sharper tailoring of appeals.

4. Concentrate also on market areas and on distributors that have the best potentials. If the specific types of buyers being promoted consider the old brand as speciality in shopping behaviour, exclusive distribution agreements may obtain dealer support.

5. Offer special bonuses or other rewards for pushing of the product by distributors and their sales personnel.

6. Limit the always costly personal sales calls to only the best outlets or buyers. Substitute more telephone or mail ordering for personal calls.

7. Utilise more economical wholesale channels by shifting to agents that are shared with other products.

8. Trade down the product to lower price buyers through price reductions made possible by austerity actions.

MONITORING PRODUCT PERFORMANCE

As a result of the emphasis upon NPD as a major competitive strategy, the risks of failure have become substantial. In addition, the continuing stream of new offerings poses serious threats to the products they seek to replace, and so puts a premium upon careful monitoring of product performance to secure early warning of any problems and permit remedial action to be taken.

In determining the product's state of health profitability, sales volume and market share are the usual criteria. Of course, profitability may be measured in a number of ways, including the following:

- An operating margin on sales
- A return on investment (ROI) for each product line
- A contribution to advertising and promotion above all fixed and variable costs above a minimum level
- A ratio of direct costs to sales price above a minimum level
- A return on assets (ROA).

Sales volume provides both an absolute and a relative measure of performance, and most firms would wish to consider both before making specific marketing decisions, e.g. to boost promotion, extend distribution, cut price etc. Thus one needs to monitor the industry sales/market demand for the product to provide a yardstick with which to measure one's own comparative performance. However, in some product areas with very high fixed investments, management may fix a minimum sales volume below which it is unattractive to stay in that market. This does not mean that firms will drop immediately any product that falls below such a minimum sales volume as much will depend upon whether the resources can be transferred to other uses and how quickly. In the short term even sick products make a contribution to fixed and operating costs, and one needs to be certain of an equivalent or larger contribution from other uses of one's resources before making any change.

The importance of market share as an indicator of both performance and profitability has been discussed in Chapter 4 and appears to be used by an increasing number of companies for monitoring individual products. While the conventional wisdom is that one should seek to dominate a market so that one can exercise leadership over it, it requires only a moment's reflection to realise that if all firms believed this then all industries would be monopolistic. Of course a great deal depends upon how one defines a market and it is quite clear that small firms may concentrate all their energies upon a small but discrete market segment and dominate it while only achieving a fraction of industry sales for the product as a whole.

In addition to the three usual criteria of profits, volume and share, Baker and Hart (2007) identify several other factors that management use in assessing product potential, which are summarised in Table 15.6.

Obviously the ideal product will be complementary to one's other products and markets, will have low cash needs, be technologically advanced, use freely available materials and components and be unlikely to attract any adverse public or governmental attention.

In our previous discussion of the management of products at different stages in their life-cycle, there was an implicit assumption of a smooth progression through the four stages. In reality this is unlikely to occur for individual offerings, and the purpose of monitoring is to permit remedial action to be taken at any stage of a product's life.

TABLE 15.6 Factors used to evaluate whether a deletion candidate should be retained

Internal evaluation factors

1. Resource related:
   - Availability of a new product
   - Effect of the elimination on recovery of overheads
   - Reallocation of resources to other opportunities
   - Effect of the deletion on fixed capital (i.e. plant and equipment)
   - Interchangeability (communisation) of parts, materials or packing
   - Effect of the deletion on capacity utilisation
   - Reallocation of executive and selling time
   - Effect of the deletion on working capital (e.g. stock)
   - Effect of the deletion on employment prospects of the workforce

2. Finance related:
   - Effect of the deletion on total company sales volume
   - Effect of the deletion on sales and profitability of other products in the range
   - Product's contribution to a profit centre (e.g. branch, factory, depot)

External evaluation factors
   - Product's market potential
   - Effect of the deletion on distribution (e.g. loss of shelf space)
   - Effect of the deletion on 'full-range' policy
   - Existence of substitutes to satisfy the customer
   - Effect of the deletion on company image
   - Competitive reaction to the withdrawal
   - Customer relations

SOURCE: Baker, M. J. and Hart, S. J. (2007) *Product Strategy and Management* (2nd edn). Financial Times Press

Thus it may be that the competitive reaction to a new product may be so strong that one may decide to opt out of the race while the market is still growing rapidly. Two examples of this in *Market Development* (Baker, 1983) are the vinyl floor products and body scanner cases. In the former, Delaware Floor Products realised that it had not the resources to compete with either of the major linoleum manufacturers once they had decided to enter the market and so sold its interests to one of them. Similarly, EMI neglected

further technological development of its invention and was overtaken by other companies who also had a much better understanding of the market for X-ray equipment. EMI, too, sold out long before the market for body scanners reached maturity. If EMI had been less complacent and monitored product developments better, it may well have retained its leadership – a salutary lesson that monitoring performance is an essential activity to be performed continuously.

Chapter summary

In this chapter we have only scratched the surface of the issues involved in formulating and implementing a product policy. Hopefully, however, we have succeeded in communicating the belief that the product is at the very heart of the marketing process and deserves greater attention than it appears to have enjoyed in recent years. That said, we have also tried to demonstrate that the product has to match market needs,

that the functions of supply and demand are mutually interdependent and that neither is of much consequence unless it stimulates a reaction from the other. (There are just as many if not more demands which suppliers do not consider it worth their while to satisfy as there are products which consumers are unwilling to buy.)

A review of the role of the product, user needs and product characteristics and the

definition of the 'product', was followed by a short discussion of services. This explored some of the reasons for the growth of services in advanced economies, and the characteristics that are usually used to distinguish services from physical products. It was concluded that while the same marketing principles apply to both, in particular one needs to modify the marketing mix to allow for the balance between tangible and intangible elements in the sales offering.

The need for a product policy was outlined, with an emphasis on the importance of having a portfolio of products, preferably at different stages in their life-cycle.

Because of competitive pressures, and in recognition of our maxim that 'the act of consumption changes the consumer', more and more firms are turning to product differentiation as a means of sustaining or improving their position. This has resulted in growing interest in the process of NPD and the normative approach to this has been described and discussed, as have organisational structures to promote the process.

Following our adoption of the product life-cycle as the basic analytical and planning framework, we looked next at the implications of this for the product variable. Our review suggests that product considerations will be important throughout, but are most critical in the introduction and decline phases. Notwithstanding this generalisation, we consider it important to monitor the product's performance on a continuous basis and the chapter concluded with a brief overview of approaches to this.

Recommended reading

Baker, M. J. and Hart, S. J. (2007) *Product Strategy and Management* (2nd edn). Hemel Hempstead: Pearson.

Cooper, R. G. (1999) New product development, in Baker, M. J. (ed.) *Encyclopedia of Marketing*. London: International Thomson Business Press.

Cooper, R. G. (2001) *Winning at New Products: Accelerating the Process from Idea to Launch* (3rd edn). New York: Perseus.

Gabbott, M. and Hogg, G. (1997) *Marketing: Contemporary Services Marketing Management*. London: International Thomson Business Press.

Hart, S. (2003) New product development, in Baker, M. J. (ed.) *The Marketing Book* (5th edn). Oxford: Butterworth Heinemann.

Kahn, K. B. (ed.) (2004) *The PDMA Handbook of New Product Devel-

opment* (2nd edn). New York: John Wiley & Sons.

Palmer, A. (2003) The marketing of services, in Baker, M. J. (ed.) *The Marketing Book* (5th edn). Oxford: Butterworth Heinemann.

Trott, P. (2004) *Innovation Management and New Product Development* (3rd edn). New York: FT/Prentice Hall.

REFERENCES

Abbott, L. (1955) *Quality and Competition*. New York: Columbia University Press, p. 9.

Ansoff, H. I. (1957) Strategies for diversification, *Harvard Business Review* (September–October).

Ansoff, H. I. (1965) *Corporate Strategy*. New York: McGraw-Hill.

Ansoff, H. I. (1968) *Corporate Strategy*. Harmondsworth: Penguin.

Aspinwall, L. (1958) The characteristics of good theory, in Lazer, W. and Kelley, E. (eds) *Managerial Marketing* (rev edn). Homewood, IL: Richard D. Irwin.

Avlonitis, G. (1980) An Exploratory Investigation of the Product Elimination Decision-making Process in the UK Engineering Industry, unpublished Ph.D thesis, University of Strathclyde.

Avlonitis, G. A. (1983) The product elimination decision and strategies, *Industrial Marketing Management*, **12**: 31–4.

Baker, M. J. (1983) *Market Development*. Harmondsworth: Penguin.

Baker, M. J. and Hart, S. J. (2007) *Product Strategy and Management* (2nd edn). Financial Times Press.

Baker, M. J. and McTavish, R. (1976) *Product Policy and Management*. London: Macmillan – now Palgrave Macmillan, Chapter 5.

Bateson, J. E. G. (1977) Do we need service marketing? in Eigler, P. (ed.) *Marketing Consumer Services*. Boston, MA: Marketing Science Institute.

Bennett, R. C. and Cooper, R. G. (1982) The misuse of marketing: an American tragedy, *McKinsey Quarterly* (autumn): 52–69.

Blois, K. (1982) *Organisational Structure and Marketing Policies in Service Firms*. Paper presented at the 11th Annual Conference of the European Academy for Advanced Research in Marketing (April).

Brown, S. (2001) Torment your customers, *Harvard Business Review* (October).

Copeland, M. T. (1923) Relation of consumers' buying habits to marketing methods, *Harvard Business Review* (April).

Corey, E. R. (1975) Key options in market selection and product planning, *Harvard Business Review* (September–October).

Donnelly, J. H. Jr and George, W. R. (eds) (1981) *Marketing of Services*. Chicago, IL: American Marketing Association.

Drucker, P. (1963) Managing for business effectiveness, *Harvard Business Review*, **42**(May/June).

Evans, J. R. and Berman, B. (1982) *Marketing*. New York: Macmillan.

Gardner, C. A. (1986) Dissertation proposal, George Washington University, Washington DC.

Goodfellow, J. H. (1983) The marketing of goods or services as a multidimensional concept, *Quarterly Review of Marketing* (spring): 19–27.

Guiltinan, J. P. and Paul, G. W. (1982) *Marketing Management: Strategies and Programs*. New York: McGraw-Hill, pp. 40–2.

Gummesson, E. (1979) The marketing of professional services: an organisational dilemma, *European Journal of Marketing*, 13(5): 308–18.

Hayes, R. H. and Abernathy, W. J. (1980) Managing our way to economic decline, *Harvard Business Review* (July–August).

Johne, A. (1982) Innovation, Organisation and Marketing of High Technology Products, unpublished PhD dissertation, Strathclyde University.

Johnson, S. C. and Jones, C. (1957) How to organise for new products, *Harvard Business Review* (May–June).

Kotler, P. (1965) Phasing-out weak products, *Harvard Business Review* (March–April): 108–18.

Kotler, P. (1978) Harvesting weak products, *Business Horizons*, 21 August: 15–22.

Levitt, T. (1960) Marketing myopia, *Harvard Business Review* (July–August).

Levitt, T. (1974) *Marketing for Business Growth*. New York: McGraw-Hill.

Levitt, T. (1976a) The industrialisation of service, *Harvard Business Review* (September–October).

Levitt, T. (1976b) The augmented product concept in Rothberg, R. R. (ed.) *Corporate Strategy and Product Innovation*. New York: Free Press.

Luck, D. J. (1972) *Product Policy and Strategy*. Englewood Cliffs, NJ: Prentice Hall.

Luck, D. J. and Ferrell, O. C. (1979) *Marketing Strategy and Plans*. Englewood Cliffs, NJ: Prentice Hall.

Markin, R. (1982) *Marketing Strategy and Management*. New York: John Wiley.

Michael, G. C. (1971) Product petrification – a new stage in the life cycle theory, *California Management Review*, 9(fall): 88–91.

Miracle, G. E. (1969) Product characteristics and market strategy, *Journal of Marketing* (January).

Riesz, P. (1980) Revenge of the marketing concept, *Business Horizons* (June).

Rogers, E. (1983) *Diffusion of Innovations* (3rd edn). New York: Free Press.

Rothe, J. A. (1970) The product elimination decision, *MSU Business Topics*, 18(autumn): 45–52.

Rothwell, R. (1995) Towards the fifth-generation innovation process, *International Marketing Review*, 11(1): 7–31.

Rothwell, R., Gardiner, P. and Schott, K. (1983) *Design and the Economy*. London: The Design Council.

Shostack, G. L. (1982) How to design a service, *European Journal of Marketing*, 16(1): 49–63.

Stanton, N. J. (1981) *Fundamentals of Marketing*. New York: McGraw-Hill.

Talley, W. J. (1964) Profiting from the declining product, *Business Horizons*, 7(spring): 77–84.

Thompson, H. V. (1962) *Product Strategy*. London: Business Publications, p. 33.

Wasson, C. (1974) *Dynamic Competitive Strategy & Product Life Cycles*. St Charles, IL: Challenge Books.

Wickham, R. G., Fitzroy, P. T. and Mandry, G. D. (1975) Marketing of services: an evaluation of the theory, *European Journal of Marketing*, 9(1): 59–67.

Wind, Y. and Mahajan, V. (1982) Designing product and business portfolios, *Harvard Business Review*, (January–February): 155–65.

Yorke, D. A. (1990) Interactive perceptions of suppliers and corporate clients in the marketing of professional services: a comparison of accounting and legal services in the UK, Canada and Sweden, *Journal of Marketing Management*, 5(3): 307–23.

NOTES

1. As Levitt (1976a) has shown, virtually all services are associated with physical/objective factors that are necessary to the delivery of the service. Thus the opulence of the bank, the cleanliness of the operating theatre and the comfort of the beauty parlour will all have an important influence on the perception of the service rendered. It is for this reason that we prefer not to deal with services as being completely distinct from physical products.

2. This was first introduced in Chapter 9 when discussing the general influence of product characteristics on choice behaviour.

Packaging

Making silk purses out of sows' ears.   ANON

After reading Chapter 16 you will be able to:

✔ Explain the four roles played by packaging in marketing.

✔ Describe the five criteria to be considered in developing a package – appearance, protection, function, cost and disposability.

✔ Spell out the steps to be followed in designing a pack and achieving a balance between the five functional criteria.

INTRODUCTION

In Chapter 9, when discussing 'How do buyers choose?', it was argued that both individuals and organisations are often faced with situations in which two or more competing offerings appear equivalent in terms of their performance characteristics and the cost benefits associated with their acquisition and use. Under such circumstances, even relatively small perceived differences may result in the prospective buyer preferring one product to another. One element of the marketing mix that offers considerable scope for creating a 'just discernible difference' or 'determinant factor' is packaging, and in this chapter we shall look first at the functions of packaging, then at the factors involved in developing a pack, and finally at the use of packaging in the marketing mix. Although packaging has an important role to play in the marketing of all types of product, it is clear that its overall influence is greatest in the field of fast-moving consumer goods (FMCGs) and such products will tend to dominate the discussion in this chapter. That said, it should not be overlooked that design features which comprise the 'packaging' of many industrial goods, e.g. use of colour on machinery, operator comfort features etc., play an increasingly important part in many industrial buying decisions.

DEFINITIONS

While there are many books concerned with technical aspects of packaging, comparatively few of these deal with the managerial aspects of the function which are of prime importance to the marketer. One of the few that does, Briston and Neill (1972), offers three definitions of packaging as follows:

1. Packaging is the art, science and technology of preparing goods for transport and sale.
2. Packaging may be defined as the means of ensuring the safe delivery of a product to the ultimate consumer in sound condition, at the minimum overall cost.
3. Packaging must protect what it sells, and sell what it protects.

In the standard reference work edited by Frey (*Marketing Handbook*, 1965), packaging is defined in terms of the role it plays in marketing and divided into four categories as follows:

1. Primary packaging is the 'essential container enveloping the product [which] remains with the product from the time of its manufacture or preparation at least through distribution to retailers, and very often continues through the entire life of the product'.
2. Secondary packaging refers to the additional containers and wrappings that are added for protective or marketing requirements.
3. Display packaging is packaging intended for displaying the product at the point of sale.
4. Shipping packaging is intended primarily for protecting goods in transit and storage.

All four categories of packaging are of major importance in marketing, bearing in mind that the manufacturer is concerned not only with protecting their goods until they are safely delivered to the final user, but also with their relationships with intermediaries in the channels of distribution. Well-designed packaging performs a number of distinct purposes, each of which will vary in importance for these different persons in the distributive chain from producer to user, and a review of these will indicate a number of ways in which packaging may be used as both a tactical and strategic variable in the marketing mix.

It should be noted that while the above references appear dated, in fact very little of any substance has been written about the use of packaging in the marketing mix since they appeared. While explicit recognition is given to the important role that aesthetic design plays in new product development and of packaging as a point-of-sale reminder and selling aid, this recognition is rarely supported by further discussion or evidence in marketing textbooks. Undoubtedly this will change in the same way that customer service has become a topic for extended review now, whereas 10 or so years ago it received only cursory mention.

One exception to the above generalisation is *The Marketer's Guide to Successful Package Design* (Meyers and Lubliner, 1998), to which some reference will be made later. Meantime we will depend on the original sources cited earlier.

PACKAGING CRITERIA

Briston and Neill (1972) distinguish five criteria that have to be considered in developing a package:

1. Appearance
2. Protection
3. Function
4. Cost
5. Disposability.

The appearance of a product is of vital importance to the vast range of FMCGs that are sold through self-service outlets. Given that most retailers will carry three or four different brands of a given product, the package provides a critical visual cue at the point of sale, acting both as a reminder (most purchases of convenience goods are unplanned in the sense that the shopper does not enter the outlet with a prior intention to buy specific products, but relies on the display to act as a signal or prompt to suggest or recall specific needs) and a distinguishing feature between the product and closely competitive offerings. In addition to providing a distinctive and appealing means of identification, the pack must also provide the user with information concerning its contents. Some of this information may be required by law, while the remainder must communicate not only the identity but also facts concerning method of use etc.

Protection of the contents is probably the single most important criterion involved in pack design and construction (Allen, 1982). Damage may arise from physical and/or chemical causes, of which the most important are:

- *Chemical:*
  - Interaction between the container and its contents
  - Ingress of vapours or liquids
  - Ingress of micro-organisms
  - Loss of liquid or vapour.
- *Physical:*
  - Compression/impact/vibration/puncturing
  - Effect of temperature
  - Effect of light
  - Attack by insects/rodents etc.
  - Pilferage/tampering.

During 1982 the importance of packaging as a means of protecting a product was strongly emphasised when several people died in the USA as a result of illegal tampering with a number of well-known packaged products. In the first instance, cases were confined to a brand of painkiller to which a lethal ingredient was added, but the publicity given to the incident sparked off a spate of copycat incidents that culminated in the UK with claims that poultry on sale in a number of chain stores had been infected with a poison so that all the merchandise had to be withdrawn and stringently tested. In 1984 Mars was threatened by a group of animal rights activists who stated their intention of poisoning the company's lines of confectionery. Although a hoax, sales plummeted. A similar claim about Lucozade in November 1991 forced the company to withdraw millions of bottles for fear that they had been contaminated.

Cases such as these have led to renewed interest in ensuring that packaging is tamper-resistant and to a reversal of the trend towards simplicity, easy opening and cost/material reduction. Nowadays packaging suppliers emphasise security against tampering, but as Allen (1982) observed, 'Most packaging suppliers were careful to specify that their products achieved tamper-evidence or tamper-resistance, not tamper-proofing'. No pack can be tamper-proof, but precautions can be taken with many types of packaging to ensure that it is obvious if an attempt has been made to violate its integrity. These range from heat-seal banding of bottlenecks, through print which is removed from its substrata when the label is pulled off, to a tear-off strip attached to plastic screw caps.

A major area of concern that exemplifies well the dilemma between security of contents and simplicity in use is provided by the packaging of products which may be harmful if used incorrectly, particularly by children. Thus, the British Pharmaceutical Society recommends that all prescription drugs should be sold in child-resistant containers (CRCs), which are difficult for small children to open but are easily opened by adults. Examples of such packs are the 'press-and-turn' closure found on many pill bottles, and lids that can only be opened after lining up matching marks on the lid and body of the container.

According to Briston and Neill (1972), packaging performs two basic *functions*:

1. Those concerned with its end use
2. Those concerned with its behaviour on the packaging/filling line.

Of the end-use factors, the most important are seen as display, ease of opening, convenience and dispensing. By *display* is meant making the contents visible to the prospective user rather than appearance of the pack itself which has already been touched upon. While it is not always possible to use packaging which displays the contents, e.g. where a light-resistant pack is used to protect the contents, such as unexposed photographic film, from damage, the majority of users like to be able to examine an object prior to purchase. This instinct is firmly grounded in the injunction not to buy 'a pig in a poke' and frequently creates a conflict between the seller, who is anxious to protect their stock from damage, and the buyer, who is loath to buy something which they have been unable to inspect closely, such as books or magazines sealed in shrinkwrap. In circumstances such as these, it may be necessary to have a display or demonstration model available, with the remainder of the stock being sold in sealed containers.

The question of *ease of opening* has already been reviewed when describing the need to protect products from being tampered with or misused. The problem of ease of opening is a very real one and has become acute in the case of many products which use new packaging materials such as plastic and foil pouches and foil-sealed plastic containers such as those used for yoghurt or portions of butter, jam etc. Similar problems of opening may be experienced with tear-off sealing strips on liquid containers and can be a source of considerable frustration to users.

Many of these new approaches to packaging have been developed in an attempt to achieve the third function of *convenience*, often to the extent that product and package have become completely integrated, as is clearly the case with packaging in aerosol containers and TV dinners on a foil or plastic tray. Similarly, dispensing the product is closely related to ease of opening and convenience and provides numerous opportunities for manufacturers to differentiate their product through close attention to these features.

The second basic group of factors which the manufacturers must take into account when making a decision on packaging is concerned with its *behaviour* on the packaging or filling line. It follows that the greater the standardisation and the more basic the pack the greater are the production economies open to the producer. Most packaging equipment and machinery is extremely sophisticated and therefore costly. Conversely, such standardisation may be in direct conflict with the desire to cater for user needs and has led to considerable emphasis upon contract packaging.

In *Market Development* (Baker, 1983) I included a case study which describes the launch of the wide-mouth bottle in the UK. As is so often the case, the innovators concentrated their initial selling-in efforts on the largest potential users of the new pack, and only after a singular lack of success did they turn their attention to the small breweries. The latter were quick to see that the new pack offered them an opportunity to distinguish their product at the point of sale from that of their main competitors, whose products were sold mainly in cans with the balance in conventional bottles, and adopted the innovation enthusiastically. Looking back on this experience, and with the benefit of hindsight, the marketing director explained the initial lack of success to the fact that the big breweries had very large investments in their existing packaging plants and could not afford to make this obsolete prematurely by taking up a new type of pack.

This dilemma faces many manufacturers, especially of FMCGs. On the one hand, packaging offers an opportunity to differentiate their product at the point of sale, but, on the other, it can represent a significant on-cost and so encourages the producer to standardise their packaging to achieve the maximum economies of scale. One solution to such an impasse is to subcontract part of one's output to an outside agency.

Writing in *Marketing* in 1982, Richard Lawson estimated that 15–20% of all FMCGs were packed by outside contractors, rising to 20–25% for food, 50% for aerosols and 80% for portion packs. Lawson observed:

> The business is likely to continue to grow as manufacturers pay closer attention to segmented markets and as the resulting production runs become shorter. This is because it is uneconomical for manufacturers to put in their own expensive packing machinery if it is not used more or less continuously.

For relatively short runs, the only way they can get the benefits of economies of scale is to go to a specialist packing contractor whose equipment is used to service a number of manufacturers. This has clearly been the case.

Lawson goes on to describe a number of specific situations where using the services of a contract packer may be particularly advantageous. These may be summarised as:

1. *New product development* (NPD): as noted earlier, the capital cost of a specialised packing plant can represent a significant element in the total cost of production. By using a contract packer, one can experiment with a variety of sizes and designs before taking a final decision.
2. *Production of sample packs:* e.g. for sales promotion purposes.
3. *Cross-branding promotions:* i.e. where one pack contains a brand from another manufacturer, e.g. a sachet of Bick hamburger relish in a pack of Bird's Eye hamburgers.
4. *Multipackaging:* where products are offered in non-standard packs for promotional purposes or as 'banded' i.e. joint, offers.
5. *Portion packing:* i.e. miniature containers of jam, butter etc.
6. *Demand seasonality:* where demand fluctuates according to the season of the year the manufacturer may install only base-line capacity and contract-out peak demands.
7. *Exporting:* export packaging is often different from that used in domestic markets. Depending on the scale of foreign sales, it may be more economical to subcontract the packaging rather than change one's own facilities. Frequently such packaging may be undertaken in the export country itself.

It seems clear that faced with shorter runs due to increased competition and an accelerated rate of NPD, not to mention the changes in packaging technology and materials, manufacturers will depend increasingly upon packing contractors for some or all of their requirements.

The importance of careful assessment of cost–benefit is obviously a major factor underlying all packaging decisions. Briston and Neill (1972, p. 20) identify four areas where packaging is of significant importance to the marketing of the product and packaging costs must be closely controlled:

1. Where the cost of the packaging is high relative to the product costs, e.g. cosmetics, toiletries and specialty goods.
2. Annual expenditure on packaging materials is high: household cleaning products, tobacco and cigarettes, and food products.
3. The unit product cost is high: electrical appliances, watches, specialty chemicals and wines/spirits.
4. A large number of items are handled: automobile spare parts, private label products etc.

Cost-control procedures for packaging are very similar to those used for the manufacturing process as a whole and demand a fine balance between perceived value added, losses due to inadequate packaging and the actual costs incurred.

The final criterion which it was suggested should be borne in mind when developing packaging was the *disposability* of the pack. This factor has become of particular importance in recent years due to increased public awareness of the need to protect the environment from litter and pollution caused by discarded packaging, accompanied by concern as to the wastage implicit in disposing of much packaging material. While comparatively few consumers would actually reject a product because its packaging was not actually biodegradable or capable of being recycled (but probably still a sufficient number to warrant serious consideration as a distinct market segment!), the potentially bad effects caused by litter bearing distinctive brand names warrants careful consideration of ways of avoiding such criticism and will accelerate the search for new materials which will reduce or eliminate the problem. Meantime, bottle banks, wastepaper collection and incentives to recycle tinplate and aluminium containers provide a partial solution.

Although Frey's discussion of criteria to be taken into account in developing a package differs in detail from those proposed by Briston and Neill, there is a high measure of agreement, as can be seen from Frey's (1965) statement of the 'Characteristics of a good package', which should be:

1. *Economical:*
   - to manufacture (on standard equipment by regular suppliers)
   - to fill (on standard equipment within the plant)
   - to move (on conventional carriers at normal cost)
2. *Functional:*
   - in transit (for protection)
   - in stores (for merchandising)
   - at home (for convenience)
3. *Communicative:*
   - of brand (to distinguish from competitors)
   - of product (to identify contents)
   - of usage (to point out special uses)
4. *Attractive:*
   - in colour (appropriate to nature of product)
   - in design (readily distinguishable from competitors)
   - in graphic impact (to gain attention and hold interest).

DEVELOPING THE PACK

According to Nancarrow et al. (1998), there are broadly seven occasions when marketers become involved in pack design:

1. Launch of a new product or variant
2. Revitalising a dated/tired pack
3. Repositioning a product (changing what it competes with and/or its functional or symbolic benefits)
4. Changing its target market
5. When cost reductions in packaging are required
6. When legal or regulation requirements demand it
7. When new packaging technology becomes available.

Whereas a great deal of packaging development is concerned with modifying, improving and updating existing packaging, it will be useful to assume that one is starting from scratch with an entirely new product. By adopting this assumption (as we did when discussing NPD), we will take into account all the steps and procedures/techniques involved in the complete process and so provide a framework for deciding which parts

are relevant when considering whether to modify an existing pack.

In broad terms the sequence to be followed is similar to that for all other problem-solving situations:

1. Problem recognition
2. Statement of objectives
3. Collection of relevant information
4. Assessment of alternatives
5. Selection of a course of action
6. Implementation
7. Evaluation and feedback.

In the case of a completely new product, the need to design a pack that will complement the product and enable it to satisfy the five criteria reviewed in the preceding section is clear-cut, and the major problem is deciding on the relative emphasis to give the pack vis-à-vis the other mix elements.

To a large extent the questions to be considered are the same as those which will be asked in developing the new product itself, i.e. Who will buy the product? When and where will they buy it? How will the product be consumed and what role will the pack play in dispensing, protecting and storing the product in use? What information needs to be conveyed on the pack – by law – for purposes of brand identification, to ensure correct use etc.? What packaging are competitors using? What needs does the channel of distribution have? Are we going to package ourselves – what constraints does this impose – or do we intend to subcontract?

With an existing product, determining the cause of lacklustre performance is not always easy, and while giving the packaging a 'face lift' may bolster declining sales, it will be insufficient to make good serious deficiencies in other elements of the marketing mix. In turn, setting objectives will usually require one to specify some order of priority for the five criteria (appearance, protection, function, cost and disposability) – e.g. if economy or cost reduction is the prime objective, then basic packs, as used by ASDA for their own-label brands, will be preferred; if protection, then perhaps cost factors will be subordinated, e.g. packing malt whisky bottles in stiff cardboard cylinders.

Faces of Betty Crocker

The US is the most ethnically diverse nation in the world. The population includes 14% of Anglo-Saxon ancestry, 13% of Germanic ancestry, 12% of African ancestry, 10% of Hispanic ancestry, and 2% of Asian ancestry. It is estimated that by the year 2050, one-half of the US population will be African American, Hispanic American, Native American, and Asian American. Companies are updating their symbols and images according to increasing diversification in the population and changes in the lifestyles. An example is the case of General Mills Inc. updating Betty Crocker, the white-bread and mayonnaise symbol pictured on the package. Since 1921 when Betty was originally pictured as a fair-haired, white housewife, her look has been changed seven times in 75 years in order to match the product's image with their target market's ethnic background and lifestyles. Findings from Source Effect studies show that people like and trust their own. For example, when they identify with the picture showing a person on the package of the brand, they may respond better to the brand. A company manager stated that Betty Crocker has always reflected the faces of its customers and the company will continue to do the same in years to come. The last update required General Mills to modify Betty's look in order to fit her to the 1990s' perfection: a love of cooking and baking, commitment to family and friends, resourcefulness and creativity in everyday tasks. The 1990s' Betty is a brunette with neither white nor black skin colour and looking less of a housewife, than an employee of corporate America.

SOURCE: Zafer Erdogan, personal communication

With regard to collecting relevant information, the *Marketing Handbook* (Frey, 1965) cites nine factors which have to be taken into account, each of which may encompass a number of subfactors:

1. *Size:*
   - Contents
   - Trade customs
   - Price
   - Consumer convenience (portability, use, storage)
   - Dealer convenience
   - Available packaging machinery
2. *Shape:*
   - Tradition
   - Cost
   - Space requirements
   - Utility
   - Eye appeal
3. *Material:*
   - Protective quality
   - Cost factors
   - Sales appeal
   - Tradition and fads
   - Impression of quality
   - Transparency
4. *Construction:*
   - Costs
   - Protection of contents
   - Utility
   - Sales appeal
5. Closure:
   - Durability
   - Ease of opening
   - Ease of closing
   - Aid to use of contents
   - Attractiveness
   - Capacity for carrying copy
   - Cost factors
6. *Surface design*
7. *Legal requirements*
8. *Packing*
9. *Distribution.*

Most of these topic headings are self-evident and need little elaboration, but it may be helpful to say a little more about design and the economics of packaging (cost factors), as these dimensions are common to all the others.

Reference has already been made to the fact that often the pack constitutes the just discernible difference which attracts attention at the point of sale and prompts purchase. Bearing in mind that the average supermarket is likely to have more than 30,000 products on display at any one time, it is clear that outstanding design is essential if it is to capture the customer's attention.

In his contribution to the *Encyclopedia of Marketing* (1999), Peter Dart of the Added Value Group focuses discussion of packaging and design on the value added to branded products. Ten key themes are identified as the means to achieving this objective.

Dart contends that packaging and design provide an excellent mechanism for changing category rules. Specific examples he cites include the case of Haagen Dazs who caused a reappraisal of the premium ice cream market when they decided to package their product in small cardboard tubs rather than the traditional large plastic containers. Similarly, Pedigree Pet Foods created a new super premium brand which enabled them to command a 200% price premium by packaging the product into small flexible aluminium trays.

> Refills, systems, secondary usage containers, easier to open, easier to store, directable, concentrated, dilute, beer that comes out with a head (as if from draught), pumps, airsprays, microwaveable, small portions, big portions – the world is exploding with packaging innovations. And as the pace hots up consumers are demanding more, better, faster than ever before. (p. 52)

Dart cites a number of specific examples where the design of the packaging has added significantly to the brand's equity. These include: the shape of the container (Toilet Duck), a distinctive opening device (Grolsch), the packaging material (Ferrero Rocher), the packaging material finish (Absolut Vodka), any other distinctive physical features, e.g. the shape of the capsules in Elizabeth Arden's Ceramide Time Complex Capsules, the colour of the packaging (Marlboro), the logo style (Coca-Cola), the use of a symbol (Woolmark), the use of a personality (Colonel Saunders).

Dart also sees an opportunity to take advantage of the demand for more environmentally friendly packaging. This may take many forms and he cites the following examples:

- *Less bulk:* simply using less material
- *Removal of secondary packaging:* why sell tooth-

paste in two containers when it is perfectly OK sold in one?
- *Concentration:* concentrated detergents now use less than half the packaging material compared to before
- *Reusable:* Many products are now sold in a 'first time' box/tin/jar, which can then be replenished via a refill pack
- *Secondary usage* (especially important in developing markets): design the packaging for its original purpose and for a secondary purpose (e.g. a storage jar)
- *Recyclable:* design the material and its construction so that it can be collected back in and either reused directly or reprocessed
- *Bulk or home delivery:* the ultimate non-use of packaging, but not yet commonplace.

Producers of packaging materials are sensitive to these concerns and are constantly innovating to produce better solutions. While steel packaging represents a smaller proportion of all packaging than it did 50 years ago, its use continues to grow as a result of innovation and new designs. According to British steel producer Corus:

> We offer a variety of steel grades that are suitable for numerous different can shapes: choose from flat, tall or tapered cans, round or square, trays or bowls. Corus Packaging Plus continuously innovates, creating new shapes and new looks, and helping to enhance the shelf visibility of your products. We invented the square *Le Carré* can – a breakthrough innovation for food applications. Its slim square shape is highly distinctive, giving it unique possibilities for decoration and lithography, and ensuring it takes up less space both in transportation and on the shelf. *Le Carré* also has a peelable end with a ring made of polymer-coated steel, making it easy to open.
>
> In another ingenious development, some of our steel packs can now be warmed up in the microwave or oven, which enables the food to be cooked more evenly throughout. The steel pack remains rigid and solid, so it is easy to handle. (www.coruspackaging. com/en/markets/food/food/be_inspired).

Numerous examples of such innovations can be found at this website and those of other producers of packaging materials.

The influence that packaging has upon

consumer perceptions of the product itself was highlighted in *Marketing* (1982), which quoted an A.C. Nielsen survey in the US in which 46% of a representative sample of consumers said they had discarded or returned a product because of defective packaging in the previous twelve months. Of these dissatisfied consumers, 19% said they would never buy the same brand again, and 24% said they would 'shop more cautiously' or 'buy a different type of package'.

In another American survey, consumers were asked to list the package characteristics of most importance to them. The answers were: storage life of the unused portion; ability to recognise the contents by looking at the package graphics; resealability and ease of storage.

An article by Sara Macdougall in the same issue of *Marketing* (1982), reported the results of a UK consumer attitudes survey commissioned by INCPEN (the Industry Committee on Packaging and the Environment). The research carried out by Market Behaviour showed that consumers found bulky packs irritating, especially when rigid cartons were found to be only three-quarters full, as were cereal and soap boxes. Again it was believed that superfluous packaging costs unnecessary money. Examples given included tubes in boxes, board sleeves on beer cans and margarine tubs, and triple layers of packaging for multipack KitKats.

While consumers' concerns were found to be primarily functional, the economic and aesthetic aspects of packaging were also important. These criteria were often found to conflict with each other. Consumers' awareness of the benefits of packaging did not prevent a significant number of them from expressing dissatisfaction with some aspects.

If anything, the situation has worsened rather than improved with the growth of 'green marketing' and a growing concern amongst consumers for environmental protection and the conservation of non-renewable resources.

Chapter summary

In this chapter we have been concerned with two broad issues:

1. The role of packaging as a strategic element in the marketing mix
2. The factors to be considered in developing a package.

With respect to the first issue, we considered the basic roles played by packaging – primary, secondary, display and shipping – and their importance in protecting the product in distribution and use as well as acting as a source of information and brand identification for prospective buyers.

Next we reviewed the five criteria to be considered in developing a package – appearance, protection, function, cost and disposability. It was noted that current concerns with environmentalism have focused increased attention on packaging and especially the disposability and protection criteria.

Finally, we returned to the role played by packaging as a strategic element in the marketing mix where it may become the 'just noticeable difference' or JND factor, which enables intending consumers to differentiate between products or services with very similar performance characteristics (cf. Chapters 9 and 13).

To conclude, we quote from the Introduction to Meyers and Lubliner's 1998 book referred to earlier:

The right kind of package links the consumer's mental process to an image already created by advertising, a personal experience, or a friend's referral and then triggers a buy decision. For those products that are not advertised and thus rely entirely on the package for creating a product image, the challenge is even more compelling. The right kind of package dispels uncertainty; it informs and educates; it appeals to the heart and mind of the prospective buyer, who makes a choice in less than ten seconds. The right kind of package says 'Take me home; I'm worth the money.'

Recommended reading

Baker, M. J. (2006) Chapter 13, Packaging in *Marketing: An Introductory Text* (7th edn). Helensburgh: Westburn.

Dart, P. (1999) Packaging and design, in Baker, M. J. (ed.) *Encyclopedia of Marketing*. London: International Thomson Business Press.

Meyers, H. M. and Lubliner, M. J. (1998) *The Marketer's Guide to Successful Package Design.* Chicago, IL: NTC Business Books.

REFERENCES

Allen, M. (1982) Designs for top security, *Marketing*, 9 December.

Baker, M. J. (1983) *Market Development*. Harmondsworth: Penguin.

Briston, J. H. and Neill, T. J. (1972) *Packaging Management*. London: Gower Press.

Dart, P. (1999) Packaging and design, in Baker, M. J. (ed.) *Encyclopedia of Marketing*. London: International Thomson Business Press, pp. 368–75.

Frey, A. W. (ed.) (1965) *Marketing Handbook* (2nd edn). New York: Ronald Press.

Lawson, R. (1982) Opting for an outside job, *Marketing*, 9 December.

Macdougall, S. (1982) Images to catch the eye, *Marketing*, 5 August.

Meyers, H. M. and Lubliner, M. J. (1998) *The Marketer's Guide to Successful Package Design*. Chicago, IL: NTC Business Books.

Nancarrow, C., Wright, L. T. and Brace, I. (1998) Gaining competitive advantage from packaging and labelling, *British Food Journal*, **100**(2).

Pricing policy and management

A cynic is a man who knows the price of everything, and the value of nothing.
OSCAR WILDE

After reading Chapter 17 you will be able to:

✔ Explain the economic theory of price and its role in achieving a balance between supply and demand.

✔ Describe the concept of elasticity.

✔ Suggest the limitations of price theory as an explanation of real world behaviour, but its contribution to understanding policy and procedure.

✔ Spell out the objectives of price policy and distinguish particularly between profit and sales-oriented objectives.

✔ Define and describe three basic approaches to pricing – cost-plus, flexible mark-up and marginal-cost pricing.

✔ Discuss the role of price as an element in the marketing mix.

✔ Review the pricing strategies available to the firm.

INTRODUCTION

In economic theory the concept of price is of central importance as the mechanism through which supply and demand are adjusted in order to ensure that resources are allocated to those uses which will maximise overall satisfaction. Prices and price policy are also of major importance to the businessman for, as Kuhlmeijer (1975) has pointed out, price is the only marketing strategy variable that generates income. All the other variables in the mix – advertising, product development, sales promotion, distribution and packaging – generate costs. Hopefully these activities will generate or sustain demand, but price, while also affecting demand, is a direct determinant of the pool of revenue out of which marketing and other costs will have to be recovered. But, while price is a very flexible marketing tool, it is also very visible to both customers and competitors alike, to the extent that the distinguished economist Fellner (1951) has described it as 'the blunt instrument of competition'.

Under conditions of perfect competition the seller cannot be a price-maker, but is a price-taker. At any price above that prevailing in the marketplace he will sell none of his output, while to sell below the going market price would be irrational, as it would result in a lesser level of profit than that obtainable by accepting the market price. However, as we have seen in earlier chapters, few if any markets correspond precisely to those in which competition is deemed to be perfect by the theoretical economist. Instead, we are more likely to find a state of oligopoly or competition between the few, with a very large proportion of total output being accounted for by a relatively small number of firms, with the balance of supply being accounted for by a large number of small firms. Under these conditions price competition is usually unattractive and has led to the anonymous observation that price competition is like cutting your competitor's throat and bleeding to death yourself. Indeed, it is often claimed that the unpopularity of price competition led to the emergence of non-price factors as a basis for competition and it was this which led to an emphasis upon a marketing orientation.

In recent years, however, the role of price has received increased attention due to competition from the emerging economies, especially China and India. During the last quarter of the twentieth century, many multinational firms outsourced much of their manufacturing to low labour cost countries, e.g. Nike. However, little if any of these cost savings were passed on in lower prices to customers. Today, the situation has changed completely as low-cost producers like China are using their lower costs to penetrate markets with highly competitive prices.

In this chapter we shall examine some of the theoretical foundations to the theory of pricing as a basis for examining broad pricing objectives open to the firm. Next we shall examine the way in which prices are determined and discuss the three broad-brush approaches which have been observed in practice – marginalism, cost-based approaches and trial and error. Finally, we shall turn to an assessment of the role of price in the marketing mix.

THEORETICAL FOUNDATIONS

One of the earlier and still popular definitions of marketing is 'identifying the needs of consumers and satisfying them at a profit'. If this is so, and many practitioners have argued strongly in favour of such a basic definition in preference to the more diffuse and broadly based ones which emphasise mutually satisfying exchange relationships, then clearly the nature of demand is the primary concern of the marketer. In theory, demand concerns the relation between quantity and price and considers the demand for a product as a function of its price, the prices of substitutes and complements, consumers' tastes and incomes. Assuming that these latter determinants of demand (income, consumer tastes and the price of substitutes) are held constant, then the law of demand indicates an inverse relationship between price and quantity with the result that demand curves have a negative slope, implying that the higher the price the smaller will be the quantity demanded (see Chapter 5).

In developing their theory of demand economists have evolved a number of very useful concepts that help the practitioner understand better how demand and therefore price may influence freedom for action. A basic and very important distinction made by economists is that between short-run and long-run demand. *Short-run demand* refers to existing demand, with its immediate reaction to price changes, income fluctuations etc., whereas *long-run demand* is that which will ultimately exist as a result of changes in pricing, promotion or product improvement, after enough time is allowed to let the market adjust itself to the new situation. The importance of this distinction is that it proscribes the competitive options available. In the short run the basic question is whether competitors will react to the fall in demand by changing their prices in an attempt to maintain their market share, with the almost inevitable result that everybody else will follow suit and so maintain their market share, but at a lower margin of profit. In the long run, of course, structural change becomes possible and companies may either enter or leave the market depending upon whether demand is expanding or contracting, while both consumers and suppliers may explore the possibility of substitute products as an alternative to the product for which demand has changed. Joel Dean (1951) proposes two groups of factors which may give rise to the distinction between long- and short-run changes in demand:

1. *Cultural lags in information and experience.* A price change today starts a chain of adjustment in customers' attitudes and competitors' prices that may not be completed for years, even if nothing further occurs. This is partly a matter of market information. There may be delay in learning about changes in relative prices among substitutes, but there is also delay in acting on these new prices because use patterns are sticky.
2. *Capital investment required of buyers to shift consumption patterns.* For example, the mass consumption of frozen food required an investment by producers and consumers in new refrigerators designed with double- or triple-sized freezer compartments. Products that require a large initial investment in consumption equipment quite commonly meet sticky and price-intensive buying habits in established markets. In such cases, industry's promotional effort in expanding sales may aim at selling the equipment rather than the product.

A second and very important distinction in demand theory is that between *industry* and *company demand*. By definition an industry demand schedule reflects the relationship of price to the quantity that will be bought from all firms. Of course, the usefulness of the industry demand schedule as a benchmark for evaluating the demand available to any individual seller depends very much upon the degree to which prospective buyers perceive the output of the different firms as close substitutes for each other. To the extent that suppliers can differentiate their product in the minds of potential users, they can create a demand schedule which is particular to themselves. As we saw earlier in Chapter 2 when discussing competition, a major difficulty associated with product portfolio planning and market share analysis is determining which firms and products are in direct competition with one another. Similarly, one of the main reasons underlying the emphasis upon non-price competition, and particularly the practice of product differentiation, is that suppliers are attempting to create a unique position for themselves in the minds of potential buyers and thereby establish a monopoly over their demand.

Another concept from the economic theory of demand which is of particular usefulness to practitioners is the concept of *elasticity*. As originally conceived, the concept of elasticity refers only to price/sales ratios (price elasticity of demand), but it has now become generalised to apply to each demand determinant such as consumer income, advertising expenditures etc. Thus, in the abstract, elasticity is the ratio of the relative change in the dependent variable (demand) to the relative change in an independent variable (price, consumer income). Thus, demand is said to be inelastic when the relative change in the independent factor is greater than the relative change in the quantity demanded, and elastic when it is less than the relative change in the quantity demanded. Graphically, these differences are reflected in the slope of the demand curve, with totally inelastic demand being represented by a vertical line and infinitely elastic demand by a horizontal line. These differences are indicated in Figures 17.1 and 17.2 respectively, while 17.3 represents the type of demand curve typically found in which elasticity will vary according to price as discussed in Chapter 5. As can be seen from Figure 17.3, a minority of users have a very

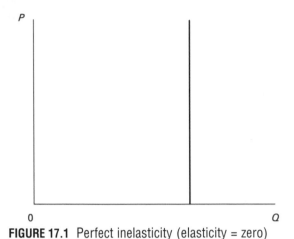

FIGURE 17.1 Perfect inelasticity (elasticity = zero)

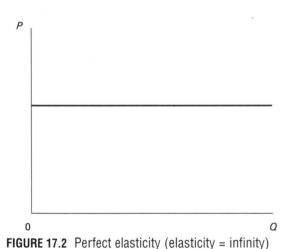

FIGURE 17.2 Perfect elasticity (elasticity = infinity)

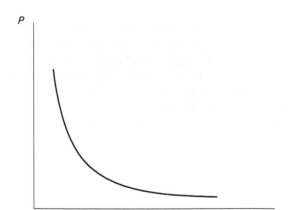

FIGURE 17.3 Unit elasticity

strong demand for the product and therefore price is inelastic for them. However, as price falls, more and more users will become willing to buy units of the product and demand becomes very elastic relative to price. This tendency continues until the market approaches saturation, at which point even drastic reductions in price are unlikely to result in very much more demand so that the price elasticity once again is inelastic.

Another very important dimension of demand is known as *cross-elasticity*. Cross-elasticity of demand measures one of the most important demand relationships – namely the closeness of substitutes or the degree of complementarity of demand. A high cross-elasticity means that the commodities are close substitutes for each other (Ford and Toyota), while a zero cross-elasticity means that they are independent of each other in the market (TVs and washing machines). Finally, a negative cross-elasticity means that the goods are complementary in the market in that one stimulates the sales of the other (cars and petrol).

A final demand theory concept of great usefulness to the practitioner is the distinction between *direct* and *derived demand*. By derived demand is meant that the demand for one product is the result of the more fundamental or direct demand for another product. Thus, the demand for all manufacturing equipment is ultimately determined by the demand for the products which that equipment is designed to produce. Similarly, the utilisation of such manufacturing equipment in turn determines the level of demand for basic raw materials such as steel.

The second major area of economic theory related to demand, from which practitioners can derive some useful concepts, is that related to cost. As with demand, the first and perhaps most important distinction is that drawn between the *short-run* and *long-run costs*. In the short run some of the variables in a problem may change but not all of them. But, in the long run virtually all the economic variables in the problem may change with the exception of those which are related to the overall growth of an industry or group of industries. Thus, short-run costs are those associated with changes in the utilisation of fixed plant or other facilities, whereas long-run cost behaviour encompasses changes in the size and kind of plant. The distinction between the short and long run leads naturally to the distinction between variable and fixed costs. Thus, variable costs are all those which do vary as output varies, whereas fixed costs are usually defined as all those costs which do not vary with output.

From these definitions it follows that the total cost of any given output in the short run is equivalent to the sum of all the fixed and variable costs of the firm, from which it follows that the average cost is the total cost divided by the output. A third type of cost of particular importance to marketers is the *marginal cost*, which measures the exact rate of change of total cost as output changes. Finally, there is the *opportunity* cost, by which is understood the sacrifice of alternatives as the result of making any given decision. Thus, in money terms it takes the profits from alternative ventures which are forgone by using resources in a particular way. (For a fuller discussion of these costs and their use in budgeting the reader should refer to Chapter 23.)

Two additional concepts which are central to economic price theory and of importance to marketers are those concerned with profit maximisation and market structures. We have already reviewed in some detail theories of competition and market structure in Chapter 2 and so will not review concepts of perfect and imperfect competition in this chapter. However, these ideas are absolutely fundamental to an understanding of the pricing alternatives open to the marketers, and the reader should review Chapter 2 in conjunction with the present chapter.

The assumption of profit maximisation is an essential axiom on which the economist's theory of price rests. Basically this assumption states that entrepreneurs strive always to earn larger profits and are therefore motivated by the desire to maximise profit. To do so the entrepreneur will behave as a marginalist and seek to achieve that price–output combination at which marginal cost equals marginal revenue. This assumption of profit maximisation has been subject to much criticism, as it presumes an ability to forecast accurately both demand and cost in a manner which is usually extremely difficult, if not impossible, in the real world. Further, as we shall see when discussing pricing objectives, it is clear that many entrepreneurs are motivated by other goals related to sales, security etc.

LIMITATIONS AND CONTRIBUTIONS OF PRICE THEORY

As an explanation of pricing in the real world, price theory suffers from a number of limitations, which may be summarised as follows:

1. The theory usually rests on the assumptions of profit maximisation which, as Stephen Enke (1977) has pointed out, does not provide the entrepreneur with a single and unequivocal criterion for selecting one policy from another in the face of future uncertainty. Similarly, as Kotler has pointed out, the problem of pricing over the product life-cycle requires a more sophisticated model than one which has only a single criterion.
2. The theory does not distinguish clearly between long- and short-run effects of price changes. Haynes (1974) states that traditional theory does not deal adequately with the dynamics of pricing: the theory has little to say about the effect of today's prices on future profits and the usual graphs for short-run pricing show today's demand and cost curves and suggest that managers price to equate marginal cost and marginal revenue. However, when an entrepreneur is seeking to penetrate a market and build up an image of low price, he may well prefer to sacrifice current profit for future profit and the theory does not deal with this problem.
3. The theory does not face the problem of uncertainty and assumes that entrepreneurs know their demand and cost functions. There are grave statistical problems which handicap the determination of actual demand and cost functions for new and established products.
4. The theory fails to view the firm as an organisation in which pricing decisions are influenced by a variety of persons with varied objectives and motives.
5. The theory assumes that the only significant group to consider in the pricing of a product is the firm's customers. But, in reality, several parties have to be considered simultaneously, including rivals, suppliers, distributors, government and other business executives.
6. The theory assumes that price is the businessman's chief policy instrument, even when it is admitted that he may sometimes have others to

rely upon such as product quality, sales prom-otion and distribution activities.

7. The theory regards price solely as a device for obtaining financial objectives, as viewed by economists, namely pricing decisions should reflect cost and demand functions and balance them to the firm's greatest advantage. What is overlooked by price theory is that price can be used as a communication device to communic-ate facts to the market participants about the firm, its products and its capabilities in the manner that might increase sales, raise prices or reduce costs. These communication benefits achievable by price are often central to the prof-itability of business.

Despite all these criticisms, and the perceived limitations which they place upon the use of price theory, it still would seem that the theory has some contribution to make to price-setters and is basic to an understanding of price policy and procedures.

In the analysis of how an individual firm sets its prices, price theory is helpful to the extent that it sets forth the general forces which affect pricing. In addition, it assumes the isolation of separate influences on prices where there are many influ-ences operating simultaneously, and it brings to light a number of questions that the price-maker should take into account.

Price theory provides a useful standardised terminology for the discussion of cost and demand concepts. Oxenfeldt (1961) states that the theory has produced a highly penetrating and useful analysis of the manner in which costs are affected by the volume of output, and developing the cost concept and the manner of each kind of cost are of great value to pricing executives in enabling them to set prices at the right level. Joel Dean (1951) asserts that the main contribution to practical pric-ing of theoretical analysis is the kind of demand and cost relations and showing how these func-tional relations should be used to indicate the most profitable price.

In addition, the discussion of market structures provides useful guidelines for pricing executives. In the first place, it should focus their attention upon the importance in any price decision of the similarity of products offered by their rivals and the number of sellers offering similar products. Second, it places a heavy emphasis on the selection

of pricing strategies and on the recognition that most of the time they are matching wits with others who are intent on outsmarting them: that is, their competitors presumably are operating on the basis of carefully considered strategies designed, at least in part, to eliminate them as a competitor.

PRICING OBJECTIVES

A recurring theme of this book is the need for the firm to articulate clearly what its precise objectives are. In that pricing is but a means to the overall aim of an organisation, it is clear that pricing objectives are but a means to an end and therefore should be consistent with the overall objectives of the firm.

Like all other elements of the marketing mix, price should serve and help attain the firm's objec-tives. In the short run price has a direct and immediate influence on the firm's short-run prof-itability through its effect on sales volume, which in turn affects sales revenue and possibly unit cost of production and marketing as well. Further, in the medium to long run there is an indirect connec-tion between prices and the firm's profit objectives as prices affect the firm's cash flow, its inventories, its customers' inventories, its brand image, its quality image, the competitiveness of its markets, the likelihood of government regulation and customer awareness of, and concern with, price.

In discussing the multiple implications that price has for a firm's goal achievement, Alfred Oxenfeldt (1975) sets out a number of hierarchies that should help executives construct a list of goals that their firms can pursue through the intelligent use of price.

The first hierarchy, reproduced as Figure 17.4, indicates the ultimate objectives of most firms that he defines as 'value judgements on the part of a firm's top management and large owners. They are the outcomes that those persons want "simply because they want them". That is, they are not desired because they lead to some other results. They are ends in themselves'.

Oxenfeldt then proceeds to develop each of the four generalised ultimate business objectives showing how pricing strategy impinges upon them. However, before looking at pricing strate-gies ourselves, it would be helpful first if we were

Ultimate business objectives

FIGURE 17.4 Hierarchy of business objectives
SOURCE: Oxenfeldt, A. (1975) *Pricing Strategies.* New York: AMACOM, p. 43

to examine the general objectives in somewhat greater detail.

Again, it is important to distinguish between the short and long run, particularly as we have already argued that short-run objectives may sometimes contradict long-run objectives. For example, maximising long-run profits may be achieved by restraining profits in the short run with a lower price, a higher product quality, or a more extensive promotional campaign than the one that would maximise short-run profits. Because of the inevitable uncertainty that surrounds the future there is a tendency for most pricing methods to concentrate on the short rather than the long run. Thus, Lawrence Fisher (1966) offers the following list of short-run pricing objectives:

1. To penetrate and pre-empt the market for a product by charging a low price
2. To cream the market and obtain early profits and liquidity by charging a high price
3. To assist in phasing out an obsolescent product by making it unattractively expensive
4. To discourage competition from entering the market
5. To avoid customer and political criticism
6. To support a company image
7. To encourage market expansion by a low price / high volume policy
8. To avoid unduly provocative action which could lead to prices falling to a level inconsistent with long-term profitability.

Clearly, while these are proposed as short-run objectives, only one of them, 3, is intrinsically

incompatible with a long-run pricing objective, and even this may be seen as such in an indirect way in that disposing of an obsolescent product enables one to divert resources to new and potentially more profitable ends.

An extended listing of 24 possible objectives in setting a price appears in Table 17.1.

TABLE 17.1 Possible objectives in setting a price

1. Target return on investment
2. Target market share
3. Maximum long-run profits
4. Maximum short-run profits
5. Growth
6. Stabilise market
7. Desensitise customers to price
8. Maintain price-leadership arrangements
9. Discourage entrants
10. Speed exit of marginal firms
11. Avoid government investigation and control
12. Maintain loyalty of middlemen and get their sales support
13. Avoid demands from suppliers
14. Enhance image of firm and its offerings
15. Be regarded as fair by customers
16. Create interest and excitement about the item
17. Be considered trustworthy and reliable by rivals
18. Help in the sale of weak or other items in the line
19. Discourage others from cutting prices
20. Make a product visible
21. Spoil market to obtain high price for business
22. Build traffic
23. Maximum profits on product line
24. Recover investment quickly

Irrespective of the time perspective, however, it is generally agreed that a business firm is an organisation designed to make profits and profits are the primary measure of its success. As Joel Dean (1969) points out, social criteria of business performance usually relate to the quality of products, rate of progress and behaviour of prices. But these are tests of the desirability of the whole profit system within which profits are the acid test of the individual firm's performance. This being so, it will be helpful now to examine in more detail some profit objectives.

PROFIT OBJECTIVES

The whole of the early theory of the firm, and even the bulk of the modern development of it, identifies the profit motive as aiming for the maximum attainable amount over any given time period. The principal of total profit maximisation demands that price should be set at the level at which a small change in total cost would just equal the change in total revenue. As Kotler (1972) has pointed out, advocates of the thesis that firms always seek to maximise their profits above any other goal depend on one or more of three arguments:

1. Profit maximisation is the formal purpose for which companies are established.
2. The competitive pursuit of maximum profits creates the greatest economic welfare.
3. Profit maximisation provides management with a relatively unambiguous criterion for business decision-making.

Kotler then cites Henry Ford II (1962), who expresses succinctly what has now become known as the Friedmanite economic doctrine.

> There is no such thing as planning for a minimal return less than the best you can imagine, not if you want to survive in a competitive market. It is like asking a professional football team to win by only one point, a sure formula for losing. There is only one way to compete successfully – all out. If believing this makes you a greedy capitalist lusting after bloated profits, then I plead guilty. The worst sin I can commit as a businessman is to fail to seek maximum long-term profitability by all decent and lawful means. To do so is to subvert economic reason.

However, as Gabor (1977) and Gabor and Granger (1973) have argued, there are at least four ways of interpreting what is meant by maximising profits. First, there is the absolute interpretation which means that capital would be poured into a firm until the increase in total profit due to the last increment was equal to the interest charge on that capital, irrespective of any other more favourable investment opportunity. The second interpretation is that one maximises the mark-up rate; the third that one maximises the rate of return on only that part of capital which belongs to the owners of the firm; and, fourth, that one maximises the rate of return on the total assets of the firm irrespective of the origin of the funds. Gabor concludes that this latter is the most appropriate objective and also makes a telling point when he observes that maximising profits has usually been interpreted by businessmen as the desire to achieve larger profits. Thus he observes 'a larger profit will always be preferable to a smaller one'. This is what we meant by profit maximisation. It follows that it is not the same thing as striving for excessive profits at the expense of all other considerations.

There is a large amount of empirical evidence to support Gabor's contention and this has led to the emergence of an alternative thesis of profit-seeking behaviour which has been termed 'satisficing' as opposed to 'maximising'. The view that entrepreneurs seek to make satisfactory profits rather than pursue a goal of profit maximisation owes much to the seminal work of Simon (1952). In one of his early contributions, Simon (1959) observes that the notion of satiation plays no role in classical economic theory, while it enters rather prominently in the treatment of motivation in psychology. In most psychological theories the motive to act stems from drive, and action terminates when the drive is satisfied. Moreover, the conditions for satisfying the drive are not necessarily fixed, but may be specified by an aspiration level that self-adjusts upward or downward on the basis of experience. Simon (1959) argues that to explain business behaviour in terms of this theory we must expect the firm's goals to be not maximising profit, but attaining a certain level or rate of profit, holding a certain share of the market or a certain level of sales. Firms do try to satisfice rather than to maximise.

Baumol (1971) argues that the businessman, knowing his own limitations and the limited accuracy of the data and calculation procedures available to him, adopts a more modest goal. He wishes to obtain conditions that are thoroughly viable, but which offer no assurance of producing for him the best of all possible worlds. Thus, the failure to scan all the relevant possibilities before reaching a decision, far from constituting an imperfection in the businessman's procedures, is a logical consequence of the nature of his aspirations.

Cyert and March (1963) state that when firms satisfice they do not try to find that course of action which brings them as close as possible to a particular objective. Instead they set a minimum level of performance in each of a number of different fields, say, a return of 10% on capital employed, a market share of 25% and a production running at 90% of existing capacity. These minimum levels of performance are often described as 'aspiration levels'.

Two things usually seem to happen. First, the firm takes no non-routine decisions at all as long as the aspiration levels set for a product, department or, indeed, for the whole firm are being achieved (management by exception). Only if the firm fails to earn the required rate of return on capital employed, or to reach the required market share, will special action be taken. So long as all aspiration levels are being met it will seem unnecessary. The firm may or may not be exceeding the minimum level of achievement which it has set for itself, but, so long as it is not achieving less, managers will be content to leave things as they are. Second, if any aspiration level does cease to be met, the firm will then take some remedial action. In taking this action it will not seek to optimise anything: it will make no attempt to find the best solution.

From the foregoing discussion it is clear that many, if not all, firms will pursue a policy at variance with that predicated by classical economic theory. This is not to say that firms do not set themselves profit objectives, nor that they do not strive to increase the overall level of profit earned. Rather, it is to argue that they are likely to state their overall objective in more general terms. Frequently these terms or objectives are related to sales goals, and it is these which we shall now review.

Box 17.1   *Threat or opportunity?*

While most companies think of the emerging economies in terms of the threats posed by their low-price/high-value products, some of the world's leading manufacturers of consumer goods see them as a market opportunity. In an article in *The Times* (10/12/05), C. Varl Mortished described how Unilever is marketing Omo in Brazil as an exemplar of effective marketing practice.

Adjusted for purchasing power the dollar spend of consumers in Asia, Africa and Latin America was $15 trillion in 2000, roughly equal to the spending power of North Americans and Europeans, Unilever says. By 2010 consumers in developing and emerging markets will have raced ahead of the developed world.

To exploit this opportunity, Unilever has adopted a different strategy from most of its global competitors. While the latter tend to concentrate their efforts on the affluent minority, Unilever is seeking to cater for all socioeconomic groupings with a particular emphasis on the lowest paid.

In the middle of Heliopolis, a notorious slum in São Paulo, Unilever has opened the Omo Community Laundry where people can sign up for two-hour slots on factory fresh washing machines for free.

This is about selling soap even if not a single packet is vended or given away at the Omo Laundry – the women bring their own powder. The mission is to sell a wholesome and desirable world of perfumed fragrance and pristine white linens, a world a million miles from the *favelas*, that no slum-dweller could possibly afford.

The strategy is working. Clean clothes make people feel good about themselves and Unilever's Omo (Persil in the UK), sells for 15–20% more than Ariel, its main rival marketed by Procter & Gamble. While P&G slashed prices by 30% to try and win share from Omo, Unilever has retained its 75% share of the Brazilian market and dominates the distribution channels by emphasising its brand values and the feel-good factor.

Local knowledge and campaigns designed to exploit their insights into consumer behaviour are also paying off in other developing markets in Africa and Asia, which increasingly represent Unilever's centre of gravity. Harish Manwani, head of Unilever for Asia and Africa, explained how its strategy is not only to defend market share but to build markets from the bottom by creating new customers. So, when Unilever launched Sunsilk in India, it quickly realised that $2 bottles were too expensive and started to sell the shampoo in sachets for 2 cents. Once it had established what the consumer could afford, Unilever designed a manufacturing process to produce the 2-cent sachets at a satisfactory margin. Further, because Indians oil their hair, Unilever removed the conditioning agent from the shampoo as this reduced its performance and made a useful cost saving in the process.

In many countries, and especially China, where global brands are new and attitudes to them fluid, getting in at the bottom and establishing brand recognition with affordable products appears an attractive long-term strategy.

SALES-ORIENTED OBJECTIVES

W. J. Baumol (1959) is generally recognised as having first suggested that firms often seek to maximise the money value of their sales, i.e. their sales revenue subject to a constraint that their profits do not fall short of some minimum level which is just on the border-line of acceptability. In other words, so long as profits are at a satisfactory level management will devote the bulk of its energy and efforts to the expansion of sales. Such a goal may be explained perhaps by the businessman's desire to maintain his competitive position which is partly dependent on the sheer size of his enterprise, or it may be a matter of the interested management, since management's salaries may be related more closely to the size of the firm's operations than to its profits, or it may simply be a matter of prestige. It is also Baumol's view that short-run revenue maximisation may be consistent with long-run profit maximisation, and revenue maximisation can be regarded as a long-run goal in many oligopolistic firms. Baumol also reasons that high sales attract customers to the popular product, cause banks to be receptive to the firm's financial needs, encourage distributors and make it easier to retain and attract good employees.

However, the sales revenue maximisation theory has been criticised by Ragoff and Lynn (1972), who state that it is probably inefficient and leads to fat in operations. When sales are growing there is less motivation for cost control and there might be a tendency to let things slide, to approve questionable expenditure, to postpone decisions to terminate unproductive personnel etc. However,

in an earlier paper, Lynn (1968) had suggested that unit volume is an especially important pricing goal where profit requirements are not high and where cost and demand combine to permit relatively ample gross margins. The attainment of high unit volume appeals to firms in a number of different situations:

1. The product has a high level of visibility to consumers.
2. A threshold of sales is needed to make a firm a significant element in an industry.
3. High unit sales may facilitate the recruiting and the retention of desirable dealers.
4. Records of unit sales volume are publicised so management cannot afford to ignore unit volume.
5. Brand loyalty or store loyalty once obtained is strong.
6. Repeat sales are important.
7. Organisational growth is sought.

Either sales revenue or unit volume is usually the criterion used for making comparative assessments between one firm and another competing in the same industry in the form of a statement concerning their respective market shares. As we have seen earlier, when discussing portfolio planning models, the assessment of market share is difficult. Nonetheless, as Oxenfeldt (1959) claims, market share is a convenient goal because it differentiates the changes in sales due to a firm's action from those due to external forces. Further, it is a fair and reasonable measure, as it is related to total industry sales and not to the performance of the best competitors only, and is more relevant as an index for measuring market effectiveness, because it eliminates most of the influence of forces on which marketing people have little or no control compared to both sales and profit measures.

Although market share goals now enjoy considerably popularity with top management, they possess a number of disadvantages, as Chevalier and Carty (1974) have pointed out:

1. Market share used as a performance index does not itself reveal the cost at which it has been gained, 'buying market share' through huge discounts and promotion, or the profit at which it has been lost.
2. Market share disregards potential knowledge about companies' idiosyncrasies, because it assumes that they are comparable in many qualitative characteristics such as management ability, cash flow availability or advertising effectiveness. It assumes too that outside forces affect them in the same way, whereas it is well known that the impact of a recession or a regulation on companies' share is not uniform, and depends on their previous marketing actions which more or less prepared them to face the new constraints.
3. Market share figures may be biased performance indices if the market or company sales definition does not correspond to the responsibility of the manager.
4. Market share is not a universal way to state objectives in the sense that its feasibility is linked to the stage of the life-cycle of the product. Market share may not be used for a new brand in a new market; in this case, the innovator company is the only seller and primary and secondary demand are equal. Sales, profits, or even distribution objectives may seem more appropriate under such conditions. Despite this, market share is often used for a new brand in an existing market in order to stress the need to capture business from competitors and reach a minimum sales level to break even or to take advantage of possible economies of scale.

As we have seen in Chapter 2, it is the pursuit of the economies of scale and the so-called 'experience effect' that prompt many firms to set market share objectives. The pursuit of such a strategy requires one to be prepared to accept negative results in the short run in the expectation of long-run profit maximisation.

In addition to the foregoing major goals that are most often found as the basis for a firm's pricing strategy, one may also discern a small number of other objectives. For example, some firms may pursue an image goal in the belief that high prices will be associated with high quality or prestige and thereby ensure acceptance in a market. In other industries, where demand can fluctuate frequently and sometimes violently, a price leader may emerge which perceives its role as one of keeping prices stable. In such industries price stability may be seen as a corollary for earning a target return on investment. Third, in small firms it is often found that mark-up is a major goal as it provides a convenient guide for decision-making and can be justified by reference to other objectives such as profits or ethics. It is also prevalent among wholesalers and retailers who have difficulty in making an accurate allocation of many operating expenses to specific products. These problems combine to encourage the use of workable rules of thumb, and attainment of conventional mark-up is one of these rules. Finally, some pricing decisions are affected by ethical considerations in which the businessman's personal views mediate decisions based on commercial expediency.

PRICING OBJECTIVES IN PRACTICE

Despite the enormous literature on price theory, comparatively little of this is based upon empirical research and even less upon the implications of pricing in a marketing context. Thus, Laric (1980) comments: 'There is a relative dearth of articles dealing with strategic pricing aspects and with demand aspects.' It is hardly surprising therefore that older references such as Joel Dean's (1969) article on new product pricing policies and the Brookings study of pricing objectives are still standard citations in any work on pricing. Although the study of pricing objectives by the Brookings Institution (Kaplan et al., 1958) was first reported in 1958, it still remains the most important study of pricing objectives. The study indicates that in almost no instance did a firm state that its goal was to maximise profits by charging all the traffic would bear over the long run. In the 20 large companies which comprised the sample for the study many firms were found to have both principal and collateral goals, among which the major pricing objectives identified were:

1. Pricing to achieve a target return on investment
2. Stabilisation of price and margin
3. Pricing to realise a target market share
4. Pricing to meet or prevent competition

that is, the same as Oxenfeldt's 'ultimate objectives', cited earlier.

Pricing to achieve a target rate of return was the most common pricing goal, with two conditions generally being present when this goal was selected. First, these firms were leaders in their respective industries and, second, this objective was typical in companies with new products and low unit price, standardised and high volume items. Among the reasons offered by executives in the respondent companies selecting this goal were the following:

1. That it is a fair or reasonable objective, both in the public eye and because the firm's pricing structure is of great interest to the Justice Department
2. Industry tradition
3. It was representative of what the company thought it could get in the long run.

Another principal pricing goal often mentioned by firms was that of keeping or improving their share of the market. This objective is preferred in some companies because it relates the company's operation to the size of the market. That is, the firm may have a healthy return on investment or sales, while it is suffering from a continual shrinking of its market share. Some companies, however, may choose to limit their market share in order to avoid any confrontation with the government and the anti-trust authorities.

Stabilising prices as a goal was generally chosen by those firms that prefer to avoid price wars, even during the period of decline in demand. Furthermore, those industries characterised by having a 'price leader' generally selected this pricing objective.

Meeting or preventing competition is selected

by a large number of companies as a pricing system. It can be said that these firms have no pricing objective per se, because they cannot control the goal and the tools used to achieve it.

These findings are largely supported by other research undertaken by Pass (1971), Hague (1948–9), Haynes (1962), Barback (1964) and Hall and Hitch (1939) and leads to the almost universal conclusion that firms do not maximise their profit by charging what the market will bear, but pursue several objectives simultaneously related to objectives of profitability, sales and stability.

To conclude this review of pricing objectives, an excellent summary is given by Diamantopolous (1999) as shown in Table 17.2.

TABLE 17.2 A taxonomy of pricing objectives

PRICING OBJECTIVES

Profit
- Money profit
- Gross/net margin
- Contribution margin
- Return on sales
- Return on costs
- Return on capital employed
- Return on net worth
- Profit growth

Competition oriented
- Matching/undercutting competition
- Avoidance of price wars
- Limit entry
- Price stability
- Money profit

Volume
- Market share
- Sales volume
- Sales revenue
- Sales growth
- Capacity utilisation

Customer oriented
- Fair price levels
- Goodwill
- Value for money
- Full price range
- Price maintenance in the channel

Financial
- Cash flow
- Earnings per share
- Price earnings ratio
- Dividends

Miscellaneous
- Projection of high-quality image
- Avoidance of government intervention
- Survival/security

SOURCE: Diamantopoulos, A. (1999) Pricing, in Baker, M. J. (ed.) *The Marketing Book* (4th edn). Oxford: Butterworth Heinemann, pp. 182–97

PRICE DETERMINATION

Given that businessmen pursue objectives other than profit maximisation, it is clear that they do not follow the rule of marginalism as propounded by economists when deciding their price and output decisions. Accordingly, we shall not examine the economists' approach to marginal pricing any further, although a variant of it will be reviewed when discussing the cost approach to price determination which appears to be the method pursued by the great majority of business organisations. Basically three different approaches may be distinguished: cost-plus pricing, flexible mark-up pricing and marginal-cost pricing. We shall deal with each of these in turn. (Note that an extended discussion of costs, break-even and contribution analysis is contained in Chapter 23.)

COST-PLUS PRICING

Cost-plus pricing embraces all methods of setting prices with exclusive reference to cost and is the practice of adding to an estimated product cost an amount of money to arrive at a selling price.

As we have seen earlier when discussing the nature of costs, considerable judgement is frequently exercised in their determination and assignment. As a consequence, at least two variants of cost-plus pricing may be distinguished and it is important that one determines which approach is being followed in any given situation. These two approaches are *absorption-cost pricing* and *rate-of-return pricing*.

With absorption costing all the costs associated with the business are related to the output of manufacture and are said to be absorbed at the time the product is manufactured or sold, and the unit cost is normally arrived at by dividing the total of the production, administrative and selling expenses by the estimated volume of output. Once such a unit cost has been determined then a percentage is added to provide the business with a profit. By contrast, when using a rate-of-return approach one first seeks to estimate the total cost of a year's normal production allowing for ups and downs of the business cycle. This sum is called 'capital turnover' and by multiplying it by the goal rate of return one arrives at the mark-up percentage to be added to standard cost. This mark-up is an average, both among products and through time.

Cost-plus pricing has been criticised extensively on the following grounds:

1. It ignores demand

2. It fails to reflect competition adequately
3. It overplays the precision of allocated costs
4. It is based upon a concept of cost that is frequently not relevant for the pricing decision
5. The concept of profit as an addition to unit costs is a false one
6. It assumes that all products should absorb the fixed expenses of the business at the same rate
7. Instead of pricing being fixed in relation to the competitive requirements of the particular market, and the overhead structure of the business being attuned to those requirements, the reverse procedure is adopted, prices are adjusted to the existing overhead structure by including in each unit cost a share of fixed expenses
8. It is inappropriate during a period of cost inflation
9. The system often becomes too mechanical and decisions are made at too low a management level and often lead to friction between sales and manufacturing
10. The method takes no account of the capital backing the different lines.

To overcome some of these deficiencies, many sellers have developed a system of *flexible mark-up pricing* by which they arrive at their price by adding one of several margins to their base cost. The margin added depends upon the seller's view of demand conditions with the result that sellers add larger margins when business conditions are buoyant and lower margins during periods of recession and depression. Thus, flexible mark-ups can reflect demand, profit and competition in an indirect manner. Clearly, if one is to pursue an effective flexible mark-up pricing strategy it must be based upon extensive research of demand, competition and market activity, and a realistic appraisal of one's own strengths and weaknesses vis-à-vis these forces. Pursuit of a flexible mark-up pricing strategy is usually referred to as 'charging what the market will bear'.

THE CONTRIBUTION APPROACH

Although the economist's approach to marginal costing has been largely discounted as a basis for business pricing decisions, management accountants have developed a very useful variant of it. While this is often referred to as *marginal-cost pricing*, it is more correct to refer to it as the *contribution approach*. As Bates and Parkinson (1969) have pointed out, the philosophy underlying this approach to costing is that fixed costs are unavoidable and that what matters is to cover variable cost and make some contribution to fixed costs. Whether or not to accept an order depends on what contribution will be made to fixed costs after variable costs are covered. Thus, the approach is an attempt to take account of the fact that it is difficult to allocate fixed overhead costs to production on a basis varying with the level of output and the recognition that the resources available for meeting the fixed expenses of a business depend directly on the contribution, which is the difference between sales revenue and variable costs. It follows that the firm should seek to fix its prices so as to maximise its total contribution.

A useful product of the marginal-cost approach to pricing is breakeven analysis. A business may be said to break even when its total revenue equals its total cost and this point can be calculated via marginal-cost analysis through calculations of the contribution per unit of sales made to fixed costs and thereby determining how many units of output are necessary for a firm to cover its fixed costs and hence break even.

Readers requiring a fuller treatment of marginal-cost pricing should refer to the articles by Sizer (1969) and Johnston (1969). Between them these authors offer the following reasons for claiming that marginal-cost pricing is superior to full-cost pricing:

1. Marginal-cost pricing is more effective in the short run than full costing due to the multiproduct, multiprocess and multimarket characteristics of most business firms and the rapid rate of change in the environment which makes long run situations highly unpredictable.
2. It lends a marketing rather than a costing orientation to pricing policy.
3. Marginal cost is more relevant to pricing decisions than absorption cost because it reflects future as distinct from present cost levels and cost relationships. When making a pricing decision one is interested in the changes in costs

which will result from that decision and marginal cost represents these changes.
4. Marginal-cost pricing permits a manufacturer to develop a policy to make prices more differentiated and more flexible through time, which leads to higher sales and possibly reduced marginal costs through increased marginal physical productivity and lower input factor prices.
5. It is a practical prelude to price determination or modification and provides the courage to refuse business, to 'back-off', to withdraw from territories, and to drop products.

The two major criticisms of marginal pricing are that it may encourage price instability and that the practice is prevented by the lack of accurate demand information. Sizer (1969) discounts the argument about price instability on the grounds that there are other more powerful forces which prevent firms from making frequent and minor changes in prices.

With regard to the second criticism, whilst one accepts the difficulty of forecasting demand, one should perhaps take the view that if the contribution approach offers the benefits claimed for it then this is an even stronger argument for attempting an accurate demand forecast.

Table 17.3 provides a useful summary of the best-known pricing methods, classified according to whether they are cost-, demand- or competition-oriented.

TABLE 17.3 Pricing methods

Cost oriented	Competition oriented
■ Cost-plus pricing	■ Product analysis pricing
■ Contribution pricing	■ Value pricing
■ Target (ROI) pricing	■ Price leadership/followership
■ Price minus pricing	■ Competitive parity pricing
■ Return on costs	
Demand oriented	
■ Marginal analysis	
■ Trial and error pricing	
■ Intuitive pricing	
■ Market pricing	
■ Monopsonistic pricing	

SOURCE: Diamantopoulos, A. (1996) Chapter 11 Pricing in Baker, M. J. (ed.) *Marketing: Theory and Practice*, (3rd edn). Basingstoke: Macmillan – now Palgrave Macmillan

It now remains to consider the relative role of

pricing as a component of the marketing mix, together with a brief description of the pricing strategies which appear to be open to the company.

THE ROLE OF PRICING IN THE MARKETING MIX

As we have seen at a number of points in this chapter, the majority of studies concerned with the relative importance of price as a competitive weapon are at variance with the doctrine of economic theory in which price is the sole competitive weapon. Thus price is only one element of the marketing mix and, as numerous studies in the past 40 years have shown, its importance is likely to vary considerably according to a wide range of situational and environmental factors.

In Udell's (1964) study exploring the relative importance of the different elements of the marketing mix considered by American businessmen as most important to their success, pricing was only ranked sixth in order of importance. This finding was confirmed in the UK by Pass's (1971) study, but contradicted by the findings of a further study undertaken by Robicheaux in 1975 (cited in Kotler, 1980). More recently Dr Hanaa Said (1981) undertook a large-scale investigation of pricing

policies and practices in UK industry and came up with findings very similar to those of Robicheaux. This can be seen from Table 17.4 in which the findings of the four studies are reproduced together.

While many factors account for the differences in these findings, it seems reasonable to assume that the inflationary and recessionary trends which became so marked in the middle 1970s would have had a significant effect upon the perceived importance of pricing in the marketing mix.

In a major literary review of articles published in the years 1964 to 1980 dealing with pricing, Michael Laric (1980) summarised the situation by suggesting that prices will tend to increase in importance when:

1. The item is offered for the first time (a new task-buying situation)
2. The company needs to raise prices (a return to modified rebuy situation)
3. Competition reduces prices and makes direct offers to one's buyers
4. The products involved are directly input into the end product of the buyer and their cost is therefore fixed per end product
5. The buyer sells to a government agency which is primarily concerned with price.

TABLE 17.4 A comparison of the Said, Robicheaux, Pass and Udell studies

	Said study 1981	Robicheaux study 1975	Pass study 1971	Udell study 1964
Pricing	1	1	6	6
Customer services	2	2	4	5
Product research and development	3	4	1	1
Product services	4	–	3	–
Sales management	5	3	7	3
Physical distribution	6	6	8	11
Advertising and sales promotion	7	9	5	4
Marketing research	8	7	2	2
Marketing cost, budgeting and control	9	5	11	9
Distribution channels control	10	10	9	8
Extending customer credit	11	11	12	10
Public relations	12	12	13	12
Organisational structure	–	8	10	7

SOURCE: Said, H. (1981) *The Relevance of Price Theory to Pricing Practice: An Investigation of Pricing Policies and Practices in UK Industry,* Ph.D dissertation, University of Strathclyde

Conversely, price will tend to be less important when:

1. The item is bought on a regular basis (routinised rebuy pricing)
2. The seller has a high/unique reputation and the product's failure to perform may cause severe handicaps to the buyer
3. The purchase represents an overhead on direct cost to the buyer
4. The cost of the item can be easily concealed in an overall budget, as in the case of a small machine within a large budget
5. In government markets when the budget was not yet appropriated.

An important dimension of many of these generalisations is that they reflect the perception of the prospective purchaser, i.e. the price elasticity of demand, and thus reinforce the desirability of undertaking research to determine how buyers perceive price, rather than by attempting to set prices through the addition of predetermined mark-ups to one's own costs.

More recent evidence on the use of pricing in the marketing mix is contained in an article by Barbara J. Coe (1990), in which the author reports the findings of an eight-year study into six SIC industries covering accessory equipment (3573), installations (3721), fabricating materials and parts (2819), corrugated and solid fibre boxes (2653), paints (2851) and ready-mix concrete (3273). The issues addressed included:

1. What is the strategic role of pricing in the marketing mix of industrial firms, and has it changed during 1980–8?
2. What are the general and specific pricing objectives, and have these changed during 1980–8?
3. What pricing approaches are used, and have these changed during 1980–8?
4. How do external and internal factors impact the pricing decision within the industrial firm, and has the importance of each changed during 1980–8?
5. What other marketing strategies play an important role in the marketing mix of industrial firms, and have these strategies changed during 1980–8?

Professor Coe's findings make dismal reading and are a confirmation of Hayes and Abernathy's (1980) indictment of American management 'managing its way to economic decline'.

According to Coe, having retreated from aggressive product development strategies to hold and build market share in the face of foreign competition, American business resorted to aggressive pricing strategies. But her research reveals these too have been dropped in exchange for

a self-defeating focus on internal demands for short-term profits. Driven by a quick-fix mentality, fuelled, in part, by internal politics, many in American management have ignored competitive realities in the marketplace and heeded only demands for quick profits. Management appears to be in a three-dimensional 'Catch-22' situation. First, they perceive that venture capitalists and short-term traders, both important in today's financial markets, demand quick, short-term profits. In addition, management's own compensation schemes are based on their ability to generate quick, short-term profits. Finally, management's fears concerning potential takeovers also spur demand for quick, short-term profits. Yet the sacrifice of short-term profits is seen as necessary to build a long-term strategy for survival and profitability.

As a result, pricing has ceased to be a strategy in the marketing mix of many firms.

Professor Coe's findings are summarised in Figure 17.5, from which it can be seen that in 1982 57 of the 60 respondent firms regarded pricing as a core or major support strategy (95%). By 1988, over two-thirds of the respondents did not regard pricing as an active element in their marketing mix strategy. Over the same period profit displaced competition and market share as the primary objective and the preferred pricing approach shifted from a preference for market penetration and competitive pricing (56%) to a strong preference for cost-based pricing. Concurrent with this shift was a change in emphasis from external (competitive) considerations to a preoccupation with internal factors mainly associated with short-term profitability.

Comparing these findings with those summarised in Table 17.4, it is clear that the relative importance of the mix elements varies markedly over time. That said, we should recall the point made in Chapter 9 when discussing buyer behaviour and

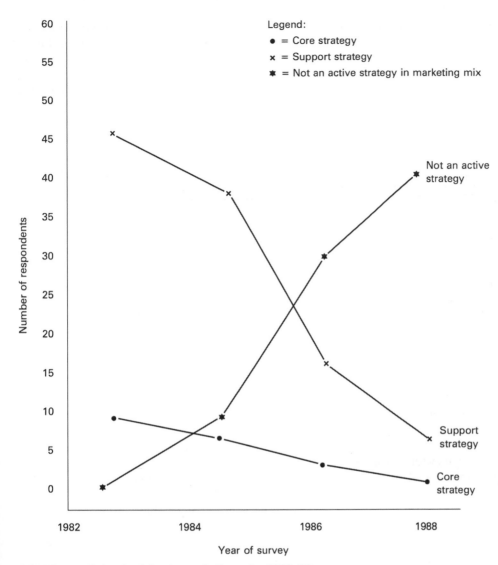

FIGURE 17.5 Role of pricing in marketing mix, 1980–88

SOURCE: Coe, B. J. (1990) Strategy in retreat: pricing drops out, *Journal of Business and Industrial Marketing*, **5**(1)

Chapter 13 that consumers' self-interest will always predispose them to look for the 'mostest for the leastest'. As such, price is an important criterion in shaping the prospective buyer's perception of value. It follows that successful firms must have an active and flexible approach to the role of price in the marketing mix if they are to maintain their competitive edge.

In his influential analysis *Price Management*, Henry Simon (1989) cites six reasons why price is of major importance to marketers:

1. For a large number of products empirical

research shows that price elasticity is about twenty times greater than advertising elasticity (Lambin, 1976, cited in Simon, 1989). That is, a 1% price change has a sales effect twenty times as big as a 1% change in the advertising budget.

2. The sales effect of a price change shows up relatively quickly (Ehrenberg and England, 1987, cited in Simon, 1989), while variations of other variables may take longer to affect sales, e.g. there are significant time lags of advertising effects, while this is rarely the case for price.

3. In contrast to almost all other marketing measures, pricing actions can be taken without

much preparatory work. A price change can be implemented immediately. Changes in product and advertising strategy take much more time. This time aspect applies also to competitive price reactions.

4. Empirical reaction elasticities of competitors are almost twice as high for a price change as for an advertising change (Lambin et al., 1975; Lambin, 1976, both cited in Simon, 1989). This result is consistent with points 2 and 3 above. At the same time, it allows for the reverse conclusion that competitors expect especially strong effects from a price change.

5. Price is the only marketing instrument that's use does not require an initially negative cash flow. An optimal value can usually be realised even in a tight financial situation (e.g. start-up companies, new products). Often this is not possible in the case of advertising or sales-force activities, which initially incur only expenses.

6. Price is the only marketing device – besides the product programme – that plays a major role in strategic planning concepts, especially in connection with the experience curve (Abell and Hammond, 1979; Henderson, 1974, 1979, cited in Simon, 1989).

Simon also lists a number of factors which reinforce the importance of price as an element in the marketing mix, including:

- Recession and inflation
- Increased competition
- Market saturation and overcapacity
- New competitors
- Consumerism
- Elimination of resale price maintenance.

Taken together, these factors reinforce the view that price is a critical element in the marketing mix. However, they also suggest why firms should seek to avoid the rigours of price competition and so have tended to emphasise non-price factors in developing marketing strategies.

PRICING STRATEGIES

Andre Gabor (1968) defined a pricing strategy as 'the application of a pricing principle to a partic-

ular situation over a certain time period'. Until recently only two broad strategic approaches to prices have been recognised, namely skimming and penetration. As the names suggest, skimming recognises that in almost all markets there is a 'hard core' of demand for whom the product in question has a particular importance. Because of the strength of their perceived need such users tend to be relatively insensitive to price and this insensitivity can be exploited through a policy of setting a very high price and thus skimming the cream off the market. By contrast, a penetration strategy is based on the assumption that if you can produce a similar product to your competitor and underprice them, then you will take away some or all of their market share. As a result of economies of scale and the experience effect, the strategist, using a penetration policy, hopes to reduce their initial cost structure to a point at which they can support the penetration price profitably.

The skimming policy may be appropriate in a number of situations and Philip Kotler (1980) identifies the following:

1. There are enough buyers whose demand is relatively inelastic.
2. The unit production and distribution costs of producing a smaller volume are not so high that they cancel out the advantage of charging what some of the traffic will bear.
3. There is little danger that high price will stimulate the emergence of rival firms.
4. High price creates an impression of a superior product.

With regard to a penetration strategy, Joel Dean (1969) sees the following three conditions as being necessary.

1. The market appears to be highly price-sensitive and therefore a low price will stimulate more rapid market growth.
2. The unit costs of production and distribution fall with accumulated production experience.
3. A low price will discourage actual and potential competition.

More recently, a number of authors have begun to suggest an alternative value-based strategy. As we have noted elsewhere, value is both a subjective and relative concept and in the case of pricing, implies that the appropriate concept is the perceived value held by the customer. This approach to value pricing was promoted by Shapiro and Jackson (1978) in an article in which they wrote: 'the marketer must determine the highest price that the customer would be willing to pay for the product'. One could view that as

Benefits *less* Cost other than price
= Highest price the customer will pay

To determine that price, the marketer needs to understand the customer's perception of benefits as well as his or her perception of the costs other than price.

The marketer also needs to remember that his or her cost is unimportant in determining the customer's perceptions. The customer cares about the marketer's price not cost. In fact, to make the statement even more accurate, the customer cares about his or her own costs much more than about the marketer's price.

More recently, Forbis and Mehta (1981) have extended this proposal and defined economic value to the customer as 'The relative value a given product offers to a specific customer in a particular application, that is, the maximum amount a customer should be willing to pay, assuming that he is fully informed about the product and the offerings of competitors'. In the view of these authors significant differences in EVC (economic value to customer) arise from the ways in which customers use and derive value from their respective reference products and may be used as a basis for segmenting a market and developing a unique advantage over their competitors. 3M and Hewlett Packard are cited as examples of companies which have established a dominant position through the use of a value-based strategy.

Such an approach would seem to have much in common with charging 'what the market will bear', which Said (1981) found to be the most widely used pricing strategy in her survey of pricing practices in UK manufacturing industry.

PRICING IN PRACTICE

In an article in the *Financial Times* (29 April, 1996),

Vanessa Houlder argued that sellers, and particularly retailers, could reap rich rewards from a detailed analysis of consumer behaviour. In essence, the article argued that while managers are well aware of the potential rewards of an effective pricing strategy (an immediate increase in profits without heavy up-front costs), David Ogilvie had accurately summarised practice when he said:

> Pricing is guesswork. It is usually assumed that marketers use scientific methods to determine the price of their products. Nothing could be further from the truth.

During the mid-1990s, as companies emerged from a prolonged recession accompanied by years of cost cutting, there was a substantial surge of interest in creative pricing as a means of expanding revenues. This was reflected by specific articles addressing the issue in the *Harvard Business Review* (Dolan, 1995), the *McKinsey Quarterly* (1995), the *Sloan Management Review* (Nagle), as well as a number of surveys by management consultancies. Houlder cites a survey by Kalchas, a London-based firm of management consultants, of 50 large UK and US companies which found that pricing issues were at or near the top of corporate agendas. Thus, the majority of the firms surveyed agreed that insufficient attention was given to revenue opportunities, especially in pricing. There was also a widely held belief that margins could be increased by several percentage points by better pricing. Similarly, the McKinsey survey offered the view that unexploited pricing and marketing opportunities exist in the order of 5% to 10% of return on sales, a finding which confirms our own observation of pricing in practice. Specifically, there is a good deal of evidence to suggest that many buyers have a discontinuity in their demand curve equivalent to a price increase of up to 10%. The logic behind this exists in the perceived risk of switching costs such that many buyers – both consumers and industrial – would not consider changing from a satisfactory existing supplier to a new and untried source for a discount of less than 10%. It would appear that psychologically a discount of 10% or more (in double figures) is sufficiently large to persuade buyers to reconsider their current buying behaviour. Certainly, in an organisational context, professional procurement managers would feel it necessary to justify in detail not switching suppliers for a discount of 10% or more. By contrast, for discounts of less than 10% generalised references to the uncertainties associated with moving from a known and satisfactory source of supply to an unknown and unproven source would be sufficient to satisfy any implied criticism.

If this simple analysis is correct, then the corollary must be that sellers enjoying strong relationships with customers could increase their prices by the order of 5% to 9% without getting them to seriously consider alternative sources.

According to the Kalchas survey, the problem is not one of a lack of familiarity with pricing options but with organisational difficulties in making pricing decisions. In part, this is attributed to the absence of formal mechanisms for setting prices and, in part, due to the insufficient use of available data. Similarly, there are often internal conflicts between finance who wish to set prices to achieve profit objectives, whereas sales and marketing wish to set prices which would achieve sales objectives.

With the increased availability of electronic point-of-sale data the opportunity to analyse consumer price sensitivity has been enhanced considerably. By utilising such data, retailers can determine the profitability of each and every product which they carry and adjust their stocking policies accordingly. Evidence of the success achieved by retailers of fast-moving consumer goods would appear to have encouraged a closer analysis of pricing policy at earlier stages in the value chain. Thus, McKinsey argued that an understanding of the true profitability of every customer and every transaction is essential to maximising profits in commodity type industries which, traditionally, tended to base their decisions on aggregated data only. Only by establishing the true cost of serving different customers does it become possible to be selective in serving those that offer the greatest profit opportunities.

Deregulation of utilities and increased competition between service companies generally has further increased the need to develop differentiated pricing strategies. In the past many such service providers offered what Houlder characterises as 'a universal service' based upon 'average cost' pricing. She observes:

As a result, telecom companies have tended to overcharge subscribers in cities and subsidise rural areas, while credit card and insurance companies have tended to overcharge the lowest risk, most attractive, customers and subsidise others. In both cases, new entrants to the market are capable of skimming off the most attractive customers – if they can get access to the relevant information.

That they can is manifestly apparent in the success of companies like Direct Line, Saga or Diamond, which offer car insurance at a discounted rate to female drivers on the grounds that they are much less prone to accidents than their male counterparts.

While the strategies of companies such as those just cited are based upon targeting and segmenting there are many other mass marketers who have adopted what have become known as everyday low price strategies. Pioneered by Procter & Gamble in the US, companies such as Asda and Esso used price as a major plank in their promotional and marketing strategies.

The adoption of such value-based strategies is that lower prices are immediately evident to everybody. By contrast, other promotions that enhance value (lower perceived price) tend only to be attractive to existing users of the product and are less than successful in getting non-buyers to change their behaviour.

Until recently, UK consumers were amongst the least price-sensitive consumers in Europe, with a survey by the Henley Centre in the mid-1990s indicating that whereas 45% of German consumers always looked for the cheapest products when shopping, only 20% of British consumers adopted this approach. However, today, it would seem clear that the British consumer has less faith in price as an indicator of quality than they had hitherto. To a large degree, this may be a self-inflicted injury in that given the increased use of price cuts and discounting and the almost perennial 'sales' offered by many retailers, consumers have become less and less confident of what is a 'fair' price. From a situation where fixed pricing was widely accepted by British consumers there is now considerable evidence of their willingness to haggle in a manner reminiscent of the Eastern bazaar.

Inevitably, and in the long run, competition on cost and prices leads to the outcome predicted in economic theory – namely, the least efficient producers will go out of business. In turn, this will lead to a concentration of power in the hands of a smaller number of larger, most cost efficient, producers. In turn, we may expect that, also as predicted by economic theory, oligopsonists will exercise a greater degree of price control and ultimately consumers will be faced with less choice and variety and higher prices.

As we have noted elsewhere, the economist Fellner described pricing as 'the blunt instrument of competition' on the grounds that it's use is immediately obvious and produces an instant reaction. In the same vein others have compared price competition to 'cutting your competitor's throat and bleeding to death yourself' on the grounds that by reducing price one is giving away a margin on every single unit one sells. For these reasons price-cutting is frequently seen as a short-term practical weapon which may be helpful for moving dated inventories or generating short-term cash flow but of limited strategic use. But, like most generalisations, there are important exceptions.

A case in point is Fuji Films' use of price to compete with Kodak in its American home market where it enjoyed a better than 80% market share. In a report in *Fortune* (27 October, 1997) Edward W. Desmond described Fuji's assault on the American homeland.

Until the spring of 1997 Fuji had priced its film a little lower than Kodak although it was clear that in what was essentially a duopolistic market they were both enjoying fat margins. This behaviour was in contrast to other world markets where Fiji competed aggressively with Kodak on a price platform. In the spring of 1997 Fuji began cutting prices by up to 25% claiming that it needed to do this in order to dispose of 2.5 million rolls of film which had been destined for Costco, one of its five largest distributors in the US, who would drop them in favour of Kodak. In Desmond's words 'When consumers saw that the familiar red, white and green boxes were a buck or two cheaper, they snapped them up' with the result that Fuji increased its share from 10% to nearly 16% while Kodak's share fell by an equivalent amount to just under 75%.

However, the fall in Kodak's stock price reflects much more than the loss of 5% market share to its rival due to its pricing tactics. Despite its still dominant position in the $2.7 billion US amateur film market elsewhere in the world, Fuji and Kodak are neck and neck with about a third of the market each. Outside the US, however, Fiji has been growing faster than Kodak and is in a much stronger overall position financially. Thus, in 1997, Fuji had a net cash position of about $4.5 billion dollars and access to borrowing at around 2.5%, whereas Kodak had more than $1 billion dollars in short- and long-term debt and could not borrow at much under 7%. In turn, these very different financial positions mirrored the different strategies of the contestants. As the established and dominant player Kodak neglected cost reductions whereas Fuji pursued such savings relentlessly. In 1984 when Kodak was invited to become the exclusive film sponsor for the Los Angeles Olympic Games Kodak refused to pay even $1 million which was far below the average $4 million for such sponsorships. As a result, Fuji was approached and eventually committed around $7 million. Desmond comments: 'No marketing investment ever brought better returns. Within months of becoming a sponsor, Fuji landed 50,000 new distributor outlets.' Given this foundation Fuji have continued to build a reputation for price, quality and sharp marketing.

Fuji has also been better able to exploit new technology. It was the first to introduce a disposable camera and it took much greater advantage of the new 24 mm Advanced Photo System Film which was developed by a consortium of Kodak/Fuji/Nikon/Canon. However, when Kodak came to launch in the US at a cost of $100 million it did so without having made enough cameras to supply dealers and before there were enough processors to develop the pictures. As a result, it had to relaunch Advantix a year later when it had rectified these errors, at a cost of a further £100 million. With the introduction of digital photography the battle of the giants has still to be resolved but it does seem clear that in the mid-90s Fuji outperformed its much bigger rival in the American market through a combination of astute marketing and the creative use of price.

Chapter summary

In this chapter we have looked at pricing in both theory and practice. Pricing plays a central role in economic theory and a number of concepts developed by economists have proved to be valuable in analysing and explaining real-world behaviour. For example, the distinction between the long and short term and the effect this has on the competitive options available to the firm in manipulating its marketing mix is very valuable, as is the concept of elasticity of demand. However, the theory possesses some severe limitations, with its assumption of profit maximisation, its failure to deal with the problem of uncertainty, its assumption that price is the businessman's chief policy instrument etc.

Having established some of the limitat-ions and contributions of price theory, we looked next at the objectives of pricing strategy. According to classical economic theory, profit maximisation is the primary objective of business, so firms should price to realise this goal. In reality, they do not, for a variety of reasons which we reviewed briefly before suggesting that firms often seek to maximise the money value of their sales through the pursuit of market share. While empirical research into pricing practice is limited, such as is available supports the findings of the study by the Brookings Institution in (Kaplan et al., 1958) which identified four major pricing objectives:

1. Pricing to achieve a target return on investment

2. Stabilisation of price and margin
3. Pricing to realise a target market share
4. Pricing to meet or prevent competition.

Empirical research also suggests that firms pursue several objectives simultaneously. In doing so, they use three main approaches to price determination – cost-plus, flexible mark-up and marginal-cost. Each of these was reviewed in some detail before examining the recent evidence on how price is used in the marketing mix.

We then looked briefly at the alternative pricing strategies of skimming and penetration before concluding that ultimately price is determined by the buyer's perception of value, before concluding with a discussion of pricing in practice.

Recommended reading

Campo, K. and Gijsbrecht, E. (1999) Pricing, in Baker, M. J. (ed.) *Encyclopedia of Marketing*. London: International Thomson Business Press.

Diamantopoulos, A. (1995) Pricing, in Baker, M. J. (ed.) *Marketing: Theory and Practice* (3rd edn). Basingstoke: Macmillan – now Palgrave Macmillan.

Nagle, T. (2005) *The Strategy and Tactics of Pricing: A Guide to Growing More Profitability* (4th edn). Englewood Cliffs, NJ: Prentice Hall.

REFERENCES

Abell, D. F. and Hammond, J. S. (1979) *Strategic Marketing Planning*. Englewood Cliffs, NJ: Prentice Hall.

Barback, R. (1964) *The Pricing of Manufacturers*. London: Macmillan – now Palgrave Macmillan.

Bates, J. and Parkinson, R. (1969) *Business Economics*. Oxford: Blackwell.

Baumol, W. J. (1959) *Business Behaviour, Value and Growth*. New York: Macmillan.

Baumol, W. J. (1971) Models of economic competition, in Townsend, H., *Price Theory*. London: Cox & Wyman.

Chevalier, M. and Carty, B. (1974) Don't misuse your market share goal, *European Business* (winter/spring).

Coe, B. J. (1990) Strategy in retreat: pricing drops out, *Journal of Business and Industrial Marketing*, **5**(1).

Cyert, R. M. and March, J. G. (1963) *A Behavioural Theory of the Film*. Englewood Cliffs, NJ: Prentice Hall.

Dean, J. (1951) *Managerial Economics*. Englewood Cliffs, NJ: Prentice Hall.

Dean, J. (1969) HBR classic: pricing policies for new products, *Harvard Business Review* (November–December).

Desmond, E. W. (1997) What's ailing Kodak? Fuji, *Fortune*, 27 October.

Diamantopoulos, A. (1996) Chapter 11 Pricing, in Baker, M. J. (ed.) *Marketing: Theory and Practice* (3rd edn). Basingstoke: Macmillan – now Palgrave Macmillan.

Diamantopoulos, A. (1999) Pricing, in Baker, M. J. (ed.) *The Marketing Book* (4th edn). Oxford: Butterworth Heinemann, pp. 182–97.

Enke, S. (1977) On maximising profits, in Watson, D., *Price Theory and its Uses* (4th edn). Boston, MA: Houghton-Mifflin.

Fellner, W. (1951) The influence of market structure on technological progress, *Quarterly Journal of Economics*, **65**(November).

Fisher, L. (1966) *Industrial Marketing*. London: Business Books.

Forbis, J. L. and Mehta, W. T. (1981) Value-based strategies for industrial products, *Business Horizons* (June).

Ford, H. II (1962) *What America expects of industry*, in an address before the Michigan State Chamber of Commerce, October.

Gabor, A. (1968) *Determining your pricing structure at home and abroad*, Marketing Industrial Products, Pera Conference, Melton Mowbray, April.

Gabor, A. (1977) *Pricing Principles and Practices*. London: Heinemann.

Gabor, A. and Granger, C. W. J. (1973) A systematic approach to effective pricing, in Rodger, L. W., *Marketing Concept and Strategies in the Next Decade*. New York: John Wiley.

Hague, D. C. (1948–9) Economic theory and business behaviour, *Review of Economic Studies*, **16**.

Hall, R. L. and Hitch, C. J. (1939) Economic theory and business behaviour, *Oxford Economic Papers*, **2**(May).

Hayes, R. H. and Abernathy, W. J. (1980) Managing our way to economic decline, *Harvard Business Review* (July–August).

Haynes, W. (1962) *Pricing Decisions in Small Business*. Lexington, MA: University of Kentucky Press.

Haynes, W. (1974) *Managerial Economics* (3rd edn). Austin, TX: Business Publications.

Henderson, B. D. (1974) The experience curve reviewed: why does it work? *Perspectives*. The Boston Consulting Group Inc.

Henderson, B. D. (1979) Strategic and natural competition, *Perspectives*, The Boston Consulting Group Inc.

Johnston, G. (1969) The pricing of consumer goods, in Taylor, B. and Wills, G., *Pricing Strategies*. London: Staples Press.

Kaplan, A., Dirlam, J. and Lanzillotti, R. (1958) *Pricing in Big Business*. Washington, DC: Brookings Institution.

Kotler, P. (1972) *Marketing Management: Analysis Planning and Control* (2nd edn). Englewood Cliffs, NJ: Prentice Hall.

Kotler, P. (1980) *Marketing Management: Analysis Planning and Control* (4th edn). Englewood Cliffs, NJ: Prentice Hall, p. 387.

Kuhlmeijer, H. J. (1975) *Managerial Marketing*. Leiden: H.E. Stenfert Kroese V.B.

Laric, M. V. (1980) Pricing strategies in industrial markets, *European Journal of Marketing*, **14**(5/6): 303–21.

Lynn, R. (1968) Unit volume as a goal for pricing, *Journal of Marketing* (October): 35–7.

Oxenfeldt, A. (1959) How to use market share measurement, *Harvard Business Review* (January–February).

Oxenfeldt, A. (1961) *Pricing for Marketing Executives*. Belmont, CA: Wadsworth.

Oxenfeldt, A. (1975) *Pricing Strategies*. New York: AMACOM, p. 42.

Pass, C. (1971) Pricing policies and market strategy: an empirical note, *European Journal of Marketing*, **5**(3).

Ragoff, D. and Lynn, R. (1972) Methods v. objectives in pricing policy, *Management Advisor* (March–April).

Robicheaux, R. A. in P. Kotler (1980) *Principles of Marketing* (4th edn). Englewood Cliffs, NJ: Prentice Hall, p. 398.

Said, H. (1981) *The Relevance of Price Theory to Pricing Practice: An Investigation of Pricing Policies and Practices in UK Industry*, Ph.D dissertation, University of Strathclyde.

Shapiro, B. P. and Jackson, B. B. (1978) Industrial pricing to meet customer needs, *Harvard Business Review* (November–December).

Simon, H. (1989) *Price Management*. Amsterdam: Elsevier.

Simon, H. A. (1952) A behavioural model of rational choice, *Quarterly Journal of Economics*, **69**.

Simon, H. A. (1959) Theories of decision making in economics and behavioural science, *American Economic Review* (June).

Sizer, J. (1969) The accountant's contribution to pricing decisions, in Taylor, B. and Wills, G. *Pricing Strategies*. London: Staples Press.

Udell, J. (1964) How important is price in competitive strategy?, *Journal of Marketing* (April).

Distribution and sales policy

Consumption is a function of availability.   MARKETING MAXIM

After reading Chapter 18 you will be able to:

✔ Explain why distribution channels develop and the role they play in linking producers and consumers.

✔ Describe the functions performed by the distribution channel.

✔ Review the forces which influence channel structure.

✔ Relate distribution strategy options to the basic marketing strategies – undifferentiated, differentiated and concentrated.

✔ Explain the trade-off between cost and control in channel selection.

✔ Distinguish between 'push' and 'pull' as distribution alternatives.

✔ Account for the decline of the role of personal selling as a marketing function.

✔ Suggest how distribution policy may vary in accordance with the stages of the PLC.

INTRODUCTION

In an article published some years ago (Baker, 1980–1), I suggested that an important marketing maxim is that 'Consumption is a function of availability' and went so far as to suggest that brand shares are a self-fulfilling prophecy. This latter suggestion was based on the following anecdotal analysis.

The basic assumption is that with 30,000 or more items to stock in a supermarket, the store manager allocates the display space available in accordance with the expected yield (profit) of each product category such that the marginal return on each will be the same. Having assigned space to the product category, the store manager will then divide this up between the brands he has decided to stock. Basically the brand stocking decision will be arrived at by taking into account the national brand share, any known local or regional variations and the retailer's policy on own or generic brands. Such an analysis could result in the following much simplified scenario for baked beans.

Baked beans are to receive 10 facings with the following shares:

- Brand A   5 facings
- Brand B   3 facings
- Own brand   2 facings

The first two customers for baked beans prefer the own brand and select it, leaving only Brands A and B available. Customers 3, 4, 5 would also prefer the own brand but, as it is not available, little Johnny wants his tea and there isn't much difference between them, they select their second choice, Brand B. Customers 6–10 inclusive would all prefer the own brand, failing which they would choose Brand B. However, as neither is available, they take the acceptable substitute, Brand A. At the end of the day the store manager notes with satisfaction that he has sold 10 cans of beans in the proportions 5:3:2 and restocks accordingly.

Clearly this interpretation maligns both the sophistication of store management and the discriminatory powers of consumers, but hopefully it makes the point that, for products which are near substitutes for one another, availability will determine consumption patterns and decision-makers are quite likely to extrapolate these when making future decisions.

However, while availability is a necessary condition for consumption, it is by no means a sufficient one and we are not seeking to re-establish the now largely discredited Say's law (formulated by Jean-Baptiste Say, 1767–1832), which holds that supply creates demand. Indeed, we would go so far as to claim that the current practice of marketing resulted directly from the realisation that the creation of a supply did not guarantee consumption and acceptance of the fact that suppliers have to compete for the customer's patronage.

But, despite its obvious importance, distribution remains a largely neglected topic in marketing. In a famous article in 1962, Peter Drucker characterised distribution as 'The economy's dark continent' and pointed out that while the distribution function accounted for between 30–50% of the total cost of manufactured goods, it received comparatively little attention compared with the other major business functions. Forty years later, very little has changed – distribution activities account for substantial costs and provide extensive employment, but in the UK, few marketing academics, or practitioners, have given the subject much attention. This neglect is even more surprising when one considers that much of the early marketing literature has a distribution focus.

Perhaps distribution remains unexplored because it lacks the interest and excitement associated with the other marketing functions – especially product development and promotion. Yet, while lacking in glamour, effective distribution is a sine qua non of marketing success, as the following example shows:

In the early part of 1970, after several months and substantial expenditure, Walls withdrew from the yoghurt market and sold its fleet of chill-refrigerated vehicles to Eden Vale, its main competitors in the market. This decision meant, in effect, that Walls was abandoning the rapidly expanding chilled prepared-food market, which includes prepared salads and ready-to-serve puddings. It had been unable to obtain enough sales to warrant the high cost of distribution of these products. Underlying the poor sales performance was Walls' inability to get its chilled product distributed through enough of the high-volume outlets – the supermarkets (Guirdham, 1972).

By the same token, the tremendous success of ICI's Ambush insecticide in securing almost 50% of total sales to US cotton growers in its launch year was largely attributable to ICI signing up the most influential distributors throughout the cotton belt (Baker, 1983).

Distribution is a key policy area in the formulation of marketing strategy, and in this chapter we will attempt to cover some of the more important issues. According to Rosenbloom (1999), channel decision areas fall into six categories:

1. Formulating channel strategy
2. Designing the channel structure
3. Selecting the channel members
4. Motivating the channel members
5. Coordinating channel strategy with the marketing mix
6. Evaluating the channel members' performance.

Channel strategy refers to the broad principles through which the firm seeks to achieve its distribution objectives. Distribution objectives are usually set in terms of how, when and where the firm plans to have its products made available to its target markets.

Distribution objectives themselves may be key strategic tools under a number of circumstances. For example, for complex consumer durable products, service levels in dealerships may be a critical factor in influencing buying decisions. Other examples of distribution decisions assuming strategic importance are those where these confer some form of sustainable competitive advantage on the seller. This is often the case with very selective or exclusive distribution of prestige products, of rapid response times through the use of superior systems and technology, or novelty, as in the case of the internet. In addition, a market development strategy is essentially a distribution strategy in that it involves taking an existing product into a new location.

Channel strategy has also assumed increasing importance with the growing emphasis upon partnerships and strategic alliances giving rise to what is often termed 'supply chain management'. First we shall examine the reasons underlying the development of marketing channels and the functions they perform. This will lead naturally into a consideration of the various channels and the

factors which will influence the choice of any particular option.

As we have noted earlier, producers have only two basic options with regard to a distribution policy – they can either seek to work closely with intermediaries or else assume their functions and 'push' their product through the channel, or they can seek to establish a franchise with ultimate consumers and so 'pull' their product through the channel. Push strategies tend to lay greater emphasis upon personal selling; pull strategies emphasise advertising and promotion. Accordingly, we will look at some of the major aspects of the selling function in this chapter, while leaving advertising to Chapter 19.

Finally, in keeping with our adoption of the product life-cycle as an organising concept, we shall look at the role that sales and distribution have to play at the various stages of product development.

WHY DO CHANNELS DEVELOP?

The basic and most primitive form of economic organisation is the self-sufficient community in which the overall standard of living or quality of life depends directly upon the abilities, skills and resources available to the community. Improvements in the efficiency of such communities occur when the members recognise the benefits of task specialisation in increasing both productivity and the quality of output and adopt a basis for exchanging surpluses in excess of the producer's own needs. In time, still greater improvements are achieved through the application of technology to the production function and through the division of labour, such that individuals perform only one or a few of the many tasks involved in translating raw materials into consumable products. However, a direct consequence of the very large increments in output that result from task specialisation and the division of labour is that the production unit can supply more than can be consumed by persons with direct access to that production unit. Thus it becomes necessary to gain access to consumers who are physically distant from the production unit and this will depend upon the creation of physical means of distribution together with the development of institutions and institutional devices to serve and manage these distribution 'channels'.

Of course, improved transportation not only permits the distribution of finished goods to users, it also facilitates the movement of people and raw materials so that whole industries begin to concentrate in those areas which offer the highest comparative advantage, with classic examples being the Yorkshire woollen industry, the Lancashire cotton industry and the potteries. Such industrial concentration results in an even greater physical separation between producer and consumer and creates a concomitant increase in the dependence upon the distribution channel. As a general rule of thumb, the greater the number of consumers, the more widely they are dispersed, and the greater their frequency of purchase, the more attenuated and complex will be the channel linking producer and consumer.

Unfortunately, while the value added by production has long been recognised and accepted, the functions of 'merchants' who organise and manage the distribution channel have been poorly understood and subject to considerable criticism. Indeed, the less the physical movement and handling involved and the more indirect the channel, the more strident the criticism. Faced with such unfavourable attitudes, it is perhaps unsurprising that distribution has been regarded as the least accepted and least glamorous aspect of marketing. Since the 1980s, there have been signs that this status has changed as the balance of power between manufacturer and retailer moved in favour of the latter.

It is especially ironic that the pursuit of economies of scale in production – which is seen as laudable and to be encouraged – tends to lead to diseconomies in distribution, particularly as distribution costs are variable and only occur when manufacture is complete. In addition, and much more difficult to quantify, is the reduction in satisfaction received by consumers due to their separation from the producer. Because of this separation, producers tend to lose contact with the specific needs of consumers and lack the feedback that contact provides. The rediscovery of marketing, and the growth of consumerism, are the obvious consequences of this deterioration in contact.

From the producers' point of view, the loss of contact can become even more serious when their identity becomes submerged or lost in the identity of intermediaries in the distribution channel. While this tends to happen most often with consumer goods, e.g. Marks & Spencer, Sainsbury, Mothercare, it is also apparent in the case of many industrial raw materials and supplies where the distributor becomes the dominant force. While such a loss of identity may protect the producer from direct criticism, it also isolates them from the feedback which this provides with the result that it may be impossible to retrieve a situation where their product has become unsatisfactory.

To restore this loss of franchise with ultimate consumers, many producers have resorted to one or some combination of the following alternative courses of action:

1. Integrate forward into distribution – breweries, oil producers, shoe manufacturers
2. Shorten the channel by seeking to deal direct with consumers through a greater emphasis upon personal selling and by using modern information technology, e.g. the internet, 'tele-selling' etc.
3. Speak directly with the end consumer through their promotional effort.

However, the extent to which producers will be willing or able to manage their own distribution activities will depend ultimately upon their perception of the costs and benefits involved. Accordingly, it seems likely that given channels and forms of distribution will only survive if they are more effective in marketing the product, and to establish this one must first identify the functions which the channel performs.

FUNCTIONS OF A CHANNEL

The foregoing discussion has shown that the primary function of a channel of distribution is to provide a link between production and consumption by filling any gap or discontinuity which exists between them. Discontinuities between producers and consumers may arise from a number of causes, including the following:

1. *Geographical separation.* As noted, the application of the theory of comparative advantage has led

to considerable concentration of production on both a national and international scale. At the same time, population and economic growth have resulted in many more widely dispersed consumers wanting access to these products. Distribution creates utilities in place availability.

2. *Time.* Production and consumption rarely occur simultaneously (with the exception of personal services) and channels of distribution help even out fluctuations in supply and demand by holding stocks and through the provision of credit. These activities create time utilities.

3. *Information.* The information needs of consumers vary widely and channel intermediaries can provide a valuable service in advising producers of the needs of consumers and advising consumers of the specific characteristics of the offerings of different producers.

4. *Ownership.* In addition to making goods physically available (possession), channels also provide the mechanism whereby transfer of the legal title to ownership may be accomplished.

5. *Sorting.* The term used by Wroe Alderson (1954) to describe a number of channel functions which are implicit in creating the time, place and possession utilities described above.

According to Alderson, sorting comprises four distinct activities:

1. *Sorting out:* 'breaking down a heterogeneous supply into separate stocks which are relatively homogeneous', e.g. agricultural products
2. *Accumulation*
3. *Allocation:* 'consists of breaking a homogeneous supply down into smaller and smaller lots'
4. *Assorting:* 'building up assortments of items for use in association with each other'.

In addition to plugging potential gaps that may arise between producer and consumer due to the above factors, Alderson (1954) also shows how channels can increase consumer satisfaction through improving efficiency and thereby reducing cost, and also by reducing uncertainty through routinisation of transactions.

As Alderson observes:

Economic analysis of the factors in price equilibrium generally rests on the assumption that exchange transactions are costless. Marketing analysis directed toward an understanding of trade channels must begin with a recognition of the costs involved in the creation of time, place, and possession utilities.

Alderson proceeds to demonstrate:

The number of transactions necessary to carry out decentralised exchange is $n(n71)/2$ where n is the number of producers and each makes only one article. Since the number of transactions required is only n if the central market is operated by a dealer, the ratio of advantage is $(n71)/2$. Thus if the number of producers is raised from 5 to 25, the ratio of advantage in favour of an intermediary increases from 2 to 12. With 125 producers the ratio of advantage is 62.

Given our earlier claim that the average supermarket stocks over 30,000 different items, even allowing for the fact that these will come from significantly fewer producers, the cost advantage of dealing through such an intermediary, or assuming their functions, is immediately apparent.

With regard to routinisation, Alderson argues that this will reduce transaction costs to the minimum as it will eliminate the costs involved in searching for and approaching sources of supply on an ad hoc basis. Further, by reducing much purchase behaviour to a routine exchange, one will eliminate the uncertainty the potential buyer experiences in new buy or modified rebuy situations. Thus many buyers regard the industrial distributor or the retail outlet as the guarantee of satisfactory performance and leave it to the intermediary to undertake the search, evaluation and trial aspects of a purchase on their behalf.

Thus we can see that the functions of a channel of distribution not only improve the flow of physical goods, but also create flows in finance, information and ownership.

Box 18.1	*DHL Worldwide Express*

In 1969, Adrian Dalsey, Larry Hillblom and Robert Lynn (D, H and L) created an entirely new industry, by starting a door-to-door express service between San Francisco and Honolulu. After this first milestone, the company expanded enormously throughout the world by recognising the global need for the fast, reliable and safe delivery of goods and documents. DHL Worldwide Express is composed of DHL Airways, Inc., which serves all locations in the US and its territories, and DHL International Ltd. and its agents and affiliated companies, which serve all locations outside the US and its territories. DHL Worldwide Express is the world's largest and most experienced international air express network with service to more than 675,000 destinations in the world. DHL maintains its position as the world's leading international air express network by continually expanding and upgrading its network of offices, hubs and services, and by offering superior service through a well-trained and dedicated workforce consisting of locals who are knowledgeable about business practices and conditions to help expedite pickups and delivery schedules. The company's investment in information technology, $1.25 billion in the mid-1990s, in handling systems, automation, facilities and communications and computer technology, has also helped the company to continue to harness new technologies to streamline the shipping process and provide services that allow its customers to be more competitive, satisfied and, of course, loyal. In sum, the company's apparent single strategy throughout the world is safe, reliable and fast delivery of documents and goods by using local professionals, modes of transportation and extensive amounts of information technology, has given the company the leading position in this global industry.

SOURCE: Zafer Erdogan, based on DHL Customer Information Services

CHANNEL COMPOSITION

Channels of distribution vary considerably in their complexity, with the simplest involving a direct exchange between producer and consumer, while the most complex may involve several different kinds of intermediaries. The possible combinations and permutations are considerable for, of course, a supplier may make use of multiple channels simultaneously and not just depend upon a single approach to the market. Most of the major alternatives are illustrated in Figure 18.1.

From Figure 18.1 it is clear that the producer can have access to a variety of different intermediaries, each of whom will provide different kinds of services. Most basic textbooks devote considerable coverage to describing the similarities and differences which exist between different categories of intermediary together with an evaluation of their merits and disadvantages. We do not propose to pursue these further here as the choice of a particular kind of intermediary is more of a tactical decision than a strategic one and will be highly situation specific. Accordingly, our own focus will be upon the basic choice between direct and indirect distribution and, if indirect, the length and complexity of the channel and its functions rather than the precise designation of the intermediaries.

FACTORS INFLUENCING CHANNEL STRUCTURE

With rare exceptions, most producers will find themselves faced with a number of different channels through which they might seek to reach their target market. Some understanding of the broad influences which give rise to these different channel structures will provide a useful insight when deciding which of the alternatives to use.

In reviewing various explanations of channel structure, (see Figure 18.1) Lambert (1978) notes that there is no consensus of opinion, with some theories stressing the product life-cycle, others the characteristics of goods and still others the size of firm. Among these theories perhaps the most detailed and best known is that put forward by Bucklin (1966), which rests upon the economic relationships between channel members and the

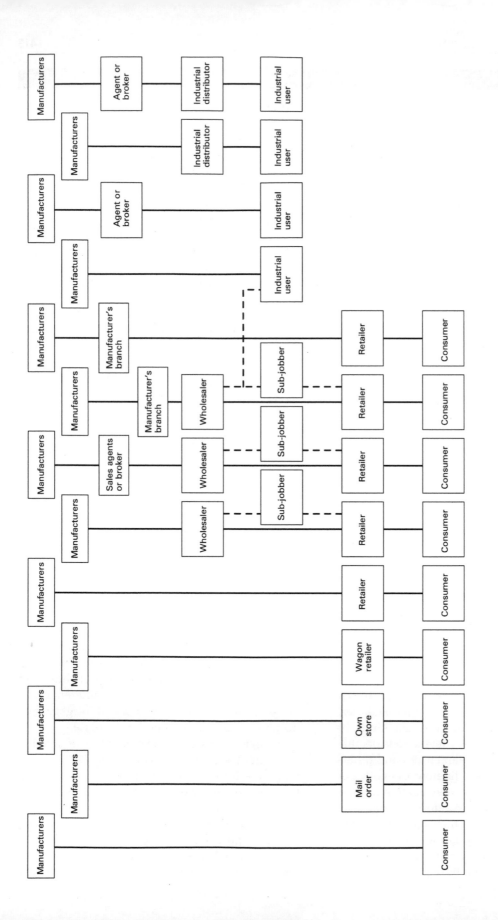

FIGURE 18.1 Alternative channels of distribution

SOURCE: Lambert, D. M. (1978) *The Distribution Channels Decision*. New York: The National Association of Accountants

concepts of substitutability, postponement and speculation.

According to Bucklin (1965), marketing functions are substitutable for one another in much the same way as the basic factors of production and, 'This substitutability permits the work load of one function to be shrunk and shifted to another without affecting the output of the channel.' He continues later: 'In essence, the concept of substitutability states that under competitive conditions institutions of the channel will interchange the work load among functions, not to minimise the cost of some individual function, but the total costs of the channel.'

Postponement and speculation are the converse of each other in that the principle of postponement 'states that changes in form and inventory location are to be delayed to the latest possible moment' (JIT) while 'the principle of speculation holds that changes in form, and the movement of goods to forward inventories, should be made at the earliest possible time in the marketing flow in order to reduce the costs of the marketing system', e.g. through economies of scale.

Based upon these three principles, Bucklin argues that consumer demand will determine what services are required and what value is placed upon them, and this will result in the evolution of the most efficient and cost-effective channel structure. Thus for convenience goods ready and widespread availability is a sine qua non and we are likely to find the producer using multiple channels involving both direct and indirect sales to achieve the maximum market coverage. Conversely, for many industrial goods and consumer shopping goods, the variation in consumer demand will lead to greater postponement so that precise needs can be articulated and will frequently result in shorter channels and a greater dependence upon personal interaction between buyer and seller.

However, as producers and distributors jockey for position to satisfy the ultimate customer, one must anticipate an ebb and flow in the competitive standing of the channel members. Lambert (1978) provides a useful synopsis of Bruce Mallen's (1973) analysis of the competitive forces that are likely to result in structural change in the channel, as follows:

1. A producer will spin off a marketing function to a marketing intermediary(s) if the latter can perform the function more efficiently than the former.
2. If there are continual economies to be obtained within a wide range of volume changes, the middleman portion of the industry (and perhaps individual middlemen) will become bigger and bigger.
3. A producer will keep a marketing function if the producer can perform the functions at least as efficiently as the intermediary.
4. If a producer is more efficient in one market, the producer will perform the marketing function; if in another market the middleman is more efficient, then the middleman will perform the function.
5. If there are not economies of scale in a growing market, more firms may be expected to join the channel.

Important decisions involved in choosing a channel structure include (Rosenbloom, 1999):

1. The length of the channels
2. Intensity at various levels
3. The types of intermediaries involved.

Intensity refers to the number of intermediaries to be used and is usually described in terms of:

1. Intensive distribution involving as many outlets and intermediaries as possible
2. Selective distribution where intermediaries are chosen according to their ability to meet certain important criteria
3. Exclusive distribution where only one distributor will be appointed to serve a given sales area.

According to Rosenbloom, the most widely used performance criteria for evaluating channel members' performance are:

1. Sales performance
2. Inventory maintenance
3. Selling capabilities
4. Attitudes
5. Competitive products handled
6. Growth prospects.

Of course, changes in the competitive standing of producers and distributive intermediaries will be subject to the complex interplay of the environmental forces reviewed in Chapter 7 and underlines the importance of monitoring these if one is to select the most efficient channel.

CHANNEL CHARACTERISTICS

While channel characteristics receive some attention in the B2B literature, they are largely ignored in the B2C literature, which tends to emphasise product and brand choice. In the view of Michaelidou et al. (2005), the proliferation of non-store channels – catalogues, direct mail, the internet etc. and the growth of home shopping – suggest that channel characteristics deserve closer consideration in terms of their impact on consumer behaviour.

Such limited research as has been done indicates that factors like risk aversion, self-confidence, variety seeking, convenience orientation, flexibility and demographics differ measurably and significantly between shopping modes. In the absence of conceptual models, Michaelidou et al. suggest that channel characteristics offer a useful basis for modelling channel attributes and their impact on consumer choice.

For the purpose of their theoretical paper, the authors identify five channel characteristics: involvement, perceived risk, loyalty, similarity and hedonism.

Involvement is defined by the interest and concern exhibited by the consumer in choosing between alternative channels. In turn, this will be influenced by the *risk perceived* in choosing one channel over another, e.g. are financial transactions on the internet secure? It is also likely to be affected by the degree of involvement (high or low) with the product / service concerned.

As with brand loyalty, it is hypothesised that preference for one channel over another may lead to *loyalty* towards it. In turn, *similarities* and differences between alternative channels may encourage or inhibit switching. Finally, *hedonism* is a measure of the enjoyment experienced by the shopper from patronising different channels.

These five primary characteristics are combined with four secondary factors to create a conceptual

model for analysing the influence of channel characteristics on purchase behaviour. Given that these are 'driven' by the product characteristics, it is clear that sellers need to give careful consideration to such a model when taking channel decisions.

SELECTING THE DISTRIBUTION CHANNEL

Thus far, the analysis of the factors governing the functions and structure of distribution channels has laid most emphasis upon cost efficiency, particularly as distribution represents such a significant proportion of the final cost to the consumer. However, we have also referred to 'effectiveness' and consumer satisfaction, both of which tend to be of a subjective and qualitative nature. To some extent, cost efficiency and maximising consumer satisfaction are conflicting objectives and lead to the classic dilemma in choosing channels of distribution – the trade-off between cost versus control.

Louis Stern (1965) defines channel control and its implications succinctly when he writes:

> Channel control [signifies] the ability of one member of a marketing channel for a given product (or brand) to stipulate marketing policies to other members. For example, in a simple channel where a buyer interacts directly with a seller, the party gaining control in the bargaining process either through the use of sheer economic power, political or legal means, superior knowledge, more subtle promotional aids, or other methods, obtains a major advantage in all aspects of their relationship. When marketing policies may be stipulated by any one party, this may have a marked influence on the efficiencies of both. Their goals may not be totally compatible; therefore, by complying with the dictates of buyers, for example, sellers may frequently be forced to alter their methods of operation in a manner that is not often profitable for them.

Obviously there are many situations where the seller will have to accept an inevitable discrepancy in bargaining power between themselves and their customer, but equally there are many other situations where a creative marketing approach may minimise or eliminate control over one's affairs. This is particularly true of the distribution function where it may be possible to retain a larger measure of control by performing channel functions oneself rather than using the more cost-effective services of an intermediary, e.g. in the level of servicing and/or maintenance provided, of the inventory held etc. In turn, by providing greater user satisfaction one may be able to secure a higher price and so offset the additional costs.

As noted earlier, when selecting a channel of distribution, one must pay particular attention to the environmental situation, to the product and market characteristics and the company's own strengths and weaknesses. While these factors have been the subject of extensive discussion in earlier chapters, it will be helpful to summarise the major points to be considered and provide some elaboration of them here in general terms.

- *Environmental:*
  - Market structure: number and location of both suppliers and users
  - Market conduct: degree of concentration and nature of competition
  - Market performance
  - Legislation/regulation
  - Institutional infrastructure: what channels are available and what are their distinguishing characteristics

- *Product characteristics:*
  - Class of product
  - Bulk/volume
  - Price/value
  - Durability/perishability
  - Seasonality
  - Service requirements

- *Market characteristics:*
  - Benefits looked for
  - Geographic location
  - Discernible segments

- *Company strengths and weaknesses:*
  - Size
  - Competitive standing
  - Goodwill – how much with whom
  - Service and technical abilities.

Consideration of these factors will inevitably lead one to consider the relative merits of our three basic strategies: undifferentiated, differentiated and concentrated marketing with their associated distribution strategies: intensive, selective and exclusive distribution.

As we have seen, an undifferentiated strategy rests on the assumption of user homogeneity and/or an implicit acceptance that one has no prior ability to segment a market and so must appeal to all of it. Either way, maximum distributive coverage is called for, that almost invariably will require one to use the services of intermediaries to secure it.

By contrast, differentiated marketing implies an ability to segment a market and to cater for the varying needs of the different segments. In these circumstances some segments are likely to be more important to a given producer than others, and so justify a direct approach, while intermediaries may be used to reach more dispersed segments or those with particular needs best served by another channel member, e.g. a manufacturer of industrial equipment might sell direct to major users and through distributors or agents to increase geographical coverage.

Finally, concentrated marketing calls for highly selective distribution. It also implies a smaller supplier, hence the concentration on only one segment, and so will require the use of intermediaries in all but the most geographically concentrated markets. However, with the advent of the internet even the smallest suppliers can, theoretically, obtain access to all those linked to it – a major factor underlying the growth of e-commerce (see Chapter 24). The implications of these three strategies for distribution are summarised succinctly in Evans and Berman's (1982) overview of distribution planning reproduced below as Table 18.1.

In their textbook Gaedeke and Tootelian (1983) provide a very useful summary table of the factors which are likely to influence the length of the channel and, therefore, the number of intermediate functions to be performed between production and consumption. These data are reproduced in Table 18.2.

However, notwithstanding the implications of these generalisations, there are numerous instances where channels will differ from the normative prescription. Such variation may reflect a conscious decision to adopt a different approach to distribution in order to position the firm in a distinctive way, i.e. using distribution as the key

TABLE 18.1 Intensity of channel coverage

Characteristics	Exclusive distribution	Selective distribution	Intensive distribution
Objectives	Strong image, channel control and loyalty, price stability	Moderate market coverage, solid image, some channel control and loyalty	Widespread market coverage, channel acceptance, volume sales
Channel members	Few in number, well-established, reputable stores	Moderate in number, well-established, better stores	Many in number, all types of outlets
Customers	Few in number, trend setters, willing to travel to store, brand loyal	Moderate in number, brand conscious, somewhat willing to travel to store	Many in number, convenience oriented
Marketing emphasis	Personal selling, pleasant shopping conditions, good service	Promotional mix, pleasant shopping conditions, good service	Mass advertising, nearby location, items in stock
Examples	Automobiles, designer clothes, caviar	Furniture, clothing, watches	Groceries, household products, magazines

SOURCE: Evans, J. R. and Berman, B. (1982) *Marketing*. New York: Macmillan

variable in a competitive strategy, or it may simply reflect inertia or neglect. Like so many other areas of activity, while the underlying trend may be towards homeostasis or equilibrium, the state may never be reached and conditions will approach then swing away from the central state rather in the manner of a pendulum.

In the sphere of retailing these fluctuations have been characterised as a 'wheel' in which different approaches will dominate from time to time only to be displaced by alternative forms until the wheel comes full circle. The concept of a 'wheel of retailing' was first proposed by Professor Malcolm McNair (1958) of the Harvard Business School and hypothesises that:

new types of retailers usually enter the market as low-status, low-margin, low-price operators. Gradually, they acquire more elaborate establishments and facilities, with both increased investments and higher operating costs. Finally they mature as high-cost, high-price merchants, vulnerable to new types who, in turn, go through the same pattern.

Hollander's (1960) article provides an excellent summary of the evidence for and against the theory and concludes that, while it is not valid for all retailing, it does 'describe a fairly common pattern in industrialised, expanding economies'. Certainly, firms like Marks & Spencer, Tesco and Comet would seem to conform to the hypothesis and the critical question must be: 'If the management of these organisations can recognise the applicability of the theory to their development to date – will they be able to avoid the seemingly inevitable outcome?'

Reference to retailers such as Marks & Spencer, Tesco, Comet and the like provides a useful link with the point made early in the chapter that, as a result of the attenuation of distribution channels, many retailers (and industrial distributors) have become the dominant channel member. In that this book is written from the perspective of producer organisations this immediately raises the question as to what implication this has for producers and what actions can they take.

FORMULATING A DISTRIBUTION POLICY

From the preceding discussion, it has become clear that a very large number of factors may influence the structure of distribution channels between manufacturers and consumers. It has also become

TABLE 18.2 Summary of factors influencing channel length

Channel consideration	Favouring long channels	Favouring short channels
Market or customer characteristics		
1. Size of purchasing unit	Small	Large
2. Number of customers	Many	Few
3. Location of customers	Geographically dispersed	Geographically concentrated
4. Customer knowledge	Considerable and widely dispersed	Limited and concentrated
5. Installation and servicing assistance	None required	Help required
Producer characteristics		
1. Size of firm	Small	Large
2. Length of time in business	New to market	Old and established in the market
3. Financial resources	Limited	Abundant
4. Location to the market	Not centrally located	Centrally located
5. Control over marketing programme	Unimportant	Important
6. Overall resource position	Weak	Strong
7. Market coverage desired	Intensive	Exclusive
8. Managerial capabilities	Weak	Strong
9. Market information availability	Limited	Abundant and expensive
10. Power	Weak	Strong
11. Policy toward pushing product	Passive	Aggressive
Environmental characteristics		
1. Number of competitors	Many	Few
2. Number of resources controlled	Few	Many
3. Economic conditions	Recessionary	Booming
4. Entry and exit of producers	Easy	Limited
5. Economic customs and traditions	Stable	Dynamic
6. Location of competitors	Geographically dispersed	Geographically concentrated
7. Laws and regulations	Tight	Loose
8. Competition among customers	Weak	Strong
9. Market to be served	New	Old
Product characteristics		
1. Perishability	Low	High
2. Fashionability	Low	High
3. Size of product	Small	Large
4. Value of product	Low	High
5. Weight of product	Light	Heavy
6. Complexity of product	Technically simple	Technically complex
a Special knowledge for sale	None	Considerable
b Installation	Not necessary	Required
c Maintenance	Not required	Frequent or regular
d Service	Not required	Frequent or regular
7. Risk of obsolescence	Low	High
8. Age of product	Old	New
9. Production process	Standard	Custom built
10. Order size (quantities purchased)	Small	Large
11. Appearance of product	Undifferentiated (homogeneous)	Differentiated (heterogeneous)
12. Type of product (buying characteristics)	Convenience good	Speciality good
13. Type of product (market)	Consumer good	Industry good
14. Time of purchase	Seasonal	Non-seasonal
15. Timing of purchase	Frequently	Infrequently
16. Regularity of purchase	Regular	Irregular
17. Profit margin	Low	High
18. Width of product line	Narrow	Broad
19. Availability requirements	Delayed	Immediately
20. Number of products per line	Few	Many
21. Product lines	Unrelated	Related
22. Number of alternative uses	Many	Limited

SOURCE: Gaedeke and Tootelian (1983), adapted from Brady, D. L. (1978) *An Analysis of Factors Affecting the Methods of Exporting Used by Small Manufacturing Firms.* University of Alabama, pp. 39–41

clear that the weighting given to any particular factor will vary over time due to changes in the environment and/or in accordance with the perception of the individuals or organisations who comprise the channel. Thus, while it may be possible to define and describe theoretically 'optimum' channels in terms of objective cost factors, the perception of producers, intermediaries and consumers may all conclude that such an 'optimum' arrangement will not optimise their own objectives and yield the desired satisfactions. For example, selling through Marks & Spencer by a textile manufacturer might ensure that the customer gets excellent value for money, but may be seen as inimical to that manufacturer's wish to retain some direct control over the marketing of their output. The question is then, how does the manufacturer resolve this dilemma by assigning their own subjective weights to the key criteria? How does one establish a distribution policy?

Before attempting to answer this question, it is important to stress a point made earlier that theoretical solutions are very often only intended to clarify the factors and their relationships which need to be taken into account. In doing so it will be necessary to make certain assumptions that will clean up the data and reduce the noise in the system, and the greater the number of assumptions and the simplification of the data, the more likely it becomes that the theoretical solution will depart from the empirical reality. Thus most textbooks describe issues of policy formulation for the mix element as if one were starting with a clean sheet of paper and had complete freedom of choice. But throughout this book we have tried to bear in mind that most businesses are already in being, are part of existing industry/market structures and enjoy established and continuing relationships with both suppliers and customers. Only occasionally do new organisations come into being to introduce a new product into the market and rarely will such an occurrence have much impact upon the prevailing industry/market structure. Even less often will a new market be created.

It follows then that many distribution decisions will be heavily influenced and proscribed by current relationships and commitments. Salient among these will be the existing and accepted channel structures and a basic policy decision will be whether to 'push' or 'pull' the product through a channel. Luck and Ferrell (1979, p. 188) recognise the importance of the decision when they comment:

A fundamental strategic decision will be whether to pull the product through the channel by concentrating on final purchasers or whether to push it through by gaining the cooperation of middlemen. A decision to push or to pull the product will determine whether to aim messages or where to send sales people.

Of course push and pull are not mutually exclusive alternatives, as elements of both are required in almost every buying/selling situation. Reverting to the simple hierarchy of effects models discussed in Chapter 9, it is clear that awareness/interest must precede desire and action. As a working generalisation impersonal means of communication (essentially advertising) will be most cost-effective in creating initial awareness and interest while personal communication (essentially salesmanship) will be most effective in translating interest into desire and action. The reason that this should be so is that as a prospect moves through the stages their interest will prompt questions particular to their own state of knowledge and precise needs, all of which cannot be anticipated or covered by impersonal sources unless they assume encyclopedic proportions. By contrast the salesman will be able to respond directly to questions and so reduce the uncertainties experienced by persons contemplating a new or unfamiliar purchase. In addition, the salesman can reinforce the prospect's own reasons for considering purchase and so overcome real or imagined obstacles to purchase. Clearly then, it is a matter of emphasis and the producer's decision will hinge upon their perception of where the leverage exists in the channel vis-à-vis their own resources and bargaining power.

Where the producer wishes or has to use the services of an intermediary, then both the intermediary and the final customer may be the object of promotional activity, but the intermediary will become the primary customer and the object of the direct selling effort. Further, the distinction and emphasis between push and pull will tend to turn on whether the intermediary is willing to work with the producer or has to be 'coerced' to do so. I use the word 'coerced' advisedly because the producer may be able to buy cooperation through incentives to distributors (a 'push' tactic), but there will be circumstances where such efforts will be matched by competitors and the producer will have no option but to see if they can exert pressure on (coerce) the intermediary by developing a franchise with the ultimate consumer. Given that use of an intermediary has excluded personal selling by the producer to the ultimate customer by definition it is obvious that development of such a franchise will depend upon impersonal 'selling' or advertising/promotion – a 'pull' approach.

Many authors imply that there are basic differences between consumer and industrial products when developing distribution/promotion strategies and deciding whether to push or pull the product through the channel. I am not of this opinion as there are as many examples of industrial goods producers having to stimulate primary demand amongst end users in order to get the intermediaries to carry their line (see, e.g., Corey, 1956) or to incorporate it in their own product as there are consumer goods examples. The decision criteria and the principles are the same.

As intermediaries occupy such an important link in the chain between production and consumption, and because they are likely to be the focus of the producer's personal selling effort when he uses them, it will help to round out this chapter if we look briefly at the sales function here while leaving the subject of promotion to the next chapter. First, however, it will be useful to define and describe the concept of vertical marketing systems (VMSs) as a possible response to the conflict and control issues which figure so large in setting distribution policy.

VERTICAL MARKETING SYSTEMS

Up to this point, the discussion of distribution channels has conformed with the traditional view that members of such channels are autonomous and independent organisations which are pursuing their own individual objectives. Where these objectives are not congruent there is the potential for conflict and, to try and avoid this, the channel members with the greatest leverage will seek to superimpose their goals over other members and assume control of the channel. Thus, as we have seen, conflict and control are major issues in select-

ing a distribution policy. Further, and implicit in the word 'superimpose', there has been the expectation that channel conflict will be resolved by competition rather than cooperation.

In many cases competition between channel members leads to inefficiencies and lost profit opportunities. To avoid this, an alternative, more cooperative, form of organisation has begun to emerge in recent years and has been designated the vertical marketing system (VMS). According to the Westburn *Dictionary of Marketing* (2002), a VMS is 'A marketing channel which has achieved some degree of vertical integration involving some central control of operational practices and programmes.' Nylen (1990) elaborates on this definition, by suggesting that VMSs differ from conventional channels in four important respects:

1. VMSs use centrally prepared marketing programmes
2. Whether or not the members of a VMS are independent of each other their activities are directed by this central programme
3. In a VMS, marketing functions are assigned to units on the basis of efficiency and effectiveness rather than on the basis of traditional roles and precedent
4. The members in a VMS accept closer control than is usual in a conventional channel, with the result that VMSs tend to be more stable.

Following the publication of a paper by Bert C. McCammon Jr (1970) it has been customary to recognise three main types of VMS – administered, contractual and corporate. The difference between the three kinds of system is determined primarily by the means used to exercise control over the members. In an administered system a channel leader (sometimes termed the channel captain) has sufficient power to persuade the other members of the benefit of cooperation. In order to enjoy this power the leader will normally be the organisation that enjoys the strongest customer franchise. For most food products this now means the major multiples will set the lead, although major brands like P&G, Lever Bros, Heinz etc. will be able to moderate this power and are likely to give the lead in the channels which involve the smaller retailer chains and independents. Either way the leader of an administered VMS will be expected to spell out the terms of trade within the channel (discounts, allowances, trading areas etc.) in order to provide the incentives necessary to keep the channel intact.

The second type of VMS is the contractual system in which the relationships between members tend to be more formalised and spelt out in official contracts. Three main kinds of contractual VMS may be distinguished – retail cooperatives, wholesale cooperatives and franchises. Retail cooperatives occur when independent retailers take the initiative to band together and set up their own wholesaling intermediary. Conversely wholesaler cooperatives occur when smaller wholesalers band together to secure the benefits of bulk buying power through pooled purchases as well as the benefits of professional advice, joint branding and advertising etc. commonly associated with both kinds of cooperative.

Franchises occur where the owners of products or services license others to wholesale or retail them under the franchiser's name in exchange for the payment of a fee. Car dealerships, fast food outlets and soft drinks like Coca-Cola are probably the best known example. Franchises also depend upon a contractual relationship, but differ from retail and wholesale cooperatives which are forms of backward integration by intermediaries whereas franchises are cases of forward integration by producers.

Finally, corporate VMSs exist where a firm integrates vertically, either backwards or forwards, and so becomes responsible for the product/ service from its initial conceptualisation/production right through to its consumption and after-sales service.

Nylen (1990) summarises the advantages and disadvantages of VMSs as follows:

- *Advantages:*
  - Distribution economies
  - Marketing control
  - Stability, reduction of uncertainty
- *Disadvantages:*
  - Loss of incentive
  - Investment requirements
  - Inflexibility.

Nylen continues to suggest that the choice between VMS and conventional systems depends largely on the answers to six questions.

1. What level of power does the firm have?
2. What is the potential for economies?
3. How much marketing cooperation is needed?
4. Are appropriate channel members available?
5. Is there potential for competitive differentiation through the channel system?
6. Is there a competitive threat from integrated systems?

The growth of interest in VMSs is a reflection of the increased strategic emphasis given to channels of distribution during the 1990s. In turn this has seen the growing emphasis on relationships and networks and the partnerships and strategic alliances associated with them.

Clearly, the answers to these questions (like so many in marketing) will call for both formal analysis and the exercise of judgement.

PERSONAL SELLING

In many situations deciding what to exclude or ignore is even more difficult than deciding what to include and recognise. So it is with the subject of personal selling. Repeated reference to the present needs of the organisation and the exhortation to practise 3-in-1 marketing can leave no doubt as to the importance of the sales function and yet it is consigned here to only a section within a chapter. In part such a decision is justified on the grounds that the basic objective of selling is to exercise personal influence over buying behaviour and the latter subject was treated more fully in Chapter 9; in part it is because the goals of personal selling are the same as for other forms of promotion which will be treated at greater length in Chapter 20. Overriding both these considerations, however, is my own belief that marketing is selling and thus the subject of the whole book.

This latter view is not entirely a popular one because there is a great deal of truth in the cynic's view that the term 'marketing' was coined to avoid the undesirable connotations which have built up around the term 'selling'. These latter are reflected in the stereotype which Gaedeke and Tootelian (1983) report from a survey of business students taking a first marketing course in response to the question 'What do you associate with the word "salesman"?' In rank order the ten most popular replies were: (1) pushy; (2) fast talker; (3) aggressive; (4) commission; (5) money; (6) dishonest; (7) helpful; (8) persistent; (9) cars; (10) well dressed. In addition many exponents of marketing see it as a much extended and more sophisticated function than selling, and there can be no denying this if we consider the scope of a modern marketing book or course compared with a modern book on the sales function. On the other hand if you look at a book on selling written before or immediately after the Second World War you will likely find that it deals with many of the issues of customer identification and motivation which are seen now as the province of marketing not selling. It is also as well to remember that if you go back that far you will find little or nothing on corporate planning and strategy and it is planning and strategy which are considered central to the marketing function. In other words there is good reason to believe that if we hadn't changed the name the selling 'product' would now bear a remarkable resemblance to the 'marketing' product in its composition and performance, against which must be set the possibility that the change of name was essential to gain the penetration and acceptance which 'marketing' now enjoys. Whatever the reasons there can be little doubt that personal selling is now regarded as a sub-function of marketing and the great majority of writing and thinking about it is concerned with the tactical use and management of personal selling rather than regarding it as a major strategic weapon.

While few people would deny the effectiveness of personal selling in any of its traditional functions – identifying and locating potential customers, establishing contact, determining precise needs and presenting the product so that it will be seen to meet these, handling objections, closing the sale and providing after-sales service – the real and apparent importance of the function has declined for several reasons. First, personal selling is labour-intensive and time-consuming and so represents a significant on-cost. Accordingly, as markets have grown in size and numbers, producers have looked for economies in selling cost in exactly the same way as they have pursued economies in distribution. Indeed the major economy in distribution contained in Hollander's (1960) simple formula is the economy in the number of personal contact points reinforced by the specialisation of the various channel interme-

diaries. Second, several of the salesmen's functions can now be performed more efficiently and cost-effectively by other means – particularly marketing research to establish market size and characteristics, and advertising to create awareness and customer identification as well as to provide basic information on product characteristics, price and availability. Third, there is a tendency to think of selling as being performed solely by manufacturers and to forget that channel intermediaries – distributors, agents, wholesalers, retailers etc., also perform personal selling functions and must take into account exactly the same factors as the manufacturer's sales force:

- Definition of sales territories
- Setting sales targets/quotas
- Determination of sales call frequencies by customer type – new prospects, established accounts
- Interface with promotion
- Development of a compensation plan
- Evaluation of selling effectiveness.

Thus a great deal more personal influence or selling is involved in moving products from producers to consumers than immediately meets the eye.

SALES AND DISTRIBUTION EFFORT THROUGH THE PRODUCT LIFE-CYCLE

Decisions as to the most appropriate sales and distribution strategy at different stages in a product's life-cycle will be heavily influenced by the same considerations which we discussed in looking at the product variable, particularly at the launch stage. Clearly if we have a radically new product a great deal will depend upon our expectations of the resistance it might encounter and the degree of protection we enjoy from direct competition. Where the degree of protection is high, a selective and controlled distribution effort is likely to have most appeal, as by restricting supply the producer will limit their own risk exposure, i.e. through restricting investment in production and marketing activities. In addition, a selective approach will enable them to focus their attention on those prospects with the greatest interest/need for the product which will be of particular value where the product is complex and requires considerable learning in use by the buyer and/or where the product is of a kind where additional product development is expected to be necessary based upon early usage experience (see, for example, the textile machinery case histories in *Market Development*, Baker, 1983). Finally, by restricting supply the seller will be able to secure higher prices and so maximise margins.

On the other hand, where a new product is felt to have only limited advantages over its competitors and/or its features can easily be copied, then the seller will usually wish to secure the widest possible distribution to reach the target market(s) as quickly as possible. To achieve this it will be necessary to offer intermediaries direct incentives (discounts) for stocking the product as well as to persuade the intermediary that one is investing in advertising and promotion to ultimate consumers to stimulate awareness and interest and help pull the product through the channel. In the case of many branded consumer products, the manufacturer will be forced or will wish to limit the geographical availability of a product:

- to limit the launch risk
- because of finite marketing resources
- because concentration of effort is likely to result in deeper penetration
- because a launch confined to a particular geographical market may be regarded as a trial run and enable them to iron out any bugs in the product or its marketing strategy/plan
- because documented success in the market will prove a powerful argument for gaining dealer and consumer acceptance in other geographical areas.

Once a product has achieved recognition and acceptance then sales will take off, but, as we noted earlier, this will be as much a function of the bandwagon (increased supply) effect as of the contagion (increased demand) effect. Indeed the ultimate constraint upon the volume of sales must be the volume of production and it is likely that manufacturing and physical distribution will be seen as key strategic functions by corporate management while selling and promotion will operate in support of them. To achieve this end many producers, who may well have marketed

direct during the launch phase, will want to work through intermediaries to ensure the widest possible distribution of their product. Given that the market opportunity will now be apparent to almost everybody, there should be no shortage of intermediaries willing to handle the product and the important decision is to select those who offer most synergy to the manufacturer.

With the onset of maturity the major concern must be to maintain the maximum availability of the product. However, by this stage of the PLC, one will have been able to make informed judgements about both the attractiveness of different market segments as well as the effectiveness and efficiency of different channels in reaching them, and may well want to phase out some of the markets and intermediaries. Also, while distribution will remain an important function, familiarity with the product is likely to lead the manufacturer to give more emphasis to product improvement and advertising and promotion to maintain the interest of both final users and intermediaries.

Much the same approach will also apply to the decline stage, where the manufacturer is seeking to make a phased withdrawal at minimum risk and cost to themselves and with the least inconvenience to users and distributors. Of particular importance at this stage is the manufacturer's policy on the provision of spare parts and maintenance, both of which will be an integral part of their distribution effort.

Ohmae (1983, p. 256) provides a compelling example of how many Japanese companies have varied their distribution policy over the product life-cycle in order to penetrate and then dominate markets:

> In the early stages of such a strategy, (penetration) the company in question still needs to achieve price competitiveness; hence, securing the economies of scale is likely to take precedence over building brand awareness. For this reason, such a company will be prepared to play the role of OEM (original equipment manufacturer) and rely parasitically on distributor sales rather than waste its resources prematurely on international marketing and sales. This enables it to gain, as quickly as possible, the volume base needed to generate manufacturing profits and thus become a recognised global competitor although not yet a completely functional company. Once it has attained

the required economies of scale, such a company will gradually terminate its OEM supplier role and distributor arrangements and shift to establishing its own brand and its own distribution network.

Examples of companies which have followed this strategy include Honda, Seiko, Sharp, Casio, Sony, Hitachi, Nikon and Yamaha, to mention but a few.

Chapter summary

In this chapter we have seen that while distribution policy and decisions may lack the glamour and visibility of some other elements of the marketing mix nonetheless they are of central importance to marketing strategy and management. In part this importance is due to the fact that between 30% and 50% of the total cost of manufactured goods is accounted for by the distributive function. But even more important is the fact that it is the distribution channel which acts as the link between producer and user. However, while physical distribution has successfully overcome the spatial separation of manufacturer and consumer the development of marketing may be largely attributed to the failure of distribution channels to overcome the psychological separation of the parties.

To overcome the physical separation of producer and user a variety of intermed-iaries may be involved and, while many critics question the value added by them, it seems clear that such intermediaries will only prevail when they are more cost-effective than direct links. However, the use of and dependence upon intermediaries frequently faces the producer with a need to trade-off the cost savings which may be possible with the loss of control which may accompany them. Accordingly, the choice of distribution channel will call for a careful evaluation of the environment, of product and market characteristics and the company's strengths and weaknesses leading to the selection of either an undifferentiated, differentiated or concentrated strategy. Similarly the producer will have to decide whether to work closely with distributors and 'push' the product to the consumer or, alternatively, seek to temper the influence of the intermediary by develop-ing a franchise with the end-user which will 'pull' the product through the channel.

The discussion of distribution led naturally to a review of the role of personal selling. In part the inclusion of this topic in a chapter on distribution was prompted by the view that the greater part of personal selling is done by distributors rather than manufacturers. However, it was also suggested that the strategic aspects of selling are inextricably a part of marketing, and so pervade the book as a whole, while selling itself is essentially a tactical activity most closely associated with distribution policy.

To conclude, the chapter has examined the most appropriate sales and distribution strategies at different stages in the product's life-cycle. In the next chapter our attention will turn to issues of promotion policy and management.

Recommended reading

Coughlan, A. T., Anderson, E., Stern, L. W. and El-Ansary, A. I. (2006) *Marketing Channels* (7th edn). Upper Saddle River, NJ: Prentice Hall.

Ennis, S. (1995) Channel management, in M. J. Baker (ed.) *Marketing: Theory and Practice* (3rd edn). Basingstoke: Macmillan – now Palgrave Macmillan.

Rosenbloom, B. (1999) Channels of distribution, in M. J. Baker (ed.) *Encyclopedia of Marketing*. London: International Thomson Business Press.

Rosenbloom, B. (2003) *Marketing Channels: A Management View* (7th edn). Mason, OH: South Western College Publishing.

REFERENCES

Alderson, W. (1954) Factors governing the development of marketing channels, in R. M. Clewett, *Marketing Channels for Manufactured Products*. Homewood, IL: Irwin.

Baker, M. J. (1980–1) Maxims for marketing in the eighties, *Advertising*, **66**(winter).

Baker, M. J. (1983) *Market Development*. Harmondsworth: Penguin.

Baker, M. J. (1998) *The Dictionary of Marketing and Advertising*. London: Macmillan – now Palgrave Macmillan.

Brady, D. L. (1978) *An Analysis of Factors Affecting the Methods of Exporting Used by Small Manufacturing Firms*. University of Alabama, pp. 39–41

Bucklin, L. P. (1965) Postponement speculation and the structure of distribution channels, *Journal of Marketing Research*, **2**(1).

Bucklin, L. P. (1966) *A Theory of Distribution Channel Structure*. University of California: Institute of Business and Economic Research.

Corey, E. R. (1956) *The Development of Markets for New Materials*. Boston, MA: Harvard University Press.

Dictionary of Marketing (2002) Helensburgh: Westburn Publishers.

Drucker, P. (1962) The economy's dark continent, *Fortune*, (April).

Evans, J. R. and Berman, B. (1982) *Marketing*. New York: Macmillan.

Gaedeke, R. M. and Tootelian, D. (1983) *Marketing: Principles and Applications*. St Paul, MN: West Publishing.

Guirdham, M. (1972) *Marketing: The Management of Distribution Channels*. Oxford: Pergamon Press, p. ix.

Hollander, S. C. (1960) The wheel of retailing, *Journal of Marketing*, **25**(July): 37–42.

Lambert, D. M. (1978) *The Distribution Channels Decision*. New York: The National Association of Accountants.

Luck, P. J. and Ferrell, O. C. (1979) *Marketing Strategy and Plans*. Englewood Cliffs, NJ: Prentice Hall.

McCammon, B. C. Jr (1970) Perspectives for distribution programming, in L. P. Bucklin (ed.) *Vertical Marketing Systems*. Glenview, IL: Scott, Foresman.

McNair, M. P. (1958) Significant trends and developments in the postwar period, in A. B. Smith (ed.) *Competitive Distribution in a Free, High-level Economy and its Implications for the University*. Pittsburgh, PA: University of Pittsburgh Press.

Mallen, B. (1973) Functional spin-off: a key to anticipating change in distribution structure, *Journal of Marketing*, **37**(3).

Michaelidou, N. (2005) Characteristics of marketing channels: a theoretical framework, *The Marketing Review*, **5**(1).

Nylen, D. W. (1990) *Marketing Decision-making Handbook*. Englewood Cliffs, NJ: Prentice Hall.

Ohmae, K. (1983) *The Mind of the Strategist*. Harmondsworth: Penguin.

Rosenbloom, B. (1999) Channel management, in M. J. Baker (ed.) *Encyclopedia of Marketing*. London: International Thomson Business Press, pp. 407–19.

Stern, L. W. (1965) Channel control and interorganisation management, in P. D. Bennett (ed.) *Economic Development*. Chicago, IL: American Marketing Association.

Promotion policy and management

Don't hide your light under a bushel.   SERMON ON THE MOUNT

After reading Chapter 19 you will be able to:

✔ Describe the nature of the communication process.

✔ Explain how advertising appears to work in consumer decision-making and distinguish between high- and low-involvement buying situations.

✔ Justify the view that the primary goal of advertising is to influence attitudes and suggest alternative strategies for achieving this.

✔ Identify possible advertising objectives.

✔ Discuss the issues involved in developing a promotional strategy.

✔ Describe and evaluate five basic approaches to setting the advertising budget.

✔ Suggest methods for measuring advertising effectiveness.

INTRODUCTION

In Chapter 18 we noted that considerable suspicion has long existed about the value added by sales and distribution activities. In the case of promotional activities, and particularly mass-media advertising, the suspicion and criticism is even more acute. Taken together sales, distribution and promotion are frequently regarded as unnecessary and cost-creating functions which contribute little or nothing to consumer satisfaction – a viewpoint neatly encapsulated in Ralph Waldo Emerson's frequently quoted assertion that:

> If a man build a better mousetrap then, even though he live in a wood, the world will beat a path to his door.

Emerson was wrong. He was wrong because he did not appreciate that 'better' is a comparative statement and can only possess meaning for the consumer in terms of their current knowledge and expectations. Only if the whole population satisfied the assumptions on which the theory of perfect competition rests would 'the world' possess a homogeneous demand and so perceive the mousetrap as better. The mere existence of a marketing function is testimony that this is not the case. But Emerson was even more wrong in his assumption that the act of creation of a better product would in and of itself result in a demand for it. Awareness of the existence of a product and knowledge of its price, performance and availability are all necessary prerequisites for the creation of demand, and awareness and knowledge require the communication of information to bring them into existence. There is also the important fact that where physical and objective differentiation between goods is small or non-existent – as we saw in Chapters 9 and 13 when discussing how buyers choose – subjective factors such as image may become determinant. A major role of advertising is to create and develop such subjective associations.

As we saw in Chapter 18, physical availability and personal selling are both effective means of communicating the existence of products, but, in that they depend upon the potential consumer being exposed to the product stimulus, e.g. by seeing it at a trade exhibition or in a shop window, or a face-to-face contact with a salesman, they tend to be limited in coverage and expensive to achieve. By contrast, impersonal channels of communication using various broadcast and print media have almost universal coverage and on a cost per contact/exposure basis are very inexpensive to use.

As the creation of awareness and the dissemination of information are essential components of effective demand it would seem sensible to use the most efficient and cost-effective means of achieving this. In this chapter we shall seek to show that almost invariably this will require the use of indirect and impersonal sources of communication to some extent. In recent years, however, a new channel of communication has evolved that has had a major impact on the role of impersonal sources of communication and greatly increased the potential for more direct and personal communication. This new channel is the internet.

Some reference to the role of communication was made in Chapter 9 when discussing models of buyer behaviour, but before turning to examine the managerial implications, it will be helpful to summarise some of the key ideas that may be derived from the extensive body of theory related to communication which have immediate application to the practice of promotion in marketing. Specifically, it will be helpful to review:

1. The nature of the communication process
2. Further implications of selectivity in perception, attention and retention
3. The nature of memory span and 'forgetting'.

Based upon the insights from such a review, it becomes possible to identify realistic communication objectives and the optimum promotional mix for achieving them. Clearly, selecting an optimum mix requires careful consideration of the cost and effectiveness of the promotion and we shall examine both the question of setting a promotional budget and the pre-testing and post-testing of communication to establish this. First, however, it will be useful to provide some definitions of key terms.

THE NATURE OF THE COMMUNICATION PROCESS

This topic is given extensive coverage in Chapter 15 of *Marketing* (Baker, 2006) and the reader should refer to this for a survey of the theoretical under-pinning of marketing communications.

In his book, Wilbur Schramm (1955) defines communication as 'the process of establishing a commonness or oneness of thought between a sender and a receiver'. Thus the simplest model of the communications process would consist of only three elements:

Sender → Message → Receiver
(Source   Signal   Destination)

However, until thought transference becomes possible such a model is inadequate, for it ignores the necessity to translate ideas into symbols so that they can be transmitted. To allow for this we must introduce encoding and decoding elements into the model, which will then appear as:

Sender → Encoder → Message → Decoder → Receiver

As Schramm points out, the model can accommodate all types of communication, so that in the case of electronic communication the encoder becomes a transmitting device – microphone, teletype etc. – and the decoder a receiver–radio or television set, telephone etc. In the case of direct personal (face-to-face) communication, then one person is both source and encoder while the other is decoder and destination and the signal is language. It follows that if an exchange of meaning is to take place, then both source and destination must be tuned in to each other and share the same language. Put another way, there must be an overlap in the field of experience of source and destination (Figure 19.1).

We must also recognise that all communication is intended to have an effect and introduce the notion of feedback into our model of communicat-ion, for it is through feedback that the source learns how its signals are being interpreted. In personal communication feedback is often instantaneous through verbal acknowledgement or gesture, but in impersonal communication through the mass media it may have to be inferred from other indic-ators, e.g. audience size, circulation, readership or monitored by sampling opinion.

The final element in Schramm's model is the channel or, more correctly, channels, for messages are rarely transmitted through a single channel. Thus in personal communications it is not merely the words which convey the message but the intonation of our voice and the gestures which accompany them. Similarly, in the print media we lend emphasis by italicising keywords, by use of different typefaces, underlining etc.

The marketer's version of Schramm's model employs slightly different terminology, but contains the following elements (Shannon and Weaver, 1962):

Who...   *says what...*   *how...*   *to whom...*
Communicator   *Message*   *Channel*   *Audience*

with what effect...
Feedback

Kotler (1972) defines these basic elements as follows:

- *Communicator:* the sender or source of the message
- *Message:* the set of meanings being sent and/or received by the audience
- *Channels:* the ways in which the message can be carried or delivered to the audience
- *Audience:* the receiver or destination of the message.

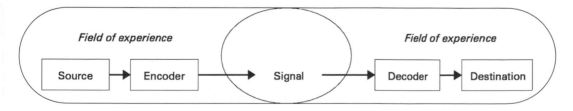

FIGURE 19.1 Overlap in the field of experience of source and destination
Source: Schramm, W. (1955) *The Process and Effects of Mass Communication*. Urbana, IL: University of Illinois Press

From his model, Schramm derives four basic 'conditions of success in communication … which must be fulfilled if the message is to arouse its intended response'. These are:

1. The message must be so designed and delivered as to gain the attention of the intended destination.
2. The message must employ signs which refer to experience common to source and destination, so as to 'get the meaning across'.
3. The message must arouse personality needs in the destination and suggest some ways to meet those needs.
4. The message must suggest a way to meet those needs which is appropriate to the group situation in which the destination finds himself at the time when he is moved to make the desired response.

Consideration of these four requirements should strike a receptive chord in the memory of the reader who is methodically working their way through the book, for they echo closely points discussed in Chapter 9 concerning hierarchy of effects models in consumer behaviour. In fact Schramm's four conditions are similar to Strong's basic AIDA model – awareness, interest, desire and action. It will be useful, therefore, to recapitulate on this earlier discussion, but specifically in the context of marketing communications.

While the basic model of communication was developed by Wilbur Schramm in 1955, the nature and importance of marketing communications has changed significantly in recent years. One reason underlying this change is that increasingly marketing communications have emerged as the only sustainable long-term means of differentiating between products and services in the marketplace. In parallel with the increased importance attached to marketing, communications

> has moved our thinking way beyond the simple distinctions between advertising, public relations, sales promotions and similar categorisations of the various tools available to us. Not only are the tools themselves significantly enhanced with the availability of new and emergent forms of media, associating devices such as product placement and sponsorship, but their application has changed with

the development of the internet, electronic point of sale, virtual advertising and ambient media. (Yeshin, 1998, p. 11)

In light of these changes, there is increasing emphasis being given to integrated marketing communications or what formerly used to be identified as the promotional mix.

Integrated marketing communications (IMC) has been defined by the American Association of Advertising Agencies as:

> A concept of marketing communications planning that recognises the added value of a comprehensive plan that evaluates the strategic roles of a variety of communications disciplines and combines them to provide clarity, consistency and maximum communications impact through the seamless integration of discrete messages.

A major factor underlying the growing interest in IMC is that while distinctions between different promotional and communication tools may be important to the sender, they are of comparatively little relevance to the receiver or consumer, who is more concerned with the content of the message than its source or provenance. It represents, therefore, a customer-driven market orientation which is central to the marketing concept. Among the factors behind this changed approach Yeshin cites information overload, the growth of global marketing, the growing importance of visual or non-verbal communication as television viewers can access foreign-language programmes in cable TV, and the speed of information access. As a result of these trends, attitudes towards the conventional promotional mix have changed in favour of IMC. Yeshin cites the following as driving forces behind this growth of interest:

> Value for money; increasing client sophistication; disillusionment with advertising; disillusionment with agencies; power shifts towards retailers; green issues.

One of the best-known textbooks in the USA dealing with 'promotion' as the fourth P of the marketing mix appeared in its third edition (2003) with the title *Advertising and Integrated Brand Promotion*. In the Preface to the fourth edition, the authors (O'Guinn et al., 2006) comment:

Some people questioned that title: 'Isn't it supposed to be Advertising and Integrated *Marketing Communication*?' We were convinced then that advertisers and agencies alike were focused on the brand and integrated *brand promotion* (IBP), and that integrated marketing communication (IMC) was really a thing of the past, and probably the wrong term in the first place. Our perspective proved to be correct. Advertising and promotion is *all* about the brand, and industry is pursuing brand awareness and competitive advantage with an ever-expanding array of advertising and promotion brand building techniques.

Like all sellers, the authors are seeking to differentiate themselves from their competitors in suggesting that IBP has replaced the 'fad' for IMC. Our view is that both perspectives deserve recognition. Borden's original conceptualisation of the marketing mix included branding, personal selling, advertising, promotions and packaging, and argued for their integration, so neither IMC or IBP is a novel concept. What is different is that due to the difficulty of maintaining a competitive advantage based on physical or objective factors, and the growth of service industries, emphasis on the subjective and emotional factors has grown in importance. As O'Guinn et al. note, heavy users of advertising and promotion like Procter & Gamble identify their core competitive capability as 'branding'.

The British Direct Marketing Association (BDMA) defines direct marketing as 'An interactive system of marketing which uses one or more advertising media to effect a measurable response and/or transaction at any location.' While direct marketing principles have changed comparatively little since they were first developed by mail order companies in the nineteenth century, the need to position oneself carefully against competitors and target specific customers and customer groups has greatly increased interest in the medium. However, it is the electronics revolution and developments in computer hardware and software which have fully released the potential of direct marketing.

Yeshin (1998) cites a number of fundamental changes in both consumer attitudes and behaviours which have contributed to the growth of direct marketing. These may be summarised as:

1. The desire for experimentation

2. Convenience of shopping at new kinds of outlets
3. The focus on the home
4. Societal change – more women in employment, changes in the composition of the family, demographic change etc.
5. The progressive growth of the service sector and a recognition that services, particularly financial services, do not require expensive retail outlets
6. The increasing costs of reaching fragmented audiences
7. An increasing ability to target specific consumers and segment markets more effectively
8. The growth of a cashless society
9. Improvements in information technology.

While direct marketing often lacks the ability to create and develop brand images in the way that media advertising can, it possesses significant advantages over the scatter gun nature of most advertising media. Yeshin summarises some of these advantages as:

1. Targeting
2. Relationship-building with individuals
3. Interactivity
4. The ability to motivate specific responses
5. The creation of detailed databases containing transactional information
6. Measurement of effectiveness leading to greater predictability of response
7. Control over level of investment and growth
8. Testing and experimentation.

HOW DOES ADVERTISING WORK?

The question of how advertising works is perhaps of less significance to the line manager than are the questions what can advertising do and how much will it cost to do it? That said, some understanding of what may be taking place in the 'black box' is necessary if the line executive is to judge when or when not to use advertising, and also to judge the recommendations of the advertising specialist. However, it must be admitted immediately that theoretical explanations of how advertising works are by no means complete or universally accepted. Further, in common with many other areas of research in marketing, there have been relatively few significant additions to our knowledge in the past 30–35 years, although there has been considerable refinement of concepts and ideas borrowed from other behavioural sciences. Thus, in seeking to provide some answers to our question, it is difficult to better the explanation provided by T. Joyce of the British Market Research Bureau published as long ago as 1967, and this source will provide the framework for the discussion here (see also *Marketing*, Baker, 2006). At the same time, reference will be made to an article by Smith and Swinyard (1982), which contains a comprehensive review of more recent research and proposes an 'integrated information response model' which seeks to synthesise concepts from a number of areas.

In a nutshell, the nature of the problem and the basis for controversy centres upon the question of whether attitudes cause or change behaviour or whether behaviour results in the formation of attitudes. Clearly, if attitude formation or change always precedes behaviour, this will be the primary focus for promotional activity. Conversely, if attitudes develop out of experience, they will be of secondary importance and the primary effort will be concentrated on encouraging and reinforcing behaviour favourable to one's product (purchase and consumption).

Hierarchical models of the kind discussed in Chapter 9 rest upon the assumption that each step is a necessary (but not sufficient) antecedent of the following step. In that liking and preference are attitudinal states, such models assume that attitudes precede purchase, but much of the evidence seems to point to the opposite conclusion. Thus Smith and Swinyard cite a number of studies of the correlation between attitudes and behaviour that indicate scores between 0.00 and 0.30, leading to the conclusion that it is more likely attitudes will not be related to actual behaviour than that they will!

As an alternative to the traditional learning model – cognition → affect → conation, Krugman (1965) developed the so-called 'low-involvement model', which posits the sequence cognition → conation → affect. According to Krugman, advertising for trivial products is of so little interest to consumers that they do not become actively involved in processing the information, which over time and through constant repetition may well

change the receiver's cognition without awareness. Accordingly, when faced with a purchase situation, the consumer may select a product without having formed any specific attitude towards it. Only after consumption and actual experience will attitudes be formed. Clearly, such a model (which has been empirically validated) provides powerful support for critics of advertising like Vance Packard (1957), who would argue that advertisers are indeed hidden persuaders who condition consumers to act without conscious evaluation of their actions. In defence, one might point out that the effect only applies to 'trivial' products that do not merit a high level of involvement and that in any event the purchase does not represent commitment but only a trial with limited risk to the consumer. In so far that learning from direct experience is likely to give rise to much more strongly held beliefs than will learning from indirect experience, i.e. from the claims of advertisers, one might also argue that if advertising can encourage people to try products without conscious pre-purchase evaluation and attitude formation one runs a very real risk that if the product does not live up to expectations a trial will lead to rejection and that it will be very difficult to persuade the consumer to change this belief subsequently by further advertising.

On balance, however, the low-involvement model would not seem to require us to reject the more traditional hierarchical models of the awareness → interest → desire → action (cognition → affect → conation) kind. The low-involvement model provides a useful explanation of how advertising seems to work in a particular context, and it is this context – mass consumption convenience goods of low unit value – where most of the advertising expenditure and action is concentrated. That said, advertising also has an extremely important role to play in communicating information about the characteristics, performance and availability of goods which are complex, specialised and of high unit value and, presumably, may be classified as high involvement. In these cases logic and perceived risk both require the prospective customer to develop attitudes and beliefs prior to trial and possible adoption. Further, in the case of both low- and high-involvement situations, much advertising is designed to reinforce attitudes, beliefs and behaviour rather than to change them.

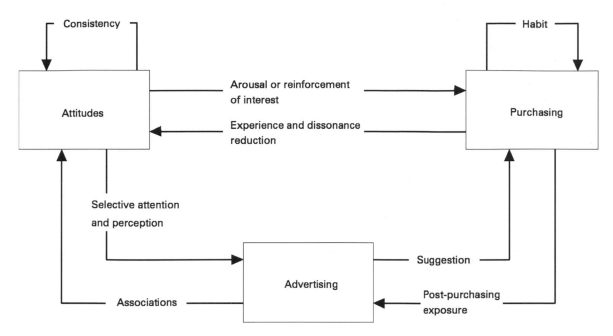

FIGURE 19.2 How advertising may work

Source: Joyce, T. (1967) *What Do We know about How Advertising Works?* London: J. Walter Thompson Company Ltd

In the light of these arguments, the model proposed by Joyce appears to be as good a working representation of the way advertising works as it was in 1967 and it is reproduced here as Figure 19.2, together with Joyce's own explanation of its construction and interpretation.

We might take as our starting-point a simple model of advertising consisting just of two arrows joining the three boxes – an arrow from 'advertising' to 'attitudes' showing that advertising changes or reinforces attitudes by investing the product with favourable associations, and an arrow from 'attitudes' to 'purchasing' showing that favourable attitudes lead to interest in the product being aroused when there is an opportunity to buy it or to a reinforcement of a purchasing habit.

However, it seems that it would also be correct to put in arrows going the other way. Purchasing may influence attitudes, partly as a straightforward reflection of product experience, but partly (perhaps even before the product is consumed) by the drive to reduce dissonance, which leads to favourable attitudes in justification to oneself of the decision. Equally, the impact of advertising on the consumer is very much affected by attitudes in the sense of

preconceptions: both attention and perception are selective and this selectivity is affected by attitudes.

It also appears legitimate to put in arrows linking advertising and purchasing directly. We have considered the possibility that advertising may partly work by suggestion, a process in which attitudes need not necessarily function as an intermediary. Also there is evidence that the fact of having bought a particular product may in some circumstances heighten attention to advertisements for that product, again as a part of the phenomenon of the drive to reduce dissonance.

Finally, it seems appropriate too to introduce two 'loops' in the system. We have considered a certain amount of evidence that there is a drive towards consistency among attitudes even when advertising stimuli and purchasing situations are absent, and we therefore put in a loop around 'attitudes'. Also, we have recognised that much purchasing is habitual and apparently unaffected by advertising or by attitude changes, at any rate below some sort of threshold level. This is represented by a loop around purchasing.

The precise direction of the arrows and the labelling of arrows and boxes is perhaps less important than the general impression conveyed by the diagram, which is surely correct – that the advertising/purchasing system is a rather complex system of interacting variables. The model itself is tentative, but this general conclusion seems unlikely to be overthrown.

From the foregoing discussion it is clear that advertising 'works' in a number of different ways and that one must be careful to define the exact context in which advertising is to be used before one will be able to determine what may be possible. Such analysis should be an integral part of the marketing audit and will give clear indicators as to what constitutes a reasonable advertising objective which, in turn, will determine what budget or appropriation is necessary and how the effectiveness of the advertising effort may be measured.

We agree entirely – advertising works in many different ways. Writing in the *International Journal of Advertising*, Tim Ambler (1998) acknowledges the ongoing debate, and particularly the criticisms of Ehrenberg, but argues that we need a much better understanding of how the human brain works before we will be able to answer the question 'How does advertising work?' That said, Joyce's model identifies the key constructs, their interaction and relationships and so provides a useful framework for thinking about the subject in a strategic way. Those concerned with the development of promotional campaigns per se will obviously need recourse to more specialised advice.

PROMOTION OBJECTIVES

In a number of places we have given considerable support, both implicit and explicit, to the concept of hierarchies in behavioural response and particularly to Maslow's (1943) hierarchy of needs and Lavidge and Steiner's (1961) 'hierarchy of effects'. Despite the fact that such hierarchies are a logical and inevitable consequence of the definitions used in formulating them, as we have seen they have not found universal favour and, as Boyd et al. (1972) point out, they have been criticised on at least two counts. First, in that sales are the ultimate objective of marketing efforts it seems reasonable that critics should be dissatisfied with promotional objectives which emphasise moving prospects up a hierarchy (awareness, recall, interest etc.) without attempting to quantify the end-result sales.

Second, certain behavioural scientists contended that little evidence supported the hierarchy of effects itself that is, learning does not necessarily lead to attitudinal change, nor does attitudinal change lead to behavioural change. Thus, advertising goals formed on the basis of changes in intermediate variables – such as recall or comprehension – may be of questionable value.

With regard to the first criticism, it is only natural that advertisers should want to be able to quantify and measure the sales effect of their advertising investment. It is very doubtful, however, if many advertisers (if any at all) would go to the lengths necessary to establish the possible/probable/likely effect of advertising upon sales. In 1970 Robert Buzzell and I took advantage of a natural experiment in attempting to establish that there is a positive correlation between advertising expenditure and sales. Our findings, which were reported in the *Journal of Advertising Research* were claimed by the editor to constitute the first 'proof' that advertising creates sales, but neither Buzzell nor I would be so foolhardy as to attempt to claim any particular, quantifiable advertising : sales effect.

The circumstances of our natural experiment were that the auto workers' union had taken industrial action against Ford in the USA immediately prior to the annual new-model launch in 1969. In the absence of new models to sell, Ford abstained from advertising and husbanded its budget for use when the strike was settled. Faced with the prospect of a delayed new-model launch by Ford, the other major auto manufacturers cut back their own advertising budgets in order to maintain a reserve for combating Ford when its campaign was mounted. Our analysis clearly showed that the reduction in sales was greater than would have been the case if advertising had no influence on the primary demand for cars (i.e. cars were available [place] with attractive features [product] and competitive prices so it was only the fourth p [promotion] which had been changed). However, while it was possible to distinguish a direct relationship between reduced advertising expenditures and declining sales, it was clear that there was a distinct 'lag' in the effect (lending force to the argument that advertising should be considered an investment like R&D, and capitalised) and it would have been necessary to continue the 'experiment' much longer and then repeat it several times before one would have dared propose a formula to express the advertising : sales effect. Faced with such an 'academic' proposal, any sensible marketing man would tell you not to be a 'damned fool' as the lost sales revenue in establishing a relationship, which everyone implicitly accepts, could hardly be compensated for by the quantification of an effect which would be unlikely to occur again due to changes in both the environment and the other elements of the marketing mix. On these grounds alone we reject the arguments of critics who in attempting to appear pragmatic only reveal almost total insensitivity to the realities of competition and the marketplace.

With regard to the second criticism the outcome has been more productive, for it has resulted in substantial evidence to support the theoretical view. Thus, it has been shown that advertising can influence attitudes and that attitudes predispose people to behave in a particular way from which it is a logical step to propose that attitudinal change may be a surrogate for purchase behaviour (sales) so that setting advertising objectives in terms of attitudinal change is both appropriate and effective. As Boyd et al. (1972) point out:

Attitudes have the operationally desirable quality of being measurable, albeit with difficulty and some lack of precision. Attitudes also have long been the object of investigation by behavioural scientists, and a considerable body of knowledge has resulted from their studies and models. Today's psychologists believe that attitude includes both perceptual and preferential components; i.e. attitude is an inferred construct. When one refers to an attitude he means that a person's past experiences predispose him to respond in certain ways on the basis of certain perceptions. Attitudes, therefore, may be viewed as a variable which links psychological and behavioural components.

Since attitudes reflect perceptions, they inevitably indicate predispositions. Thus, they permit advertising strategists to design advertising inputs which will affect predispositions to respond or behave.

Perhaps even more important than hypothesising the link between attitudes and behaviour, and focusing research upon it, has been the development of a whole battery of powerful techniques for measuring and stimulating both attitudinal and behavioural change. Thus while formal quantification of the precise relationship between advertising and behaviour still eludes us, it has become possible to measure attitudes and attitude change from which behavioural changes can be inferred. In keeping with our earlier assertion that objectives should be quantifiable so that we can measure our progress towards achieving them, it seems entirely reasonable to accept that the primary goal of advertising is to influence attitudinal structures. If this is the case then, as Boyd et al. show, the manager has five broad strategy alternatives:

1. Affect those forces which influence strongly the choice criteria used for evaluating brands belonging to the product class
2. Add characteristic(s) to those considered salient for the product class
3. Increase / decrease the rating for a salient product class characteristic
4. Change perception of the company's brand with regard to some particular salient product characteristic
5. Change perception of competitive brands with regard to some particular salient product characteristic.

Some elaboration of these rather cryptic statements seems called for.

Strategy 1 is most appropriate to those situations where the advertiser is seeking to stimulate demand for the product by increasing its saliency in the minds of potential customers vis-à-vis other competing product classes. In order to do this it is clear that as a minimum the advertiser must have a clear appreciation of the needs of the target market in terms of the choice criteria used to discriminate between the competing products[1] (i.e. the weighting attached to/given to the various product characteristics and benefits discussed earlier in Chapters 14 and 12 respectively). This need profile can then be matched with that of the product and the purpose of the advertising will be to try and increase the saliency of those features in which the product enjoys some advantage over its rivals. In seeking to influence the weighting given to the various choice criteria which consumers use in developing their own scale of preferences it is important to recognise that many products are used in a specific context or as part of an 'event'. It follows that the most effective way of influencing decisions on particular products may well be to link them with the context or event and seek to modify attitudes towards the latter rather than the product which is an ingredient or part of the event.

Strategies 2 and 3 represent the basic alternatives which are available when a mismatch exists between the product and customer profile. Strategy 2 consists of adding a salient characteristic either physically, e.g. auto-focusing in cameras, solar power for calculators, numerical control to a machine tool – or, mentally by emphasising an existing feature of the product not considered salient hitherto, e.g. adults using baby powder. This strategy is particularly appropriate to the mature stage of the life-cycle by which time consumer attitudes to choice criteria will have become well-established.

Strategy 3 involves much the same approach as Strategy 1 in that it seeks to modify the consumer's perception of the saliency of specific product characteristics, i.e. rather than the saliency of the product class itself compared with other product classes. To some extent attempting to alter the saliency of a characteristic is akin to Strategy 2, but it is felt to differ significantly in the sense that Strategy 2 offered a 'new' benefit whereas Strategy 3 is seeking to reorder existing preferences. The latter is much more difficult to do and only likely to succeed where there are marked differences in terms of the characteristic between competing products within the class.

Strategies 4 and 5 are similar to Strategies 2 and 3 except that here the advertiser is not so much concerned with modifying the consumer's perception of the ideal product so that their new perception will shift towards the actual product but rather the reverse, i.e. they will seek to show how and why the actual brand corresponds (or not) to the ideal. Strategy 4 is perhaps the most traditional approach as it often comprises simply extolling the virtues of the manufacturer's brand as the ideal product. By contrast, Strategy 5 has only come into prominence in the increasingly competitive climate of recent years when pointing out the deficiencies of the opposition (knocking copy) has become commonplace.

Boyd et al.'s discussion of promotion objectives focuses upon achieving changes in potential users'

perceptions and attitudes and in doing so it fails to give explicit attention to the problems discussed earlier of actually achieving awareness of one's communication in a very noisy and confined environment. It also fails to recognise that many advertisers are quite happy with the consumer's existing perceptions and attitudes in so far that they favour them and so are concerned with reminding and reinforcing rather than changing these. It would seem therefore that to Boyd et al.'s five strategic objectives we should add three R's:

- Recognition (awareness)
- Reminder
- Reinforcement.

To some extent the creation of awareness is implicit in Boyd et al.'s first strategy as the inference is that one has to bring a new product to the prospect's notice before they can rank order it in their overall scale of preferences. However, the emphasis is upon achieving changes in the rank order rather than the initial recognition which, by implication, might be dismissed as a low-order objective. While it is true that awareness or recognition is but the first rung on the ladder, it is also clear that the great majority of communications go completely unnoticed. With odds of the order of 99 to 1 against recognition, this would seem to be a worthwhile objective in its own right. Establishing recognition also possesses the distinct advantage that it is easy both to define and measure its existence and changes in it and thereby satisfies the ever-present managerial wish to quantify both objectives and their achievement.

Once awareness has been accomplished, learning theory predicates that it will be necessary to repeat the stimulus in order to achieve learning and the creation of habitual behaviour, and that in doing so it will be necessary to reinforce the suitability of the response to the initial stimulus. A great deal of advertising of all types of goods and services is conceived and designed solely with the objective of reminding and reinforcing users in their existing patterns of behaviour and thereby inculcating a natural resistance to change.

Selection of an appropriate promotion objective will depend heavily on all the considerations we have discussed in connection with the other mix elements. Rather than repeat these yet again, we

TABLE 19.1 Advertising objectives

Objectives related to awareness:

- to inform people the product exists
- to gain or regain awareness
- to create or recreate awareness
- to buy awareness
- to create awareness in a specified section of the market.

Objectives related to trial:

- to gain trial
- to tempt people to try the product
- to stimulate trial
- to gain trial among a specified section of the population.

Objectives related to education/informing (distinguished from messages because of their more factual, objective bases):

- to educate people to the use of the product/an additional use of the product
- to educate people to the serving of the product
- to communicate a particular change in the product
- to show the multiple uses of the product
- to announce the variety availability
- to establish the varieties available
- to demonstrate the convenience of the product
- to give factual information about the product
- to show people how to get the best performance out of the product.

Objectives related to attitudes:

- to reinforce the early favourable attitudes
- to make attitudes more favourable to a particular product
- to sustain favourable attitudes
- to improve a particular attitude to the product
- to establish favourable attitudes
- to modify existing attitudes
- to improve existing negative attitudes
- to enhance certain attitudes in the target population.

Objectives related to loyalty:

- to retain loyal customers
- to encourage loyalty
- to keep building loyalty.

Objectives related to reminding:

- to remind people that the product exists.

Objectives related to branding/image building:

- to build an image for the product
- to improve the image of the product
- to establish the product as unique
- to establish the brand and position it in a particular way, for example as warm and friendly
- to retain a product quality image
- to maintain a favourable image of the product or manufacturer
- to create a brand leader in a particular market
- to create an image equal to that of the main competitor
- to establish branding
- to gain general image improvement
- to promote the corporate image and the qualities associated with the company products
- to advertise the brand
- to associate a product with the manufacturing company
- to create the right impression of the company among a particular section of the population
- to position the product for an additional section of the market
- to reassure existing users of the product
- to retain and reassure existing users of the product.

Objectives of conveying a specific message:

- to say that the product has a particular quality
- to establish particular associations with the product
- to convey the idea that the product is 'value for money'
- to get across the idea that the product tastes good
- to support the taste and quality claim for the product
- to convey the idea of a 'modern' product/one which is used by 'modern' people
- to state the advantages of the product compared with the competition
- to get across the idea of a unique product
- to get across the 'newness' of the product
- to say how much people like the product
- to convey a particular theme, for example real fruit
- to create warmth and friendliness for the product
- to emphasise the goodness of the product
- to convey the taste of the product
- to say something of the manufacturer
- to give the consumer a reason for buying the product.

SOURCE: Corkindale, D. and Kennedy, S. (1974) *The Evaluation of Advertising Objectives*. Marketing Communications Research Centre, Cranfield School of Management, Report 10 (November)

would prefer to emphasise the major implications of our model of buyer behaviour, namely that promotion will play a major role in:

1. Creating awareness

2. Conditioning perceptions (of the facts)

3. Suggesting subjective associations and benefits which will prove determinant when there is an apparent objective parity between two or more competing alternatives.

Box 19.1   *Marketing microprocessors: the role of promotion*

Since its inception in July, 1968, Intel has been the leader of microprocessor technology. Its 1998 revenues totalled US$26.3 billion. Intel chips power 90% of all personal computers in the world. The twentieth-century's digital revolution owes itself to microchips.

In the early days, Intel needed to educate the market concerning chips, and was conducting corporate training sessions on how to use the microprocessor. Intel appealed to engineers and their managers by promoting the idea they could speed up the time-to-market by using microprocessors. New and revolutionary products that are ahead of their time need intensive promotion and marketing.

Intel's co-founder Gordon Moore predicted in 1965 that chips would double in power and halve in price every 18–24 months. Moore's observation, now known as Moore's Law, described a trend that has continued and is still remarkably accurate. It is the basis for many planners' performance forecasts. In 26 years the number of transistors on a chip has increased more than 3,200 times, from 2,300 on the Intel 4004 in 1971 to 7.5 million on the thumbnail size Pentium® II processor today.

Intel has differentiated itself in the rapidly changing technological environment by its advertising campaign 'Intel inside', and has staved off competition from Motorola, IBM, and several clone companies. Although users do not see the processors that computers use, the 'Intel inside' labels tell them what is powering their machines. This is a way of increasing consumer awareness of components supplied by original equipment manufacturers and enhances brand loyalty in what is otherwise an engineered commodity market. Today, Intel is worth more than IBM, thanks to its technological and marketing capabilities.

SOURCE: Oburai, P. based on *Time*, 29 December, 1997–5 January, 1998; annual reports and company website, www.intel.com

---

To some extent all promotional activity will be directed to these ends, and the specifying of an explicit objective will rest upon a careful evaluation of each and every situation on its own merits. What is important is that the choice objective be stated clearly and unequivocally, for only by doing so will it become possible to establish realistic budgets and measures for assessing effectiveness.

In concluding this section, in Table 19.1 we present the listing of advertising objectives Corkindale and Kennedy (1974) derived from their extensive research into advertising in the UK in the early 1970s that has not been bettered since.

PUBLICITY

The great attraction of publicity is that it is exposure of an organisation and/or its products in the media *without payment* to the media owner. In a sense then publicity is 'free'. However, most favourable publicity is the direct result of the organisation using public relations – either in-house or bought in – to craft and communicate newsworthy information for use by the various media. At the same time it must be recognised that a major role of public relations is to combat *negative* publicity that may arise as a result of product failure, a lack of response to customer concerns and complaints, exploitative or antisocial behaviour etc. Clearly, to do so calls for commitment to and investment in the activity, so that publicity is rarely 'free' unless it occurs serendipitously due to the media picking up a 'good story'.

Perhaps the main point to make about publicity, both negative and positive, is that the subject has no direct control over it. It is entirely at the discretion of the media to decide what information it wishes to carry and, in the case of both, this will depend very much on what other 'news' is available. In the UK in recent years, the government has come in for considerable criticism for announcing controversial measures and decisions to coincide with major news stories in the hope that they will receive little publicity and so go largely unnoticed by the public. The timing of such releases of information is seen as being heavily influenced by the government's PR advisers.

Because the organisation cannot control negative publicity, it is vital that it has a policy on how to react if this occurs. Denial, or a failure to respond, almost invariably results in an escalation of the story as other media pick it up. Indeed, there are many cases where a quick response to a perceived failure can actually enhance the organisation's reputation, as was the case when Perrier withdrew its product from the market immediately when it was found that some bottles of water had been contaminated. Once the cause had been found and explained, Perrier was reinstated without any apparent loss of market share. The management of publicity is clearly a major function of public relations.

DEVELOPING A PROMOTIONAL STRATEGY

Once the firm has established the intended objectives for its promotional activities it becomes possible to consider the strategies available for their achievement.

By virtue of the strategic analysis that precedes the formulation of a marketing plan and the selection of a marketing mix, the planner/manager will have already established the market segment to be addressed, and the manner in which their brand(s) is to be positioned within that segment. As a consequence, they should have a clear picture of the intended audience, of the benefits which are important to that audience, of their present purchasing behaviour and their reaction to price inducements. In other words, whether through market research and/or prior experience, the manager will have considerable information on the other major elements of the marketing mix – product, place and price.

While this might appear to make advertising

something of a residual, requiring much less attention than the weighty consideration given to, say, product development, this is very far from the case. In *Competitive Marketing*, O'Shaughnessy (1984) illustrates this forcefully in a table, reproduced as Table 19.2.

With six major factors – target audience, goals (objectives), message appeal, message format, media and vehicle mix and scheduling – and the major elements associated with each, O'Shaughnessy offers 4,320 different combinations and permutations. If we were to include the 63 advertising objectives set out in Table 19.1 in place of O'Shaughnessy's four 'goals', then the options would escalate to 68,040 and this is long before one begins to choose between different media.

Given this level of complexity, it is unsurprising that the development of advertising campaigns is almost invariably delegated to the specialist advertising agencies that have developed to fill this function. In terms of O'Shaughnessy's table, it is likely that the advertiser's primary input will be the articulation of the specific goals or objectives which they hope to achieve with secondary inputs on the characteristics of the target audience and the factors which will have a bearing upon the message appeal such as their positioning vis-à-vis the competition, buying criteria etc. The remaining activities are sufficiently complex to require weighty textbooks in their own right (see Recommended reading in Chapter 9). For a broadly based description of the advertising industry, agency selection, the characteristics of various advertising media, the reader should consult Chapter 18 in *Marketing* (Baker, 2006), which contains an extended discussion of the growing

TABLE 19.2 Advertising Strategy

Target audience →	Goals →	Message appeal →	Message format →	Media and vehicle mix →	Scheduling
Consumers/customers	Convert	Unique selling proposition (USP)	Dogmatic	TV	Concentrated
Gatekeepers	Increase	Image	Emotional	Radio	Continuous
Opinion leaders	Attract	Positioning vis-à-vis competition	Reason-giving	Direct ad	Intermittent
Others	Maintain	Buying criteria		Magazines	
		Others		Newspapers	
				Outdoor	

SOURCE: O'Shaughnessy, J. (1984) *Competitive Marketing: a Strategic Approach.* Winchester, MA: Allen & Unwin

importance of the use of direct marketing methods in place of the mass communication associated with media advertising

Before leaving the subject of promotional strategy, it is important to reiterate the point made previously, namely that promotion will play a major role in:

1. Creating awareness
2. Conditioning perceptions (of the facts)
3. Suggesting subjective associations and benefits which will prove determinant when there is apparent objective parity between two or more competing alternatives.

SETTING THE PROMOTIONAL BUDGET

Empirical observation indicates that firms use one or other of five basic approaches to setting the promotional budget. These may be characterised as:

■ Percentage of sales
■ Competitive parity
■ What we can afford
■ Fixed sum per unit
■ Task and objective.

The variety of methods in use arises largely from the fact that, while ultimately advertising is intended to increase sales or, at worst, prevent one's competitors from reducing them, it is almost impossible to develop a direct measure of the advertising to sales effect. (The obvious exception is direct advertising and marketing that we discuss later.)

In his book, Dr Simon Broadbent (1970) recommends that the advertiser should seek to answer four questions when setting a budget:

1. What can the product afford?
2. What is the advertising task?
3. What are competitors spending?
4. What have we learned from previous years?

As Broadbent notes, one or other of these questions will usually dominate and so give rise to one or other of the basic approaches listed above. But, that said, there is considerable merit in seeking to answer each of the questions as objectively

as possible as a cross-check on their relative importance.

With regard to the question of what a product can afford, Broadbent emphasises the intrinsic paradox when he says 'the advertising budget is often based on a sum which assumes that sales are fixed – yet the object after advertising is to affect this sales figure'. Another common and dangerous assumption is that advertising expenditures are a residual on-cost, with the result that advertising expenditures are seen as having a much more direct influence on profit than do other costs and so become more vulnerable to cutting, as profits come under pressure which may be precisely the time when increased advertising effort is called for. Of course, cash availability must represent the ultimate constraint on what the product can afford, but, as we noted previously, the assessment of cash availability is likely to be very different if one considers that advertising is a long-term investment in market share as opposed to a short-run, variable and residual marketing expense.

With regard to the question of the advertising task, this should be the outcome of a careful analysis of the role promotion is to play in the overall marketing mix which will be strongly influenced by our knowledge of the way advertising works and the particular context in which it is to be used. Taken together, these considerations will lead to the formulation of advertising objectives, in the manner discussed in the previous section, which Broadbent sees as leading to three specific questions:

1. What media are likely to be chosen?
2. At what cost do they reach the target?
3. What number of exposures to the target might achieve the specified effect?

Clearly, what is required here is a broadbrush review of the key characteristics of the various media available as a basis for selecting between them, rather than the preparation of a detailed media plan which is the responsibility of the advertising manager and the agency within the policy guidelines contained in the marketing strategy. A much simplified résumé of the main features of the major media is contained in Table 19.3.

TABLE 19.3 Strengths and weaknesses of major media

	Strengths	Weaknesses
TELEVISION	Broad reach Creative opportunities for demonstration Immediacy of messages Entertainment carryover A compelling medium Negotiable costs Frequent messages	Little demographic selectivity Commercial clutter Short advertising life of message Decreased viewing in summer Some consumer scepticism towards claims made High cost
Network	Association of prestige with programming	Long-term advertiser commitments
Local	Geographic selectivity Association with programs of local origin and appeal Short notice to schedule	High reach more difficult on independent stations High cost for broad geographic coverage Ad can be preempted
RADIO	Low cost High frequency Immediacy of message Short notice to schedule Relatively no seasonal change in audience Highly portable medium Negotiable costs Short-term advertiser commitments Entertainment carryover	No visual treatment Short advertising life of message Background sound Commercial clutter
Network	Lower absolute cost for national coverage	Difficult to accumulate reach of a large audience No geographic flexibility Limited demographic selectivity Limited programming variety Clearance problems Variation in audience by market
Local	Excellent demographic selectivity Good geographic flexibility Personality identification	High cost for broad geographic coverage
MAGAZINES	Good reproduction, especially colour Permanence of message Demographic selectivity, reaches affluent audience Regional Local market selectivity Special interest possibilities Readership not seasonal Relatively long advertising life (one week, one month) Informational Editorially compatible environment Secondary readership Merchandising programmes	Long-term advertiser commitments Slow audience build-up Limited demonstration capacities Less compelling than other major media like television Lack of urgency Long closing dates Not a frequency medium (unless used specially with multiple units in same issue)
NEWSPAPERS	Geographic selectivity and flexibility Short-term advertiser commitments News value and immediacy Advertising permanence Readership not seasonal High individual market coverage Local retailer–dealer identification Merchandising programmes Short closing	Little demographic selectivity High absolute costs for national representation Limited colour facilities Variable colour reproduction Different local and national rates Little secondary readership

SOURCE: Fajen, S. R. (1978) More for your money from the media, *Harvard Business Review* (September–October)

The third question 'of competitive parity' is often regarded as a 'cop out', but, as Broadbent (1970) explains, knowledge of competitors' advertising spend is a vital input to one's own thinking. First, there is the crude but useful rule of thumb that: 'the sales expected for our product are the same share of the market as our advertising share'. Certainly if all the advertisers use a percentage of sales and/or fixed sum per unit approach to budgeting this will be the case. Second, an analysis of competitive expenditure will often reveal that there is an accepted ratio of advertising to sales, although this ratio is likely to vary according to the market structure and one's competitive standing, i.e. a dominant market leader will usually experience scale effects for their advertising while a small adversary will have to accept a higher advertising to sales spend in order to achieve a minimum threshold level of advertising. Of course it is always possible that the market leader will use a similar advertising : sales ratio as their smaller competitors as both a competitive weapon and a barrier to entry. Irrespective of whether you are a leader or a follower, knowledge of one's competitors' promotional strategy is a vital input to one's own planning.

Finally, there is the important question of what have we learned from previous years. By now the reader will be more than familiar with my overriding belief that a great deal of marketing can be explained in terms of a relatively small number of options or alternatives. The difficulty, challenge and excitement of managing the marketing function arises from the contextual complexity in which the variables interact and the speed with which these variables change. Thus, while it is possible to develop useful generalisations about

decisions and courses of action, detailed planning and implementation must always be situation-specific and so will depend upon the experience of the manager in their particular industry/market. It follows, therefore, that decisions on future advertising strategy and expenditure should be heavily influenced by our highly specific past experience. Broadbent goes further and advocates that not only should one use previous experience as a guideline for future action, but one should actively experiment with different advertising 'treatments' to determine their effectiveness.

Ideally the provision of answers to our four questions should result in the setting of an appropriation that corresponds to the task and objective method most authors (including myself) advocate as the most effective method. Essentially, the task and objective approach consists of a series of iterations, whereby the decision-maker:

1. Sets an objective
2. Specifies what is necessary to achieve this in terms of media coverage and cost
3. Compares the theoretically desirable budget with the resources actually available
4. If compatible, implement
5. If not compatible, either revise the objective and/or secure new resources.

As noted at the beginning of this section, such a procedure may still result in the advertiser selecting, say, 'competitive parity' as the key decision factor and claiming to budget on this basis. Therefore one should be careful not to dismiss the method as lacking in objectivity until one has determined what other considerations were taken into account.

Box 19.2   *Boosting returns on marketing investment*

The above title was given to an article that appeared in the *McKinsey Quarterly* in 2005 by David C. Court, Johnathan W. Gordon and Jesko Perrey. In the authors' view, the traditional model of marketing is being challenged by a number of trends, including a decline in the

effectiveness of mass advertising, a general proliferation of media and distribution channels, declining trust in advertising, multitasking by consumers, and digital technologies that give users more control over their media time.

In the 1960s and 1970s, mar-

keters in consumer product industries emphasised mass advertising and justified the spend in terms of sales growth and brand-building using generalised models of recall and impact. These practices were adopted in the 1980s and 1990s by industries like pharmaceuticals, retailing and telecommunications and, initially, worked well for them too. But fragmenting media, and changes in consumer behaviour as a result of the trends outlined earlier, point to the need for a new model and better methods of calculating and measuring ROI on marketing expenditures.

The authors estimate that by 2010, TV advertising could be only 35% as effective as in 1990. To cope with these changes, marketers need to apply investment fundamentals to the marketing function, i.e. clarifying the objectives of investments, finding and exploiting points of economic leverage, managing risk and tracking returns. In other words, better metrics.

EFFECTIVE ADVERTISING

Some years ago J. Harvey, the international confectionery and foods marketing director, and his colleague David Woods, were asked to prepare a set of guidelines to ensure that the very best of their advertising practices, procedures and experiences should be gathered together for the benefit for all those responsible for the development of Cadbury Schweppes advertising around the world. Like many other examples and sources cited in this book that date back 20 years or more, ideas and principles contained in them have withstood the test of time remarkably well. This is certainly true of Harvey and Woods' *Principles of good brand advertising*, in which they wrote:

> Advertising is only one of the many elements in the successful marketing of our products. The first rule of good advertising, therefore, is that it should be entirely consistent with the company's business philosophy and marketing objectives. In broad terms, these can be summarised as follows:
> - We aim to make products which satisfy consumer needs, and not simply those we find convenient to make.
> - We are in business to achieve continuous, long-term, profitable growth.
> - We will be good stewards of the reputation for quality and value which the company and its products have already built in the minds of our consumers.
>
> The role of good brand advertising in our Company can be simply defined:
>
> Good advertising creates awareness, favourable attitudes, and a preference in the consumer's mind for one particular brand; it thereby helps persuade her to try it and continue to use it.

In support of this policy statement, the authors identified eight principles of effective advertising, namely:

1. It regards the consumer as sovereign
2. It satisfies the consumer need with a competitive advantage
3. It contains one dominant promise
4. It relates the promise inextricably to the identity of the brand
5. It avoids distractions
6. It is credible
7. It must stand out
8. It is legal, responsible, and in keeping with the identity of the company.

In developing an advertising strategy, the first step is to establish the brand positioning. To do this one must summarise how the consumer currently sees the product and how the seller would wish them to see it. In turn, this must be compared with the positions of competing products to ensure that the chosen position is both clear and unique as well as relevant for the future. In order to develop a brand position, it is vital that one can both visualise and profile the intended consumer. It is to these that the advertising message is to be directed and it follows that the more precisely they are defined, the more likely it is that the communication will reach the intended target.

As was seen in Chapter 9 when discussing consumer behaviour, modern society is characterised by information overload. As a consequence, we depend heavily upon the subconscious processes of selective attention and perception to screen out information that is not seen as relevant to conscious action. In order to break through these defences, it is clear that an effective message must communicate a benefit of immediate relevance to

Given the restrictions imposed on mass media advertising of tobacco-based products, companies such as Philip MorrisUSA Inc., owners of the dominant Marlboro brand, have turned increasingly to direct marketing methods. Its tactics include 'buzz' marketing at live events, a website, price promotions and direct mail to create a viral marketing campaign that has created a brand community of over 26 million smokers. Given that smokers feel increasingly excluded by the population at large, the loyalty generated as a member of the Marlboro brand community is enormous and

regularly reinforced by the award of Marlboro Miles with every pack purchased. Miles can be used to buy a wide range of prizes offered by Marlboro including special trips to the Marlboro ranch in Montana for luxury vacations.

According to *Business Week* (31 October, 2005):

Built by company field reps who stake out bars, as well as through internet sign-ups and calls to an 800 number, the Marlboro database populates events with smokers who often feel under siege in an increasingly smoke-free world.

By these tactics Marlboro has developed a more effective promotional impact than was possible through mass media advertising. *Business Week* estimates that Marlboro is earning margins of 28%, 'twice the current operating margin of well-run companies like General Electric and Exxon-Mobil, and also well beyond Proctor and Gamble's 19% margin this year'.

From these margins Marlboro is able to attract new customers through in-store promotions, price cuts and other deals, which gives Philip Morris up to 80% of display space in stores like Wal-Mart.

the target audience. Only through detailed research is it likely that one will identify the unique and distinctive feature that will set the brand apart from the competition. But, as our discussion of hierarchical effects models has shown, while gaining attention is notoriously difficult, once achieved it must be reinforced immediately to convert attention into interest. In other words, one must provide justification through the provision of supporting evidence that you are capable of delivering the claimed benefits of satisfaction. It is these distinctive and differentiating properties that together go to make up the brand identity.

Finally, the choice of the channel of communication is critical to ensure that the intended message is received and interpreted correctly by the intended audience. Achieving this is the purpose of media strategy which is a complex art covered at considerable length in major advertising textbooks.

MEASURING ADVERTISING EFFECTIVENESS

Given the specification of clear advertising objectives and the allocation of a budget for their achievement, it is only natural that one should

seek to measure how effective the advertising has actually been in securing the desired results. That said, the preceding examination of how advertising works should have made it clear that this is a subject in its own right and that we can only scratch the surface here.

At the outset, it is important to distinguish between pre-testing and post-testing promotion, as these have quite different roles to play. As the term suggests, pre-testing is used to try and establish the effectiveness of one or more elements of the promotional method prior to its full-scale use with the target audience, while post-testing seeks to quantify the extent to which the advertising objective has actually been achieved after implementation of the promotional programme.

The benefits and value of pre-testing were suggested in our earlier example of the nature of selective perception (Chapter 9), in which it was shown that a campaign conceived to encourage parents not to smoke in front of children was not perceived as conveying this message by members of the target audience. Indeed it was a demonstration of the singular lack of effectiveness of this expensive and highly thought of (by health educationalists and other advertising professionals) campaign established by post-testing that convinced the sponsors of the very real benefits that could accrue from pre-testing on a small scale. Thus, in advocating the task-and-objective approach, pre-testing would have an important role to play in specifying precisely what message and media would provide the most cost-effective way of realising the overall objective.

With regard to post-testing, the major decision will revolve around what is an appropriate measure of the agreed objective. As we have seen, the most frequently desired objectives will tend to correspond closely with our perception of the prospect's location on our hierarchy and our attempt to move them towards the ultimate goal of a satisfied repeat purchaser:

- Awareness = recall product identity
- Interest = recall advertising content
- Desire = attitudes
  buyer intentions
- Action = purchase/sales
  reinforcement.

For a low-involvement product, perhaps our hierarchy would appear as:

- Awareness = subconscious knowledge =
  recognition at point of sale
- Interest = trial = sale and conscious use of
  advertising
- Desire = beliefs about product
  repeat purchase = reinforcement
- Action = habitual behaviour
  brand loyalty = reinforcement

With regard to specific measures of sales, attitudes, beliefs, behavioural interest, awareness and recall, Corkindale and Kennedy (1974) provide the following useful summary table (Table 19.4).

A newer, sophisticated approach to measuring advertising effectiveness was reported in *Marketing Week* in May 1990 when AGB Nielsen Media Research announced a new development which it claimed could demonstrate not only whether a particular TV campaign had worked, but which viewers bought more products as a result of the advertising and how the budget should be deployed to bring the best sales results. AGB's claim is based on the use of technique called data fusion which involves the integration of two existing data sources. Ideally the answer to many

research questions is to use single-source data, in which a representative sample of consumers can be surveyed in terms of their purchasing behaviour related to their reading, viewing and listening habits. However, attempts by Central Adlab and Nielsen and HTV's Statscan to set up sufficiently large panels to provide such data proved to be prohibitively expensive, and had to be abandoned.

To overcome this problem, BMRB (the research and consultancy agency) launched its Target Group Ratings service in April 1990 which is based on the fusion of TGI (which measures product usage) and BARB (which measures viewing). The aim of Target Group Ratings is to enable advertising agencies to plan campaigns more accurately by selecting programmes watched by the users of their products rather than by more broadly defined demographic groups. However, the AGB service differs in that its primary purpose is to aid campaign evaluation by quantifying the effect of advertising on sales.

The AGB method also uses BARB data, but fuses it with information from its own TCA panel which measures product purchases in 6,500 homes. *Marketing Week* (June, 1990) reported:

> By developing a computer model of TV viewing behaviour, based on the individual viewing patterns of housewives on the BARB panel, AGB can now predict when an individual housewife on the TCA panel is likely to be watching ITV or Channel 4. From this, it can work out the number of times she is likely to have seen a particular commercial.

The model depends on certain key demographic characteristics and viewing claims, such as the fact that non-working women are much more likely to watch TV during the day than those who are out at work.

In a test on a new FMCG, the fusion model showed that among heavy viewers who saw a commercial an average of 8.6 times their purchases increased by 44% compared with an increase of only 29% by light viewers who saw the commercial on average 2.7 times during the campaign. The analysis also showed that advertising primarily increased trial of the brand and sales to occasional buyers rather than increasing the purchase rate of regular buyers, demonstrating that the ads were much more effective with some demographic groups than others.

TABLE 19.4 Means of assessment of advertising objectives

SALES
Own – ex-factory
Sales of complementary products
Audits – home (and/or diaries)
■ Outlets
Total marketing – via DTI
　　　　　　– via pooling of all makers
Share = own total + published total, or pooling by all
　　　manufacturers
Share of sales through own outlets
Gains/loss special panel analysis
Penetration surveys
Special analysis of panel data (lapsed users etc.)
Omnibus – surveys to measure 'trial'
Cost per item sold

TRADE
■ Special investigation of dealer behaviour
■ Trade survey (of attitudes)
■ Monitor dealer response
■ Salesmen's reports
■ Interim comparison (of outlet's performance)

ATTITUDES
■ Usage and attitude surveys (U & A)
■ Surveys for advertising model (St James)
■ Syndicated attitude survey (API)
■ Corporate image survey
■ Image study

BEHAVIOUR
■ U & A survey by research agency
■ Survey of buyer behaviour by own field force

ADVERTISING CONTENT
24-hour recall
Omnibus – on recall
■ Recall survey
■ Shopper survey of awareness

CONSUMER REACTION
■ Discussion groups — formative / evaluative
■ Depth interview
■ Pre-test
■ Post-test – product oriented
■ Letters from consumers

AUDIENCE ACHIEVEMENT
■ Media research (before)
■ TV ratings achieved
■ Press – forecast OTS
■ Cost/1000 – forecast
　　　　　　– actual
■ Reading and noting scores
■ Comparative expenditures (MEAL)

EXPERIMENTAL AREAS
■ Advertising weight tests via area tests
■ Advertising content tests via area tests

COUPON RESPONSE
Coupon enquiry

SOURCE: Corkindale, D. and Kennedy, S. (1974) *The Evaluation of Advertising Objectives.* Marketing Communications Research Centre, Cranfield School of Management, Report 10 (November)

Chapter summary

Like distribution, promotion and particularly mass-media advertising, is often regarded as a cost-creating function which adds little or nothing to the value of the product. In this chapter we have sought to dispel this misconception by showing that not only is advertising the most cost-effective means of informing potential consumers about the existence of a product and generating interest in it, but it also adds value by enhancing the subjective merits of the product or service.

To this end we have reviewed the nature of the communication process and examined alternative explanations of the way in which advertising is claimed to work. While research indicated a low correlation between attitudes and behaviour (which are central to the traditional hierarchical models of advertising effect) it was suggested that this may be due to the fact that much of the reported research has been concerned with what Krugman (1965) termed 'low-involvement goods'. Accordingly, our own preference was to accept the model proposed by Joyce in 1967, which recognises that while advertis-

ing may 'work' in a number of different ways, attitudes play an important role and are susceptible to influence through advertising.

Following a discussion of how individuals use selective perception, attention and retention to survive in an overcommunicated society, considerable attention was given to the selection of promotion objectives as an essential precursor to setting the advertising budget. Five basic approaches to the latter problem were proposed and complemented by a summary of methods for estimating how effective such expenditure had been.

Recommended reading

Broadbent, S. (1999) Advertising in M. J. Baker (ed.) *Encyclopedia of Marketing*. London: International Thomson Business Press.

Crosier, K. (1995) Marketing communications in M. J. Baker (ed.) *Marketing: Theory and Practice* (3rd edn). Basingstoke: Macmillan – now Palgrave Macmillan.

Crosier, K. (2003) Promotion in M. J. Baker (ed.) *The Marketing Book* (5th edn). Oxford: Butterworth Heinemann.

Fill, C. (2005) *Marketing Communications: Engagement, Strategies and Practice* (4th edn). Harlow: FT/Prentice Hall.

Yeshin, T. (1998) *Integrated Marketing Communications*. Oxford: Butterworth Heinemann.

REFERENCES

Ambler, T. (1998) Does advertising affect market size? Some evidence from the United Kingdom, *International Journal of Advertising*, **17**(4).

Baker, M. J. (2006) *Marketing* (7th edn). Helensburgh: Westburn.

Boyd, H. W. Jr., Ray, M. L. and Strong, E. C. (1972) An attitudinal framework for advertising strategy, *Journal of Marketing*, **36**(April): 27–33.

Broadbent, S. (1970) *Spending Advertising Money*. London: Business Books.

Buzzell, R. D. and Baker, M. J. (1970) Sales effectiveness of automobile advertising, *Journal of Advertising Research*, **12**(3): 3–8.

Corkindale, D. and Kennedy, S. (1974) *The Evaluation of Advertising Objectives*. Marketing Communications Research Centre, Cranfield School of Management, Report 10 (November).

Court, D. C., Gordon, J. W. and Perrey, J. (2005) Boosting returns on marketing investment. *McKinsey Quarterly*, **2**.

Fajen, S. R. (1978) More for your money from the media, *Harvard Business Review* (September–October)

Joyce, T. (1967) *What Do We Know About How Advertising Works?* London: J. Walter Thompson Company Ltd.

Kotler, P. (1972) *Marketing Management* (2nd edn). Englewood Cliffs, NJ: Prentice Hall.

Krugman, H. E. (1965) The impact of television advertising: learning without involvement, *Public Opinion Quarterly*, **29**(3): 349–56.

Lavidge, R. J. and Steiner, G. A. (1961) A model for predictive measurements of advertising effectiveness, *Journal of Marketing*, 25 October.

Maslow, A. H. (1943) A theory of human motivation, *Psychological Review*, **50**.

O'Guinn, T. C., Allen, C. T. and Semenik, R. J. (2006) *Advertising and Integrated Brand Promotion* (4th edn). Mason, OH: Thomson South-Western.

O'Shaughnessy, J. (1984) *Competitive Marketing: A Strategic Approach*. Winchester, MA: Allen & Unwin.

Packard, V. (1957) *The Hidden Persuaders*. Harmondsworth: Penguin Books.

Schramm, W. (1955) *The Process and Effects of Mass Communications*. Urbana, IL: University of Illinois Press.

Shannon, C. and Weaver, W. (1962) *The Mathematical Theory of Communication*. Urbana, IL: University of Illinois Press.

Smith, R. E. and Swinyard, W. R. (1982) Information response models: an integrated approach, *Journal of Marketing*, **46**(winter): 81–93.

Yeshin, T. (1998) *Integrated Marketing Communications*. Oxford: Butterworth Heinemann.

NOTE

1. The implicit assumption is that we are concerned with product classes which are reasonably close substitutes for one another, for example alternative forms of entertainment, of transportation or forming metals or constructing buildings etc.

Part 4

IMPLEMENTING MARKETING

Customer care and service

Customer care can incorporate anything that an organisation does for and on behalf of its customers.

DAVID CARSON

After reading Chapter 20 you will be able to:

✔ Define and describe customer service and customer care.

✔ Discuss the nature and importance of customer service and customer loyalty.

✔ Explain how customer services can be classified as pre-transactional, transactional or post-transactional and the uses of this classification.

✔ Suggest how service activities may be used strategically to differentiate and position products and services.

✔ Define the concept of total quality management (TQM) and discuss some of the issues and problems associated with its implementation.

✔ Suggest how to price services.

✔ Discuss how to measure service quality.

✔ Illustrate, through a case study example, how service may be used in formulating a marketing strategy.

INTRODUCTION

In the first edition (1985) we wrote:

> In our model of buyer behaviour no explicit reference
> was made to the role of service in motivating specific
> choice decisions. Similarly, little direct reference is to
> be found to customer service in the major marketing
> textbooks although it is frequently mentioned in
> connection with specific marketing activities – partic-
> ularly physical distribution. However, in an increas-
> ingly competitive environment it seems reasonable to
> assume that as the potential for product differentiat-
> ion is eroded one should give added consideration to
> the provision of services which will enhance both the
> physical performance of products and their perceived
> value in the customer's eyes. Even more important,
> through the provision of support services the supplier
> has the opportunity to increase the strength of the
> bond with his existing customers and so reduce the
> risk of their 'switching' to alternative suppliers.[1]

More than 20 years later it is clear that this was a
prophetic forecast as customer service (CS) and its
associated total quality management (TQM) are
high (if not top) of most companies' agendas. As
predicted, the erosion of physical differences
between competing products has required
customers to depend increasingly upon a broader
definition of 'fitness for purpose' which embraces
the services associated with the purchase and
consumption of a product or service. (It should be
noted here that we are not concerned with the
marketing of services per se, which has become a
fashionable subfield of marketing in its own right –
see Chapter 23 in *Marketing: An Introductory Text*
(Baker, 2006), but with service as an element of the
marketing mix.) Customer concern with the
augmented product, which includes the associated
service elements, has resulted in a spate of publications dealing specifically with service as an
intrinsic element of the firm's competitive offering. It follows that while the inclusion of such a
chapter was commented on by reviewers of the
first edition as an 'innovation' it now represents
but a brief introduction to an extensive literature.
Hopefully, it covers the key issues and will
encourage reference to the specialist texts by those
who are persuaded that service, like marketing
research, must be added to the simpler 4Ps version

of the marketing mix when devising successful
marketing strategies.

In this chapter we provide a brief review of the
ways in which service activities may be used to
enhance consumer/user satisfaction for both
products and services. The chapter opens with a
discussion of customer satisfaction, customer care,
customer service and customer loyalty and with
consideration of the view that such services may
be associated with three distinct phases of the
buying process – pre-sale, sale and post-sale. The
scope for customer service in both the industrial
and consumer market will be examined, together
with an evaluation of the use of service at both the
strategic and tactical level, in which it will be
examined as part of the broader TQM concept. The
chapter concludes with a discussion of pricing
services, the measurement of service quality, and
the use of service as marketing strategy.

CUSTOMER SATISFACTION

It used to be that customer satisfaction was seen as
a sufficient objective to ensure repeat purchase. In
today's competitive marketplace this is no longer
the case. Indeed, pioneering work by Xerox in the
early 1990s demonstrated that if satisfaction is
ranked on a scale of 5 to 1 with 5 representing
completely satisfied, then persons scoring 4 –
which most would think reflected a fairly high
level of satisfaction – are six times more likely to
defect that those scoring 5.

In an article in *Fortune* Thomas A. Stewart (1997,
p. 70) summarised a number of reasons why 'a
satisfied customer isn't enough'. According to
Stewart there are only two certain strategies for
customer loyalty and retention: neuter competition or satisfy customers completely:

> One way to create uncompetitive markets is to limit
> customers' choice. Patents do this, as do regul-
> ations, airport landing rights, broadcast licences,
> mergers that tip-toe past the sleeping dogs like
> justice, and the like. You can also maim the Invisible
> Hand by making it inconvenient or expensive for
> customers to switch. Frequent flier firms are a great
> example, so powerful that few airlines even try to
> make flying pleasant. Location is another: I prefer
> Burger King to McDonald's, but when my choles-

terol is too low I go to McDonald's because it's closer. De facto standards also raise switching costs. The ubiquity of Windows, the dollar, and gasoline powered cars make it harder to switch to Macs, the lire, or electric vehicles.

By contrast, many major brands are seen as very close substitutes for one another and loyalty to a particular brand appears to depend on a combination of smaller factors rather than any big single advantage. According to Mintel International, quality and price are the two most important determinants of a company's reputation, followed by customer service, responsiveness to complaints, and the behaviour of contact personnel. To the extent that quality and price can be benchmarked, they have increasingly become a necessary but not sufficient condition for competitive success. In today's marketplaces it is the performance of individuals who deliver services that provide the just noticeable difference and the foundation for customer loyalty associated with superior performance.

Depending on context, opportunities to remind customers that they are receiving superior performance may be either explicit or implicit. Stewart cites the case of Southwest Airlines as an organisation that constantly reminds its customers of the explicit benefits they receive.

> Southwest delights its customers by making and keeping a promise to be cheap and fast, and the airline doesn't miss a trick when it comes to reminding you of it. With its casually dressed employees, colour coded and tattered boarding cards, sheep shearing boarding process, and lack of food, Southwest seizes every opportunity to point out to passengers the frills it eliminates.

By contrast, superior performance in international hotel chains is more often than not implicit and unobtrusive. Loyalty is usually developed by establishing the precise needs of individual guests and then ensuring that these are both anticipated and provided for every time a customer makes a booking. Delivery of such service calls for extremely sophisticated databases that are continually updated, extensive training and empowerment of service delivery personnel to create and deliver enhanced service whenever the opportunity presents itself.

CRM OR CSM

In Chapter 2 brief reference was made to the perceived need for a different approach to the practice of marketing which led in 1992 to the publication of a seminal article in the *Journal of Marketing* by Fred Webster. The ideas discussed in 'The changing role of marketing in the corporation' were neither new nor original but, as with Levitt's 'Marketing myopia' (1960) and Porter's 'Competitive Advantage' (1985), Webster crystallised thinking on the need for an alternative to the marketing management school of thought, and its replacement with a model that we now know as 'relationship marketing'. Webster, like Levitt and Porter, was the tipping point.

At roughly the same time Reichheld (1996) was pointing to the nature and importance of customer loyalty and it was not long before relationship marketing and customer loyalty management were combined into the concept of *customer relationship management* (CRM). In my view the notions of relationship and management are antithetical – management is about exerting control over something; relationships are about mutual accord and agreement to enter into exchanges that give the desired satisfaction to both parties a win–win rather than a win–lose outcome. The purpose of the relationship is mutual *satisfaction* and it is this that should be the primary motivation of the seller. Accordingly, we believe that *customer satisfaction management* (CSM) would be a better and more accurate descriptor in that the critical success factor is the satisfaction experienced by the customer, the essence of the marketing concept. If one maximises the customers' satisfaction, then loyalty, repeat purchase and positive word of mouth will be the sellers' reward.

Of course, in proposing that sellers maximise customer satisfaction, we are not suggesting the seller foregoes the profit that is the deserved reward for delivering the satisfaction looked for by the customer. Far from it. The 'invisible hand' is intended to encourage freedom of choice while simultaneously ensuring that scarce resources are used in such a way as to maximise the overall satisfaction obtained from them. What we are seeking is the achievement of our definition of marketing as 'mutually satisfying exchange relationships'.

According to Stewart (1997):

- Satisfied customers tell an average of five other people about their experience
- It costs five times as much to create a customer as to keep one
- 68% of customers who switch suppliers do so because of poor service rather than price or quality problems
- 98% of dissatisfied customers never complain to the company they are disappointed with
- But, the average dissatisfied customer will tell nine others; 13% will tell 20 or more people.

If customer service leads to customer satisfaction and competitive success, the question is 'What service leads to this satisfaction?' While there is no single or simple answer, there are at least three solutions in Copeland's (1923) 'classification of goods' – convenience, shopping and specialty – and Porter's generic strategies – cost leadership, differentiation and focus. Both these classifications/analytical frameworks derive directly from an understanding of the basic market forces of demand and supply. It is perhaps because they seem so obvious and familiar that they rarely get the attention they deserve. To begin with, effective demand reflects a combination of need (desired satisfaction) and disposable income. In turn, Maslow's hierarchy of needs indicates that the greater our disposable income, the higher the order of need we can satisfy – survival, social, status and self-actualisation. The importance and relevance of this is apparent in the concept of price elasticity and was exemplified in our discussion of Ford and GM's strategies in the US car market between 1910 and 1930. The same forces also underpin the analysis of Baker's Box.

It is important to remember, however, that while a customer may profess to be 'satisfied', this does not mean they could not be even more satisfied by another offering. While 90% of US car buyers say they are satisfied with their purchase, only 45% will repurchase from the same supplier the next time they enter the market. At least four situations may account for this:

1. Sellers don't fully understand customers' needs
2. Sellers don't fully understand their own performance
3. Sellers lack commitment to customer service
4. Sellers are the victims of customer service 'myths'.

Further, a great deal of customer service is mechanistic and technology-driven. Later, we extol the benefits achieved by British Airways with its Executive Club. However, its sophisticated technology was insufficient to prevent a mailshot to its most profitable customers who regularly flew on Concorde being addressed by the name of the internal file in which their data was stored – 'Dear Rich Bastard'.

As for customer satisfaction myths, the most prevalent of these are:

- Price is the only thing that matters
- We're already at 99%
- Our customer service department handles that
- We understand their needs
- Customers won't involve us
- We can't afford to give customers what they want.

By contrast, companies with a record of satisfying customers:

- Let customers define service values
- Exceed customer expectations in key areas – not all areas
- Segment, target and position
- Invest in staff education, training and systems.

And companies with a superior record:

- Listen to the voice of the market and respond accordingly
- Communicate a clear vision of what quality and satisfaction mean throughout the organisation
- Establish measurable standards of service performance
- Monitor performance against standards continuously.

In other words, successful firms put theory into practice.

CUSTOMER CARE

Early editions of this book contained a chapter called 'Service'. Given the lack of attention in most other textbooks dealing with marketing strategy, this was something of an innovation. Perhaps inevitably, however, many people confuse the discussion of service as an element of the marketing mix with 'the marketing of services' as a special case of the application of the marketing concept. It is for this reason that the chapter is now entitled Customer Care and Service. According to Chaston (1990), the term 'customer care' embraces:

1. The product knowledge and interpersonal skills of the employees who interact with customers.
2. The type of service required by the customers and their perceptions of how the organisation fulfils their expectations on quality.
3. The organisational structure of the company that determines the efficiency with which services (products) are delivered at all phases, from the point of initial contact through to the customers' post-purchase evaluation of the service [product] received.

In the opinion of Carson (1999):

Customer care can incorporate anything that an organisation does for and on behalf of its customers.

What form this takes will depend upon a multiplicity of factors, such as the nature of the product or service, the industry, the competition and the expectation of consumers.

This view is encapsulated in Figure 20.1 first developed by Carson and Gilmore in 1989.

Ideologically, marketing is all about customer/consumer orientation and the organisation of the seller/supplier's activities to meet the customer's needs efficiently and effectively. As such, the idea of customer care ought to be central to the practice of marketing. It would seem, therefore, that the highly specific interest now shown for the topic, which has merited a separate section on it in this book, implies that customer care has not received the attention it deserves, a view endorsed by Donaldson (1995, p. 330). In this section we consider this proposition through a discussion of the origins and nature of customer care and the marketing activities designed to create and deliver it.

In David Carson's (1999) view, 'The origins of customer care and satisfaction stem from attempts

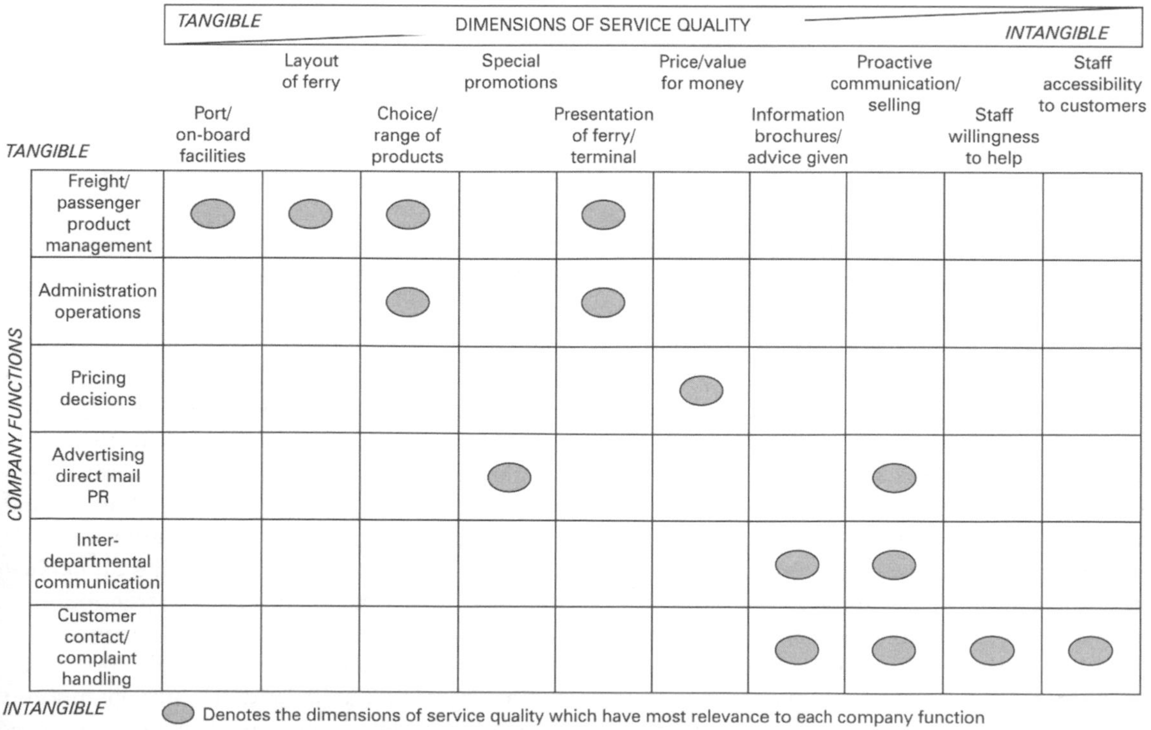

COMPANY FUNCTIONS	TANGIBLE ← DIMENSIONS OF SERVICE QUALITY → INTANGIBLE									
	Port/ on-board facilities	Layout of ferry	Choice/ range of products	Special promotions	Presentation of ferry/ terminal	Price/value for money	Information brochures/ advice given	Proactive communication/ selling	Staff willingness to help	Staff accessibility to customers
Freight/ passenger product management	●	●	●		●					
Administration operations			●		●					
Pricing decisions						●				
Advertising direct mail PR				●				●		
Inter- departmental communication							●	●		
Customer contact/ complaint handling							●	●	●	●

INTANGIBLE   ● Denotes the dimensions of service quality which have most relevance to each company function

FIGURE 20.1 A model for quality improvement in Sealink Stena

SOURCE: Carson, D. and Gilmore, A. (1989) Customer care: the neglected domain, *Irish Marketing Review*, 4(3): 49–61

by marketers to enhance the dimensions of after sales service.' Such after-sales service was traditionally associated with industrial goods and consumer durables, where advice on use or application, maintenance or repair were essential elements of the life-cycle cost and the total package bought by the customer. In many cases, after-sales service was (and is) the only effective means of differentiating between the offerings of competing suppliers. For example, in the late 1950s/early 1960s, when the author was a steel salesman, both the price and specification were fixed so that the only means buyers had of differentiating between competing sellers was on the basis of the quality of the service offered. In addition to obvious dimensions such as quality, reliability, delivery etc., this extended to offering extensive technical advice to users to ensure they obtained the maximum value from their purchase. It is this 'added value' that is now seen as the major benefit offered by customer care programmes.

Originally, and as the phrase implies, added value was seen as something additional to the basic product offering. It was this distinction which prompted Levitt and others to distinguish between the core product – the object that would meet the consumer's basic *need* – and the augmented product that was designed to meet the specific *want* of particular customers through the addition of benefits and values looked for by them. Under this concept, the added values were bundled in with the core product or service as opposed to being offered separately in the form of service contracts, provision of spare parts etc.

Customer care is a natural consequence of increased competition and the search for a sustainable competitive advantage through segmentation, targeting and positioning. It is also inextricably linked with the concept of relationship marketing through which the seller seeks to establish a long-term, mutually satisfying exchange relationship with the buyer as opposed to regarding each contact with the customer as a one-off transaction (see Chapter 1). Such a perspective is one of commercial common sense, for it has been estimated that it costs five times as much to create or win a customer as it does to keep one through the continuing supply of a quality product or service backed up by appropriate customer care. If each sale is regarded as a one-off

transaction, then it is likely the seller will seek to make a profit on the initial sales which requires them to recover all the 'capital' costs incurred in identifying, prospecting for and selling to that customer. If these costs are five times as great as those incurred in maintaining an ongoing relationship, then it is not difficult to see how and why the transactional approach will lead to a higher price and a perception of lower added value.

By contrast, if the seller takes a long-term view then they will seek to spread the costs of their initial capital investment, incurred in creating the customer, over a series of transactions for frequently purchased consumer goods and through a life-cycle approach for durable products which are purchased infrequently but require upkeep and servicing through their useful lives. However, the economics of relationship marketing make it clear that there will always be an initial capital cost involved in entering or creating a new market and that it will require customer loyalty and repeat purchase to recover or amortise these costs. It is for this reason that the established seller always has an advantage over the newcomer. Only if a new entrant is offering additional benefits or values, perceived as important by the buyer, will the seller be able to get the buyer to change his or her behaviour and, possibly, pay a premium price for the added value. It is for this reason that innovation and new product development has assumed such importance as a competitive strategy.

WHAT IS CUSTOMER CARE?

In its widest sense, customer care embraces everything an organisation does to establish and sustain a relationship with its customers. In its narrow sense, it is any activity or action which adds value to the relationship so that an organisation's customer care programme may consist of a listing of a series of highly specific activities. This is particularly so when a firm publishes an explicit statement of its customer care programme. In a sense this distinction between the concept of customer care, embracing all aspects of the customer relationship, and its implementation through a series of specific functions, is very similar to the distinction between the marketing concept and the marketing function. At one level, customer care is a state of mind which permeates the thinking of the selling organisation. At another level, it is a highly focused and closely defined set of activities designed to add values and satisfaction important to specific customers.

Donaldson (1995, p. 331) makes an important distinction between the concepts of customer loyalty, customer satisfaction and customer care. As he points out, a customer may be loyal due to the absence of competitive alternatives. However, this does not automatically mean they are satisfied, such that if a new competitor enters the market with an improved or better product/service customers are likely to switch to them. Loyalty is always fragile in buyer : seller relationships if for no other reason than that, ultimately, the customer's loyalty is first to him or herself, then to their family and then to their employer. As Donaldson observes: 'Customer loyalty can be measured but it is earned and cannot be delivered.'

Similarly, as we discuss later, customer satisfaction may be measured and delivered but it is essentially a subjective concept and so specific to each individual. Accordingly, satisfaction is 'a measure of customer responsiveness to marketing stimuli in a given competitive environment' (Donaldson, 1995). It is a consequence or result of all aspects of the seller's interaction with the customer including the service/care elements of the exchange. While some authors distinguish between customer service and customer care, Donaldson considers them to be the same and defines them 'as all those activities provided by the seller which have value for the buyer thus increasing customer satisfaction and encouraging patronage and loyalty between the parties' (Donaldson, 1995, p. 332).

As an activity, Carson (1999) sees customer care as a concept that encompasses at least four kinds of distinct activity, which he explains as follows:

1. *Customer service:* Generally includes advice and information for customers regarding the technical specifications of a product or service and after-sales back-up arrangements and procedures. To emphasise this point, Christopher (1986) writes that 'ultimately customer service is determined by the interaction of all those factors that affect the process of making products and services available to the buyer.'

2. *Product quality:* Relates to standards and measures set to ensure a product conforms to specifications and is therefore fit for its purpose and safe to use.
3. *Service quality:* Refers to the company / customer interface and relationship, focusing on the customer's experience during the process of the transaction.
4. *After-sales service:* Covers after-sales enquiries and complaints, together with repair and maintenance procedures.

Clearly, the current scope of customer care goes much beyond the original idea of after-sales service, which is only one of several elements in the above taxonomy. As conceived here, customer care includes all activities from anticipation and identification of the intended customer's need, through initial contact, to negotiation, sale and consumption. The organisational implications of this concept are important. Like marketing as a whole, it requires people within an organisation, with specific organisational responsibilities, to take a holistic view and see how their contribution fits into the overall interface with the customer. Workers on a production line are just as involved and concerned, possibly more so, in ensuring customer satisfaction, through building quality into the product, as is the salesperson or service engineer in ensuring that the customer gets what they want. Indeed the concept of TQM underlines the importance of designing and building satisfaction into a product or service in the first place.

Customer satisfaction is very much a subjective concept and its achievement is difficult because it is particular to every individual customer. At one level it is not too difficult to specify what the customer wants in terms of performance factors and what price/value they will place upon different performance levels (cost/benefit). But, as we saw in Chapter 9, the composite model of buying behaviour makes it clear that prior learning and experience leads to the formation of attitudes and the phenomenon of selective perception. Thus, the same objective 'facts' are likely to be interpreted differently by different individuals. One consequence of this is that we develop different expectations, and satisfaction is essentially a measure of the degree to which performance matches or exceeds expectations. For example, you book into a

5-star luxury hotel at a cost of £250 per night. The environment is superior and elegant, the service is discreet and attractive, the food is excellent. But, for £250 per night that's the least you would expect so the overall experience is probably 'satisfactory' or 'very satisfactory' on the customer questionnaire you are asked to complete on departure. If you're used to this type of hotel it is very rarely that you will tick 'excellent' or 'superior'. You only do this if performance exceeds expectations. Contrast this with spending a night in a two-crown bed-and-breakfast establishment in the Outer Hebrides for £25 including dinner. You have a very comfortable room with a wonderful view and an en-suite bathroom with lashings of hot water. Your wet walking gear disappears on arrival but is clean and dry by the time you leave in the morning. You have lobster and fresh raspberries and cream for dinner and a breakfast in the morning that will keep you going all day. There is no questionnaire to complete but the experience so exceeds your expectations that you write and thank the landlady, you write to the Scottish Tourist Board saying what a wonderful place it is, and you, foolishly, tell everyone the same thing, so next time you want to make a reservation it's fully booked. Satisfaction is complete!

The implications are obvious – the higher the expectation the more difficult it becomes to exceed

them and the harder the supplier will have to work to ensure they meet the required standard. In doing so, it quickly becomes apparent that one must distinguish clearly between the tangible/objective aspects of an object and the intangible/subjective elements associated with it. Carson and Gilmore (1989, p. 52) provide a helpful diagram summarising these two dimensions of customer care, reproduced as Figure 20.2 below.

The implications are clear. Even though individuals may interpret tangible elements somewhat differently from one another, they are still comparatively easy to measure. A 1.6 litre, 4 cylinder petrol engine is likely to be common to most mid-range family saloon cars, while features like overhead cams and number of values are also easy to compare between one model and another. But, in selecting a motorcar we are likely to take into account the whole range of tangible and intangible elements listed in the figure. Furthermore, as the model of buyer behaviour makes clear, when products appear objectively the same then we will have to resort to less tangible, subjective elements to enable us to discriminate between competing products. It follows that the objective and tangible elements which are amenable to specification and, therefore, to rules and procedures are the necessary conditions for being considered as a supplier.

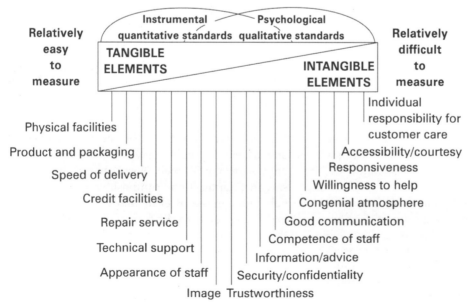

FIGURE 20.2 Dimensions of customer care

SOURCE: Carson, D. J. and Gilmore, A. (1989) Customer care: the neglected domain. *Irish Marketing Review*, 4: 52

But, it is the subjective and intangible elements, which are less easy to define and/or standardise, that are most likely to influence the intending buyer's perception and so determine their final decision. It is recognition of this, combined with the difficulty of maintaining objective performance superiority for long, which has thrown into sharp relief the importance of customer care.

It is clear from Figure 20.2 that the less tangible elements of an exchange relationship are largely services, the performance of which will depend very largely on the individual supplying them. As Levitt (1976) demonstrated, it is possible to reduce the human element on many service activities through specific techniques and practices e.g. standardised portion control in fast food outlets, or the development of formal procedures for the service supplier to follow, e.g. the preparation of quotations, billing and guarantee provision in Kwik Fit establishments. It is also possible to train people to achieve and sustain a high level of service delivery, and it was the implementation of such a programme in British Airways which has enabled it to claim to be 'The World's Favourite Airline'. In the final analysis, however, it all comes down to the individual performance of the service provider and it is their behaviour which will usually determine whether or not one's satisfaction meets or exceeds expectations. It follows that the training, motivation and supervision of service delivery personnel is central to any customer care programme.

In addition to training and motivating service personnel, it is also very important to pay careful attention to what, otherwise, might be considered 'trappings', i.e. elements of the service delivery package which, in and of themselves, are complementary to the service but not of its essence. Service organisations are often judged by their appearances. The huge banking hall of the past, intended to communicate the security and probity of the bank, has now come to be seen as intimidating to many private customers who prefer the more friendly atmosphere of the local building society office. Many parents might be concerned about their children's predilection for 'junk food' but can have no qualms whatsoever about the spotless hygiene of McDonald's or similar outlets. Clean delivery and service vehicles, smart livery and uniforms all provide tangible evidence of the supplier's professionalism and tangible concern for their customers.

The creation of the kind of 'esprit de corps' that motivates every individual in the organisation to give of their best has come to be seen as the responsibility of 'internal marketing'. As the phrase suggests, internal marketing consists of regarding employees as 'customers' and configuring the organisation to ensure that the needs of individual employees are understood and satisfied. This requires considerable management attention and effort if it is to be achieved. Otherwise there can develop a tendency for an 'us and them' mentality to develop where the frontline contact personnel

Box 20.1 — Caring for customers

In the UK, the AA (Automobile Association), proudly proclaims itself to be the nation's 'fourth emergency service', reinforcing the message with advertisements that depict its employees giving assistance to motorists in distress

Unfortunately, long-time member David Barker suffered a massive heart attack when driving, and was taken to hospital where he died. Subsequently, his relatives went to recover the car but were unable to restart it. Finding his AA membership card in the glove box, they phoned it seeking assistance. However, when the operator learned that Mr Barker had died, she advised them that his membership had expired too, so that assistance would only be given if someone rejoined, and then she hung up.

Subsequently, a spokesman for the AA apologised and recognised that under the circumstances it should have provided service as requested. As reported in the *Daily Mail* (4 January, 2006), he then said: 'It is inevitable in large organisations that sometimes we don't meet our own high standards and we are taking up the issue with the operator involved.' Perhaps one would have been more impressed if the AA had accepted the blame for not having trained its service personnel properly in the first place.

come to be seen as somehow more important, better or superior to the back-room personnel who support them. Total quality management has a major role to play in this internal marketing activity.

In this section we have looked briefly at some of the factors that have resulted in customer care receiving more explicit attention than in the past. Essentially, this interest is a direct consequence of three major environmental trends:

1. Increased competition
2. The rapid elimination of objective differences between competing suppliers
3. The growing importance of services, which now account for two thirds or more of all consumption in advanced economies.

As a result of these trends, sellers have had to pay much more attention to the less tangible elements of the exchange relationship, and add value to the core product or service through the provision of additional benefits.

In order to provide and deliver superior customer care, the organisation must motivate and train *all* its employees to understand the importance of creating and delivering satisfaction. In doing so, however, it is important to bear in mind that satisfaction is the extent to which a product or service meets or exceeds one's expectation. Accordingly, one needs to offer sufficient satisfaction to encourage people to buy, but not so much that the reality cannot possibly live up to the expectation.

CUSTOMER SERVICE

As noted in the Introduction, until recently comparatively little attention has been given to the role of customer service, with the result that there are no definitive statements as to the nature and scope of its functions. In one of the few British books on the subject, Christopher et al. (1979) define customer service as 'a system organised to provide a continuing link between the time that the order is placed and the goods are received with the objective of satisfying customer needs on a long-term basis'. Many would consider this too narrow a definition, as it excludes the fact that the provision of services may be highly instrumental

to the actual placing of an order. This view would seem to be shared by an American Management Association (AMACOM) research study in which the authors comment: 'Many buyers today regard service support as a major criterion for vendor selection' (Blenel and Bender, 1980).

To some extent this lack of agreement probably arises from the fact that many customer services are inextricably linked with other aspects of the marketing function and so are not seen to enjoy an existence apart from that function. For example, the provision of pre-sale information may properly be considered part of the promotion variable and seen as the responsibility of the salesman or the advertising function. Indeed the very title of Christopher et al.'s book links service with distribution.

However, the evidence from the AMACOM study shows clearly that product servicing is already a major and often independent function in its own right and is likely to assume even greater importance in future. On the first point, Blenel and Bender (1980, p. 12) state that:

> More people in the US today are engaged in technical and customer service than in industrial sales, with service organisations ranging in size from the independent repair person to corporate divisions with tens of thousands of employees.

With regard to the second point, the authors draw attention to the fact that the increased technological sophistication of many capital goods is now so great that it is beyond the competence of the user's own technicians and that they have to depend upon the manufacturer to supply the necessary service. Such dependency is clearly to the supplier's advantage and has become a deliberate policy of many manufacturers.

The broadened perspective of customer service is reflected strongly in Blenel and Bender's (1980) statement of the basic goals of service which they see as threefold.

'The first mission of service is to protect the company's customer base', a task which it accomplishes by ensuring that goods and services are delivered on time and in accordance with specification and supply and continue to supply those benefits for which they are purchased in the first place.

Box 20.2   *Importance of frontline service*

A survey by Bain & Company, the international consulting firm, into the factors underpinning persons evaluation of a shopping experience highlighted the importance of service.

In the case of a *great* shopping experience, 56% of loyal respondents mentioned 'service', 31% 'product', and 13% 'atmosphere'. For non-loyalists, 70% cited 'service' and 30% mentioned 'product'. For a *bad* shopping experience, 87% of loyalist cited 'service' and 13% 'atmosphere'. For non-loyalists 88% said 'service', and 12% mentioned 'product'.

It is clear that service dominates people's perceptions of both good and bad experiences, and noteworthy that no respondents chose 'price' as a major factor in either great or bad shopping experiences.

As noted previously:

Service's second mission is to enhance the product's saleability, since product performance alone is no longer the only consideration of most purchasers. Many buyers today regard service support as a major criterion for vendor selection. If technology, price, delivery, and quality are comparable among vendors, *service can be the determining factor*. It can play a major role in keeping a company competitive, especially as it affects life-cycle costing and product life.' (p. 17, emphasis added).

'The third mission of service, from the marketing perspective, is to generate income.' Blenel and Bender comment that while many services such as installation, maintenance, training etc., were often provided at no charge, revenues from such activities can now account for up to 30% of a corporation's total revenue. Of course such services were never provided 'free', but were built into the original price to the benefit of the less efficient and less well-organised firm and the detriment of those with better internal standards of training and maintenance. By costing these services separately, the supplier is able to build up a much better understanding of their customers and concentrate on those who offer the best prospects for a mutually satisfactory long-run relationship. We return to this issue later.

It is clear that, stated in these terms, customer services are equally relevant to both consumer and industrial products, although in general the latter are emphasised more than the former. In my opinion this is due more to organisational convenience than any basic difference between the two categories of goods. As a working generalisation, the more complex the product the longer its working life and the greater the financial outlay upon it the greater the need for customer service, from which it follows that consumer durables like cars, washing-machines and televisions will need attention just as much as forklift trucks, pickling plants and computer display terminals. Similarly, the major determinant of whether or not a firm will provide service directly to customers will depend upon much the same considerations that govern its choice of channel of distribution. (Indeed the close link between service and physical distribution strategies is apparent throughout Christopher et al.'s book.)

Accordingly, rather than preserve the traditional dichotomy between industrial and consumer goods that is supported by Blenel and Bender, we prefer to follow the distinctions based upon performance characteristics and user needs that has underlain all our analysis so far. By doing so it becomes possible to see how merchandising has been developed by manufacturers as a major service function which provides additional benefits to the retailer, who is the immediate customer, while enabling the producer to ensure that his products are displayed to the best advantage at the point of sale. Further, by following such an approach it is likely that consumer goods manufacturers will be encouraged to consider the experience of their industrial counterparts when assessing the contribution service policy may make to marketing strategy for consumer goods markets.

Box 20.3   *Value-added service*

As sales of new products, the main source of profit for many manufacturing companies, begins to slow, Caterpillar Inc. has begun to develop service business to maintain growth. Currently, Caterpillar's biggest problem has been keeping pace with the demand for earth-moving equipment and heavy-duty engines. However, CEO James Owen, with a doctorate in economics, is well aware that this basic business is extraordinarily cyclical and forecasts that the US market for large truck engines will peak in 2006, and the mining sector in 2009.

To counter the slowdown, Owen is seeking to make acquisitions in high-growth markets like China, encouraging dealers to run down inventories now to sustain future capacity and sales, and raising prices to take advantage of the buoyant demand.

Services, however, are the key to Caterpillar's strategic shift. The Peoria (Illinois) company has three service divisions today – Financial Services, Logistics and Remanufacturing – that account for 15% of Caterpillar's revenues and perhaps 20% of its net income.

These are forecast to increase to 20% of sales and as much as 30% contribution by 2010.

Remanufacturing is the newest of the service units and was set up in 1973 because one of Caterpillar's major customers, Ford, wanted a source of rebuilt engines. Despite its profitability, remanufacturing was regarded as a sideline until the late 1990s when its potential to profit again and again from the same goods was properly appreciated. In addition, by selling rebuilt products at a discount it headed off competition from makers trying to break into the lucrative after-market. With a plant in Shanghai, Caterpillar has the potential to establish a strong position in a growth market unable to afford new equipment, with remanufacturing having the highest growth and earnings potential in the years ahead.

SOURCE: Based on an article by Arndt, M. (2005) Caterpillar sinks its claws into services, *Business Week*, 5 December

CUSTOMER LOYALTY

At a seminar held in Edinburgh in 1996, organised by the Direct Marketing Association, and over which the author presided, a variety of expert speakers presented their views on the subject of customer loyalty. To begin, John Kemp of Tarp Europe Limited, an international management consulting/research company, defined customer satisfaction as 'The state in which customer needs, wants and expectations through the products' or services' life are met or exceeded, resulting in repurchase, brand loyalty and willingness to recommend.' Based on their own industry-specific data, Tarp confirmed that a surprisingly high proportion of customers experience problems. Topping the list was 69% of respondents who had experienced a problem with their last travel and leisure visit and 45% for their most recent vehicle repair. Forty-four per cent of consumer telecommunications customers had experienced problems within the past three months, 41% with financial services and 28% with utilities. Over a one-year period 49% of customers had experienced problems with industrial products and 40% with retail products. Despite experiencing these problems, many customers did not complain – 83% for retail products, 61% for financial services, 58% for travel and leisure, 56% for utilities, 38% for vehicle repair services, 29% for consumer telecommunications, and 12% for industrial products. These findings lend strong support to the contention that rather than voice their dissatisfaction, many customers merely take their business elsewhere. Of even more concern, perhaps, is the fact that many customers, ranging between 33% and 77% were not happy with business' response to their complaints, leading Tarp to conclude that a badly handled complaint can lose more customers than no action at all.

In a presentation, Peter Mouncey, the Automobile Association general manager group marketing services, identified five key points which the Association believes build loyalty:

1. A dedication to providing world class service – ensuring this is delivered to meet the defined needs of members and competently measured against their parameters. A customer-focused culture.
2. A detailed understanding of the brand and how this relates to the service and product mix – now and in the future. A commitment to the brand across the organisation and measurement tools to attract performance.
3. Marketing communications which inform and reflect the needs and expectations of the company's members.
4. Utilising the buying power of the AA to provide members with an increasing range of exclusive offers and price advantages for other AA and third party products.
5. A database strategy which enables the AA to finally target its products and services based on an increasing level of understanding of the company's members, customers and their individual needs.

In September 1994 Lord Marshall, then chief executive of British Airways, stated: 'Customer service innovation and the achievement of customer loyalty will form the competitive battle-ground of the twenty-first century for the major carriers.' This sentiment was echoed by Professor Adrian Payne of the Cranfield School of Management when he said 'The quality and history of our relationship is perhaps the only source of competitive advantage that ultimately cannot be copied.'

As background to the importance of British Airways' Executive Club, Chris Tilling, senior manager relationship marketing, provided some interesting statistics. To begin with, British Airways flies over 30 million people a year but less than 1 million people contribute more than 35% of BA's turnover and 50% of premium brands revenue. More to the point, BA knows who they are and where they live. Further, members fly more than non-members – an average of around 40 times a year and 37% of members said that they would have chosen another airline if they had not been an Executive Club member. While air miles are clearly an incentive for BA Executive Club members, frequent travellers identify 'hassle-free' travel as the benefit they most desire. Among the benefits the Executive Club offers that contribute to this, the number 1 benefit spontaneously mentioned by all members is lounge access, followed by air miles, seat choice, priority waitlist, and dedicated reservation lines. For all these services, the benefits received are rated as fairly or very satisfactory by over 80% of users, with less than 10% expressing dissatisfaction with any of them.

In conclusion, Executive Club is seen as delivering vital commercial objectives to BA, driving more than one-third of their revenue and growing. It underpins genuine decision-making and loyalty, while feedback from members drives both product development strategy and ideas. Finally, database investment is seen as critical in order to effectively target the right products to the right people at the right time.

Box 20.4   *Customer satisfaction – never mind the rhetoric*

In a panel discussion at the Royal Society of Arts (RSA), Philip Cullum, deputy chief of the National Consumer Council, stated:

> Apparently, it was Mahatma Ghandi who coined the phrase, 'The customer is king'. But the world moves on. Ghandi's claim has now been topped by some much more modern gurus – the people at Burger King. They tell their customers, 'We may be the King but you, my friend, are the almighty ruler.'
>
> The question is: How true is the rhetoric about companies loving their customers? From the council's view, the evidence is mixed. While there are many success stories:
>
> But, in our research, we've heard lots of horror stories too – often about some of the biggest UK businesses. Consumers mention the same sectors time and again: financial services, the utilities, electrical retailers, garages … And if you think the consumers are perhaps being a bit unfair just remember that the official figures suggest that the car servicing industry rips us all

off to the tune of £4 bn a year. In financial services, where world-class profits aren't matched by world-class quality, things have got so bad that the regulator has a programme called Treating Customers Fairly.

Cullum then observed that, despite the clear benefits of treating customers fairly, companies 'still seem to neglect their own self-interest by providing a lousy service'. Three particular examples of this are:

1. Companies are impersonal and described as 'distant, clinical, and uncaring'. Call centres, automated telephone systems and cold-calling are universally disliked and customers react badly when companies don't take ownership of problems. Banks and credit card companies were bottom of the list on this count.
2. 'The second complaint is that many businesses are incompetent.' Companies react slowly, patronise their customers and seem incapable of getting even simple things right.
3. 'Last, but not least, consumers complain about businesses saying one thing, then doing another. All too often, companies take a short-term perspective, focussing on today's sale at the expense of longer term damage to their reputation for mis-selling.'

While one must remember that a Consumer Council is likely to be a focus for complainants, it is clear that many firms are still failing to walk the marketing talk. The opportunities and benefits for those who do are obvious – the difference between a satisfied Starbucks customer and a dissatisfied one in terms of customer lifetime value (CLV) is about $2,800, while a satisfied BMW customer has an estimated CLV of $143,500.

SOURCE: RSA *Journal*, February 2006

To begin with, customer loyalty was measured in terms of satisfaction and retention. With better data and increased understanding, the emphasis has now moved on to measurement of the actual value of individual customers. Such analysis has indicated that many customers cost more than they are worth and so should not be encouraged to remain loyal, or, alternatively, be encouraged to switch to less costly services. Research by McKinsey and Co. (Coyles and Gokey, 2002) also identified a trend they termed 'migration', in which less satisfied customers spend less before possibly defecting to other suppliers. This trend was apparent in 16 industries studied and was dominant in two-thirds of them. Accordingly, the authors argue that by identifying customers who are spending less, one may take steps to halt or reverse this decline and increase customer value.

Box 20.5   **Loyalty cards**

In an article in *The Times* (4 June 2005), Sarah Butler and Michelle Henery summarised the benefits of using loyalty cards to both customers and retailers.

According to Mintel, 65% of people over 15 have at least one loyalty card and 11% of the population use four or more. However, 49% of respondents to their survey preferred lower prices – a factor that may have caused ASDA to drop AsdaClub in 1999 after a pilot in 19 of its stores, and to adopt 'everyday low prices' (ELP) as its basic strategy. This view is also shared by Morrison, Waitrose and John Lewis's supermarket, suggesting that firms with everyday low prices find cards expensive relative to the benefits received.

By contrast, Tesco is thought to spend about £20 million a year on its scheme and give away about 0.86% in margin to the 11 million households who use the card. On the other hand, interpretation of the data on its customers, including their names and addresses, has enabled it to fine-tune its strategy, as well as expand effectively into financial services and home shopping.

On average, loyalty cards offer a 1% discount but Boots Advantage Card offers a 4% discount to 14 million holders, which can rise to as much as 6% for regular users who get additional offers and vouchers. Despite the high discount, Boots are reported as saying: 'The Advantage Card drives sales. It has been running for eight years and one of the reasons is it drives fantastic footfall and customer loyalty.' It is also effective because points can only be redeemed on selected items, most of them higher margin, own-label goods.

Loyalty cards seem to work well in encouraging retention for a limited proportion of customers. They are less effective in attracting new customers, and find it hard to compete with price discounts. That said, about a quarter of rewards are never claimed, and the detailed information on buyer behaviour might cost as much, or more, to collect through other forms of market research.

THE SCOPE OF CUSTOMER SERVICE

Having advocated that conceptually it is not advantageous to compartmentalise marketing when considering customer service policy, it is clear that the scope of the service function will differ considerably according to the context. This variation is illustrated well in the two organisation charts reproduced as Figures 20.3 and 20.4 which relate to durable and consumer goods respectively and make it clear that the notions of customer service and customer relationship management are not new!

La Londe and Zinszer (1976) suggest a useful approach to classifying the elements of the service function when they assign them to the

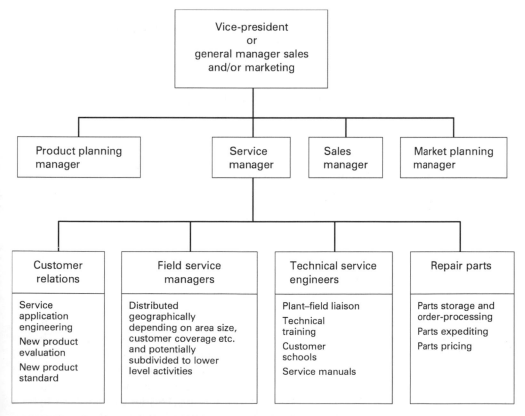

FIGURE 20.3 Composite service organisation for durable goods industries

SOURCE: Reprinted from Gannon, T. A. (ed.) (1972) *Product Services Management*. New York: American Management Association, p. 76

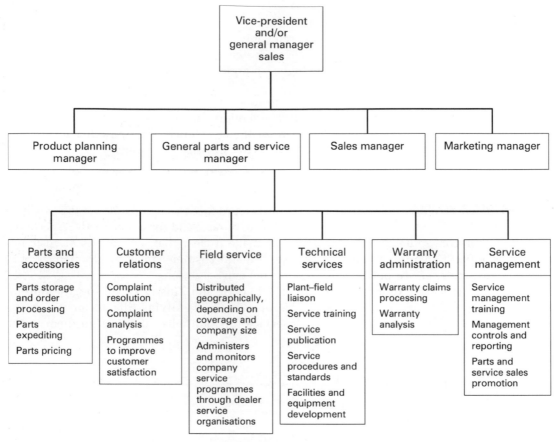

FIGURE 20.4 Composite service organisation for consumer goods industries

SOURCE: Reprinted from Gannon, T. A. (ed.) (1972) *Product Services Management.* New York: American Management Association, p. 76

pre-transaction elements, the transaction elements and the post-transaction elements. As summarised by Christopher et al. (1979), these are:

The pre-transaction elements of customer service relate to corporate policies or programmes, e.g. written statements of service policy, adequacy of organisational structure and system flexibility.

The transaction elements are those customer service variables directly involved in performing the physical distribution function. The most commonly quoted elements within this group are:

1. Product availability.
2. Order cycle time – average and consistency.
3. Order status information.
4. Order preparation.
5. Order size and order frequency.

The post-transaction elements of customer service

are generally supportive of the product while in use. For instance, product warranty, parts and repair service, procedures for customer complaints, and product replacements.

As noted, we would wish to extend the pre-transaction elements to incorporate the provision of services that will predispose the prospective user to buy from the source providing the service. Thus many companies will supply information and advice to inquirers free of charge even though they may not have purchased the company's brand of product to which the information relates, e.g. data on the use or application of materials such as paints, lubricants, insecticides etc. Similarly, in both the industrial and consumer markets, companies will often undertake survey work to advise potential customers of the benefits which will accrue from purchase, e.g. analysis of office productivity, energy-saving and insulation surveys, need for wood treatment by firms like Rentokil.

A particular example from my own experience selling tin plate supports this point. Tin plate is essentially a homogeneous product manufactured to a precise specification. At the time in question (late 1950s, early 1960s), there were only two suppliers in the UK market and the price was fixed, with the result that the only factors distinguishing the two suppliers were their marketing and service. Because of the difficulty of achieving a significant long-term advantage on these two dimensions, customers exhibited considerable inertia and adopted the simple purchasing policy of buying from the two companies in proportion to their output – a ratio of $2:1$. In the early 1960s demand declined due to competition from new packaging materials, just as new production facilities came on-stream, resulting in excess tin-plate capacity and there developed the first real competition between the two suppliers in over twenty years. In this climate I undertook a survey of over 200 specifications used by a major tin-box manufacturer and with the help of the operations research section was able to show how these could be reduced to six basic specifications which would cover all the end-use specifications. By doing this the buyer would be able to secure maximum bulk discounts and effect major savings on their raw-material purchases. The company was delighted with this proposal and as a token of its appreciation transferred 50% of its business from our competitor to ourselves.

In addition the promise of service on and after purchase may also be used very effectively to encourage active consideration of a supplier's product and secure it a place on the 'ladder' in the mind of the would-be purchaser. Whether these activities are classified as public relations, advertising, missionary selling or whatever, they clearly comprise elements of customer service and should be treated as such in the development of a service policy.

In the case of La Londe and Zinszer's 'transaction elements', the emphasis is again on physical distribution elements that are designed to ensure the product is available as and when required. Given the frequently voiced complaints about delays in the delivery of many British manufac-

tured goods in both domestic and foreign markets, this aspect of service cannot be emphasised enough. One should also remember our maxim that consumption is a function of availability! However, the importance of physical distribution should not be allowed to distract attention from other important service elements associated with a sale. Of particular importance are:

1. Financing the sale
2. Installation
3. Demonstration and/or training in use.

With 'large ticket' items both industrial and consumer buyers may need to spread payments over some future time period. Because of its expertise and knowledge of its prospective customers, a manufacturer or distributor may have a much better feel for their creditworthiness than do the traditional sources of credit. Thus sellers may be able to use their own credit rating and their 'bulk borrowing' capacity to offer advantageous credit terms to their customer. In addition, the purchaser may find it more convenient to combine the actions of raising credit and completing a purchase into a single transaction. Credit and financing policy may well be the responsibility of the accounting/finance function, but it still comprises an important customer service which needs to be integrated into the firm's marketing strategy.

Installation may be simple – plugging in an appliance in the home or office – or complex, fitting kitchen units or double glazing, commissioning a power station. Either way the customer benefits from the provision of such a service (which may well be an important source of revenue to the supplier), while the seller has the reassurance that the product is more likely to prove satisfactory when properly installed than would otherwise be the case. Much the same consideration attaches to demonstrating correct usage and providing training where necessary. In the absence of this, the customer may well misuse the product and fail to obtain the desired output from it thus increasing the possibility of dissatisfaction and the need for more expensive post-transaction services. (See, for example, the textile machinery cases in *Market Development*, Baker, 1983.)

The provision of services of this kind can do much to reduce the risk perceived by a prospective purchaser and can constitute a major source of preference for one supplier over another.

In the post-transaction stage, the seller has a responsibility to ensure that the customer receives the desired and promised benefits. To do so they must establish a mechanism whereby customers may receive advice and service to keep the product working – both of which will have an important effect in reducing post-purchase dissonance and in confirming the buyer in the correctness of their original decision. Such satisfaction will also ensure that the supplier will have a strong likelihood of remaining the preferred source when a replacement decision has to be made.

Suppliers must also develop a policy and mechanism for handling customer complaints. While buyers are offered extensive protection under the law, relatively few will pursue a complaint this far and prefer to adopt the simple expedient of not buying from that source again. In so far as we have defined marketing as 'selling goods that don't come back to people who do', failure to deal efficiently and sympathetically with complaints amounts to a negation of the marketing concept. Worse still, dissatisfied customers are likely to tell others of their dissatisfaction and negative word of mouth can be just as harmful as positive word of mouth is helpful.

Evidence to support the view of the negative impact of poor service was provided in an article by Daniel Finkelman and Anthony Goland (1990) entitled 'How not to satisfy your customers'. The authors' opening paragraph endorsed the views expressed above:

> Today, a company's ability to ensure satisfaction with the entire 'customer ownership experience' is critical to its long-term success. As years of investment have, at least, made many firms competitive in both costs and quality, their ability to create a clear advantage based on either has been substantially reduced. Hence, the new battleground for the 1990s: providing the most satisfying ownership experience for customers – from the time shopping begins, to the buying experience itself, to the point of delivery, through the period during which the product is owned and used, and even to the customer's ultimate disposal of the product.

Finkelman and Goland cite numerous studies to support the view that customer satisfaction leads to loyalty and a high likelihood of repurchase, while dissatisfied customers are likely not to complain or repurchase. However, if complaints are resolved quickly then the likelihood of repurchase increases dramatically. Figures 20.5 and 20.6 illustrate that 'A large portion of what makes up customer satisfaction for a given company or product may be entirely unrelated to product quality'. Figure 20.7 indicates that, in the case of consumer durable and industrial equipment, if product quality accounts for half of the customer's satisfaction then the remainder is attributable to a variety of service elements.

Detailed discussion of the establishment of such service policies and mechanisms is clearly beyond the scope of this book and the reader should consult the Recommended reading at the end of the chapter for information on these.

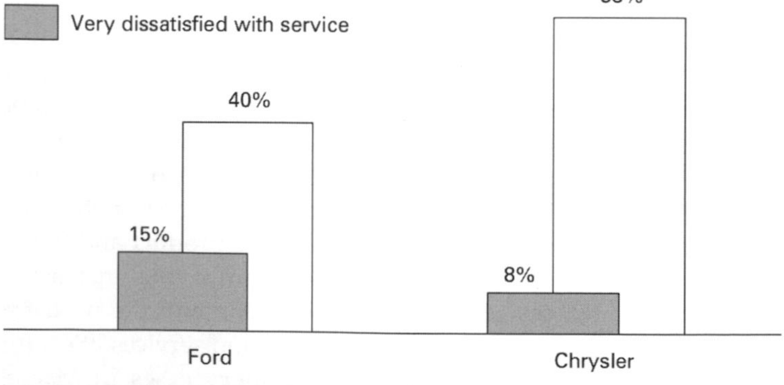

THE STRATEGIC USE OF CUSTOMER SERVICE

In discussing the reasons underlying the growing importance of the service function, Blenel and Bender (1980) observe that 'Besides technology, there are two other driving

FIGURE 20.5 Repurchase loyalty to the retailer (new vehicle sales)

SOURCE: Finkelman, D. and Goland, A. (1990) How not to satisfy your customers, *McKinsey Quarterly* (winter)

Why industrial companies lose customers

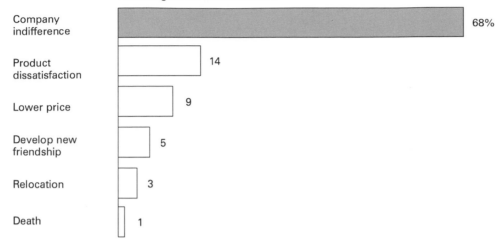

Percentage of all lost customers

Company indifference	68%
Product dissatisfaction	14
Lower price	9
Develop new friendship	5
Relocation	3
Death	1

Why customers purchase from a specific service company

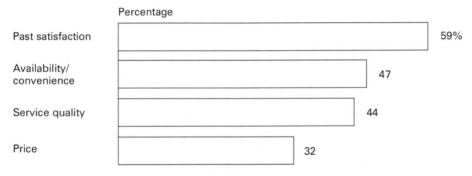

Percentage

Past satisfaction	59%
Availability/ convenience	47
Service quality	44
Price	32

Main reason for switching banks

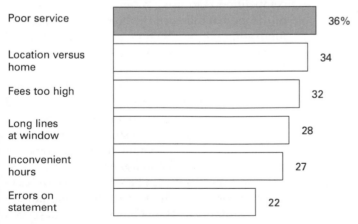

Top box answer, percentage of respondents

Poor service	36%
Location versus home	34
Fees too high	32
Long lines at window	28
Inconvenient hours	27
Errors on statement	22

FIGURE 20.6 The value of customer satisfaction

SOURCE: Finkelman, D. and Goland, A. (1990) How not to satisfy your customers, *McKinsey Quarterly* (winter)

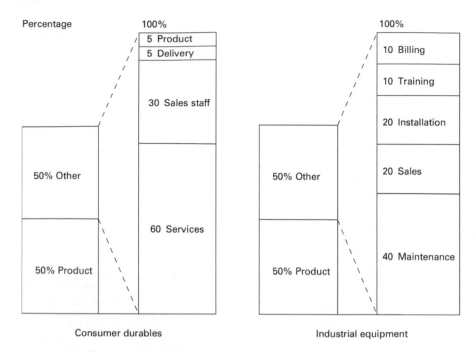

FIGURE 20.7 The relative importance of customer satisfaction factors

SOURCE: Finkelman, D. and Goland, A. (1990) How not to satisfy your customers, *McKinsey Quarterly* (winter)

forces of service's growth – consumerism and legislation. Consumers today are not only more knowledgeable, they also have more alternatives.'

Consumerism has been characterised, correctly in my view, as 'the shame of marketing' for clearly if suppliers were truly marketing-oriented then consumers should have little cause for dissatisfaction with their efforts. By the same token the spate of legislation to protect consumers which has come into existence in recent years in most countries is an indictment of the supplier's willingness to respond voluntarily to such overt dissatisfaction.

Of course, ensuring consumer satisfaction starts well before and goes far beyond the provision of customer service in a technical sense. That said, it is clear that, to a lesser or greater extent, the provision of customer service constitutes an integral component of the bundle of benefits anticipated by a purchaser. Thus in Chapter 2 we argued that products and services are part of the same spectrum by which suppliers transfer benefits to users such that for the purpose of strategic planning one could reasonably consider them to be the same. Nonetheless as one progresses along the spectrum from pure good to pure service, the service element

increases from negligible to virtually complete and it follows that the strategic importance of customer service will vary in the same way.

Having said that, it is apparent that one way of developing a differentiated marketing strategy which will set one apart from the general run of competition is to use a different product : service mix from that followed by the majority. Flour and lubricating oil may be pure goods but BeRo and Castrol have successfully positioned themselves by providing advisory services in support of their products. Similarly, as Ted Levitt (1972) has shown, the industrialisation of service has enabled suppliers to control and guarantee the quality of many personal services and so enhance their value to consumers (e.g. automatic telling machines in banks, McDonald's hamburgers).

It must also be remembered that service back-up may constitute the key strategic variable in certain situations. Thus Ohmae (1983) describes the case of Toyota, who recognised service as a critical factor to forklift customers and so chose it as the main basis of competition. This was an important strategic decision, since it entailed high fixed costs – so high that Toyota's subcritical competitors could not afford to match its investment. Today Toyota's forklift business has an awesome service network; the company boasts that it can despatch a service car to any part of Japan within two hours. As a result, despite its rather conventional product and pricing schemes, Toyota's share of this service-hungry industry continues to climb (p. 131).

As with other aspects of marketing planning, the critical questions with regard to developing a service strategy are:

1. What do customers want?
2. What do we and our competitors provide?
3. How can we improve our offering and differentiate it from our competitors?
4. What will this cost and what benefits can we anticipate from this?

With regard to the first question, Kotler (1980) quotes a Canadian survey in which buyers of industrial equipment ranked 13 service elements in the following rank order:

1. Delivery reliability
2. Prompt quotation
3. Technical advice
4. Discounts
5. After-sales service
6. Sales representation
7. Ease of contact
8. Replacement guarantee
9. Wide range of manufacturers
10. Pattern design
11. Credit
12. Test facilities
13. Machining facilities.

It is perhaps significant that faced with a list of features in rank order, the respondents emphasised general rather than specific service attributes, which suggests that only if you perform satisfactorily on these will additional service factors become determinant.

Blenel and Bender (1980) take a much broader and pragmatic view and state:

In the authors' experience, customers differ in what they most value from service. The majority consider that the most important function is to maintain the equipment so it operates well. This implies availability of spare parts, well-trained technicians, up-to-date instruction manuals, and liaison between company and customer.

The next most-valued quality is a continued sales presence after the major sale. All too often service technicians must perform the after-sale function to ensure that the customer has the required re-supply items. To see that the customer gets proper and continued attention, management must make a firm decision on which unit of the company is responsible for a re-supply of expendable materials or parts, else service, unprepared though it may be, can be stuck with the task.

The third most-valued quality is that service be first-rate and that it be easily accessible. The finest advertising campaign cannot convince the public that a sow's ear is a silk purse. Performance, not promise, is what is demanded. Even good equipment is often downgraded unfairly when the service organisation gives it poor support.

From these comments, it is clear that one may generalise about the broad dimensions of service, but in the particular the most obvious way to determine what is required and how strong the requirement is (Would you pay more for it? How much?) is to undertake research among one's customers and compare the results with the existing provision (Question 2) to see how well they match up. Only when such an analysis has been completed does it become possible to evaluate possible changes in the service strategy.

Based on their research Christopher et al. (1979) propose six areas in which they believe that customer service decisions differ significantly from other decision areas. While not accepting this view, as several of the 'distinctions' would seem to apply equally to other aspects of marketing, their listing is helpful in specifying factors which must be taken into account when devising a service strategy. It almost goes without saying that 'Customer service is part of the total market offering of the firm' but the second of their propositions 'Service is perceived asymmetrically; good service is expected as a normal concomitant of business relationships; weak service becomes a highly visible negative signal' reinforces the importance of giving as much attention to service as to the other elements of the marketing mix and of developing specific service policies.

Another important proposition, which I would qualify with the word 'often' is 'Customer service is directly concerned with relationships with market intermediary firms, rather than to final customer'. It follows that the needs of the intermediaries in the distribution channel must be given specific attention, for they may well differ radically from the needs of the final customer and call for distinct service policies for each.

Finally, Christopher et al. draw an important distinction between the short- and long-run implications of customer service. In the short-run service failures may result only in lost orders due to stockouts, or to reduced margins because of the need to replace defective parts or offer compensation. In the long run, repetition of such failures can put the whole organisation at risk, as customers switch to alternative sources of supply. Conversely, careful attention to service in the short run can be a powerful force in developing habitual buying behaviour and customer inertia. However, such advice begs the question as to precisely what service the supplier should provide and how they should charge for this. Before examining this issue, however, it will be useful to look at service as an integral part of the much wider concept of TQM.

TOTAL QUALITY MANAGEMENT (TQM)

TQM is well understood as a vision or concept – the challenge and the difficulty lies in translating it into action.

A concern for quality is enlightened self-interest. All the evidence indicates that quality reduces costs, adds value and is often the just noticeable difference (JND) that differentiates between success and failure at the point of sale. Erickson (1991) reports the findings of research conducted during the 1980s by Opinion Research Corporation, which showed that corporations ranking below average on nine key dimensions of perceived quality tend to have far lower price–earning ratios than firms with strong reputations in those areas.

However, the problems with TQM tend to emerge when its principles are extended beyond the 'hard' and objective functions such as manufacturing into the 'soft' areas which involve interpersonal relationships and the provision of services. Erickson argues that 'The way to make quality improvement

effective in such areas as customer service, marketing, and R&D is by having a clearly articulated strategy that ties all these efforts together and focuses the corporation – including top management – on strategic quality improvement. The way to ensure top management's commitment to quality is to embed quality in areas of unquestionable top management priority – the fundamental goals and priorities of the corporation.'

In order to achieve this, it is argued that those responsible for the formulation of corporate strategy should change the parameters of the planning matrices that have had such a major influence on strategic business management for the past 30 years or more. Rather than emphasise the dimensions of industry maturity and competitive position (refined during the 1980s by the inclusion of concepts of competitive advantage and intensity), it is proposed that the planning matrix for the 1990s 'should allow organisations to articulate their objectives against the level of customer satisfaction that they strive to achieve, as well as how their competitors respond to similar challenges' (Erickson, 1991). Such a matrix is shown in Figure 20.8.

To use this matrix, Erickson suggests the firm should classify and plot the attributes of its total offering in three major categories – threshold attributes, performance attributes and excitement attributes. Performance attributes are essential aspects of the product or service and, as indicated in our composite model of choice behaviour (Chapter 9), will be the primary basis for discriminating between alternatives, with 'better' performance always being preferred within any given price bracket. By contrast, threshold attributes are those in which additional improvements result in little added customer satisfaction and so have little or no economic value. However, excitement attributes are defined as 'features of a service or product that consumers don't expect and in which a modest improvement above the competitive norm can provide significantly enhanced customer satisfaction and economic benefit'.

As the result of competition, performance and excitement attributes (which may be thought of more as subjective values – BR in our model of choice behaviour) may lose their distinctiveness and become threshold attributes. As and when this occurs the firm will have to develop and introduce new attributes if it is to maintain its competitive

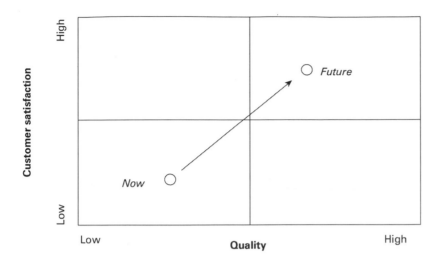

FIGURE 20.8 A quality-driven planning matrix: strategic response
SOURCE: Erickson, T. J. (1991) Beyond the quality revolution: linking quality to corporate strategy, *Prism* (1)

standing. To achieve this calls for sophisticated measurement techniques and a creative understanding of customers in order to monitor and anticipate change, together with tools for quality improvement. As Erickson notes 'Quality improvement tools can play a critical role in helping a firm enhance performance, lower the cost of a product, reduce lead time, and even identify new attributes and opportunities to satisfy the customer, as well as to set priorities.'

Writing in the same issue of *Prism*, Diane Schmanlensee (1991) emphasises the point that as quality improvement has spread from manufacturing to services, so the concept of quality and its measurement have changed. Like 'satisfaction', quality is something particular to the consumer and it is their perception, not the supplier's, which matters. Perceived quality will depend heavily upon expectations such that an organisation with a modest reputation delivering good service may be rated higher than an organisation with a superior reputation delivering equally good service. In the first case, expectations, and so value-added, are exceeded; in the second case they fall short, and will be reflected in lower service rating. The challenge is obvious – improved service levels increase expectations and increased expectations call for still further improvements in service levels.

In order to track and respond to customers' expectations and perceptions firms have had to develop a battery of 'soft' measures to complement the familiar 'hard' measures that quantify objective performance measures. Schmanlensee comments:

A soft measurement is something that cannot be timed or weighed or calibrated. It is neither tangible nor physical. Rather, it is concerned with individual attitudes, beliefs, and opinion. Soft measurement allows you to hear the clear voices of your customers, employees, managers, and intermediaries. And those voices are critical not only in understanding how well you are doing, but also in determining what you should be doing next.

Of course none of this is new to the marketer, for whom AIO (attitude, interest and opinion) measurement has been a key technique in identifying market opportunities for several decades. What is new is that the total quality concept has provided a bridge between the traditionally hard measures of manufacturing and the soft measures of sales and marketing. In doing so, it has underlined the interdependency of the functions, and done much to break down the traditional divisions between them in a less threatening way than was seen to be the case when exhorting companies to become market-oriented.

PRICING SERVICES

From the previous section it is evident that certain services may be regarded as an integral part of the product offering and their provision must be regarded as an essential cost of doing business. Clearly, such costs should be incorporated in the selling price, but what criteria should one apply to determine whether services should be priced jointly or separately? James Hauk (1970) provides a useful checklist:

1. Do customer needs differ significantly?
2. Do needs vary in proportion to the size of the order?
3. What is the magnitude of service cost?
4. Is it to the interest of the seller to have all buyers use the service offered?
5. What is the company's major market target?

Where customer needs are homogeneous, it makes sense to incorporate the price of associated services into the price of the product – otherwise one should offer the services separately at a price, i.e. a service contract. Similarly, if the need for service varies with the size of order, a joint price will ensure that clients receive what they pay for; if a fixed service is required irrespective of order size, it is more equitable to charge for the service separately (or give a discount).

The third criterion seeks to relate the magnitude of the service cost to the total cost. Where this is high those customers who do not need the service would be unlikely to choose a supplier who added the service cost to the product cost and separate pricing would be appropriate. Conversely, where the service costs are small related to total cost, buyers may not perceive them and will be willing to accept a joint price.

In many cases suppliers will wish to install their products and retain responsibility for their maintenance and repair. By incorporating the service price in the selling price, the supplier will limit sales to those clients willing to accept these terms and so avoid possible dissatisfaction arising from incorrect installation and maintenance. As noted earlier, such a policy also enables the suppliers to develop long-term relationships with their customers and so enhance the likelihood of securing new and/or replacement sales.

Finally, the seller should consider whether the target market is price sensitive – in which case services should be priced separately – or service conscious when joint pricing is to be preferred.

In cases where services are priced separately, exactly the same considerations apply as to the pricing of the product itself – namely what is the demand for the service, how price-sensitive is it and what are the costs of providing any given level of service? However, one must also allow for the fact that the product and service are in joint demand and be prepared to modify the price for one or the other in order to optimise total revenue, e.g. you may install equipment at or below cost if it promises an attractive earnings stream from the long-term supply of services.

MEASURING SERVICE QUALITY

In the spring 1991 edition of *Survey*, Diana Brown of the Royal Mail and Roger Banks of Research International described some of the measures used by the Royal Mail to monitor the implementation of its TQM process 'Customer First'. Unlike many quality assurance programmes, 'Customer First' is not concerned solely with the quality of the service itself; it is seen as a way of working throughout the business based on the needs of both internal and external customers. To measure the effectiveness of this service quality two kinds of indicator are used – hard and soft.

One of the most important 'hard' measures is the end to end (E2E) programme devised by Research International, which measures the time taken from pillar box to doormat. This E2E measurement system is able to provide highly localised and diagnostic feedback. However, it measures only one aspect of quality – speed of the delivery. To complement this information, Royal Mail also undertakes nationwide image studies to establish how its customers feel about the business. While this information is helpful in enabling Royal Mail to position itself against other large organisations such as BT and British Gas, it is of little practical help to staff in each of Royal Mail's 64 districts around the UK.

In the words of the authors:

What was required was a comprehensive measure of performance on a range of quality issues that actually matter to business and personal customers – a measurement system that operated at the local level. And one which provided clear, unequivocal and practical guidance on how staff could consolidate in areas of strength, and improve in areas of weakness. The name of this measurement system is the Customer Perception Index (CPI).

Based upon qualitative group discussions with a cross-section of customers to establish key quality issues, a large, nationally representative survey was undertaken to determine their relative importance. The CPI represents the third stage of the research and comprises a continuous mail survey of some 320,400 personal and business customers each year.

Reports of the survey findings are circulated every three months to each of the districts and cover both hard and soft measures as well as comparative measures relating current to prior performance. What helps distinguish CPI from much similar market research is the effort made to action the findings by providing advice and support to district head postmasters so they can apply them at the local level.

THE INDUSTRIALISATION OF SERVICE

In 1976, the *Harvard Business Review* published 'The Industrialization of Service' by Theodore Levitt. As with many of his seminal articles, Levitt was ahead of the game in identifying an important emerging trend – the growing importance of services in the advanced economies as the newly industrialising countries (NICs) took over the supply of many manufactured products at more competitive prices than domestic producers. Using Britain as an example, Levitt argued that if the advanced economies failed to manage service delivery efficiently and effectively, then the higher labour costs generally associated with service provision would lead to a loss of international competitiveness and a decline in standards of living.

In the case of Britain, he wrote: 'In Britain, "to serve" remains to this day encrusted with immemorial attachments to master–servant pretensions that dull the imagination and block the path to service

efficiency.' Happily, we appear to have grown out of this mindset, but a recent holiday in Ireland suggests it is alive and well there! So, what needs to be done? Essentially, Levitt's argument is that as it is the people who cause problems with service delivery, we should, as far as possible, remove them from the equation. To do so we need to 'industrialise' services, and Levitt proposes three ways in which we may do this: via hard technologies, soft technologies and hybrid technologies.

In the case of hard technologies, one substitutes 'machinery, tools, or other tangible artifacts for people in the performance of service work'. As examples he cites electrocardiograms, consumer credit cards, airport X-ray surveillance equipment, automatic car washes, automatic toll collectors, automatic clothes and dishwashers, non-iron fabrics etc.

'Soft technologies are essentially the substitution of organised preplanned systems for individual service operatives'. As examples, he cites: supermarkets and other self-service establishments, fast-food restaurants like McDonald's, where portion preparation and control are highly automated, package tours, various kinds of insurance and investment schemes etc.

The third category, hybrid systems, combines both hard equipment and systems 'to bring efficiency, order, and speed to the service process'.

Levitt's argument is, essentially, that while the Industrial Revolution was enabled by the deskilling of craft specialisations, this has yet to occur in many service occupations. This is most apparent in the case of the professions, where entry is restricted by qualification. Clearly, practitioners need to be knowledgeable about their subject and, hopefully, skilled in its application but, in many cases, customers might be better served by the elimination of some restrictive practices and the industrialisation of the services they offer. To do so calls for *management*.

SERVICE AS A MARKETING STRATEGY

Writing in *Industrial Marketing Management* in 1990, M. P. Singh, a business manager for the Reliance Electric Company, provides a compelling case history of how his company has used 'offering the best service in the market as its marketing strategy to significantly increase its market share and profitability'. A synopsis of this case history provides a fitting conclusion to this chapter.

This case history reinforces many of the points made thus far. First, and perhaps most important, to succeed in business one must have a competitive edge which enables prospective customers to distinguish and prefer your offering to that of your competitors. Second, in assessing competitive offerings buyers will consider first performance factors and fitness for purpose. Having satisfied themselves that the offering will perform the functions for which it is required, buyers will compare offerings of similar functionality in terms of their cost–benefits, i.e. which offering represents the best value. If more than one offering passes this test, the buyer will have to resort to other less objective criteria in order to decide between the available alternatives. Third, service provides both objective and subjective values and enhances customer satisfaction, leading to preference and loyalty.

Singh's description tends to stress the pre-transaction and transaction elements. While these are vital, we would conclude this chapter by speculating that as more and more companies use service as a strategic element in the marketing mix it will be the post-transactional elements which will become determinant.

Box 20.6 — Service as a marketing strategy

The case study concerns the Mechanical Group of the Reliance Electric Company, a leading supplier of power transmission equipment with world sales in excess of $1.5 billion. The Mechanical Group (MG) manufactures and markets mechanical power transmission products directly to large original equipment manufacturers (OEMs) and select users, and through distributors to other OEMs and users in USA, Canada, Mexico and Brazil. The distributors account for 'an overwhelmingly large portion of the total sales', which are mainly in the US market, and are connected with MG by computers for both information and transaction.

'The severe recession of 1982 in the US industrial economy threw the MG sales into a tailspin, and the bottom line showed big losses.' Singh describes the recession as the culmination of a series of adverse environmental and competitive trends of the kind discussed in Chapters 6 and 10 – particularly technological change and increased international competition. Singh also cites 'The traditional thinking of relating mass production to lower costs' as causing problems for marketers in that it 'resulted in 20%–30% excess capacity throughout the industrial sector of the US'. (Additional evidence that the pursuit of market share can have negative consequences, despite the fact that possession of a dominant share confers significant strategic advantage.)

Singh's analysis also lends support to our composite model of buyer choice behaviour when he distinguishes four stages in the evolution of markets which call for different emphases in marketing strategy as 'different factors assume dominant importance in customer-purchase decisions'. To begin with technology is most important but, as technology diffuses and becomes more widely available, so cost assumes dominance to be succeeded by quality as cost differentials disappear. Finally 'when the market leaders can offer the same (similar) costs and quality, the issue of service emerges as the dominant factor affecting the purchase. Most of today's markets are in this stage now'.

Having taken decisive action to recover from their tailspin through attention to the classic mix elements (downsizing to reduce the breakeven point, increased sales and promotional efforts, accelerated plans for product improvement and NPD) MG recognised that something else was required to restore their competitive edge. 'Serving customers better' emerged as the preferred strategy.

To implement this strategy it was necessary first to define what 'service' is. Based upon feedback from customers and internal consultation MG decided that 'Service could be measured by the ease, speed, and accuracy with which the customers can:

1. Get assistance from any employee
2. Understand all policies and sales programmes
3. Get all the needed technical information about products and their applications
4. Get all the needed commercial information
5. Make the purchase
6. Update themselves about the status of any order if there are any delays or problems expected with the shipment (ideally, there should not be any delays or problems)
7. Stock and identify the products
8. Get post-purchase service like credits and return of merchandise etc.'

Singh describes how MG developed the practices and procedures necessary to achieve these objectives and the outcomes, which included steady increases in market share, the best profits and ROI for its industry and reported customer perceptions that they delivered the best service in their market.

Chapter summary

As noted in the Introduction to this chapter, comparatively little has been written about the role of service as an element in the marketing mix. To some extent this apparent neglect may arise from the fact that many customer services are inextricably linked with other aspects of the marketing function and so are not seen to enjoy an existence separate from that function. While this is undoubtedly true, the perspective of this chapter has been that the growing importance of service as a differentiating factor in the firm's strategy is such that it merits explicit treatment in its own right.

Our analysis suggests that service plays an important role in both establishing and sustaining the relationship between supplier and user. Anticipation of the user's needs and the manner in which they will 'consume' the product over time will constitute a vital input to the original design and manufacture of the product. Similarly, advice or assistance with installation and use will increase the likelihood that the product will deliver the promised performance and so provide the satisfaction which the consumer is looking for.

In turn these considerations will have a significant influence upon pricing and distribution decisions – should one set the initial price low and earn one's profits from the provision of service over the product's life-cycle or should one make one's profit on the initial sale and leave the provision of service to a third party? Clearly, there is no single or simple answer to such a question for as our analysis of the other elements of the marketing mix has shown time and again, such decisions tend to be situation-specific. That said, there is considerable evidence to suggest that in many markets, particularly for mature products, the service element will be a major factor in distinguishing between success and failure.

Recommended reading

Carson, D. J. (1999) Customer care and satisfaction, in M. J. Baker (ed.) *Encyclopedia of Marketing*. London: International Thomson Business Press.

Christopher, M. (2003) Customer service and logistics strategy, in M. J. Baker (ed.) *The Marketing Book* (5th edn). Oxford: Butterworth Heinemann.

Donaldson, W. (1995) Customer care, in M. J. Baker (ed.) *Marketing: Theory and Practice* (3rd edn). Basingstoke: Macmillan – now Palgrave Macmillan.

Reichheld, F. (2001) *The Loyalty Effect: The Hidden Force Behind Growth, Profits and Lasting Value*. Boston, MA: Harvard Business School Press.

Shaw, C. (2004) *Revolutionise Your Customer Experience*. Basingstoke: Palgrave Macmillan.

REFERENCES

Arndt, M. (2005) Caterpillar sinks its claws into services, *Business Week*, 5 December.

Baker, M. J. (1983) *Market Development*. Harmondsworth: Penguin.

Baker, M. J. (2006) *Marketing* (7th edn). Helensburgh: Westburn.

Baker, M. J. (2006) *Marketing: An Introductory Text* (7th edn). Helensburgh: Westburn Publishers..

Blenel, W. H. and Bender, H. E. (1980) *Product Service Planning*. New York: AMACOM.

Brown, D. and Banks, R. (1991) Customer first, *Survey* (spring).

Butler, S. and Henery, M. (2005) *The Times* (4 June).

Carson, D. J. (1999) Customer care

and satisfaction, in M. J. Baker (ed.) *Encyclopedia of Marketing*. London: International Thomson Business Press, pp. 550–61.

Carson, D. and Gilmore, A. (1989) Customer care: the neglected domain, *Irish Marketing Review*, **4**(3): 49–61.

Chaston, I. (1990) *Managing for Marketing Excellence*. Maidenhead: McGraw-Hill.

Christopher, M., Schory, P. and Skjott-Larsen, T. (1979) *Customer Service and Distribution Strategy*. London: Associated Business Press.

Copeland, M. T. (1923) Relation of consumers' buying habits to marketing methods, *Harvard Business Review* (April).

Coyles, S. and Gokey, T. C. (2002) *Customer Retention is Not Enough*, McKinsey and Co.

Donaldson, W. (1995) Customer care, in M. J. Baker (ed.) *Marketing: Theory and Practice* (3rd edn). Basingstoke: Macmillan – now Palgrave Macmillan, pp. 330–45.

Erickson, T. J. (1991) Beyond the quality revolution: linking quality to corporate strategy, *Prism* (1): 5–21.

Finkelman, D. and Goland, A. (1990) How not to satisfy your customers, *McKinsey Quarterly* (winter).

Gannon, T. A. (ed.) (1972) *Product Services Management*. New York: American Management Association, p. 76.

Gilmore, A. and Carson, D. (1993) Enhancing service quality: a case study, *Irish Marketing Review*, **6**: 64–73.

Hauk, J. (1970) The role of service in effective marketing, in V. P. Buell and C. C. Meyel (eds) *Handbook of Modern Marketing*. New York: McGraw-Hill.

Kotler, P. (1980) *Marketing Management* (4th edn). Englewood Cliffs, NJ: Prentice Hall, p. 375.

La Londe, B. J. and Zinszer P. H. (1976) *Customer Service: Meaning and Measurement*. Chicago, IL: National Council of Physical Distribution Management.

Levitt, T. (1960) Marketing myopia, *Harvard Business Review* (July–August)

Levitt, T. (1972) Production-line approach to service, *Harvard Business Review* (September–October).

Levitt, T. (1976) The industrialization of service, *Harvard Business Review* (September–October): 63–74.

Ohmae, K. (1983) *The Mind of the Strategist*. Harmondsworth: Penguin.

Porter, M. E. (1985) *Competitive Advantage: Creating and Sustaining Superior Performance*. New York: Free Press.

Reichheld, F. F. (1996) *The Loyalty Effect*. Boston, MA: Harvard Business School Press.

Schmalensee, D. H. (1991) Soft measurement: a vital ingredient in quality improvement, *Prism* (1): 49–57.

Singh, M. P. (1990) Service as a marketing strategy: a case study at Reliance Electric, *Industrial Marketing Management*, **19**.

Stewart, T. A. (1997) A satisfied customer isn't enough, *Fortune*, 21 July.

Webster, F. E. (1992) The changing role of marketing in the corporation, *Journal of Marketing* (October).

NOTE

1. It will be recalled from Chapter 8 that switching costs play an important role in competition.

Developing a marketing culture

The way we do things around here.   ANON

After reading Chapter 21 you will be able to:

✔ Explain why strategy should determine organisational structure.

✔ Describe the characteristics of the five basic business orientations – technology, production, sales, financial and marketing – and how these condition the conduct of the firm's business.

✔ Define the concepts of organisational climate, corporate personality and corporate culture, and show how these shape and mediate the firm's strategy and behaviour.

✔ Spell out what is involved in the development of a marketing-oriented organisation.

✔ Review some of the obstacles to the translation of theory into practice through effective implementation.

INTRODUCTION

In Chapter 1, we expressed the view that while some may still hold to the view that marketing is an art or craft which can be only mastered by experiential learning, the reality is that with increased professionalism there is a distinct need for formal education in the subject. We also argued that with growing recognition of the role of marketing it makes sense to train young people for careers in the function. To do so, it seems sensible to capture the extensive body of knowledge that mirrors the distilled experience of skilled and successful practitioners and record this in texts of this kind which can be used in such education and training. In the preceding chapters this is what we have attempted to do – always recognising that the treatment must be partial and eclectic and can provide only a broad overview of the subject. However, the point has now been reached in which we must address the critical question of how to put this knowledge into practice.

To begin with, it is important to consider the relationship between a firm's structure and its strategy. As we shall see, ideally, the strategy should dictate the most appropriate organisational form to ensure its effective implementation. However, with the exception of the green-field 'start-up' (which is a basic assumption of the textbook writer) organisations already possess an organisational structure, and the challenge is how to protect, modify or grow them to achieve the organisational purpose. At the outset most organisations' structures are dominated by one or other of the five basic business functions. Accordingly we are accustomed to think of firms as having a predominantly production, finance, sales or whatever orientation. From the outset this book has taken the view that while all the business functions contribute to the firm's performance, this will be enhanced if it is marketing-oriented and customer-driven. Peter Doyle (1992) lends considerable support to this view, as well as providing a useful diagram to help distinguish between the financial and marketing orientations. In addressing the question: What are the excellent companies?, Doyle comments: 'The market-led approach which seeks market leadership through superiority in meeting customer needs is often associated with Japanese companies, the profit-led

one with British and US ones', and cites an earlier study in which he found that in answer to the question: Does the statement 'Good short-term profits are the objective' describe your company well?, 87% of British companies and 80% of US companies responded 'yes', against only 27% of the Japanese companies. The essence of the distinction between a marketing and financial orientation is aptly summarised in Figure 21.1.

The question we address is: how do we diagnose the existence of a particular bias in the firm's orientation? Existence of a dominant bias is reflected in the concepts of corporate climate and personality which, during the 1980s, became increasingly seen as a single phenomenon termed 'corporate culture'. We look at all three concepts as the basis for suggesting how one might develop a marketing-oriented organisation. Central to this objective is the articulation of a broad vision to which the members of the organisation can subscribe, and its translation into a clear mission and specific objectives which will guide and motivate them.

Finally, we explore some of the issues to be faced in implementing marketing.

ORGANISING FOR MARKETING

The question of whether an organisation's strategy should dictate its structure or whether its structure should dictate its strategy has been the subject of much discussion between academics and practitioners alike. As with most debates, polarisation of the issues is a useful if not necessary step to tease out and make clear the arguments for and against the respective positions. In the strategy vs. structure argument, one of the leading exponents, if not the initiator of the debate, is Alfred Chandler Jr (1962), whose seminal contribution – *Strategy and Structure: Chapters in the History of the American Industrial Enterprise* – has provided the stimulus for extensive inquiry into the issue. As Baligh and Burton (1979) note in their very useful review of the impact of the marketing concept on the organisation's structure, 'Chandler presented the original ideas'.

In our definitions of SMP in Chapter 4, we have already cited Chandler's definition of strat-

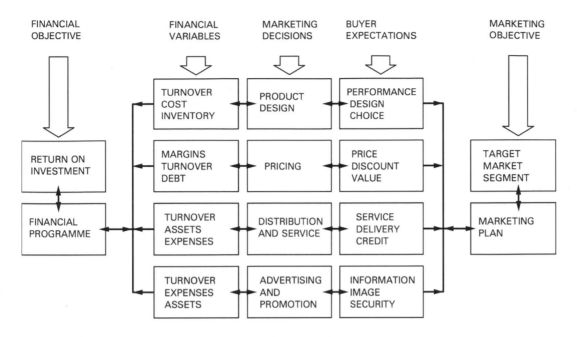

FIGURE 21.1 Financial versus marketing orientations

SOURCE: Doyle, P. (1992) What are the excellent companies?, *Journal of Marketing Management*, 8(2)

egy: 'Strategy can be defined as the determination of the basic long-term goals and objectives of an enterprise; and the adoption of courses of action and allocation of resources necessary for carrying out these goals.' As Baligh and Burton note, this definition (along with most others) reflects 'an outside orientation for choosing what to do, i.e. which products or services to provide and how to market them', in other words, a marketing orientation. Baligh and Burton continue to cite Chandler's definition of structure: 'Structure can be defined as the design of the organisation through which the enterprise is administered' and his hypothesis: 'The thesis deduced – is then that strategy follows structure', which leads them to conclude that 'The thesis says that the internal organisation logically follows from the outside environment chosen from those available to the organisation. Neither can be optimised alone, they must be set relative to one another. This has been the statement of the proposition for some time.'

Of course, and as the existence of a debate recognises, such a clear-cut claim is overly simplistic except perhaps as a long-term objective or principle one would like to move towards. In the real world, and in the short to medium term, firms have to put up with the structures they have and the attitudes and experience of the individuals who comprise the organisation, fill its roles and perform its functions. It follows that strategy formulation will be coloured by the perception and interpretation of the people comprising the organisational structure and they can vary quite dramatically depending upon their basic business orientation.

BASIC BUSINESS ORIENTATIONS

In the conduct of business at least five distinct functions are involved, namely research and development, production, sales, finance and marketing linked together by the human resource management (HRM) function. In the nature of things, one or other of these functions is likely to be dominant and thus lead to the whole business being oriented towards that function. In his book, McKay (1972) provides a useful summary of the key features of each of these orientations as follows.

TECHNOLOGY ORIENTATION

An emphasis upon research and development or technology is to be found in many companies and comprises the following key features:

1. Emphasis is on research and engineering per se, with little recognition of economic consider-ations.
2. Market criteria to guide research and develop-ment are inadequate or non-existent.
3. The product is considered the responsibility of the technical organisation with little product planning influence from marketing.
4. There is a tendency to overengineer products to satisfy internal inclinations or even whims, beyond what the customer needs or is willing to pay for.
5. Basic development, product, and facility decis-ions are often made between engineering and manufacturing management, without market-ing participation.

PRODUCTION ORIENTATION

This is the classic orientation in economies where demand exceeds supply. McKay identifies seven principal characteristics:

1. The factory floor is considered to be the business.
2. The focus and emphasis are on making products.
3. Little attention is given to marketing research and product planning.
4. There is a tendency to base price on cost and cost alone, with value and competitive consid-erations largely ignored.
5. Cost reduction efforts may sacrifice product qual-ity, product performance and customer service.
6. The role of the sales organisation is to sell what-ever the factory chooses to make.
7. If customers aren't happy, the salesmen are told to go out and get some new ones.

SALES ORIENTATION

McKay comments that this is often confused with a marketing orientation because it places heavy emphasis on customer considerations;

however, it has fundamental differences. Its major features include:

1. The focus is on volume, not on profit.
2. The prevailing point of view is that the customer should be given whatever he wants, regardless of the cost to the business.
3. There tends to be weak linkage between true customer needs and wants and the planning of products to be offered.
4. Pricing, credit, and service policies tend to be loose.
5. Production scheduling is overinfluenced by subjective estimates from the field force.
6. Market guidance of engineering and manufac-turing is commonly inadequate.

FINANCIAL ORIENTATION

McKay comments 'this orientation prevails frequently without being clearly recognised. Its dominance may be indirect, through the influence of the accounting, auditing, and treasury personnel on general management decisions.' In the 1980s this orientation was much more pervasive than it used to be and has been severely criticised by authors such as Hayes and Abernathy (1980), who believe that this orientation has been responsible for much of the loss in economic vigour in many Western industrialised economies in the post-war period. The key features of the orientation are:

1. The emphasis tends to be on short-range profit at the expense of growth and longer range profit.
2. Budgeting and forecasting frequently pre-empt business planning.
3. Efficiency may outrank effectiveness as a management criterion.
4. Pricing, cost, credit, service, and other policies may be based on false economy influences and lack of marketplace realism.
5. The business focus is not on the customer and market but on internal considerations and the numbers.

MARKETING ORIENTATION

The basic features of this orientation are:

1. The focus is on the marketplace – customers, competitors and distribution.
2. A commercial intelligence system monitors the market.
3. It requires recognition that change is inevitable, but manageable in the business arena.
4. The business is committed to strategic business and marketing planning, and to creative product planning.
5. The emphasis is on profit – not just volume – with growth and profit kept in balance.

Clearly, each of the foregoing summaries is a stereotype. Nonetheless they contain a sufficient element of truth to indicate that an excessive bias to any one of them will significantly affect the way in which the firm interprets and responds to its environment. It follows that if we can diagnose the prevailing orientation in an organisation, then we will be in a good position to predict how it might respond to competitive pressures and also to advise how it ought to respond. In attempting such a diagnosis/prognosis, considerable insight and help can be gained from the findings of the field of study generally known as organisational behaviour or human behaviour in organisations (HOBO).

A fundamental principle of survival and progress is specialisation. In economics, task specialisation and the division of labour are seen as critical to the improvement in productivity necessary to sustain growth and enhance standards of living. In the evolutionary process it is specialisation which enables organisms to adapt to changing conditions and survive. In research it is specialisation which provides the focus and the expertise which prompts discovery and invention. Clearly, specialisation is a good thing. Unfortunately it can also be wasteful and impede progress – one man's tunnel vision is another's single-mindedness of purpose! Recognition of this is implicit in the concept of synergy – the so-called $2 + 2 = 5$ effect.

The purpose of this brief homily is to warn of the dangers of specialisation to the neglect of a more broadly based perspective, despite the fact that specialisation is often essential at the outset of one's career. Indeed, the acid test that distinguishes between successful functional managers and those responsible for the overall direction and control of an organisation is the ability to generalise and

perceive the linkages between superficially disparate functions or bodies of knowledge. In Chapter 9 when we discussed buyer behaviour, we observed that there were at least four major disciplinary based explanations of choice behaviour. The trouble is that none is an adequate explanation of the real world, and so we needed to develop a composite model applicable to issues of both individual and group/organisational buying behaviour.

A similar division is apparent in the existence of a subfield of knowledge designated human behaviour in organisations. Once one has created the subfield, there is an inevitable tendency to specialise in the particularities and lose the potential insights which might occur if one considered ideas and concepts related to the individuals who comprise the groups. It was such a consideration that prompted the author to pursue the thought that if the attitudes and personality of an individual coloured his or her reaction to innovation and new products, the same might also be true of organisations. In doing so, we identified the concept of organisational climate developed by Taguiri and Litwin (1968), which has now received much wider recognition in the concept of corporate culture. Taguiri and Litwin pointed out that a concept such as organisational climate was an operational necessity as behavioural scientists shifted their attention from the individual to the organisation which plays such an important role in all our lives in an industrial society. As they observed:

> Concepts such as climate are needed especially to explain behaviour outside the laboratory, in settings where the environment cannot be experimentally controlled or where the situation cannot be held constant.

Intuitively, the concept of climate is familiar and is reflected in everyday expressions such as 'the climate of opinion', 'the industrial climate' etc. However, precise definition presents a number of problems and in *Marketing New Industrial Products* (Baker, 1975) we reviewed a number of attributes (pp. 85–6), which lead Taguiri and Litwin to offer the following definition:

> Organisational climate is a relatively enduring quality of the internal environment of an organisation that (a) is experienced by its members (b) influences their

behaviour, and (c) can be described in terms of the values of a particular set of characteristics (or attributes) of the organisation.

Closely allied to the idea of organisational climate is that of corporate personality and, taken together, the two concepts suggest that firms will exhibit a certain consistency in their response which will enable one to predict how they will react to particular circumstances. In a famous study of how firms in two industries (engineering and textiles) responded to their environment, Burns and Stalker (1961) coined the terms 'organic' and 'mechanistic' to describe the two radically different responses they detected. In their own words:

There seemed to be two divergent systems of management practice. Neither was fully and consistently applied in any firm, although there was a clear division between those managements which adhered generally to the one, and those which followed the other. Neither system was openly and consciously employed as an instrument of policy, although many beliefs and empirical methods associated with one or the other were expressed. One system, to which we gave the name 'mechanistic', appeared to be appropriate to an enterprise operating under relatively stable conditions. The other, 'organic', appeared to be required for conditions of change. In terms of 'ideal types' their principal characteristics are briefly these:

In mechanistic systems the problems and tasks facing the concern as a whole are broken down into specialisms. Each individual pursues his task as something distinct from the real tasks of the concern as a whole, as if it were the subject of a subcontract. 'Somebody at the top' is responsible for seeing to its relevance. The technical methods, duties, and powers attached to each functional role are precisely defined. Interaction within management tends to be vertical, i.e. between superior and subordinate. Operations and working behaviour are governed by instructions and decisions issued by superiors. This command hierarchy is maintained by the implicit assumption that all knowledge about the situation of the firm and its tasks is, or should be, available only to the head of the firm. Management, often visualised as the complex hierarchy familiar in organisation charts, operates a simple control system, with information flowing up through a succession of filters, and decisions and instructions flowing downwards through a succession of amplifiers.

Organic systems are adapted to unstable conditions, when problems and requirements for action arise which cannot be broken down and distributed among specialist roles within a clearly defined hierarchy. Individuals have to perform their special tasks in the light of their knowledge of the tasks of the firm as a whole. Jobs lose much of their formal definition in terms of methods, duties, and powers which have to be redefined continually by interaction with others participating in a task. Interaction runs laterally as much as vertically. Communication between people of different ranks tends to resemble lateral consultation rather than vertical command. Omniscience can no longer be imputed to the head of the concern. (pp. 5–6)

While one can characterise an organisation as being organic or mechanistic, overall it should be clear from our earlier statement of basic business orientations associated with the various functions that these will tend towards one or other of these polar opposites. Thus we could represent the various functional subsystems of an organisation as lying on a continuum similar to that depicted in Figure 21.2.

Such a diagram prompts at least two observations:

1. The competing claims of the various functions will lead to most firms occupying an intermediate position between the two extremes.
2. Overall effectiveness will depend heavily upon the extent to which the separate functions can be integrated together.

Many organisational theorists are of the opinion that both the effectiveness and efficiency of the various functions will be optimised if they assume the structural characteristics appropriate to their location on the spectrum. Thus Lawrence and Lorsch (1967) have suggested four levels of formalised structure (see Figure 21.3).

FIGURE 21.2 Organisational subsystems continuum

Structural characteristics	Formalised structure*			
	1	2	3	4
Average span of control	11–10 persons	9–8 persons	7–6 persons	5–3 persons
Number of levels to a shared superior	7 levels	8–9 levels	10–11 levels	12 levels
Time span of review of subsystem performance†	Less than 1 each month	Monthly	Weekly	Daily
Specificity of review of subsystem performance	General oral review	General written review	One or more general statistics	Detailed statistics
Importance of formal rules	No rules	Rules on minor routine procedures	Comprehensive rules on routine procedures and/or limited rules on operations	Comprehensive rules on all routine procedures and operations
Specificity of criteria for evaluation of role occupants	No formal evaluation	Formal evaluation – no fixed criteria	Formal evaluation – less than 5 criteria	Formal evaluation – detailed criteria – more than 5

* Scores from low to high formalised structures
† Based on shortest review period

FIGURE 21.3 Scales of structural characteristics

SOURCE: Lawrence, P. R. and Lorsch, J. W. (1967) Differentiation and integration in complex organisations, *Administrative Science Quarterly*, 12(1): 1–47

If this is so, then special devices will be necessary to achieve the overall coordination and integration desired, and much emphasis has been given to matrix structures, project teams, new venture management and the like. More recently, Johne (1982) has discovered that a particularly important aspect in his sample of successful firms was the ability of individual managers to 'change gear' and switch from organic to mechanistic roles and back again as the task demanded. From personal experience and observation, this latter interpretation seems best to explain why some managers perform much more successfully than others who appear to be stuck in a single mode especially in the marketing and general management functions. Such an ability would seem to be particularly important if one is to practise 3-in-1 marketing as recommended earlier.

During the 1970s international competition intensified with Japan, West Germany, and a number of NICs like Korea, Hong Kong and Singapore scoring significant gains against traditional trading nations like the UK and USA as well as penetrating their domestic markets in a major way. The lacklustre performance of American firms led to the criticisms of commentators such as Hayes and Abernathy (1980) and the search for increased competitiveness epitomised by the success of Peters and Waterman's *In Search of Excellence* (1982). The major consequence of this evaluation and analysis was recognition of the importance of a marketing orientation and the creation of customer-driven organisations. For many, this required a change to an alternative orientation to sales, finance, production etc. and so focused attention on the nature of corporate climate/personality within the enlarged concept of corporate culture.

According to the American Sociological Association (Schwartz and Davis, 1981), 'the concept of "culture" is defined in terms of the shared beliefs, norms and traditions within the organisation'. Schwartz and Davis (1981) endorse this, and explain that 'Culture … is a pattern of beliefs and expectations shared by the organisation's members. These beliefs and expectations produce norms that powerfully shape the behaviour of individuals and groups in the organisation.' In other words, corporate culture defines 'how we do things around here'. As such, it is clearly a powerful force in determining what are accepted principles and practices and so will tend to reject or exclude persons who do not subscribe to these values.

This is not an appropriate place to discuss the issues of organisational change. That said, it is clear that if our diagnosis indicates that the organisation is not marketing-oriented (which is not the same as observing that it lacks a formal marketing function and the trappings associated with it), then the key issue is: how do we change the orientation? This question, too, is largely beyond the scope of this book, although we return to it in the final section of this chapter on implementation. We look next at some of the steps involved in developing a market-oriented organisation.

DEVELOPING A MARKET-ORIENTED ORGANISATION

Our earlier review of the strategy vs. structure argument indicated that ideally organisations should be structured in the manner which enables them best to implement their chosen strategy. In turn our discussion of strategy has provided strong support for the Arthur D. Little principle that strategy should be condition-driven and so represent a match between the firm's resources and competencies and the external environmental opportunities available to it. It follows then that the firm's structure should be oriented towards its external environment or markets – that it should be market-oriented – and it is because of this emphasis that we have chosen to make little if anything of the distinction between corporate and marketing planning in this book.

However, it must be recognised that an emphasis upon marketing and marketing planning can have undesirable effects if it is seen to threaten or diminish other functional specialisations. Accordingly, it is important to distinguish carefully and clearly between a market orientation and the marketing function. In so far as a market orientation requires one to look outward to the needs of one's customers, all members of the organisation should be required to adopt such a perspective. However, in encouraging them to do so one should remember that one employs functional specialists because of their expertise and so not dismiss lightly alternative interpretations which a finance or production person may place

upon data from the marketplace. To assume that the marketing function has a monopoly of insight or wisdom when it comes to interpreting the market would be as mistaken as regarding any other function as infallible.

What we need to achieve then is a state of mind in which the marketing function is seen as providing essential intelligence and information on which to base decisions after taking into account the views of other functional specialists. It is no accident that much of the success of the Japanese in world markets can be traced to their efficient implementation of corporate plans for which all have accepted collective responsibility. While collective responsibility may imply consensus, this is not necessarily the case and the important factor is that once a course of action has been decided on then all will support it fully. Achieving such commitment will clearly be easier if people have been consulted and involved, even though their personal opinion may not have prevailed. It would also seem reasonable to assume that the likelihood of agreement will be improved if all employees can be persuaded to put the customers' needs first in their thoughts – which is not the same as asking them to become marketers. Indeed, it may be true that the success of a marketing department/function is inversely related to its visibility, in that the more marketing can be integrated with the other functions the less it will be seen to enjoy a separate and possibly 'threatening' existence of its own. This has certainly been a major trend during the 1990s. As we saw in Chapters 1 and 2, marketing's 'mid-life crisis' was precipitated by a view that formal marketing departments had outlived their usefulness. But, as we pointed out, this is not the same as saying that marketing has outlived its usefulness. On the contrary the importance of marketing has increased and it is for this reason that it needs to be diffused throughout the whole organisation.

Offering such opinions is easy – putting the ideas into practice is difficult. Much advice and assistance is to be found in the extensive organisational behaviour literature mentioned earlier (see also Recommended reading), but is beyond the scope of a book of this kind. The important thing is to be sensitive to the problem and to accept that inculcating a market(ing) orientation in an organisation is a different task from organising the marketing function.

McKay (1972, pp. 33–76) provides an extensive analysis of the factors that influence the design of a marketing organisation, which is worth detailed study. As a first step, McKay argues that one must clearly define the scope of marketing in terms of its purpose and responsibility to the business as a whole, e.g.:

1. To formulate and recommend to the general manager long- and short-range marketing plans for the business in terms of products, customers, sales channels and prices.
2. To formulate, execute and measure marketing programmes to achieve these plans, and to integrate performance of these activities with other functions of the business.

To fulfil such terms of reference, one will have to take into account all the elements in the marketing mix, set out in Chapter 14, as well as make decisions about the actual structure of the marketing function itself and its relationship with other functional areas. To accomplish this McKay proposes a five-step process:

1. Determine the work to be done
2. Establish the structural form (e.g. product- or market-centred)
3. Design individual positions
4. Wrap up and document the organisation proposed
5. Communicate and implement the organisation plan.

With the growth of interest in corporate culture, there has developed a parallel interest in the view that a culture develops out of a vision which, in turn, will enable an organisation to define a clear mission and objectives. The best definition of (corporate) vision known to the author is that given by Bennis and Nanus (1985):

What is a vision? A vision should state what the future of the organisation will be like. It should engage our hearts and our spirits; it is an assertion about what we and our colleagues want to create. It is something worth going for; it provides meaning to the people in the organisation, in the work that they are doing. By its definition, a vision is a little cloudy and grand; if it were clear, it wouldn't be a vision. It is a living document that can always be added to; it is a starting place to get more and more levels of specificity.

Now beyond that, when the vision statement is close to completion, the questions that also have to be asked in any organisation are: What is unique about us? What values are true priorities for the next era? What would make me personally commit my mind and heart to this vision over the next ten years? What does the world really need that our organisation can and should provide? and What do I really want my organisation to accomplish so that I will be committed, aligned and proud of my association with the institution?

From this definition, it is clear that they see it as providing an aspiration, sense of purpose and broad direction in which to travel. Others attach somewhat different meanings, and/or confuse the concept with mission or strategic intent, concepts we discussed in some detail in Chapter 4.

In *Frontiers of Excellence* Robert Waterman (1994) claims that it is a company's organisational arrangements which influence its performance. Specifically:

- They are better organised to meet the needs of their *people,* so that they attract better people than their competitors do and their people are more greatly motivated to do a superior job, whatever it is they do.
- They are better organised to meet the needs of *customers* so that they are either more innovative in anticipating customer needs, more reliable in meeting customer expectations, better able to deliver their product or service more cheaply, or some combination of the above.

In the Epilogue, Waterman (1994, pp. 282–4) reviews the patterns he believes help to explain long-term success:

First, and maybe most important, is the fact that the companies that remain successful break themselves into small, fairly autonomous units. This has the effect of shoving the market mechanism for making decisions down into the hierarchy and keeps the upper echelons from doing dumb things.

[Second, is] the will and the ability to organise 'downward' rather than 'upward' ... the companies that stay healthy organise to please their customers and to motivate their people.

A third factor is the ability to switch smoothly and easily from normal bureaucracy (using the word in its nicest sense) to what I have called 'adhocracy' [i.e. the ability to set up cross-functional project teams or task forces to tackle particular problems].

The last factor is sheer staying power and the will to commit to long-term plans.

IMPLEMENTING MARKETING

A recurrent theme throughout this book has been that the processes and techniques associated with marketing strategy and management are a necessary but not sufficient condition for competitive success. Any manager or organisation which is not familiar with the concepts and ideas discussed this far is bound to be at an immediate competitive disadvantage compared with someone who is. However, unless you have opened this book at this page purely by chance, the likelihood is that you are but one of several thousands who have read it from the beginning, one of hundreds of thousands who have read a book or books on marketing

strategy, or one of millions who have read the works of Peter Drucker, Igor Ansoff, Peters and Waterman or Michael Porter. In other words, the knowledge, and the wisdom and experience it represents, is widely available to all. This being so, it is clear that knowledge alone is insufficient for success and the critical factor that discriminates between levels of performance is the quality of implementation.

While this fact has been explicitly recognised in numerous studies of competitive success published in the 1980s, few of these studies offer much by way of advice of how to put theory, or even currently useful generalisations (CUGs) to work in practice. True, there are books on leadership and numerous autobiographies detailing how successful businessmen like Buck Rogers (IBM), Lee Iacocca (Chrysler), John Harvey-Jones (ICI) or Jack Welch (GE) 'made it happen' in their organisations. While interesting, and often inspirational to read, most of these books are short on specific advice on how to do it and, especially, in the particulars.

It was recognition of this gap in the literature that prompted Nigel Piercy (1991) to write *Market-led Strategic Change: Making Marketing Happen in your Organisation*. As he stated in the Preface:

Box 21.1   *Innovation – people and leadership*

As it becomes increasingly difficult to maintain a sustainable competitive advantage, innovation remains the most effective means of doing this. Traditionally, people think of innovation in terms of new products and processes but, in the final analysis, innovation comes down to people and leadership. An article in *Fortune* (February 2006) by Fred Vogelstein, 'Mastering the art of disruption', cites Steve Jobs as a model CEO for the twenty-first century, taking over the role performed so effectively by Jack Welch at General Electric in the twentieth century.

Heading up Apple Computers and Pixar, the animated

movie house, Jobs is named as being unrivalled in the art of disruption:

Many entrepreneurs talk about turning ideas into products that change the world. Yet the landscape is littered with first movers who ended up finishing last. In so many cases, being out in front just makes you a target for deep-pocketed rivals. Think back to the early PC manufacturers or the spreadsheet – and word processing – software makers. Can you recall any of them? Does VisiCalc ring a bell? XyWrite? Probably not. But Microsoft's Excel and Word are still with us.

Jobs' success as an innovator lies not just in his ability to take technology and turn it into good-looking, easy-to-use products, but in his capacity to do it faster than others and continually keep in front of the followers. When iPod was first released in 2002 it had a monochrome screen and 5 gigabyte hard drive. In 2006 it has a colour screen and a 60 gigabyte hard drive at roughly the same price.

'What other business would obsolete a successful product like the iPod mini after only 18 months to introduce the nano?'

The primary goal of this book is to provide managers with a number of new practical tools for evaluating the marketing performance of their organisations and, as a result of that evaluation, for identifying how best to improve marketing performance.

First, you have to know what marketing is, and what you want it to do for you. As Piercy acknowledges, you don't have to read books or attend courses on marketing in order to be successful in business, in much the same way as you don't need to be able to define prose to use it in communication. That said, one has only to consider that enormously successful marketer Henry Ford I to appreciate that while he intuitively knew what the market wanted in 1908, by 1918 he was losing touch with it and by 1925 had been upstaged by General Motors, who discovered the importance of differentiated as opposed to undifferentiated marketing. Perhaps some knowledge of consumer behaviour and product life-cycles might have helped Ford with his problem! For most people, therefore, some formal introduction to the nature, scope, processes and techniques of marketing would seem to be a worthwhile foundation for successful practice.

That said:

What we cannot do is to provide an easy managerial 'quick-fix'. The sad truth is that there are no easy answers. We can provide new tools, and we can identify the issues and areas where they can be used, but actually using them, and achieving the objective of making our marketing work, is likely to be uncomfortable, painful, messy, imperfect, unpopular, and just plain difficult. There is really no escaping this conclusion. (Piercy, 1991, pp. 17–18)

So what is one to do? Piercy suggests that in very simple terms there are two kinds of manager – transactional and transformational. *Transactional* managers operate on the basis that if you do something for them they will do something for you (pay you). By contrast, *transformational* leaders (like the four cited earlier) have the ability to motivate people to achieve their vision of the organisation's potential and future. This they do by managing the context so that people have a sense of direction, a wish to make things happen and are allowed – and encouraged – to make things happen. Of course,

such charismatic and transformational leaders are in short supply.

Accordingly, Piercy's aim is to help managers better evaluate, manage and design the context that is needed to make marketing happen in organisations. He summarises the central issues to be confronted by managers in managing the context of marketing as being:

- A focus on customer satisfaction (by painstaking example and substantial action, not the easier option of advocacy, 'quick-fix' programmes, and lip-service by us to others).
- Getting marketing strategies and programmes together (explicitly, in integrated form, and linked to actions in the marketplace – no implicit, grandiose, managerial ego-massaging which sounds impressive in meetings and reports, but leads nowhere in the reality of the marketplace as far as the customer is concerned).
- Organising to show we believe in marketing to customers, that we want and intend for it to happen, and to remove at least some of the most blatant organisational barriers to serving customers, which seem to exist everywhere.
- Collecting and communicating information and intelligence about customers, competitors, the changing environment, and our performance, to help shape – and if necessary change – the way executives perceive, and hence cope with, their market environment.
- Designing critical decision-making processes (namely in our case strategic marketing planning and marketing budgeting) to achieve the effects we want both in the company and in the market.
- Facing up to the realities in implementing marketing strategies early enough, honestly enough, and explicitly enough that it is possible to do something about barriers, and adapt our strategies to match the realities of what we can actually do as an organisation.

Each of these issues is dealt with in detail by Piercy (as, hopefully, they are in this book), with the difference that he emphasises the context, whereas most conventional books emphasise the content. Of course, Piercy does detail the content, but in addition, he provides numerous diagnostic questionnaires developed from research at the Cardiff Business School into how managers implement marketing in practice, supplemented by feedback from using these questionnaires with practising managers.

As Piercy notes in his penultimate chapter:

> The real marketing problems for virtually all organisations are incredibly obvious and straightforward. The real problems are not about the lack of sophisticated marketing skills and techniques. They are about the following obvious and basic issues:
>
> ■ The attitude of our company, its culture, our managers, and our employees to the paying customer, and the results in how we treat that paying customer. Not what we say – what we do.
> ■ The incredible competitive power which comes from something as simple as listening to the customer and getting better at doing the things that matter most to the customer.
> ■ Getting the marketing act together, so the fine words and strategies are turned into the practical delivery of service and product to the customer.
> ■ Organising ourselves to make it easier to make marketing happen, not creating barriers and obstacles to effective marketing.
> ■ Intelligence that challenges our underlying strategic assumptions and how we look at the world (i.e. the customer), so we stay in touch and get better at coping with the changes, threats, and challenges in the outside world.
> ■ Managing processes like marketing planning and resource allocation to get 'ownership', commitment, and action – because our people want and are determined to make marketing happen.
> ■ Taking the issue of marketing implementation, and the strategic organisational change it creates, seriously enough that we plan it, resource it, and make it part of our strategic thinking in the first place.

In 1997 the second edition of Nigel Piercy's *Market-Led Strategic Change* appeared. Unlike many new editions in which the author merely updates the detail, Piercy's second edition represents a radical change, implicit in its subtitle being changed from *Making Marketing Happen in your Organisation* to *Transforming the Process of Going to Market*. The change is not merely cosmetic, as indicated by the title of the first chapter 'Whatever Happened to Marketing?' – it sort of went away into a corner and sulked. In this opening chapter, Piercy (1997, p. 5) observes:

Some readers may still wonder why I have dropped the use of the word 'marketing' in many places in the book and in my work with executives:

■ 'Going to Market' instead of 'Marketing';
■ 'Market Strategy' instead of 'Marketing Strategy';
■ 'Market Led' instead of 'Marketing Led', and so on.

The reason is simple. It is not a ploy to save paper and ink. It is simply because markets are more important than marketing, and we should say so. It is also because markets and customers are the responsibility of *every* manager in a company, not the 'property' of marketing specialists.

There is another reason also – basically traditional marketing is dead in the water.

The days of the large corporate marketing department, with its market research surveys and brand managers and an obsession with advertising, have gone – if indeed they ever existed for most companies. In a prize-winning paper in 1995, Antony Brown of IBM (cited in Piercy, 1991) observes:

> There are now two types of corporation: those with a marketing department and those with a marketing soul. Even a cursory glance at the latest *Fortune 500* shows that the latter are the top performing companies, while the former, steeped in the business traditions of the past, are fast disappearing.

As we noted in Chapter 2, Brown's comments mirror those of many other commentators on 'marketing's mid-life crisis' in the early 1990s. In our view, this represents a return to the original marketing concept as a philosophy of business and management of the marketing function as a practice. Piercy endorses this when he says: 'Marketing' belonged to marketing specialists, but 'going to market' is a process owned by *everyone* in the organisation – the 'part-time marketers, (Gummesson, cited in Piercy 1991), the chief executive, cross-functional teams, – and that is how we have to learn to manage it.' To achieve this Piercy states:

> The things a manager really needs to get a handle on, in the process of going to market, are:
> ■ *Customers* – understanding customers and focusing on the market offering we make to them and what it produces in customer value, satisfaction and loyalty

- *Market strategy* – choosing market targets and a strong market position based on differentiating capabilities to create a robust and sustainable value proposition to customers and networks of critical relationships
- *Implementation* – driving the things that matter through the corporate environment to the marketplace. (p. 9)

In the final chapter of his second edition, Piercy (1997, pp. 620–1) puts forward 'an agenda for market-led strategic change' in which he states that the real problems faced by an organisation are not about the lack of sophisticated skills and techniques but about a number of obvious and basic issues. He summarises these as:

- Recognising and accepting that traditional marketing is no longer the way forward – to cope with the challenges facing the company now we have to focus on the *process of going to market* and get better at coordinating and managing that process;
- The attitude of our company (its culture and values, the behaviour of managers and employees) and how it results in our treatment of the paying customer – not what we *say* but what we *do*;
- The massive power for competitiveness and innovation which comes from something as simple as *listening to the customer* and getting better at doing the things that matter most to the customer;
- The problems of building and sustaining *customer focus* in an organisation which would rather focus on internal needs than customer priorities;
- *Demystifying and clarifying our market strategy* – distinguishing between creative strategising and formal planning; making clear choices about market and segment targets; applying our differentiating capabilities to define our value proposition to the customer; and identifying the key relationships we will have to manage to deliver that promise;
- Turning the strategy into a structured and coherent *marketing or market plan*;
- *Getting the marketing act together* – so that the fine words in the market strategy and the plan turn into the real delivery of the value proposition to the customer;
- *Organising* ourselves to make it easier to go to market, not creating barriers and obstacles, in companies that have weak marketing organisations or no marketing organisation, and where new shallow and alliance based organisations are emerging;
- Managing key *processes* by planning and resource allocation to build 'ownership', commitment and action – because our people are determined to make things happen;
- *Market sensing* to build real management understanding of the market, not market research to build piles of reports, and to challenge our assumptions, not confirm them;
- Building *partnership* between sales and the other owners of the process of going to market (including marketing departments where they are still around, but much more besides), to drive market strategy through to the customer relationship;
- Taking the issue of *implementation* and the *organisational change* it creates seriously enough that we plan it, resource it and make it part of our strategic thinking in the first place, and using internal communications and internal marketing as ways to manage market strategy in the new environment we face;
- Learning from the *experiences* of other companies in how you deal with these issues for real.

In Nigel Piercy's book you will find much useful and practical advice on implementing marketing. That said, one must remember the earlier caution that there are no 'quick fixes'. One of the reasons that the Harvard Business School perseveres with its case method approach is the recognition that case studies provide both content and context. The case method enables managers (actual or potential) to apply their knowledge and experience to the solution of specific problems, subject to the scrutiny and criticisms of their peers. By simulating the decision-making process in a wide variety of contexts, participants learn diagnostic, analytic and communication skills, all of which are crucial to effective implementation. But even the Harvard Business School recognises that 'wisdom can't be told', it is something one acquires by combining knowledge with experience. Accordingly, even highly practical books like Nigel Piercy's cannot implement anything for you – they can only suggest options and possibilities which may help in practice. What it requires is a 'stakeholder philosophy in which every member of the organisation is involved in and committed to its

success. A classic example of a company that has achieved this is Unipart.

Box 21.2   **Stakeholder philosophy**

A classic example of the application of a stakeholder philosophy to a company and its transformational effect is Unipart. Led by Strathclyde MBA graduate John Neill, Unipart was the subject of a management buyout in 1987. Since then Neill has implemented his belief that a stakeholder philosophy is the best way to run a business. In an interview reported in *Strategy* – the newsletter of the Long Range Planning Society (April 1997) – John Neil referred to the findings of the RSA Tomorrow's Company Inquiry of which he has been a member, to define what he understood by a stakeholder approach, namely the understanding that companies derive value from relationships with customers, suppliers, employees, investors and the community.

At the time of the buyout, Neill described Unipart as a successful marketing division with a third-rate manufacturing operation. Its core values could be summarised as: short-termist, low productivity, high cost, power based, adversarial, confrontational, unionised, distant from the community, remote from the workforce, with a focus on price and little competitive edge. It was clear to

Neill that in order to be able to compete with the Japanese and German suppliers it would be necessary to develop a long-termed, shared destiny relationship based on trust with the company's stakeholders.

For Neill the turning point in the company's fortunes was winning a contract to supply fuel tanks to Honda in the UK. To fulfil this order Unipart sent a team of six people to Japan to benchmark Honda's Japanese supplier Yachiyo Kogyo. As a result of what they learned in Japan there was a complete change in both management and production methods enabling Unipart to match and even exceed both quality and productivity standards at Yachiyo.

Another important element in the transformation of Unipart was the involvement of every employee in a two-day customer service seminar You Make the Difference, followed by a second programme entitled Putting Customers First. Further, Neill's commitment to creating a learning organisation is reflected by his establishment of Unipart U – a company university – in 1993. Offering around 180 different courses taught by Unipart managers and staff,

Unipart U has become an integral part of ensuring that Unipart stays at the leading edge of competitive performance.

Integral to the learning organisation approach was the offer of an individual contract of employment for every employee based on a concept of partnership and collaboration in place of the old adversarial and confrontational atmosphere.

In addition to its internal relations Neill gave equal attention to the external stakeholders, customers, suppliers and the community. But, in spite of his success in almost doubling turnover in the period 1987–1995 and trebling profitability, Neil is not complacent, pointing to a 1993 Andersen Consulting Lean Enterprise Report, which showed that on every key performance measure the Japanese were twice as good as their British counterparts except on quality where they were 100 times better. It is for this reason that Neill is committed to Peter Drucker's observation that 'Knowledge is the only meaningful resource today'. It is this which underpins the establishment of Unipart U and his commitment towards becoming a world-class global competitor.

Chapter summary

In this chapter we have explored some of the organisational implications of becoming marketing-oriented and customer-driven.

First we considered the view that strategy should determine an organisation's structure. In most cases, however, this reasoning is circular for the simple reason that it is largely existing organisations that are concerned with strategy and planning so it would be surprising if their strategic decisions were not heavily influenced by what they already are. As we have seen, planning is the process for determining how we should get from where we are to where we want to be, based upon a careful evaluation of both the internal factors (including our current orientation and organisational structure) and changes in the external environment in which we have to operate. Clearly, if the change in the external environment threatens our current organisation and objectives, we will have to reconsider them or else accept the threat to our continued survival.

Much evidence suggests that with increased competition firms which are oriented towards the market are more likely to succeed than organisations that are more oriented to internal concerns such as R&D, production, finance or sales. Some diagnostic tests were suggested to help determine the firm's current orientation and advice was offered on how to develop a market-oriented organisation.

Central to the task of developing a successful organisation is the definition of a vision which will motivate members to strive for its achievement. Such a vision helps define the corporate culture, and it is from this that we derive the specific mission and objectives that underpin the firm's strategy.

Ultimately, however, success is not only a matter of analysis, evaluation and planning, it is a matter of implementation. In the final section we considered some of the factors which needed to be taken into account and concluded that while 'wisdom can't be told', knowledge is an essential foundation for successful practice.

Recommended reading

Piercy, N. F. (2003) Marketing implementation, organisational change and internal marketing strategy, in M. J. Baker (ed.) *The Marketing Book* (5th edn). Oxford: Butterworth Heinemann.

Piercy, N. F. (2001) *Market-led Strategic Change: Transforming the Process of Going to Market* (3rd edn). Oxford: Butterworth Heinemann.

REFERENCES

Baker, M. J. (1975) *Marketing New Industrial Products*. London: Macmillan – now Palgrave Macmillan.

Baligh, H. H. and Burton, R. M. (1979) Marketing in modernisation – the marketing concept and the organisation's structure, *Long Range Planning*, **12**(April): 92–6.

Bennis, W. and Nanus, B. (1985) *Leaders: The Strategies for Taking Charge*. New York: Harper & Row.

Burns, T. L. and Stalker, G. M. (1961) *The Management of Innovation*. London: Tavistock.

Chandler, A. Jr (1962) *Strategy and Structure: Chapters in the History of the American Industrial Enterprise*. Cambridge, MA: MIT Press.

Doyle, P. (1992) What are the excellent companies?, *Journal of Marketing Management*, **8**(2).

Hayes, R. H. and Abernathy, W. J. (1980) Managing our way to economic decline, *Harvard Business Review* (July–August).

Johne, F. A. (1982) Innovation, Organisation and the Marketing of High Technology Products, Ph.D dissertation, University of Strathclyde, Department of Marketing.

Lawrence, P. R. and Lorsch, J. W. (1967) Differentiation and integration in complex organisations, *Administrative Science Quarterly*, **12**(1): 1–47.

McKay, E. S. (1972) *The Marketing Mystique*. New York: American Management Association.

Peters, T. and Waterman, R. (1982) *In Search of Excellence*. New York: Harper & Row.

Piercy, N. (1991) *Market-led Strategic Change: Making Marketing Happen in your Organisation*. Oxford: Butterworth Heinemann.

Piercy, N. (1997) *Market-led Strategic Change: Transforming the Process of going to Market* (2nd edn). Oxford: Butterworth Heinemann.

Schwartz, H. and Davis, M. S. (1981) Matching a corporate culture and business strategy, *Organizational Dynamics*, summer.

Taguiri, R. and Litwin, G. H. (eds) (1968) *Organisational Climate*. Cambridge, MA: Harvard Business School.

Vogelstein, F. (2006) Mastering the art of disruption, *Fortune* (February).

Waterman, R. (1994) *Frontiers of Excellence*. St Leonards, NSW: Allen & Unwin.

CHAPTER 22

The (short-term) marketing plan

Planning is everything, the plan is nothing.

GENERAL DWIGHT EISENHOWER

After reading Chapter 22 you will be able to:

✔ Explain the role of the short-term marketing plan within the strategic planning process.

✔ Describe and justify a normative framework for marketing planning.

✔ Set out the conditions to be satisfied if an organisation is to produce a marketing plan successfully.

✔ Outline the key elements of a formal marketing plan and provide reasons to support their inclusion.

INTRODUCTION

Up to this point, our main concern has been with the broad sweep of strategic thinking and analysis in order to spell out the basic parameters within which the firm must operate. In addition, we have been concerned to stress the inevitability of change and the importance of continuity. Thus we do not see marketing and a marketing orientation as separate or divorced from production and a production orientation, or technology and an R&D orientation, but rather as essential elements of an organic institution attempting to cope with the varying pressures of quite different time horizons.

In the short term, survival is the name of the game and the preoccupation of management is to extract the maximum return from their existing resources and opportunities largely through tactical manipulation and manoeuvring. However, if the firm is to survive then it must have some expectation or concept of the future for which it is seeking to survive – it must have a sense of purpose and direction and it is for this reason that we have advocated so strongly the need for and the benefits flowing from SMP. Clearly, once we have defined our present status and our future aspirations then we are in a position to make plans to move us from where we are to where we want to be. This is the purpose of the marketing plan, and the primary task of (marketing) management.

As a key document in the implementation of marketing strategy, it will be useful to set out the essential components of a marketing plan, for this will serve to review and reinforce some of the key strategic elements already discussed, as well as review the kinds of issues with which the marketing manager has to grapple. It should also be reiterated that the development of a marketing plan is seen as a formal process and that its product should be a clear written statement available to all responsible for its implementation.

That said, it is important to repeat the caveat made in Chapter 4 that plans should not be regarded as immutable or as a managerial straitjacket. Rather they represent one's aspirations and means of achieving them in light of the knowledge one possessed at some time in the past. Accordingly, as one progresses and new information comes to light, one should be prepared to revise and modify both the plan and its implementation

to allow for these changes. In the absence of a plan, and a clear statement of the information and assumptions on which it is based, it is difficult to see how one can diagnose and explain change, for one does not possess a benchmark or reference-point for assessing the direction and magnitude of the change for which one has to allow. It is for this reason that in Chapter 3 we advocated strongly the need for both deliberate and emergent strategies. The marketing plan should be a living document, not a museum piece. A written plan provides such a point of reference and so allows one to make judgements as to the action to be taken when reality is different from one's expectations, as well as being able to assess the actual progress made.

A FRAMEWORK FOR MARKETING PLANNING

In Chapter 4 we introduced a number of frameworks for strategic marketing planning, including the model developed by Malcolm McDonald (1982). This was presented as Figure 4.4 and is reproduced below as Figure 22.1 for the sake of convenience and in a slightly modified form. The modifications, which were introduced in a joint article by Leppard and McDonald (1991) are contained in the box relating specifically to the marketing plan. Commenting on the model of the marketing planning process, the authors have the following to say:

> Although the marketing planning process can be represented diagrammatically, [see Figure 20.1], it is not necessarily the straightforward, linear sequential operation that the diagram suggests. In reality, all the stages are highly interactive and the planning process requires the flexibility to move backwards and forwards from the general to the specific. Sometimes it is even possible for some stages in the planning process to be dealt with concurrently.

Marketing plans can also vary in their time scale and degree of complexity, both of which will be dependent upon the nature of the host company and its business.

Another variable is the degree of formality of the plan. Should it be formalised as Camillus (1975) advocates, thereby making executives 'communic-

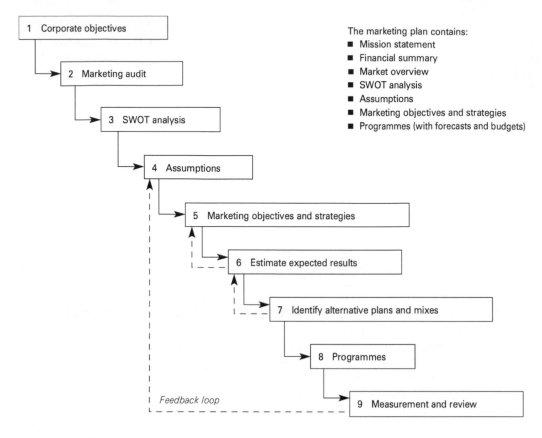

The marketing plan contains:
- Mission statement
- Financial summary
- Market overview
- SWOT analysis
- Assumptions
- Marketing objectives and strategies
- Programmes (with forecasts and budgets)

FIGURE 22.1 The marketing planning process

SOURCE: Leppard, J. W. and McDonald, M. H. B. (1991) Marketing planning and corporate culture: a conceptual framework which examines management attitudes in the context of marketing planning, *Journal of Marketing Management*, **7**(3)

ate, think ahead and so on'? Or should companies heed the warning of Ames (1970), who found that 'an overemphasis on format and procedure leads to a lack of substance and innovative thinking'?

Clearly, marketing planning has to be tailored to suit the style and situation of the company, while steering a course between the Scylla of good intentions and the Charybdis of bureaucracy.

Nevertheless, it is possible to describe a marketing planning process that is more or less universally accepted:

1. There is an information-gathering stage, which addresses itself to the company's internal operations and its external environment (the marketing appreciation or audit discussed in detail in Chapters 7–10).
2. The major strengths, weaknesses, opportunities

and threats are identified from the marketing audit (the SWOT analysis – Chapter 11).
3. Basic assumptions are made about the company and its situation.
4. Marketing objectives are set for the business, taking into account steps 1–3.
5. Strategies are devised about how best to attain the marketing objectives.
6. Programmes are formulated that identify timing, responsibilities and costs.
7. The marketing plan is monitored and reviewed at regular intervals.

Leppard and McDonald's (1991) article is based upon empirical research into the actual use and application of marketing planning in a sample of British companies. Probably their major finding is that marketing planning is more than a simple set of procedural steps and that its successful application depends upon a set of underlying values and assumptions. Only in more developed and mature organisations is one likely to find a culture capable of sustaining these values. From their analysis, the authors conclude that:

A company will only be able to produce a complete marketing plan if:

1. It has the required body of knowledge, the bulk of which is concerned with understanding planning, marketing and various conceptual analytical marketing 'tools'.
2. It can translate this knowledge into practical working skills and procedures.
3. Adequate resources are allocated to the planning process in terms of people, time and back-up support.
4. There is an adequate data bank and data retrieval system.
5. The plan or planning process is perceived as necessary and not wasteful of time and effort, i.e. there is a belief in planning.
6. There is a corporate plan to provide a context for the marketing plan.
7. Personnel are willing to own up to problems or disclose where existing situations could be improved.
8. Roles are made clear regarding who does what.
9. Facts outweigh opinions.

10. Senior executives value and pay due cognisance to the information that emerges from the planning process, to the extent that they will act upon it.

Overall it would seem that such a company sees marketing to be an important function and addresses the implications of being marketing-oriented in a mature and rational manner.

On the basis of these conclusions, it is clear that successful marketing planning calls for a major commitment on the part of an organisation if it is not to degenerate into the 'trappings' described so vividly by Ames (1970) in his explanation of the apparent failure of marketing in industrial companies.

Before leaving Leppard and McDonald's framework for marketing planning, it is worth highlighting the modifications proposed for the actual marketing plan contained in Figure 22.1. Compared with the earlier model (Figure 4.4), the following additions have been made:

- Mission statement
- Financial summary
- Market overview
- Forecasts.

The importance of an explicit mission statement was discussed in Chapter 4, and its inclusion in the formal marketing plan is now regarded as providing both the context and direction for all that follows.

Box 22.1 **Ten key stages in marketing planning**

1. *Executive Summary*
2. *Background*
   A short description of the company, its current markets, products and performance. The purpose, structure and content of the plan.
3. *Mission Statement*
4. *Marketing Appreciation*
   A. Macro-environmental analysis
   - PEST (political, economic, social and technological factors)
   - Key issues
   B. Micro-environmental analysis
   - Industry/market
   - Competitors
   - Customers
   C. Self-analysis
   - SWOT analysis (strengths, weaknesses, opportunities, threats)
5. *Conclusions and Key Assumptions*
6. *Strategic Objectives*
7. *Core Strategy*
8. *Key Policies*
   - Product
   - Price
   - Place
   - Promotion
9. *Administration and Control*
10. *Timing*

In Chapter 23, we shall examine some of the financial indicators that help to monitor and control the firm's performance. The inclusion of a summary of these financial targets and appropriate performance indicators is vital to enable line management to determine how effectively they are implementing the plan. Similarly, a market overview or situation analysis is important to provide both context and perspective to the detailed action plans derived from management's analysis of the situation and the tasks which face them over the period of the plan.

Finally, the inclusion of forecasts in association with the budgetary process is necessary to enable management to monitor implementation and determine if variances are due to changes from the forecasts (assumptions), or to competitive activity.

What, then, should the short-term marketing plan contain?

ESSENTIAL COMPONENTS OF THE SHORT-TERM MARKETING PLAN

While there is considerable variation in the recommendations of various authors as to the detailed content of the marketing plan there is little or no disagreement that its essential components are:

- Executive summary
- Situation analysis (or market overview):
  - External environmental audit
  - Industry audit
  - Customer Audit
  - Internal evaluation (market audit)
- Conclusions and key assumptions
- Objectives
- Core strategy
- Key policies:
  - Product
  - Price
  - Place
  - Promotion
- Administration and control
- Communication
- Timing.

In general the information to be contained in each section should be along the following lines.

EXECUTIVE SUMMARY

With the recent developments in information technology, the potential for information overload has grown alarmingly and most managers are having to become increasingly selective in terms of what they read. For this reason alone it is essential that any complex document should be prefaced with a clear and concise summary of the key issues contained in the main body of the document. While executive summaries are generally prepared for managers who are not directly concerned with the subject of a report, either as a specialist or as someone responsible for the detailed implementation of its findings, one should not overlook their value to such persons in providing an overview which will help guide more detailed analysis.

Writing executive summaries demands the exercise of considerable judgement. On the one hand they must not be too long or else they will fail on the conciseness criterion, while if they are too short they may be discarded as superficial and lacking in conviction. To some extent these conflicting requirements can be reconciled through judicious cross-referencing so that persons requiring substantiation of a point or argument can turn to the appropriate section in the main body of the report, e.g. 'It is unlikely that any new sources of raw materials can be brought on stream within the next five years so that costs may be anticipated to increase by 5% per annum over the period, net of inflation (para. 3.1.1–3.4.2).'

SITUATION ANALYSIS

As discussed in this and preceding chapters, a situation analysis should proceed from the general to the particular and from the external to internal. Given that one cannot possibly evaluate every single factor that may affect the firm, it is particularly important that one not only justifies those which are included in the analysis, but also that one outlines the reasoning which led one to exclude others. For example, one might list all those eventualities which are thought to have an individual likelihood of occurrence of 0.05 or less. In doing so, one reminds oneself of influences that need to be taken into account, specifies a criterion for not doing so and informs third parties that one has not overlooked certain possibilities, but merely discarded them on the grounds of irrelevance or unimportance.

Having painted a general scenario summarising one's expectations about the overall environment one should undertake an analysis of potential changes in one's industry and markets, whether arising from external pressures or the interplay of competitive forces. In doing so, particular attention must be given to the market segments in which the firm competes or expects to compete.

Finally, the situation analysis should be completed by an audit of the firm itself summarising its major strengths and weaknesses in relation to the threats and opportunities identified in the two preceding stages.

Following the advice given in Chapters 7–11, the situation analysis should cover:

- A macro-environmental analysis covering the political/legal, economic, social and technological (PEST) factors common to all firms
- A clear definition of the market, its structure and the basis of competition
- A profile of the customers to be served in terms of their needs and wants as defined by the attributes and benefits looked for, the values and beliefs associated with them, and the underlying emotions and motivations that condition the perceptions of all of these
- An internal analysis of the company covering its assets, resources and competencies and identifying its strengths and weaknesses vis-à-vis the opportunities and threats existing in the target markets (a SWOT analysis).

CONCLUSIONS AND KEY ASSUMPTIONS

While the conclusions from a SWOT analysis may seem self-evident, it is vital that they be made explicit and set out in a comprehensive list. As a result of this discipline, it will be easier to identify the gaps in one's knowledge and either to draw inferences which will make these good or else to state assumptions which reflect one's expectations about future and uncertain events.

In *Marketing* (Baker, 2006), we discuss the importance of formulating assumptions and

making them explicit at some length. Part of that discussion is drawn on here.

McKonkey (1988) argues that the formulation of assumptions should proceed in orderly steps and proposes the following sequence:

1. Isolate those future events that are most likely to have a significant effect on the company's business.
2. Evaluate as accurately as possible the probable effects of these events.
3. Determine whether an assumption is necessary; if so, formulate the assumption.
4. Record all assumptions.
5. Continuously track the validity of all assumptions.
6. Revise the assumptions and plans, and take corrective action when assumptions prove to be incorrect.

From this, it is clear that assumptions represent our best guess as to the future state of affairs at the time we are drawing up or revising our strategic plan. With the passage of time, these future events become nearer, and the information available to us becomes more certain. It follows, therefore, that we should monitor the accuracy of our original assumptions and be prepared to adjust our plans to reflect changes in them.

When formulating assumptions, it will also be helpful to try and quantify how likely or probable it is that a given assumption will materialise. Initially most people are more willing to express the likelihood of an outcome in qualitative or verbal terms such as 'very likely', 'likely', 'unlikely', or 'very unlikely'. When pressed, however, it is surprising how wide a discrepancy may exist between two different people's expectations of a given outcome when required to quantify this. Thus one person may consider an event 'likely' when it is better than an evens (50/50) chance, whereas another would consider it 'likely' only if the odds were 3 to 2 on (0.75 or 75% probability). For planning purposes, it is vital that all the decision-makers share the same scale of values, albeit that these values will be subjective (i.e. particular to each individual decision-maker) rather than objective, in which case there would be a known or certain outcome for a given event.

In addition to formulating probability estimates, McKonkey also recommends that one should assign a confidence factor, especially when dealing with highly critical assumptions upon which major investment decisions may be made. In this context 'confidence' refers to the amount of confidence the manager has in the data on which his probability estimate was made so that even though a manager might consider that a given event was very likely (90% chance of occurrence) if he had no facts on which to base this assumption then it would have a low confidence value. Under such circumstances – a strong 'hunch' that such and such would happen – the manager would be likely to increase his efforts to secure more and better information to test his belief.

As noted earlier, only if we make our assumptions explicit will we be able to diagnose the possible causes of variances between actual and planned performance.

OBJECTIVES

Objectives (discussed at length in Chapter 4) should be stated for both the long and short term. As we have seen, long-term objectives tend to be broadly worded statements of intent which point the direction in which the organisation is headed. Conversely, the short-term objectives should be closely defined and explicit goals set to be attained through implementation of the short-term plan. These should represent steps to move the firm from where it is to where it wants to be. On a year-to-year basis long-term objectives may vary very little, but short-term objectives require continuous reappraisal and updating.

CORE STRATEGY

In Chapters 2 and 3 it became clear that while there is only a limited number of competitive strategies there is a much larger number of 'labels' attached to them. While it matters little which label one uses, it matters a great deal that the core strategy should be made crystal clear in a statement such as the following:

The firm will achieve its objective of 5% increase in the XYZ market during the coming financial year through increased market penetration using a pull strategy based on lower prices and increased promotion.

Once stated in these terms, the remainder of the plan becomes a detailed statement and explanation of how this core strategy is to be implemented.

KEY POLICIES

Although the core strategy will usually make it clear which of the mix variables is to be emphasised, this in no way reduces the necessity to set out policies for all the others. Only by developing the fullest possible statement will it become possible to judge whether one's plan is internally consistent. For example, our core strategy stated above could easily be seen as inconsistent unless we can show that economies of scale in production and distribution will enable us to cut costs so that we can lower prices and increase the promotional spend. Thus we need to look at the interaction of each of the mix variables to ensure that they reinforce rather than counteract one another. Much of Part III was concerned with an in-depth survey of these considerations in terms of each of the 4 Ps.

ADMINISTRATION AND CONTROL

In this section of the plan it must be set out who is to be responsible for implementing the proposals contained in it, together with a clear statement of areas of responsibility and authority. Lines of reporting and control must be spelt out as must the type and frequency of measures which will be used to monitor performance. While separate budgets for the major mix policy areas will have been included in the discussion of these, the administration and control section is the one in which they should be integrated into a complete budget for the marketing function.

COMMUNICATION

This heading is not often found in books on market

planning, probably on the grounds that formal lines of reporting should be contained under the administration heading. Our reason for suggesting that communication merits separate treatment rests on the observation that business, like military, failures frequently arise from failures in communication. In turn, such failures may arise from a lack of communication or from miscommunication.

Lack of communication may be a simple case of someone forgetting to tell you or else wrongly assuming that you already possess the information in question. Checklists of information required, written plans and formal reporting systems should overcome this deficiency. Much more serious is the situation where the information does not exist because no one has identified the need for it and taken steps to acquire it. Clearly, this is the responsibility of the marketing information system and the marketing research function, but, in the same way that Borden tacked on marketing research as the final element in his marketing mix, so most marketing planners make no explicit provision for spelling out a programme of information gathering and dissemination. In that communication is a two-way process, it is essential that the firm have clear policies for both gathering and disseminating information and it is our belief that these should be set down in this section of the plan. We also believe that this is the appropriate place within the plan, on the grounds that all which precedes it represents an action plan based on past information, whereas the communication section is concerned with making good gaps in the past information as well as acquiring the new data needed for future plans.

It is also felt that by giving the marketing research function a separate identification, it will increase others' awareness of it and so reduce the potential for miscommunication.

TIMING

While sequences and timings will have been set out for various activities in the preceding part of the plan, this heading provides the opportunity to consolidate these into a single, comprehensive timetable.

APPENDICES

As with any report, a careful course has to be steered between information overload in which salient points become lost in unnecessary descriptive material, and insufficient detail to give conviction to the reader. An obvious way to avoid this is to consign detailed analysis to appendices and cross-reference these in the main body of the report. Examples of topics best dealt with in this way are:

■ Calculations of market size, trends and market share
■ Details of market research
■ Sales forecasts under different assumptions
■ Financial forecasts, e.g. cash flow, break even etc.

Chapter summary

In this chapter we have been concerned with the issues involved in developing a short-term marketing plan. In general, we subscribe to General Eisenhower's maxim that 'Planning is everything, the plan is nothing'. But, in offering this advice, Eisenhower certainly did not intend us to infer that plans have no value. As we have seen, an overemphasis upon formal planning in the 1970s resulted in it becoming distanced from those whose primary responsibility it should have been. The result was that line management felt no ownership for these plans, which became increasingly complex and detached from the realities of competition and the marketplace.

Clearly, a middle road must be found. Those responsible for implementation must be involved in planning. At the same time, their efficiency and effectiveness will be enhanced if they are familiar with the techniques and procedures described in this book. Finally, the output of the planning process needs to be captured in the preparation of a formal plan to act as both guide and reference point in moving the organisation from where it is, to where it wants to be.

In this spirit we have reviewed a framework for strategic marketing planning first introduced in Chapter 4. As our discussion made clear, planning is a continuous and cyclical process and formal plans are attempts to define specific courses of action within meaningful time periods – the shorter the time period the greater the certainty about the assumptions on which the plan rests and the more precise the actions called for. Experience suggests that these actions may be set out in a formal plan and we then reviewed the essential components of such a document.

There is a wide variety of aids to formal planning, from generalised checklists such as those proposed by Aubrey Wilson (1982) to highly detailed work books such as those by Stapleton (1987) and Makens (1989). More recently, the *Marketing Manual* (Baker, 1998) is a comprehensive and step-by-step workbook specifically designed to enable the reader to prepare a marketing plan of their own. These should be referred to by those wishing to amplify the outline of a marketing plan provided here.

Recommended reading

Baker, M. J. (1998) *The Marketing Manual*. Oxford: Butterworth Heinemann.

McDonald, M. H. B. (1999) Developing and implementing a marketing plan, in M. J. Baker (ed.) *Encyclopedia of Marketing*. London: International Thomson Business Press.

McDonald, M. H. B. (2003) *Marketing Plans: How to Prepare Them; How to Use Them* (5th edn). Oxford: Butterworth Heinemann.

REFERENCES

Ames, B. C. (1970) Trappings versus substance in industrial marketing, *Harvard Business Review* (July–August): 93–102.

Baker, M. J. (1998) *The Marketing Manual*. Oxford: Butterworth Heinemann.

Baker, M. J. (2006) *Marketing* (7th edn). Helensburgh: Westburn Publishers.

Camillus, J. C. (1975) Evaluating the benefits of long-range planning systems, *Long Range Planning* (June).

Gofton, K. (1984) The Fed loses its reserve, *Marketing* (August).

Leppard, J. W. and McDonald, M. H. B. (1991) Marketing planning and corporate culture: a conceptual framework which examines management attitudes in the context of marketing planning, *Journal of Marketing Management*, 7(3).

McKonkey, D. D. (1988) Planning in a changing environment, *Business Horizons* (September–October).

Makens, J. S. (1989) *The 12-day Marketing Plan*. New York: Thorsons.

Stapleton, J. (1987) *How to Prepare a Marketing Plan* (4th edn). London: Gower.

Wilson, A. (1982) *Aubrey Wilson's Marketing Audit Checklists*. New York: McGraw-Hill.

Implementation and control

Efficiency is doing things right, effectiveness is doing the right things.

PETER DRUCKER

After reading Chapter 23 you will be able to:

✔ Suggest why profitability alone is an insufficient measure of a firm's performance and potential.

✔ Explain the difference between fixed and variable costs and how these behave over time.

✔ Undertake a breakeven analysis.

✔ Describe other cost concepts and their use in diagnosis.

✔ Explain and exemplify the nature and use of contribution analysis.

✔ Define and describe the concepts of cash flow and net present value.

✔ Suggest how management ratios may be used to diagnose a firm's financial health.

✔ Justify the importance of control in implementing marketing strategy.

INTRODUCTION

The primary objective of strategy formulation, and the development of plans for its implementation, is that one wishes to exercise control over an organisation and its activities and so give it direction and purpose. However, the degree of control which management can achieve will vary enormously. As we saw in Chapter 7 when discussing the marketing environment, the ultimate constraint upon a firm's freedom of action must be the social, economic, cultural, political and technological framework within which it must operate, for while the firm may have some influence upon these factors, it is unlikely that it will be able to control them. Thus the purpose of environmental analysis is to determine what opportunities are available to the firm to be exploited and what threats are to be avoided. Once these boundary conditions have been established, the decision-maker is in a position to select the strategy they feel will best enable them to achieve the organisation's corporate objectives and from this articulate policies for integration of the marketing mix elements in the most effective way.

In principle, management of the marketing function is under the control of the organisation and this will be reflected in the establishment of specific objectives supported, wherever possible, by quantified targets for achievement. But, in setting down such objectives and targets in one's marketing plan it is always necessary to bear in mind that achievement will depend upon performance by the individuals responsible and the absence of any significant change in the assumptions upon which the targets and objectives are based. Recognising that most of these assumptions will relate to external factors beyond the firm's direct control, it is clear that objective measures of performance will only be possible provided one can quantify any changes between the assumed and actual conditions in the marketplace. Given such information, one will be able to establish how well the organisation is performing, what factors may account for any under- or overperformance and what modification may be necessary to correct or take advantage of discrepancies between planned and actual achievement.

At various places in our discussion of the management of the marketing function, we have considered appropriate objectives for the major mix elements and also suggested ways in which the achievement of these may be assessed. Basically, all the methods reviewed possess the common aim of seeking to quantify the benefits flowing from, or expected to flow from, incurring costs or expenditures on different kinds of marketing activities with the ultimate objective of selecting that combination or mix which will yield the maximum return for any given outlay.

In this chapter, our primary concern is with those techniques and approaches which will enable one to assess the overall contribution of the marketing function to corporate success. To this end, the main focus will be on costs and the way these behave in relation to output or volume and profit. Attention will also be given to the concept of cash flow and net present value, as these are of vital importance in assessing the advantages and disadvantages of different courses of action; this leads naturally to an examination of the relevance of various summary measures of performance such as return on investment (ROI) and payback. In that one's assessment of competitive standing will depend upon an appreciation of financial standing, some reference will also be made to methods of assessing an organisation's financial health from its published statements through the computation of a series of management ratios.

THE MEASUREMENT OF MARKETING PERFORMANCE

> Marketing can be described as the origination and acquisition of cash flow and therefore critical to any company whether explicitly or implicitly. And yet, CFOs frequently see marketing as the last bastion of unaccountable spending, and thus an easy target in times of corporate belt-tightening. (Clark et al., 2005)

These opening sentences of a recent article in the *Journal of Strategic Marketing* reflect well current views on marketing's contribution to corporate well-being and the measurement of that contribution, especially in financial terms. Indeed, the measurement of marketing performance, or marketing *metrics*, has been the number one priority of the Marketing Science Institute (MSI) in the USA for several years, and figures prominently in discussions of marketing among other management professionals. As a research organisation, MSI is largely funded by business organisations who are invited to contribute to its agenda, and help set the priorities for research funding on a biennial basis. In consequence, its listings are a good reflection of what are seen to be the most important issues to be addressed by marketing management.

Of course, marketing's (in)ability to quantify the financial return on investment in marketing activities is forever immortalised in Lord Leverhulme's observation about his company's advertising budget: 'Half my expenditure on advertising is wasted; the trouble is I don't know which half.' Given that his company was very successful, and that success was largely based on effective advertising, Leverhulme apparently was prepared to spend twice as much as he thought necessary to ensure that he kept on being successful.

The problem with quantifying the sales return on a given investment in advertising is not a trivial one. Indeed, the only way that one can establish this accurately is by varying one's ad spend and then measuring the sales results. While scientists may recommend controlled experiments in the laboratory, there are few managers who would consider this a realistic suggestion as a guide to competitive behaviour in a real market. And, even if they considered it for a moment, their inability to control their customers' and competitors' behaviour would soon dissuade them from trying. Indeed, one of the very few studies that has established a link between advertising and sales was undertaken by the author in 1970 when working with Bob Buzzell at the MSI. The editor of the *Journal of Advertising Research*, in which the results were published (Buzzell and Baker, 1970), said that it was the first such 'proof' that he knew of.

However, this study was based on a 'natural' experiment in which none of the participants were willingly involved – the shut-down of one of the big three auto manufacturers by the Auto Workers Union in pursuit of their annual pay claim. Every year the workers would put in a pay claim that was resisted by the employers as unreasonable and unaffordable. To emphasise their bargaining power, the workers of one of the major manufacturer's would be called out on strike. As the manufacturers knew well in advance whose turn it would be, and that the strike itself would occur in

August at the beginning of the new model year, they adapted their marketing plans accordingly. Obviously, the firm experiencing the strike would not advertise heavily the new models it hadn't got to sell, and would reserve its promotional budget for a new model launch when the strike was over. At the same time, while the other two would increase their expenditure to advertise their new models, they would do so at a lesser level than they would have done if there had been three major competitors in the market. They would also wish to hold back some of their budget so that their efforts would not be overwhelmed when the third company re-entered the market.

By analysing industry advertising and sales data, Buzzell and Baker (1970) were able to show that there was a significant decrease in sales volume over a period of several months, paralleling the reduction in overall promotional expenditure. While marketing management was undoubtedly pleased at this confirmation of what they already knew, it is highly unlikely that executives in any other industry would have volunteered to participate in a similar 'experiment' to confirm that the same relationship was true for their industry too!

While this example illustrates the problems of measuring advertising effectiveness in terms of sales, it is not a reason for not trying to develop better measures of marketing performance. In fact, considerable effort has been put into this since the 1990s, when marketing experienced its so-called 'mid-life crisis', largely as a result of its inability to come up with acceptable measures of its contribution to firm performance. To begin with, the emphasis was on what measures were actually used by managers, but the Clark et al. (2005) paper, referred to earlier, is one of the first to explore the reasons *why* managers do it. Before considering this, however, it will be useful to summarise the findings into the marketing metrics that are currently available.

PROFITS AND PERFORMANCE

In the final analysis, perhaps the simplest and most basic way of judging the effectiveness of a business organisation is by examining its profitability, both in absolute terms and as a return on the capital employed. To assess profit (or loss) we need to look at two parameters – revenue and costs – and it is immediately apparent that while we may have almost complete control over our costs, revenue represents the market's assessment of the value of the goods or services that we offer to it. Clearly, in deciding whether it is worthwhile to incur costs through creating a supply of anything, one needs to have some feeling for the nature of a demand schedule that indicates the quantity which will be consumed at any given price. Much of the content of this book has been concerned directly with this problem and, if nothing else, should have made it clear that predicting future purchase behaviour is a complex and difficult task. Given the uncertainty involved in forecasting demand, it is unsurprising that many managers feel happier dealing with production and supply, for here there are assured and reliable methods of measuring output and cost and exercising direct control over them. The current emphasis on marketing metrics represents a focused attempt to redress this balance.

Further, as we have attempted to show in several places, the greater the external turbulence and uncertainty, the greater the inclination for corporate management to reduce risk by adopting a short-term outlook and giving particular attention to milking their past investment. Such milking tactics give added weight to the importance of controlling costs and lead to the development of a financial orientation of the kind described in Chapter 21. In and of itself, careful cost control is a necessary and laudable objective, but without a proper appreciation of the nature of costs and the way in which they vary according to the volume of output, one may easily be tempted to adopt measures which in the short run will reduce costs (and so appear to increase profits) but in the long run will prove counterproductive as they discourage future sales. A simple (and true) example will help make the point.

A major international hotel group had a policy of rotating its managers between different hotels in order to broaden their experience. Based upon their performance, good managers got promoted to bigger and more important hotels and less successful managers got demoted and possibly

fired. The group was concerned that its overall performance and standing was declining in comparison with that of its major competitors.

A consumer survey revealed that many former clients had switched to competing hotels that they felt offered better value for money and when questioned on how they assessed this indicated a wide range of factors including decor, facilities, service, quality of food etc. Clearly, these were all the responsibility of the hotel management and raised the question as to how a policy of promoting the most successful managers could result in such poor management at the top.

Analysis revealed that internally managerial performance was judged by the bottom line of the accounts (i.e. the profitability) and probing soon indicated that, in the short term, the quickest way to enhance profits is to cut costs. Investigation showed that managers who were being judged as successful were enhancing their profits through cost avoidance – didn't redecorate or refurbish, cut the number of personnel, provided less food in the restaurants etc. Now hotels, in common with all businesses, depend heavily upon repeat purchase, which, as the quality of the product declined, began to fall away, resulting in a diminishing revenue. But, as long as you could cut costs faster, you still appeared to be making better profits. Eventually, of course, such a policy will lead to the inevitable conclusion, but what happens if you promote the 'successful' manager before profits actually dip? Well, his successor will finish up the scapegoat and the better a manager he is, the worse his performance will seem. On taking over a rundown establishment with a dwindling customer base, the good manager will realise that he will have to improve the product before he can win back any customers. To do so will require expenditure and take time and it is not difficult to see how, at the end of his tour, he will be judged 'unsuccessful' and demoted while handing over a concern ripe for 'milking'.

While a little poetic licence has been used to stress the point, it is clear that the hotel group's control system was having almost the diametrically opposite effect to that desired because it was depending upon a single criterion – profit – and in computing this it failed to inquire into the nature of the costs involved or the purposes for which they were incurred. To avoid such problems, one must have a clear understanding of the nature of costs.

COST ANALYSIS

Conventionally, costs are divided into two types – fixed and variable – but it will be helpful to distinguish a third and intermediate category, which may be labelled semi-fixed, semi-variable, or 'mixed'.

In defining and classifying costs, the major criterion is their behaviour in relation to a given output over time. Again by convention as accounts are usually prepared on an annual basis, then costs which do not change from year to year will be considered fixed, while those which do and/or fluctuate with output will be considered variable. Semi-fixed costs are those which can be changed during the accounting period, but usually result in a step function due to an intrinsic lack of divisibility, e.g. the acquisition of an additional member of staff. In economics the distinction between fixed and variable cost is defined more precisely by reference to the definition of the 'short run' and the 'long run'. In the short run, plant capacity cannot be altered, although of course output may be varied through changes in other factor inputs, such as hours worked and efficiency/productivity. By contrast, in the long run, capacity may be changed as well as the rate of output. Examples of

the three kinds of costs in a marketing context might be:

Fixed	*Semi-fixed*	*Variable*
Salaried staff	Additional staff	Commissions
Advertising approp.	Merchandisers	Distribution costs
Ad hoc surveys		
Marketing research budget		Sales promotion
Premises		Service costs
Vehicles		Financing/ credit

Diagrammatically these may be represented as in Figure 23.1.

As John Howard (1963) has pointed out, cost behaviour may be dealt with in at least three different ways. First there is the *accounting approach*, which is:

> much the simplest since it consists in classifying accounts into fixed, variable, and semi-variable by means of inspection and judgement. Because of its subjective nature, the method is open to serious criticism. Thus, the user of the cost data derived by the accounting method should investigate the logic used in classifying the accounts.

Advice with which we agree totally. Specifically, Howard suggests that such an approach may be

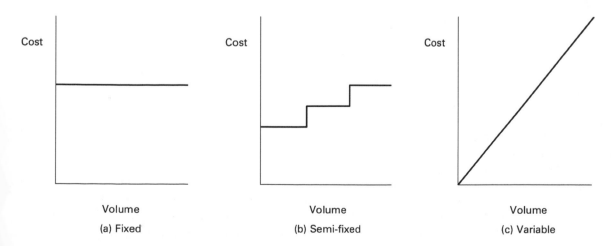

Cost — Volume
(a) Fixed

Cost — Volume
(b) Semi-fixed

Cost — Volume
(c) Variable

FIGURE 23.1 Cost curves

acceptable where three conditions exist, namely: wide fluctuation in production, detailed accounts that have been kept in the same way for a number of years and stable economic conditions. In recent years, the volatility of the economic conditions has highlighted the deficiencies of many traditional accounting practices and particularly the subjective nature of cost allocation. As a consequence, a much more explicit treatment of costs has become apparent, including the use of the alternative statistical and engineering approaches.

In the *statistical approach*, much the same conditions need to apply as for the successful application of the accounting method, but a much greater degree of accuracy may be achieved by determining how costs vary with output, using techniques such as regression analysis, thereby permitting clearer definition of variable costs. In turn clearer definition of variable costs enables more precise identification of fixed costs.

Where the conditions do not satisfy the three criteria set out, the *engineering approach* will be appropriate. Essentially this method represents a return to basic principles as one first spells out the physical relations involved in creating output, i.e. the combination of plant and equipment, labour and materials, and the costs associated with their use.

As we have noted on numerous occasions, the great majority of business is transacted by existing organisations that already comprise a collection of resources which represent their fixed costs. As a result, the minimal objective must be to generate sufficient revenue to cover these fixed costs and any additional variable costs which may be necessary to generate that revenue. In other words a firm will want to 'break even'. However, in order to establish its breakeven point, the firm will probably need to compute a number of calculations using different assumptions about the behaviour of both costs and revenues. In undertaking such an analysis, the breakeven chart provides a simple but powerful tool to help clarify the relationships.

Most representations of breakeven charts, including the one given here, adopt the simplifying but usually incorrect assumption that variable costs are constant per unit of output and so may be represented by a straight line as in Figure 23.2. In reality one expects the economies of scale and experience discussed in Chapter 8 to come into

operation, which would result in a curvilinear variable cost curve, as shown in Figure 23.3.

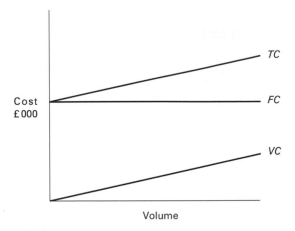

FIGURE 23.2 Simplified breakeven chart

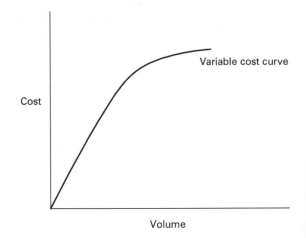

FIGURE 23.3 Curvilinear variable cost curve

Clearly, accurate representation of the variable cost schedule and curve is of much greater importance when making strategic decisions, when one will wish to explore the implications of additional increments in fixed costs in the light of one's expectations about the price elasticity of demand. Within the short term, and with a given fixed cost, declining variable cost is less likely and a straight line will be an acceptable compromise, particularly as it is likely to suggest a higher breakeven than will actually be required. In order to plot the breakeven point, first one will need to compute the total cost curve as shown in the following schedule and in Figure 23.4.

Output	Fixed cost	Variable cost	Total cost
1	10,000	1	10,001
100	10,000	100	10,100
1,000	10,000	1,000	11,000
2,000	10,000	2,000	12,000

(This schedule assumes a single product. In a multiproduct firm each product would have to be assigned its 'share' of the fixed costs in order to determine its individual breakeven point. As noted previously, cost classification is often subjective in nature while allocation is arbitrary. It is for these reasons that we prefer the contribution or marginal approach, discussed later in the chapter.)

In the case of an existing product, one will probably have some feel for the price elasticity of demand and will certainly know the going market price for competitive products. On the basis of this knowledge, one can construct a revenue curve by the simple expedient of calculating volume × price and, by plotting this curve, determine the breakeven point at its intersection with the total cost curve. Thus, if it is assumed that in the case of our theoretical product, the going market price is 8, our product is closely comparable to our competitors, who are numerous, we have adequate distribution and promotion and demand is buoyant, it is reasonable to assume we can sell all our output at this price with the outcome plotted in Figure 23.4.

On the other hand, where the product is new, knowledge of the total cost curve will provide a useful starting point for constructing a demand schedule and selecting a price–volume relationship that will meet the firm's profit objectives best.

OTHER IMPORTANT COST CONCEPTS

While the concept of fixed and variable cost is probably the best known and most widely used in making marketing decisions, there are a number of other cost concepts to be found in the economic and accountancy literature, and a brief review of them may prove useful. Perhaps one of the best accounts of the relevance of cost analysis to marketing decision is that published by John Howard as long ago as 1963 and our summary draws heavily on this source.

To begin with, Howard provides an excellent summary table which is reproduced in Table 23.1.

The distinction between outlay and opportunity cost is a particularly important one, but probably enjoys greater observance in theory than it does in practice. In essence, an outlay cost is an actual expenditure, whereas an opportunity cost represents the value which would be placed upon a factor in its most productive alternative use. While the outlay and opportunity cost may often

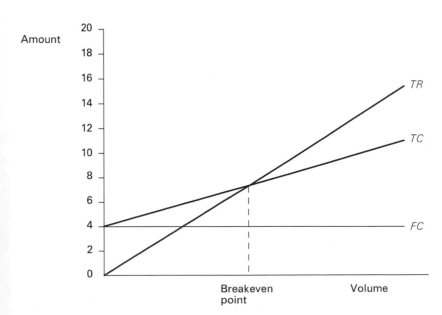

FIGURE 23.4 Breakeven point

TABLE 23.1 Cost distinction

Concepts		Basis of distinction
Outlay	Opportunity	Nature of the sacrifice
Future	Historical	Degree of anticipation
Short run	Long run	Degree of adaptation to present output
Variable	Fixed	Relation to output
Incremental	Marginal	Type of added activity
Traceable	Common	Traceability to a part of the company
Direct	Indirect	Traceability to different products

SOURCE: Howard, J. A. (1963) *Marketing Management* Homewood, IL: Irwin, p. 173

be the same, e.g. when evaluating a future investment, they can also differ significantly, particularly when considering the redeployment of resources. A case in point which we have already touched on is the treatment of 'dogs' in the product portfolio where their status as pets may well prevent objective assessment of their true position. If one considers the actual outlay it may not seem unreasonable, particularly by comparison with other products and the overall profitability of the firm. The trouble is that the below-average performance of the dog will depress the overall profitability of the firm by dragging it down to its level, whereas consideration of the earnings which would flow if the same investment were made in its most productive alternative use might give a totally different picture. As Howard emphasises: 'Opportunity cost is always the appropriate concept.'

As a consequence of the rampant inflation of the 1970s and 80s and economic turbulence in the 1990s, the obvious but neglected distinction between historical and future costs has become much more apparent. In that decisions only involve future costs, it is important that historical costs only be used as indicators and even then treated with great caution. Such advice is especially pertinent to the new product development (NPD) process where one of the most frequently cited causes of failure is 'higher costs than anticipated', which is usually equivalent to saying that one budgeted one's projections using past cost data without adjusting them for likely changes between the commercial analysis and launch phases. Conversely, one should be careful not to discontinue new products prematurely because their costs appear too high, as these may fall quite

dramatically due to the scale and experience effect as the market 'takes off' (Sizer, 1979).

The concepts of traceable – common and direct and indirect – costs are closely related. As the terms imply, traceable costs can be allocated directly to the activity engendering the cost whereas common costs are those which arise from or in support of a number of activities simultaneously and contribute indirectly to them all. For purposes of judging the comparative performance of activities, e.g. different products in the product line, the more clearly one can trace the costs involved the better the evaluation. A full description of techniques for assigning costs is given by Howard and is to be found in any basic cost accountancy text.

We have left the concepts of incremental versus marginal cost until last because these provide a natural lead into the subject of contribution analysis which is the method preferred by most marketers. Defined precisely, the marginal cost is that which will be incurred by adding one more unit of output to the existing output. In the same way that one more straw will break the camel's back so one additional unit of output may create the need for an increase in fixed investment or some other discontinuity in the cost, but, so long as the income derived from the sale of the marginal unit exceeds its marginal cost, its production and sale should be undertaken to maximise profits (see Figure 23.5).

While the concept of marginal cost strictly is confined to increases in output, it tends to be used loosely to cover what properly should be termed 'incremental cost' which relates to any added activity and can encompass the addition of several

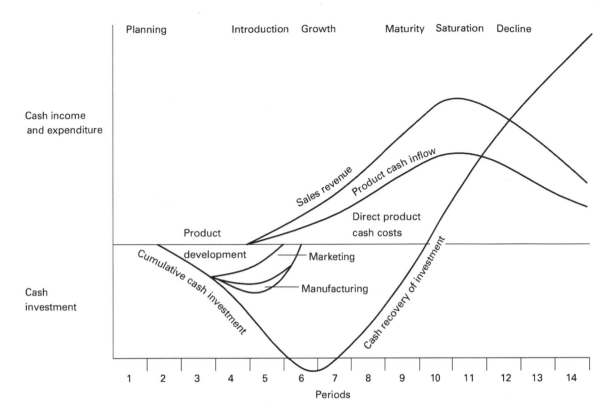

FIGURE 23.5 Investment life-cycle of hypothetical new product

SOURCE: Sizer, J. (1979) *An Insight into Management Accounting*, Harmondsworth: Penguin, p. 394

units rather than one. The latter situation relates to most changes in marketing activity and so will be the appropriate concept to use.

CONTRIBUTION ANALYSIS

Perhaps the simplest way to highlight the difference between the conventional and contribution approaches to accounting is by means of a simple example.

The general manager of Sporting Promotions Ltd has called a meeting with his accountant, production and sales managers to discuss problems related to stocks of goods carried forward from the previous year's trading which he considers to be worthless. The two lines in question differ quite significantly. Line A, which has sold successfully for many years, consists of a cricket score book in which enthusiasts can keep their own record of their championship team's performance.

The covers of the book are embossed with the team's name and the season, but otherwise are completely standard. Internally, the first 12 pages consist of information about the county, its performance last season, and the players signed for the coming season together with the fixture list, while the remaining 84 pages are preprinted but completely standard for all 17 counties. Sales are usually handled through the club itself. Once the season is over, these score books are out of date with regard to the printed information and, while some could still be sold at a reduced price as ordinary score books, the company considers this might cannibalise future sales and declines to do so. While the blank pages could be reused, the costs involved in remaking the books closely approximates a new print run and is not considered worth the effort.

Line B consists of an extensive range of booklets covering all the teams in the football league. Basically the books all serve the same purpose, which is to provide information about the league fixture list and the club's past performance and future prospects. Space is also provided so that a record may be kept of the cup and any other special games in which the team may be involved. However, the basic product is 'packaged' in a number of different formats and sizes and can be personalised for use as 'give aways' by firms to their customers as well as being sold through sporting good and confectionary, tobacconist and newsagent (CTN) outlets.

At the meeting, the following information is tabled, summarising the performance of the two lines:

	Line A Cricket		Line B Football	
Sales	100,000		220,000	
Cost of goods sold				
Labour	30,000		100,000	
Material	30,000		60,000	
Fixed overheads	40,000		40,000	
Total cost	100,000		200,000	
Stock at cost	10,000		20,000	
	90,000	90,000	180,000	180,000
Gross margin		10,000		40,000
Selling and admin exp.		15,000		35,000
Profit (Loss)		(£5,000)		£5,000

Faced with these figures, the accountant argues that both lines should be discontinued immediately, as his figures show that the cricket line is a loss-maker and the profit on the football line is hardly worth the effort. The sales manager disputes this and states that it is the cricket line that has made the loss and the football line is showing a profit, which he is confident will increase next year. The production manager admitted the gross margin on the football line was better, but argued that all the specials disrupted his production schedule and that the cricket line was more homogeneous and easier to control.

The general manager pointed out that as the stock is worthless, both lines show the same loss of £15,000 each and suggests that it would be more helpful to consider the contribution of the two

lines that consist of the sales for each line less their direct variable cost:

	Line A		Line B	
Sales		100,000		220,000
Labour	30,000		100,000	
Material	30,000		60,000	
		60,000		160,000
Contribution		40,000		60,000

From this analysis, it is clear that both lines make a very significant contribution to the fixed (overhead) and semi-fixed (selling and administration) costs of the company and that to drop either line immediately would only exacerbate the situation unless other new products can be brought on stream immediately using the same fixed assets. It is also apparent that the cricket lines make a bigger contribution per unit of sales than do the football lines and it is open to question whether the fixed and semi-fixed cost allocations are appropriate. For instance, there are only 17 cricket clubs to call on but there are 130 UK football league teams, not to mention the other sales outlets used and the wide range of options available. Similarly, the fact that the football lines require more hand-finishing (higher unit labour cost) and so make less use of machinery does not necessarily justify an equal allocation of fixed costs between the two lines.

Clearly, in deciding how to proceed, the management team needs much more information on the reasons why sales were less than forecast and what the prospects are for the coming year, e.g. if it was a very wet cricket season with well below average attendances, what the likelihood is of this occurring again etc. That said it is also clear that the contribution analysis gives a much better picture of the comparative performance of the two lines and emphasises the need for much more careful budgeting and cost control, particularly in terms of the criteria used for allocating the fixed and semi-fixed costs.

Leland Beik and Stephen Buzby (1973) suggest that the contribution approach will be of even greater value as a control mechanism, when the analysis is extended beyond the product line to the different market segments in which it is sold. This is illustrated in Tables 23.2 and 23.3 below, the first of which provides a breakdown by product type

TABLE 23.2 Breakdown by product type

	Company total ($)	Full keyboard ($)	Deluxe ten key ($)	Basic ten key ($)
Net sales	10,000	5,000	3,000	2,000
Variable manufacturing costs	5,100	2,500	1,375	1,225
Manufacturing contribution	4,900	2,500	1,625	775
Marketing costs				
Variable:				
Sales commissions	450	225	135	90
Variable contribution	4,450	2,275	1,490	685
Assignable:				
Salaries – salesmen	1,600	770	630	200
Salary – marketing manager	100	50	25	25
Product advertising	1,000	670	200	130
Total	2,700	1,490	855	355
Product contribution	1,750	785	635	330
Non-assignable:				
Institutional advertising	150			
Marketing contribution	1,600			
Fixed joint costs				
General administration	300			
Manufacturing	900			
Total	1,200			
Net profits	400			

TABLE 23.3 Product characteristics and product benefits segments

	Company total ($)	Full keyboard		Deluxe ten key		Basic ten key
		Bank seg. ($)	Non-seg. ($)	Mfg. seg. ($)	Non-seg. ($)	Retail seg. ($)
Net sales	10,000	3,750	1,250	2,550	450	2,000
Variable manufacturing costs	5,100	1,875	625	1,169	206	1,225
Manufacturing contribution	4,900	1,875	625	1,381	244	775
Marketing costs						
Variable:						
Sales commissions	450	169	56	115	20	90
Variable contribution	4,450	1,706	569	1,266	224	685
Assignable:						
Salaries – salesmen	1,600	630	140	420	210	200
Salary – marketing manager	100	38	12	19	6	25
Product advertising	1,000	670	–	200	–	130
Total	2,700	1,338	152	639	216	355
Segment contribution	1,750	368	417	627	8	330
Non-assignable:						
Institutional advertising	150					
Marketing contribution	1,600					
Fixed joint costs						
General administration	300					
Manufacturing	900					
Total	1,200					
Net profits	400					

for the company's line of adding machines, while the second exhibit carries the analysis a stage further and distinguishes the segments at which the products are targeted in terms of their characteristics and product benefits:

- Full keyboard   =   Banks
- Deluxe ten key   =   Manufacturing firms
- Basic ten key   =   Retailers

In the case of the first two segments, customers other than the prime targets also buy the machines (labelled 'non-seg.') and the analysis enables one to compare the comparative performance of the primary customer vis-à-vis the others. From such a breakdown, it becomes clear that the bank segment is showing a poor return for the marketing effort expended on it, which calls for further investigation and explanation that could well lead to changes in the marketing strategy. Without such an analysis, the disparity between the prime customers and the rest may well have gone unremarked.

CASH FLOW AND NET PRESENT VALUE

When considering the concept of the product portfolio (Chapter 5), reference was made to the differing cash needs of products at different stages of their life-cycle. From this discussion it should be clear that a full understanding of the nature of cash flow is vital to the whole process of marketing planning, for otherwise the enterprise may be put at risk due to expenditures exceeding revenue in the short to medium term without adequate provision for such an imbalance.

Strictly speaking, the calculation of cash flow is one of three methods used by financial accountants to assess and quantify the likely return from a possible investment (the others being the marginal or contribution approach discussed in the preceding section and the conventional calculation of profits after the deduction of overheads attributable to the project). Texts on financial and management accounting stress that cash flow is not the same as profit and will only become the same when a business is finally wound up. It follows that using cash flow to measure the worth of an investment may give quite a different picture from the calculation of profit. (A clearly worked example highlighting the difference between the two measures can be found in Taylor and Shearing, 1974.) Specifically, profits are likely to exceed cash flow in the early years of a project, but fall below it in later years due to the inclusion of depreciation.

Because the different approaches may yield different results, it would seem prudent to use them all before deciding which is most appropriate to the particular circumstances of the firm and its decision-makers. However, as suggested earlier, in the case of new product development (NPD) it is considered particularly important that one should seek to specify as clearly as possible a sales forecast and expected revenues for comparison with one's budget for the launch of the product. Initially the cash flow will be negative as the manufacturer has to invest in inventory, secure distribution, promote the availability of the product etc., while sales will take time to build up. As noted in Chapter 15, with low-learning products or 'fashion' goods, there may be only a short time lag between introduction and volume sales, but in the case of high-learning products the introduction phase may extend over many years and require considerable underwriting which will have to be funded by the positive cash flow from established products and/or other sources.

Due to the fact that many investment projects will have lives extending over many years, it is important that one discount the cash flow or future earnings stream to establish its net present value. As Taylor and Shearing (1974) point out, the two major problems involved in discounting cash flows are (a) to decide on the period over which the calculations are to be made, and (b) to assess the appropriate rate of interest or discount to be used. However, once decisions on these two parameters have been made, and one can always compute a number of alternatives and subject them to a sensitivity analysis, the actual calculation is straightforward as the appropriate discount factors are readily available in published tables. For example a 5% interest rate has the following factors:

Year 1	0.9524
Year 2	0.9070
Year 3	0.8638
Year 4	0.8227

The application of discounted cash flow analysis in selecting a product portfolio, which also incorporates a Bayesian approach to handling uncertainty concerning future outcomes, is described fully in an article by Gottlieb and Roshwalb (1966) and is recommended reading for anyone wishing to pursue this topic further.

However, before leaving the topic of cash flow analysis, it is worth mentioning that such calculations are frequently used to determine the payback period for different projects. Payback is a very simple concept, as it merely states how long it will take to recover one's initial investment in a project. Under conditions of inflation and uncertainty, such as existed in the UK (and elsewhere) in the late 1970s and early 1980s, the temptation to invest only in projects with short-term payback periods became almost overwhelming, resulting in the inadequate investment in R&D and long-term strategic projects which has been commented on in several places in this book. As with most summary statistics, one must be careful not to place too much reliance on a single measure without full consideration of all its implications – advice which also applies to the use of management ratios when assessing the general financial health of an organisation. Payback is calculated by the simple formula:

$$\text{Payback} = \frac{\text{Net investment}}{\text{Average annual operating cash flow}}$$

The payback period is often used in determining whether an investment can be recouped within its economic life, but can be misleading unless one builds into the calculations an amount equivalent to the opportunity cost of using the funds, e.g. purchase of a machine tool with a life of six years at a cost of £50,000 and current interest rates of 15% should be calculated as follows:

Year	Opening balance	Earnings @ 15%	Cash flow	Closing balance	
1	50,000	7,500	12,500	45,000	
2	45,000	6,750	12,500	39,250	
3	39,250	5,888	12,500	32,638	
4	32,638	4,896	12,500	25,034	= payback
5	25,034	3,755	12,500	16,289	
6	16,289	2,443	12,500	6,232	

From this calculation, it can be seen that the crude payback indicates payback in four years, but the calculation of the opportunity cost of the investment, assuming interest rates will remain steady on average 15%, shows that it will record a net loss of £6,232 when the machine has to be scrapped.

The position is even more complicated when the cash flow varies, which is usually the case, when payback can give quite erroneous indications of the merits of alternative investments.

MANAGEMENT RATIOS

Insofar as marketing is primarily concerned with competitive activity, it follows that one should seek to learn as much as possible about those with whom one is competing. In that all registered organisations are required to lodge annual statements of their accounts with the Registrar of Companies and public companies publish them widely, evaluation of such statements should comprise an essential ingredient in one's strategic planning. It goes without saying that one should also apply the same evaluation to one's own accounts in order to assess the health and progress of the organisation. In doing so, one should be sensitive to the six reasons set out in Table 23.4 why such comparisons may be of limited value when conducted on an individual basis. However, as Sizer (1979) also points out, there are a number of consolidated returns such as Interfirm Comparisons, Business Monitors, The Times 1000 etc., which provide a useful yardstick of competitive achievement.

A major tool for such evaluation is the use of ratio analysis. As noted above, management ratios are summary statistics and must be treated with caution. Their main value lies in the fact that ratios express relative rather than absolute values and so make it possible to compare results over time. Most books on financial management and control suggest a pyramid of ratios similar to that reproduced in Figure 23.6. The apex of the pyramid is the most basic measure of performance – ROI – and each lower level measures the component parts that go to make up or influence the summary measures on the level above. Thus if ROI is unsatisfactory, this may be because profit on sales is inadequate or it may be that while profit

TABLE 23.4 Reasons why comparisons of individual annual statements of accounts may be of limited value

1. At the present time the accounts are prepared on a historical cost basis.

2. There are a number of permitted accounting rules for dealing with particular items of revenue, expenditure, assets, and liabilities. As no 2 companies employ exactly the same set of accounting rules, the rates of return of any 2 companies may not be intrinsically comparable.

3. If a company is a subsidiary of a large group, it is often difficult to separate the financing of the subsidiary from its trading activities.

4. If the company is a member of a vertically integrated group of companies, where the end products of one company become the raw materials of another company, the transfer prices from one company to another may not be market prices and the profits of individual companies in the group may not be meaningful.

5. In a vertically integrated group of companies, one company in the group may accept an export order at a loss, but for the group as a whole the order may be profitable. A comparison with the company accepting the export order at a loss would be of limited value.

6. In a group of companies a single product line might be produced by several subsidiary companies, each of which also produces several other products, while the parent company absorbs all research and development costs.

SOURCE: Sizer, J. (1979) Investment life-cycle of a hypothetical new product, in J. Sizer, *An Insight into Management Accounting*. Harmondsworth: Penguin, p. 185

margins on sales are satisfactory, the actual volume of sales is too low in relation to the capital employed. Whichever appears to be the cause, one can then work downwards through the pyramid until the root cause or causes is found. A full discussion of how to use ratios in this way is to be found in R. M. S. Wilson's *Management Controls and Marketing Planning* (1979) or John Sizer's *An Insight into Management Accounting* (1979).

For those unable to consult these or similar sources, the main ratios and their uses are:

1. *Measures of liquidity:* i.e. of the funds available for use in the business:

- The current ratio $= \dfrac{\text{current assets}}{\text{current liabilities}}$

This ratio measures the extent to which the firm is able to meet claims upon it from its creditors. A ratio of 2 : 1 is generally regarded as 'about right' in that the firm could experience a severe (50%) reduction in its current assets and still meet its liabilities and continue trading. While a higher ratio would no doubt please creditors, it could well indicate poor control as it might consist of excessive inventories which could be difficult to dispose of in an emergency and/or too generous a credit policy. In the latter case a need to call in payment may well reflect a general downturn in trading conditions and an inability of the debtors to pay up.

- The 'acid-test' ratio $= \dfrac{\text{liquid assets}}{\text{current liabilities}}$

'Liquid assets' comprise cash + marketable securities + receivables and the acid test measures the firm's ability to cover its current liabilities in a real crisis.

- Stockturn $= \dfrac{\text{annual sales}}{\text{average stock}}$

or $= \dfrac{\text{average stock} \times 12}{\text{annual sales}}$

- Receivables $= \dfrac{\text{debtors/receivables} \times 12}{\text{sales}}$

A measure of the length of credit extended to customers.

- Payables $= \dfrac{\text{creditors/payables} \times 12}{\text{sales}}$

A measure of the credit extended by suppliers.

2. *Measures of profitability:* While the pursuit of profit has been much qualified as a corporate objective in recent years, there can be no doubt that it still remains the primary aim of the business organisation. John Sizer cites Peter Drucker's *The Practice of Management* (1954), which points out that profit serves three purposes:

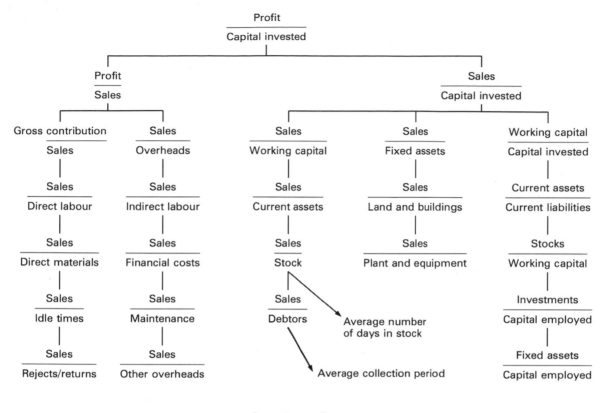

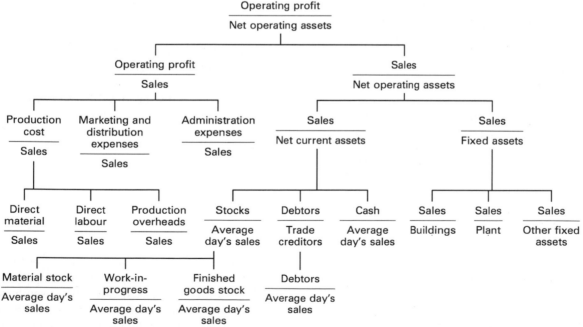

FIGURE 23.6 Control and operating ratios

SOURCE: Sizer, J. (1979) *An Insight into Management Accounting.* Harmondsworth: Penguin, p. 394

1. It measures the net effectiveness and sound-ness of a business's effort.
2. It is the premium that covers the cost of stay-ing in business – replacement, obsolescence, market and technical risk and uncertainty. Seen from this point of view it may be argued that there is no such thing as profit; there are only the costs of being and staying in busin-ess. These are the costs of survival. The management of a business has to provide adequately for these costs by generating sufficient profit.
3. It ensures the supply of future capital for innovation and expansion, either directly, by providing the means of self-financing out of retained profits, or indirectly, through prov-iding sufficient inducement for new outside capital in the form which will optimise the company's capital structure and optimise its cost of capital.

While most if not all managers would agree to these three propositions, because of the qualificat-ion of the profit objective alluded to, there is no single method of computing a firm's profit or its profitability and the statistic is subject to consider-able ambiguity. Perhaps the most obvious comment is that profit per se is meaningless unless it is related to the magnitude of the resources used in generating that profit which suggests that one should first compute:

- *The return on investment (ROI):* Depending upon the authority consulted, several methods are suggested for calculating this ratio. The most basic expression of it (and the top ratio in the pyramid) is:

$$\frac{\text{Net profit}}{\text{Capital employed}}$$

But while Sizer would define this precisely as profit after taxation and interest and after deduction of

$$\frac{\text{Profit attributable to minority and}}{\text{Equity shareholders' investment}}$$

preference shareholders

many other sources are much less explicit and suggest the ratios:

$$\frac{\text{Net profit (after tax)}}{\text{Total net assets}}$$

and

$$\frac{\text{Net profit (after tax)}}{\text{Fixed assets}}$$

- *Gross profit* (or gross margin)

$$\frac{\text{Gross profit}}{\text{Sales}}$$

This ratio emphasises the contribution of sales to the selling, general and administrative expense and thus subjects them to close scrutiny, particularly when compared with:

- *Net profit*

$$\frac{\text{Net profit}}{\text{Sales}}$$

- *Earnings per share (EPS)*

$$\frac{\text{Profit attributable to equity shareholders}}{\text{Number of equity shares}}$$

This ratio is much favoured by investors and financial analysts as a performance measure, and is usually reported in conjunction with share prices as a:

- *Price–Earnings (P–E) ratio:*

$$\frac{\text{Price per share}}{\text{EPS}}$$

From the above selection of ratios it should be obvious that one can compute an almost infinite number of ratios. As noted earlier, the usefulness of such ratios will vary considerably and their main value lies in highlighting changes in direc-tion which can then be subjected to closer and more careful scrutiny.

THE BALANCED SCORECARD

The notion of a 'balanced scorecard' was developed by Robert S. Kaplan and David P. Norton in a series of articles in the *Harvard Business Review* (1992, 1993 and 1996) which were subsequently synthesised in *The Balanced Scorecard* (1996):

> The Balanced Scorecard (BSC) provides managers with the instrumentation they need to navigate future competitive success.

Drawing on the analogy of flight instrumentation, the BSC proposes a comprehensive set of performance measures across four perspectives: financial; customers; internal business processes; and learning and growth.

From 1850 to about 1975, competition in the industrial age was based on the economics of scale and scope using physical assets. Thereafter a shift to the information age occurred and with it the need to mobilise and exploit intangible assets in the manner predicted by Peter Drucker who said that information age organisations are built on a new set of operating assumptions:

- Cross-functional rather than specialised functional skills
- Links to customers and suppliers
- Customer segmentation
- Global scale
- Innovation
- Knowledge workers.

While traditional financial measures are still needed, they record past events and are inadequate for guiding future development. The BSC complements these with measures of the drivers of future performance and is intended as a strategic management system.

Perspective	General Measures
Financial	ROI and economic value added
Customer	Satisfaction, retention, market and account share
Internal	Quality, response time, cost, new product introductions
Learning and Growth	Employee satisfaction and information system availability

The balanced or corporate scorecard is an approach to measuring corporate performance by weighting both financial and non-financial measures. The financial measures comprise all those described earlier in this chapter.

Among the non-financial measures may be numbered both internal and external yardsticks. Most important among the *external* measures are those relating to customers, covering such issues as acquisition, retention, profitability, service levels and perceived satisfaction etc. Other important external measures would include those relating to social responsibility and community relations. The *internal* measures tend to emphasise HRM matters such as employee satisfaction, retention, cost/profit etc., together with measures of the efficiency and effectiveness of internal business processes.

A pivotal issue critical to the development of a balanced scorecard is the identification of the key performance indicators appropriate to the firm in question. While benchmarking (Chapter 8) may identify critical success factors or key performance indicators for competing organisations, they may be neither as relevant nor as important for one's own company. Other issues that need to be taken into account include:

- Distinguishing means from ends
- Measuring what is easiest to measure
- Managing what gets measured
- Paralysis by analysis
- Appropriate qualitative measures, e.g. 'satisfaction'.

It is also important to remember that, as with strategic planning itself, the whole exercise will be worthless if measurement and analysis does not lead to specific actions.

The underlying logic of using a balanced scorecard approach is that it requires the analyst to identify and understand the cause–effect relationship. It is from such analysis that the *drivers* which determine the desired results may be identified. The perceived importance of marketing metrics is confirmed by the fact that the Marketing Science Institute of Cambridge, Massachusetts identified this as its top research priority for the periods 1998–2000 and 2000–2002, based on feedback from the corporate sponsors that fund its programmes.

MARKETING SPEND – EXPENSE OR INVESTMENT?

A major problem with most marketing expenditure is that it is treated as an expense to be written off in the year in which it is made. As a result of this treatment, it is frequently difficult to justify the effectiveness of this expenditure. It also has the tendency to make marketers adopt a short-termist approach to selling and objectives based on comparative parity with competitors rather than long-term strategic decisions designed to build customer loyalty and build the brand. While this topic was the subject of a major article by Adrian J. Slywotsky and Benson P. Shapiro in the *Harvard Business Review* in 1993, the concern with marketing metrics that has been a dominant theme in the new millennium indicates that much needs to be done if senior management is to be persuaded that marketing expenditures should be treated as investment.

In their article Slywotsky and Shapiro (1993) argue that:

> Companies can gain a competitive advantage over more established rivals by treating marketing expenditures the same way they treat capital outlays: as investments that drive revenues over time.

As the authors point out, if factories were built following the same kind of thinking that underpins many marketing decisions, they would have to be built on an instalment plan. Instead, it is accepted that having decided on the benefits that will flow from building a new factory, the capital investment is made upfront and amortised over its expected life, with long-term revenues and profits looked at in terms of ROI.

> Building a customer base demands the same assumption as building a factory: investment drives revenue, not the reverse … The nature of the customer development process involves a lag between action and results. Investment thinking makes this lag time clear and understandable. Expense thinking confuses cause and effect. Even worse, it can let unrealistic sales projections determine the marketing budget.

Slywotsky and Shapiro are concerned particularly with the challenges facing new entrants to a market where there are established competitors

with significant market shares and high brand equity. Recognising that the latter are themselves the consequence of cumulative marketing investment over time, the question is how can a follower displace the dominant firm? First movers and early entrants have the advantage of making customers aware of the existence of the new category, and defining it in terms of initial customer preferences. As is freely acknowledged, winning customers in established markets can be an expensive and risky business and many fail in the attempt. But, as the examples of Glaxo's Zantac and Philip Morris' Marlboro show, it is not impossible and can be enormously profitable.

In the case of Zantac, it was taking on Smith-Kline's Tagamet, which had held a virtual monopoly since its launch in the late 1970s. Most analysts believed that, at best, Zantac would gain no more than a 10% share but in six years it had gained 50% while Tagamet had fallen to 23%. Glaxo achieved this by targeting known side effects of Tagamet. SmithKline could not respond directly to this as many people had experienced side effects and so was forced 'to spend huge sums to point out, in essence, "We're not that bad."' In the case of Marlboro, with a 1% market share and an advertising budget to match, the breakthrough was achieved through a highly effective advertising campaign featuring the iconic cowboy. In both examples, the followers were able to reposition their brands in consumers' minds, as recommended in Ries and Trout's well-known *Positioning: the Battle for your Mind* (1986). To do this accurate targeting is critical.

Slywotsky and Shapiro recommend focusing on three groups that 'create maximum value for the marketing investor':

1. Customers who have low acquisition costs: 'switchables'
2. Customers generating the most returns: 'high-profit customers'
3. Customers contributing to long-term growth: 'share-determiners'.

Basically, switchables are customers who are sufficiently unhappy with their current suppliers that they are willing to consider alternatives, but they need to be distinguished from 'garage sale' switchers who always go to the cheapest source. By

Key yardsticks

Rate of return

Operating ratios

Payout ratios
Interest coverage

Debt–equity ratios
Debt service

Present value

Key strategies

Conduct of operations

Deployment of assets
Market selection
Pricing strategy
Cost effectiveness
Operating leverage

Disposition of profits

Dividends to owners
Interest to lenders
Reinvestment of profits

Financing strategy

Types of equity
Types of debt
Financial leverage

Investment strategy

Types of investments
Emphasis and
development

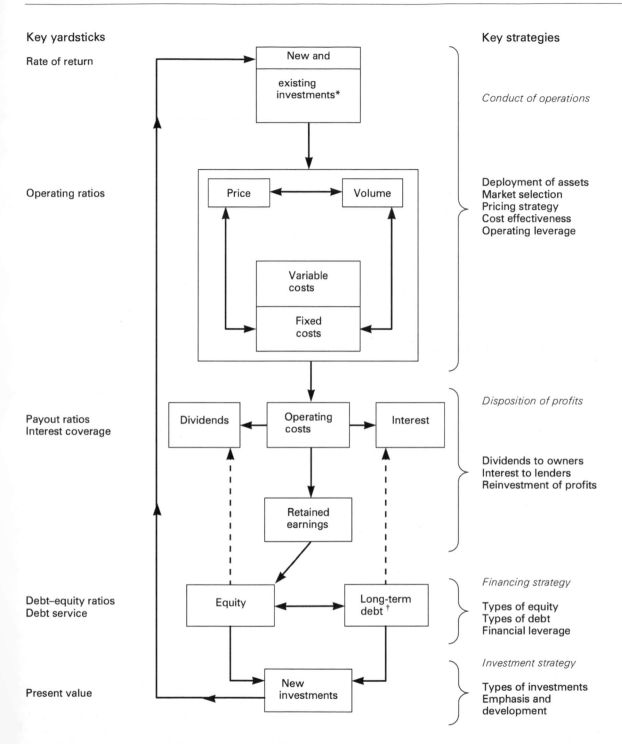

* Assumes an amount equal to depreciation invested here
† Assumes continuous rollover, with no reduction through repayments

FIGURE 23.7 The business system: an overview

SOURCE: Helfert, E. A. (1982) *Techniques of Financial Analysis* (5th edn). Homewood, IL: Irwin

contrast, high-profit customers are not overly concerned with price and cost less to service than other customers. They can only be identified through detailed analysis of the customer database. The third group, share determiners, are those likely to have the 'greatest impact on the company's long-term position. They may cost a lot to acquire, but they deliver higher returns than many other customers because of the duration and extent of their influence.' For example, Glaxo targeted doctors in training, and Toyota 18–25-year-old car buyers on the principle that they were the 'customers' of the future.

Having identified the target group, the critical tactics are to have an unmatchable message and continuity of investment.

Chapter summary

The Importance of Control in Marketing

The foregoing discussion of financial controls and measures may seem somewhat misplaced in a book on marketing strategy and management, particularly as it is so selective and essentially superficial. However, the intention is not to provide a primer in managerial accounting, but to emphasise the basic point that finance and control are integral parts of the marketing function and that marketing managers must have a sound understanding of both if they are to discharge their duties effectively. The truth of this claim is clearly indicated in Figure 23.7, which is a diagrammatic representation of the business system.

Recommended reading

Davis, J. (2007) *Measuring Marketing: 103 Key Metrics Every Marketer Needs*. Singapore: John Wiley & Sons (Asia).

Kaplan, R. S. and Norton, D. P. (2006) *Alignment: How to Apply the Balanced Scorecard to Corporate Strategy*. Boston, MA: Harvard Business School Press.

McDonald, M., Ward, K. and Smith, B. (2005) *Marketing Due Diligence: Reconnecting Strategy to Share Price*. Oxford: Butterworth Heinemann.

Ward, K. (2003) Controlling marketing, in M, J. Baker (ed.) *The Marketing Book* (5th edn). Oxford: Butterworth Heinemann.

Wilson, R. M. S. (1999) Marketing budgeting and resource allocation, in M, J. Baker (ed.) *Encyclopedia of Marketing*. London: International Thomson Business Press.

REFERENCES

Beik, L. and Buzby, S. (1973) Profitability analysis by market segments, *Journal of Marketing*, 37 July: pp. 48–53.

Buzzell, R. D. and Baker, M. J. (1970) Sales effectiveness of automobile advertising, *Journal of Advertising Research* 12(3): 3–8.

Clark, B. H., Abela, A. V. and Ambler, T. (2005) Organizational motivation, opportunity and ability to measure marketing performance, *Journal of Strategic Marketing*, 13(4): 241–59.

Drucker, P. (1954) *The Practice of Management*. New York: Harper & Row.

Gottlieb, M. J. and Roshwalb, I. (1966) The 'present value' concept in evaluating new products, *New Ideas for Successful Marketing*, Proceedings of the American Marketing Association, World Congress, Chicago, pp. 387–400; reprinted in D. Maynard Phelps (ed.) (1970) *Product Management: Selected Readings*. Homewood, IL: Irwin.

Helfert, E. A. (1982) *Techniques of Financial Analysis* (5th edn). Homewood, IL: Irwin

Howard, J. A. (1963) *Marketing Management*. Homewood, IL: Irwin, p. 207.

Kaplan, R. S. and Norton, D. P. (1996) *The Balanced Scorecard*. Boston, MA: Harvard Business School Press.

Ries, A. and Trout, J. (1986) Positioning: the Battle for Your Mind. (1st rev. edn). New York: McGraw-Hill

Sizer, J. (1979) *An Insight into Management Accounting*. Harmondsworth: Penguin.

Sizer, J. (1979) Investment life-cycle of a hypothetical new product, in J. Sizer *An Insight into Management Accounting*. Harmondsworth: Penguin.

Slywotsky, A. J. and Shapiro, B. P. (1993) Leveraging to beat the odds: The new marketing mindset, *Harvard Business Review* (September–October).

Taylor, A. H. and Shearing, H. (1974) *Financial and Cost Accountancy for Management* (6th edn). London: Macdonald & Evans.

Wilson, R. M. S. (1979) *Management Controls and Market Planning*. London: Heinemann.

CHAPTER 24

Current issues and future trends

What has been will be again, what has been done will be done again, there is nothing new under the sun. ECCLESIASTES 1

INTRODUCTION

As has been commented on in Chapter 1 when describing the scope and coverage of this book, the writer is faced with a major dilemma as to what to include and what to exclude. This decision becomes increasingly difficult with successive editions as new ideas emerge. Wherever possible these new ideas have been incorporated into the text but there still remain a number of current issues which are felt to be of sufficient importance to deserve at least a passing reference. Accordingly, in this chapter we will address first the impact of information technology (IT) on marketing and, particularly, the rapidly developing field of e-commerce, which is a logical extension of it.

It has been claimed that changes in information and communication technology, and specifically the internet, have given rise to a 'new economy'. The nature and substance of this claim are examined in some detail, as is the view that there is a need for a new paradigm of the domain of marketing that recognises the transition from manufacturing-based economies to those that are based on services. For reasons we explain in some detail, we reject both these claims but feel they are sufficiently important to be brought to the attention of readers who may think otherwise.

Another major trend that deserves some recognition is the social responsibility of organisations, both for the environment in which they operate and towards the customers that they serve. This responsibility is reflected in the place of ethics in marketing and the impact of marketing on the environment. Short sections have been included on these topics.

Finally, while frequent reference has been made to global competition we have given no explicit discussion of it. In part this is because international competition is seen as calling for the same principles and practices that apply to competition in general. Obviously, one will need to adjust one's strategy and marketing mix to accommodate differences in culture, behaviour, regulation etc. but these are issues of degree not kind. That said, the attention given to 'globalisation' is so extensive that some thoughts on the matter seemed to be called for. Accordingly, we examine some of the general issues involved in global marketing and particularly the role of emerging economies.

INFORMATION TECHNOLOGY AND MARKETING

According to Buzzell and Sisodia (1999, p. 225):

> Among the key developments have been the measurement of retail sales via scanning, outfitting field sales forces with laptop computers, utilisation of planning software by product managers, utilisation of electronic order entry systems, and – most recently – the use of the internet for communications and transactions between suppliers and customers.

In turn, these changes have been made possible by a number of key developments in information technology, including:

1. *Processing:* more powerful, smaller and less expensive
2. *Data storage:* greater capacity, easier access, lower cost
3. *Display:* greater resolution, less bulky and less costly
4. *Software:* easy to use, more versatile
5. *Networks:* increased capacities at lower cost
6. *Wireless systems:* from voice to data.

After discussing the application of IT to the management of the mix elements, Buzzell and Sisodia give particular attention to the growth in direct marketing. They cite Hair and Keep (1997, pp. 231–2) for the consensus of expectations regarding electronic marketing:

- Improved market information for sellers
- Improved market information for buyers
- Enhanced interactivity and interconnectivity between buyers and sellers
- Emergence of new market intermediaries
- Expanded technology-based channels of distribution
- Additional technology-based consumer services
- More worldwide sourcing
- Increased emphasis on building customer loyalty
- Safeguards for security and buyer–seller confidentiality.

Buzzell and Sisodia (1999, p. 235) also believe that the use of advanced IT in marketing has led to several important organisational changes. These include:

- Flattening of structures: As with other functional areas, marketing is being affected by reductions in middle management ranks.
- Decentralisation of marketing activities: More marketing decisions are now being made by front-line (i.e. customer contact) personnel empowered with information tools. In some companies, regional sales offices are taking over many marketing tasks.
- Greater use of cross-functional teams: Some companies have reorganised their marketing divisions into customer-centred themes, which go beyond major account management in that they include personnel from other functional areas.

They also identify two future trends, the first of which is that the quality and quantity of marketing data are now such that its possession does not confer any competitive advantage. It is the quality of a company's knowledge bases and the systems based on them that will become more important in the future. Second, the development of upgraded computing and communication infrastructures, which will allow for two-way communication and be broadband, will enable consumers to interact

directly with suppliers. As noted earlier, this new distribution channel is likely to have significant impact on existing structures.

ELECTRONIC COMMERCE – THE FUTURE IS HERE TO STAY[1]

INTRODUCTION

Electronic commerce (e-commerce) is more than the popular image of shopping on the internet. Rather it refers to all commercial transactions based on the electronic processing and transmission of data (including text, sound and image and video). This includes electronic data interchange (EDI), electronic funds transfer at point of sale (EFTPOS), electronic banking, digital cash and other electronic payment systems, as well as the popular conception of commerce transacted over the internet. This can be business-to-consumer (B2C), business-to-business (B2B) (hubs), consumer-to-business (C2B) and consumer-to-consumer (C2C) (exchanges, e.g. eBay and Trademe). Many consider e-commerce to be too narrow and that we should be talking about electronic business, as it is a way to do business (Figure 24.1). While it mirrors existing issues that come with traditional paper-based commercial transactions, as a medium for conducting business it also presents significant issues that include security (cryptography), tax collection, privacy and the legal status of electronic documentation, cross-border jurisdiction and consumer protection. Additionally, there is still much to be sorted out with reference to legal issues. The case of Napster from 1999–2001 is a case in point. The resulting increase in peer-to-peer (P2P) exchanges continues to prove too difficult to control and enforce. Spamming has attracted much attention and the introduction of local laws, new protocols and anti-bot measures, such as the use of graphic passwords rather than textual, has improved the situation.

There is no doubt in the minds of industry observers and commentators that e-commerce is here to stay. The challenge for many firms is how to migrate their customer base online by adding value. While industry's marketing managers and individual consumers are grappling with the implications for future trade and relationships, academics are equally busy trying to define and delineate it. For many companies, internet tech-

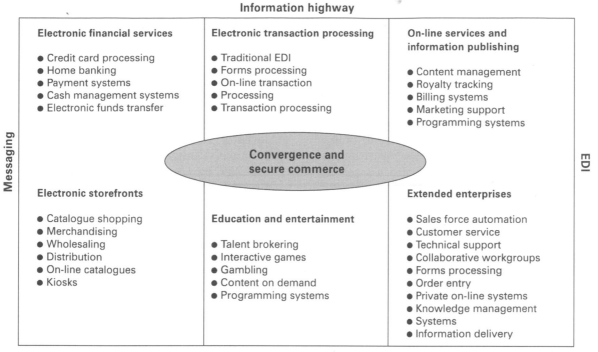

Information highway

FIGURE 24.1 E-commerce enabled business functions
SOURCE: KPMG (1999) *Electronic Commerce Research Report.* London: KPMG

nology has enabled them to create and leverage the 'three nets'. The *intranet* is the use of internet technology within the firm and allows companies to share real-time information among its employees. Different levels of access and a secure section mean complete control of sensitive corporate information. On the one hand, it becomes a central repository for company information, procedures and protocols and on the other hand allows the senior management team to share planning and control information regardless of physical location or time. The *extranet* also uses internet technology but shares this access with select strategic partners, e.g. suppliers and buyers. This adds a significant level of sophistication to such functions as logistics and materials management. Finally, the *internet* allows the company to have a presence on the global stage. With the number of websites now in existence and being added to daily, search engine optimisation has become a necessity. It is no longer enough simply to fill *meta tags* with a series of company buzz words. Search engines are more sophisticated and drill down through sites to establish links between the meta tags, the URL

(uniform resource locator or web address), the title and most importantly, the entire site content.

Having secured a top ranking spot, i.e. page one, on a search engine, the site must also be capable of being read on a number of different media. In the beginning, a 480 × 640 monitor was our prime concern. Now, with high resolution monitors, personal digital assistants (PDAs) and wireless technology, many more interfaces need to be catered for. In parallel with these changes is a shift in online consumer profiles. Where this was once dominated by males aged 18–35, the online population now more closely resembles and reflects the general population. Children, teens, young professionals, empty nesters and the grey market are all avid users and online buyers. That said, there is still a digital divide between those who have access and those who do not. This can be at an individual level, people who choose not to go online, to a national level where less developed nations simply do not have the funding and therefore infrastructure. There is also the issue of culture, geography, topography and lifestyle.

Regardless, a high percentage of users continue to go online to send and receive email, gather news, use a search engine, check the weather and surf for 'fun'. The main activities are banking, travel arrangements, online auctions and purchasing a range of products. Consumer behaviourists are increasingly interested in online search, evaluation and purchasing behaviour as well as the formation and managing of online relationships with customers. Moving customers through their decision-making process can be managed very effectively.

Worldwide, the value of online business 10 years ago (1996) was $2.7 billion. It was forecast to reach $10.2 trillion by the end of 2006 and that figure will be out of date by the time this book is read! The driving force is the exponentially increasing capabilities of the converging technologies of computing and telecommunications. What was a great disadvantage – the distance from, and time to, major markets – is immaterial in the instant world of global digital networks, where the minimisation of the barriers of time and distance result in efficiency gains in the business demand chain. The democratic nature of the internet has allowed individuals, small and medium-sized enterprises (SMEs) and large corporations alike to easily participate in electronic commerce.

As noted, email, with its facility for sharing electronic documents, files and applications, is the internet application most commonly used for commercial purposes. However, more sophisticated applications are also becoming prevalent. The web (WWW or W3) is being used as a marketing tool to disseminate product information, deliver support services, create dialogue, support relationships or as a vehicle for direct selling.

The likely impacts of electronic commerce are difficult to quantify but include:

- An increase in the retail and distribution use of RFID (radio frequency identification) and the internet
- Easy and cost-effective access to the global market for both producers and consumers
- Greater number of merchants on the internet. Cost of set-up can be as low as a few hundred pounds
- An increase in global consumers. Anyone with

a computer, an internet connection and a credit card can become a global consumer
- Greater effectiveness in the delivery of services and support
- Greater accessibility to distant markets
- Significantly reduced supply times
- Shortened product cycles
- Simplified ordering processes and reduced inventory
- Producers and consumers are brought closer together by allowing them to communicate directly, without the intervention of traditional intermediaries such as importers, exporters, wholesalers and retailers
- Lower transaction costs
- Lower barriers to entry (trade and economic)
- Net outflow of cash from an economy in the absence of a suitable international regulatory framework
- Improved access to information for the consumer
- A move towards products that are typical of a 'knowledge' economy (financial and other services, software, travel, entertainment and high-value niche market goods) and hence well suited to e-commerce.
- The ability to move from mass production of lower value products to the mass customisation of higher value 'customised' products developed in direct consultation with the final customer
- The ability, in theory, to shift from one national UK market of 56 million to 56 million markets of one
- The collapsing of space, time and distance – then is now and there is here.

AREAS OF GROWTH

While the size of this online consumer market is growing, it is still only a fraction of the overall consumer market. Contrary to the popular view, the area of most rapid growth in electronic commerce – and the area with the most immediate potential – is in business-to-business (B2B) transactions. There are several reasons for this.

1. B2B electronic transactions are usually a continuation of an existing business relationship already underpinned by a high degree of trust and supported by established contracts.

2. Moving a traditional relationship to an electronic one is regarded as a means of making efficiency gains through the application of technology, rather than a move into e-commerce.
3. Due to the larger volumes, e-commerce can most easily and visibly deliver efficiency gains, particularly through demand chain integration, automating the buying process, and superior support service.

The development and spread of a modern telecommunications infrastructure that can support the high bandwidth needs of electronic commerce applications will determine the growth and rate of adoption for many countries and is of particular concern to developing countries.

Security has been and always will be an issue, particularly with consumers. Consumers are comfortable and willing to give their credit card numbers to complete strangers when completing a purchase via a telephone call, yet hesitate to send their credit card details over the internet to a well-established web-based vendor using secure encryption technology. There is the additional problem of effective protection for consumers who purchase goods or services from overseas traders who fail to meet the guarantees or comply with the standards available in their own country. Finally, there is the potential for consumers to be exposed to unfair marketing practices and fraud. Significant advances have been achieved in the cat and mouse game of online transactions. ISPs (internet service providers) and ASPs (application service providers) are offering more sophisticated encryption technologies and banks are offering higher levels of protection. Banks often cooperate and develop a common gateway to offer secure online transactions, and companies such as DPS (Direct Payment Solutions) have established a reputation for integrity of operation as well as secure peace of mind to purchaser and vendor alike. That said, a more secure operation is viewed as a challenge to many hackers and fraudulent dealers.

OTHER ISSUES/BARRIERS

There are a number of other issues that may pose

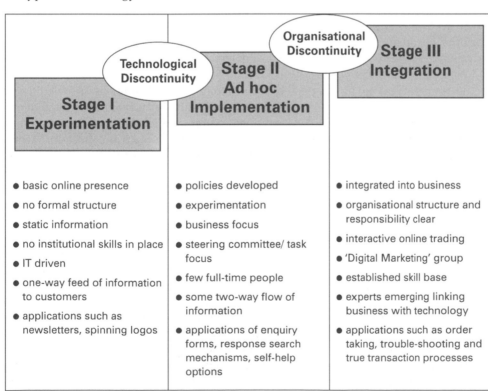

FIGURE 24.2 Adoption and implementation of e-commerce

SOURCE: Nolan Norton Institute (www.nolannorton.com)

barriers to the development of e-commerce. These include:

- The ability of businesses to comprehend and leverage the many and varied opportunities that e-commerce represents.
- The availability of the skills and knowledge required to develop and implement a successful e-commerce initiative, especially in the areas of website design, content creation, technical skills and internet marketing skills.

Although the Nolan Norton Institute identified three stages an organisation goes through in terms of its adoption and implementation of e-commerce (Figure 24.2), perhaps the cost of entry will determine the eventual uptake by various product categories, product–market mixes and indeed countries themselves.

All this aside, the electronic future is bright, sustainable and here to stay.

THE NEW ECONOMY

One of the reviewers of the manuscript for this new edition commented that the treatment would benefit from 'a new economy perspective'. Given that reviewers are anonymous, it wasn't possible to clarify just what this person had in mind, although it was clear that no specific comment had been made on this issue. Perhaps the comment was prompted by the inclusion of a complete chapter, 'Marketing Strategies for the New Economy', in Walker et al.'s (2005) fifth edition of *Marketing Strategy*. Accordingly, while the nature and implications of this term are discussed implicitly in a number of places, this section seeks to define the new economy and examine its relevance to marketing management and strategy.

The term 'new economy' appears to have been used first in 1995 when *Newsweek* used it to describe the transition of the advanced, industrialised economies from a manufacturing base to one founded on information and knowledge. This transition was precipitated by competition from the newly industrialised economies of Southeast Asia and the emerging economies of Brazil, Russia, India and China – the so-called BRIC economies. With lower material and labour costs,

these countries were able to use price as a competitive weapon and this encouraged many major corporations to outsource their inputs from these countries as well as relocating their own manufacturing in them.

To sustain employment, and compensate for the loss of jobs in manufacturing, academics, business leaders and policy-makers advocated the move into a 'knowledge-based' economy, and many sources appear to use this term as if it is synonomous with 'new economy'. In our view, this is incorrect, as all economies, whatever their stage of economic development, are based on knowledge. What distinguishes between them is how advanced the knowledge is at their disposal, how skilled their citizens are in using that knowledge, and how sophisticated are the assets and resources available to facilitate output and productivity.

In Chapter 10, we discussed the nature and importance of internal marketing and 'human capital' 'in the shape of competencies, ideas, brands, relationships and networks, strategic alliances and the like' that are based on knowledge. Knowledge is the fruit of experience and research and may be either implicit or explicit. Implicit knowledge has not been codified and published and is intrinsic to the individual or organisation that possesses it. By contrast, explicit knowledge has been codified and published and so, in principle, is available to all. Implicit knowledge is a source of competitive advantage and differentiates the owner from competitors. But explicit knowledge is in the public domain and, unless protected by intellectual property rights (IPR), cannot in itself be a source of differentiation and competitive advantage. On the other hand, when adopted and used by others, especially if they enjoy a lower cost base, it can become a competitive weapon for use against those who created the knowledge/technology in the first place. Sony, who acquired a licence to use the technology embedded in the transistor for the trivial sum of $25,000, is a frequently cited example. It follows that to talk of 'knowledge-based' economies is next to meaningless unless one distinguishes clearly between the degree of sophistication of that knowledge base and bears in mind that knowledge is a commodity that is readily transferred.

Undoubtedly, knowledge was a major factor contributing to the conditions that led to the identification of a 'new economy' but, as subsequent events were to prove, the state was more illusory than real. During the late 1980s and early 1990s, a sustained period of steady growth and low unemployment in the USA, as well as many other countries, prompted the view that a new economic paradigm had emerged and that the fluctuations of the business cycle had become a thing of the past. Specifically, developments in information and communication technology (ICT), combined with globalisation and the development of global markets, were seen as the source and drivers behind this new state.

Perhaps the best-known and most frequently cited ICT development was the creation of the internet and the dot.com boom that accompanied it. Less frequently mentioned are developments in physical transportation and distribution (containerisation, pipelines for oil and gas, air travel etc.), satellite communication and digital technology, all of which combined to reduce the physical separation between producers and consumers and create a truly global market.

Now, a decade or more after the identification of the new economy, a more balanced evaluation of the implications and impact of ICT is possible. Such an analysis 'What we learned in the New Economy' by Jennifer Reingold appeared in the March 2004 issue of *Fast Company* (http:www. fastcompany.com/magazine/80/neweconomy, accessed 02/08/2006). Specifically, Reingold identifies six beliefs that underpinned the view that a new economy had really arrived with a more balanced and detailed view that she calls 'cold reality'.

The first belief 'The internet changes absolutely everything ' is only partially true. Yes, there are completely new businesses like Amazon, Expedia and eBay that owe their existence, and success, to the internet. But there are also many other 'dot.gones' that failed miserably as a result of the same misplaced optimism that resulted in the tulip bulb mania of the 1630s, the South Sea bubble of the early 1700s and many similar finacial disasters that have occurred since, culminating most recently in the Nasdaq bubble. Between 1996 and 2000, the Nasdaq went from 600 to 5,000 as more and more dot.com companies were floated to gullible and greedy investors. And then the bubble burst. The stock market plummeted from 5,000 to

2,000 in a matter of months and, by 2002, it bottomed out at 800, with millions unemployed in a major recession. (See http://www.stock-market-crash.net/ nasdaq. htm for a detailed account.)

As Stock Market Crash!Net (www.stock-market-crash.net) comments: the new economy is:

> a buzzword that describes the new, high growth technology companies that are expected to revolutionise the economy, and trounce old economy companies.
>
> At the height of every financial bubble, people will claim that 'We are in a New Economy', or some variation. The New Economy was the term used in the 2000 bubble. In 1929 people claimed that 'We are in a New Era'. The main theory of the New Economy was that the business cycle was dead and that all of the old economic rules don't apply ... Needless to say, the New Economy was a farce, and traditional economic principles still hold.

What has become clear is that the internet is an alternative channel of communication and distribution that complements (and may displace) pre-existing channels. Thus many of the successful businesses using the internet are those that have incorporated it into a previously successful bricks-and-mortar business. As Reingold observes, the effective use of the internet depends on what you sell. 'The internet gives an edge to products with unpredictable or fragmented demand', where carrying stock may be both risky and costly (books/Amazon, PCs/Dell). But it can also increase transportation costs for physical products, which is why P&G is unlikely to use it for selling detergents. But, this is not an issue for travel services or online auction businesses.

Another belief is that spending on IT has fuelled an unstoppable productivity boom that has ended the business cycle. Again, it is clear that investment in IT has resulted in a significant growth in productivity but, as history shows us, major technological breakthroughs have this propensity but are also subject to diminishing returns. Further, some applications diffuse more quickly than others as innovations take the path of least resistance and are adopted first in those situations that offer the most immediate payback or 'relative advantage'. Reingold (2004) reports an analysis by the McKinsey Global Institute that found that:

more than three-quarters of the US net productivity gain came from only six sectors: retailing, securities brokerage, wholesaling, telecom, semi-conductors, and computer assembly, which together make up just under one-third of GDP. Other sectors spent with equal abandon but never saw the pay-off.

As for the business cycle, this is as much about competition as new technology, and the impact of the emerging economies makes it unlikely that we have seen an end to fluctuations in demand and supply.

Proponents of the new economy stress the importance of the first mover advantage, but the evidence amply demonstrates that it is 'better to do it right than first'. If you are a first mover and correctly identify an attractive market opportunity, then your success will surely attract others to want to enter the market. Only if you are already big and successful is it likely that you will be able to fight off the competitive threat. More often than not innovative, entrepreneurial firms find it easier to license their IPR or sell out to the established players in the market.

Another belief about the internet is that it gives the consumer 'new, limitless power'. Given the existence of websites where you can research and comparison shop for almost anything, this claim is more robust than many others. However, to benefit from the information available, you have to shop online, which only a minority do. In addition, the consumers' power will be moderated where sellers can effectively differentiate their products and services from their competitors and so offer greater value. Reingold cites Shopping.com whose research shows that while 50% of its customers choose a retailer whose price is in the lowest quartile, a retailer with a five-star rating is 35% more likely to win a sale than one with three stars. Also, five-star products win twice the sales per visit of their three-star rivals. Clearly, perception and emotional factors still have a role to play in buying decisions.

Finally, many believed that the new dot.com technology would result in the demise of established businesses and their replacement by new ones. In reality, while some new businesses have emerged, the main source of growth in ITC applications has been their adoption by established businesses and integration into their strategies and operating systems.

From these comments, it is clear that the internet has had an impact on marketing strategy and this was identified by many commentators in the early 2000s including Michael Porter. In the seventh edition of my introductory textbook *Marketing* (Baker, 2006) we commented as follows:

MARKETING STRATEGY AND THE INTERNET

Writing in the *Harvard Business Review*, Michael Porter (2001) made an important point that is still frequently overlooked – the internet is an enabling technology, the impact of which has been greatest in industries 'constrained by high costs for communicating, gathering information, or accomplishing transactions'. While e-commerce has permeated large organisations, and spawned a generation of dot.com organisations, proportionately its impact has been greatest on SMEs. This is because in a global market the economies of scale in manufacturing that gave rise to the multinational corporation have been largely eroded due to advances in other technologies, the widespread availability of cheap labour in emerging economies like the Southeast Asian 'tigers' and, more recently, countries like India and China. As a result, economies of scale are now mainly to be found in marketing expenditure on selling, promotion and distribution.

As we have seen, for an effective demand to exist, a customer must be aware of the existence of a good or service that might meet their need, and be able to gain access to it – consumption is a function of availability. With the advent of the internet and the web, even the smallest organisation can make itself known to a world market at negligible cost. This ability greatly increases the scope of competition through a levelling effect, which significantly reduces the potential for sustaining a competitive advantage, with a marked impact on industry structure. As we saw in Chapter 2, structure, conduct and performance are inextricably linked to one another, from which it follows that all organisations must be sensitive to the potential effects of the internet on their strategy.

Indeed, it was this issue that prompted Porter, one of the world's leading authorities on competitive strategy, to explore the internet's implications for strategy. While written some years ago on a topic notorious for the rapidity of change, many of his observations have either come about or remain valid. Most importantly, Porter argues that the internet has not made strategy obsolete but needs to be incorporated into one's strategy to complement existing ways of doing things. As with any innovation, its introduction encourages experimentation, which can lead to mixed and sometimes misleading messages from the marketplace. Accordingly, one should not rush to conclusions but should monitor trends to detect those which are likely to survive.

Thus, during the launch phase, many firms used and continue to use price as a competitive weapon. As has been evident in numerous failures, it is questionable how long individual firms can sustain this, especially as many of the start-up costs have been subsidised or set off against stock. While competitive prices are attractive when the buyer knows the precise specification of the desired product or service, backed up by a reputable brand, economic rationality would predict that you would buy from the lowest cost supplier – the *Da Vinci Code* or the latest Harry Potter are the same everywhere. On the other hand, if you are not quite sure what you would like to read, browsing a bookshop adds value and so can command a higher price. Indeed, with most shopping goods, and all specialty goods, the shopping experience *is* an integral part of the exchange. So while the price-conscious segment may grow, as the research from Shopping. com reported earlier shows, higher premiums may be obtained from less price-sensitive customers seeking additional services and experiences.

Porter observes:

Indeed the internet has given rise to an array of new performance metrics that have only a loose relationship to economic value, such as pro forma measures of income that remove 'nonrecurring' costs like acquisitions. The dubious connection between reported metrics and actual profitability has served only to amplify the confusing signals about what has been happening in the marketplace.

As a consequence, the inflated stock prices of the dot.com bubble did not reflect real economic value, which Porter observes is 'nothing more than the gap between price and costs, and is reliably measured only by sustained profitability'. This is the acid test, and the two drivers that determine profitability are industry structure and sustainable competitive advantage. As has become apparent, in many cases the internet did not alter existing structures, and/or was unable to confer a sustainable advantage in that its benefits were available to all that adopted it.

This outcome confirms Porter's prediction that his model of the five competitive forces would still prevail, and that one would still need to review these on an individual industry/company basis in order to determine the likely impact of the internet on competition. He perceived the potential positive impacts as consisting of a dampening of the bargaining power of channels, reduced barriers to entry and increased operating efficiencies. However, potential negative impacts were increased bargaining power, lower barriers to entry, a more open system reducing proprietary advantages, increased competition from a larger market, and reduced variable costs, e.g. on promotion, which would emphasise the importance of fixed costs and prompt price competition. eBay is an example of the potential of the positive impacts, while competition in auto retailing illustrates the negative impacts.

The rush into the internet was based, according to Porter, on the assumption that its use would increase switching costs and create strong network effects with important first mover advantages for strong new economy brands. These assumptions were flawed. Other new technologies have made switching much simpler and network effects only create a barrier to entry if they are proprietary to one company. Few can achieve this and it has also been difficult to establish strong internet brands.

While most of the attention on the impact of the internet has been focused on the B2C market, its use was pioneered in B2B markets where it has had major effects on procurement and the use of outsourcing. While supply partnerships are often promoted as offering a 'win–win' outcome for both parties, it is clear that this is not always the case. Dominant sellers/buyers will still seek to obtain concessions from their 'partners', leading to instability in the supply chain and opportunities for new competitors. Similarly, while outsourcing can reduce costs in the short term and increase flexibility, in the long term it can lead to homogeneous inputs, a lack of distinctiveness and increased price competition – in a word, 'commoditisation'.

The digital marketplace creates the opportunity to automate corporate procurement and offers buyers:

low transaction costs, easier access to price and product information, convenient purchase of associated services, and, sometimes, the ability to pool volume. The benefits to suppliers include lower selling costs, lower transaction costs, access to wider markets and the avoidance of powerful channels'. (Porter, 2001).

However, the nature and extent of these potential benefits will vary in terms of the existing industry structure and the products involved, emphasising the importance of the structure/conduct/performance model introduced in Chapter 2. It must also be remembered that it is in the nature of competition that successful firms may be expected to develop new strategies to cope with the changing competitive environment. It follows that an innovation like the internet represents a major opportunity but only if it is integrated effectively into the firm's operations.

Porter reiterates that the only sure way to achieve a sustainable competitive advantage is by operating at a lower cost or commanding a premium price. These may be obtained in two ways – operational effectiveness and strategic positioning. He sees the internet as:

arguably the most powerful tool available today for enhancing operational effectiveness. By easing and speeding the exchange of real time information, it enables improvements throughout the entire value chain, across almost every company and industry.

But these benefits are available to all and are easily copied. In consequence, it is more difficult to maintain an operational advantage so, if anything, strategic positioning and flexible implementation have become even more important.

Porter comments:

Strategy goes far beyond the pursuit of best practices. It involves the configuration of a tailored value chain – the series of activities required to produce and deliver a product or service – that enables a company to offer unique value. To be defensible, moreover, the value chain must be highly integrated.

As we saw in Chapter 2, when it is, competitors need to be able to replicate it all to compete directly.

In Porter's opinion, confirmed by events, many internet pioneers have:

competed in ways that violate nearly every precept of good strategy. Rather than focus on profits, they have sought to maximise revenues and market share at all costs, pursuing customers indiscriminately through discounting, giveaways, promotions, channel incentives, and heavy advertising.

This is a destructive zero-sum form of competition and a 'race to the bottom'.

Much of Porter's diagnosis has been confirmed by events. While the internet has created opportunities for new kinds of companies to develop, comparatively few have been 'successful' *and* profitable on a large scale. The major beneficiaries have been SMEs that can now access a global market without incurring the huge promotional costs that previously precluded this. As an enabling technology, it has the potential to confer significant benefits but these are available to all. Failure to integrate the potential of the internet into one's ongoing strategy and operations can only result in a loss of competitiveness.

From this review, it would seem that, in the strict sense in which the term 'new economy' was originally used, it was just another fashionable flash in the pan that has gone the same way as many other managerial fads and 'silver bullets'. As Santayana observed: 'Those who forget history are doomed to repeat it'. It is for this reason that we prefer to depend on established theory and knowledge that has stood the test of time, rather than fall into the trap of only reporting the most recent thinking on the subject, most of which remains to be validated in practice. Since the first edition appeared, some of the topics and trends discussed in the penultimate chapter have become sufficiently established to be incorporated into the main body of the text; some have disappeared and some are still evolving and are considered to be 'current issues and future trends'. Obviously, this is a matter of judgement and there is no scarcity of other books that emphasise topical issues – whether these will survive the test of time is another matter! So, to conclude, we refer to another extract from *Marketing* (2006). This topic was also alluded to by another reviewer who, on reflection, thought it might be too early to merit inclusion. As I have already 'gone public' on the issue of this 'new paradigm of marketing', repetition here will not go amiss.

A NEW MODEL OF MARKETING?

An article by Stephen L. Vargo and Robert F. Lusch (2004) in the *Journal of Marketing* has prompted extensive debate about the need for a new model, or paradigm, of the domain of marketing. At the Australia and New Zealand Marketing Academy conference held in Freemantle, WA, in December 2005, a special session lasting half a day was given to arguments for and against the adoption of this new model. In the absence of agreement on the subject, it is clear that it would be premature to argue for or against the model when documenting the evolution of the accepted wisdom about marketing. On the other hand, when discussing current trends and future issues, an overview of the arguments is clearly important for those new to the subject of marketing.

The article that precipitated the debate is entitled 'Evolving to a new dominant logic of marketing' and in the Abstract, Vargo and Lusch write:

> The purpose of this article is to illuminate the evolution of *marketing* thought toward a new dominant logic … Briefly, *marketing* has moved from a goods-dominant view, in which tangible output and discrete transactions were central, to a service-dominant view, in which intangibility, exchange processes, and relationships are central.

The authors then stress that their interpretation of 'service-centred' should not be equated with current conceptualisations of services as a residual, i.e. not a tangible good; something to add value to a good – value-added services; or service industries like healthcare and education. They state:

> Rather, we define services as the application of specialised competences (knowledge and skills) through deeds, processes, and performances to the benefit of another entity or the entity itself … Thus, the service-centred dominant logic represents a reoriented philosophy that is applicable to all *marketing* offerings, including those that involve tangible output (goods) in the process of service provision.

To justify and sustain the case for a new model or paradigm of marketing involved a closely argued case running to 17 pages of text, and supported by four pages of references. Given the numerous warnings elsewhere in this textbook concerning selectivity and bias, the reader is warned that the following summary of what I consider to be the important issues is a personal one and that, if you find them interesting or provocative, you should read the original yourself and form your own judgement.

Vargo and Lusch's analysis starts with a summary of the evolution of marketing thought that reflects the overview provided in Chapter 1. As the latter mirrors that to be found in most standard marketing textbooks, then we are agreed on the point of departure, and know 'where we are'. The need for a new 'worldview' or dominant logic is predicated on the proposition that 'Marketing inherited a model of exchange from economics, which had a dominant logic based on the exchange of "goods", which usually are manufactured output. The dominant logic focused on tangible resources, embedded value and transactions.' However, this view is not seen as appropriate today.

Over the past 50 years or so the focus on resources as 'stuff' that is to be acquired and used by humans – what we would normally think of as natural and physical resources – has changed to a view that incorporates intangible and dynamic functions calling for human ingenuity and appraisal. 'Everything is neutral (or perhaps even a resistance) until humankind learns what to do with it. Essentially, resources are not; they become.' (Zimmerman, 1951, in Vargo and Lusch, 2004).

To explain this distinction, Vargo and Lusch introduce the distinction between *operand* and *operant resources*. Operand resources are those on which some act or operation has to be performed to produce an effect, while operant resources are those that produce effects. Increased interest in operant resources 'began to shift in the late twentieth century as humans began to realise that skills and knowledge were the most important types of resources'. Although prior reference had been made to the work of Malthus (1798), and his conclusion that the continued growth of population would result in the exhaustion of natural resources, no explicit link is made by Vargo and Lusch to numerous forecasts in the 1960s of the inevitable truth of this prediction, unless humankind could make them go further. Thus it was publications such as the Club of Rome's report *The Limits to Growth* (Meadows et al., 1972) that precipitated the recognition of the primacy of operant over operand resources.

The logic and importance of this is manifest in Vargo and Lusch's statement that:

> Operant resources are often invisible and intangible; often they are core competences or organisational processes. They are likely to be dynamic and infinite and not static and finite, as is usually the case with operand resources. Because operant resources produce effects, they enable humans both to multiply the value of natural resources and to create additional operant skills.

If, then, this primacy is the defining characteristic of the new 'service-centred logic', few would challenge it; whether they would describe it as a service-centred logic is another matter. Vargo and Lusch believe that this perceived shift (hint: they perceive it, I'm not sure yet) has important implications for marketing and they start with an examination of the 'goods versus services' school of thought.

Traditional marketing is seen as focusing on operand resources, is goods-centred and concerned with the notion of utility(ies). Service-centred marketing is seen as comprising four elements, which are summarised as:

1. Identify or develop core competences, the fundamental knowledge and skills of an economic entity that represent potential competitive advantage.
2. Identify other entities (potential customers) that could benefit from these competences.
3. Cultivate relationships that involve the customers in developing customised, competitively compelling value propositions to meet specific needs.
4. Gauge marketplace feedback by analysing financial performance from exchange to learn how to improve the firm's offering to customers and improve firm performance.

This view is grounded in and largely consistent with resource advantage theory.

It is customer-centric and market-driven.

Vargo and Lusch then proceed to compare the two views and identify six differences between them, all centred on the operand/operant distinction. These attributes are then analysed in the

context of eight foundational premises (FPs). These premises are:

1. The application of specialised skills and knowledge is the fundamental unit of exchange.
2. Indirect exchange masks the fundamental unit of exchange.
3. Goods are distribution mechanisms for service provision.
4. Knowledge is the fundamental source of competitive advantage.
5. All economies are service economies.
6. The customer is always a coproducer.
7. The enterprise can only make value propositions.
8. The service-centered view is customer oriented and relational.

Each of these premises is discussed and evaluated in some detail.

FP1 recognises the importance of task specialisation and the division of labour (discussed by us in Chapter 1) as depending on exchange for their existence. The principle issue debated is the narrow focus on tangible output with exchange value, and the role and contribution of service activities in creating and enhancing that value. In my view, the arguments deployed pay insufficient attention to the reasons for the original emphasis on the 'product', and the present emphasis on the 'service'. As a result, it presents a polarised, 'black-and-white' explanation that is inconsistent with a wider knowledge/understanding of economics, which is presented as a monolithic and internally consistent discipline devoid of schisms and alternative explanations.

FP2 addresses the issue of the physical and psychological separation that developed as a consequence of the Industrial Revolution and led to the development of complex marketing systems to link the factory with the customer. The existence of these systems is seen as masking the fundamental nature of the exchange process, which, according to Vargo and Lusch is that: 'People still exchange their services for other services. Money, goods, organisations, and vertical marketing systems are only the exchange vehicles.' But, ask yourself, in most low-involvement transactions, have you the slightest interest in who, precisely, was responsible for the creation of the good for which you are paying money?

FP3 follows automatically from FP2, which depends on the premise that 'Goods are distribution mechanisms for service provision.' It is claimed that:

> Goods are not the common denominator of exchange; the common denominator is the application of specialised knowledge, mental skills, and, to a lesser extent, physical labour (skills).

This is truly a heroic premise, and while the authors may cite a handful of distinguished academics as their authority, I am not convinced that the man on the Clapham omnibus quite sees it that way.

FP4 that 'Knowledge is the fundamental source of competitive advantage' is superficially uncontentious but the premise omits specific reference to the qualification contained in their quotation from Day (1994, in Vargo and Lusch, 2004) that such advantage will only accrue if you can 'make it work'. Otherwise, as my old boss used to say, knowledge is just so much luggage that has to be carted about – you can buy books full of knowledge by the container load and finish up with only the headache of where to store them.

FP5 that 'All economies are service economies' might be true if you accept the authors' earlier premises. But a more balanced and less controversial claim might be appropriate if one considers the relative proportions of effort expended on products and services in different national economies. Ultimately, of course, if you take the view that natural resources have no value until they are 'serviced' by humans, then the premise is tautological or true by definition.

Much the same arguments apply to FP6 that 'The customer is always a coproducer', for without consumption there is no exchange – a fact recognised by Adam Smith when he stated that 'The sole end and purpose of production is consumption.' This fact was self-evident to him at the time when he emphasised the need to increase the output of physical goods if the operants were not to fall victim to the Malthusian controls of disease, famine and war, all of which would have eliminated surplus operants while stabilising the operands.

FP7 is uncontentious. Value, like beauty, lies in the eye of the beholder. Truly, 'The enterprise can

only make value propositions' – it is the customer who will determine if value actually exists.

Finally, FP8 states 'The service-centered view is customer oriented and relational.' But, if you review the discussion of the 'three eras' explanation of the evolution of modern marketing in *Marketing* (Baker, 2006), and substitute 'production' for 'goods-centred', then the next step is *marketing*. You may also recall my own 1973 definition of marketing as 'The creation and maintenance of mutually satisfying exchange relationships' – no mention of goods or services, or of the mix of goods and services that give rise to satisfaction, nor to the obvious corollary, that satisfaction implies perceived value. The problem, as I have argued at length elsewhere, is that the marketing *concept* was hijacked by the marketing management school of thought in the USA, who then promoted marketing as something to do *to* customers rather than *for* customers. Only when it was realised that this didn't work were the true intentions of the marketing concept – customer-oriented and relational – implemented.

In sum, I believe that the logic of the service-centred approach reflects the logic and intentions of the marketing era, as distinguished from the production era that preceded it. Where I have difficulty with Vargo and Lusch's proposal is that in order to recognise the importance of services/operant activities, they seem to think it is necessary to deny the role of physical resources and technology in creating physical objects that are necessary to realise the value of those service activities. In other words, without operand or physical resources to work with we would soon all die of starvation.

In their discussion, the first issue appears to concern the degree of customisation incorporated into physical goods. I have to confess to having some difficulty in following their argument, especially in terms of their definition of 'normative qualities'. According to Vargo and Lusch: 'The goods-centered view implies that the qualities of manufactured goods (e.g. tangibility), the separation of production and consumption, standardisation, and nonperishability are normative qualities (Zeithaml, Parasuraman and Berry, 1985, in Vargo and Lusch, 2004).' As a consequence, 'From what we argue the *marketing* perspective should be, the qualities are often neither valid nor desirable.'

I have great difficulty in accepting this claim, which is almost as bad as the academic economist's view that to purchase on the basis of emotional beliefs, rather than giving precedence to price, is 'irrational'. In the great majority of purchase decisions, our survival does not depend on buying anything – we can always take it or leave it. Furthermore, the existence of producers attempting to satisfy picky customers has led to greater choice and variety than has ever existed before. What the authors see as the service-centred view of exchange is what, since 1987, has been known as 'mass customisation', in which producers like Dell involve customers directly in specifying the attributes and features they desire in their computer. Now, with a complex product such as this, if I know precisely what I want, then I can become a co-producer, but what if I can't? Or what about my motorcar when I only wish to order a limited number of 'extras' because otherwise the standard model meets virtually all my needs? Or what about canned vegetables? The activities involved in getting these to my preferred retail outlet are extensive, complex and expensive. There is a huge variety on offer, and keen competition between suppliers of the same product category. And, if you are dissatisfied with the manufacturer's attempt to satisfy your need, you can always go to the farmer's market and buy 'the real thing' for a much higher price. Or, better still, why not become a producer yourself and find out if the time involved improves your overall standard of living?

To be fair, many of the attributes of the service-centred view recognise that marketing should be about 'mutually satisfying exchange relationships', in which both producer and consumer have a role to play and in which, as we argued in Chapter 1, supply should be determined by demand. In my opinion, these are the distinguishing features of the marketing concept and a marketing orientation, which has taken rather longer to put into practice than one would have liked. On the other hand, those organisations that have bought into the concept and are marketing-oriented are more successful. Ultimately, natural selection and the 'invisible hand' will prevail. In this sense, Vargo and Lusch may be seen as seeking to accelerate the process and, as they say, they

are looking for 'reorientation rather than reinvention' (p.14).

To achieve this reorientation, they argue that:

> A service-centered college curriculum would be grounded by a course in principles of *marketing*, which would subordinate goods to service provision, emphasising the former as distribution mechanisms for the latter.

Clearly, this would call for a radical restructuring of textbooks like this, which will become imperative if the service-centred view advocated by Vargo and Lusch does indeed become the dominant paradigm. By now you should have gathered that I doubt if it will.

As with any debate, the proponents have to exaggerate their case to make their point. So we would agree that the marketing management concept has paid insufficient attention to the wants of consumers. On the other hand, it has done very well in catering to their needs. What is called for is more fine-tuning to ensure that the goods and services created cost-effectively by producers/sellers match ever more closely the needs of buyers/consumers. As we have said, mass customisation has recognised the benefits of doing this, as has the emphasis on customer relationship management and getting closer to the customer. But producers have an important role to play too. Giving the customer what they (think) they want is not necessarily the way to ensure the optimum utilisation of scarce physical resources (cheaper air travel and more global warming?). In solving the basic economic problem of maximising satisfaction through the use of scarce resources, both producer and consumer have an equal role to play. Handing over 'dominance' to users does not appear to be the best way to achieve this.

So much for my views. In the same issue of the *Journal of Marketing* (2004), there are also invited commentaries from some much better known marketing scholars. You should read these too if you intend to study marketing in greater detail. For the time being, however, the jury is out and only time will tell if this topic will be 'promoted' and become the organising principle for any future editions of this book.

ETHICS IN MARKETING

While ethical issues have always existed in the domain of marketing, it is only in recent years that they have begun to attract explicit attention in mainstream marketing textbooks. Indeed, the contemporary interest in ethics would seem to be closely related to the emergence of relationship marketing as the dominant paradigm in place of the marketing management model, with its focus on the transaction which preceded it. Under the latter representation, the transaction has often been seen as an adversarial model in which business seeks to 'win' at the expense of the consumer. It was this perception that gave rise to the consumerist movement of the 1950s and 60s, epitomised by books such as Vance Packard's *Hidden Persuaders* (1957).

Nowadays, it is widely accepted that marketing is all about mutually satisfying exchange relationships in which both parties gain the satisfaction and benefits they are seeking. It is also accepted that 'relationship' implies a long-term and continuing association whereas 'transaction' refers to a one-off, or single exchange, albeit that a sequence of transactions may lead to a relationship. For a relationship to succeed there is an assumption that certain principles of behaviour will be accepted and observed and it is these which constitute the ethical dimension of the association.

According to N. Craig Smith (1999, p. 905):

Marketing ethics can be defined as both the study of the moral evaluation of marketing and the standards applied in the judgement of marketing decisions, behaviours and institutions as morally right or wrong. It refers to a discipline and the subject matter of that discipline, the 'rules' governing the appropriateness of marketing conduct. It is a subset of business ethics, which in turn is a subset of ethics or moral philosophy. More simply, marketing ethics is about the moral problems of marketing managers. It includes, for example, the ethical considerations concerned with product safety, truth in advertising, and fairness in pricing. It is an integral part of marketing decision-making.

As noted earlier, questions of what is right and wrong in business relationships have been discussed and debated for centuries and Smith cites the Roman philosopher Cicero who examined the moral duties of merchants in his *De Officiis* as an early example. These questions found expression in the concept of social responsibility as an issue for corporate decision-makers, and in classes with titles such as 'Business and Society', during the 1960s and 70s. Within the subject of marketing, ethical issues were most often identified with specific topics, with truth in advertising being one of the earliest and most widely discussed themes. Product safety also attracted

---

Box 24.1 *Online shopping*

While the attractions of online shopping receive much favourable publicity, research into the topic indicates that many people suffer from frustrating experiences, which have the potential for a negative impact on the seller's reputation. According to the 2005 Holiday Shopping: Online Customer Experience survey conducted by Allurent, 82% of respondents said they would be less likely to return to a site that had frustrated them; 55% said such an experience negatively impacted their overall opinion of that retailer; and 33% said that a frustrating online experience would make them less likely to buy at that retailer's physical store.

Among the critical issues that give rise to a negative online shopping experience are:

- Poor site navigation
- Insufficient product information
- Inadequate browsing facilities
- Problems with checkout
- High shipping costs
- Inventory problems
- Pricing.

Factors that enhance the experience are simple checkout procedures and detailed product information, such as product zoom, 360 degree product views and online videos. While 81% of respondents see shopping online as convenient, only 57% said it was trouble-free and 29% that it was fun. (For more details see: www.allurent.com.)

considerable attention, particularly after Ralph Nader's (1965) *Unsafe at any speed* drew widespread attention to product defects in GM cars during the mid-1960s. Similarly, an increasing concern for the environment and the birth of the 'green' movement focused concern on products and processes damaging to the environment, such as the use of CFC as a propellant in aerosol products.

The latter is an excellent example of the need for both improved consumer education and regulation of business practice. Traditionally, buyers and sellers have been regarded as being on an equal footing, with the onus resting on the buyer to ensure that they received what they bargained for. Thus the common law concept of *caveat emptor* (let the buyer beware) assumes that if goods are openly available for sale, then it is the buyer's responsibility to decide whether or not they wish to buy. With the increased availability of manufactured goods following the Industrial Revolution, and the insertion of intermediaries in channels of distribution between producer and consumer, legislation (the Sale of Goods Act 1892) was enacted to give greater protection to consumers and ensure that goods were fit for the purpose for which they were sold.

During the twentieth century, the growing complexity of goods and services required a significant expansion in legislation to provide consumers with protection in terms of their basic rights, as spelt out by President Kennedy in his first consumer address to Congress in 1962 namely:

1. *The right to safety:* to be protected against the marketing of goods that are hazardous to health or life.
2. *The right to be informed:* to be protected against fraudulent, deceitful or grossly misleading information, advertising, labelling or other practices, and to be given the facts needed to make an informed choice.
3. *The right to choose:* to be assured, wherever possible, of access to a variety of products and services at competitive prices and in those industries in which government regulations are substituted, as assurance of satisfactory quality and service at fair prices.
4. *The right to be heard:* to be assured that consumer interests will receive full and sympathetic

consideration in the formulation of government policy and fair expeditious treatment in its administrative tribunals.

While the emergence of consumerism, and the need for legislation to protect consumers, has been designated 'the shame of marketing' on the grounds that a business discipline founded on the concept of mutual satisfaction should have no need for imposed regulations, most reasonable people would agree that, in the real world of rapid technological innovation and change, the market is too imperfect a mechanism to ensure producers will always act ethically to protect their long-term interests. Equally, in a competitive marketplace the formulation of rules and regulations, through legislation and industry codes of practice, provides a baseline for minimum standards of performance common to all.

Clearly, if legislation exists, breaches are illegal and can be dealt with by legal processes. That said, there will always be controversy about marginal cases and grey areas where interpretation will differ according to the individual's point of view. The nature and extent of these grey areas will become even more difficult where clear guidelines don't exist, as is often the case with legislation. In a survey of marketing practitioners to determine what constitutes the most difficult ethical problem, Chonko and Hunt (1985) identified the following 10 issues in rank order of frequency of citation:

1. *Bribery* (most frequently cited; includes gifts from outside vendors, 'money under the table', payment of questionable commissions)
2. *Fairness* (manipulation of others, corporate interests in conflict with family interests, inducing customers to use services not needed)
3. *Honesty* (misrepresenting services and capabilities, lying to customers to obtain orders)
4. *Price* (differential pricing, meeting competitive prices, charging higher prices than firms with similar products while claiming superiority)
5. *Product* (products that do not benefit consumers, product and brand copyright infringements, product safety, exaggerated performance claims)
6. *Personnel* (hiring, firing, employee evaluation)
7. *Confidentiality* (temptation to use or obtain classified, secret or competitive information)

8. *Advertising* (misleading customers, crossing the line between puffery and misleading)
9. *Manipulation of data* (distortion, falsifying figures or misusing statistics or information)
10. *Purchasing* (reciprocity in supplier selection).

As Smith (1999) observes, many of these issues are not unique to marketing and apply to all managers. That said, as issues in the domain of business generally, they all impinge and impact upon the marketing function itself. Smith concentrates on those issues he considers specific to marketing, namely:

- Marketing research
- Target marketing
- Product policy
- Pricing
- Distribution
- Personal selling and salesforce management
- Advertising and sales promotion.

Some of the key topics/issues that he identifies are as follows:

Marketing research: Research integrity – the potential conflict between scientific/ professional objectivity and business/commercial obligations. The rights of respondents – to choose, to safety and privacy (anonymity), to be informed (lack of deception) and to respect.

Target marketing: As this involves the selection of particular individuals this can give rise to problems of inclusion – intrusion of privacy, stereotyping, exploitation of vulnerable persons – and exclusion such as the withholding of products or services from disadvantaged subgroups.

Product policy: The major ethical issues in product policy are:

- product safety
- 'questionable' products, that are harmful, in bad taste, or not considered socially beneficial
- 'me-too' products and product counterfeiting
- environmental impacts of products and packaging
- deceptive practices in packaging or product quality specifications

- planned obsolescence
- arbitrary product elimination
- service product delivery (Smith, 1999, pp. 912–30).

Pricing: Like product issues, pricing is subject to extensive regulation on issues such as price fixing, price discrimination, predatory pricing and deceptive pricing.

Distribution: Most issues in distribution relate to the exercise of channel power whereby the larger and more powerful members in a channel use this power to exact an unfair advantage from their suppliers and/or customers. A particular topic of concern here is the power of multiple retailers. Franchising has also been cited as an area subject to abuse.

Personal Selling: Smith (1999, p. 917) suggests that conflicts can arise in three distinct areas or interfaces: between salesperson and customer, salesperson and company, and competitors. These are summarised as:

Salesperson: customers
1. The use of gifts and entertainment
2. Questionable/psychological sales techniques
3. Overselling
4. Misrepresentation
5. Account discrimination/favouritism
6. Conflicts of interest.

Salesperson: company
1. Equity in evaluation and compensation
2. Use of company assets
3. Falsifying expense accounts and sales reports
4. Salesperson compliance with company policy.

Salesperson: competitor
1. Disparagement
2. Tampering with a competitor's product
3. Spying
4. Exclusionary behaviour
5. Discussing prices.
(These activities are generally illegal).

Advertising and sales promotion: The basic issue here is truth in advertising. This may involve a deliberate intention to deceive (deception) or unintentional (misleading). In most countries the advertising profession has sought to retain responsibility for self-regulation, preferring this to excessive regulation through legislation. To this end regulating bodies such as the Advertising Standards Authority in the UK publish detailed codes of practice and have formal procedures for receiving and dealing with complaints.

The above summary clearly identifies specific areas of particular concern to marketers. The key problem in handling ethical issues is that there are often no hard and fast rules concerning individual or corporate behaviour. Where society has a clear view on what is acceptable/unacceptable these views are enshrined in legislation which is enforceable through the process of law. Where the interpretation of moral values, such as those contained in various religions, is left to the individual, then it is unsurprising if the boundaries between right and wrong become blurred or fuzzy. Offering a client a cup of tea would hardly be regarded as bribery, or occasionally using office stationery, as theft. On the other hand, a weekend in the Ritz, or hiring out your company car to someone else would probably be regarded as wrong. As the concern for ethical behaviour in marketing grows, it may be expected that philosophical issues such as these will receive more formal attention. As to whether this increased attention will permeate the treatment of the various subfields as identified above or become focused in specific courses on marketing ethics remains to be seen. To conclude, however, Smith (1999, p. 924) proposed the following maxims for determining whether or not your marketing is ethical:

- The golden rule: Do unto others as you would have them do unto you.
- The media test: Would I be embarrassed in front of colleagues/family/friends, if my decision was publicised in the media?
- The invoice test: Are payments being requested that could not be fully disclosed within company accounts?
- Good ethics is good business: The belief that good ethics is in the long-term best interests of the firm.
- The professional ethic: Would the action be viewed as proper by an objective panel of professional colleagues?
- When in doubt, don't.

GREEN MARKETING

Ecological concerns now represent a significant factor to be taken into account in environmental planning. Further, they are now of global concern as the number of natural disasters attributable to climatic change appears to grow every year, e.g. droughts and floods attributed to El Nino, atmospheric pollution associated with burning of the Indonesian forests etc. Because of the global nature of the causes of these problems, they have been the subject of a series of environmental summits at which both the developed and developing nations seek to agree limits to pollution, deforestation etc. that have resulted in ozone depletion and the greenhouse effect.

Unfortunately, while there is widespread public support for more environmentally friendly behaviour, individual consumers are less inclined to modify their own consumption behaviour to achieve this end. In the absence of regulation, which resulted in the withdrawal of CFC propellants in aerosol sprays, decisions about the suitability of 'green' products rests very much with the individual. Nonetheless, the number of individuals who are prepared to modify consumption behaviour and express a preference for green products is sufficiently large to constitute an important market segment. According to Georges Haour (1997), it is difficult to define precisely what is a green product because:

> Depending on the region, the culture and the time, criteria for *green-ness* indeed differ. They may include 'organically grown' fruits and vegetables, no preservatives, lower ecological impact in use of materials, or upon processing and usage (i.e. lower energy consumption, no toxic substance used), long-life products, as well as returnable or minimum packaging.

It follows that the range of products promoted on a green platform varies widely. Haour cites the case of the Canadian supermarket chain Loblaws which has introduced a 'green line' which now counts for well over 100 products, including things such as phosphate-free detergents, energy-efficient light bulbs, unbleached coffee filters, reusable cloth nappies in place of disposable diapers etc.

Packaging materials have been a major area of interest on the basis that the most ecological packaging is no packaging at all. But, as Haour points out, one needs to make a full evaluation of materials and energy content, as well as transport, storage and preservation requirements of a given package in terms of the total product–package system before it is possible to determine whether disposable packaging is preferable to recyclable packaging or vice versa. In addition, as he points out:

> Analyses of the same system will yield different results depending on local conditions such as availability and price of materials, energy and transport. All these vary substantially from country to country.

Variety and choice are also seen as a contributory factor. Thus a reduction in the number of brands available in the supermarket would significantly reduce the storage and display space and the energy required, particularly for refrigeration. Other savings might also arrive through more efficient logistics management and a more effective use of transportation.

Haour concludes that: 'Reconciling ecology with economy makes complete ethical and business sense. Indeed, ecological solutions favour optimal use of energy and materials, minimising waste, transport and storage costs.' From this point of view, then, green marketing represents a significant opportunity – always provided that it isn't used against you!

According to a report published by *Key Note* (2005; www.keynote.co.uk), green and ethical (G&E) products only account for a small percentage of total consumer expenditure but represent significant niche markets. *Key Note* found that: 'For the majority of consumers, price overrides ethical considerations as a key factor in their decision-making.' Consequently, G&E concerns are more strongly expressed by the affluent.

Fair trades have been growing rapidly and consumer pressure groups, boycotts and legislation are having an impact, e.g. the introduction of the congestion charge in central London has reduced traffic by 25%. In general, however, the government has taken a laissez-faire approach. On the other hand, more companies now have corporate social responsibility (CSR) policies which cover G&E issues.

Box 24.2 *Is enlightened self-interest unethical?*

A recent article in *Fortune* (28 November, 2005) by Geoffrey Colvin says 'don't blame Wal-Mart' and argues that, despite growing criticism of its practices, Wal-Mart isn't evil – it is just caught up in the global economy.

Colvin's article (2005) was prompted by the release of a documentary film *Wal-Mart: the High Cost of Low Price*, which catalogues many of the criticisms of Wal-Mart's practices that have enabled it to become the world's largest corporation. While these criticisms are held by many, Colvin points out that it is the plunging cost of computing power and telecommunications, and a global labour market, that have enabled Wal-Mart and other companies like it 'to create previously impossible business models that give customers what they want. This trend is not going to stop.'

While Wal-Mart is chastised for driving small retailers out of business, Colvin observes accurately 'Wal-Mart can't drive anyone out of business. Only customers can do that, and millions happily drive right past those little stores because they'd rather pay lower prices.' In other words, it boils down to enlightened self-interest.

In the new global economy, workers all around the world compete and companies established in affluent, postindustrial countries can no longer afford to pay uneconomic labour costs or, as is increasingly becoming clear, excessive pension and medical costs. This new reality does not condone illegal practices or exploitation, and firms and people guilty of such acts will be punished. That said, the message is clear, people everywhere must adapt to the new order that is coming and not seek to shift the 'blame' to those who are already doing so.

For 2002, the Co-operative Bank estimated expenditures of £1,170m. on food; £1,473m. on green household goods; £3,309m. on charitable donations; £187m. on personal goods including cosmetics not tested on animals; £2,582m. on ethical boycotts; £1,568m. on local shopping; £3,3886m. on ethical banking; £3,510m. on ethical investment etc., giving a grand total of just under £20 billion.

A survey in 2004 indicated that 55% of females and 42% of males would recycle and are concerned about G&E issues. Overall, however, consumer attitudes are 'ambivalent'.

A major factor appears to be availability, e.g. the stocking of fair trade goods like coffee and bananas in supermarkets which has led to considerable growth. More publicity, books and reports are also helping to increase awareness of the issues.

For example, a report by the National Consumer Council (NCC) *Rating Retailers for Health* examined each of the supermarkets' influence on a healthy diet, based on factors like the salt content in own-label processed foods, quality of nutrition labelling and advice, and emphasis given to junk foods vis-à-vis healthy foods. The main finding was that the supermarket's policy had a major impact, e.g. Morrisons have 25% more salt in sliced bread and sausages than do the Co-op; Tesco give three times as much shelf space to junk foods and snacks like crisps, biscuits and sweets compared with fresh fruit, while in Marks & Spencer equal space is given to the two categories. Marked out of 10 the results were:

- Waitrose   6.5
- Sainsbury   5.5
- Co-op   5.0
- Tesco   3.5
- ASDA   3.0
- Morrisons   2.0

The growth of sales of organic foods has slowed significantly in recent years but has still grown from £110 million in 1995 to £1,120 million in 2004, with about 10% of the population claiming to buy on a regular basis.

The Key Note report concludes:

Incorporating eco-friendly aspects such as community development and pollution-free activity and establishing a longer term approach to profit and development, will become increasingly attractive as market assets for companies either genuinely interested in seeking more ethical production or a more market-oriented 'green rinse'.

CORPORATE SOCIAL RESPONSIBILITY (CSR)

The ethical and environmental issues reviewed in the preceding sections are increasingly addressed together in discussions of corporate social responsibility (CSR).

During the Cold War, ideological views were polarised between communism and capitalism as alternative models of political and economic organisation. With the collapse of communism in the Soviet Union in the late 1980s, it became clear that when comparing the two ideologies, the prevailing version of capitalism was that known as 'Anglo-Saxon', which Milton Friedman describes as 'the business of business is business'. According to this credo, anything that is not illegal goes and the objective of corporate management is to maximise shareholder value. Social issues are of little or no concern.

However, this is not the only version of capitalism and it soon became apparent that many other very successful economies were practising what is known as the Germanic-Alpine model, which originated in Bismark's Germany in the 1860s. Prior to that time, Germany also subscribed to the Anglo-Saxon model, derived directly from Adam Smith's view of the market as an invisible hand best suited to achieve an equilibrium between demand and supply. However, it became clear to Bismark that this model had given rise to social unrest due to the excessive power of big business exploiting powerless consumers. To secure re-election, steps had to be taken to curb this power through the intervention of the state acting on behalf of the consumer (electorate) in regulating the worst excesses of totally free markets. While social democracy, as this approach came to be known, is identified mainly with liberal/democratic/socialist ideals, whereas the 'free market' is associated with conservative/republican politicians, the latter parties of 'big business' cannot afford to ignore the power of the consumer. Accordingly, 'regulators' have been appointed to oversee many industries formerly in public ownership or dominated by a small number of oligopolists, e.g. utilities, telecommunications.

The problem with regulators is that many of them tend to be reactive rather than proactive and so only become involved when consumers complain about anti-competitive practices. Further, many industries, and especially professional services, are self-regulated and many doubt that they always act on behalf of the customers' best interests. Either way, there is a growing body of opinion that argues business organisations should demonstrate greater social responsibility and that, in the long run, those that do will perform better than those that do not.

The need for large firms to take social issues on board when formulating strategy was the subject of a recent article in *McKinsey Quarterly* (2005) by Ian Davis, in which he wrote:

> The problem with the 'business of business' mind-set is rather that it can obscure two important realities. The first is that social issues are not so much tangential to the business of business as fundamental to it ... from a defensive point of view, companies that ignore public sentiment make themselves vulnerable to attack ... The second point that the 'business of business is business' outlook obscures for many companies – the need to address questions about their ethics and legitimacy – is related to the first. For reasons of integrity and enlightened self-interest, big companies need to tackle such issues, with both words and actions. It is neither sufficient nor wise to say that it is for governments to set laws and for companies simply to operate within them.

In this context, Davis sees much CSR activity as 'too limited, too defensive, and too disconnected from corporate strategy'. The reason for this is that CSR was a reaction to a series of anti-corporate campaigns in the late 1990s, reinforced by protests about globalisation that failed to address the real issues.

To begin with, big business should not be defensive, given the 'huge and critical contribution' it makes to modern society, which needs to be identified and explained. Secondly, for strategic purposes, companies need to do more than react to social issues as they evolve. As predicated by the normative theory of macro-environmental or PEST analysis (as discussed in Chapter 7), firms need to anticipate change and build this into their future strategy. Such anticipation is central to corporate management and not a task to be delegated to the public or corporate affairs department.

According to Davis, a new approach is called for, with three main strands:

> First, business should introduce explicit processes to make sure social issues and emerging social forces are discussed at the highest levels as part of overall strategic planning. Second, big business must recognise that it has a contract with society and manage it actively. And, third, it should seek to shape the debate on social issues through the standards of integrity and transparency it adopts and promotes.

Basically, Davis's proposals boil down to the adoption and implementation of a marketing orientation. Business exists to serve the needs of society and the better it succeeds in doing so, the greater its potential rewards. Support for these views is to be found in another McKinsey report (*The McKinsey Global Survey of Business Executives: Business and Society*, www.mckinseyquarterly.com. article downloaded 27/01/2006) into the role of business in society, based on a survey of 4,238 executives – more than a quarter of them CEOs or other C level executives – in 116 countries. The principal findings were:

> Business executives across the world overwhelmingly believe that corporations should balance their obligations to shareholders with explicit contributions 'to the broader public good.' Yet most executives view their engagement with the corporate social contract as a risk, not an opportunity, and frankly admit that they are ineffective at managing this wider social and political issue.

While 16% agreed with the Friedmanite approach that business should 'focus solely on providing the highest possible returns to investors while obeying all laws and regulations', 84% believe that 'business should generate high returns to investors but balance with contributions to the broader public good'. However, support varied by country, with 90% in India supporting the 'public good' dimension compared with only 25% in China.

Overall, 68% are 'generally' or 'somewhat'

positive about the broad impact of business on society, with 16% 'neutral' and 16% 'generally or somewhat negative'. However, 76% of executives think their own organisation is making a positive contribution. Interestingly, there is quite a difference between the tactics actually used by the companies and those considered to be most effective. While media and public relations (49%) and lobbying of governments and regulators (48%) are used most frequently, increasing transparency about the risks of products and processes (36%); developing and implementing practices on ethics and other corporate responsibility issues (e.g. human rights, the environment) (35%) are seen as the most *effective* tactics to use. Almost three-quarters (74%) believe the CEO or chair should take the lead in managing the sociopolitical agenda.

In terms of the issues most likely to have the most impact, positive or negative, on shareholder value over the next five years, job losses and offshoring were mentioned in the top three by 41% of the respondents. Other issues were:

- Political influence and/or political involvement of companies 29%
- Environmental issues, including climate change 28%
- Pension and retirement benefits 28%
- Privacy and data security 26%

Ethical issues in advertising and marketing were tenth in terms of number of mentions with 10%.

GLOBALISATION AND MARKETING STRATEGY[2]

Since the early 1980s 'globalisation' has been a recurrent theme in textbooks, reports and articles dealing with international competition. Indeed, often without any clear understanding or agreement as to what globalisation involves, the word and its attendants 'global strategy/marketing' have come to be seen as a sine qua non for competitive success. The origins of this preoccupation with global marketing may be traced back to a forceful article entitled 'The globalisation of markets' (1983a), in which Ted Levitt argued:

> A powerful force now drives the world toward a single converging commonality, and that force is

technology. It has proletarianised communication, transport, and travel, making them easily and cheaply accessible to the world's most isolated places and impoverished multitudes. Suddenly no place and nobody is insulated from the alluring attractions of modernity. Almost everybody everywhere wants all the things they have heard about, seen or experienced via the new technological facilitators that drive their wants and wishes. And it drives these increasingly into global commonality, thus homogenising markets everywhere.

The result is a new commercial reality – the explosive emergence of global markets for globally standardised products, gigantic world scale markets of previously unimagined magnitudes.

According to Levitt, countries (Japan) and firms (Coca-Cola), which have appreciated this trend, enjoy enormous economies of scale in production, distribution and marketing, and, by using price as a competitive weapon, are able to devastate the competition. This trend is accelerated by the NICs' desire for modernity, as a result of which they have run up enormous external debts, and made the old patterns of international trade obsolete. As a consequence, the multinational corporations that have dominated the scene for so long are giving way to the global corporation:

> The multinational and the global corporation are not the same. The multinational corporation operates in a number of countries, where in each case it adjusts with accommodating care and therefore high relative costs to the presumptive special conditions of the particular country. In contrast, the global corporation operates with resolute constancy and therefore at low relative costs as if the entire world (or major regions of it) were a single, largely identical entity; it does and sells the same things in the same single way everywhere.

Since Levitt's article appeared, there has been a continuous stream of articles in both academic and managerial journals that have both supported and rejected his view. For those living in a borderless world, it is the only way to go, for others, including marketing guru Philip Kotler (1984), it is trying to turn the clock back 30 years or more and bend demand to suit supply, when all the current thinking is stressing the need to bend supply to suit demand.

WHAT IS GLOBALISATION?

Some clues as to the nature of globalisation and global strategy have already been provided in the quotation from Levitt in the previous section of this chapter, particularly when distinguishing the global corporation from the more familiar multinational. In making this distinction, Levitt departs from the definitions offered by Hout et al. (1982) in which they analyse the nature of global competition and suggest that 'From a strategic point of view, however, there are two types of industries in which multinationals compete: *multidomestic* and *global*.' For succinctness and clarity it would be difficult to improve on Hout et al.'s definitions:

In *multidomestic* industries a company pursues separate strategies in each of its foreign markets while viewing the competitive challenge independently from market to market. Each overseas subsidiary is strategically independent, with essentially autonomous operations. The multinational headquarters will coordinate financial controls and marketing (including brand name) policies world-wide and may centralise some R&D and component production. But strategy and operations are decentralised. Each subsidiary is a profit centre and expected to contribute earnings and growth commensurate with market opportunity ... In short, the company competes with other multinationals and local competitors on a market-by-market basis.

A *global* industry, in contrast, pits one multinational's entire world-wide system of product and market positions against another's. Various country subsidiaries are highly interdependent in terms of operations and strategy. A country subsidiary may specialise in manufacturing only parts of its product line, exchanging products with others in the system. Country profit targets vary depending on individual impact on the cost position effectiveness of the entire worldwide system – or on the subsidiary's position relative to a key global competitor. A company may set prices in one country to have an intended effect in another ... Strategy is centralised and various aspects of operations are decentralised or centralised as economics and effectiveness dictate. The company seeks to respond to particular local market needs, while avoiding a compromise of efficiency of the overall global system.

As Jolly (1997) has pointed out, it is sometimes easier to define something by establishing what it is *not*. To begin with, despite Komatsu's injunction to 'think local, act global', global strategy does not demand standardisation in product–market strategy on the assumption of a single, homogeneous, border-free marketplace. Despite attempts to liberalise world trade, the world is still comprised of a large number of independent countries of vastly differing size, economic philosophy and stage of economic development, not to mention cultural and societal values and aspirations. Ultimately, all are guided by the principle of self-interest and the idea of a borderless world and a commonality of world interests is a very long way from the reality. As we shall see, however, this does not mean that within each of these independent sovereign states there are not subgroups or market segments that do resemble one another sufficiently to permit the execution of a standardised product–market strategy. Whether this qualifies as 'global marketing' is another matter.

The other end of the spectrum of approaches to global strategy is reflected in ABB's exhortation to 'think global, act local'. While some have assumed, given ABB's size and breadth of operations, that this means a global strategy requires one to be of sufficient size to operate in a majority of the world's markets, it does not. Globalisation and global strategy are, like 'marketing' itself, to do with a state of managerial thinking which is concerned with *how* it will execute its business to achieve its goals and objectives rather than *where* it will operate. The latter is a secondary issue which flows from the first.

In light of this, Jolly (1997) argues that:

To qualify as pursuing a global strategy, a company needs to be able to demonstrate two things:

- that it can contest any market it chooses to compete in
- that it can bring its entire worldwide resources to bear on any competitive situation it finds itself in, regardless of where that might be.

Two basic concepts are contained within this definition – *selective contestability* and *global capability*. The concept of selective contestability is central to successful marketing practice with its core principle of segmentation, targeting and positioning. Irrespective of whether the organisation is operating in a regional, national or global market the ability to disaggregate generic markets for earth moving equipment or carbonated beverages into meaningful submarkets or segments is at the very heart of devising a competitive strategy. Given an array of market segments one must then target one or more which offer the best match with the seller's strengths, ambitions and, above all, distinctive competencies. Then, given the identification of the target market, wherever it may be in the world, one must devise and develop a marketing strategy to compete effectively within it. What differentiates the global company is its willingness and ability to consider the whole world as a potential market and act accordingly.

It is this latter ability – to be willing and capable of operating anywhere in the world – that is represented by the concept of global capability and results in recognition as a global brand. The idea of a global brand goes far beyond the firm's physical presence in a number of different national markets as it reflects the existence of a global customer franchise and the perception of a cluster of values and benefits specific to that brand. It is this universal recognition that also enables one to distinguish between the firm with a presence in numerous national markets pursuing a focused strategy in each (a multidomestic strategy) from the true global player with the synergy associated with a global brand like Ford, Coca-Cola or Levi's.

Given these two dimensions of globalisation, Jolly acknowledges that it is still difficult to differentiate clearly between multidomestic and global strategy. To do so, one should assess a company in terms of five attributes – the higher it scores on each the more it may be considered a global competitor. These five attributes are:

1. Possessing a standard product (or core) that is marketed uniformly across the world
2. Sourcing all assets, not just production, on an optimal basis
3. Achieving market access in line with the breakeven volume of the needed infrastructure
4. The ability to contest assets as much as products when circumstances require
5. Providing all functions (or competencies) with a global orientation, even if they are primarily local in scope.

Clearly, these call for some elaboration.

The first attribute is essentially one of standardisation in both the product/service and its marketing mix and represents what most people would regard as a global strategy as articulated by Levitt (1983).

Given that global sourcing of supplies is itself a comparatively recent phenomenon its extension to embrace all the assets utilised by the organisation is a major step successfully attempted by a relatively small number of true multinational corporations. Ironically, if one were to pursue this to its logical conclusion, one might well find that nationalistic factors might well result in one finishing up with an essentially multidomestic operation due to local requirements on capital ownership, employment etc.

The third attribute of market success in line with breakeven volume means that the global competitor must be of sufficient size and generate sufficient volume/revenue in each of the markets in which it competes to justify the marketing investment needed to compete effectively. Inevitably, and especially when this involves developing a global brand, this attribute tends to limit global strategy to the large player.

Much the same qualification attaches to the fourth attribute of contesting assets as this reflects the firm's ability to match its principal competitors in gaining access to and control over assets critical to its successful operation, e.g. technology, low-cost supplies etc.

The final attribute – a global orientation – is probably the most difficult to achieve and to measure as it reflects the 'mental set' of those responsible for devising a strategy as well as all those responsible for its execution and delivery.

In light of this discussion and review, while it may be possible to distinguish between strategies that are global or domestic, with multidomestic strategies occupying an intermediate position between the two ends of the spectrum, it should be clear that none of these strategies is *intrinsically* superior to another. One should not be surprised at this conclusion, as the essence of competition and choice is the existence of alternatives and it is these which create the need for different approaches or strategies. Further, given the inborn variability of human drives and motivation, even before they have become modified by socialisation and learning, it seems likely that variety and choice are unavoidable determinants of consumption and buyer behaviour.

The spectrum of competitive strategies

Global ⟵— Multidomestic —⟶ Local

If this contention is true, then it follows that in any given national market one is quite likely to find firms pursuing any one of the three strategies successfully and simultaneously. Indeed, if one considers the pages of any serious management paper or magazine (*Financial Times, Wall Street Journal, Business Week, The Economist, Fortune* etc.) one is struck more by the variety than the similarity. While Peters and Waterman (1982) may well have identified eight attributes common to successful companies, we all now appreciate that, in the words of the song, 'It ain't what you do, it's the way that you do it.'

THE DEVELOPMENT OF GLOBAL MARKETING

The main impetus behind 'global marketing' undoubtedly came from the US and its growing involvement in international trade from the 1970s on. Unlike many other countries, the USA was largely a self-sufficient economy and foreign trade played an insignificant role in its economy until the early 1960s. Since then it has assumed growing importance with significant import penetration leading to an adverse balance of payments and major loss of market share in many industrial and consumer goods markets.

Faced with this level of competition in its home market, it is hardly surprising that US firms have had to fight back, and in doing so have come to recognise the need to compete in the world market. In doing so, however, they have chosen the line of least resistance and selected the least sophisticated approach – an undifferentiated marketing strategy.

An *undifferentiated* marketing strategy is one of three basic marketing strategies (the other two being differentiated and concentrated). An undifferentiated strategy exists when the supplier offers the same or undifferentiated product to all persons or organisations believed to have a demand for a product of that type. Three sets of circumstances suggest themselves as being suited to an undifferentiated strategy:

- the introduction of an innovation
- the mature / decay stage of the product life-cycle
- commodity marketing where the conditions most closely approximate the economist's model of perfect competition.

When introducing a new product into the marketplace, especially a radically different product, several factors may predicate an undifferentiated strategy. For example, it is widely recognised that much of the risk attendant upon a new product launch is uncertainty as to the scope and nature of demand, which may result in a perceptual mismatch between supplier and potential user. Inertia and commitment to the known and safe product or process make it difficult to forecast just what interpretation prospective users will make of the benefits offered by the innovation. Under such circumstances, a broad approach may be preferable to an attempt to pre-identify receptive customers as a basis for market segmentation and the development of either differentiated or concentrated strategies. Similarly, by the time the product is moving into its decline, it is safe to assume that the users / consumers are strongly committed to the product and so there is little need for special marketing effort. In the third case, the essential homogeneity of the commodity militates against either a differentiated or concentrated strategy.

By contrast, a *differentiated* strategy exists where the supplier seeks to supply a modified version of the basic product to each of the major subgroups which comprise the basic markets. In doing so he will develop a different marketing mix in terms of the product's characteristics, its price, promotion and distribution, although attempts will often be made to standardise on one or more of these factors in the interests of scale economies (usually distribution, e.g. car dealerships, consumer durables etc). Such differentiation is only possible for very large firms that can achieve a sufficient volume in each of the segments to remain competitive.

The third basic strategy is *concentrated,* in which the producer deliberately selects one of the major market segments and concentrates all their efforts upon it. It should be noted that this approach is different from user self-selection, which amounts to an undifferentiated strategy. In the latter case, the subsets of the market are not clear – the supplier does not possess profiles of different market groupings or segments, and so cannot devise a targeted or concentrated strategy for matching output to the needs of one segment. By contrast, in the case of a concentrated strategy, the supplier has been able to define highly specific market segments but has chosen to concentrate their efforts on only one of them. Such a strategy is particularly appropriate to the small producer that is unable to develop a range of differentiated products suited to the needs of the different segments which comprise the total market.

From these definitions it is clear that, with rare exceptions, demand is not homogeneous and therefore it is possible to disaggregate or segment demand curves, be they local, national or international. It is also accepted that by seeking to cater for the distinctive (or differentiated) needs of consumers, one is adopting a marketing orientation, whereas to convert people to buy what we can make is a production or sales orientation that is intrinsically more expensive to execute than making what one can sell in the first place. All this is not to say that an undifferentiated marketing strategy cannot be enormously successful as evidenced by Henry Ford's famous Model T. As Ford recognised, there was an enormous potential demand for the radical innovation, the motorcar, if only he could make it cheaply enough to bring it within the reach of the market. This he did with enormous success through product standardisation and scale economies, but he eventually ignored what I have characterised (Baker, 1980) as a marketing maxim 'The act of consumption changes the consumer.' In other words, possession of a Model T satisfied the basic needs of a motorist but it also made them aware of ways in which cars could be improved. It is a matter of history (see Sloan, 1964) that General Motors recognised this in 1923 and introduced a strategy of product differentiation which enabled them to usurp Ford's number one status – permanently.

Indeed, the evidence of economic history and marketing itself is that one tends to move from an undifferentiated strategy, to a differentiated strategy to a concentrated strategy. This is certainly apparent in the case of the product life-cycle where the new product is introduced in an undifferentiated format by an innovator. As demand for the product grows, so other suppliers seek to climb on the bandwagon by introducing variants of the original product and so both stimulate and enable the exponential growth of the market. As the market nears maturity, so competition settles down and tends to resolve itself into an oligopoly of suppliers more or less equally matched in terms of size and cost structure, surrounded by a constellation of very small producers filling the interstices or niches in the market through the pursuit of a highly specialised and concentrated strategy. Eventually, the market begins to decline so that some of the larger producers will withdraw, leaving a single major producer in an undifferentiated market.

It is ironic that Levitt and others should see today's technology leading to convergence, when all the evidence is that at last it provides the opportunity for the majority to 'do their own thing' and self-actualise. Consider what Alvin Toffler had to say on the subject as long ago as 1984:

> Take mass production. Nothing was more characteristic of the industrial era. Yet we're already moving from a mass production, mass consumption economy to what I've called a 'de-massified' economy. In traditional mass manufacturing, factories pour out a stream of identical objects, by the million. In the Third Wave sector, mass production is replaced by its opposite: demassified production – short runs, even customised, one-by-one production, based on computers and numerical controls. Even where we turn out millions of identical components, they are frequently configured into more and more customised end products. The significance of this can't be overestimated. It's not simply that products are now more varied. The processes of production are themselves transformed. The smokestack – that symbol of the industrial, assembly-line society – is becoming a relic. We still think of ourselves as a mass production society, yet in the advanced sectors of the economy, mass production is already an outmoded technique. And the idea that we can keep our old mass manufacturing industries competitive indefinitely is based on ignorance of what is actually happening on the factory floor. The new technologies make diversity as cheap as uniformity. In fact, in many industries, it's customise or die. This is exactly the opposite of what was required in the Second Wave economy. In fact, it is almost a dialectical return

to pre industrial, one-of-a-kind production, but now on a high technology basis. And exactly the same trends are visible in the distribution system, too, where we see more and more market segmentation, direct mail targeting, specialty stores, and even individualised delivery systems based on home computers and teleshopping. People are increasingly diverse and, as a result, the mass market is breaking into small, continually changing sectors.

TOWARDS A RECONCILIATION

There is a long tradition of polarising arguments in a debate, both to define the parameters of boundaries of the argument and to expose the uncommitted to the alternatives open to them. While Lorenz (1984a) reports that Levitt 'admits to exaggeration' and that 'All I'm really trying to do is to stress the need for companies to examine the growing *similarities* between consumer preferences, as well as the *differences* which still persist', one must be concerned that many readers of the original *HBR* article may accept his advice as gospel. (If you read the version in *The Marketing Imagination* (Levitt, 1983b), then the close juxtaposition of a chapter entitled 'Differentiation of everything' may alert you to the paradox.) A similar phenomenon occurred in the early 1960s when many managers became disillusioned with the marketing concept because they accepted uncritically an extreme version of it (Lorenz, 1984b). (See Ames, 1970) for a discussion of the difference between the 'trappings' and 'substance' of marketing.)

It would be equally regrettable if one were to accept Kotler's dismissal of the potential of a global strategy. After all there are many multinational companies which owe their success to pursuing a global strategy in the sense defined by Hout et al. Further, the competitive threat posed by Japan and many NICs that are following its example testify to the potential which such a strategy offers.

As with most things, neither extreme is likely to command much support and majority opinion will opt for the middle ground, which recognises that there are at least three basic strategies available. When introducing a product to a new market, an undifferentiated strategy is frequently the most appropriate, particularly when one lacks a clear

profile of those most likely to be early adopters. Similarly, in the late maturity and decline phase of the product life-cycle, consumption will have become habitual and those who have not switched to the new substitute product are, by definition, undifferentiated in their loyalty and resistance to change. By contrast, markets develop and grow as much in response to the increased availability of variants of the original innovation as to the sheer increase in supply created by new entrants to the market. Thus, in the growth and early maturity phase, as firms jockey for position, differentiation is essential, otherwise the product will degenerate into a commodity, in which case suppliers can only react to the market when they really wish to exercise a degree of control over it.

The third alternative, concentration, may be appropriate at the introduction of a new product if you have a clear picture of the likely initial users (which must imply you perceive differences between different categories of users) but most often emerges at the mature phase when smaller suppliers fill the niches in the market with highly differentiated products.

None of these strategies is mutually exclusive and each may be appropriate under given and different circumstances. Indeed, for many companies with a portfolio of products, it may be necessary to practise three quite different strategies simultaneously, as was demonstrated in *Marketing and Competitive Success* (Baker and Hart, 1989). That said, in advanced economies, and given the current stage of technological development, if one can only pursue one option, then Toffler's assessment would seem to suggest that differentiation must always be preferred by a marketer.

THE NEXT GLOBAL STAGE

The heading of this section is taken from the title of a book by Kenichi Ohmae published in 2005. Kenichi Ohmae is an international authority on the subject of globalisation and its implications for business strategy, and the author of several books on the subject including *The Borderless World* (1999). The following is a summary of the key ideas in his latest book.

In Ohmae's view, the global economy has four innate characteristics:

1. The global economy is *borderless* in terms of the four key factors of business life – communications, capital, corporations and consumers.
2. Many activities of the global economy are *invisible*, in the sense that they are performed on computer terminals rather than in public places/premises.
3. This potential is enabled by *cybertechnology* that allows huge amounts of data to be transferred almost instantaneously.
4. Performance is *measured in multiples* that reflect expectations about the value to be earned from exploiting future business opportunities.

This economy differs from the traditional notion of a region defined by national boundaries with the world consisting of an assembly of autonomous nation states. In the borderless global economy, resources, and especially excess money, are not confined to their place of origin but can follow attractive opportunities wherever they may be. And the factors that define these owe more to behavioural economics outlined in Chapter 3 than they do to the rational economic model. Under the new economic paradigm, natural resource endowment is not a prerequisite for prosperity, as the success of Finland and Ireland has shown. While domestic wealth is not necessary, investment is, and the world's excess capital will flow to those regions that appear to offer the best future opportunities. It follows that a large domestic market is no longer a requirement for an organisation to be able to compete effectively on a global scale.

In the borderless world, the important geographical and economic unit is the *region*. In some cases this will coincide with political units that define nations with borders but, often, they will comprise areas within a country – Porter's idea of clusters. Alternatively, the region may comprise an area which crosses borders. In all cases, successful regions need to be flexible and able to adapt as circumstances dictate. Added to this, regions need good marketing and be driven by a will to succeed.

While some critics see globalisation as a drive towards convergence, homogenisation and 'Americanisation' (much as Levitt originally proposed it), the reality of globalisation is that it emphasises the fallacy of self-sufficiency and the interdependence of human beings, both of which require the operation of free markets if we are to optimise the satisfaction to be gained from scarce resources. Given that these beliefs underpin the practice of marketing, the transition from national markets to a global one may require some rethinking about implementation but should not be seen as challenging the basic principles on which marketing is based.

Guerilla tactics

The November 2005 issue of the Australian magazine *Marketing* contained an article, 'The new face of marketing', that summarised some of the new tactics being employed by marketers. Among these were:

1. *Roaching:* 'a highly targeted means to promote a brand through initiating positive word-of-mouth advertising via peer-to-peer interaction with opinion leaders and early adopters.'

   Roaching is most effective with consumer goods and involves a representative of a brand starting up a conversation with a prospect about the brand and its attributes and benefits, often offering a trial of the product itself, e.g. a drink in a bar.

2. *Ambush Marketing:* 'is concerned with the strategic placement of marketing/promotional material at any events that attract media attention' but without paying to do so. Ambush marketing is particularly attractive to small organisations with limited promotional budgets, but users have to be careful not to create negative reactions 'by getting in the way', e.g. like spam on the internet. There may also be repercussions from the official sponsors of events.

3. *Podcasting:* consists of creating content on specific topics that can be downloaded on a computer and transferred to a portable music player or mobile phone automatically. This enables broadcast messages to be listened to when the audience wants, offering much greater flexibility than traditional radio, or by adding value to niche print

media through the inclusion of audio/video content.

4. *Branded content:* was pioneered by BMW North America in 1996 through the creation of a series of short web-based films in which 'advertisers adopt an ownership position with regard to their brand's identification, leveraging and assignment of its intellectual property'. The attraction of branded content is that as audiences gain more control over the media they are exposed to, web-based content is more likely to be sought out by people with a direct interest in the product.

5. *Word of mouth (WOM):* while the phenomenon of WOM has been well known for decades, word of mouth marketing (WOMM) is about ways to stimulate and amplify the consumer's natural tendency to tell others of their experiences. What is required are 'shapers' – people with many contacts who have persuasive, extrovert personalities and are considered to be credible sources of information without appearing to have too much knowledge. WOM appears to work best with products 'involving risk, complexity, social consumption,

experiential, or just being outright streets ahead of the competition.'

For WOM to work it has to be genuine, i.e. you have to believe what you are saying, otherwise it can be unethical and have negative consequences. When delivered online to social networks, WOM can have epidemic effects and is known as *viral marketing*.

The major problem with using WOM is identifying the shapers or 'opinion leaders'.

Chapter summary

In this chapter we have explored a number of current issues which may, or may not, have a significant impact on future marketing thinking and practice. These have included information technology and the development of e-commerce, together with the associated claim that their influence heralds the birth of a 'new economy'. As my quotation from *Ecclesiastes* suggests, I don't think so!

We also reviewed the ideas of Vargo and Lusch (2004) published in the *Journal of*

Marketing, in which they call for a new model of marketing. This has prompted extensive discussion and, in this case, we believe the jury is still out.

Ethics, green issues, and corporate social responsibility (CSR) are all subjects of wide debate. A brief overview of the issues is given and I anticipate they will be of increasing importance in the future.

Finally, we looked at globalisation which is both a product of trends in information and communications technology (ITC) and a

driver of the other issues discussed in this chapter. While no particular attention has been given to the topic of 'Emerging Economies' this is largely due to my belief that 'Marketing is Marketing – Everywhere' an extended discussion of which is to be found in *Vikalpa* (**30**(3), 2005) based on the keynote address I gave at The International Conference on Marketing Paradigms for Emerging Economies held at the Indian Institute of Management, Ahmedabad, 12–13 January, 2005

Recommended reading

Buzzell, R. D. and Sisodia, R. S. (1999) Information technology and marketing, in M. J. Baker (ed.) *Encyclopedia of Marketing*. London: International Thomson Business Press.

Douglas, S. P. and Craig, C. S. (1999) Global marketing, in M. J. Baker (ed.) *Encyclopedia of Marketing*. London: International Thomson Business Press.

Hamill, J. and Ennis, S. (2003) The Internet: the direct route to growth and development, in

M. J. Baker (ed.) *The Marketing Book* (5th edn). Oxford: Butterworth Heinemann.

Peattie, K. and Charter, M. (2003) Green marketing, in M. J. Baker (ed.) *The Marketing Book* (5th edn). Oxford: Butterworth Heinemann.

Schlegelmilch, B. (1998) *Marketing Ethics: An International Perspective*. London: International Thomson Business Press.

Smith, N. C. (1999) Marketing ethics, in M. J. Baker (ed.) *Ency-*

clopedia of Marketing. London: International Thomson Business Press.

It is also recommended that you read *Business Week, The Economist, Financial Times, Fortune* and similar publications. Much useful information is also to be found at the websites of the major consulting companies, e.g. www.bain. com and www.mckinsey.com.

REFERENCES

Ames, C. B. (1970) Trappings versus substance in industrial marketing, *Harvard Business Review* (July/August).

Baker, M. J. (1980) Maxims for marketing in the eighties, *Advertising*, **66**(winter).

Baker, M. J. (2006) *Marketing* (7th edn). Helensburgh: Westburn.

Baker, M. and Hart, S. (1989) *Marketing and Competitive Success*. London: Philip Allen.

Buzzell, R. D. and Sisodia, R. S. (1999) Information technology and marketing, in M. J. Baker (ed.) *Encyclopedia of Marketing*. London: International Thomson Business Press, pp. 225–37.

Chonko, L. B. and Hunt, S. D. (1985) Ethics and marketing management; an empirical investigation, *Journal of Business Research*, **13**: 339–59.

Colvin, G. (2005) Don't blame Wal-Mart, *Fortune*, 28 November.

Davis, I. (2005) What is the business of business?, *McKinsey Quarterly*, **3**.

Hair, J. H. and Keep, W. W. (1997) Electronic marketing: future possibilities, in R. A. Peterson (ed.) *Electronic Marketing and the Consumer*. Thousand Oaks, CA: Sage.

Haour, G. (1997) Environmental concerns: are they a threat or an opportunity?, in Dickson, T. (exec. ed.) *Mastering Management*. London: Financial Times, pp. 609–12.

Hout, T., Porter, M. E. and Rudden, E. (1982) How global companies win out, *Harvard Business Review* (September–October).

Jolly, V. (1997) Global strategies in the 1990s, in Dickson, T. (exec. ed.) *Mastering Management*. London: Financial Times, pp. 572–7.

Kotler, P. (1984) reported by C. Lorenz, The overselling of world brands, *Financial Times*, 19 July.

KPMG (1999) *Electronic Commerce Research Report*. London: KPMG.

Levitt, T. (1983a) The globalization of markets, Harvard Business Review (May–June).

Levitt, T. (1983b) *The Marketing Imagination*. New York: The Free Press.

Lorenz, C. (1984a) The overselling of world brands, *Financial Times*, 19 July.

Lorenz, C. (1984b) Why new products are going global, *Financial Times*, 16 July.

Malthus, T. (1798) *An Essay on the Principles of Population*.

Meadows, D. H., Meadows, D. L., Randers, J. and Behrens, W. W. III (1972) *Limits to Growth*. New York: Potomac Associates.

Nader, R. (1965) *Unsafe at Any Speed*. New York: Grossman.

Nolan Norton Institute (www.nolannorton.com)

Ohmae, K. (1999) *The Borderless World: Power and Strategy in the Interlinked Economy*. New York: HarperCollins.

Ohmae, K. (2005) *The Next Global Stage: The Challenges and Opportunities in Our Borderless World*. New Jersey: Wharton School Publishing.

Packard, V. (1957) *Hidden Persuaders*. Harmondsworth: Penguin Books.

Peters, T. and Waterman, R. (1982) *In Search of Excellence*. New York: Harper & Row.

Porter, M. E. (1979) How competitive forces shape strategy, *Harvard Business Review* (March–April).

Porter, M. E. (2001) Strategy and the internet, *Harvard Business Review* (March): 62–78.

Reingold, J. (2004) What we learned in the New Economy, *Fast Company* magazine (80) (March): 56ff. (www.fastcompany.com).

Sloan, A. P. (1964) *My Years with General Motors*. New York: Doubleday.

Smith, N. C. (1999) Marketing ethics, in M. J. Baker (ed.) *Encyclopedia of Marketing*. London: International Thomson Business Press.

Toffler, A. (1984) *Previews and Premises*. London: Pan.

Vargo, S. L. and Lusch, R. F. (2004) Evolving to a new dominant logic of marketing, *Journal of Marketing*, **68**(1): 1–17.

Walker, O. C. Jr., Mullins, J. W., Boyd, H. W. Jr. and Larréche, J. C. (2005) *Marketing Strategy* (5th edn). New York: McGraw-Hill Irwin.

NOTES

1. This section on electronic commerce was contributed by Dr Kenneth R. Deans, Department of Marketing, University of Otago, Dunedin, New Zealand.

2. This section develops themes originally aired in Baker, M. J. (1985) Marketing (4th edn). Basingstoke: Macmillan – now Palgrave Macmillan.

| # Recapitulation

Chance favours only the prepared mind.   LOUIS PASTEUR

INTRODUCTION

This book has been concerned with a description and analysis of the application of strategic planning to the marketing function, and the translation of the resultant marketing strategies into operational plans. Thus we have looked at the nature of strategy in general and marketing strategy in particular, and have recognised that marketing is constrained by the environment within which its activities must be performed. Within this overriding constraint, we have acknowledged that the particular performance of the individual organisation will depend upon its ability to identify and satisfy the highly specific needs of individual customers and that the degree of success it will enjoy will depend in turn upon its ability to differentiate itself in the minds of prospective customers from the offerings of its competitors. Success in achieving this will be determined by its degree of understanding of the way in which buyers choose, and the extent to which it can put this knowledge to good effect by identifying and developing profitable market segments.

Once the firm has decided upon its basic objectives in terms of the products and markets which it intends to deal in, it must develop an internally consistent set of policies for the management of its marketing mix. Part III of the book has been concerned specifically with a review of the management of the marketing mix and the four Ps – product, price, place and promotion – building upon the assumption that the reader is already familiar with the descriptive aspects of these topics. Finally, we have just looked at the problems associated with implementing marketing and the need for monitoring and controlling the marketing function in order to provide the feedback that closes the circle of marketing strategy and management. In this concluding chapter, we shall seek to tease out those ideas that we consider provide the framework for the development of marketing strategy and the management of the marketing function. In doing so we are conscious that, while oversimplification can be dangerous, our earlier discussion of selective perception and retention, and the concept of memory span, provides a forceful argument for restricting our own listing of CUGs to a parsimonious number. To this end, first we examine some predictions about marketing in the future. Next we look at the four elements that comprise the 'virtuous circle of best marketing practice'. We then review the contribution of marketing to competitive success. This is expanded into a set of 'maxims for marketing' and we conclude by proposing a 'Baker's dozen' of key concepts.

VISION 2010

Vision 2010 is a research report published by the Economist Intelligence Unit and written in cooperation with Andersen Consulting (1997). The purpose of the report is to profile the successful business enterprise of the future and it analyses the forces of change that are making vertically integrated organisations increasingly redundant. Their replacements are likely to be leaner enterprises drawing on a network of external relationships. The findings of *Vision 2010: Designing Tomorrow's Organisation* are based on approximately 350 survey responses supplied by board level and senior executives at global multinational and national corporations, reinforced by personal interviews with about 50 top executives. Finally, a group of business leaders participated in a focus group to discuss the issues raised by the survey questionnaire.

The key findings from the survey were:

1. Companies are preparing for more change, and it will be rapid and challenging. Competition will continue to increase, with the emphasis changing from vertically integrated operations based on capital and raw materials to smaller and more manoeuvrable knowledge-based companies.
2. The key drivers of business strategy are:
   - Customer demands for higher quality and service
   - An ability to attract and retain the best people
   - International competition
   - New and rapidly changing technologies.
3. Change will be driven by multiple factors inside and outside the company.
4. Companies are looking for new sources of competitive advantage beyond their core competencies.
5. Executives will use a wide spectrum of organisational models and management tools to cope with change. The emphasis on mergers and acquisitions, joint ventures, outsourcing and strategic alliances will continue to grow.

In the past, with fewer secure sources of raw materials dominated mainly by cartels, vertical integration and control of the whole value chain was seen to be vital. In the future, knowledge is seen to be the only source of sustainable competitive advantage. As the rate of change continues to accelerate, speed in the collection, assimilation, dissemination and utilisation of knowledge has become critical. Networks, both formal and informal, further accelerate information exchange, while the global economy now operates on a 24-hour basis. For example, Satyem Computers based in Hyderabad is India's largest software company. With customers distributed around the world, software engineers work a 24/7 shift system.

Ultimately, the virtual corporation of the future may well consist of a small management group who control the firm's knowledge base. If this is the case then 'it follows that the remainder of a conventional company's operations is so much baggage, to be picked up or discarded as business opportunities dictate' (p. 15). Based on its knowledge of market opportunities and customer needs on the one hand and suppliers and partners on the other, the team will use electronic linkages to outsource all its requirements and create a value added package.

In its survey, respondents were asked to identify the relative importance of various factors both today and in the year 2010. In the case of both the forces affecting business strategy and the key factors driving competitive advantage, there were only minor changes in the rank ordering but overall a very significant increase in the perceived importance of them. Thus, in terms of forces affecting business strategy, 85% ranked customer demands for higher quality and service first, followed by the ability to attract and retain best people (80%), new and rapidly changing technologies (75%), and international competition (74%). In terms of key factors driving competitive advantage, relationships with suppliers and customers was ranked first (90%), followed by people and human resources (86%), core competencies (85%), flexible organisational structure (80%), high productivity (79%), and technology (78%). Of all the factors, flexible organisational structure (42% to 80%) and procurement and supply chain management (30% to 57%) showed the largest swings.

In general, a regional analysis of survey replies showed remarkably little variation.

Forging strategic alliances, which enable cooperation with competitors and organisations both in one's own and other industries, are seen as a key aspect of competition in the 2000s. Based on the survey and the advice of several alliance specialists, *Vision 2010* suggests the following checklist:

1. Be sure of top management support
2. Think through broader strategy and alliance objectives with care
3. Determine whether the company is ready to learn from the alliance and help the alliance learn from it
4. Select partners with great care and ensure that they fit in terms of:
   - Strategic goals and objectives
   - Brand compatibility
   - Size and profitability
   - Business styles and practice
   - Chemistry and culture
5. Negotiate with an open mind

6. Put a top quality executive in charge with a clear but flexible mission
7. Obtain commitment at all operating levels.

Factors driving the search for strategic alliances include:

- The pursuit of growth
- Products and service improvement
- Acquisition of new competencies
- Leveraging existing competencies
- Owning an industry standard.

Among the factors militating against successful strategic alliances are:

- Dominance of a partner
- Difficulty in establishing win–win relationships
- Limited freedom of manoeuvre
- Incompatibility in corporate strategies and cultures
- Distortion of core strategies
- Demands on management time
- Shortage of good partners.

Among the key benefits identified with outsourcing were:

1. Lower costs for outsource process (68%)
2. Improvement in overall business performance (62%)
3. Sharpened business focus (57%)
4. Access to external expertise/skills (53%)
5. Improved quality and efficiency of outsource process (52%)
6. Competitive advantage (44%)
7. Creation of new revenue sources (18%).

The emphasis upon strategic alliances and outsourcing reflects the view that competition is less between companies and more between supply chains. Given that conventional wisdom dictates individual companies must concentrate on their core competencies, the scale of global competition means that few, if any, companies can control all the elements from the sourcing of raw materials through to after-sales service. Arising from this increased interdependence is a need both to define and measure accurately key performance indicators.

The other major force motivating the focus on core competencies is recognition that in the vertically integrated organisation rigid hierarchical structures tend to be the order of the day, with the result that there is often a significant physical and psychological distance between those responsible for the formulation of strategy and those responsible for its implementation. To overcome this, it is essential that those responsible for strategy formulation get closer to the customer and this has become much more likely in the more focused, flatter and horizontally structured organisations that emerged throughout the 1990s. As we move towards 2010, both the key and associated findings have proved to be remarkably prescient. The need to capture tacit knowledge and foster a learning environment are critical to future success.

According to Ikujiro Nanaka and Hirotaki Takeuchi (1995), Western companies, and particularly the financially driven Anglo-Saxon ones, overemphasise hard explicit knowledge but neglect tacit knowledge. Explicit knowledge is the kind that can be written down and communicated formally, whereas tacit knowledge exists in people's minds and is based upon their experience, judgement and subconscious feelings. Converting tacit knowledge into explicit knowledge is a major challenge for learning organisations. It is the source of distinctive skills and competencies and the only sure foundation for developing a sustainable competitive advantage.

THE 'VIRTUOUS CIRCLE' OF BEST MARKETING PRACTICE

During 1983 the Institute of Marketing, the University of Bradford Management Centre and Industrial Market Research Ltd joined forces to undertake a major investigation into the role and practice of marketing management in the UK. Based upon the response of over 1,800 senior marketing executives, Hooley et al. (1983) concluded that: 'The best companies and the most successful managers combine an unwavering commitment to classic marketing principles with a significantly heightened sensitivity and responsiveness to environment signals.' These factors are depicted diagrammatically in what Hooley et al. call the 'virtuous circle of best marketing practice', shown in Figure 25.1. While the survey is now

FIGURE 25.1 Virtuous circles of marketing practice

dated, the evidence considered in this book indicates the conclusions are still sound, as is idea of a virtuous circle. From the study it is possible to isolate certain key features which characterise the more successful organisations. These features, which are illustrated in Figure 25.1, provide clear guidelines for improved marketing effectiveness.

The key elements in this virtuous circle may be summarised as follows:

1. *Marketing orientation*

Despite radical changes in the environment, a marketing orientation still offers the best likelihood of commercial success.

> The key to marketing success is the development of clear-cut and competitively defensible market position. This is based upon the isolation of a market segment or segments where an organisation's distinctive capabilities and competencies find a match with unsatisfied consumer needs. The best performing companies demonstrate an unwavering focus upon the marketplace and relate all their major operating decisions to the dictates of customer needs.

Market research is seen as an essential prerequisite of the identification and selection of suitable market opportunities, but it is believed that far too few firms make use of this essential marketing tool.

2. *Organisational flexibility and adaptability*

Flexibility and adaptability in a firm's systems, attitudes and structures are also seen as vital to survival in a turbulent environment. Thus, 'successful companies recognise the need for a flexible planning system which can encompass a wide range of possible scenarios'.

Flexibility also arises from the development of product portfolios which allows the firm to spread its risks across different markets.

3. *Heightened environmental sensitivity*

The UK survey confirms and supports the findings of Ansoff (1968), Argenti (1974) and others that survival depends upon the development of suitable environmental scanning systems to enable the firm to monitor and respond to the 'speed, complexity and discontinuity of change' (a view confirmed in Chapter 7 of this book and elsewhere).

4. *Increased marketing professionalism*

'The best organisations show a commitment to the training of their personnel and a willingness to experiment with new ideas and concepts.' In other words, a 'seat of the pants' approach to marketing is no longer sufficient to cope with current conditions.

While Hooley et al. were concerned primarily with the role and practice of marketing management, one would expect that if marketing plays such an important role in the corporation's overall strategy (as is claimed in this book), any survey of corporate success would also show support for these factors. In one of the most influential management books in recent years, Peters and Waterman (1982) provide such confirmation. Although the eight attributes they define as characteristic of the excellent and innovative company cover the whole range of general management, getting 'close to the customer', 'productivity through people' adaptability and flexibility are all seen as central to success.

MARKETING AND COMPETITIVE SUCCESS

Throughout the 1980s and 90s, and now in the early 2000s, competitiveness has been a major preoccupation of managers and academics alike. Extensive research has been undertaken on the topic and numerous books and articles on the subject produced. Of necessity, the treatment of the topic in the summary of a book of this kind can only be eclectic and the reader should be aware that this is the case.

In Chapter 2 we summarised the main thesis of Michael Porter's *The Competitive Advantage of Nations* (1990). A major conclusion of this study of the performance of national economies was that, while a generous endowment of physical resources is an undoubted advantage, history appears to show that it is the human factor which is critical to sustained competitive success. Indeed, the emergence of the industrial revolution in Britain and the Japanese economic miracle following the Second World War appear to owe much to a determination to overcome a scarcity of physical resources. This is especially the case through involvement in international trade as a means of exporting human skills as 'value added' in exchange for imports of raw materials and commodities.

In Chapter 2 we also reported some of the findings of the study undertaken by Professor Susan Hart and myself and published as *Marketing and Competitive Success* (MACS) (1989). This study attempted to address the criticisms levelled against many earlier analyses – particularly that such studies tended to be partial and/or anecdotal. In our study we deliberately set out to analyse a sample of industries, covering those in the growth and mature/decline stages of development – the so-called 'sunrise' and 'sunset' industries. Further, we collected data from both successful and unsuccessful firms judged against the performance criteria appropriate to their own industry.

Based on data collected in the mid to late 1980s, it was clear that all our samples possessed an important and distinctive characteristic – they had all survived the recession of the late 1970s and early 1980s. It also became clear that the great majority were aware of the claimed benefits of strategic planning and of the techniques and procedures of the kind discussed in this book. Inevitably we are drawn to the conclusion that it is the quality of implementation which differentiates between more and less successful firms. Knowledge of the kind contained in this book is a necessary but *not* sufficient condition for success.

During the late 1980s James Lynch et al. of the University of Bradford Management Centre undertook a follow-up study to that reported in the previous section. Funded by the Economic and

Social Science Research Council (ESRC), the objective of the study was to explore the effectiveness of British marketing and, in particular, the activities and attitudes of the more successful organisations (Lynch et al., 1988).

Following a series of preliminary depth interviews with senior marketing executives a questionnaire was mailed to 5,416 firms from a list provided by Dun & Bradstreet and marked 'for the attention of the Chief Marketing Executive'. The effective mailout was 5,121 which, after a follow-up, yielded 1,380 replies (27%) 'broadly representative both in size and standard industrial classification (SIC) of British Industry, including both manufacturing and service sectors'.

The major conclusions were that:

1. There is no magic formula which will guarantee marketing effectiveness: 'The key to success, it would appear, may be not so much in what is done but in how it is done'. This finding clearly confirms those of MACS.
2. 'In broad terms, the survey suggests both a rise in the perceived importance of marketing's role in organisational success in the last five years and a growing appreciation of the major marketing concepts'. However, the improvement is not universal and leaves much scope for further progress.

In their analysis, Lynch et al. (1988) isolated the 'better performers', who comprised approximately 12% of the sample and reported better performance than their competitors across a range of financial and market-based measures, and then compared these with the remainder:

Detailed analysis of the research results suggests that the key differentiators between the top performers and the rest are probably not so much issues of strategy or tactics as questions of commitment, cultural consistency and leadership where marketing is concerned. In specific terms, the top performers show a greater marketing grasp and a stronger and more clearly worked-out commitment to marketing principle.

To assess their general orientation to business, respondents were asked to select one of three statements 'which best describes the marketing approach of your company'. As Table 25.1 shows, almost two-thirds selected the third option which

TABLE 25.1 'Which of the following best describes the marketing approach of your company?'

	Total sample (1,346) (%)	Better performers (162) (%)	Others (1,184) (%)	Better performer variation from others (%)
Make what we can and sell to whoever will buy	16.3	9.9	17.1	−42
Place major emphasis on advertising and selling	18.2	16.0	18.5	−14
Place major emphasis on prior analysis of market needs adapting our products and services to meet them if necessary	65.5	74.1	65.4	+15

NOTES:

1. Percentage figures are column percentages
2. 'Better performer variation from others' shows the extent to which the two groups differed. The variation is calculated by dividing the better performers' percentage by that of the others. Where the better performers adopt a particular answer more often a positive variation is noted, where they adopt one less often a negative variation results. The 'flags' show the extent of the variation

SOURCE: Lynch, J., Hooley, G. and West, J. (1988) *The Effectiveness of British Marketing, A Report to the ESRC*. University of Bradford Management Centre

reflects a marketing orientation, while 18% chose a selling orientation emphasising advertising and selling, with the remaining 16% favouring a production orientation.

This pattern is confirmed in the response to the statement that 'Marketing is seen as a guiding philosophy for the whole organisation', as shown in Table 25.2.

Additional attitudinal statements indicated that:

- There is a stronger level of marketing commitment on the part of the chief executives of the top performing organisations
- The top performers reported significantly more aggressive objectives over the past five years than their less successful counterparts, with much greater emphasis on growth and expansion
- Top performers are more likely to have adopted a longer term marketing objective rather than short-term financial goals
- Top performers attach much greater importance to marketing training.

In terms of organisational structure the key findings are summarised in Table 25.3.

In terms of operational practice – what the firms actually do in the marketplace – several important differences emerged, which are summarised in Table 25.4.

TABLE 25.2 'How well does the following statement describe the role of marketing in your company?'

	'Marketing is seen as a guiding philosophy for the whole organisation'			
	Total sample (1,125) (%)	Better performers (148) (%)	Others (997) (%)	Better performer variation from others (%)
Exactly	29.4	41.2	27.6	+49
To some extent	48.9	43.9	49.6	−11
Not at all	21.7	14.9	22.7	−34

SOURCE: Lynch, J., Hooley, G. and West, J. (1988) *The Effectiveness of British Marketing, A Report to the ESRC*. University of Bradford Management Centre

TABLE 25.3 Top performer organisation

- More likely to have a marketing department
- More likely to have marketing represented directly at board level
- More likely to adopt a market-based organisational structure
- Work more closely with the other functional areas:
  - Finance
  - Production
  - Sales
  - R&D

TABLE 25.4 Top performer marketing activities

- A greater input from marketing to overall strategic planning
- Greater tendency to formal long-term marketing planning
- More aggressive marketing objectives
- Prepared to attack the whole market and take on any competition
- More prepared to take a calculated risk
- Superior quality, high-price positioning strategies
- Build competitive advantages through reputation and quality
- More active in new product development to lead their markets

Based upon their analysis, Lynch et al. conclude 'that it is possible to isolate four basic orientations towards marketing on the part of respondents to the survey'. Taking the function and philosophy as the two key dimensions of their classification, the four categories are represented diagrammatically as in Figure 25.2, and are defined as follows:

1. *The sales supporters* (9%): demonstrated a very narrow view of marketing's role and sphere of influence within the organisation. For this group, marketing, where it exists at all, is perceived as essentially a support function to the central task of making the sale.
2. *The unsures* (24%): appeared to be in a state of flux and some uncertainty concerning marketing's role in their organisation. The unsures see marketing to some extent as a sales supporting function but it is also believed to have some involvement in identifying and meeting customer needs.
3. *The departmental marketers* (26%): are characterised above all else by the belief that marketing is a departmental activity confined to the activities of the marketing people in the organisation.
4. *The marketing philosophers* (41%): clearly distinguish between philosophy and function and, very significantly, 91% of the CEOs of these firms see marketing as the guiding approach for the whole organisation (vs. 53% amongst the departmental marketers, 45% among the unsures and 25% among the sales supporters).

The researchers conclude that these categories reflect an evolutionary pattern of organisational marketing effectiveness. We judge that organisat-

ions initially see marketing as a simple adjunct to selling (the sales supporters). This narrow view often changes over time to a wider but more uncertain sense of marketing's broader potential (the unsures). In those organisations where additional evolution occurs, the next stage gives greater prominence to marketing but confines it strictly to the activities of the marketing people in the business (the departmental marketers). The final stage involves the recognition that marketing is more than just a function. It is an attitude and a philosophy which should guide all the organisation's activities and is centred upon customer focus, competitive advantage, environmental sensitivity and a healthy commitment to the financial bottom line (the marketing philosophers).

Lynch et al.'s findings support those of Peters and Waterman, Baker and Hart and many others in their emphasis upon a number of basic principles and excellence in their implementation. From an analysis of marketing practice certain themes occur and re-occur with a frequency which seems to suggest that there is a nucleus of concepts and ideas that have near-universal validity. Indeed, the robust and durable nature of these CUGs is such that they may be articulated as a series of maxims for marketers.

MAXIMS FOR MARKETERS[1]

In reviewing what I consider to be among the most important of these 'marketing maxims', it appears that the early development of marketing thought and practice has been characterised by a predilection for overstatement. Whereas such

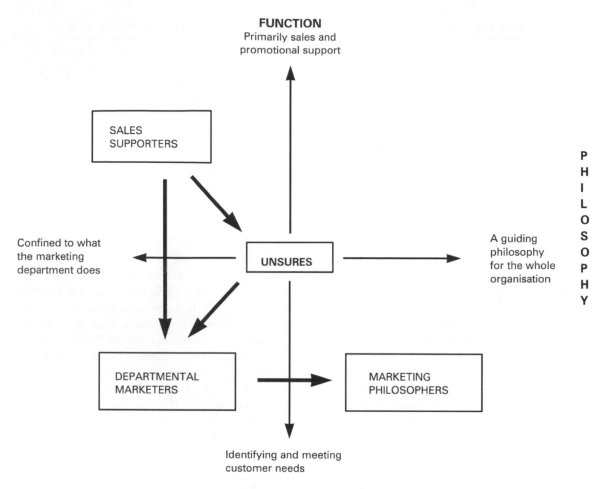

FIGURE 25.2 Marketing approaches and evolutionary patterns

overstatement may have been necessary in the 1950s and 60s to distinguish the new marketing orientation from the sales and production orientations that preceded it, during the 1970s and 80s such hyperbole became misleading to the point of being counterproductive and underlines the need for a clear statement of just what marketing is really all about.

Maxim 1   Marketing is both a philosophy of business and a business function

It seems to me that many of the difficulties which hinder understanding and acceptance of the marketing concept derive from a failure to distinguish clearly between marketing as a state of mind concerning the optimum approach to business,

and the activities whereby such ideas are translated into practice.

It is probably true to say that successful entrepreneurs have always been marketing-oriented, in the sense that they have recognised that success depends upon having the right goods at the right price at the right place at the right time. More important still, they have recognised that what is 'right' depends upon the consumers, for it is they who cast their money votes in the marketplace and thereby exercise their sovereignty. For a variety of reasons, which I discuss below in the context of other maxims, the emphasis in recent years has moved away from the 'what' and 'where', and the 'when', to the 'who', and 'why', and the 'how', and it is this change of emphasis which has led to the stress on the marketing function and marketing practice and, particularly, upon personal selling and promotion. To a large degree the latter activities appear to be the antithesis of product design and development, and the efficient management of production and distribution, which dominated earlier phases of post-Industrial Revolution market development, all of which appear objective and quantifiable. By contrast, selling and advertising appear to be subjective and non-quantifiable, and it is hardly surprising that this strong difference should alienate managers brought up in the scientific school of management. In turn, this alienation against marketing practice has tended to prejudice acceptance of the marketing concept, despite the intuitive attraction of this approach – thus, as the need for marketing has grown greater so also has antipathy to the means whereby concept should be translated into practice.

The main reason why there has been a need for a change in marketing practice is to be found in:

Maxim 2 The act of consumption changes the consumer

On reflection, the validity of this maxim is so obvious that it hardly seems worth stating. Unfortunately many successful entrepreneurs have ignored the implications of this principle, and often with dire consequences. Probably the most eloquent and well-known analysis of this phenomenon is Ted Levitt's Marketing myopia (1960), in which he makes the trenchant observation that 'every declining industry was once a growth industry' – you have to rise before you can fall. To rise you have to be able to recognise a market opportunity – to know what the customer wants – in other words, to be marketing-oriented. However, the seeds of self-destruction and failure are built into every successful product, for it introduces the user to standards and aspirations hitherto dormant and unsatisfied. Railways made it possible to move people and freight across continents with a speed, economy and comfort unknown in the days of horse-drawn traffic and beyond the capabilities of canals and rivers. But, while the railway moguls became complacent, their customers began to perceive certain disadvantages in this new mode of transport, not least of which was the need to travel when it suited the railways, and to start your journey from their premises, not your own.

The internal combustion engine, cars and lorries, provided the flexibility and convenience which the consumer was looking for, and Henry Ford knew exactly what he was doing when he set out to mass produce a basic car at a price nearly anyone could afford.

Indeed, Henry Ford was so successful that not only did he stimulate an enormous expansion in the market, but in 20 years he moved from an insignificant share of the market to a dominant position with over 60%. Unfortunately Henry Ford forgot the insight which gave rise to this success, and he failed to observe that once everyone had a Model T, many wanted something better. The product planning committee of General Motors understood this, and they were also sensitive to:

Maxim 3 Downward-sloping demand curves reflect differences in preferences and purchasing power. To this one might add the corollary that 'The vast majority of demand curves for products and services slope downward'

Now the mistake of the tyro economist (and of Henry Ford) is to assume that those with the strongest demand and/or most purchasing power would behave in exactly the same way if the price were reduced, i.e. they would continue to consume the same volume of the product as before, now that it had become available to more users at a lower price. For some goods this may be so, but, for most, those with the strongest preferences (inelastic demand) will look for a differentiated product. The explanation for this is to be found in Maxim 2. When new products are introduced, both supply and demand tend to be relatively small and prices high, due to the absence of economies of scale in production, distribution and marketing, coupled with the innovator's desire to capitalise his investment in R&D early in the life of the innovation. Because of its relatively high price, only those with a very strong preference and/or high levels of disposable income are able to afford supplies. As awareness of the product grows and demand expands, producers are able to 'slide down the demand curve', offering lower prices as they achieve scale economies. By this time the early buyers have become familiar with the product, and look for improvements in it. In other words, willingness to pay different prices implies a desire for different product configurations. General Motors understood this, and evolved the concept of market segmentation, providing different types and qualities of motorcar at different prices.

Two further maxims derive directly from the rapid growth of supply and demand associated with any successful NPD:

Maxim 4 The greater the separation between producer and consumer, the greater the propensity for distortion in communication between them

Maxim 5 The more sophisticated the demand, the less self-evident it becomes

As markets grow, there is a tendency for concentration to develop on the supply side, as the more efficient firms eliminate their less efficient competitors. Once achieved, such concentration is usually self-sustaining, as it provides scale economies in production and marketing. However, as noted earlier, a dominant position can result in complacency and loss of touch with the consumer, and it is this which can lead to a failure by the supplier to be aware of and respond to the changing needs of his customers.

By the same token, broad basic needs – food, drink, shelter, clothing, transportation etc. – are easy to detect and even to quantify in general terms. But, in the particular, this is far from the case, and in a free market suppliers expend considerable energy and ingenuity in attempting to create differentiated supplies which will appeal to a non-homogeneous collection of potential buyers.

Separation and sophistication both predicate the need to monitor carefully and continuously the nature of demand, and underline the need for marketing research.

As a consequence of Maxim 2, the act of consumption changes the consumer – plus competition and concentration – we may identify:

Maxim 6 Change is inevitable – to which, parenthetically, we might add 'and difficult to predict'

The validity of this maxim is particularly well-exemplified by one of the few genuine marketing

concepts – the idea of the product life-cycle. Although the concept of a product life-cycle has been subject to much criticism, I believe this arises from attempts to use it, often unsuccessfully, to develop specific sales forecasts, rather than regarding it for what it is – a generalised predictive device of the way in which the sales of successful products will grow, stabilise and stagnate. The emphasis upon 'successful' is important, for one obviously cannot anticipate a period of rapid growth for a deficient product which is doomed to failure from its inception. Similarly, just as the length of any given phase of a biological life-cycle will vary according to the species, so will it vary according to the type of product under consideration.

It is also important to remember that, while change is ultimately inevitable, it is possible to influence the shape of the 'normal' product life-cycle through deliberate action. Thus, much of my own research has been concerned with ways and means of speeding up market penetration by better pre-identification of the best prospects for new products. In the same way, many others have proposed methods of extending the mature phase through policies of incremental product improvement and market extension, and there is even a modest literature on avoiding the debilitating effects of old age through programmes of planned euthanasia.

The reason why all managers should have a framed diagram of the product life-cycle on their desk or office wall is to remind them that sooner or later, for better or worse, the status quo will change. It is the manager's responsibility to be sensitive and to plan for this eventuality. Better still, he should consciously seek to influence and control the future – an assertion which leads to:

Maxim 7 Marketing is accountable for the present and responsible for the future

One of the worst effects of the excessive enthusiasm for 'marketing' in the 1960s and 70s was the emphasis it placed upon marketing's role in anticipating and planning for the future. A direct consequence of this was to play down, or even undermine, the sales function, which, hitherto, had been the mainstay of most marketing effort. This tendency still prevails, and it is not without significance that selling and sales management is not to be found enjoying the same status as other marketing functions such as advertising, marketing research, public relations etc., in the curricula of business schools and professionally oriented courses. This attitude is irresponsible, for today is yesterday's future, and if we want to claim the privilege of planning the future we must be prepared to accept accountability for it when it arrives. Clearly, in the short term it is necessary to sell what you can make – widely derided as the antithesis of the marketing concept – in order to realise the capital invested in production facilities, so that this may be reinvested in new facilities to produce new products. It follows that the marketer must achieve a balance between the time and effort expended upon monitoring change in the marketplace and translating this into plans for future action, and maximising the return from the present product–market mix.

In order to maximise sales it is necessary to give full attention to the facts discussed in the introduction to Chapter 18, namely:

Maxim 8   Consumption is a function of availability

This maxim is essentially a restatement of the now largely discredited Say's Law that 'supply creates demand'. Despite the inevitable logic of the proposition that one can only consume products and services that are available, many commentators assert that seeing markets as supply-led is to ignore consumer sovereignty, with the result that they neglect production and distribution while stressing advertising and sales promotion. Of course, the mere creation of supply is not in itself a sufficient condition to ensure consumption, and it is for this reason that the marketing concept has so much to offer in reminding us that consumer preferences change, and that we need to keep a careful check of these changes, and modify our output accordingly. That said, however, it is clear that many potential sales are lost through non-availability, and that the less distinctive the product the greater the probability that such non-availability will result in consumers changing their preferred supplier. This is not only true of convenience goods like detergents, baked beans etc., where brand shares are frequently a self-fulfilling prophecy (i.e. retailers stock brands

in the proportions of their reported brand shares, so that, assuming total stocks for a given period roughly equate sales, it is not surprising that actual brand shares mirror predicted brand shares) it is also true of standardised industrial materials (basic chemicals, steel etc.), components and supplies, especially when made to a well-recognised specification. Indeed, a number of surveys of industrial buyers have shown that quality and reliability are much more important determinants of buyer preference than the economists' preferred discriminator – price. This leads us to:

Maxim 9   In a true-choice situation it is the subjective marketing factors which are determinant

Most analyses of buyer behaviour, whether they be industrial buyers or ultimate consumers, are agreed that purchasing is an essentially rational process in which the potential buyer seeks to discriminate between possible solutions to his felt need through the application of objective criteria. Of these objective criteria, performance characteristics and the cost–benefit of any given purchase are considered first. However, given the potential to create excess supplies in the advanced industrialised economies, there is frequently intense competition between suppliers of near-identical products, such that price and performance factors do not point to any clearly preferred alternative. Under such circumstances, the potential buyer is still faced with the need to make a choice, and his wish to appear rational requires that he find a criterion to justify his eventual selection. Given that objective and measurable factors have been exhausted in arriving at the short list from which a choice is to be made, it is the subjective elements which condition the final selection, and it is the subjective elements which are most sensitive to marketing activities. This is especially true of promotional activity, whether it is by impersonal communication through the media, or personal communication by salesmen, or word-of-mouth recommendation by opinion leaders.

Unfortunately this determinant role of marketing only comes into operation when all else is equal, a fact which is increasingly overlooked by those who seem to regard marketing as a panacea for all other deficiencies – in product design, in product quality, in price and in availability.

Marketing is only one factor, albeit a critical one, in ensuring commercial success. In proposing nine marketing maxims I have tried to isolate what I consider to be key considerations in the philosophy and practice of marketing, and to emphasise that true success can only occur where those responsible for the direction of the enterprise are marketing-oriented, and ensure that the marketing function is fully integrated with the other key business functions – R&D, production, finance and control.

A BAKER'S DOZEN OF KEY CONCEPTS

In the preceding section we have looked at a nucleus of ideas that occur over and over again in any discussion or analysis of the real essence of marketing. These 'maxims' (as we have designated them) summarise some of the more important philosophical underpinnings of the marketing concept and their acceptance is essential to the development of a marketing orientation. However, as this book has attempted to show, above all else marketing is something which you do and in this final section we identify thirteen key concepts which are seen as intrinsic to the effective practice of marketing, namely:

1. Generic product definition
2. The product life-cycle
3. Limited strategic alternatives
4. Business portfolio analysis
5. The marketing audit
6. Selective perception
7. Customer diversity
8. Market segmentation and positioning
9. Differential advantage
10. The marketing mix
11. Integrated marketing planning
12. Control and feedback
13. 3-in-1 marketing.

To some extent, these key concepts are an extension of the marketing maxims, the essential difference being that they represent a sequence of operational guidelines for marketing managers.

Generic product definition is a term coined by

Kotler and Levy (1969) to encapsulate the most basic marketing principle of all – that one should define market opportunities in terms of the underlying need to be served rather than in terms of the product currently available to serve that need. (Kotler and Levy's article in the *Journal of Marketing* was also the first to suggest a set of key concepts which apply to all types and kinds of marketing.) To paraphrase Levitt (see Maxim 1), who first counselled firms to think of themselves as being in the transportation business rather than in railroads, in entertainment rather than movies, and energy rather than oil, 'people buy drills, but they need holes'. Clearly, with the development of laser technology, conventional twist drills may soon become a thing of the past – has the hole-making industry reflected on the implications of this? Or, to take another example, consider those doyens of consumer goods marketing, the detergent manufacturers. Have Unilever and Procter & Gamble reflected on the fact that consumers don't particularly want detergent; their real objective is clean clothes so that an ultrasonic 'washing-machine' which requires no detergent would serve their needs just as well as would disposable or non-soil clothing.

It follows that the starting-point for all strategic marketing planning must be a clear and explicit statement of the benefit or satisfaction which the customer is seeking and this is so whether the customer is a firm or an individual and irrespective of whether the means of delivery is a product or a service.

As was seen in Maxims 2 and 6, a clear corollary of identifying the long-term and enduring needs of the customer is the *product life-cycle* concept which underlines forcefully the inevitability of change and the fact that while basic needs continue almost indefinitely, the means of satisfying them change continuously. Not only do products come and go, but there is a clearly discernible pattern to the life of every successful product as it passes from introduction, to growth, maturity, decline and withdrawal. So consistent is this pattern that it provides a clear set of guidelines for managing the product as it progresses from birth to decay. Thus while it cannot predict the duration or strength of any individual phase, it should sensitise the planner to the need for carefully monitoring the sales performance of his product so that he can identify changes at an early stage and take the appropriate managerial action.

Limited strategic alternatives is a simple idea which postulates that there is only a small number of basic strategies open to a firm:

- Do nothing – peaceful co-existence
- Direct competition – price
- Indirect competition – product differentiation, promotional differentiation, distribution differentiation
- Innovation – changing the rules of the game
- Withdrawal.

The concept indicates that only rarely will it be possible to pursue a do-nothing strategy successfully due to the continuous change taking place in the market (see Maxim 6). Similarly direct or price competition is only feasible when the firm possesses a significant cost advantage and is willing to use this to secure a dominant market share and further economies of scale. Tactically, however, smaller firms may use price as a competitive weapon in the knowledge that the major suppliers are unlikely to offer a similar discount on their much larger sales volume.

In an attempt to avoid direct competition most firms have chosen to compete indirectly through differentiation of the other elements of the marketing mix – product, promotion and distribution. Through indirect competition the firm hopes to secure a monopoly over a segment of the market and so be able to exercise a degree of control over that segment, particularly in terms of price policy.

However, monopolies arising from indirect competition are often uncertain, fragile and short-lived, and this encourages many firms to pursue a strategy of innovation in the hope of establishing a genuine monopoly with a radically different product or service.

The fourth key concept – *business portfolio analysis* – is a natural extension of the preceding concept in that it recognises that while there is only a limited set of strategic alternatives these are not mutually exclusive. While it is true that there are many firms that survive and even prosper on the basis of a single product they are either very large – electricity generation, telecommunications – or very small with a particular niche in the market that no one else would wish to

compete for. For the majority of firms, survival and prosperity depend upon their having a range of products at different stages in their life-cycle so that as old products are withdrawn new ones are introduced to replace them. As a consequence, the multiproduct, multimarket firm with a portfolio of products at different stages in their life-cycle may well be pursuing all the strategic alternatives simultaneously with a broadly based portfolio model such as the Boston Box or Shell's directional policy matrix providing the framework for its strategic planning.

An essential ingredient to such strategic planning is the *marketing audit* or SWOT analysis through which the firm seeks to identify threats and opportunities in the external environment as a basis for maximising its own corporate strengths and minimising its weaknesses. In undertaking such an audit, and indeed in every aspect of marketing, one must be continuously aware of the nature and effects of *selective perception*.

The importance of this phenomenon was underlined in the discussion of how buyers (and sellers) make decisions, from which it became clear that we all tend to interpret 'facts' in terms of our own background, experience and value systems with the result that different individuals are likely to place quite different interpretations on a given piece of objective information. Accordingly one must be ever sensitive to the dangers of the self-reference criterion and of assuming that the rest of the world sees, believes and acts in the same way as ourselves. We must recognise that because of *customer diversity* there is rarely, if ever, a homogeneous demand for the product.

However, the fact that individuals do differ from one another does not mean that there are no similarities between them, and a key activity for the marketing planner is the identification of groupings of consumers which are sufficiently alike and of sufficient size to constitute a worthwhile market in their own right. As was seen in Chapter 12, there are many diverse approaches to *market segmentation*, but behavioural differences resulting from selective perception stand out as a major source of customer diversity.

Given that markets can be segmented or subdivided on the basis of a variety of different criteria the objective of the marketing planner must be to position himself so that his offering will be seen as matching most closely the distinctive needs of the segment for which he has chosen to compete. To do so effectively the seller's product or service must be seen as offering some *differential advantage* over those of his competitors. In our model of buyer behaviour it was seen that objective, physical and measurable differences are to be preferred, but it also recognised that such differences are also the easiest to match or copy. Thus in many markets, particularly industrial and institutional markets, products and services are objectively the same and differentiation between them must depend upon intangible and subjective factors such as design, quality, reputation or branding and, increasingly, service.

In order to cater for the distinctive needs of different market segments and maximise such differential advantage as one possesses, the marketer will need to develop a unique combination of the basic marketing ingredients – product, price, place and promotion. In other words, one must create a *marketing mix* which is perceived as both different and better by a sufficient number of prospective users to comprise a worthwhile market in its own right. To achieve such a marketing mix it is vital that the firm practise *integrated marketing planning*, for it is only by doing so that synergy can be created and a competitive edge be achieved and maintained. While systems and procedures are important, our discussion of managerial orientations and organisational structures indicate that successful implementation is most likely to occur when all members of the organisation subscribe to a philosophy of customer satisfaction – a marketing orientation – and that this is reflected in the values, mission and objectives (corporate culture) of the organisation.

But the road to hell is paved with good intentions. Sophisticated marketing planning procedures are irrelevant and useless unless stringent efforts are made to monitor performance through *control and feedback* mechanisms. It is through such mechanisms that the planner is able to detect what is working and what is not, and so make the continuous adjustments necessary to maintain the integrity of the operation and ensure its successful continuation.

And, finally, we return to *3-in-1* marketing, which is a plea to marketers to remember that while long-range strategic marketing planning is challenging, creative, demanding and exciting it will be of no avail if we lose sight of the need to manage the short- and medium-term future efficiently and effectively. Thus we must pay much more attention to the cinderellas of marketing – selling and distribution – for these are the means whereby we will recoup our past investments and earn the profits on which the future will depend.

REFERENCES

Ansoff, I. (1968) *Corporate Strategy*. Harmondsworth: Penguin.

Argenti, J. (1974) *Systematic Corporate Planning*. Sunbury on Thames: Thomas Nelson.

Baker, M. J. and Hart, S. J. (1989) *Marketing and Competitive Success*. London: Philip Allen.

EIU/Andersen Consulting (1997) *Vision 2010: Designing Tomorrow's Organisation*. New York: Economist Intelligence Unit/Andersen Consulting.

Hooley, G. J., West, C. J. and Lynch, J. E. (1983) *Marketing Management Today*. Cookham: Institute of Marketing.

Kotler, P. and Levy, S. J. (1969) Broadening the concept of marketing, *Journal of Marketing*, **33**(January).

Levitt, T. (1960) Marketing myopia, *Harvard Business Review* (July–August).

Lynch, J., Hooley, G. and West, J. (1988) *The Effectiveness of British Marketing, A Report to the ESRC*. University of Bradford Management Centre.

Nanaka, I. and Takeuchi, H. (1995) *The Knowledge Creating Company*. Oxford: Oxford University Press.

Peters, T. and Waterman, R. (1982) *In Search of Excellence*. New York: Harper & Row.

Porter, M. E. (1990) *The Competitive Advantage of Nations*. London: Macmillan – now Palgrave Macmillan.

NOTE

1 This section draws heavily on Baker, M. J. (1980) Maxims for marketing in the eighties, *Advertising*, **66**(winter).

Index

A

B